Electronic Publishing

UNLEASHED

William R. Stanek &
Lee Purcell, et al.

SAMS
PUBLISHING

201 West 103rd Street
Indianapolis, IN 46290

Copyright © 1995 by Sams Publishing

FIRST EDITION

International Standard Book Number: 0-672-30752-9

Library of Congress Catalog Card Number: 95-70108

98 97 96 95   4 3 2 1

Interpretation of the printing code: the rightmost double-digit number is the year of the book's printing; the rightmost single-digit, the number of the book's printing. For example, a printing code of 95-1 shows that the first printing of the book occurred in 1995.

Composed in AGaramond and MCPdigital by Macmillan Computer Publishing

Printed in the United States of America

Trademarks

Publisher and President Richard K. Swadley

Acquisitions Manager Greg Weigand

Development Manager Dean Miller

Managing Editor Cindy Morrow

Marketing Manager Gregg Bushyeager

Acquisitions Editor
Grace Buechlein

Development Editor
Mary Inderstrodt

Software Development Specialist
Wayne Blankenbeckler

Production Editor
Kristi Hart

Copy Editors
Marla Reece
Tonya Simpson

Technical Reviewer
Bob "rab" Bickford

Editorial Coordinator
Bill Whitmer

Technical Edit Coordinator
Lynette Quinn

Formatter
Frank Sinclair

Editorial Assistants
Sharon Cox
Andi Richter
Rhonda Tinch-Mize

Cover Designer
Jason Grisham

Book Designer
Alyssa Yesh

Production Team Supervisor
Brad Chinn

Production
Mary Ann Abramson, Angela D. Bannan, Carol Bowers, Michael Brumitt, Charlotte Clapp, Terrie Deemer Ayanna Lacey, Kevin Laseau Paula Lowell, Donna Martin Brian-Kent Profitt, SA Springer, Tina Trettin SusanVan Ness, Suzanne Whitmer

Indexer
Greg Eldred

Contents

Foreword

When computer-book publishing was born in the early 1980s, everyone immediately realized that an amazing publishing phenomenon had occurred. In the space of a few short years, the industry went from zero books and zero revenue to thousands of books and hundreds of millions of dollars in revenue. Bookstore shelves were packed with computer books; retailers created best-seller lists dedicated to this new baby; hundreds of hard-working editors, proofreaders, layout artists, and sales people found new jobs; and hundreds of people who had rarely given any thought to publishing suddenly found that they were authors—authors of computer books.

What few people realized in those early days, however, was that this new industry was carrying along with it the seeds of a profound change in publishing itself. It all started innocently enough—the editors, almost all of whom had no publishing experience, did their editing on PCs, working on word-processing files submitted by authors who were, of course, also working on PCs. From there the process became traditional, using typesetting and manual layout.

The next step was neither immediate nor easy, but inevitable. In our company (which at first comprised the separate companies of Que and Sams, later united to form the nucleus of Macmillan Computer Publishing), the change was precipitated by necessity. Que's *Quick Reference* series was designed to have a certain layout and an exact number of pages. The complexities in using the traditional methods to always arrive at that exact page count were too daunting, so we set up the series director with a Macintosh in her office and she laid out the series in PageMaker. And so our company had its first totally electronically published product. The advantages in time, cost, and flexibility were so obvious that we soon converted our entire system. The time was 1988–89.

From that time until now, the tools of electronic publishing have grown immensely sophisticated and have transformed the face of all publishing, although that transformation is only half-done at best. The authors of this book have clearly and ably described these tools and how they are used to get great results. In other words, they show you how to *publish electronically*—how to create print product using electronic tools. But more than that, they have taken us into the next dimension of electronic publishing—how to create electronic product.

Macmillan Digital USA was founded in November, 1994, to create electronic product as part of Macmillan Publishing's overall mission to publish outstanding reference product. One unit works to create multimedia product for distribution on CD-ROMs; another unit maintains a presence on the World Wide Web and on consumer online subscription services such as America OnLine and CompuServe. The goals of both groups ultimately are the same—to bring desired and necessary information to people when and how they want it, in a way that makes learning easy, enjoyable, and more digestible.

Online publishing is in its infancy. There are substantial technological and systemic restrictions on widespread and rapid dissemination of information in any form other than textual, and textual information is still better suited to a printed book than to a screen. Convenience, accessibility, and searchability are advantages that online publishing has over print, but it remains to be seen how valuable those advantages are perceived to be. Certainly, anyone with a good knowledge of technology, as explained in this book, can create a raft for his or her ideas and launch that raft on the great river of bits flowing throughout the world—can become an electronic publisher. But online publishing as a business will exist only when consistent value can be placed on the intellectual product that is published, and the value can be converted into currency. Until that time, the authors who can sell their ideas in other media will continue to do so.

The online world as a communications tool, on the other hand, is unrivaled. Part of that communication is about ideas that are published in other media, print or CD-ROM. People can easily find out about books and software, can extensively sample the offerings, can make direct inquiries to the publisher or author, and can order the product, all online. If they choose, they can help the publisher create an individual profile to alert them about future products and chat sessions and forums. The online world is alive with information that anyone with the tools and the knowledge can tap into at any time, even if it is not yet a business.

Multimedia CD-ROM production is a business, one that is both exploding and struggling. The explosion is one of creativity, with thousands of new products coming to the market— many ingenious and well-conceived, others not so. The explosion in title output is all the more amazing considering the cost of production and the availability of shelf space. It is like the gold rush of 1849. Certainly there is gold "in them th'ar hills," and some will strike it rich and stay rich, others will strike it rich and lose it all, others will make just enough to pay the high cost of surviving in the gold fields, and many others will never make it. What's the key? Good ideas well executed. And good execution requires an intimate knowledge of the tools and how to use them. Books like this one make an outstanding contribution.

Another way to look at multimedia production is that it is just a way of preparing for the future. No one knows what the technology will be five years from now, but it's a good bet that it will involve some sort of widespread broadband delivery system. In that environment, people will want (and will pay for, either directly or through advertising) multiple-media, interactive entertainment and information. Starting now, on the CD-ROM distribution method, prepares for that future.

Print will not go away. In some instances it will be replaced by multiple-media interactive product, but mostly it will just be supplemented and enhanced. And the methods of producing print product will continue to evolve. Certainly for reference information, the authors of the future will be producing not just word-processing documents, but documents that are designed with an SGML-type tagging system that will make the information flexibly searchable and organizable. The publisher will then be able to easily decide which medium or media to use to publish the information, whether in print or electronic form, online and live, or in physical form and static. The decision can be based on the market and the suitability of the information to the medium, not on the restrictions of the technology.

Ultimately, publishing technologies bring freedom and power, an environment in which ideas prevail. That is the goal and the natural endpoint of the great revolution that is in progress. The people who know the tools will be the builders of that future.

Lloyd J. Short
President
Macmillan Digital USA
August 15, 1995

About the Authors

Roger Bindl is a consultant, electronic publishing developer, and owner of HADRON Data Graphics. He has extensive background in telecommunications and personal computers. Major corporations he worked for include General Telephone Company, Alcatel Network Systems, Telxon Inc., and the Pulsecom Division of Harvey Hubbell. Throughout his telecommunications career, he promoted integration of personal computers into the business environment. This process began in 1980 with VisiCalc, word processing and database tools for planning, forecasting, and expense tracking. The integration expanded in the early 80's with the online electronic OAG (Official Airline Guide), MCI Mail, and work process automation using Basic language programming and other software tools.

His experiences in the telecommunications industry include digital multiplexers, ISDN- and SONET-based fiber optic systems. Personal computer work encompasses the environments of Macintosh, DOS, and Windows. Software integration grew from the staples of word processing, spreadsheet, and friendly databases to authoring, multimedia, database development, communications, image editing, video capture and edit, animation, audio, online services, publishing, and so on.

Integration, exploration, and curiosity lead Roger to his current role of consultant and developer. He's president of HADRON Data Graphics. HADRON specializes in electronic publishing, and focuses on authoring with Microsoft's Multimedia Viewer. They use and implement various authoring and multimedia development tools in developing electronic publications.

Mitch Gould, co-author of *Windows 95 Multimedia Programming* (M&T Books, September 1995), was the first book author to cover Autodesk 3D Studio with a 1991 book, *Mastering Animator*. He has worked as an information designer at LotusDevelopment Corporation, AT&T's Distributed Multimedia Technology Development lab, the Georgia Tech Research Institute, and BellSouth Services. ADAM Software turned to him for documentation of its award-winning release of ADAM, an interactive atlas of the human body. In 1994, his Digital World testimony against violence in multimedia attracted the attention of Popular Science, and he received a scholarship to attend the Multimedia BootCamp at Microsoft headquarters. He is currently developing strategies for intelligent agents as a user interface in broadband interactive TV.

Ewan Grantham's first three computers were a Timex/Sinclair 1000, a Commodore 64, and a PDP-11. Not surprisingly, he now specializes in building GUI front-ends for client-server systems, designing data warehouses, and creating multimedia presentations and training for clients. In addition to his work on this book, Ewan was also a contributing author on Sams Publishing's *Windows 95 Unleashed, Programming Windows 95 Unleashed,* and the forthcoming *Access 95 Unleashed.* He currently is authoring the book *Microsoft Office 95 Unleashed,* and has a monthly column on multimedia in *Windows 95 Journal*. Ewan can be reached on CompuServe at `74123,2232` or through the Internet at `74123.2232@compuserve.com`.

David Gulbransen has been involved with electronic publishing for over five years. His past works include contributions to *Tips And Tricks of Internet Gurus*, *The Macintosh at Indiana University* (CD-ROM), and the World Wide Web site for BlueMarble Information Services. In addition to freelance WWW development, David is currently employed by the Indiana University School of Fine Arts and is developing a variety of electronic teaching resources. Some of his current projects included a WWW site for the School of Fine Arts and an electronic imaging lab to allow multimedia CD-ROM production. David also enjoys sneaking some free time in to trade the computer screen for the silver screen.

Much to **John Kovalic's** surprise, he was born and educated in England, where he first started sketching muskrats that looked more like badly-drawn ewes with the hives. This talent he soon turned to cartooning, and his now-syndicated comic strip, "Wild Life," has been running since the late 1970s. He is also an award-winning editorial cartoonist and frequent computer and technology writer for the Wisconsin State *Journal*, the morning newspaper of Madison, Wisconsin. His e-mail address is `muskrat@msn.fullfeed.com`, and on the World Wide Web, he can be found at `http://www.msn.fullfeed.com/muskrat`. Please do not feed him.

Bill Mann is a veteran writer and software developer. Some recent works include *Edutainment Comes Alive!* (by Sams) and Desert Frog Screen Scenes (Desert Frog Software). He and his family are preparing to face their first New Hampshire winter, after nine years in Phoenix, Arizona.

Bill Montemer is a multimedia producer and programmer. He specializes in New Media in all its forms, and is currently developing software engines and children's educational content to drive them.

Lee Purcell is a technical writer, journalist, musician, and private pilot who lives a stones throw from the Otter Creek in the state of Vermont. Despite many hours of staring at the creek, he has yet to see an otter. His previous book for Sams Publishing, *Super CD-ROM Madness!*, has been translated into three languages. In between book projects, he designs online help systems, writes hardware and software manuals, and helps clients adapt information for use on the Web. You can address comments and queries to Lee through CompuServe at `71160,2041`.

Lance Rose, Esq. (`elrose@well.com`) is a writer and attorney. He is of counsel to Lewis & Roca in Phoenix, Arizona, and co-chair of its Intellectual Property and Technology Group, serving the high-technology, information, and media industries. Clients of the firm include software developers and publishers, online services, electronic publishers, trade associations, and other providers and users of high-technology and information products.

Mr. Rose is the author of the book *NetLaw*, the legal guide for online service providers, and he writes regularly for *WIRED Magazine* and *Boardwatch Magazine*. He speaks regularly at national conferences on the law of the Internet and online systems, and he was chairman of the "Business and Legal Aspects of the Internet" conference sponsored by the National Law Journal in 1994 and 1995. He is also moderator of the "Networks and Online Systems" conference area on the Lexis Counsel Connect online service. Mr. Rose is a charter member of the New York Media Association, honorary member of the Association of Shareware Professionals, founding member of the Society for Electronic Access, and a member of the Association of Online Professionals.

Marj Rush-Hovde recently received her Ph.D. in Rhetoric and Composition from Purdue University. She currently teaches a variety of professional writing courses and serves as a consultant to an organization developing a World Wide Web page.

William R. Stanek (william@aloha.com) is the publisher and founder of The Virtual Press, a non-traditional press established in March 1994. As a publisher and writer with over 10 years experience on networks, he brings a solid voice of experience on the Internet and electronic publishing to the book. He has been involved in the commercial Internet community since 1991 and was first introduced to Internet e-mail in 1988 when he worked for the government. His years of practical experience as an ADP and Network Manager are backed by a solid education, Master of Science in Information Systems and a Bachelor of Science in Computer Science. His press publishes electronic books under four imprints: Virtual Mystery, Virtual Fantasy, Virtual Science Fiction, and Virtual Truth. He maintains several World Wide Web sites including: The Writers Gallery, The Internet Publishing Information Center, The Electronic Packaging Center, The Internet Consulting Center, and The Virtual Press Headquarters (http://www.aloha.com/~william/vphp.html). His Electronic Packaging center designs electronic publications—magazines, newsletters, newspapers, and books—for clients. His Internet Consulting Center tailors Internet business strategies to meet client's needs and helps them through every step of their Internet connection and marketing deployment.

He served in the Persian Gulf War as a combat crew member on an Electronic Warfare aircraft. During the war, he flew on numerous combat missions into Iraq and was awarded nine medals for his wartime service including one of our nation's highest flying honors, the Air Force Distinguished Flying Cross. He has written many books, articles and essays. His book length projects include nine fiction titles and three nonfiction titles. When he's not writing or working, he spends time with his family, his favorite time of the day being story time when he reads to the youngest.

Ray Werner is a member of the adjunct faculty at Ivy Tech State College in Indianapolis, Indiana, where he teaches Desktop Publishing and other computer-related subjects. He is the author of several computer books, including *BBS Secrets, CorelDRAW! 5 For Dummies Quick Reference, Harvard Graphics for Windows for Dummies Quick Reference, You and Excel, Word for Windows for Dummies, The First Book of CorelDRAW! 3*, and *50 Ways to Get Your Money's Worth With Prodigy*. Ray has also contributed to several books, including *PC World Word for Windows 6 Handbook* and *Windows Gizmos for the Internet*.

Introduction

Over the years, human knowledge has advanced by fits and starts. The curious and unpredictable species that invented the printing press so that ideas, laws, and events could be preserved and transmitted between generations is the very same species that in the 4th Century cheerfully burned down the great library of Alexandria, Egypt, the largest repository of human knowledge that existed at the time. Knowledge has been alternately sanctified and devalued; the ownership and control of it has been a central theme in human history since the beginning of time.

Present-day methods for storing and recapturing the experiences and collective information resources of our culture rely more and more frequently on the computer and digital methods of storage. Electronic publishing—the process by which information is organized and presented for computer display—has advanced from a little-understood curiosity to a mainstream medium of communication.

Imagine a worldwide library linked by speed-of-light connections and encompassing every source of information collected by every culture on earth. Electronic publishing has already given us the framework for such a structure; HTTP servers on the Internet connect hundreds of thousands of documents through a complex matrix, linking data, programs, and other resources within a global network known as the World Wide Web. This huge virtual knowledge base is growing daily and providing access to every conceivable form of information. The electronic publishing tools to create and produce documents, data, and knowledge bases to place within this structure have become available and accessible to nearly anyone. The promise of this new method of communication is immense; governments, businesses, educational institutions, and private citizens have flocked to participate, making the Internet the fastest growing communication medium in history.

Another communication medium borne out of the development of the audio compact disc, the CD-ROM, has become the electronic papyrus of the '90s. Inexpensive to produce, capable of storing large volumes of digital data in every form, the CD-ROM has moved into prominence as a distribution medium for interactive multimedia productions and electronic books. The availability of inexpensive CD recorders might do for electronic publishing what the laser printer did for desktop publishing. Soon everyone will have one and people will be exchanging compact discs like kids exchange POGS.

The interlocking and recombining of ideas and information—as supported by electronic publishing—could dramatically change the way we educate our children, learn new skills, develop understanding and tolerance of other cultures, and gain appreciation for art, film, and literature. In the course of writing this introduction, I consulted the *1996 Grolier Multimedia Encyclopedia* to see if I could determine when the library at Alexandria was destroyed. A keyword search using *library* and *Alexandria* turned up more than a dozen matches. Prowling through the contents of these search results revealed a host of related information. An entry about the history of books mentioned that book collecting has been going on since the Ptolomies of Egypt started the practice in the 2nd century B.C. The Tibetan *Book of the Dead* is generally considered to be the oldest surviving book, although there have been earlier fragments and pieces of other books unearthed—too little remained of them to reconstruct the contents. The *Book of the Dead*, which was often read to those who were dying, served as a guide and magical sourcebook, a kind of instruction manual for existing in the afterlife.

A side trip to the history of libraries mentioned that Eumenes II, who ruled the centuries-old Greek kingdom of Pergamum, perfected techniques for producing vellum—a predecessor to paper—by dressing the skins of sheep and goats. Vellum pages were sewn together and covered by wooden boards. According to records of the time, Eumenes II supervised the construction of a library that ranked among the most impressive in the world. Public libraries didn't originate until the 17th century; earlier libraries were private, but that didn't matter much because at the time few people could read.

A bit more searching and I came across an entry that indicated that the library and academy at Alexandria were destroyed at the end of the 4th century; alchemists who had been working there trying to figure out new ways to turn lead into gold fled the area and migrated throughout the Near East. Nonetheless, they were hounded and persecuted by various governments for years and associated with black magic.

This interesting trail through the encyclopedia not only yielded the detail I was looking for (the period in which the library was destroyed), but a good deal of other information on books and libraries that lent perspective to my understanding of how books and libraries have evolved and how human knowledge has been transmitted in different cultures. Each search through a multimedia document of this type can uncover and present surprising details and closely related subject matter. Information is more fluid and it can be organized to unfold details in ways that stimulate curiosity, open up parallel paths of inquiry, and provide elaborate interrelationships between subject areas.

Electronic Publishing Unleashed explains the concepts, tools, and principles that underlie the digital information revolution. You'll find examples of what others have done in this area and suggestions as to what you might do (and how you can do it). This field is still young, and the time is ideal for shaping and influencing generations of communicators armed with electronic tools and filled with ideas that might change the world.

Overview

Part I, "Fundamentals of Electronic Publishing," establishes the groundwork upon which electronic publishing tools and technologies have been built. Freed from the constraints of moving paper-based information by conventional means, electronic publishers are quickly adapting to new forms of media that transmit ideas swiftly and silently. Part I provides many examples of different applications of electronic publishing, explores the terminology and concepts associated with the technology, and takes a look at the tools that can be employed to produce electronic publications. Guidelines for selecting a medium for distributing your electronic work are provided. Part I concludes with a discussion of the career opportunities for prospective electronic publishers.

Part II, "Organization and Design of Electronic Documents," examines the structural aspects of different forms of electronic documents, from help systems to HTML documents. By providing useful design criteria and workable models for document structuring, this series of chapters provides a practical approach to making the transition from print publishing to electronic publishing. The chapters examine the fundamental characteristics of hypermedia linking, explore the techniques for presenting information for onscreen use, and suggest ways in which multimedia elements can be effectively incorporated in an electronic document. Part II concludes with a discussion of the steps that document developers follow when creating electronic works.

Part III, "Publishing on CD-ROMs," offers guidelines and practical advice for using CD-ROMs as the delivery medium for electronic publications. The chapters compare the pros and cons of CD-ROMs for various types of publishing and provide detailed examination of the different data types (such as audio, video, computer data) as stored within current compact disc formats. Hardware tools, such as the new generation of CD recorders, and software applications, such as premastering tools, are discussed and compared. Techniques for incorporating multimedia elements into a CD-ROM project are presented, and the role of CD-ROMs in the business environment, including disc arrays and CD recorders, is examined. Part III concludes with a look at the issues faced by title developers in the CD-ROM industry, including copyright issues, pre-release testing, and marketing.

Part IV, "Online Publishing and the Internet," provides a practical view of one of the fastest growing platforms for electronic publishing, the World Wide Web. From an overview of the Web, including a perspective for publishing within this medium, Part IV advances through a focused look at the markup languages, HTML and SGML, as used for producing complex platform-independent documents. The use of multimedia elements in online documents, and the setup and use of Web servers, gateway scripts, and helper applications is also discussed. The increasing reliance on electronic publications for transmitting information in LAN and WAN environments is covered, as well as the techniques for advertising and protecting documents that you place on the Web.

Part V, "Projects," moves from the realm of the theoretical into the real-world production of several different forms of electronic documents. Step-by-step hands-on procedures lead you through the creation of your own personal multimedia résumé, a newspaper designed for Internet access, and an interactive magazine distributable on floppy disk. You also learn the fundamental procedures for creating more elaborate electronic documents, such as an interactive encyclopedia. Part V concludes with a description of how to produce and publish a comic book designed for electronic access. Within the range of projects covered in this part of the book, you will likely find one to suit your personal interests and to test your developing electronic publication skills.

Part VI, "Implementation," presents a number of essential considerations that should be faced by anyone contemplating the release and distribution of an electronic publication. You will learn how to fully test a publication prior to release, how to obtain user feedback during development, and how to introduce the world-at-large to your newly launched document. Part VI includes tips for achieving success in your publishing and marketing efforts, as well as a careful examination of the laws and regulations surrounding copyrights and intellectual property rights.

Part VII, "Appendixes," rounds out the book with a valuable set of resources, including a list of the tools and applications commonly used for electronic publishing, a number of CD-ROM titles of interest to developers and publishers, and a full compilation of the HTML commands used for constructing Web pages. Appendix D describes the contents of the CD-ROM included with this book, and provides tips for accessing and using the CD-ROM.

Who Should Read This Book

We've deliberately created a work that leads to hands-on involvement with the processes and techniques for creating electronic publications. Anyone interested in personally learning how to construct a modest or an elaborate electronic publication should find material in this book to satisfy their aspirations.

The prospective audience easily covers a broad range: educators, librarians, publication managers, book publishers, newspaper and magazine publishers, technical writers, public relations specialists, marketing and sales professionals, retail mail-order firms, information professionals in government organizations, communicators in public and non-profit groups, research firms—literally anyone interested in learning about the ways the electronic publishing can effectively and inexpensively communicate ideas.

One of the appealing aspects of the technology is that it is not limited to programmers or "gearheads." Anyone who can use a word processor can easily construct an electronic publication in portable document format. If you can master a few embedded codes, you can build a Web page in HTML. With a bit more perserverance, you can structure an infobase for use on CD-ROM. Electronic publishing is for *everyone*. We hope this book leads you to success in the electronic publishing field.

PART

I

Fundamentals of Electronic Publishing

From Atoms to Bits: Electronic Publishing Emerges

1

by Lee Purcell

IN THIS CHAPTER

When you hear the slap of that rolled-up newspaper hitting your front porch at 5:45 a.m., it's a less-than-subtle reminder that we still depend on paper as the primary medium for written communication. Acres of trees are felled and pulped to provide us with the privilege of reading the sports' scores in the morning and learning about the latest plane crash or terrorist act. Paper has weight and substance, and it takes the concerted effort of many individuals to bring information to our breakfast tables in this manner—the loggers, the paper-mill employees, the newspaper staff, the printers, the truck drivers who distribute the bundled newspapers to drop points where bleary-eyed adults and kids pick them up and then—in cars or on bicycles or on foot—deliver the printed product to your doorstop. Then, once you've learned that the Red Sox beat the A's and your mutual fund dropped a couple of points, the paper goes out to the recycling bin where it's trucked around some more and hopefully turned into something useful.

Elementary school lessons taught us that paper, like all matter, is composed of atoms. The newspapers dumped on our front porch, the books filling our libraries, the magazines lined up in newsstands—collectively, we're looking at millions of tons of atoms. Without any profound analysis, it clearly takes a large expenditure of energy to move the atoms upon which we store information.

The digital information revolution suggests a different means of accomplishing the same goals. Instead of moving information around by moving heavy, intractable masses of atoms, we're starting to move it as *bits*. Bits are electronic signals that serve as swift, nearly weightless representations of the physical world. As a single unit, a bit doesn't convey any more information than a traffic signal; it is either on or off. Grouped by the millions, bits can form representations of sounds, images, and words. Bits travel at the speed of light through the air and through fiber-optic pathways. Even conveying bits through the millions of miles of twisted-pair copper cables that encircle the earth achieves near-instantaneous transfers.

Bits can be copied easily without any degradation of the original source. They can be stored on a variety of optical and magnetic media. They can be manipulated in sophisticated ways that are generating entirely new art forms. A half-ounce CD-ROM can contain the equivalent of several hundred thousand printed pages or a digital version of a full-length feature film.

In his recent book *Being Digital* (published by Alfred A. Knopf, 1995), the founding director of MIT's Media Lab, Nicholas Negroponte, describes bits as "the DNA of information." He uses the bits versus atoms analogy to illustrate a global trend: the rapid, unstoppable movement toward a digital future in which companies compete in vastly different ways. As he describes it, "The information superhighway is about the global movement of weightless bits at the speed of light. As one industry after another looks at itself in the mirror and asks about its future in a digital world, that future is driven almost 100 percent by the ability of that company's products and services to be rendered in digital form."

This book, *Electronic Publishing Unleashed*, examines the different forms that information can take when it is transformed into bits. In the same way that desktop publishing gave anyone with a computer the ability to produce high-quality books, newsletters, brochures, and references, electronic publishing lets anyone repackage and reorganize information for inexpensive distribution on a multitude of digital channels, including the Internet, your own personal BBS, or a personally produced CD-ROM. You can design your electronically published creation to be played back on a bare-bones character-based video terminal, a full-featured multimedia workstation, or the paperback book-sized screen of a handheld personal digital assistant. In fact, you can often easily process the same information to be presented in all of these forms. One of the wonderful advantages of storing information in digital form is the ease with which you can manipulate, reshape, and exchange it.

This book also talks about the tools and techniques involved in becoming an electronic publisher. You'll find many examples of how to gain experience with this emerging technology, whether your goal is to produce a CD-ROM to explain quantum physics to high school students or to develop an interactive catalog containing solar energy devices to distribute on the Internet. Even if your goals are more modest, such as producing an interactive version of your résumé or a home page to announce your presence on the Internet, you'll find procedures within this book to support your efforts. If you become intrigued by some of the possibilities suggested, you will also find abundant cross-references to other books and materials to contribute to your mastery of electronic publishing.

Electronic publishing is both something new and something rooted deeply in the earliest traditions of communication. We're witnessing the emergence of what might be considered a hybrid technique for communication, a technique that borrows on nearly every other form of communication. Over the last 2000 years, the human family has moved from communicating through song and dance and storytelling around the campfire to the written word. We've gone from handwritten pages to the printing press to the desktop computer to networked computers. We can now distribute information to points all around the planet in a matter of seconds. Electronic publishing opens up completely new channels of communication. Using a single information medium, we can combine the precision of the written word with the immediacy and emotion of dance or song or spirited speech. An electronic document may contain more than words—sounds, images, animation, video, and hypertext links extend the range of experience and let you structure information in complex yet comprehensible ways.

The Push and Pull of Information

The interactive nature of electronically published works lends itself well to both learning and entertainment. Writers and researchers, when describing the differences of new media, such as interactive multimedia on CD-ROM, indexed databases, and online books, often use the terms "push" and "pull." Broadcast media, such as television and radio, push information at you. You receive information packaged in forms to grab your attention and hold it—to keep you from clicking the channel button on the remote. You are force-fed commercials between segments of news or entertainment. Sitcoms have laugh tracks to remind you when to laugh, dramas contain built-in pauses for regular commercial breaks, and the news comes packaged in short attention span sound bites. Outside of your ability to turn off the broadcast or to switch channels, you play the passive role of a viewer or listener.

In contrast, electronic publishing puts the selection of information and the viewing controls in your hands—you "pull" what you want or need from a vast range of available selections. In research centers, such as MIT and Interval, programmers are working to develop intelligent agents to siphon, filter, and sift through huge bodies of information to find the things you are looking for and deliver them to you in simple, accessible ways. Well-designed, hypermedia documents provide depth and perspective to subject matter and let you examine information at several different levels. Your role in this context is an active one—you become an explorer navigating through a multilayered information matrix, free to choose or reject whatever you encounter. Designing information to work in this kind of framework takes different skills than writing a book, producing a technical reference, or even creating a training video.

It takes imagination and foresight to anticipate the different ways the audience might respond to electronically published media and to provide a structure for exploration that feels both comfortable and open-ended. Many early efforts to move information into this domain have missed the mark—users struggled to orient themselves, grappling with user interfaces that might have served well for special-purpose computer applications but made things unnecessarily confusing within an electronic book or reference.

Every form of media that has been introduced has undergone a period of development during which communicators learned how to best use it. Until Edward R. Murrow began using television as an "eye" to examine news events from the front lines, the concept (though obvious now) was largely ignored by television producers. Similarly, electronic publishing overturns some of the basic concepts common to other communication media. For example, film and television production groups think in terms of shows that run 30 minutes or an hour and a half. How long does a CD-ROM-based interactive multimedia journey into the Amazon rain forest run? You might spend an hour exploring content describing the various species of birds in the region, and another two hours reading narratives written by early explorers of the Amazon river. You might spend 20 minutes more examining maps of the surrounding territory and jumping to photographic images linked to the maps. Unlike reading a book or watching a movie, interactive works don't necessarily have a beginning or an end, and the *running time* extends only as long as the viewer's interest. This fundamental difference in presenting material still hasn't been fully absorbed into the consciousness of the developer community.

The software and hardware tools required to accomplish electronic publishing have dropped within the reach of mere mortals, both in terms of price and in respect to the effort required to make them operate effectively. Applications designed for constructing hypermedia documents have improved dramatically and no longer require years of training to use. Access techniques have improved as well. You can now easily generate full indexes of the contents of thousands of pages that can be accessed with swift, sophisticated proximity search engines—without having to do any programming or scripting. Computer performance and modem communication have improved significantly; it is now practical to present more intricate and complex information, whether you download it from a service or access it from a CD-ROM.

Information in digital form can be reshaped in countless ways and communicators continue to find exciting, innovative techniques for doing so. Maybe you'll develop your own unique method for entertaining, educating, or enlightening based on the tools and techniques described in this book. You'll see some of the possibilities and explain how you can become an active participant in the rapidly growing field of electronic publishing.

A Working Definition of Electronic Publishing

I was tempted to discreetly bypass this section, because coming up with a clear definition of electronic publishing runs smack into the same kind of wall that chokes industry spokespersons who are trying to define multimedia. It's like trying to define a new biological organism while the organism wriggles away from your description by mutating into a new form every twenty minutes. By the time you've completed the definition, you're looking at an entirely new beast. As with multimedia, everyone seems to have their own notion of what constitutes electronic publishing, and these notions sometimes run at cross purposes.

To focus our efforts in this book, however, it makes sense to establish at least a framework from which to view electronic publishing. What are the characteristics that distinguish electronic publishing from other forms of computer-based information delivery?

First and foremost, electronic publishing is a medium for creating and distributing computer-based information in a compact and accessible format. Not bad, but exactly what constitutes "computer-based information?" We know that if we're talking about computer-based information, we're talking about digital storage, and we can store almost anything digitally (text, images, speech, music, video, animation). Then again, if we're talking about sound and music and animation, isn't this the same as multimedia?

This is where we need to draw a dividing line. For the purposes of this book, electronic publishing is the extension and enhancement of materials designed for the printed page to make them accessible using a computer. This gives us the latitude to include many types of multimedia enhancements to pure document formats, such as creating a dictionary that includes buttons to audibly pronounce individual words. Multimedia can certainly be considered a part of electronic publishing (hmm, multimedia hasn't been defined yet, has it?), but not the most important part. Maybe we better try again.

Electronic publishing is a medium for presenting conventional print-based media, such as newspapers, magazines, catalogs, encyclopedias, technical references, and almanacs, in a form that the reader can view and use on the computer. Part IV contains a comic strip project that demonstrates how that conventional medium can be transformed as well. Maybe that's the distinguishing characteristic: the fact that we're adapting and enhancing conventional media for computer access. This lets us include things like the Grolier *Multimedia Encyclopedia* and *Guinness Disc of Records*; Microsoft's *Cinemania* (a compilation of film reviews and cinema information from several different sources); Voyager's *The Complete Maus* (a computer adaptation of a Pulitzer-winning graphic novel by art speigelman that deals with the Holocaust experience); Apple's *En Passant* online catalog; and similar titles.

We can probably exclude materials where the relevant content is based on non-print resources. Games such as LucasArts Dark Forces and ID Software's DoomII are action-based adventure games and perhaps a third cousin removed from electronic publishing. Titles based on documentaries or films may come close to our electronic publishing definition, but in the end they're much more related to pure interactive multimedia. Discovery Communication's CD-ROM titles, such as *Normandy: The Great Crusade* and *In the Company of Whales*, are closer to online documentaries than electronic publishing examples.

We still haven't paid too much attention to those examples of electronic publishing that reside on the Internet or in the BBS realm. Basically, anything you can put on disk or CD-ROM can be placed in downloadable form on a network. The corollary is true as well: many kinds of information available on the Internet, including documents constructed in the HTML format common to Web browsers, such as Mosaic and Netscape, can be stored on CD-ROM and viewed using the same browsing tools. You can use other viewing tools, such as Adobe Acrobat and FrameMaker Viewer, in similar dual roles, providing a window to CD-ROM-based material or network downloadable files. In addition, a host of new search-and-retrieval tools let you probe the contents of an information base and extract data that you need. Whether the data resides on a CD-ROM or on a network file server, you can find information that you are searching for in a matter of seconds. Some of these tools are presented in later chapters; they provide more ways you can structure and organize digital information.

In many cases, you can download electronic versions of computer journals, books, magazines, references, company brochures, or legal documents which you can then store on hard disk, diskette, tape, or any other storage medium. For example, Peach Pit Press has released a free electronic version of its book, *Aether Madness: An Offbeat Guide to the Online World* (by Gary Wolf and Michael Stein) that you can download from the World Wide Web (`http://www.neo.com/Aether/`). The fascinating and idea-saturated alternative news magazine, *Utne Reader*, now has an online version called *Utne Online*. Macmillan Computer Publishing (as you might expect) also provides a Web site where you can download samples of many current books. You'll see many more examples of downloadable books and magazines throughout this book.

At some point the lines in our fumbling definition of electronic publishing begin to blur. Microsoft's *Complete Baseball* consists of a CD-ROM-based reference that users update with current statistics through downloaded data from a network. Time Warner recently released Kurt Vonnegut, Jr.'s novel *Slaughterhouse-Five* as an interactive work with clips from the movie, video interviews with Vonnegut, and many other multimedia elements. As such, even though it's based on a novel, it seems to swing closer to interactive multimedia than our definition of electronic publishing, because the video and film aspects are so prominent. Another example,

3D Landscape, a CD-ROM title produced by Books That Work, takes the traditional book approach to home landscape design one step further. You can click and drag different types of plants and trees around a computer model of your yard, put them through computer-simulated growth patterns to see how they will look in five or ten years, and examine the characteristics of different species through search techniques. Is this a work of electronic publishing or a whole new model for presenting practical information?

This somewhat artificial division between electronic publishing and interactive multimedia breaks down pretty quickly under some scrutiny, but from a practical standpoint, another way to look at it is this: Electronic publishing is a way in which small companies and individuals can present creative, multilayered, content-rich information to anyone who has a computer. We'll leave the full-scale definition of interactive multimedia to the large studios and giant communication megaliths with the resources to fill rooms with Silicon Graphics workstations, pay licensing fees to top recording artists, and recruit animators from Hollywood studios. Greg Roach and his staff at HyperBole Studios can afford to pay union-scale wages to a dozen actors to perform in one of his virtual cinema productions; you probably can't.

Nevertheless, you can do an amazing variety of things on a moderately high-performance computer, and using channels, such as the Internet or some innovative CD-ROM marketing, you can inexpensively reach an audience of millions with your electronically published work. In this book, you'll look at the practical and exciting prospects offered by new hardware and software tools and provide hands-on experience with the development process.

If you're still confused as to what electronic publishing is (and isn't), keep reading; I guarantee that by the end of this book you will have constructed your own definition and understanding of this elusive, still-evolving computer enigma.

The Evolution of Electronic Publishing

The origins of electronic publishing can be traced to a stream of discoveries and inventions. Charles Babbage's work on mechanical calculating engines in the early 1800s certainly had an influence because this work laid the foundations for the modern computer. Babbage himself used concepts originated by Joseph Marie Jacquard, who, in the late 1700s, used punch cards to control looms to weave complex fabric patterns. As James Burke pointed out in his book *The Day the Universe Changed*, microchips would not have been devised without a succession of experiments to uncover the nature and the principles of magnetism—a process that took hundreds of years and involved thousands of individual experiments. The development of the transistor at Bell Labs in 1948 began the rapid move toward miniaturized electronic circuits. A host of other discoveries and inventions led to our ability to create electronic documents. Some of the most noteworthy of these originated in the previous century.

Long-Distance Communication

Remember the telegraph? You probably don't, unless you were around during the Civil War. The telegraph was a quantum leap forward in communication, the first practical method for transmitting messages as electrical impulses.

Previous methods of communicating long-distance—smoke signals, drums, signal flags, and so on—depended on the messenger directly reaching the eyes or ears of his or her audience. Signal flags and smoke signals are useless in a heavy fog, and even the resounding rhythms of war drums can be drowned out by a good thunderstorm. With the telegraph, suddenly a message could be delivered to someone beyond the line of sight or out of the range of hearing. Relying on a code that converted words to strings of short and long clicks or light flashes, the telegraph required an alert operator at each end of the communication line. An operator at one end of the line converted the message to a string of signals, usually tapping out the codes on a telegraph key. Another operator at the other end had to figure out what these signals—in the form of dots and dashes—were saying.

Although the principles and components of the telegraph were developed by a number of individuals, Samuel Finley Breese Morse won acclaim (and is usually credited as the inventor) after demonstrating a working prototype to members of Congress in 1844. Telegraph offices quickly sprang up across the country; the electromagnetic signals generated by the telegraph key could be inexpensively routed through a single conductor cable with earth supplying the ground and closing the circuit. The power of this long-distance method of communicating was irresistible to a generation that had previously depended on moving messages by horseback and ships. Telegraph lines began snaking across the mountains and prairies until in October of 1861, the eastern and western branches of the transcontinental telegraph came together in Salt Lake City. Only a handful of citizens in this rough-edged and sparsely populated city witnessed this event.

Burke goes on to discuss how the telegraph figured prominently in the Civil War as a means of relaying details of troop strengths and the outcomes of battles. Abraham Lincoln used to cross the White House lawn and enter the War Department telegraph office to receive incoming news from his field generals about conditions and front-line events. Lincoln described the telegraph office as the place he went to "escape his persecutors."

Modern remnants of the telegraph still exist, although instead of using wires to transmit messages, radio signals relayed through communication satellites act as the carrier. The Telex was devised as a means of using telegraphy techniques to transmit and receive printed messages, but more recent forms of electronic communication have made this method of sending messages largely obsolete.

From Looms to Punch Cards

Most references that chronicle the history of computers acknowledge the intellectual contribution of French inventor Joseph Marie Jacquard, who devised a system for using punched cards for producing textile patterns on an automatic loom. Despite resistance from certain factions—notably the silk workers of the time—designers improved and refined the automatic loom during the early 1800s which became a principal reason that the textile industry prospered during this period. The idea of storing complex patterns symbolically on a card was a strong one, and an idea that two other inventors did not overlook. Charles Babbage tried to use punched cards for mechanically performing mathematical calculations, and though he failed to complete his dream machine, his writings and prototype devices served as stepping stones for later researchers.

An American inventor, Herman Hollerith, adopted the use of punched cards to drive equipment used in compiling the results of the U.S. census in 1890. He continued refining his tabulating equipment over the years and eventually formed the company that was to evolve into the world's largest computer corporation, IBM. In 1946, the University of Pennsylvania constructed ENIAC (Electronic Numerical Integrator And Calculator) out of a huge assembly of vacuum tubes. A select group at IBM became interested in the technology and decided there might actually be a market for these electronic versions of calculating machines. A development program led to the release of the IBM 701 in 1953, and sales of this unit soon exceeded those of the earlier released UNIVAC. Punched cards remained in use for many more years as a simple, though tedious, means of recording and storing data.

ASCII as a Common Denominator for Text

The mainframes and minicomputers of the 1960s and 1970s were a proving ground for techniques to encapsulate text in a format the computer could digest and disseminate. ASCII, the American Standard Code for Information Interchange, originated as a way to convert alphanumeric characters and a range of control characters to a code that would occupy seven bits of computer storage per character. This left one bit remaining out of a byte, the 8-bit unit that is the building block of most computer data processing and storage standards. The extra bit provides a convenient way to perform error checking, so that when computer data is transferred over noisy telephone lines, seven bits typically carry the data in the form of ASCII characters, and the eighth bit stores a parity value—the sum total of the other seven bits considered as an odd or even value.

ASCII encoding and decoding provided a neat and efficient means for both converting data entered into the computer by keyboard and for displaying textual information on a computer terminal. ASCII quickly became the dominant method for encoding text to be stored and distributed on the computer and has become so widely entrenched that, despite some inherent difficulties in its use, it persists even now. However, for communication and data-handling operations, microprocessors frequently rely on eight bits (a byte) as a standard unit of storage. The problem is that many word processing programs that rely on more sophisticated techniques for storing and presenting formatted data. Although they may use the eight bits of the ASCII code for basic character storage, they often use the eighth bit for their own purposes.

Moving messages through large-scale networks, such as the Internet, that have been set up to transfer and interpret messages consisting of seven-bit ASCII creates problems. Specially designed utilities enable you to convert eight-bit data into a seven-bit code to transfer through the Internet and then change it back again once it is received at the other end, but obviously this is a less than ideal way for transferring information. The fact that data to be sent as a message may also consist of computer programs, conventionally stored and transferred in eight-bit units, additionally complicates the communication process.

Widespread use of ASCII enabled early forms of electronic publishing to develop and achieve consistency; electronic publishers could easily store and distribute any document consisting purely of text on diskette or place it on a Bulletin Board System (BBS) where other users could download it for use. The disadvantage, obviously, is that large blocks of monospaced text are hard to read and even though the information you are looking for may be embedded somewhere within this unformatted jungle, finding it may not be worth the effort. The standardization provided by ASCII was, however, the first step in making electronic document exchange widespread. Competing standards, such as EBCDIC (Extended Binary Coded Decimal Interchange Code), dwindled over time and linger only as relics in older mainframes. Extended, more fully developed versions of ASCII include additional characters necessary for languages other than English and permit the use of specialized characters, such as copyright and trademark symbols, and line-drawing symbols.

Methods for Searching and Indexing

Recognizing the difficulty in pinpointing specific information within a mass of text, researchers at IBM began working on methods for indexing and rapidly searching large blocks of text. Way back in 1959, Hans Peter Luhn and a group of fellow researchers came up with a scheme called Keyword in Context (KWIC) indexing, a technique that builds automatic indexes out of title strings. Although machine-generated indexes have enjoyed favor because of their compilation speed, most professional indexers recognize the deficiencies of this method of providing access to written material. You'll still find many automated approaches to indexing; generally, tools that give the indexer the ability to create and control the index entries serve the reader far better than fully automated approaches.

The fact that the computer rapidly performs repetitious comparisons makes it ideal for performing searches, which can be structured using the same logical operations that form the basis for computer processing. If you turn a search program loose to locate particular patterns within a block of data, it can compare and match millions of characters and return the results in a matter of seconds. This simple facility results in one of the most impressive benefits of electronic publishing: the ability to quickly locate individual words or phrases buried in numerous documents or files.

Although you might not personally be able to easily read through 400 pages of ASCII text, the computer can rapidly search through this same data and locate occurrences of the words "Washington" or "Bing cherry" or "Potomac" in milliseconds. The ASCII representations of these words are just groups of bits forming a pattern that the computer can identify with unerring precision. This capability, combined with some other computer-processing tricks that are discussed later in this book, forms the heart of search-and-retrieval software utilities, which are still extremely important in the electronic publishing scheme of things.

Hypermedia Is Born

Text is useful, and you can store many valuable kinds of information in textual form; however, the reach of communicated messages expands considerably when you can add graphics, sound, and motion to the digital data basket. Combining different forms of data into a single mix is, in simplest terms, the definition of multimedia. *Interactive* multimedia enables you, the viewer, to control the course of this mix of media, usually by pointing to and clicking on-screen icons or typing short commands. Creating interactive multimedia productions used to be a task reserved for skilled programmers, but the tools to create presentations of this sort have been simplified significantly. Instead of writing code to perform operations, you create, move, and link objects shown graphically on the display. Objects represent sounds, music, segments of video, graphics, blocks of text, and so on. You can create complex interactive works by assembling chains of object-based information and designing paths for your reader to move through the information.

As was the case with desktop publishing, interactive multimedia and electronic books gained an early lead on the Macintosh platform. The complexities of combining graphics, sound, animation, and video were more easily mastered within the Macintosh environment. Because Macintoshes were already equipped for multimedia playback, consumers generally encountered fewer problems when playing back multimedia content from CD-ROM or disk. The earliest and most impressive authoring tools appeared on the Macintosh, and the first widely distributed electronic books were launched with Apple computers in mind. The most recent generation of machines on the PC platform include better integrated multimedia components. Operating system support for multimedia, as appears in Windows 95, should help improve the acceptance and use of multimedia tools on the PC platform.

Kodak's work on the Photo CD standard, a technique for storing and retrieving photographic images on compact disc, achieved significant exposure in the first book packaged with a set of interactive CD-ROMs, *From Alice to Ocean*. Based on a 1700-mile journey by Robyn Davidson across the Australian outback, the compact discs contain brilliant photographs by Rick Smolan, a well-respected photojournalist on assignment for National Geographic. Portions of Robyn's book, *Tracks*, appear along with Rick's photographs documenting the harrowing journey of one woman, four camels, and a dog through some of the most desolate and challenging landscapes on earth. *From Alice to Ocean* became a landmark example of the power, flexibility, and scope of the CD-ROM as a communication medium, and it holds up well even today when compared to more recent titles.

When electronic publishers structure digital data in a format in which the viewer can interactively jump between segments, play music, listen to speeches, or watch animated clips, the term *hypermedia* is sometimes used to describe the result. Techniques for creating hypermedia documents are central to the software designed for electronic publishing.

Making Formats Portable

Plain, monospaced blocks of text are difficult to read, and they fail to fully communicate organization and underlying meaning in written information. Differences in computer displays and graphic handling, however, have caused problems in displaying different fonts, diagrams, page layouts, and other information in a form that viewers using different computers can transfer between them. This is one of the reasons why bland ASCII text has persisted for so long as the common exchange medium of online information; bland or not, it has served as a common denominator that can be displayed on almost any terminal or computer display.

Recognizing this problem, companies such as Adobe and Frame Technology Corporation have devised *portable* formats, methods of storing and displaying intricate page layouts, including multiple fonts and diagrams, in a form in which users on any computer can read them. This approach generally requires two components: a tool to create the document and format it, and another tool, sometimes called a reader, to display the document on each of the different supported platforms.

Similar techniques have improved document display on the Internet and other online services. World Wide Web browsers are essentially readers that interpret and display coded document files in a form that lets viewers on any computer enjoy the benefits of various sized fonts, different types of page layouts, and embedded graphics. Browsers and readers have uses both in online situations (where users view or download documents from services) and for exchanging information on diskette, CD-ROM, or magnetic tape.

Summary

The progression from recording information on strips of goatskin to storing it as patterns of bits upon an optical or magnetic medium has taken thousands of years. If you decide to create your own electronic documents, you'll be working with software tools that let you manipulate bits in a staggering number of ways. Although the temptation to use every tool available can prove irresistible to newcomers of this technology, the underlying content inevitably separates a successful electronically published document from a failure. In the chapters that follow, we'll provide guidelines that help you recognize the techniques that separate a quality electronic publication from an inferior work and demonstrate the ways you can apply these principles to your own work. The journey of a thousand electronic pages starts with a single bit.

Glowing Examples

2

by Lee Purcell

Like it or not, digital printing is slowly replacing conventional printing; you can now find an electronic version of almost any kind of paper-based publication. Interested in newspapers and magazines? You can log on the Internet and access the Electronic Newsstand for your favorite news and periodicals. Or, you can pick up a copy of Medio Magazine on CD-ROM and enjoy live interviews and music along with written articles. Do you have a fondness for recipe books? These have been one of the longest running forms of electronic publishing. Among the very earliest programs for the first-generation personal computers, such as the Altair, Osborne 1, and Tandy TRS-80 machines, were electronic versions of recipe books. Some of the new ones can literally talk you through the recipe.

References of all kinds have been adapted to the hypermedia model, particularly encyclopedias. Dozens of them out there now fill the prismatic surfaces of CD-ROMs with millions of words of text that can be searched in numerous ways, most of them containing multimedia tidbits as well. According to *Wired* magazine, sales of CD-ROM versions of encyclopedias surpassed sales of print versions in 1993. Interested in professional journals? Perform computerized bibliographic research from CD-ROM using PsycLIT, a reference tool for psychologists and students. Many other journals have been transformed into an electronic format as well. For a medium that has only been in existence a dozen years or so (at least beyond the walls of academia and industry), electronic publishing has developed and flourished in a variety of useful niches, virtually anywhere that the need for information and entertainment exists.

This chapter explores the range of materials you can find on CD-ROM. Keep in mind, however, we're focusing on a moving target (as is everything in the realm of computers). New categories and different kinds of information arise in electronic form every day. We can call these examples of electronic publishing *glowing* examples because, to a large degree, they are displayed on computer monitors where the image appears as an electron beam strikes a phosphor coating, making it glow.

Books

For several centuries, books have been the mainstay of human knowledge. The reluctance to give up the tactile properties and physical sensations associated with books may be one of the strongest reasons that electronic publishing hasn't made even faster inroads than it has. Anyone who is a book lover has probably had something similar to the following experience. You're traveling along a country road while on vacation and discover a 19th century colonial home converted into a used bookstore. A step across the threshold opens up the senses—there's that smell of old books, a mix of binding glue and aging paper with a trace of printer's ink. The heft and texture of each book adds to the pleasure, as does the sense that each book represents a portal into an unknown world from 10 or 25 or 100 years ago.

The cold blink of your computer display doesn't quite make an adequate replacement. So far, our efforts to make computer displays compact and readable and as satisfying as books have failed miserably. In *Being Digital,* Nicholas Negroponte speculates that someday computer displays may be flat, malleable, light-weight objects with crisp displays, something that you could comfortably bring to bed for late-night reading, but today, they are not. Even the smallest Personal Digital Assistants are cumbersome and much harder to read than a book.

Electronic books, however, can do many things that conventional books cannot do. They can pronounce words for you (useful for those French phrases that you've always been too embarrassed to inject into a conversation). They can be layered—through hypertext or hypermedia links—to explain concepts that you may not understand or provide details deeper than the mainstream narrative. The same electronic book can effectively serve both the novice and the expert, something that can't be done well in a conventional book. They can add dynamic aspects to communication that are impossible in a printed book, such as showing the movements of a dance or letting you hear a 50-year-old blues guitar piece. They can offer different paths to move through their contents (providing context and perspective to the information and—in the case of intelligent agents or guides—lending a definite viewpoint to the journey).

Improved tools and utilities for authoring electronic books offer multiple options for combining and structuring contents and ideas: you can take a chronological perspective of events, set up intricate networks of searchable keywords, align material to a particular character's viewpoint, relate the present to the past or future, or come up with entirely original methods of organization. You can create as many paths through a single work as suits the subject, and clearly the context and organization can have a profound effect on how a viewer responds to and assimilates the information. Electronic books can even give you the opportunity to see and hear the author commenting on his own work, as in the Voyager title, *The Society of the Mind*. Author Marvin Minsky pops up in a series of short video snippets to interject new ideas about the subject. These comments on the contents of his book and related ideas add another dimension to the material.

As was the case with early desktop publishing, electronic publishers often want to take advantage of every conceivable design option. Instead of dazzling combinations of fonts, however, we're now seeing complex and convoluted interfaces and links that twist and turn through every corner of an electronic publication. Three clicks into a document and you're lost. As electronic publishers gain some maturity with this new medium, you can expect to see simpler and more elegant interfaces; those that provide straightforward guidance and direction through the content, with fewer distracting visual elements, usually succeed over the Las Vegas strip approach with flashing neons and entrances beckoning you from every direction. Keep this in mind while working on your own designs; discretion and simplicity should guide your judgment.

Electronic books are probably the largest single category of this new medium; to do justice to the range of this subject, we'll look at electronic books through several subcategories: fiction, encyclopedias, specialized references, and even theatrical drama. (I improvised on this last category to include an interesting entry by Attica Cybernetics covering the works of Shakespeare; it does an excellent job of pointing out the changes and evolution of the English language over a several-hundred-year time span.)

Interactive Fiction

Imaginative works of fiction have satisfied the long-standing human craving to engage in storytelling, a desire we can trace to folktales, myths, and legends as far back as we can go in history. One of the most popular forms of storytelling, the novel, recently has been resurfacing in electronic form—the approaches to interactive fiction of this sort have varied widely. In some cases, the electronic version adds color and depth to the original work. In other cases, the electronic additions become excess baggage, making the original work ungainly and cumbersome. As with all forms of electronic publishing, you have to remember that we're dealing with techniques of communication that have developed over the last few years. The early examples of film, characterized by very short reels covering subjects like train robberies and couples kissing, didn't exactly foretell the importance of cinema as a communication medium. Likewise, techniques for presenting information and ideas in electronic publishing will improve as the medium gains acceptance and practitioners acquire skills.

Trouble is My Business

Raymond Chandler's fictional detective Philip Marlowe ranks up there with American cultural icons Lou Gehrig and Marilyn Monroe, and a fair number of people might even believe that Marlowe actually drew breath and caught lead on the mean L.A. streets. *Trouble is My Business* is a collection of several Chandler novels interwoven with film clips from various spin-off movies, letters to and from Chandler, and biographical information about the author. Figure 2.1 shows themain menu for this title.

FIGURE 2.1

Marlowe's desk is used as a backdrop for menu operations.

This electronic work opens with an animated segment of Marlowe himself driving up to the seedy backstreet area harboring his business office while a brassy, 1940s-era jazz theme plays in the background. He casually shoots the pistol out of the hand of a trench coat-clad female nemesis lurking in the shadows and navigates the shadowy stairway to his office where he pulls open the top drawer to reveal a whisky bottle rolling gently back and forth. Nice animation, nice opening. This sequence, about a minute long, captures the flavor of the Philip Marlowe persona, a character that scores of mystery writers have been trying to capture in their own fiction. Robert Parker has probably come the closest with his Boston-based Marlowe alter-ego, Spenser. (This is not an accidental resemblance—Parker has actually completed a pair of unfinished Chandler works, suggesting that maybe he has paid some attention to Chandler's work.)

The components of this collection of interactive novels are quite simple. You have the full text of eight Chandler novels, including *The Big Sleep, Farewell, My Lovely, The Lady in the Lake, Playback, The Simple Art of Murder, The Long Goodbye, The High Window,* and *Trouble is My Business.* If you're ambitious, you can read straight through the collection, though you might get tired scrolling through the individual chapters. Most chapters have audio control buttons embedded in the text; you can click the play button and have someone read short segments to you if your eyes get tired reading the computer text.

You will find interactive links to film clips of many of the Marlowe-based cinema works embedded in the text if you want to take a detour and see how it was done in the movie. You can also bring up a period-correct map of Los Angeles and click colored blocks to view significant landmarks and architecture from the Chandler novels. When Chandler writes, "The muzzle of the Luger looked like the mouth of the Second Street Tunnel" in *The Big Sleep,* you can display a shot of the Second Street Tunnel to see what it actually looked like, as shown in Figure 2.2.

FIGURE 2.2.

The Second Street Tunnel, looking like the muzzle of a Luger.

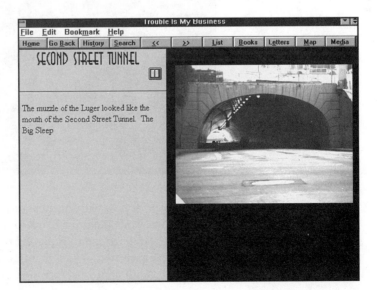

A sampling of letters from Chandler gives some insight into the mind of the author who started out writing pulp fiction and eventually gave life to a character who still elicits smiles and appreciation from a jaded late twentieth-century audience.

I doubt that anyone will actually read all eight novels from cover to cover on his or her computer display, but any Chandler fan will appreciate the color and depth offered by this electronic version of his work. Developed by Bryon Preiss Multimedia and distributed by Time-Warner Interactive, this CD-ROM shows some of the ways electronic publishers can extend a book using multimedia elements. Byron Preiss Multimedia used Microsoft's Multimedia Viewer to create the work.

Slaughterhouse-Five

You can now experience, in multidimensional splendor on your computer display, one of the novels that catapulted Kurt Vonnegut, Jr. to fame. *Slaughterhouse-Five* combines science-fiction time travel with grisly World War II realism, enlivened with Vonnegut's inimitable commentary. Vonnegut himself appears in a series of video clips (see Figure 2.3), describing the origins of the novel's protagonist, Billy Pilgrim, in an actual person—a chaplain's assistant—whom he characterizes as the "most innocent person I ever knew."

FIGURE 2.3.

Vonnegut commentary on innocence.

The interactive version of *Slaughterhouse-Five* plays with the time-travel theme that runs through the book. You can choose to view this title in a Linear or Random fashion. The Random option has you skipping around in time and space and thus piecing the story together out of a string of disassociated parts. The Linear navigator, as you might expect, starts on page 1 and moves sequentially through the book. Both approaches include music, sound effects, and interactive links to film clips and other material. Every page is a surprise. A section about the lead character working as a reporter starts with sound effects, the chatter of manual typewriters, and phones ringing in an office. A segment about an accident in an elevator includes the mechanical squeal of elevator pulleys. For another type of book, this approach might be annoying, but for Vonnegut's scene-by-scene rambling, the effects enhance the narrative flow. Short animations, silly poems, bomb blasts, dialog snippets, sketches, moody photographs—all of these different elements are skillfully mixed together to produce a book that reaches out to all the senses. This is how the Monty Python troupe might compose a novel; you don't just read it—it keeps reaching off the page to tweak you on the nose. This is also not to diminish the underlying serious content; Vonnegut makes his points through irony and humor. Figure 2.4 shows a typical page.

FIGURE 2.4.

A drunken Billy Pilgrim searches for the steering wheel of his car.

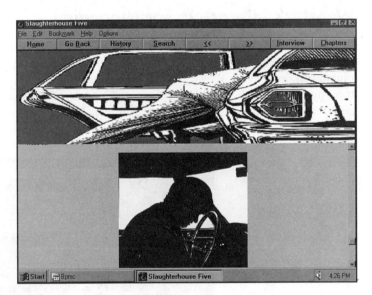

Some readers might be offended by the manner in which this book fills in details that the reader's imagination might better supply, but—in the same manner as a film represents an interpretation of someone else's story—this interactive work adds a layer of textures and patterns and ideas, and, if anything, the treatment opens new imaginative pathways. I suspect that Vonnegut is pleased with the results of this title.

Encyclopedias

Microsoft's Bookshelf informed me that the term *encyclopedia* originated from a Greek phrase that meant to receive continuing education in the liberal arts and sciences; somehow this phrase was transmuted into a New Latin word, enkuklopaedia, by copyists of Latin manuscripts. In English, the term emerged with the meaning "a general course of instruction." It was then applied to a generalized English reference work in 1644.

In its present-day interactive form, the encyclopedia has demonstrated for many the feasibility of the CD-ROM as a storehouse for information. Most of the online services also offer some type of interactive encyclopedia, although for the typical connect time charges you're probably better off to buy a CD-ROM and do your research offline. Encyclopedias are frequently bundled with CD-ROM drives, and it's pretty safe to assume that most people who have used a CD-ROM drive have spent a bit of time browsing an interactive encyclopedia.

In a crowded, competitive market, developers of CD-ROM-based encyclopedias have worked energetically to distinguish their products through improved interfaces and search capabilities, flashy embedded multimedia effects, and guided paths through collected works. The following two examples of interactive encyclopedias highlight some of the new features.

Webster's Interactive Encyclopedia

The Oxford, England-based multimedia developer, Attica Cybernetics, recently released the *Webster's Interactive Encyclopedia*, which puts a fresh face on the normally bland icon-based multimedia interface. As shown in Figure 2.5, the main screen for this product displays large, three-dimensional objects to key the viewer to functions such as searching (a magnifying glass) and scanning the index (a Rolodex-style card file). These generously sized icons are repeated throughout the encyclopedia and serve as attractive visual landmarks for navigation.

FIGURE 2.5.

Oversized navigation icons provide quick viewer orientation.

Although the articles in this encyclopedia are a bit shorter than those that appear in some of the competitor's works, the overall organization and presentation of the topics deserves recognition, and the search facility is rather unique. After you enter the search terms and run the search, the display shows the search results in two columns, both scrollable. You can scroll through the left column which shows the actual articles with the search terms highlighted, or use the list on the right, which contains just the entry names, to scan and navigate to promising topics.

As befits an English-designed encyclopedia, a search using the term *tea* generated 108 matches (see Figure 2.6). Cruising through the list of topics provides a mini-history in the use, cultivation, and significance of tea in trade and historical events (such as the Opium Wars). Similar searches through other topics yield a wide selection of closely correlated topics, demonstrating that the linking and organization within this work has been carefully orchestrated.

FIGURE 2.6.

A search on the term tea.

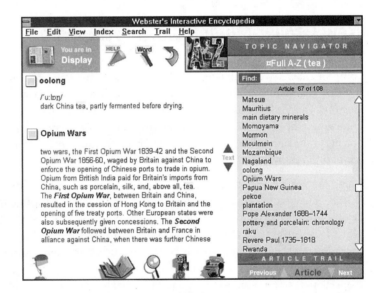

The help system also bears notice. Clicking the help icon doesn't bring up a help screen, but rather an audio description of the interface, delivered by a woman with a crisp English accent and a somewhat stern, no-nonsense tone of voice. This approach takes a bit longer than it might take to read a series of help screens, but it tends to personalize the product and actually does a better job of orienting the viewer to the interface, because you don't have a help screen in your way as you listen to the description of the interface. Many interface designers might argue with the efficiency and compactness of having a narrator provide the help, but I find that this type of approach adds warmth and makes the product more accessible. If you're going to use multimedia elements, you have an excellent opportunity to give your work some personality and help the viewer relate to it in a more human way.

Accessing the Topics listing yields a scrollable set of thumbnail images, letting you navigate the encyclopedia through collected groups of articles. Clicking any subject icon then brings up the familiar two-column screen with full articles on the left and a navigable list of entries on the right.

The overall work has a decidedly British bent. It gives considerable attention to things such as a several-minute-long audio clip of a speech by British field marshal General Montgomery as he primed the troops for the coming battle in North Africa. April Fools' Day is disdainfully described as "the first day of April, when it is customary in Western Europe and the United States to expose people to ridicule by a practical joke, causing them to believe some falsehood or to go on a fruitless errand." Rather than detract from the encyclopedia, the British flavor adds a unique perspective and gives you the chance to look at the world through English eyes. The clean interface, thoughtful topic linking, and powerful search mechanisms make this encyclopedia a good example of how to simplify access to more than 30,000 individual topics.

New Grolier Multimedia Encyclopedia

One of the earliest producers of reference materials on CD-ROM, Grolier continues to create comprehensive, well-balanced works that take advantage of some of the best aspects of multimedia. Solidly grounded in a well-respected print encyclopedia, *The Academic American Encyclopedia*, Grolier has extended the single-dimensional page with video clips, sound, and animation (the quantity of multimedia material is not overwhelming, but it provides tasteful accents to the source reference). You can navigate through the 21 volumes of material in a number of different ways.

Using the Knowledge Tree, you gain access to articles grouped by six categories: The Arts, Science, Geography, Society, History, and Technology. A Multimedia Map Index highlights key historical events with animations supported by voice-over narration. The Knowledge Explorer Index gives ten-minute tours of subjects that you might think would resist being encapsulated in such short pieces—such as Architecture, but the handling of this material is quite well done and offers a good introduction to the topics, especially for children. A timeline, a requisite part of every multimedia encyclopedia, lets you locate articles by skimming through the years from prehistory to present day. Grolier also does a particularly good job of inserting hypertext links that let you jump from article to article and explore extended chains of thought.

Grolier also implements its search engine well; a *search engine* is the mechanism for hunting through the volumes to locate articles that contain particular keywords. You can either scroll through an alphabetic list of keywords or set up a search sequence containing one or more words. On a reasonably fast machine, most searches take only a few seconds. The speed at which you can locate information is one of the strongest advantages of electronic publishing.

Figure 2.7 shows two of the entry points for navigating the encyclopedia: the Map Index and the Timeline.

FIGURE 2.7.

Navigation entry points, the Map Index sorted by region and the Timelines by era.

You can also search through a categorized list of illustrations and select a series for display. This illustrates another unique characteristic of electronic publishing: you can make comparisons by placing retrieved information, such as pictures, side by side. For example, if you've ever wondered how a domesticated Burmese cat differs from an American shorthair cat, you can retrieve and compare illustrations of them. Figure 2.8 shows the two in all their feline glory.

FIGURE 2.8.

Burmese and American shorthair cats displayed side-by-side for comparison.

Much recent discussion of the electronic information age has centered around the notion of "point of view." So-called objective reporting of information inevitably has a cultural bias and a generally unstated point of view that is cloaked in whatever terms the prevailing mode of thought (as determined by the gatekeepers of the information) deems appropriate. Because electronic publishing places at our fingertips enormous quantities of information, which can be difficult to sift through and evaluate, researchers have been working on ways to locate information using intelligent agents or guides, whose point of view can be predicted or programmed. For example, depending on your personal perspective, you might want to use a Noam Chomsky guide to filter a set of topics.

Grolier introduced a feature, known as Pathmakers in the 1995 edition of its encyclopedia, that lets you tap into articles selected by prominent figures in different fields. For example, Stephen Jay Gould (evolutionary theorist and natural history writer) offers a connected progression of ideas and articles that illustrate his interests and background. Kurt Vonnegut, Jr., another Pathmaker, provides context and insight to literary accomplishments and society's foibles. If you know and respect the commentator, their insights and impressions can lend credence and context to a progression of information.

The myth of objectivity is gradually giving way to a perspective that recognizes that widely differing points of view can exist on the same subject. A Native American's account of the nineteenth century Westward Expansion won't include the same positive, manifest-destiny adjectives as a typical nineteenth-century settler. Being able to easily contrast and compare differing points of view is another great advantage of electronic publishing. When authoring your own electronic works, consider techniques for including divergent points of view to increase the depth and breadth of the information being presented.

Special-Purpose References

Encyclopedias make good general search tools, but they are designed for breadth of knowledge rather than depth. If you want to probe deeper into a subject area, you need a special-purpose reference, and many of these are appearing in CD-ROM format. Special-purpose references include such things as bibliographic references to psychology works, business phone directories for North America, guides to the trees of the northeastern United States, and dental hygienists' training guides. One of the leading categories of electronically published references is database material released by corporations or government agencies; organizations from NYNEX to NASA have taken advantage of the compactness of the CD-ROM as a storage medium.

For example, if you need to know the origin of the word "replicate," you probably wouldn't find it in your interactive encyclopedia. A quick search through the Microsoft Bookshelf dictionary, however, reveals that the term is derived from the Latin word "replicare," which means to fold back. Microsoft Bookshelf, discussed in the following section, serves as a special-purpose reference to word history and meanings (with an encyclopedia thrown in as well).

Microsoft Bookshelf

Although Microsoft Bookshelf is not a recent product (it's been available for several years), it still ranks as one of the best examples of how a select body of information can also be highly accessible. On one CD-ROM you get a dictionary, a thesaurus, a book of quotations, a compact encyclopedia, an atlas, a chronology, and an almanac.

Once installed, Bookshelf becomes easily accessible from anywhere in Windows—a three-button Bookshelf toolbar floats at the top of the desktop and remains there regardless of what application you are running. One click and you can open either the encyclopedia or the dictionary. Early computer-based references were often not worth the effort to use them; by the time you could start the application, work through the menus to fire off a search, and get back the grindingly slow results, you could have pulled the print version of your dictionary off a shelf and read half of it. Not so with Bookshelf. It opens quickly, has extensive linking, and will win any speed competition with a print-bound reference hands down. With multitasking and faster processing, earlier cumbersome online references have achieved their promise—they've become a faster, better means of gaining information.

Microsoft has used the several years since the introduction of Bookshelf to refine and polish the interface, search engine, and the links throughout the collection. If you plan to design any type of integrated reference set, take a look at Bookshelf first to see how the masters have done it. Figure 2.9 shows a page from the dictionary.

FIGURE 2.9.

MS Bookshelf dictionary page.

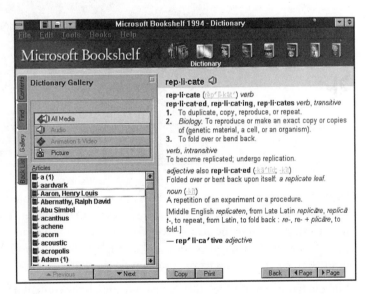

Microsoft Cinemania

Cinemania won't teach you anything about the migration habits of the Great Grackle or the primary export product of the tiny nation of Belize (it's sugar, if you're curious). As a special-purpose CD-ROM-based reference, it is dedicated to just one subject: the American cinema. It covers this subject in almost every way imaginable and serves as an effective source book and guide to every aspect of filmmaking.

Cinemania combines film reviews from silver-screen observers such as Leonard Maltin, Roger Ebert, and Pauline Kael with details and descriptions from a number of other references, such as HarperCollins' *The Film Encyclopedia.* If you're fascinated by film, you can easily spend days swimming through this material without ever touching bottom.

Cinemania opens with appropriate fanfare and a composite graphic that hints at each of the great Hollywood studios without resembling any one of them too closely (see Figure 2.10).

FIGURE 2.10.

The opening screen of Cinemania.

With this product design, Microsoft also provides another object lesson on how to create a complex interactive work that doesn't totally disorient the viewer. You initiate searches by clicking a Find button from the main screen. You can display an alphabetical listing of topics, movies, people, or all of these together and scroll through to find an entry. You can also type in a term in the search edit box and let the program do the work.

You can follow a number of different paths through the content. If you're interested in awards, you can view the Academy Awards victors from 1927 to the present. A slot-machine-like gadget also lets you make random selections of movies—handy before a trip to the video store. The ListMaker feature lets you assemble a list of interesting films to rent or check out in the late-night program listings.

You can sample much of the multimedia content—film clips (usually short), photographs (many nice crisp black-and-white shots mixed with the color ones), audio snips from movies (usually entertaining)—through the Gallery, a scrollable list of items individually identified by icons.

Cinemania offers a reasonable balance between entertainment, serious film history, and cinematic trivia. As a mainstream commercial product, it plants the goalposts that other developers will have to reach to successfully release a product of this type.

Online Books on the Internet

Even a fairly large book can be compressed into a compact computer file. In file form, books can be distributed at the speed of light to anyone with access to a computer. These two simple facts have led to a number of different organizations and individuals placing works of literature onto the Internet where readers can freely download them. As you might suspect, most of these works are in the public domain; that is, no one holds any type of copyright on them. However, other copyrighted works are available for reading but not distribution and other variations of the copyright theme. If you download materials of this type, check any associated notes or warnings to make sure you understand what factors affect the printing or distribution.

The Gutenberg Project, a largely volunteer effort to convert existing works to a digital format for worldwide dissemination, includes many classic works of literature. The address of the Gutenberg Project is

```
http://jg.cso.uiuc.edu/PG/
```

> **NOTE**
>
> You will see several Web addresses similar to this one for the Gutenberg Project throughout this chapter and the rest of the book. Where the address is inserted in the text in parentheses, use only the mono typeface address; do not include the parenthetical marks when you enter an address. For more information on Web addresses, see Chapter 19, "The World Wide Web."

Among the titles that appear in the Gutenberg List of Literature are

Nathaniel Hawthorne's *The Scarlet Letter*
Thomas Hardy's *Tess of the d'Ubervilles*

Norman Coombs's *The Black Experience in America*

Joseph Conrad's *Heart of Darkness*

Samuel Langhorne Clemens' *Tom Sawyer Detective*

George Elliot's *Middlemarch*

Henry James' *The Turn of the Screw*

Jack London's *The Call of the Wild*

John Milton's *Paradise Lost*

D.H. Lawrence's *Sons and Lovers*

Virginia Woolf's *The Voyage Out*

Henry David Thoreau's *Walden*

The list goes on and on; the Gutenberg List of Literature could keep you supplied with reading material for the next dozen years. This is not the only place on the Net where you can find literary works. Several similar projects, mostly associated with universities, exist at various locales such as the following:

The Data Text Library in the United Kingdom

`http://www.datatext.co.uk/library/index.html`

Project Bartleby at Columbia University

`http://www.columbia.edu/~sv12/index.html`

Electronic Text Center at the University of Virginia

`http://www.lib.virginia.edu/etext/ETC.html`

Foreign language works, online magazines, and shorter works are represented as well. How do you find out where all of this good stuff resides? Certain people make it a practice to cruise the corridors of Internet libraries and compile access information for others to use.

John Ockerbloom is one of these people. In concert with other individuals, he has created a Web page called The On-Line Books Page (`http://www.cs.cmu.edu/Web/books.html`) that serves as an index to the many types of publications available online. The listing includes a searchable index (by author or title), a browse utility, links to other directory pages, and occasional special exhibits, such as "Banned Books On-Line" and "A Celebration of Women Writers."

Commercial producers of online publications are also represented. Eastgate is one company that produces hypertext fiction. As with other forms of hypertext, you can navigate through the contents by accessing links, which are jumps to other points in the document. Rather than a single narrative flow, links and jumps can lead you through a number of different paths. You explore a book, rather than just reading it. You'll learn more about how to set up different paths in Chapter 7, "Organizing Information."

You can also sample works and read short reviews of individual pieces through the Web. Many of the hypertext works cost about as much as a hard-bound book ($20 seems an average price); it's clearly more difficult to create a hypertext work—the author not only writes the words but creates the links. It is also much more difficult to lay out the structure of a book that extends in a multitude of directions rather than a single linear path.

If your system is not set up to run a Web browser, you can also download many books from Gopher sites or FTP sites. In a large number of cases, we're talking about massive quantities of ASCII text. Formatting is minimal—monospaced fonts are normal. You can, of course, import the text into a word processor and apply your own fonts; you could even set up a macro to automate this process, but there is no way around the fact that pure ASCII text is not the most readable way of delivering information on the planet.

Some of the more modern works are set to run under a reader utility, such as Adobe Acrobat, and these include the benefits of a formatted page layout and genuine use of fonts.

Copyrighted Works Freely Distributed

As an organically grown communication medium, the Internet has attracted many advocates of open information exchange, including established authors who provide access to their copyrighted works without trying to impose a fee (but also, it should be added, without relinquishing any of their copyright protections). The message is: "Read and enjoy, but don't abuse or attempt to resell my work."

Science-fiction writer Bruce Sterling is one author who vocally encourages the free distribution of much of his work on the Internet. He describes his work distributed online as "literary freeware," followed by the admonition "Not For Commercial Use." Obviously not worried about reducing the volume of his book sales, Sterling represents one of the far-thinking individuals intent on resisting the transformation of the Internet into a corporate-controlled commercial channel.

Sterling's work frequently projects the excesses of our current technology into chillingly rendered portraits of future civilization. *Heavy Weather*, published by Bantam Books in 1994, depicts a future where environmental degradation has surpassed everyone's expectations, leading to the privatization of global resources and the collapse of governments around the world. Massive changes to weather patterns, triggered by man's industrial wastes influencing atmospheric conditions, have created a planet plagued by severe storms and catastrophic climactic events. Set not that far in the future (2030), this novel casts a grim pall over our attempts to control planetary processes with our technological tools and arrogance.

You can gain access to a home page devoted to information about Bruce Sterling that contains links to speeches, reviews, and other material. Of particular interest is the full text of a speech, "The Virtual City," given in Houston, Texas on March 2, 1994 to the Rice Design Alliance. Sterling examines the design processes that have shaped our cities and culture over the last 100 years and discusses the role of science fiction in letting us view and contemplate the direction of our culture. The address for the Sterling home page is

```
http://riceinfo.rice.edu/projects/RDA/VirtualCity/Sterling/index.html
```

For a complete discussion of copyright issues associated with CD-ROM publishing, refer to Chapter 18, "Title Development, Production, and Distribution."

Press Releases

Sending color photographs of products and glossy folders filled with additional product literature can be expensive. Not only is the printing and postage expensive, but the process of updating all of the printed materials on a regular basis adds another ongoing expense to companies and public relations agencies that distribute product information. On the other hand, the CD-ROM is lightweight, and it can contain not only press releases and photographs, but multimedia testimonials from satisfied customers and animated comparisons of product features.

With computers or backup media, companies can easily store the source files and update them quickly as required. The only limiting factor is that your audience must be equipped with a CD-ROM drive to view product information in this form. Even this restriction is fading swiftly, however, as somewhere around 80 percent of all currently shipped business computers include a built-in CD-ROM drive. The CD-ROM makes a good deal of sense as a promotional tool for product information, and this type of use promises to become more prevalent.

Kodak Digital News Kit

With the release of its Digital News Kit in March 1995, Kodak provides a tremendous amount of product information in an easily accessible framework. Much of the material is "printed to disc" using Adobe Acrobat, and the CD-ROM includes an installer for the Adobe Acrobat reader and a limited version of Adobe Type Manager. Besides simple product announcements, the CD-ROM includes detailed information on Kodak-developed technologies in the form of online white papers and comprehensive product specifications. As Kodak mentions in its description of the Digital News Kit, use of Adobe Acrobat gives editors the ability to cut and paste text directly into any Mac or Windows-based word processing program.

As you might expect from the company that devised the dominant method for storing high-quality digital images, Kodak also includes an assortment of photographs on disc, ranging from product shots to historic images. Editors and publishers using Kodak images in their works can incorporate low-resolution formats as placement graphics while preparing a document layout, and then as high-resolution images for final reproduction. Figure 2.11 shows that legendary hallmark of foolproof photography, the Instamatic camera.

FIGURE 2.11.

A page from the Kodak Digital Press Kit. Reprinted courtesy of Eastman Kodak Company.

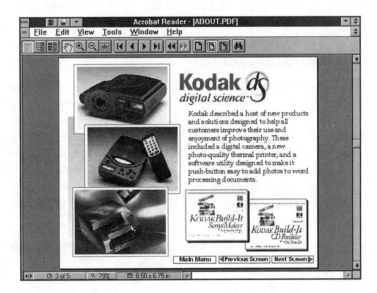

Paper-based press kits seem like an anachronism in the digital age. It costs a lot to send a bundle of glossy photos and shiny folders and paper through the mail. By comparison, it costs very little to send a lightweight CD-ROM, and even less to send a stream of bits from one destination to another. Electronic publishing promises to keep making inroads in this area as more companies find creative ways to package information digitally.

Magazines and Journals

It's easier to start up an online magazine or journal than to start up a traditional paper-based equivalent. You don't have to sign up investors to handle the enormous start-up costs, you don't have to worry about shelling out tens of thousands of dollars for the monthly print runs, and you don't have to rent an office to house your staff—they can be spread out across the world, anywhere that a fiber optic line can reach.

You *do* have to think about achieving the high production values to satisfy a generation bred on MTV, and you do have to figure out a way to get compensated for publishing in electronic form, but the startup is manageable even for a one-person publishing house. With the Internet as your delivery medium, your potential audience is immense—you can place your publication in an accessible place ("If you build it, they will come.") and wait for the readership to grow. Of course, it's not that easy, but a cross-section of the new publications being introduced in electronic form cuts across every social strata and covers every conceivable subject. Some examples follow.

PC Magazine on CD

During a recent trip to Barnes and Noble, one of the largest bookstores in the Burlington, Vermont, region, I was scanning the magazines in the computer section and came across a cover with the shiny tracks of a compact disc beaming through a transparent window. Picking it out of the rack, I noticed it didn't have pages like the other magazines—the entire thing was a magazine-sized package for a CD-ROM containing a year's worth of *PC Magazine* articles and additional feature stories. Sitting like the proverbial wolf in sheep's clothing amidst the other magazines, the CD-ROM version of *PC Magazine* may not yet be the vehicle to clear the racks of paper-based magazines, but this approach to publishing has some definite benefits and advantages over traditional publishing.

The short installation utility, which runs under Windows, enables you to choose from among three modules to install; each requires between 2.5MB to 3.5MB of disk space. Like most current CD-ROM applications, it places those items that need to run fast on hard disk, a factor that can take up quite a bit of disk space if you install very many CD-ROM applications. Once installed, it includes an icon that lets you remove the hard-disk resident files—something you may want to do to reclaim the storage space after you've read all the articles.

> **NOTE**
>
> The capability to remove files (sometimes called uninstalling, to the chagrin of many English teachers) has become increasingly important in the multimedia environment. Microsoft is actively pitching disk-conservation practices by developers; in fact, to earn the right to display the Microsoft Windows 95 logo on their packaging, each company's application must include an uninstall feature.

Once installed, when you launch the *PC Magazine* icon, a video replica of Editor Michael J. Miller appears on-screen before a backdrop of the *PC Magazine* cover. If your speakers are turned on, this Hobbit-sized figure explains how to access different parts of the issue and gestures toward the elements shown on the backdrop, like a pint-sized weatherman pointing out a cold front moving into Nebraska. Although it may sound a bit hokey, this short video introduction provides a warm and personable touch to the normally "cool" (in McLuhanesque terms) medium of the computer.

Browsing and navigating through this online version of the magazine is fairly fluid, although you may spend a lot of time double-clicking the Windows Control Menu to clear windows that pop up everywhere. The search function, however, is where the electronic version leaves its paper ancestor in the recycling bin. Using a powerful search engine, you can search for articles and keywords in a variety of ways, something that has never been easy in the advertisement heavy print form of the magazine. To sweeten the deal, publisher Ziff-Davis includes all articles from the previous year linked to the same search mechanism. If you want to know about the latest graphics card technology, you can locate all related articles in seconds. If you need some information about Web browsers, you can set up a search and find what you need almost instantly. For a writer (or anyone who appreciates a fast way to sort through computer-related articles), this feature easily justifies the price of the CD-ROM edition.

The electronic version of *PC Magazine* retains much of the look and feel of its print-based forebear. You have options that make this delivery medium more flexible than a printed magazine, such as the option to select the font to use when you read an article.

PC Magazine on CD-ROM has a price tag of $17.95, not totally out of line when you consider the normal shelf price for a single issue is $3.95 and each CD-ROM is a quarterly edition. You still don't escape advertising, but the ads are less obtrusive, and you gain the benefit of being able to access demos of many top-notch products. To view many of the demos, you need to install them to your hard drive. Most have polite uninstall features to remove them when you're done viewing, but moving massive quantities of data over to hard disk for viewing kind of defeats the purpose of distributing on CD-ROM. It is possible to ensure quick playback without littering someone's hard disk; demo developers should use these techniques.

The presentation is not perfect—I found myself frequently adjusting the volume control of my speakers because one narrator would practically be whispering and the next would be shouting like a boot-camp training instructor. Demos, many of them produced using Lotus ScreenCam, sped by so quickly that they were gone before I could find the Pause button. Others had a rough-edged, amateurish quality that emphasizes the point that just because you have the tools to create animated screen sequences and voice-overs doesn't mean you necessarily know how to use them. This is clearly still a new medium, and it will take some time for people to apply some polish to their audio-visual presentation techniques. Even these early efforts look promising, though, and I'd buy the issue for the search capabilities alone.

First Floor: The Magazine Rack

Mecklermedia's InternetMall has floors, just like Gimball's and Macy's. On the First Floor, you can thumb through the magazine rack. Here is just a short sample of what you can find.

3W Magazine
http://www.3W.com/3W/
Describing itself as the Global Networking Magazine, *3W Magazine* promises to focus on Internet issues while avoiding jargon-laden descriptions.

Ability Network
http://www.nstn.ca/cybermall/first.html
Canada's predominant publication dealing with cross-disabilities.

American Homebrewers Association
http://branch.com/zymurgy/zymurgy.htm
Don't spill any suds on your keyboard; these guys cover brewing technology at its finest.

American Journalism Review
http://branch.com/zymurgy/zymurgy.htm
This monthly magazine offers observations on the nation's media, as well as an abundance of links to other journalism-related sites.

Deliriously Serious SoftWorks
http://www.tricon.net/Comm/synapse/index.html
Published on CD-ROM, this one includes music, animations, design tips, and more.

Iceland Review
http://www.centrum.is/icerev/
So that you don't forget they're up there, these guys offer news, nature books, T-shirts with Icelandic motifs, and a monthly business newspaper.

Silly Little Troll Publications
http://pobox.com/slt
Billed as a freelance-written, general-interest online magazine, this one deserves a look just for its name.

Strobe Magazine
http://www.iuma.com/Strobe/
An independent music magazine with an assortment of art, commentary, reviews, and other eclectic stuff.

Tech Review Magazine

`http://web.mit.edu/techreview/www/`

Almost 100 years old, this publication springs from the brain trust at MIT. Not content to deal with simply technological breakthroughs, they consider the effects of technology and policy issues.

Many of these referenced publications occupy small sites; they may even be gone by the time you try to access them. The point is that the Internet has provided fertile ground for electronic publishing. With a world full of readers and viewers to reach, you may be able to succeed with a niche publication that would die an early death on a conventional magazine rack. One of the greatest strengths of electronic publications is the ability to reach a diverse, heterogeneous audience inexpensively no matter where you are located geographically. Shades of McLuhan's Global Village....

Starting an Online Magazine: *mobilis*

Mainstream print magazines generally cost hundreds of thousands of dollars to launch. Online magazines can be started for far less, a factor that has encouraged many new electronic publishers to enter the field with unique, specialized publications. One example is *mobilis: the mobile computing lifestyle magazine.* The premier issue in July 1995 included an extensive interview with Andy Hertzfeld, member of the core design team for the Apple Macintosh. Hertzfeld's new design efforts for General Magic include the Magic Cap operating system, designed for the ultimate portable machines, personal digital assistants. I talked with publisher John Jerney about his startup experiences, and the following sidebar contains a portion of that interview.

INSIGHTS FOR ONLINE PUBLISHING WITH JOHN JERNEY

Q: How did your prior career experiences get you interested in online publishing?

A: One of my goals as an author has always been to have as many people as possible read my material. This is especially true when you consider the amount of work that goes into a typical magazine or book. Online publishing, especially through systems such as the World Wide Web, enables you to reach a potentially massive audience and, through self-publishing, maintain ultimate control of your work. Online publishing does, however, involve trade-offs, including lack of control in terms of demographics. The good news is that while the current audience on the Web or Internet is a subset of all the people you would typically like to reach, it is a motivated audience and, in reference to magazines, has the nice characteristic of being self-qualifying to a degree.

Q: What were your experiences during the startup phase while working out the processes and mastering the tools?

A: I would characterize our early development on the Web as Cro-Magnon with our early tools being Stone Age caliber. Specifically, in developing our earliest prototypes in mid-1994, this meant using the UNIX text editor *vi* on HTML code downloaded from around the Net. Later, as more tools began to appear commercially and on the Net, we have continually increased our sophistication. Emerging from the same culture as the Internet, the World Wide Web has attracted a large number of cyber-citizens willing to assist even the beginning developer. However, as the Web becomes more commercialized, it is increasingly drawing interest from the leading software developers hoping to approach this new opportunity from all angles.

I have no hesitation in recommending using the resources on the Web to construct and publish online information. There are several useful home pages to help guide the motivated developer, and a whole slew of tools to help massage the information into a form worthy of presentation to the outside world. However, don't expect PageMaker style layout just yet.

Q: How have you dealt with the issue of getting compensated for your online works?

A: With so much attention placed on the amount and type of information on the Internet, revenue generation has received secondary consideration at best. However, the business model of an online publication is more important than most people are willing to admit. Hobbyists and interested volunteers will always serve as an important source of information in the online world. However, true widespread interest among both information consumers and producers will depend on a successful model for commercial activity.

mobilis: the mobile computing lifestyle magazine is based on two Internet business models, one proven and the other still evolving. The proven model involves making information freely available to any and all comers. This model clearly doesn't work for all types of information, but it is successful in general. In these terms, online publishing is similar to broadcast radio or television, where advertiser support compensates for free programming. To date, this model of revenue generation remains largely unproven. However, our early experience with *mobilis*—an advertiser supported free publication—is encouraging. By offering compelling, well designed, and original not-to-be-found-elsewhere information, combined with an environment that enables advertisers to experiment with different methods of reaching a worldwide audience, *mobilis* has begun to prove this to be a winning formula.

Q: Any advice for prospective Web publishers?

A: First and foremost, existing and prospective Web publishers should consider the psychology of their readers. Paper magazines and books, while sometimes appearing anachronistic in the new information age, are still very satisfying. And this is because successful paper publications have evolved to match the psychology of the reader. Some of these factors span all audiences; however, some are particular to the publication and type of information presented. Factors common to all readers include consistency, familiarity, and closure. Closure refers to the act of completing an action and moving on to the next item. In paper publications, turning a page or closing the back cover impart important psychological feelings of closure. In addition, readers should always know where they are, where they are headed, and how much is left before finishing. To paraphrase a basic principle of communication theory, with so much material available on the Web, making your publication easy and fun to use is essential to ensure that your signal rises above the collective noise.

You can read the latest issue of *mobilis* at this address: `http://www.volksware.com/mobilis`.

Technical References

Of all the techniques for wasting paper, technical manuals have to rank close to the top. Most of them have a life span of about six months to a year, after which the product they describe—whether hardware or software—has been revised and the manual needs to be completely updated. Hardware and software users typically don't read them; they might glance through looking for warning icons that help them avoid melting down their system cabinet or deleting all the files from a disk volume. After that, the barely opened manuals get dumped on the shelf and maybe consulted once or twice a year. I'm allowed to say these things because I've written a fair number of these paper marvels over the last 16 years, and I'm surrounded by evidence of their rapid obsolescence.

Electronically published versions of technical materials, however, offer significant advantages.

- You can design them as searchable documents, helping users pinpoint the crucial factoid that will reconfigure a piece of hardware or software, or troubleshoot a problem.

- You can design them to be portable; a shareware application downloaded from a BBS can easily come with a nicely formatted manual (using one of the portable document applications discussed in later chapters). You can also use the same facility to provide downloadable documentation for an updated software driver accessed from an online service or BBS.

- You can easily update them as needed and distribute the results in electronic form, whether as a help system, an electronic document, or a searchable database.

- Electronic documents take up far less space than printed references; this can be especially important with shelf-buckling stacks of network documentation. One CD-ROM can replace a couple of hundred pounds of technical manuals.

For these reasons, many hardware and software manufacturers are turning to electronic publishing to support their products. The Society of Technical Communication (STC) reports a sharply increased demand for technical communicators capable of designing online help systems and other forms of electronic publications. Those with the skills to support this move away from paper should fare well in the job market in years to come.

Catalogs

Retailers and mail-order companies have discovered the magic (and utility) of electronic publishing. Spiegel has a Web site (`http://www.spiegel.com/spiegel/`). L.L. Bean has an interactive catalog. Lands' End has produced a catalog for selling clothing on CD-ROM. The Internet is teeming with merchandisers of every size and shape, marketing cheese, cameras, computers, hot sex, books, and fruit baskets in the ether of cyberspace.

Electronic versions of catalogs share the same advantages of other electronic documents. They can contain multimedia elements, they can be inexpensively distributed, they can be easily modified, and they attach the cutting-edge association to the merchandiser that seems to be an important part of maintaining an image. Do interactive catalogs work?

One of the stumbling blocks to fully unleashing the potential of electronic catalogs still seems to be the order process. Digital money has been slow to catch on; many potential customers are reluctant to dispense credit card numbers to lurking bandits hiding in the shrubbery beside the information highway. Encryption techniques for transferring credit card numbers have alleviated much of the danger, but often the electronic catalog order is processed over the telephone in the conventional manner, rather than through the modem. As this changes, expect a dramatic upsurge in the popularity and use of electronically published catalogs.

One example of providing a Web presence but maintaining conventional ordering techniques is shown by Rodale Press. You can browse their collections of health and gardening books through their home page (`http://shopping2000.com/shopping2000/rodale_pre/cfij.html`), but no mechanism yet exists for ordering the books online. To order, you can use their 800 number. Although this is only slightly more difficult than clicking a button to place an order, some customers may lose the impetus to make a purchase if they're drawn away from the computer to do so. Clearly, as the techniques for the secure exchange of credit card numbers are perfected, and buyers gain more confidence in purchasing items interactively, companies like Rodale Press will probably expand their range of purchase options to include impulsive button clickers.

The ability of the Web to provide access to files of all kinds—including graphics and sound files—lets enterprising companies provide samples of their wares. For example, Windham Hill (`http://www.windham.com`) offers downloadable 30-second sound files to allow you to hear the latest music from artists such as Patty Larkin and Michael Hedges. To keep the file sizes manageable, the audio material is downsampled so that the ultimate quality is somewhat less than what you would expect on your audio CD player—roughly equivalent to FM radio quality. This technique, however, gives listeners a chance to preview new musical releases before they buy the CD. Windham Hill still relies on the trusty 800-number approach for processing orders, rather than supporting online purchases.

You can also fill in the holes in your computer library through Macmillan Computer Publishing's Web site (`http://www.mcp.com`) where more than 1100 titles are cataloged. You can search for individual books by author, title, or category. You can read sample chapters from many of the current titles, and, if you like what you read, books can be directly ordered online.

Chicago-based Spiegel's has an Internet presence as well. While not covering their full collection of products, the online catalog offerings let you select anything from clothing to the eclectic frog candlestick holders shown in Figure 2.12.

FIGURE 2.12.

Frog candlestick holders.

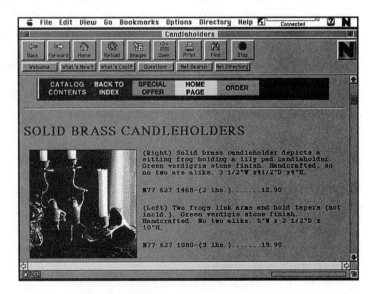

Exploring the Evolution of English

Attica Cybernetics' *Romeo and Juliet*, an interactive foray into one of Shakespeare's best-known works, may be out of place in this book about electronic publishing. As performance art, a play hovers at the outer edges of our earlier definition about what to include under the heading of electronic publishing. I include it because this title illustrates one of the most important aspects of the medium, the ability to transcend linear modes of communication and add layers of meaning around an established level of content. If you understand this technique, you can adapt and apply it to all of the other categories of electronic publishing that we've covered. Done well, it makes interactive works shine much brighter than works confined to printed pages.

The content in this case is the full version of the play, *Romeo and Juliet*. Anyone who has ever suffered through a classroom reading of Shakespeare's work, able to comprehend only every third or fourth word, will appreciate the way that *Romeo and Juliet* on disc lets them get deeper into the work by exploring the underlying meanings—both literal and figurative. With a click, you can get an explanation about a phrase or the underlying meaning of an action or an incomprehensible double meaning associated with a character's utterance. Video inserts offer commentary by articulate scholars of the theatre, including some commentary by Germaine Greer. Other segments show interpretations by actors who have appeared in various roles over more than a generation.

For example, Romeo's line in Act 1, Scene 2 that reads, "Not mad, but bound more than a madman is," might not have immediate relevance. If you click on the phrase "but bound more than a madman is," a popup explanation reveals that it was an Elizabethan custom to keep madmen tied up and shut away (Figure 2.13 shows this section of the play). When you run across a reference to "the death-darting eye of a cockatrice" a popup definition explains that this was a mythological creature, hatched from a cock's egg by a serpent, that could kill you with just a glance in your direction. These kinds of links are abundant throughout the full text of the play, and they quickly orient the reader to the less-understood aspects of the Elizabethan culture and language.

The developers even applied that common device of interactive encyclopedias, the timeline, to contribute to the understanding of the play. You can skim through the contents scene by scene using a timeline, guided by the key events that are highlighted in the middle of the display. Figure 2.14 shows the timeline display.

Shakespeare's influence on the English language is undeniable. Our everyday speech is filled with phrases and expressions that first appeared in his plays. For a fascinating look beneath the surface of a play to the customs and language that gave it life, *Romeo and Juliet* provides a powerful vehicle for investigating the roots of our communication.

FIGURE 2.13.

An excerpt from Act One of Romeo and Juliet.

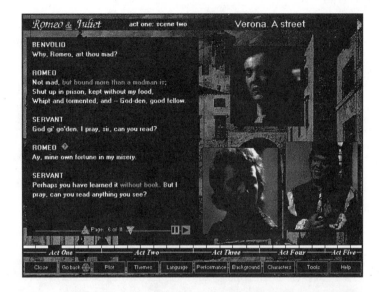

FIGURE 2.14.

Navigating with the timeline.

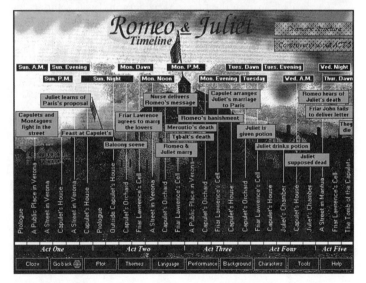

Summary

This chapter only touches on the number and variety of electronically published works that are appearing nearly everywhere you look. Keep your eyes open the next time you're browsing through the magazine rack at your favorite bookstore; I guarantee you'll find some discs mixed in among the issues of *Hot Rodder's Wild Weekends* and *The English Gardener's Fertilizer Monthly*. Notice the kinds of things you see on the Internet as you're performing quantum leaps from site to site. The next time you buy a software application, notice how much of the documentation appears in electronic form as compared to print form. If the handwriting is not already on the wall, you can expect an army of cyberspace poltergeists to be scribbling it there in the next year or two. Although this is depressing in some ways, I'd rather read my news online than to see the last few old-growth forests sacrificed for pulping into newsprint. We've been extravagant with our renewable resources and we can easily do with less paper waste in the form of yearly phone directories, junk mail advertising, 400-page catalogs, glossy 24-page catalogs, outdated product manuals, and similar expendable waste.

I might miss spreading out the Sunday paper on the living room floor so the cats can walk around on it while I'm trying to read, but I'm willing to make that sacrifice. Digital printing is here to stay, so let's work to make it as useful and effective as possible.

POSTSCRIPT

Shortly after writing the previous paragraph, I was wandering around the Web and encountered a site that was displaying one of Walt Kelly's *Pogo* comic strips. After a little more investigation, it turns out that we don't have to give up the comics after all; the comics are alive and well at the Sunday Comics Store (the sponsor of the daily *Pogo* strip; vote for the continuation of *Pogo* at

```
http://turnpike.net/emporium/G/go2pogo.index.html
```

Now if I can just figure out a way to spread out the computer display on the living room carpet...

Terms and Concepts

3

by Lee Purcell

If you're flexing your fingers in anticipation of beginning an electronic publishing project, this chapter defines the terms and concepts that you're most likely to encounter in the electronic publishing realm. Although the terminology surrounding electronic publishing is not as imposing as medical or legal jargon, much of it has been derived from a mixture of computer jargon, print publishing terms, communication terms, photography terms, and ingeniously invented terms that cover things that no one has ever thought of before. The digital domain definitely has its own vocabulary. This chapter offers a conceptual framework to prepare you for the chapters that follow—chapters that offer much detailed, practical information about producing electronic documents.

Going Digital

Information destined for the digital domain must at some point in its existence undergo a conversion. Everything—whether it is a new idea in the head of an author or the text from a centuries-old French manuscript—begins in the familiar analog world with its energy spectrums of waveforms, some of which we see as visible light, others that we interpret as sound. Whether we are dealing with an idea generated by the firing of a few thousand synapses in someone's brain or the more practical issues of how to convert a crumbling manuscript to an electronic publication, our essential goal is the same: to create in digital form some kind of representation of the analog world.

To this purpose, ingenious engineers have created laboratories full of devices to further our aim. Optical scanners can take a page from a book, convert it into a digitized image, and then additional software applications can decipher the text from this mass of character images, a process known as *optical character recognition* (OCR). If you have a sound card in your computer, it most likely contains an audio input line that goes to an analog-to-digital converter—an integrated circuit that samples the incoming sound wave and re-creates it as a string of digital values.

If you're lucky enough to have a video capture board installed in your system, you can digitize both sound and images. The high-speed circuitry in this type of board converts incoming analog data into a series of frames, each frame consisting of an image composed of a matrix of pixels. *Pixels* are picture elements, points of light and color as they appear on a display—each pixel represented by a group of bits (as many as 24 bits for displays that handle millions of colors). This approach to presenting image information digitally is not unlike the technique used by pointillist painters to create complex paintings from thousands of individual dots of color. If you capture enough of these points of color (most video cameras can record a frame in one-thirtieth of a second) and play them back in series, you create a fairly seamless re-creation of motion. The digital re-creation of a scene captured by the camera looks very much like the analog original, if played back fast enough and at high enough resolution.

As the author of an electronic publication, you might use tools to sample, rearrange, and recombine the elements of the analog world. You may link the digital sample of the crickets recorded in your backyard to the Photo CD image of a group of scouts around an evening campfire. The scanned image of an eighteenth-century farming implement may go onto your interactive "History of Agriculture" CD-ROM. A short koto piece obtained from a CD containing royalty-free music may be interwoven into the animated sequence that introduces your electronic news magazine of Japanese culture. Or, you may be directly keying in a series of short reviews of recently released jazz CDs into a program that indexes and links ASCII text.

In all these examples, you must be enter the source material and process it in such a way that it fits into a digital framework. The source material itself may originate either from materials that previously existed in familiar forms, such as books, newspapers, magazines, still photographs, film, video, or audio tape, or may be created as a wholly original work, much as a film is crafted by creating and combining all of the necessary elements. You may sometimes combine these two different types of source materials in the same work: for example, a modern narrative commentary discussing scanned images of paintings from the 17th Century.

The terms applied to these two different approaches of creating electronic publications, *republished* and *prepublished*, are defined in the next section.

Republished and Prepublished Materials

The first question that you face as the developer of an interactive electronic publication is "where does the source material come from?" If you're creating an interactive encyclopedia describing the cultures you invented in your science-fiction trilogy, *The Skylords of the Emerald Ring*, odds are that the source material originated in your head and, if published, you hold the copyright to it. You can freely provide animated illustrations of the Kanacki plants devouring hapless nomads in the Garangee wetlands without ever seeking permissions from anyone else.

However, if your objective is to convert something that has already been published or to use something—such as a piece of music—that is otherwise covered by the broad umbrella of the intellectual property and copyright laws, the process is very different. A large part of the process becomes obtaining the necessary licenses and permissions to use the material and paying any necessary fees or arranging royalties to use materials. After you do this, you can begin using the hardware and software tools to incorporate the materials into your production.

The following two descriptions define the two major divisions of source material for electronic use:

■ *Republished Materials*: These are based on source materials originating from existing works, such as the art collection of a Newport, Rhode Island philanthropist, a collection of old Dobro™ recordings, or a 24-volume encyclopedia. For these kinds of materials, the tasks involved in creating an electronic work may require scanning images, digitizing and processing old recordings, converting text on a printed page to ASCII text, or creating and linking 25,000 computer-based articles. In most cases, someone owns the rights to the material that you want to republish, and negotiating the use of the material becomes one of the tasks essential to completing the electronic version of the work. Works of this type are also sometimes called *repurposed* works.

■ *Prepublished Materials:* These are based on source materials that don't yet exist in a published form. You create the source materials directly—typically on the computer—in a format that can be most easily integrated into an electronic publication. For example, you might create a complex composite image in Fractal Painter to use in a presentation or compose an orchestral piece using a MIDI sequencer to provide mood and atmosphere to an interactive multimedia work. Prepublished materials in most cases can be directly entered into the computer using the most advantageous tools and applications. Because you are authoring directly for the intended medium, you typically don't have to perform conversions of the source material. Using prepublished materials gives you the most flexibility as a developer or author. If the material is original, you also do not have to spend time licensing or negotiating for the use of the material.

The tools and processes associated with republished and prepublished materials tend to be different. In both cases, acquiring the necessary content—whether through obtaining necessary rights or through imaginative design and creation—is probably the most critical part of the process. Once you establish the content, you can put to use the necessary tools to encapsulate it in digital form, as described in the next two sections.

Processing Republished Materials

The republishing process usually requires that you perform conversions of the source material from analog to digital form. Many hardware and software tools exist to simplify the conversion, as shown in Figure 3.1.

Scanning and Optical Character Recognition

As you can see from the diagram in Figure 3.1, the conversion step represents a major part of the process. If the source material exists in the form of a book, journal, or magazine article, the first step in the process is to convert that material to a digital form. The optical scanner is the tool of choice in many applications of this sort. Scanners can take a page of text and graphics and digitize the contents of the page, basically sampling the levels of lightness and darkness of the image on the page and creating an image file where strings of bits represent each dot that composes the image. Scanning color images requires more bits for storage than simple pages of black text on a white background—as much as 24 bits to represent each dot composing the image. Clearly, images of this sort require a significant amount of storage space; 8½×11-inch full-color images may take more than 20MB of storage. Scanner software typically lets you select the resolution of the scanning operation or allows you to scan color images as grayscale or black and white images. You may want to perform some calculations early in a project to determine how much storage space to devote to images (which will help determine the appropriate resolution for scanning).

FIGURE 3.1.

Computer components transform analog sources to digital files for republished materials.

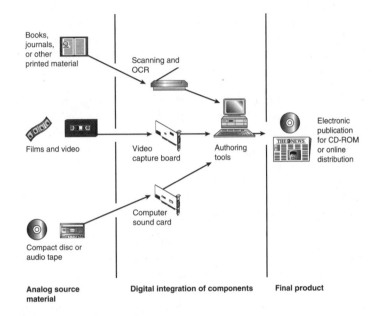

Although this level of image quality may be appropriate if you are presenting scanned photographs of famous paintings, it makes less sense for pages of text. In fact, the first thing you may want to do with a scanned page of text from a book or journal is to convert it to ASCII format, where each character is represented by a seven-bit code, making the storage requirements much more compact. Converting to ASCII formatted text is also a necessary requirement if you are going to place text within a search and retrieval program or infobase; this enables the computer to perform searches on individual words and phrases.

Many scanners include software programs to provide optical character recognition. You can also individually purchase software applications for this purpose (in many cases, more effective programs than those bundled with scanner hardware). OCR programs vary greatly in their accuracy and effectiveness. In almost all cases, you need to further process the converted text to clean up misinterpreted characters. Spell check programs can be helpful in this regard; because most word processing programs directly import ASCII text, you can open the converted text file and quickly perform a spell check to clean up most mistakes. Some OCR applications also contain the built-in intelligence to recognize words and combinations of words and perform the equivalent to a spell check during the conversion process. However, despite improvements in recognition algorithms, someone will inevitably need to proof the results of the conversion to make sure that the converted text makes sense in human terms (not only in machine terms).

> **NOTE**
>
> Most OCR applications let you save the converted text in the word processor format of your choice (Word, WordPerfect, straight ASCII, and so on), so file extensions may vary. Check the software package to make sure the application supports your word processor.

Optical character recognition will not work in all situations. You may be inputting pages that have too many graphic elements or that have numerous font changes that succeed in bewildering the OCR engine. When you encounter situations of this sort (which you'll quickly discover by the poor recognition rate when you initially try to read a page), your only choice may be to input the text directly by retyping it into a word processing program or editor. Obviously, if you're working on republishing an electronic version of 5,000 pages of source material, rekeying this text will represent a substantial part of the work involved, and it should be factored into any estimates for the project.

Another factor to consider: if you plan on using high-quality images extracted from republished material, don't count on using a scanner to obtain them. Although a scanner can do a reasonable job inputting line drawings (which are basically continuous tone images), the photographs that appear in books and magazines have been converted to half-tone images. Half-tones consist of patterns of dots created by a photographic (or computer) process to prepare an image or photograph for printing. Half-tones make notoriously poor sources for quality images—when you scan in the dot patterns you will frequently encounter clashes from the scanning technique that result in unwanted combinations of dots (swirls and halos and other unanticipated effects known as *moiré patterns*). If you need to use images in your electronic publication, try to obtain photographs of the original source material and scan the photographs directly. Photographs that have already been digitized can also be obtained in the form of Photo CD libraries that your authoring application can often directly import. Photo CD images offer a choice of resolutions, easy manipulation by your image processing applications (such as Adobe Photoshop or Fractal Painter), and convenient storage on compact disc for easy access.

> **CAUTION**
>
> Although many forms of visual art have been reprinted in individual copies or limited edition prints that are available in art galleries and so on, many are lithographic prints. Most lithographic prints have been created from four-color separations (if you look at the print through a magnifying glass, you can see the individual dots in cyan, magenta, yellow, and black). These scan badly. For scanning purposes, it's best to work from continuous tone images, such as photographs or original paintings.

Video Capture Techniques

If the demands and storage requirements of optically scanned material seem excessive, you will be completely astounded by how quickly video captures can consume all of your available hard disk space. To do justice to video captures, you need a capable digitizer installed in your computer system, a specialized board that can convert a stream of incoming video data into a series of digitized frames for use on the computer. Because the stream of data being digitized needs to be smoothly and continuously written to hard disk, you may want to configure your system with a special type of hard disk drive, known as an AV drive (for audio visual). AV drives can accept data at very rapid rates, and they also don't interrupt write operations for a process known as thermal calibration. Thermal calibration cycles can cause dropouts of video (as frames are missed) or blips (when you are doing audio recording). AV drives are a bit more expensive than normal hard disk drives but are recommended if you are going to do this type of work.

If you must reprocess existing film or video material for your electronic publication, you will probably need a fairly substantial upgrade of your equipment to support the hardware and software needed for this effort. Republishing film—if your source material has not been released on a video cassette—and converting it to digital format requires even more specialized equipment that is beyond the scope of this book. If you are seeking to convert material on film, it's recommended that you use the services of a processing house equipped for converting film. This might be helpful if you are creating an electronic documentary of your hometown and have solicited 8mm home movies of local parades and civic events from friends and neighbors. You can hand this material over to a service and get back a video cassette that you can then input into the computer. In most cases, however, works that have been released on film have already been converted to video format; you can directly input it into an installed video capture board (as long as you have the necessary rights). Several organizations and companies offer video clips of documentary or historical material that you can use in an electronic publication, but the fees for this kind of material are often steep.

If you have an installed video capture board, inputting video material is quite easy. You connect the output line from your camcorder or VCR to the input line of the video capture board, activate the software that does the recording, and start capturing. Applications, such as Adobe Premiere, can edit the video files, enabling you to cut and paste material, add special effects, add voice-over narration, and mix in animated sequences. These kinds of cinema-inspired creations can add a good deal of interest to an electronic publication, but they are time-consuming to create, require special software to play back on most platforms, and occupy a good deal of storage space. Although video sequences are appropriate for CD-ROM distribution—because of their ample storage—they often are excessive for productions planned for online distribution. When using online applications, users generally download the video material first before viewing. Current data transfer rates for online access can't support the rapid flow of data necessary to directly display video sequences.

Although video material can be a tasteful enhancement to an electronic publication, it clearly takes more resources and expertise to create this kind of material. For many types of applications, it isn't really necessary. Use your judgment when taking this step, and be sure to consider the extra expense and processing power it requires.

Sound Digitization

Your source material for sound may already exist on compact disc or audio cassette. For example, if you're actually creating a documentary of your hometown you may have access to a library of audio cassettes that contain interviews conducted by the local historical society. This audio material, consisting of the recollections of the town's oldest residents, can be successfully used as a background to period photographs (for example, a woman who was a little girl during the city hall's construction may remember the ceremony when the building opened while the bandstand in the park reverberated with brassy, triumphant music). To input this kind of material, you need a sound board installed in your computer that has the capability to sample and digitize incoming sound. Even inexpensive boards of this type can usually sample sound at CD-quality rates (44.1kHz), making this an excellent means of producing very high-quality sound from analog source material. You can further process files you create by this technique using a number of different tools that perform waveform editing—a digital replacement of the tedious cutting block and tape approach used for editing reel-to-reel tapes in days past. Using these digital tools, you can easily combine a sound clip of the woman's city hall memories with the music of a Sousa march and play the two as a digitized photograph of the city hall is displayed on-screen. Digital tools offer a greater degree of freedom when composing multimedia works than their analog predecessors.

If your source material exists on compact disc, it is already in a digital format. You could import it into a production by taking the audio outputs of your CD player and inputting them into a sound card, but you introduce some noise in the process of doing this. The sound first gets converted from digital format back to analog, and then the analog input is reprocessed into digital format again. To sidestep this interim conversion, you can use a tool from Optical Media International called Disc-to-Disk that uses your computer's SCSI bus to directly copy the digital sound information to your hard disk for further editing.

Copyright considerations are particularly important for the use of music or other recorded sound in a production. Just because you enjoy the latest release from Hootie and the Blowfish doesn't mean you can slip it in as background music in your multimedia work. If you need music for background use, you can find numerous sources of quality royalty-free music clips, many of them available on compact disc. If you have a bit of musical ability, you can also create your own musical backdrops using some of the newest computer tools, as described in the next section.

Processing Prepublished Materials

When you are using prepublished materials, you have at your disposal the full range of tools available in the digital environment to turn your imagination loose and create an engaging and informative electronic work. In many ways, working in this manner is the most effective means of producing an electronic publication, because you are generally not as concerned with the many complexities of converting materials from analog to digital form—you can work directly with tools that produce the source files that your authoring package uses to integrate the content. Figure 3.2 illustrates some of the possible paths you can follow for this kind of creation.

FIGURE 3.2.

Processing prepublished materials.

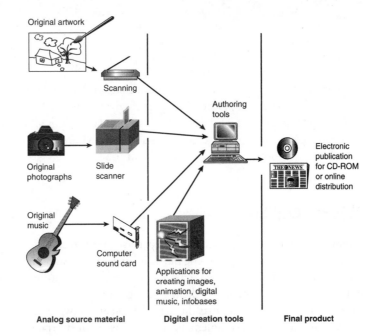

Original artwork

Scanning

Authoring tools

Original photographs

Slide scanner

Electronic publication for CD-ROM or online distribution

Original music

Computer sound card

Applications for creating images, animation, digital music, infobases

Analog source material   **Digital creation tools**   **Final product**

Including Original Artwork

As you can see from Figure 3.2, working with prepublished materials doesn't totally eliminate the analog-to-digital conversion process, because in a number of cases the unpublished source material may exist in conventional forms. For example, you may not have mastered the intricacies of Adobe Illustrator or Fractal Painter, but you may be an accomplished watercolor artist. Your painting of Half Dome in Yosemite might serve as an effective introductory image for an electronic publication describing (and mapping) the best hiking trails on the West coast. By simply scanning the watercolor you could convert it into the necessary digitized image to incorporate into your production.

Using Your Own Photography

You can include other creative forms of expression, such as photography or musical composition, in this process as well. If you have skill as a photographer, your prints or slides can be digitized and used as images in an electronic book. The level of resolution of desktop scanners has come very close to the degree of quality that commercial publishers require. You may not have the money to spend two or three thousand dollars on a 35mm slide scanner, but you can have the next best thing.

> **TIP**
>
> The next time you process a roll of film, request that the photographic images be processed onto Photo CD. If the film is put on Photo CD at the time the film is processed, images can be added to a Photo CD for less than $1.00 each. Once on Photo CD, you can access and use these images in many different authoring applications. The film developer provides the CD for the first roll developed; it's a recordable CD, and you can bring it back to have additional sessions added up to somewhere around 100 images. Playback requires a CD-ROM drive capable of reading multisession formats (most do these days).

Musical Additions

Your musical talents can provide an inexpensive means of adding the background music to an electronic publication. Because the music is intended to establish a mood or set the tone of an interactive work, it doesn't need to be as complex or dominating as a musical piece designed to hold someone's attention or get them dancing. In fact, you usually want the music to establish a texture or feeling that supports the material you are showing on the computer display, and to do this the music must complement the work without overpowering it. A few simple guitar arpeggios or a haunting melody on a flute might be simple to compose and perform, but can add an extra depth to your electronic publication.

The key addition to your system is the computer sound card. You can use any board that will sample at a 44.1kHz rate. If you're serious about the music end of production, you will also probably want to invest in some additional equipment: a mixer board, Digital Audio Tape (DAT) drive, and a high-quality microphone. But using the newer digital tools, you can accomplish an amazing amount of work with very simple equipment. For example, many of the waveform editing packages that let you manipulate the sound that you record from your sound card can enhance a piece of music or voice by adding several different types of reverb, phase-shifting, tempo changing, and other special effects. With a minimum of gear, you can achieve true professional quality results. Digital tools may not make you a musician, but they can help you compose and record music in ways that have never been possible before.

For more insights into the art and science of creating music on the computer, *Becoming a Computer Musician*, by Jeff Bowen (Sams Publishing) offers practical advice on using digital music tools.

Working in the Digital Domain

If you are developing your source material using the native tools of the computer—image processors, animation applications, hypertext editors, infobase software, tone generators, and so on—you have a remarkable degree of flexibility and power at your disposal. These are the kinds of tools that are covered in this book to explain the creative ways you can produce information and entertain an audience. Mastery of the tools is important; many of these can require a significant investment of time and energy to use. However, you gain the benefit of being able to integrate any of your creations into a wide variety of media.

The kinds of tools that perform these tasks and the concepts surrounding them are defined and discussed in the following sections.

Converting 2D Images to 3D Images

A sheet of paper covered with printed characters is limited to two dimensions: length and width. You can turn it upside down, read the characters from bottom to top or right to left or view it reversed through a mirror, and you still can't escape the basic limitations of this two-dimensional framework. Bind a few hundred of these sheets together and you've added an additional dimension, but you still view the pages one at a time in a two-dimensional way.

People are very accustomed to presenting information in this type of a medium, and in fact, many ways have been found to compensate for the fixed organization of books. The index was a revolutionary way to provide pointers to individual pages, providing quick access to the subject matter contained within any type of published work. A reference book can be more than 1,000 pages long, but using a skillfully designed index, you can find a topic in a matter of seconds.

Cross references offer another approach to expanding the fixed linear progression created by two-dimensional sheets bound together in a book or reference. Suddenly, you can jump out of the confines of one book to refer to another book, or from one section of a reference to an appendix or glossary. Both index entries and cross references are pointers or links to information contained in a published work; they serve as locators guiding you through a maze of information to your ultimate destination: a detail or subject that is the object of your search. Before electronic publishing, indexes and cross references were the best way to try to provide three-dimensional access to a two-dimensional medium.

Grouping and organizing a body of work by the terms and subjects it contains—that is, creating an index—is not a trivial task. Professional societies of indexers have been formed in the United States and Great Britain to promote and support the unique set of skills and abilities necessary to accomplish high-caliber indexing. One of the unfortunate side effects of the desktop publishing revolution has been the devaluing of the importance of indexing. Even though many computer tools can automate the job of indexing, few skilled practitioners using the tools really know how to do the job correctly. The result is poorly designed indexes. Indexes in computer manuals often frustrate the user and don't provide necessary links and pointers to the subject matter, particularly those that have been generated by an algorithm without human guidance.

Ways of Linking Information Electronically

The essential problem of finding information in a dense body of work, or a group of related works, or 100,000 cataloged works is one area in which electronic publishing has surpassed conventional indexes and cross references a thousand-fold. Electronic publishing has also added a third dimension to the printed page—any given page can contain a link to any one of millions of other pages. A document on the World Wide Web can contain a connection between a page being viewed from a server in Palo Alto, California to another page on a server stored in Cairo, Egypt. A CD-ROM containing thousands of pages of Novell's technical references on NetWare 4 can be accessed through a single table of contents that contains links to all of the subjects on disc. As an author of an electronically published work, you have the tools to create the links that correlate and connect a vast body of printed and multimedia material.

> **NOTE**
>
> Links created between corresponding text entries are called *hypertext* links. Links created between other elements, such as an icon that plays a short video clip, are called *hypermedia* links. As another variation, you'll sometimes see any link that performs this kind of action called a *hyperlink*.

The concepts that made hypertext and hypermedia possible originated in the fertile mind of Ted Nelson more than 30 years ago. The power behind these ideas has not yet been fully realized, but the source of this power supplies much of the impetus for electronic publishing. Figure 3.3 illustrates the idea of links between pages.

FIGURE 3.3.

Hypertext links can connect words and phrases in a single document, or links can form a bridge to other documents.

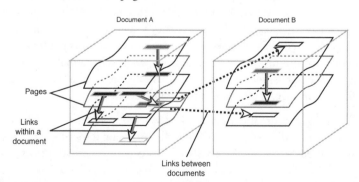

The term *interactivity* is an inescapable and omnipresent part of electronic publishing. Interactivity describes the ability to control the course of a presentation. Obviously, hyperlinks provide one means of navigating through a body of material by jumping from point to point to explore related ideas. The broader term *user interface* is generally thought of as the mechanism for controlling movement within an electronic document (or application). An interface facilitates interactivity; it's the primary means by which readers or viewers guide the direction of their inquiries—the interface includes all those control devices that let you navigate through a work. A menu is one system, a system that most computer users are familiar with, but not a particularly imaginative approach to the problem.

New Approaches to Interfaces

An interface is something that not only overlays individual applications, it can also be a window to an immense matrix of ideas and data, such as what you can find on the Internet. By its design, the interface can give shape and meaning to structures that are dense and otherwise difficult to fathom. For instance, for years there have been many tools for accessing resources on the Internet, but most of these used to be text-based tools. The burden was on the user to perceive the underlying structure and discover how to locate information within the larger structure of the network, a collection of thousands of servers, each with its own address and each with a different assortment of software tools and utilities. This approach discouraged many users who began to feel as though the effort required to navigate through this imposing morass was greater than the perceived benefit. The interface, in many cases just a blinking cursor on the command line, confused and wore them out. This situation changed dramatically with the increased popularity of the World Wide Web.

For years, many so-called computer experts thought that graphical interfaces were a waste of computer processing power. Why spend valuable processing cycles on color displays and icons and images, when the command line lets you directly and succinctly control the operation of the computer? Many stoic UNIX users still feel that way and sneer at anyone who doesn't relish memorizing pages full of command sequences. The Macintosh with its graphically based user interface opened some eyes, both literally and metaphorically. People who had spurned earlier computers were attracted to the Macintosh and could quickly master its interface and do useful work through it.

A similar evolution has taken place with the Internet. Displaying graphics not only takes a good deal of processing power, but—if you're receiving those graphics through a modem—it can take an enormous amount of connect time to receive them. The incredible improvements in the size and speed of modems changed this situation. Once a 9,600 baud modem was a huge rack-mounted device that cost thousands of dollars; now a 14,400 baud modem can fit within a PCMCIA card (about the size of a credit card) with room to spare. Suddenly it became possible to quickly and economically supply graphics to users connected to networks and services. The World Wide Web does just that; it gives to users accessing a network environment the graphical orientation familiar to Macintosh users.

Another term you will encounter in this book is World Wide Web browser, usually shortened to *Web browser*. Browsers interpret text and graphics created in a markup language as formatted pages of information with richly colored embedded images. The markup language itself is simply a method of expanding ASCII text blocks to include font variety, intricate page layouts, hypertext links to other areas, and supporting images. The author creates these document features by placing bracketed codes throughout the text. Generally, you use the HyperText Markup Language (HTML) to prepare text, graphics, and links to be viewed by a Web browser. For more information on HTML, see Chapter 20, "Using HTML."

Most Web browsers feature buttons that let you move forward and backward through a sequence of pages. You can also click a button to return to a designated Home page (the starting point for a Web sequence) or create markers that enable you to jump to specified pages. You can create your own personalized path through a sequence of pages; in a way, you can consider this a customizable interface.

Figure 3.4 shows a popular and capable Web browser called Netscape. The menu bar along the top of the window provides the basic navigational controls.

FIGURE 3.4.

A typical view from a Web browser.

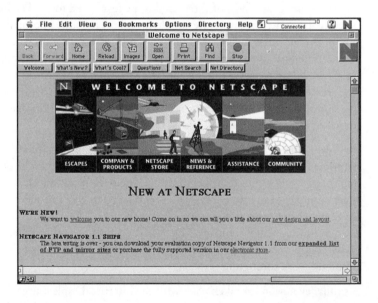

Reva Basch specializes in searching for information for clients on the Internet and other online services; her book, *Secrets of the Super Searchers*, reveals how to find what you're looking for in cyberspace. In the May 1995 issue of *Wired* magazine, she was asked what the Internet needs to make it more navigable. She replied: "There are some pretty powerful text-analysis engines out there that are being worked on. But my real dream would be a Netwide, completely up-to-date, hierarchically arranged subject indexing capability that is as sophisticated as what you find in the commercial databases. I'm not holding my breath for that. One thing that interests me is the way home pages on the World Wide Web are being used to link information. In my business, we've been asking for hypertext links to related documents for years, and it hasn't happened, except on a very limited level. And, of course, that's what the World Wide Web is all about."

Designing an Interface

As the author of an electronic publication, you select those elements—the entry points—that enable the reader or viewer to access the content. Your interface design will either enhance and clarify the information you present or it will make using the information and navigating through it more difficult. Tips and guidelines for designing useable interfaces appear throughout this book.

In a November 1993 article in *New Media* magazine, Ted Nelson characterized successful interactivity in this way: "The true interactive design is unobtrusive and clear. My favorite interactive system is a globe. A globe is not 'friendly.' A globe does not say 'Good morning, we're going to have fun today, what's your name?' It just sits there, and you learn its workings instantly, turning it and moving closer or farther away. You are not conscious of an interface." If you take a single point from this section, remember this: the less the user is conscious of the interface, the more successful you've been at your authoring tasks.

Another way of looking at interface design is to try to find ways to adapt the interface to human needs, instead of trying to force the human to adapt to the interface. Brenda Laurel, interface researcher and author of *Computers As Theatre*, described it this way in the May 31, 1993 issue of *MicroTimes* magazine: "What I'm saying is that if we want to design good interfaces that really are about global interface, and not just about global access for male business people, or people with resources, or people who speak English, or whatever, then we have to give up the idea of a universal interface. We have to think about interfaces as clay, or things that are soft, that you imprint by working with them, that are dynamic, that change as you change, that change as the subculture of which you are a member changes, etc."

Many of the tools discussed in this book are flexible enough to construct interfaces that are more accommodating to readers with different cultural backgrounds and different points of view. It's the role of the designer, or author, to find techniques for shaping electronic presentations to satisfy this goal. The computer has also proven itself as an ideal means for letting physically challenged individuals communicate, learn new skills, and express themselves creatively using a variety of computer tools. With a bit of imagination, electronic publishing can extend its reach and its audience by designing interfaces to enable access for those whose physical dexterity or mobility limitations prevent easy use of a mouse or keyboard.

Essential Traits of Authoring

Authoring is a term that has been broadened to include so many areas that is has almost lost all meaning. In simplest terms, authoring is the process of constructing an electronic document by assembling and compiling all the necessary elements. This may include acquiring information for the content (from databases, scanned documents, or converted files), as well as writing original material for electronic presentation. It also includes the process of establishing the links and framework that compose an electronic publication.

Authoring involves a wide variety of software tools and applications, including search and retrieval programs, indexing software, word processors and editors, compilers, graphics arts packages, rendering and modeling tools, presentation software, multimedia development tools, animation software, help system design tools, scripting languages, and more. The scope of authoring has expanded to include the many different tasks that are all a part of creating a complex interactive document. The skills to operate all of these different applications are rarely found in one person; this is why a successful electronic book often requires several persons, each with a different set of skills, to create the work.

> **CAUTION**
>
> If you see a package identified as an "authoring application" on the software store shelf, read the fine print before you buy it. Some of these packages may do nothing more than construct slide shows of computer graphics, maybe with a feature for adding voice-over narration to accompany the slides. Other packages may put the power of a multifaceted film company on your desktop, with features for editing video material, mixing complex sounds, creating animations in several different ways, and blending together every conceivable multimedia component. Your goal may be to provide access to information within a database or lengthy computer text, in which case your authoring tool doesn't need multimedia effects so much as a good search and retrieval engine.

The differences in fundamental tools of this sort are discussed later in this chapter in the section "The Cornerstones of Electronic Publishing."

A Working Definition of Multimedia

One of the reasons why multimedia is so hard to define is that it's changing daily. An easy way to look at it is that multimedia commingles in a cohesive manner all of the elements a computer is capable of presenting. This includes text, spoken voice, video, animated graphics, static illustrations, high-resolution photography, sound effects, or music—all linked together interactively. The *cohesive* descriptor hints at the fact that if the elements are not linked in an accessible and understandable way, the interactivity will be wasted. As you probably already know, there are as many bad examples of multimedia as there are good ones. The chapters that follow provide many examples of how to characterize quality interactive multimedia, and what separates the good from the bad.

At the simplest end of the multimedia spectrum, you'll find text-based materials that may include color graphics or sound effects. Even simple multimedia enhancements can expand the power and scope of an electronic publication in far-reaching ways.

More elaborate forms of multimedia increase the degree of interactivity and generally expand the viewer's sensory involvement. Modern flight simulator programs link control interfaces that mimic those you might find in an aircraft—including control yokes and rudder pedals—and offer real-time views of the passing landscapes through the cockpit windshield, as well as sound effects. Multimedia of this type tries to surround the participant with as many aspects of the experience as possible. Multimedia presentations that let you interactively tour an art museum may let you ask a guide questions or put your nose right up against a painting by zooming in for a close-up view.

The outer limits of multimedia exist in the virtual reality realm where the sensory involvement is so great that—in the case of some virtual reality headsets—participants suffer from motion sickness. (The *Wired* "Jargon Watch" column applied the term *Barfogenesis* to this phenomenon.) The potential in this arena is enormous, particularly as computers and their operators become more adept at re-creating the sounds and sights of the physical world. The production staff of the film *Jurassic Park* managed to convincingly bring to life dinosaurs whose habits and movements were largely open to speculation. The digital revolution provides tools to not only re-create experiences, but to imaginatively project our knowledge into re-creations of the past and the future.

Electronic publishing can include any of the elements of multimedia, but for our purpose these elements are included as extensions of the two-dimensional printed page rather than all encompassing virtual-reality experiences. Your electronic book describing the wildlife of New York City might include audio clips of chattering gray squirrels or videos of flocks of pigeons knocking the hats off tourists. If you try to extend this experience to present a three-dimensional interactive journey through Central Park, you'll need more than just electronic publishing tools (and you've ventured beyond the scope of this book).

The Cornerstones of Electronic Publishing

Before delving into the descriptions of the processes involved in creating electronic publications, you might find it useful to look at the primary applications you'll use in this field and their prospective uses. In all of these cases, the applications and their electronic output can be directed to CD-ROM, network, or online service distribution.

Electronic publishing divides into the following areas:

- **Online Help Systems:** Although everyone might not consider this to be a mainstream electronic publishing application, the arguments for including it are convincing. One of the criteria for widespread distribution of an electronic document is that the tools for reading it are easily available. Anyone with an installed copy of Microsoft

Windows (now close to half the population of the civilized world, according to some estimates) can read files in the Windows help system format. WinHelp files can be large, they can be linked to other help files, they can contain interactive graphics and other multimedia elements, and the tools to create them are easily available. In fact, if you have a word processor (such as Word for Windows) that can create Rich Text Format (RTF) files, you have the essential application for creating a Windows help file. (Beyond this, you also need a version of the help compiler for converting .RTF source files into readable help files.) Because of the ease of creating and using help files in this format, many individuals and companies distribute technical and creative works as help files, both on the Internet and through other online services.

Online help systems are increasingly replacing printed documentation for many computer products, and this trend promises to continue. The same interactive techniques that apply to other kinds of electronic documents can be used within a help system to achieve communication goals, letting the reader quickly access product information, procedures for use, and other information.

- **Portable Document Formats:** To gain the benefits of typographical variety, embedded graphics, and hyperlink navigation, portable document creation tools, such as Adobe Acrobat and WordPerfect Envoy, provide a vehicle for distributed electronic publications of many types. These types of tools often simplify creation by enabling you to "print to disk," producing a file containing the document contents in a form that users can view through a low-cost or free reader. Because documents retain their formatting and can appear on many different platforms, these tools greatly unify the distribution of electronically published works. Techniques for creating links and alternative display formats require skills beyond just printing to disk, but in most cases the required procedures are not very complex. Other entries in this field include Common Ground (Common Ground Software, Inc.) and Replica (Farallon).

- **Hypertext Tools:** The next step up the scale of complexity includes tools for creating electronic documents with extensive hypertext linking and search mechanisms. Most of these are far more intricate and also more capable than products in the portable document class. Many also include sophisticated indexing and database constructs that enable access to enormous amounts of information. Mastery of these kinds of applications often requires considerable time and training, but the results can be impressive in situations where an organization needs to distribute data rapidly across networks and on CD-ROM.

Folio Corporation's Folio VIEWS Infobase fits in this category, as does HyperWriter for Windows by Ntergaid, Inc. These packages, as well as other similar applications, offer versions scaled from simple to elaborate. Prices for different capability versions also scale upward, from $200 or so for simple versions to $3,995 and up for professional-level products.

■ **Standard Generalized Markup Language (SGML):** Born out of hundreds of hours of committee discussions, SGML represents a means of distributing ASCII-based text in a platform-independent format. The idea is to free the contents of a document from the actual presentation of it (though related applications, called transformers, can handle presentation). SGML documents can also include references to external items, such as a bitmapped image. Producing SGML documents by manual means, which consists of inserting bracketed codes within a body of text, can be a demanding (and error-prone) pursuit. Fortunately, a number of applications streamline and standardize the process, such as ArborText's Adept Editor and SoftQuad's Author/Editor.

In the past, SGML has found its main support in the military and giant corporations, but it is gaining popularity in all segments of business, education, and government. HTML, the basis of presenting platform-independent information on the Internet, is an offshoot of SGML. For more information, see Chapter 21, "Inside SGML."

■ **HyperText Markup Language (HTML):** If you've used a Web browser, you've been exposed to HTML; HTML is a method of presenting information on the World Wide Web. This language makes extensive use of hypertext linking, and links can embrace more than just other sections of a document. An embedded link in an HTML document can jump to an entirely different location, identified using the Universal Resource Locator (URL) addresses that are the prevailing identifiers on the World Wide Web.

HTML is a subset of SGML, which means to create HTML documents, you must tag text files with codes that signify the characteristics and navigational structure of the document. A number of applications have been developed to assist in this process, including SoftQuad's HoTMetaL Pro and Brooklyn North Software Works' HTML Assistant Pro. HTML has demonstrated widespread practical applications. Web use of HTML dwarfs other specialized applications of the SGML standard.

Summary

By now, you should have a good idea of the tools that can be found in a typical electronic publisher's toolkit and the way those tools are commonly used. The remainder of Part I expands the concepts and terms introduced in this chapter and applies them to the real-world environment. All of this is leading toward giving you the hands-on experience necessary to create your own electronically published masterpieces.

Media Aspects

4

by Lee Purcell

Unlike conventionally printed materials that you can hold in your hand, electronically published works in their native form are useless to you. As bits, they have no substance and no form. You can't fill your pocket with the bits composing the latest Robert Parker mystery and take them to the beach to read like you can take a paperback book. An electronic version of a book has to be delivered to you through some kind of media link. You could bring the Parker novel to the beach stored inside a Newton MessagePad and, if you could keep the sand out of the PCMCIA slot and keep the sun shining on the display at a readable angle, you could read it like a paperback. But the MessagePad has to do some work to turn the bits into the familiar words from which we construct ideas and weave stories.

The characteristic that gives electronic publishing its greatest strength—the capability of being delivered over a variety of media in swift, weightless form—also represents one of the drawbacks. You have to construct some method of delivery using some kind of hardware to access and view the electronic documents. Without the hardware, you can't see it or use it or do anything with it; the bits have to be delivered to you and translated from machine-readable formats to human-readable shapes. To do this, we rely on different forms of media. If we are on familiar terms with computers, we don't think too much about the inconvenience of having to use hardware to view electronic documents; in the same way that nearly everyone has his or her own automobile, nearly everyone has access to the computer hardware to view and use these documents.

However, the form of media we use to distribute an electronic document becomes an important consideration in determining the nature of the audience. With their universal file structure, inexpensive cost, and large capacity, CD-ROMs have (justifiably) become the darlings of cross-platform data distribution. The file system adopted for CD-ROM use and used by most developers, ISO 9660, successfully puts CD-ROMs on the desktops of UNIX, DOS, Windows, OS/2, and Macintosh users; this unified file system (discussed in more detail in Part III of this book, "Publishing on CD-ROMs") is one of the most compelling reasons for the rising popularity of CD-ROMs. One of the other reasons is the widespread availability of CD-ROM players (or drives or readers, whatever your favorite terminology). You don't need to make a major investment ($150 to $200 for a double-speed CD-ROM drive) to be able to access electronic materials on CD-ROM. As discussed later in this chapter, the cost per megabyte for data on CD-ROM is lower than any other form of distribution medium.

CD-ROMs capture bits at a particular moment of time; the information contained on them becomes outdated, and in this respect the online approaches to delivering electronic publications are far more timely. You can update an electronic document on a Bulletin Board System (BBS), online service, or on the network in an instant. The Internet continues to evolve as a universal, online library that stretches anywhere you can uncoil a telephone wire, and, in the case of wireless communications, some places where you can't. With the Internet, however, unless you are blessed with a free account through an educational institution or other organization, you pay for your connect time. Downloading the amount of information equivalent to a single CD-ROM can take many hours (depending on the data transfer rate of your online connection, between 50 to 150 hours, typically). The section titled "Advantages of CD-ROM Distribution" later in this chapter discusses this issue further.

A hybrid media has arisen out of the need for combining large quantities of information (as delivered by CD-ROM) and up-to-the-minute information (as provided by online delivery). Some journals and services offer CD-ROMs that rely on content that you can download from a network or service, such as CompuServe or the Internet. The CD-ROM provides the graphics, sound, user interface, search or game engine, and some of the content. You can then use links in the material to download additional material and store it on hard disk. The new information becomes an extension of what the CD-ROM originally contained. This approach has even been applied to artistic works. For example, the Voyager CD-ROM title *Puppet Motel*, created by Laurie Anderson and huang hsin-chien, contains a number of interactive vignettes, musical interludes, stories, 3D animated art pieces, and other mind-stimulating multimedia snippets. Once you've viewed all the material on the CD-ROM, you can link to a special Web site and download additions and extensions to the title. This hybrid approach to presenting information promises to become an increasingly important means for dealing with the advantages and disadvantages of each media type.

This chapter explores the media considerations you will face while planning to produce an electronic publication for use by others.

Publishing on Compact Disc

Design by committee usually results in flawed, heavily diluted designs that serve no single purpose very well. One noteworthy exception to that principle is the CD-ROM. Born out of Sony's experimentation into techniques for recording audio information to tape (resulting in the DAT drive), each step in CD-ROM development and evolution has shown remarkable perception both to the needs of maintaining compatibility with past standards and to the demands of accommodating storage of more than just audio data. The original compact disc standard (Red Book) was extended to include data (Yellow Book) and then extended again to include different types of data, such as video and photographic images (Green Book and White Book, respectively). Each time a change or addition to the CD-ROM standard was contemplated, a committee meeting was called—the conference table invariably included all the major hardware and software players.

The collective decisions of the various hardware and software players resulted in a single media that can bridge a number of computer platforms, each with its respective file systems. This foresight makes it possible to place an audio CD into any standard CD-ROM drive and (with the proper drivers) play back music as easily as you'd play it on the component CD player connected to your stereo system. It also makes it possible to format a CD-ROM using the ISO 9660 standard and play the mastered disc back on a Sun SPARCstation, Macintosh Quadra, Compaq Prolinea, or just about any other system you can suggest. Try this trick with a SyQuest cartridge or magneto-optical cartridge and you'll realize what a giant universal step forward this really is.

Publishing on CD-ROM used to be a major event. Only a couple of years ago, desktop CD recording systems were too expensive ($20,000 and up) and too trouble-prone to be of much use in the corporate environment. If you needed to produce a CD-ROM through a replication facility, you could expect to pay thousands of dollars for the setup charges and two or three dollars per disc for the replication (unless your quantities were in the tens of thousands, which could bring the costs down closer to $1.00).

In the last few months, however, desktop CD recording has arrived. The hardware has improved, with lightweight, reliable, inexpensive recorders available from competent manufacturers, such as Sony, Ricoh, Yamaha, and Kodak, and the software has become manageable as well. Modern CD mastering applications reduce the need to grapple with the low-level details of disc formatting; some of these applications now resemble backup or archiving utilities in their simplicity. In fact, recordable CD is rapidly replacing tape backup systems for corporate and government uses. Recordable CD provides random access to data; tape does not. Recordable CD uses a single standard format (CD-ROM), whereas tape systems use many different formats. Recordable CD has a media life of approximately 100 years; tapes last about five years before the signal levels of the magnetically recorded data begin to diminish significantly.

Producing materials for CD-ROM also offers a good deal of flexibility to electronic publishers. If you don't want to invest in your own recordable CD equipment, you can take a digital audio tape (or other removable media) containing the files for replication to a service that specializes in producing short-run compact discs (from 1 to 100 or so). Alternatively, you can take a tape or CD-ROM one-off (a single recorded CD-R disc) to a large-volume replicator to run hundreds or thousands of copies. Figure 4.1 shows the possible paths in creating an electronic publication on CD-ROM.

FIGURE 4.1.

Depending on whether you're using in-house or outside production services, the CD-recordable process can take several different directions. Courtesy of Plasmon Data, Inc.

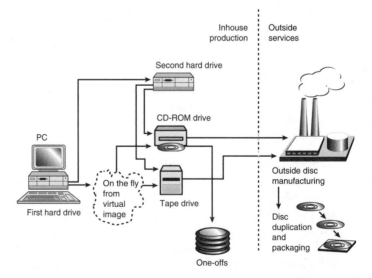

Courtesy of Plasmon Data

The same characteristics that make the CD-ROM desirable as a backup and archiving medium make it a superior medium for electronic publishing, as described in the following section.

Advantages of CD-ROM Distribution

CD-ROMs hold a lot of information. The actual data capacity varies according to the type of information stored on the disc—each of the CD-ROM formats uses slightly different error and correction codes leaving more or less room for the actual data. Pure audio data (which requires the fewest correction codes), as represented by the latest Sting or Hootie and the Blowfish album, can fill a disc with 680MB of data. Typical CD-ROM formatting consisting of computer data will max out a disc at about 650MB. If you compare this with some other forms of traditional storage media, as shown in Figure 4.2, you can see that CD-ROM excels at compressing information to an exceedingly compact (and inexpensive) form.

FIGURE 4.2.

Of the various storage methods, the CD-ROM provides the most compact and inexpensive means for storing 650MB of data. Courtesy of Plasmon Data, Inc.

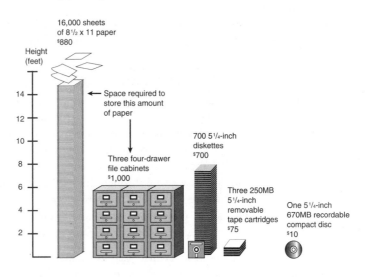

Courtesy of Plasmon Data

People tend to think online information is free. When you can download entire books from the Internet (as you can with the Gutenberg Project mentioned in Chapter 2, "Glowing Examples") or log in to the BBS of a software company, such as Microsoft, and collect several megabytes of developer information about a software application, the cost of this information seems inconsequential. Of course, the true cost depends on what you pay for connect time. If your connect time is free, the information may cost only the price of your telephone connection time. If you pay for the connect time, the cost of downloading begins to mount.

In the April 1995 issue of *CD-ROM Professional*, in an article titled "CD-ROM Versus Online: An Economic Analysis For Publishers," authors John David Wiedemer and David B. Boelio compared the costs between these types of distribution media. Some interesting facts emerged.

First, if you consider the transfer time required to download the contents of a single CD-ROM through a modem running at 9600 bps, the results are surprising. At 9600 bps, you're retrieving 1200 bytes per second or 4,320,000 bytes per hour. To download the 663,000,000 bytes stored on a single CD-ROM would require 153 hours—just hope it isn't a toll call.

The same article analyzed the relative costs of delivering 1MB of information by four different types of media with the following conclusions:

- Online costs $17 per megabyte.
- Print costs $3.50 per megabyte.
- 3½-inch diskette distribution costs $0.55 per megabyte.
- CD-ROM costs $0.0024 per megabyte.

The authors factor in representative costs to balance the equation, such as an estimated telecommunication surcharge for online connect time, the cost of a diskette and duplication charges, and CD-ROM replication fees. For the print media, the 1MB of data equates to a 400-page book (a print run of a 1,000 copies is used for the comparison).

Clearly, some eye-opening cost considerations exist in the choices available in the common media for distributing electronic publications. CD-ROM provides an economical alternative to other types of distribution media. The huge storage capacity of CD-ROM, however, presents a challenge to developers who choose this method for encapsulating their infobase, reference work, or catalog. The sheer amount of information that can be stored on CD-ROM makes it absolutely essential to provide a clear, comprehensive interface to the information and abundant navigational tools. With the potential for storing thousands of files, a user could get quickly lost without some technique for moving through this wealth of information. Creating a successful work on CD-ROM requires more than simply copying a set of files over to disc from your desktop recording system. You need to thoroughly address information access issues for this medium; tips and guidelines for accomplishing this appear in Part III of this book.

CD-ROMs, however, are not the ultimate delivery vehicle for electronic publications—they do have some problems that can hamper and frustrate developers. For one thing, CD-ROMs are much slower than hard-disk drives. Data access times for even the fastest 6× CD-ROM drives are no better than 120 milliseconds. Compare this with sub-10-millisecond hard-disk drives that have become common, and you get the idea.

If the only thing you need to access from a CD-ROM is a simple set of text files, the performance issue will probably not trouble you. However, if you design an online catalog to display full-color images of harsh weather outdoor gear containing videos of mountain climbers and audio tracks of shrieking eagles, you need to pay careful attention to a number of performance issues associated with CD-ROM; these issues are also discussed in Part III. A few simple techniques can reduce the time required to load and display different types of files and keep sound synchronized with images.

Because CD-ROM drives are slow during playback, developers have traditionally dumped onto the user's hard disk drive those files that need to run more quickly. Sometimes this may be only a handful of files occupying 700KB; other times you may be looking at 10MB of extraneous data littering your hard-disk drive.

Windows 95 guidelines recommend the zero-footprint approach to CD-ROM software installations. When possible, try to run directly from the CD-ROM without installing anything to the hard disk. When this is not possible, include an uninstall routine that removes all application files from the hard disk—including all those nasty little .DLLs and .INIs that get strewn around in Windows installations. If you're developing an electronic publication for CD-ROM, take the polite approach to the user's hard disk drive and make sure that you clean up after yourself.

Publishing on the Internet

If you plan to publish electronically on the Internet, you have a wide spectrum of choices covering everything from near-prehistoric documents composed of seven-bit ASCII text, to fully animated sound-reinforced multimedia epics with file sizes that look like distances to the nearest planet. The World Wide Web, with its robust support for formatted pages and embedded graphics, provides a natural repository for all manner of electronic publications. The price of admission for the electronic publisher is the ability to master HTML or one of the utilities that lets you create files in HTML format. HTML is simply a method of encoding files so that users can display pages in a similar manner on different platforms, and so you can generate links between both pages and different sites.

Compared to its closely related, but more complex predecessor SGML, HTML offers relatively few options, and anyone with a bit of instruction can generally master it. (One quick course to mastery is *Teach Yourself Web Publishing with HTML in a Week* by Laura Lemay, published by Sams. See Chapter 20, "Using HTML," and Chapter 21, "Inside SGML," of this book for more coverage of HTML and SGML.)

NOTE

One of the biggest reasons for the rousing success of the Web is that HTML is a true cross-platform tool; the Web browsers that display the HTML files run on all of the major computer platforms. Electronic publications in HTML form become essentially platform-independent, and anything that breaks down the communication barriers between systems of different types should be commended. You can use HTML on any sites equipped to handle Hypertext Transport Protocol (HTTP), the native communication facility for files of this type.

One of the disadvantages of operating on the Internet is that you are working with a creaky medium based on networking techniques originally engineered more than 20 years ago. The fact that it works as well as it does is to the credit of the engineers who have nursed the technology through its various stages, but the technical requirements for working with the underlying architecture of the Internet can induce shudders in even the staunchest computer users. UNIX veterans who have been brought up on TCP/IP, the protocols that structure the information flow on the Internet, scoff at the thought that anything is difficult about the technology. However, anyone who has ever tried to do anything as simple as configure a Eudora mail account on the Internet knows how grisly the details can be.

Access and use of the Internet—despite its UNIX origins—have been simplified by the addition of software layers constructed over the prickly underlying details. These layers hide the more confusing parts of this medium from those who want to use it, such as electronic publishers. The World Wide Web builds information bridges on a global scale and, if you have published something in electronic form, you can find readers in more than 30 million different places. Effective use of the Web, however, requires two essential components: an account that enables an individual to tie in to this sprawling network and hardware with sufficient bandwidth to harness the flow of data that surges from the wires.

Two protocols, Transmission Control Protocol (TCP) and Internet Protocol (IP), do the work of moving bits across the Internet. A technique referred to as *packet switching* bundles the information you are transferring into self-contained packages earmarked with an Internet address. The contents of the packet during transfer are irrelevant—if you are downloading an electronic publication from an FTP site, it gets bundled into a packet and shipped off with other packets that might contain electronic mail, application files, graphic images, or stock quotations. Depending on the size of the data file being "packetized," it may require a number of packets to transfer the file contents.

The flow of this information is directed by hardware devices called *routers*, which interpret the header information for each packet and steer it in the proper direction. When they reach their destination, the data in each packet is separated from the address and header, fragments of files are reconnected, and the information becomes available for use once again. Figure 4.3 shows how routers direct information from a workstation at one point on the Internet to a destination workstation.

Addresses on the Internet consist of strings of numbers separated by periods into four parts. The maximum number that you can use in an individual part of the address is 255. For example, a typical Internet address might be 176.134.28.5.

The routers on the Internet can determine from this string of numbers the individual network and the host computer on that network. In a manner similar to the way that telephone switching networks operate, a simple string of numbers can isolate one point within tens of thousands of networks containing hundreds of thousands of host computers. Through this miracle of electronics, a bundle of bits composing your interactive résumé, electronic cookbook, or multimedia journal can travel through a maze of copper and fiber-optic cables to reach its ultimate destination.

FIGURE 4.3.

Routers at various points on the Internet direct packets from their point of origin to their destination.

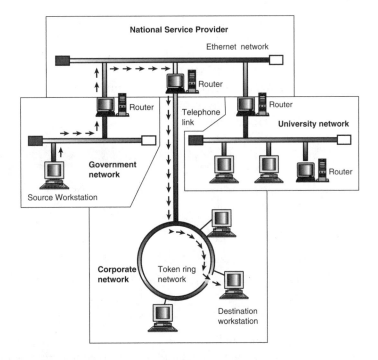

Costs Associated with Internet Access

The cost to access the Internet usually depends on two separate charges: a connect-time charge (billed by the service company itself) and a telecommunications charge (billed by the telephone company). Many Internet service providers offer bundled packages of hours. For example, the service that I use here in Vermont—TogetherNET—offers up to 30 hours of Internet access for $29 a month. Other providers have different packages, sometimes scaled by the hour, sometimes by a fixed rate for a maximum number of hours. If you have a local number to dial in to the Internet, the telecommunications charges will be minimal. However, if you need to depend on a toll call to reach the provider, the service cost can rise sharply. Once again, here in Vermont those costs can be steep: $.18 per minute or more during prime hours. In rural locations, you may be faced with similar difficulties, particularly if you want to access a telephone line that can support the 14,400 bits per second rate that is the minimal acceptable speed for dial-up Web use. Some Internet providers are offering 800 numbers (which you pay around a $6.00 per hour surcharge to use) to serve users in rural areas. If you are located in one of the 30 or so major metropolitan areas within which 80 percent of the population of the U.S. resides, you most likely have a local number to use for your access.

As an electronic publisher who wants to use the Internet as a medium for distributing documents, you have two basic choices. You can establish your own site with an Internet server (a fairly expensive proposition with a demanding setup process) or you can provide access to viewers through an established site. Depending on the services your Internet provider offers, you may be able to open a Web site within the service using an address that your service provider defines. Many Internet providers include this as a basic requirement of their services. Using this approach, you merely need to upload the necessary files to the storage location provided. If you are uploading files in HTML format, the provider must support the necessary protocol, HTTP. There also may be a fixed limit to the number and size of the files that you can make available in this manner. Some providers add a surcharge once you get beyond a certain limit, such as 50MB of information.

> **NOTE**
>
> From the perspective of Web browsers, Universal Resource Locators (URLs) represent the addresses that map links between information at different sites. URL syntax consists of several different elements: the protocol, the server name, the path, and the file. An example of an address on the World Wide Web is
>
> `http://www.cd-info.com/cd-info/CDInfoCenter.html`
>
> This represents an actual address where you can obtain information about publishing on CD-ROM.

If you place electronic publications at a site through a service provider, the site location will predetermine your World Wide Web address. You can advertise and index the contents of your Web page through a number of different techniques to ensure that your audience is aware of the existence of your work. The list of individuals and organizations who catalog and index interesting and valuable information on the Web is growing daily. With a bit of investigation, you can publicize your electronic publishing effort in numerous ways. One place to start is by registering at CERN's virtual library. The sprawling URL is

`http://info.cern.ch/hypertext/DataSources/WWW/Geographical_generation/new-servers.html`

You don't need to use the Web as the basis for electronic publishing on the Internet. You can also offer pre-prepared documents through FTP sites that your audience can download. The portable document formats, such as Adobe Acrobat or WordPerfect Envoy, are ideal for this approach, but many documents are bundled up (in compressed form) as ASCII text. Downloading files from FTP sites generally requires a little bit more work from your potential readership than accessing documents through the Web, but for those who don't have access to the Web, it may be the only method for obtaining your electronic work.

Infobases on the Web

Although much of the attention surrounding information presentation on the Web has focused on designing Web pages using HTML editors, another powerful tool is emerging as a vehicle for content delivery. *Infobases* are electronic repositories for free-form information that include extensive search and indexing capabilities with the goal of being able to locate any individual piece of data in seconds. You can distribute an infobase using any of the media discussed in this chapter—CD-ROMs, LANs, WANs, or disks—but certain utilities also let you install the infobase on the World Wide Web and provide access through any Web browser.

Software such as Folio Corporation's Infobase Web Server (discussed in the next chapter) combines the storage flexibility and rapid search characteristics of an infobase with the accessibility and familiarity of a Web browser. Internet users can tap into the infobase through the Web Server running their favorite browser and gain the benefit of sophisticated search and browsing tools, as well as a depth of content that would be difficult (or impossible) to provide using simply HTML coding. The infobase approach also lends itself well to different approaches to information access beyond the simple viewer scheme. This approach supports personalized access to information (allowing you to perform file marking and annotation) and collaborative approaches (where many people are involved in editing, updating, and restructuring the infobase). As the limitations of presenting information in page-oriented formats becomes more restrictive, expect more online publishers to adopt infobase approaches to present semi-structured information in more dynamic ways.

Publishing on a LAN or WAN

Networks on a local scale or enterprise-wide scale can provide fast, nearly transparent data access throughout companies or organizations—a perfect medium for electronic publishing. Anyone who has patiently waited for the ninety-eighth consecutive image to display on his or her Web browser through the breathtakingly slow 14,400 bps PPP link can get excited watching pages compose themselves with swift network T1 or T2 connections. Network users often take this level of nearly instantaneous data access for granted. Electronic publishers can use it to their advantage.

Almost anything you can put on CD-ROM or on the Internet you can also distribute through a LAN or WAN. See Chapter 24, "LAN and WAN Publishing," for more information. The issues become slightly different, and you are sometimes faced with confusing application licensing concerns and similar issues. Rather than buying single tools—such as Adobe Acrobat—and making them available for everyone, you will need to buy software versions designed for multiple users—such as Adobe Acrobat for Workgroups. Assuming your network distribution plans involve closed use of documents and applications—that is, you won't be allowing others outside your company to log in and access publications or data—you can generally solve most distribution issues by purchasing network-ready versions of products or tools with enough user licenses to cover the members of your workgroup.

The playback capabilities of your network users are the only limits to the type of information that you present on the network. Infobases have become popular vehicles for delivering network-based information. Workgroup applications, such as Lotus Notes, have also become popular methods of sharing database information. Other approaches merge workgroup applications and infobases; Folio Corporation has produced a product called Folio Fusion that merges the strengths of its infobase, Folio VIEWS, with the workgroup capabilities of Lotus Notes.

You also have full flexibility to distribute and present all of the other forms of electronic publications (portable document formats, CD-ROM-based files, interactive multimedia works, and so on) through the network transmission media. In many ways, a LAN or WAN is the most flexible way to deliver any form of information because of the many configuration options and the high data transfer rates.

Delivering High-Volume Information on a Network

Several innovative hardware devices have been developed that make it possible to successfully combine the speed and efficiency of LANs and WANs with the data storage merits of CD-ROMs. Jukeboxes and CD-ROM disc arrays expand the data access capabilities of network users. Jukeboxes, which manually load a requested CD-ROM from an installed selection of five to 100 discs, are less desirable in network use due to the delay in mechanically moving the requested disc into position to retrieve the contents. Disc arrays and CD-ROM servers package a number of different discs into a single cabinet and place them all under network control.

One example of a high-power CD-ROM server is Meridian Data's CD Net 556/M, an integrated system that supports up to 56 CD-ROM drives. That's enough to present more than 33GB of online information. Each individual cabinet features its own Pentium processor, and the unit contains a built-in 100MB-per-second Ethernet interface. Meridian Data is one of the earliest designers of networked CD-ROM products.

If you plan to publish to CD-ROM and also want the ability to provide recordable CD access to network users, Meridian Data also offers network-ready CD-recordable servers. These units consist of a dual-speed recorder coupled to a dedicated server that contains a huge internal cache. The high-end unit contains a large enough cache that it can buffer all of the files required for recording the CD before actually starting the recording process. Because recordable CD operations must be carried out without interruption (or the CD-R disc is ruined), this type of network recorder makes it possible to eliminate the risk of interrupting data flow because of network traffic—all of the data necessary to complete the recording is stored within the server.

If you need to produce a number of CD-ROMs across the network in a short period of time, Intaglio produces a network-compatible parallel CD recorder system. A master CD recorder controls the operation of up to 75 slave recorders, all of which can simultaneously record a compact disc. Typical recording times for a 650MB CD-ROM at double-speed rates are a little over 35 minutes. With Intaglio's system, you could record 75 CD-ROMs in that same time. As CD-ROMs become more firmly entrenched in corporations as network resources and data distribution vehicles, systems such as this will become increasingly important.

Publishing on Removable Disk Media

Unless you know your audience (as well as the equipment they are using), publishing on most forms of removable media, such as SyQuest cartridges, Bernoulli cartridges, or magneto-optical cartridges, greatly restrict your potential audience. CD-ROM titles can be successfully distributed largely because of the huge base of installed CD-ROM players on every conceivable computer type. However, if you produce an electronic book on an 88MB SyQuest cartridge, your audience could shrink to the size of a small South American country. Although removable disk media have some unique advantages, widespread delivery is not one of them.

For interdepartmental data distribution, a cartridge could serve admirably for certain kinds of information if you can predict with some certainty that your audience has the necessary playback device. This occurs more commonly in situations where equipment allocations are controlled from some central body; in such cases, removable media might be the best way to go. Consider the following examples:

■ The technical support department of your company has produced a massive infobase containing the engineering drawings, parts listings, service bulletins, application notes, and troubleshooting guidelines for all the company products, nearly 60MB of data. Quick growth has caused the existing LAN to be overburdened with data traffic, making access to the infobase too slow to be practical. However, the key support personnel all have local 88MB SyQuest drives; with its 12-millisecond data access rates, placing the infobase on several SyQuest cartridges (one for each staff member) can speed information searches and provide greatly improved information access until the network can be upgraded.

■ Your graphic arts service bureau chain, MegaArts—with locations in several major metropolitan areas—has numerous magneto-optical cartridge drives installed throughout the various locations, generally used as one method of accepting large files from customers for prepress operations. To keep the individual branch offices aligned with the company mission, corporate headquarters publishes a quarterly interactive multimedia newsletter that includes company news, showcase images from the previous quarter's work, video skits of the president doing embarrassing things after several beers at the company picnic, amusing animations produced by staff members after surviving one more crush of deadlines, and a morale-boosting message from the vice president. The branches aren't yet networked, nor are they equipped with CD-ROM drives, but you can ship 230MB magneto-optical cartridges inexpensively to each office with the contents of the interactive newsletter. This approach ensures that viewers at the destination can conveniently access the newsletter.

■ You operate a one-person desktop publishing service that performs all types of computer-based publishing, including business cards, brochures, menus, instruction manuals, price lists, newspaper ads, and so on. Most of your clients have computers, but not many them have cartridge drives of CD-ROM players. As an incentive to continuing business (and as a calling card to gain further business), you produce a monthly electronic journal and brochure highlighting your best work, giving tips to customers for preparing materials for submission, and providing some free compressed clip art that you've assembled for customer use. All of this neatly fits on a single diskette that can be inexpensively mailed to customers or prospects. Your database and query cards let you know who has PC equipment and who has Macs, so you can format the diskettes appropriately for your audience and create copies as you need them from a subdirectory containing the monthly files.

■ You are part of the sales force of a company that produces and markets high-end video-editing and effects equipment. For sales presentations designed to dazzle your prospective clients, you've created an interactive electronic brochure that includes full-screen video shots of people leaping off buildings, cars bursting through walls of fire, and kangaroos engaged in brutal kick-boxing matches with wildlife management officials. To guarantee the necessary performance during playback, the electronic brochure is loaded to individual 540MB portable hard-disk drives with 8-millisecond access rates and then connected to high-performance IBM ThinkPad portables coupled to large flat-screen displays that can be quickly set up at the customer site for presentations. The portable hard drives can be shipped to the individual sales offices prior to presentations. None of the other forms of portable media have the performance to maintain flawless playback, so the hard disk becomes the media of choice.

As you can see, in certain cases, only some forms of removable disk medium fit the bill for distributing electronic publications. In general, you should select removable media for document distribution on a case-by-case basis in circumstances in which network or CD-ROM distribution are inappropriate.

Hybrid Approaches to Publishing

CD-ROMs have won acclaim for their impressive storage capacity and economy, but they suffer from the problem of becoming outdated shortly after creation. On the other hand, online information is immediate and current, but you may spend a good deal of time trying to locate the precise information for which you are searching. Why not combine the best characteristics of each of these media into a hybrid: a CD-ROM that can perform data updates by downloading information from a service?

This idea had been germinating for some time until, in March 1994, Microsoft announced the first product of this kind, a CD-ROM product called *Complete Baseball*. *Complete Baseball* is a multimedia book about the history of the sport and its players, but it has the capability to link with a service through a modem to download daily statistics for the players and teams. As such, it becomes something like a living book, capable of refreshing itself with new information whenever necessary.

Some of the online services, such as CompuServe and America Online, are experimenting with this approach. By providing a multimedia-rich CD-ROM that includes a robust interface and a good deal of internal content, they can provide a vehicle to tap into the online service and enrich the overall experience. The constraints of maintaining a graphical interface are not as demanding if the graphics already reside on the CD-ROM and don't have to be downloaded. And, the up-to-the-minute content from the service can overcome the static nature of the CD-ROM with periodic updates.

As an electronic publisher, you can adapt this approach, using a hybrid CD-ROM with updates, in a number of ways:

- Update references annually, such as encyclopedias or almanacs, to expand the entries and adjust world population figures and data.
- Update CD-ROM-based catalogs with new price lists and additional product offerings.
- Update government databases through a brief connect session controlled by a utility on the CD-ROM.

One company, Teleshuttle Corporation, has devised a software application and service that facilitates the creation of hybrid CD-ROMs. The company offers the necessary communications software to link to a download service, the actual server where participants in the program can upload the updated information to be linked to the hybrid CD-ROM, and an application that lets the developer embed this approach—including the communications link—into his or her product. One of the early adopters of the Teleshuttle service was Vista Intermedia, which published a CD-ROM containing the World Health Organization's International Digest of Health Legislation. This 10,000-page infobase is constructed in Folio VIEWS; obviously, the information becomes outdated immediately after release. Subscribers receive a quarterly update to the CD-ROM through Teleshuttle's download service.

> **NOTE**
>
> Most hybrids work in a similar manner: They download information from the appropriate service to a storage location on hard disk. Information on the CD-ROM is not updatable, but new data to append the CD-ROM contents can be linked once it is loaded to the hard disk. The program running from CD-ROM combines the two sources of data—data stored on the CD-ROM and the downloaded data that resides on the hard disk—to create the illusion of a single, current data source.

Imaginative use of the hybrid CD-ROM can give developers and electronic publishers one more tool in their information arsenal—a tool that is guaranteed to keep their audience on top of the latest information.

Comparisons of the Different Media

Each of the media discussed in this chapter has its own unique advantages—characteristics that may make it the distribution vehicle of choice for your electronic publication—and disadvantages—those traits that may rule it out as a communication medium for you. To summarize the discussion, the following lists review the strengths and weaknesses of the different media.

Advantages and Disadvantages of CD-ROM

CD-ROM may solve your communication problems in the following ways:

- CD-ROM offers the most cost-effective means for distributing large quantities of information. Each megabyte of data costs about $0.0024 to store.

- Information on CD-ROM has a long storage life. Recordable CDs (which use a reflective gold layer inside the disc) last for about 50 to 100 years. Conventionally manufactured CDs (which use an aluminum layer, subject to corrosion) have a life expectancy of 10 to 15 years.

- CD-ROMs are compact (a little over 4½ inches in diameter) and lightweight (about half an ounce), making them ideal for inexpensive shipments by mail or express services.

- Recordable CDs can be produced right on the desktop with a hardware and software investment of about $1,500. The convenience and control offers a considerable benefit to an electronic publisher.

- Replication of CD-ROMs in large volumes is inexpensive. In quantities above 10,000, the cost per unit is about $.75. In lower runs of around 1,000, the cost per unit is about $1.00.

- The information on CD-ROMs can be merged with downloaded data from networks or services to provide more timely information.

- The large installed base of CD-ROM drives extends to millions of computer users and cuts across all platforms.

- The dominant file system for CD-ROM, ISO 9660, can be read by all the major computer platforms: DOS, Windows, OS/2, Macintosh, and UNIX.

The disadvantages of CD-ROM include the following:

- Information can go out of date quickly because the CD-ROM is a static medium and can be written only once.

- Some hardware and software expertise is required to create distributable titles on CD-ROM. Improved software applications are making things simpler, but this is still an area where newcomers may travel down many dead-end side streets before finding the main thoroughfare.

- Playback on CD-ROM is much slower—by a factor of more than ten—than other storage media, such as hard-disk or cartridge drives.

- Setup charges for replication (approximately $700) make low-volume manufacturing cost-prohibitive.

Advantages and Disadvantages of the Internet

The Internet as a medium for electronic publishing offers the following advantages:

- The potential audience is huge, numbering in the tens of millions.
- Setup for electronic distribution is reasonably simple, and you can use several different utilities to accomplish this task (HTTP, FTP, and so on).
- Replication costs are eliminated. The publisher needs to create only a single version of a publication, which can then be downloaded by literally millions of readers.
- Service costs and expenses associated with the Internet remain fairly low. Most people who want access can find an economical means of connecting to the Internet through one of many different services.
- Information can be easily updated by information providers simply modifying the source files.
- Information structured in HTML format can be accessed by many computer platforms.
- The World Wide Web supports what is basically a gigantic hypertext document with links available to any other site. You can make your electronic document part of that structure very simply, and you can also connect your document to other documents with a minimum of effort. We're witnessing the organic growth of a complex, interactive structure that can handle interrelated information in a seamless and elegant manner.

The Internet has the following disadvantages:

- Copyright protection remains a problem for electronic publishers. Once unleashed in electronic form, any document or infobase becomes subject to unlimited copying.
- Methods for obtaining revenue for published works and permitting paid subscriptions for online magazines are still in their infancy and no single method prevails. Metering systems and digital money may improve this situation, but right now it is an uncontrolled market. Many Internet users expect that everything should be available for free.
- Security issues confound information accessibility and present some risk to electronic publishers.
- More complex electronic works, especially those containing multimedia elements, require direct network links to run efficiently. Dial-up Internet access is still too slow for providing complex graphics, sound, video, or animation.
- The Internet is growing so quickly that obtaining visibility for your efforts in creating online materials can be difficult. If you're standing on a sidewalk at night in Las Vegas, waving a flashlight probably won't get you much attention amidst the blinking neon lights.

■ Threats to the open-ended growth of the Internet through government interference or privatization may irrevocably change the character of the medium in undetermined ways. Government-controlled data encryption schemes (where only the government holds the key) raise serious freedom-of-speech issues (and provide the government with the tools for high-speed electronic wire tapping of all of our communication). Commercial interests who see the Internet as one more means of peddling T-shirts, carbonated sugar water, and high-tech running shoes clearly would like to shape the medium to their particular pursuits—selling things. A quick look at commercial television demonstrates how a promising communication medium can be converted into a platform for selling dog food and laxatives.

Advantages and Disadvantages of LANs and WANs

LANs and WANs have the following advantages for the electronic publisher:

■ Your publication efforts are taking place within a controlled environment. You can effectively monitor and control distribution and access to information very precisely through rights assignments and document placement.

■ Network users represent a predictable population group. By knowing about network users and the computer hardware they use for viewing electronic documents, you can precisely structure information for your audience.

■ The data transfer rates that apply to most LANs and WANs support the distribution of very large, very complex materials. You can distribute electronic publications containing extensive multimedia elements and huge file sizes without worrying about the bandwidths for data available to your viewers (unless many of them depend on dial-up interconnections).

■ LANs and WANs support the use of collaborative tools in designing and updating electronic documents. Documents residing on the network can be living, evolving works with contributions, corrections, and comments being extended by all workgroup members. In this manner, design specifications for products, functional specifications, instruction manuals, procedures manuals, infobases on technical support issues, and similar electronic documents can be developed over a long period of time by many different people.

■ Information is dynamically updatable by modifying the source files.

■ Distribution of electronic publications is instantaneous. Once installed on the network, a document becomes globally available to anyone who needs to access it.

The disadvantages to LANs and WANs include the following:

■ If you are using specialized applications, such as portable document viewers or infobase readers, you need to obtain sufficient site licenses or workgroup versions of the products to cover everyone on the network who may be using these tools. This can be very expensive.

■ Distribution of information on LANs and WANs entails considerable network administration overhead. If you don't have network administration rights to maintain those areas of the network where the electronic publications will reside or to grant access to necessary workgroup members, you will have to work with someone who does.

■ If users at different sites within an enterprise-wide network use widely different computers, you will have to do some work to arrive at a standard format for distributing electronic publications.

■ Networks within corporations and organizations usually change over time; you will need to readdress document distribution issues on a fairly frequent basis.

■ You may also have training issues associated with getting workgroup members to use the necessary tools, find information when they need it, and navigate different parts of the network. This will initially be more difficult than simply handing someone a copy of a training manual or instruction set.

Advantages of Hybrid Approaches

The advantages of hybrid approaches to publishing include the following:

■ You can reduce the limitations of the different media types. For example, by combining CD-ROM contents with downloaded data you gain both a large data capacity and timely information. By offering a disc array of CD-ROMs on a LAN or WAN, you offer a convenient way to distribute specialized databases or similar information without requiring the network users to have individual CD-ROM drives.

■ You can overcome equipment barriers by routing electronic publications in several different directions. For example, a technical support division of a company that provides application notes on its product for customers could start with a single Microsoft Word document. That document could be provided to customers through a faxback service, in portable document format through its Internet FTP site, as an HTML document at its Web site, and as a downloadable document from its BBS. Customers who don't have a version of Microsoft Word can use the free version of Microsoft's Viewer utility to read the document.

■ With a bit of innovation and inventiveness, you can creatively combine and manipulate all of the different approaches to document delivery as well as the individual media available to design an approach that works exactly right for your audience.

Summary

Each medium discussed in this chapter handles electronic publications that have been prepared in a certain format for distribution. If you're placing an HTML document at a Web site, you need to prepare the document using an HTML editor by editing the file with the appropriate codes using a line editor, or by filtering an existing document through a macro or filter. If you are creating an infobase for distribution on a LAN, you need to work with an application that structures the information for the infobase users, such as Folio VIEWS or re:Search. If your goal is to create a portable document format publication that will be usable by everyone, applications for this purpose—such as Adobe Acrobat—have a series of procedures for creating the necessary .PDF files. Chapter 5, "Application Tools," examines some of the applications you can use for creating electronic publications and compares ease-of-use, cost factors, and applicability to different document approaches. This chapter introduced you to the primary tools used in electronic publishing. Examples presented throughout the rest of this book show you these tools in action and reinforce the basics you've learned here.

Application Tools

5

by Lee Purcell

IN THIS CHAPTER

A carpenter can't build a house without some kind of a toolkit, at the very least a basic collection of hammers, saws, and planes; similarly, you can't construct electronic publications without some fundamental application tools. These tools will vary according to your publishing intentions. The degree of expertise required to operate them ranges from absolute novice to borderline programmer. Portable document production tools, such as Adobe Acrobat, can be essentially transparent to use, as simple as printing a document. SGML production tools, however, can require a much more intensive knowledge of computer hardware and software issues. By mastering the necessary skills to build SGML documents, you gain a delivery medium that is far more flexible and more adaptable to different platform uses than basic page-flipping applications. Hypertext development tools usually fall somewhere between these two extremes.

The analogy to a carpenter's tools applies in another way as well. Just as you don't want to try to pound a nail into a board with the base of a screwdriver, you don't want to try to build a complex infobase with an application designed for presenting formatted pages on-screen. Each of the applications excels in certain types of tasks and may be less capable in other areas. You need to choose the right application toolkit for the job to avoid smashed fingers and bent nails.

But, as with all evolving technologies, sharp divisions into categories break apart when examining the feature sets of competing products; the overlap between categories can be considerable. For example, a hypertext development tool may offer export filters to produce SGML files. An application that produces portable document formats may also include an add-on utility that provides fully indexed searching and extensive hypertext linking. A humble help system may contain characteristics of all the other categories of electronic publishing. Keep in mind as you're reading that the category breakdowns are only a general way of sorting and comparing an extremely diverse collection of tools for authoring electronic works.

The overall goal, however (and a significant driving force behind the growth of electronic publishing), is to break down the barriers of both computer platforms and distribution media. Software producers are trying to enable electronic publishers to produce compact documents that they can distribute through CD-ROM, local or wide area networks, and online services to a variety of users who can play them back on all the major computer platforms. The journey has only begun, but a number of promising developments appear to be leading towards an entirely new model for information distribution, one that will significantly change the way we obtain and use information. Industry evangelists get a bit glassy-eyed and speak in reverential tones when they talk about this approaching information model, but in reality, the first generation of products for this purpose has arrived. Individuals and corporations are using these tools now and using them successfully to save money and improve information flow. Throughout this book, we'll be pointing out many examples of the ways in which electronic publishing is simplifying and improving information exchange.

This chapter covers the range of tools available, and offers some perspective as to how these tools can provide solutions to your electronic publishing goals.

The Basic Categories Revisited

Chapter 3, "Terms and Concepts," introduced the following basic categories of electronic publishing tools:

- Online help systems
- Portable document formats
- SGML tools
- HTML tools
- Hypertext tools

Within these categories, you'll find a range of features that progressively extends from products that focus on the physical appearance of the document (fonts, graphics, and page layout) to those that focus on the content of the document (data use, linking, and searching). Figure 5.1 illustrates this progression of features.

FIGURE 5.1.

Electronic publishing features range from simple portable document viewers to fully indexed infobase managers.

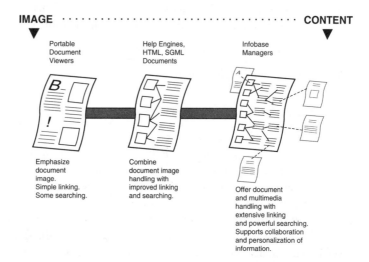

At the simplest end of the spectrum, you find tools that extend the metaphor of the printed page to the electronic realm. These work most effectively to adapt existing printed works and can generally convert the most complex aspects of the printed page to an electronic equivalent with a minimum of effort. The page elements can include intricate, high-resolution color graphics and extensive and unusual fonts. For example, in their sampler CD for Acrobat, Adobe provides examples of full-color brochures of design firms and pages out of previous issues of *Wired* magazine, both of which adapt well to on-screen display. These kinds of tools also generally include a provision for creating a table of contents with hypertext links and performing linear searches for words within a document in a manner similar to the way searches are handled in a word processing program.

At the next level, certain application tools effectively combine the characteristics of a formatted page with more elaborate search capabilities and better support for creating links between pieces of information (or "chunks," as they are often called). The Windows help engine lets the help system author set up a complex system of keywords to use in searches. HTML formatted documents extend linking of information to addressable locations throughout the World Wide Web. SGML provides a rich, extensible structure that authors can use to create platform-independent documents with many author-defined features. For a moderate development effort, tools in this category provide a good percentage of the potential power of electronic publishing.

At the high end of the scale, hypertext development tools built around the infobase model offer the most extensive options for electronic publishing. The better tools in this category let individuals personalize information through annotation and other techniques for marking or commenting on the data. Tools such as Folio VIEWS also fully support collaborative editing and updating of the information contained in the infobase, and Folio has also designed an automated retrieval tool that can query Web sites or network locations and expand the contents of an infobase with user-specified information. This is one of the first commercial applications of the intelligent agent approach to information access.

In almost all instances, these application tools require two components:

- A development application to design the page, create the links, and define search attributes
- A playback mechanism, referred to as a viewer, reader, or search engine that accesses the created files

Viewers and readers come in a variety of sizes and shapes, and are often distributed in a royalty-free form to ensure the widest possible audience. For some of the more elaborate products that contain powerful search engines, the viewer may only be distributed if the developer purchases a license based on either units sold or some other predetermined arrangement. Without a viewer or reader, the information in an electronic document is of little value because not many people will be willing to expend the funds to purchase the original development application in order to view the document contents (which can cost from a few hundred to a few thousand dollars). Some development tools, such as Common Ground (discussed later in this chapter), let the author create a compact executable file that contains the viewer as well as the electronic document, solving the entire problem very neatly.

The following sections discuss some of the most important applications in each category.

Help Systems: The Poor Person's Electronic Publishing Tool

One of the essential requirements of successful electronic publishing is ensuring a wide readership through the availability of the playback software. You would have a difficult time finding a playback platform that is more widespread than the Microsoft Windows help system—virtually everyone who is running a version of Windows has the playback equipment built right into the system.

If you open up the Windows Program Manager Help and choose File | Open (as shown in Figure 5.2), notice that a list of individual help files appears in the Open dialog box. Each help file essentially represents a standalone hypertext document that can be freely distributed; it doesn't have to be associated with a particular application. Anyone running Windows can open and read it. Windows 95 users can read both Win95 help files and Win3.1 help files.

FIGURE 5.2.

Help files are hypertext documents that can be viewed by anyone running Windows.

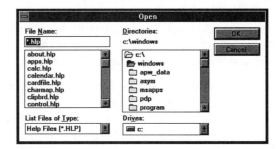

Each one of these files shown represents a portable, reasonably compact electronic document that can be read by anyone running Windows. Best of all, to create help files of this sort you only need two things:

- A word processor capable of producing Rich Text Format (.RTF) files
- The appropriate Microsoft Windows help compiler

If you've viewed the Windows help system for any of your favorite applications, you've probably noticed that it provides a remarkably full-featured set of options, including hypertext linking inside or outside the help file, popup definition windows, a search engine that supports multiple keyword strings, graphics with hot-spot links, and support for embedded objects. In other words, you have the framework for creating hypertext documents with many of the bells and whistles normally contained in expensive standalone packages—and it's *free*.

The basic creation tool is the word processor. As you might expect, Microsoft has optimized help creation for the features contained in Word for Windows. You can use any other program, however, that can create Rich Text Format files to produce the source files that provide the raw fodder for the help compiler. The help compiler is included with Windows Software

Development kits, in third-party help development packages, and as a downloadable item from Microsoft's Web site (or through other online services). Even writers who normally shy away from programming tasks can manage mastery of the help compiler. Although I wouldn't go so far as to call it simple, it's safe to say that non-programmers can learn its operation in a short period of time. You basically create a project file that provides some working instructions for the compiler and lists the RTF files and bitmapped graphics it should use as the source material. With a single command-line statement, you start the compiler working, and—with some luck—in a few minutes you have a completed electronic document in the form of a help system.

Admittedly, creating help files directly from a word processor takes some work. If you create a help system manually from a word processor, you will need to keep track of context strings (that identify topics), context numbers (that let software programmers hook into individual help topics from a running application), and other help system esoterica. Before there were any tools to assist in the development effort, Microsoft used to recommend keeping track of all these details in a spreadsheet format, which you could then continue to revise and update as the help system evolved. This is a considerable amount of work (I know—I designed several systems using this technique). Enterprising software companies improved the situation by creating utilities that automate and track the creation of topics and the use of links, and let the help author work without getting submerged in the tedium of tracking all this stuff.

One of the best tools for this purpose is RoboHelp from Blue Sky Software. Now in its 3rd generation, RoboHelp assists a help author not only in creating the help system, but also in debugging and streamlining it. It runs as an extension of Word for Windows, constructed as an elaborate set of macros with Word Basic. RoboHelp simplifies all aspects of help development, from creation of the help project file to testing the individual hyperlinks between topics. You can create Links by highlighting a line in the Word document, clicking the Links button on the RoboHelp floating toolbar (shown on the right side of the screen in Figure 5.3), and choosing the topic link from an alphabetized list that appears.

Blue Sky Software has also recently released a suite of Windows help development tools, called WinHelp Office. This package includes an expanded hyperviewer that adds searches for individual words (rather than just author-defined keywords), tools to integrate video and sound into a help system, a decompiler that can turn a help file into a Word for Windows file, and a training video.

Other help development tools that provide unique approaches to working in the help environment are as follows:

- **Doc-to-Help by WexTech Systems, Inc.** specializes in maintaining parallel versions of printed and online documentation from a single source document.
- **ForeHelp by Forefront, Inc.** provides immediate feedback as you work in an environment that resembles an operating help system. Offers graphical view of help links.

- **Help Magician Pro by Software Interphase, Inc.** lets you edit and test help links without compiling the source files. Features robust import filters and built-in spell checker.

- **HelpBreeze by Solutionsoft** supports the full range of Windows help features and bi-directional conversion of help and printed documentation. A bundled DLL lets you enhance help files with animation and slide shows.

- **OnLine View for Windows by SingaLab PTE ltd.** provides extensive multimedia development tools in conjunction with a hypermedia help engine. It features cross-platform support for multimedia files.

- **ProtoView Visual Help Builder by ProtoView Development Corporation** offers a fast, graphical means for constructing Windows help systems. It works with or without an application's source files.

FIGURE 5.3.

The RoboHelp development environment provides an efficient set of tools for creating help files.

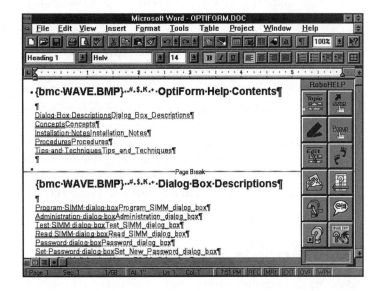

These software tools can be purchased through mail-order catalogs or retail computer outlets that including programming tools. Programmer's Paradise (1-800-445-7899) stocks most of these packages.

Windows help systems work so well that many companies and individuals have used this medium to distribute electronic books, references, training materials, and other information unrelated to any specific application. The help files detach neatly as standalone files that you can compress and mail on diskette, deliver through a BBS, or pass along through a network. As an ideal medium for creating and distributing information to Windows users, the help system engine provides hypertext capabilities and a robust authoring environment for an insignificant investment of money.

Portable Document Formats

Portable documents are designed to escape the boundaries of individual computer platforms, with their font management tools and processor constraints, and travel freely from computer to computer while maintaining their original pages' appearance. This is quite a feat, considering the complexities that have to be overcome just to present a reasonable WYSIWIG correspondence between a computer's screen display and printed output. Ideally, the eight-page brochure you create on your Macintosh describing llama treks through the Andes, complete with rich color graphics and skillful use of fonts, such as Akzidenz Grotesk Extra Bold, will display in all its splendor when Windows users view it. The techniques for ensuring that the font display and the graphics will appear the same when they appear on each computer vary a bit depending on which tool you are talking about, as described within this section.

Portable document applications are sometimes referred to disdainfully as "page-flipper" applications by infobase advocates, but most of these programs go far beyond simple screen and printer replication of a page layout. Products are usually offered in a series of tiers, with the feature sets expanding (as does the cost) for each tier that you ascend. As you get close to the pinnacle of feature nirvana, many of these programs (such as Adobe Acrobat) include powerful full-text indexing capabilities and other high-end possibilities.

These kinds of applications also offer significantly easier approaches to designing electronic publications. In many cases, you can work in your favorite application, whether a word processor or graphics application, and output to a software driver (rather than the printer) controlled by the portable document application. The result is an electronic version of the "printed" page layout viewable using readers on different platforms. If this sounds easy, it usually is, but (as with all computer software applications) you must consider certain caveats and tradeoffs as well.

The following subsections discuss several of the leading programs in this category.

Adobe Acrobat

Adobe Acrobat currently ranks as the preeminent member of a select group of portable document program producers. As the originator of the PostScript language, Adobe designers definitely have some experience in this area, and they've approached the problems of portable document exchange in a reasonable, though somewhat complex, manner. Creating and working with Acrobat files requires a suite of software applications, each with a special purpose function that handles a certain aspect of the production process.

At the most basic level you have Acrobat Reader, a tool designed to view files formatted in Adobe's Portable Document Format (PDF). Reader has no price tag and comes in UNIX, DOS, Windows, and Macintosh versions; you can download it for free, you can pass it on to your friends, and you can do anything necessary to help propagate it throughout the computer universe—this, of course, is part of Adobe's strategy. If you get the reader into the hands of each and every computer user, more and more people will buy the rest of the development tools. For your convenience, we've included a version on the CD-ROM bundled with this book. Some of the sample electronic documents appear in Acrobat format.

If you purchase the Adobe Acrobat 2.0 package, you get a couple of additional pieces of software. Acrobat Exchange lets you enhance documents with an assortment of navigational aids, such as hypertext links, bookmarks, and thumbnail images of individual pages within a document. The package also includes the PDFWriter, software that essentially replaces the printer driver of your computer to create a portable document format file. If you're operating in the Windows environment, you can use the Printer Control Panel to select the PDFWriter from the printer list. Within the Macintosh world, the Chooser allows you to select the PDFWriter—in a manner similar to Windows, it redirects the printer output to a file.

Other tools come in other packages. Adobe Catalog provides full indexed searching of text contained in PDF files. Adobe Distiller works more effectively than PDFWriter at handling PostScript output, including embedded PostScript graphics and TIFF images. Third-party plug-in utilities also enhance the utility of Acrobat. If you're working on the Macintosh, an application called PDF Navigator (produced by ARTLab) handles the task of exporting PageMaker documents to portable document format, including the addition of indexing and bookmark features. As this market develops, additional plug-ins to handle special-purpose requirements for electronic publishers will undoubtedly appear.

Adobe Reader can display the navigational framework embedded in a document using Exchange. This includes a toolbar running along the top of the window with familiar "cassette-player" controls, arrows that let you travel forward or backward through the pages of a document (as shown in Figure 5.4). You can also select a mode for viewing the contents of a document; one available mode displays a row of thumbnail images of each of the pages in a document along a scrollable view area on the left side of the window (also shown in Figure 5.4).

FIGURE 5.4.

Navigational devices in Acrobat Reader include a split screen display with thumbnail images of pages.

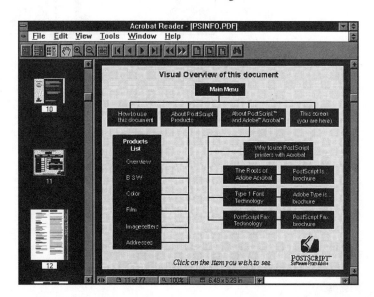

As you can also see in the previous figure, while using Exchange to develop the portable document you can create a visual hierarchy of document contents and use this tree structure as a way of guiding the reader through the document. This technique allows considerable versatility in the navigational model chosen to guide a reader—any approach that can be displayed in graphical form can be equipped with the necessary links to jump to various parts of a document.

Document hierarchies can also be reflected in a collapsible outline structure that can be displayed in the scrollable view strip beside the document windows (as shown in Figure 5.5). You can easily alternate views by switching from the display of thumbnail images to the outline format with the click of a button.

FIGURE 5.5.

Collapsible outline navigation lets you compress or expand the range of available topics.

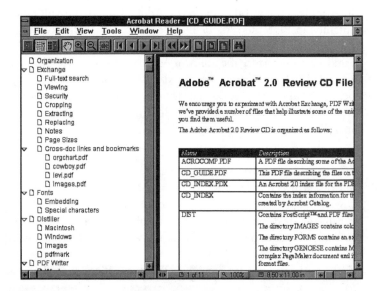

NOTE

Keep in mind that the figures we provide may differ slightly from operating system to operating system.

Another imaginative approach to the navigation issue is a built-in column navigator that lets you progressively move through an article that is set up in two or more columns. Once you zoom in to a level where the text is easily readable, a hand with a downward pointing arrow indicates a continuation of the text. Clicking the column with this modified cursor automatically advances the display down the column as you read. When you reach the bottom of the column, Reader bumps the display over to the next column and continues down with each click. At the last column at the end of the page you continue by turning the page; you can use this technique to read any type of multi-columned page layouts.

Because of the precision with which it can render complex color pages on the computer display, Adobe Acrobat has become popular with graphic artists, ad agencies, and other organizations that need to regularly proof materials intended for print output. Although the goal at this point is to simplify conventional printing processes, removing the need for producing an interim proof copy (using a color laser printer or similar output device) allows a compact electronic version of a page or set of pages to be inexpensively exchanged between parties. Using Adobe Exchange, anyone viewing the file can annotate the materials with comments. Comments get affixed to the page in the increasingly common "sticky notes" approach; they appear as small, moveable colored note pages on the larger page. Double click on a note and it opens up to reveal the message. Tools that support collaborative efforts in this manner have become an important factor in the growth of electronic publishing.

If Adobe Acrobat has any handicaps, it is that some of the best features become accessible only by purchasing a more expensive version of the product. Although the Reader can perform simple searches through documents, it lacks the horsepower for performing large-scale searches through numerous documents, such as you might find on a CD-ROM. The search capabilities that you can embed through Adobe Catalog, based on the Verity indexing software, require Adobe Exchange for use. The modest Reader cannot perform indexed searches. In fairness, this approach appears common among the applications in this category—you often do not gain access to the most useful features of the program until you opt for the more expensive version.

Because of the simplicity of creating Adobe Acrobat PDF files, you can expect to see them appearing everywhere that electronic publications are appropriate (as well as places where they are not). The academic community, in particular, has enthusiastically adopted Acrobat as a tool for communication exchange. Samples of PDF files can be found on many different online service and throughout the Internet. One place to sample this form of document (including access to the *Adobe Acrobat in Academia* newsletter) on the World Wide Web is

```
http://www.fullfeed.com/epub/index.html
```

Common Ground

Although Adobe Acrobat has defined itself as the high end of portable document publishing, Common Ground Software, Inc. with its product Common Ground has taken a different road. Jay Saltzman, the product manager for Common Ground, distinguishes his product from Adobe Acrobat in these three ways: "We've focused on ensuring document fidelity, producing exact replicas of original documents. To do this, we use the Bitstream TrueDoc technology, which stores actual outlines of each font that is used within a document in a compact format. We also emphasize simplicity and value. Common Ground includes everything in one box with a retail price of $189 and a street price of around $140. Finally, we've created a lightweight technology that produces more compact files and uses a smaller viewer than our competitors."

To produce a portable document, you create the page layout and text in the application of your choice. You then select the Common Ground as the designated printer, either through Windows Printer selection options or through the Macintosh Chooser. With this driver selected, you can choose the Print option from your application and you create a Common Ground document, with the default extension .DP. This also launches Common Ground with the new document displayed and ready for further processing, as shown in Figure 5.6. You can affix sticky notes with scrolling text fields to different parts of a page, as also shown in this figure.

FIGURE 5.6.

Common Ground application window lets you add sticky notes or bookmarks to a document.

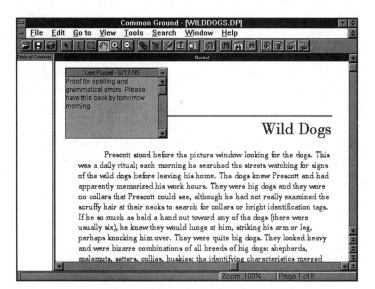

Creation of hypertext links is simple and intuitive. With the Link button activated, you highlight the text that you want to serve as the link and then navigate to where you want the link to jump and click once. You can use the equivalent to an electronic highlighter to emphasize text anywhere within the document. You can also place bookmarks (a list of pages you can jump to from the bookmark list) throughout a document to return to at a later time. Although these techniques are serviceable, every software producer seems to be relying on the same set of metaphors to serve as navigation guides in electronic documents. The paper-based model seems inescapable.

As with the Acrobat Reader, Common Ground's MiniViewer is a free product, and the company encourages the widest possible distribution of it. You can distribute the documents you create in Common Ground and the MiniViewer by any method available to a computer user: diskettes, CD-ROMs, networks, online services, BBS systems, tape, or disk cartridge. No fees are associated with distribution of this sort. The MiniViewer is also exceptionally compact, requiring less than 250KB for storage. You can also use the more elaborate ProViewer to read documents created in Common Ground. The ProViewer incorporates the Verity full-text search engine, a highly useful feature, if you want to perform extensive searches. The program creates indexes for single documents or collections of documents during the initial file creation. The search engine implementation includes the ability to provide context to search *hits* (items the search engine locates for you) by displaying the words surrounding each search hit (rather than just the document that the hit occurred in).

Searches can be extended through multiple documents by means of a feature that allows collections of documents to be defined. You first establish the documents that you want included in the collection. You can then initiate a search through the entire collection (or all collections) by choosing a button from the toolbar and specifying the search terms, as shown in Figure 5.7. The search engine then identifies documents with the specified terms.

FIGURE 5.7.

The search window in Common Ground includes a proximity option that evaluates the relation of search terms.

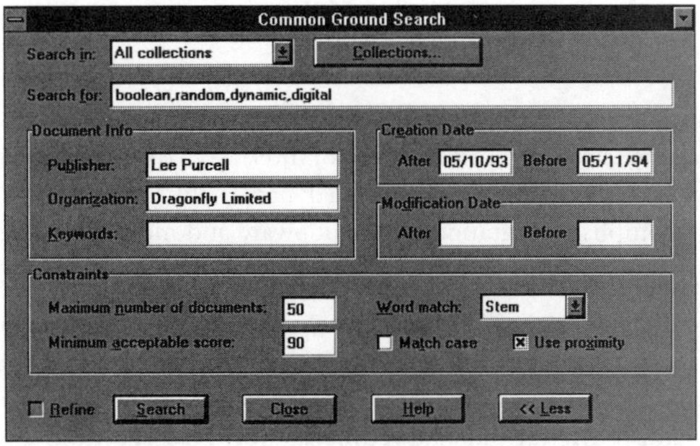

The Use Proximity checkbox shown in Figure 5.7 activates the context feature of the search engine. Search hits acquire a higher score if the search terms are within eight words or less of each other (if the terms are separated by more than eight words, a search hit is not recorded). The value you add to the box titled Minimum Acceptable Score serves as a filter to eliminate returned items from the search in which the context is inappropriate. Using the options provided in this search window, you can ensure greater precision in your search results and avoid wasting time on inappropriate search hits.

> **NOTE**
>
> Searches are performed by the reader after the document has been indexed by the author. This is entirely separate from links, which are placed by the author during document creation.

You can enable a number of security options to restrict use of an electronic document. You can prevent printing of a document or restrict the copying of text or graphics. You can also suppress the normal annotation and modification features that are usually available so that notes, links, and table of contents entries can't be added to documents. You can also restrict access to a document only to designated viewers by assigning password protection to it.

Common Ground includes features to simplify the transfer of electronic documents. One option when creating a portable file is to embed the MiniViewer into the document file to create an executable version of the file. You can launch the executable file directly without the need to install any additional viewer utility. This can be a boon in situations where the complexity of viewer installation process discourages someone from looking at a document. You also are relieved of the requirement of having to embed the fonts that you want displayed in the portable document. The technology used in this program accurately captures the font characteristics for display without actually embedding the full font data in the file. This results in more compressed document files.

You can integrate the facilities available through Common Ground into other applications through a set of application program interfaces (APIs). The viewer portion of the software is provided in both C++ libraries and a dynamic link library (DLL) so that third-party developers can accomplish integration with groupware and messaging products.

Common Ground achieves a good balance between utility and simplicity, providing a portable document production tool that anyone can use with a minimum of training. You can inexpensively distribute the compact MiniViewer, and the use of Bitstream's TrueDoc approach to font handling eliminates the need to embed fonts in a document. You can examine sample digital-paper documents and also see the "Page-on-demand" technology used in the new Common Ground Web Publishing System by accessing their Web site (`http://www.commonground.com`).

WordPerfect Envoy

WordPerfect Envoy bears many similarities to Adobe Acrobat and Common Ground. You install a print driver to produce electronic documents in the common distributable format. You can import formatted documents from a number of different source files, and then perform those modifications that prepare the document for electronic viewing and use. The features available for manipulating electronic documents also closely resemble Acrobat and Common Ground. You can create Hyperlinks to navigate internally within a document, but in this product they can't extend outside the file. You can create Bookmarks to provide access to individual pages at the reader's discretion, including a list of existing bookmarks the reader can quickly access through a menu to speed navigation. Users can attach notes to pages to personalize a portable document and annotate documents that are being worked on by more than one person.

Like Common Ground, Envoy provides an option that combines the electronic document with its own viewer utility, letting anyone open and read a document in the same manner as they would launch an application. Embedding the viewer into the document file swells the overall size of the resulting portable document file by more than 400KB. Envoy deals with fonts by letting you embed TrueType fonts or create substitutes as equivalents for PostScript Type 1 fonts. If you don't elect to embed fonts, the program carefully records the font metric values and uses them when redisplaying documents on screen with substitute fonts. A document as displayed in Envoy is shown in Figure 5.8.

FIGURE 5.8.

Envoy displays the electronic documents with headings, text, and callouts in the correct fonts.

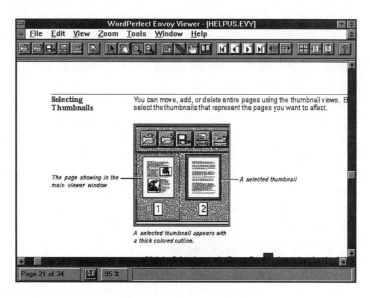

A variety of compression options for graphics lets you keep your document sizes under control. Envoy does well in handling and compressing lengthy documents; you can depend on it to create portable versions of word processor files that are more than 200 pages long. All in all, Envoy offers numerous features that make it quite capable for the large majority of portable document handling tasks.

SGML

Not so very long ago computers were brash, uncivilized machines with demanding needs that forced humans into the role of trying to think like computers. To troubleshoot some of these minicomputers and mainframes, technicians used to use a technique called "finger-boning," in which they would hand key machine code a bit at a time directly to the processor through a crude interface consisting of a series of switches. The processor responses appeared on a bank of LED read-outs. This is kind of like trying to communicate with a dolphin by playing tunes on an eight-note potato pipe.

SGML reminds me of finger-boning. You spend a lot of time trying to imagine how the computer is going to respond to a logical structure that you create and strings of codes that you feed to it. SGML stands for Standard Generalized Markup Language, and it is the result of over 10 years of committee planning with the goal to produce a platform-independent method for presenting electronic documents. The content and organization of the document is specified in a manner that it can be freely moved between operating systems and accessed by a variety of applications. If you specify something out of order, like the sequence of a chapter head and the type of paragraph that follows, the whole structure collapses. If someone does the work correctly, however, the document displays perfectly and can be shared and dynamically updated in a variety of ways.

The expertise to accomplish document creation under SGML until recently was carefully hoarded by a few highly paid consultants who earned their pay by mastering an intricate, rigorous development environment. The tools to help out in this effort were expensive and hard to use. That situation is changing with new PC-based tools that take at least some of the headaches out of maintaining and creating documents within this framework. Using SGML is not a matter of mastering a single application or learning how to format a document in particular; it requires an understanding of the entire development environment and adherence to a strict set of rules for planning and creating documents.

The three parts of any SGML document are

Declaration	A header file provides the platform-specific data that is required to access the document on a target computer.
Document Type Definition (DTD)	A hierarchical model of the document, the DTD is often presented as a tree structure that declares the various document elements and assigns attributes to them.

Document Instance   A collection of tagged text entries that represents the document contents, the instance must abide by the declared settings in the DTD.

Several tools are available to assist in each stage of this document creation process. Some companies are standardizing on sets of document type definitions, simplifying the creation of documents in certain categories, such as parts catalogs or procedures manuals. If the tools get good enough, enabling anyone to produce portable, updatable documents, SGML could continue to gain momentum, as many industry analysts think it will. Given the current set of the development environment, and the fact that you must pick and choose from an assortment of development tools rather than select a nicely integrated suite, considerable work is still left to be done before these applications are ready for mainstream use.

Some brief examples of application tools in this category follow.

ArborText's Adept Series

Tools in this set, consisting of both SGML editing and creation tools and a DTD creation application, are designed to be familiar to conventional Windows users. The SGML editor, Adept*Editor, uses drop-down menus and listboxes to assist in importing documents to convert to SGML format (based on a set of sample DTDs included with the product) or editing documents from scratch.

A design tool called Document Editor features modules that edit styles, create publishing applications within Adept, or perform editing of DTD files. Tutorials are included with this package, but a solid understanding of SGML principles is a prerequisite to performing any useful work with the tools.

SoftQuad's Author/Editor

Based on a word-processing paradigm, Author/Editor provides a simple means of entering text within the rule-based framework of SGML. You can start out working from supplied templates, and the program steers you straight if you attempt to violate any of the strictures of SGML formatting. As you're working in the editing environment, the program is linked to a specific DTD, and it uses the declarations in the DTD to ensure that the text entry stays within the guidelines.

The program includes a set of tools common to most word-processing applications: a spell-checking routine, thesaurus, macro editor, and a table creation tool. Author/Editor works in conjunction with a SoftQuad companion product called RulesBuilder. RulesBuilder creates binary versions of DTDs to be used with Author/Editor. ASCII-style DTDs cannot be used with the program. SoftQuad also offers a number of special-purpose applications that allow construction of custom SGML products and that perform style-guide related functions.

XSoft's InContext

Novice users of SGML can run off the rails fairly easily without some guidance. XSoft's InContext provides a development environment for SGML documents that lets novices learn quickly without violating the rules or producing erroneous documents. InContext reads ordinary ASCII DTD files and uses these as the basis for creation of a document instance.

A split screen includes an area to actually type in document content and an area that includes the logical elements derived from the DTD files. These logical elements represent the tags you can apply to the content; because you can only apply tags that have been defined in the DTD, you're prevented from entering anything that is out of context.

As you enter text into the content window, InContext lets you use conventional word-processing tools to check your work. A thesaurus, spelling checker, and grammar checker are included. You can import existing documents to work with in the content window, including documents that you create in a SGML framework. You can also design and apply style sheets to different elements, such as paragraph and character formatting.

InContext contains many features that should ensure its value to both beginning and experienced SGML editors.

Folio VIEWS 3.1 SGML Toolkit

Folio VIEWS, discussed more later in this chapter, is a tool to produce infobases; infobases are document repositories containing text and objects that you can rapidly search through a sophisticated indexing scheme. If you've gone to all the work of creating a set of SGML documents, the SGML Toolkit can help you make better use of the information by exporting it into infobase format.

The Windows-based SGML Toolkit includes Exoterica's OmniMark SGML processing software. OmniMark can automate the conversion process in conjunction with a SGML software driver Folio provides. It validates data before conversion, ensuring that the resulting infobase will be readable within Folio VIEWS. OmniMark can either perform conversion from one of several standard DTDs or you can adapt it to operate with a particular DTD.

HTML

Hypertext Markup Language (HTML) separates the physical appearance of a document from its structure and content. This simple characteristic has enabled HTML to drive the phenomenal success of the World Wide Web as a communication medium. Simpler in construction than its parent language—SGML—HTML lets electronic publishers independently design an information structure that can be seamlessly plugged into the larger structure that the Web provides. Individual browsers running on different platforms can interpret an HTML file (regardless of what platform it originated on), supply the formatting and links associated with it, and plug in specified graphics when so directed. All of this is accomplished through a system of tags, embedded codes that determine the structure of an HTML document by standardizing the basic, included elements. Headings, titles, paragraph types, and other elements are already defined as components of HTML; you specify these components by entering the appropriate tag for each surrounded by angle brackets. For example, the tag for title appears as `<TITLE>` in the text of your HTML document.

> **TIP**
>
> Individual Web browsers display HTML files slightly differently. Fonts, line separators, bullets, and other graphic elements vary slightly from browser to browser. Because the Web browser installs and runs on your personal computer, you can use it to view Web pages on the Internet, or (with most browsers) you can look at properly coded HTML files right on your personal computer (without connecting to the Net). You might want to assemble a collection of browsers to view HTML files that you create. This would give you the opportunity to view the variances in the file display under an assortment of browsers before actually posting a file on the Web.

HTML is evolving quickly through a series of levels, each one with a set of defined properties. At the moment most HTML files are produced in Level 2.0 format, although the full range of version 2.0 are not commonly used. To produce an HTML document, you can use a line editor or a word processor capable of generating ASCII text output. You position your tags in the correct places, add the text that constitutes the content of your document, save the file, and then test the whole thing by viewing the file in one or more Web browsers. This is the most direct way of creating a file, but it is also the most demanding. If you knew what you were doing, you could generate complex graphics simply by specifying the appropriate command statements in a PostScript file. It's easier, of course, to do this in Adobe Illustrator and let the program generate the corresponding commands as you position circles, lines, and rectangles.

In the same manner of thinking, it can be much easier to generate an HTML file using a utility that handles the tagging for you and offers some kind of framework for the file creation. Properly designed, a program of this sort can catch your mistakes and correct them, provide visual feedback to the appearance of your document (as it will be seen by a browser), and unify the file creation. Applications of this type come in a couple of varieties. Some act as extensions and filters to existing word processor applications; you create the HTML document using the conventions you are familiar with in the word processor and export it into HTML format. Microsoft's Internet Assistant for Microsoft Word is an example of this approach, as is Interleaf's Cyberleaf. Other applications serve as standalone development environments optimized for tagging and constructing HTML documents. Both approaches have individual merits and drawbacks.

The following subsections briefly describe some of the tools available for creating HTML documents. Another quick approach to mastering this standard is to pick up a copy of *Teach Yourself Web Publishing with HTML in a Week*, by Laura Lemay (Sams Publishing), and *Teach Yourself More Web Publishing with HTML in a Week*, by Laura Lemay (published by Sams.net).

SoftQuad's HoTMetaL Pro

Everyone wants a presence on the Web. HoTMetaL can put you there with a minimum of effort. As an easy-to-use HTML editor, HoTMetaL Pro provides templates, one of which includes all of the components for a Home Page on the Web. You change the text entries to fit your own description, save the file, upload to the server where you have an account, and almost magically you become part of the Web. You can include pictures of your dogs, cats, kids, wife, and goldfish and state your aspirations to challenge Bill Gates to a racquetball competition, winner take all, for the ownership of Microsoft.

HoTMetaL Pro lets you access and insert all of the necessary HTML tags into a text document using a scrollable listbox of tag names. Tags appear boldly outlined in the document, as shown in Figure 5.9, so they are easy to distinguish from the body of your HTML document. Correct your mistakes with a spelling checker. Enlarge your vocabulary with a built-in thesaurus. Preview your HTML document in your choice of selected Web browsers. The features included in this program can get even a novice HTML editor up and running in a short time.

FIGURE 5.9.

HoTMetaL tags can be applied to document text from the main application window.

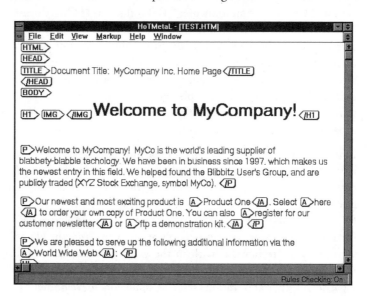

Like many programs in this category, HoTMetaL Pro includes a validation feature to ensure that your created HTML files are free from errors. You can also identify problems in other HTML files created outside of HoTMetal Pro by using the filters for HTML file import. If you get tired of looking at the tags during file creation, you can turn off the display of them to view the file content only. HoTMetaL Pro also features a publish command that prepares the HTML file for uploading by replacing the references to your hard disk (which serves as the URL during file creation) with actual URLs that will apply on the Web.

CAUTION

One minor drawback is that it is actually more strict than the actual HTML specification in what tags it requires you to use.

SoftQuad has a freeware version of this product that includes most, but not all, of the features. You are free to use it for all purposes other than commercial application; it provides a good introduction to the capabilities of the program. You lose some of the high-end features, like the built-in spelling checker, thesaurus, and HTML import filter, but you can still create error-free HTML files and experiment with different forms of Web documents.

Brooklyn North Software Works' HTML Assistant Pro

Based on a toolbar-oriented interface, HTML Assistant Pro lets you insert HTML tags into a document by pointing and clicking. The toolbar is extensible, so you can enlarge your range of commands to handle additional tasks within the program. The visual composition of the application window (shown in Figure 5.10) provides comfortable access to the program features, and HTML Assistant Pro includes a feature called Automatic Page Creator that performs like some of the wizards currently appearing in programs to guide you through procedures.

FIGURE 5.10.

HTML Assistant Pro application window provides full access to the program features.

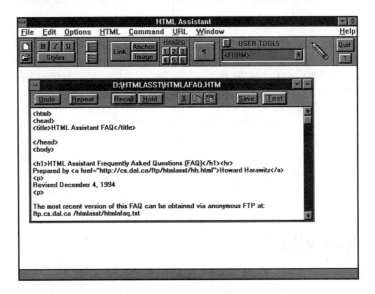

Another interesting feature is a URL Manager, an area of the program where you can store a library of URL listings with accompanying descriptions. You can access the contents of this library whenever you need to embed a URL to indicate a link to another resource. Because URL addresses are especially prone to typos and subtle errors (which render the links worthless), this feature ensures that you can create hypertext links on the Web with properly specified URLs.

The clear organization of the HTML Assistant Pro application window makes it a worthwhile tool for easing yourself through some of the more difficult aspects of producing HTML documents. Most program functions are quickly accessible through the toolbar or through a list accessed from the toolbar. Rarely do you have to go two levels deep to perform any task. This makes HTML Assistant Pro easy to navigate and a pleasure to use.

Hypertext Tools

Of all the categories mentioned so far, this one is perhaps the most nebulous. Most of the applications discussed in this chapter support some type of hypertext linking, even down to the lowliest of the portable document tools. Help systems have hypertext linking, HTML represents a global form of hypertext linking—what is different about this category?

An emerging class of information management tools now address not only electronic publishing needs, but also provide flexible, creative, and intuitive access to information. When fast access has been important, programmers have typically relied on traditional relational databases as the applications for storing electronic information. However, these types of search programs work best when the database stores the information in specific fields (which are usually of a fixed length and subject to many restrictions).

Free-form data or unstructured data, such as may appear in the electronic version of PC Magazine or 45MB of data downloaded from the LEXIS/NEXIS service, doesn't usually fit neatly into fields. Tools within this group, perhaps best represented by applications, such as Folio VIEWS, are redefining the way that information is stored and accessed. The power of these new types of tools—which we are calling hypertext tools in this chapter—rests in their ability to index terms stored within a mass of free-form data and provide dynamic techniques for searching through hundreds of Megabytes of data to isolate a fact or access a specific article. This capability may be overkill if you're planning on releasing your 100-page collection of poetry in electronic form, but it is essential if you're dealing with thousands of pages of documentation for a networking application or the parts catalog and electronic design specifications for a Boeing aircraft.

Folio VIEWS

Folio VIEWS creates infobases. Infobases represent an entirely new approach to storing and accessing information, and this approach promises to be on the leading edge for electronic publishers in the coming years. "What is an infobase?" Folio asks on the front of one of their promotional T-shirts. On the back of the shirt in a blue and green box it says, "A Place to Put Your Stuff." Around the perimeters of the box, it continues, "Get Your Stuff Together," "Get At Your Stuff," "Personalize Your Stuff." This says it better than you could in more academic terms.

The "stuff" of an infobase consists of indexed data stored in a compressed format. It can also include formatting information and multimedia objects, such as video clips, sounds, and graphics. VIEWS doesn't position itself as the final repository of information, but kind of an information interchange. You can import existing electronic documents from a variety of formats, including Microsoft Word, WordPerfect, RTF files, ASCII text, LEXIS/NEXIS data, and a proprietary pre-coded format called Folio Flat File. You can also export to Word, ASCII, or Folio Flat File, or extend your capabilities with the VIEWS 3.1 Filter Pack that provides import and export options for more than 70 database, word processing, and desktop publishing programs.

Why, you might be wondering, would you want to bring electronic publications into VIEWS in the first place? The two major reasons are accessibility and personalization. Once in infobase format, electronic documents become accessible through a fully indexed search engine that can effectively extract facts, information, article references, and other small details from hundreds of megabytes of data in a matter of seconds. The second major reason is the ability to customize the information to your own needs or the needs of workgroup project collaborators. VIEWS supports a number of techniques that let you annotate, extend, modify, mark, and otherwise add value to the mass of data in the infobase. If you are producing electronically published materials for distribution, you can extend these characteristics and the ability to personalize information to viewers of the infobase as well.

As a publishing tool, VIEWS offers particular benefits within the corporate environment, where documents and information circulate through a variety of channels with increasing reliance on electronic documents. In a June 1995 phone conversation with Curt Allen, the Executive Vice President of Folio Corporation, he described the difference between conventional databases and infobases in these words:

> "A relational database is a nice point to launch from for a lot of people. They know that a database is where you store your really important information. They know that it tends to be a mission-critical or business-critical application, and a lot of tools are built to access and use that information. What we try to point out is that a relational database is excellent for very structured information, but very poor for full-text information that constitutes the majority of business documents that we deal with. We've got support for this position from Larry Ellison at Oracle who claims that 70 to 90% of all the information we deal with doesn't lend itself to a relational database. The largest purveyor of relational technology in the world is admitting that we need something different for reference documents and business information."

The capabilities of an infobase can improve the flow and distribution of information throughout a company. Curt Allen offered this example:

> "A really good example of this is Powersoft. They were using a relational database to do their customer support, but they found that to do a search on their relational database was taking as much as 6 minutes per query. Their support times started to become a serious problem, with people on hold for long periods. We went in and replaced that system over a weekend. They had their documents nicely organized as Microsoft Word files—over 200MB—and using our import feature, they were able to import all of their support information into an infobase, it automatically built tables of contents for them, automatically built hypertext links, automatically embedded the images. Their search times went down to less than a second."

Powersoft now offers customers a CD-ROM version of their support infobase containing educational materials, white papers, service information, and application notes.

Creating and Using an Infobase

Several techniques exist for creating an infobase using VIEWS. You can start with an existing set of documents for importing. By preprocessing these files before importation, you can structure them in a way to make them more usable in VIEWS. You can define levels of headings in such a way as to automatically generate a hierarchical table of contents in the infobase. You can also determine how imported data will be segmented: by page breaks, paragraph breaks, line feeds, or other defined record breaks. A Folio utility called CREATE lets you import and structure data for an infobase.

The main reference window for Folio VIEWS (shown in Figure 5.11) provides a customizable Toolbelt along the left edge of the window that you can use for navigation, annotation, or launching searches.

Once you become familiar with the program, you can substitute icons for those commands you want most frequent access to on the Toolbelt. Launching queries through an infobase begins within the Query dialog box, shown in Figure 5.12. To simplify the search process and focus on precise results, VIEWS provides a dynamic visual display of the search hits. As you enter search terms in the edit box, VIEWS constructs a treelike graphic tabulating the number of search hits. Because this feedback occurs almost instantaneously, you can model each search in such a way that you get the desired amount of information retrieved to examine. You can also devise query templates that you can store in a file and reload to guide complex future searches.

FIGURE 5.11.

Reference window in VIEWS showing a customized Toolbelt on the left.

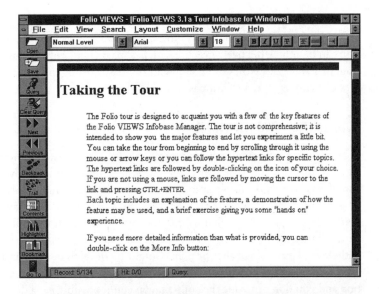

FIGURE 5.12.

Query dialog box in VIEWS lets you initiate simple or complex searches.

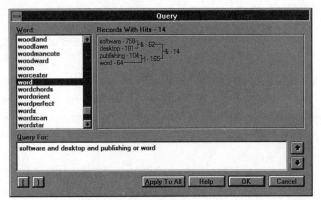

The standard assortment of personalization tools are also provided to let you customize a document to your requirements. An infobase viewer can highlight phrases in text, insert bookmarks to easily find a key piece of information, embed jumps from one part of a document to another, and follow a trail of previously viewed pages back to the source. VIEWS uses a concept known as Shadow Files, which add extensions to an existing infobase for personal use, but do not modify the core contents of a centrally stored infobase that may be on a network or stored on a CD-ROM (which, of course, can't be written). Shadow Files also provide a useful feature for collaboration efforts, allowing several people to annotate and comment on different parts of a single infobase, which might contain detail of a project proposal or the design specifications for a new product.

Folio has also produced a product called Folio Fusion that integrates the features of the popular workgroup application, Lotus Notes, with the storage and indexing strengths of VIEWS. You can be more effectively execute searches, particularly of very large collections of information, in VIEWS. A Notes filter allows an infobase creator to import large collections of Notes files and convert them to infobase format.

Chunking Information

Whether we are developing help systems or infobases, a recurrent term is used to describe the way the information is subdivided: *chunking*. Chunking is a way of breaking down large, complex constructs of information into small units that can be easily handled for searches and on-screen display. I asked Curt Allen if he saw a danger in losing context by presenting information in chunks. He replied to this and other queries in the following sidebar, "You get a decontextualization problem if you don't find a way to provide significant context to people. A pathological example of that principle might be in reference to hazardous chemical information, which is referenced using material data safety sheets. If you decontextualize the information and you don't provide the context, you could possibly get a description of a chemical and lose the hazardous warning that goes along with it because it happened to be in the next chunk."

CHUNKING INFORMATION

Q: How do you avoid this problem in Folio VIEWS?

A: What we do in the infobase is provide the entire context around the particular chunk you may be looking at. You can always scroll up or down, and you can always link back and forth, and you can always see a table of contents that shows where things fit.

Q Does information chunking make it difficult for people to use information?

A: The big problem that we have today is that there is no reusability of information chunks. Everything is built as a big monolithic product; there is not a good way for people who want to sort and sift and organize and prioritize stuff to impose their own point of view on it. That is really the benefit that we are giving to people—we allow them to take the raw material, data, and turn it into really valuable information.

Applications for VIEWS

Beyond financial and legal applications (which may be the bread and butter of electronic publishing in the corporate world), the flexibility of Folio VIEWS makes it well suited for other applications. Nintendo has created an infobase filled with games hints and tips that their support specialists use. The support specialists access actual stored images of the game screens along with the hints so they can describe the game operation clearly. If you need to know how to eliminate the nasty-tempered beaver boss, the infobase reminds you of the appropriate strategy: jump on his head five times.

Disney World is using VIEWS to coordinate activities of incoming guests and provide scheduling of their popular characters (after all, Mickey can only be in one place at one time). A commercial product constructed in VIEWS, called the Mega Movie Guide, provides a comprehensive listing of motion picture films including numerous cinema clips that can quickly access any entry. The possible applications for this tool are numerous, and its flexibility makes it likely that creative developers will find many ways to use it for electronic publishing.

re:Search

This authoring and retrieval application from re:Search International, includes a simple design environment and powerful built-in search engine with features such as proximity searches. The company has positioned the product as a delivery medium for information on CD-ROM, and their product licensing options provide several different alternatives for distributing the run-time search engine on disc. A single fee covers licensing for a specified period of time and serves as a royalty free approach for authors and developers distributing CD-ROM titles.

Hypertext links are fully supported as you construct a document, and you can also connect hypertext links with images, which do not appear as you are browsing a document, but only when you click on the link to the embedded figure. Figure 5.13 shows an image of King Tut that was accessed through a link within a document discussing in a re:Search demo database. Once displayed, the product lets you zoom in or zoom out on the graphic image. When you finish viewing it, you close the image and return to the source document.

FIGURE 5.13.

Embedded King Tut graphic can be accessed through a link in a browsed document.

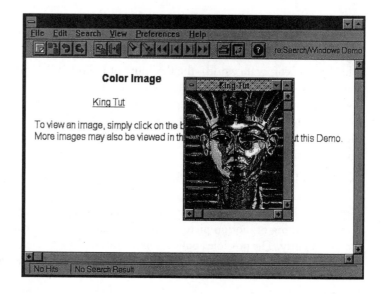

You can set up a set of specific fields for any given database and use it as an additional mechanism for performing searches. You can also conduct searches on a word-by-word basis—re:Search indexes the full-text contents of each database. You can organize the contents of a database through a DataSet, which defines a limited subset of the overall database, and then searches in a more specific fashion. re:Search International describes this product as being optimized for use with CD-ROM technology.

Users can personalize databases that they are viewing through the use of the ubiquitous Sticky Notes approach. They can affix Notes to any document where it then appears as an icon which they can be click to read. re:Search also lets you copy portions of the text to a clipboard or print selected sections.

An API toolkit is available for those who want to create applications using the underlying technology of re:Search. The functions in the toolkit support most of the features available through the DecisionWorks search and retrieval engine. The API information is documented in online form with examples for each of the functions.

Although this tool does not have the abundant features of some other applications in this category, its design simplicity, powerful search engine, and licensing policies should prove appealing to electronic publishers interested in releasing CD-ROM titles.

dataDisc QuickSearch

QuickSearch by dataDisc is a product that has its origins in the trenches of the CD-ROM service bureau business. For years, dataDisc has provided services for a number of clients and has successfully created CD-ROM based catalogs, references, medical documents, legal documents, training packages, and just about anything else you can think of in the realm of electronic publishing. They have extended their business to include software products, training, recordable media, CD-recorder bundles, and other products repackaged from OEMs. Their background and experience in this industry suggests a degree of experience with the technology that may be lacking in more recent vendors of CD-ROM-based products.

You can import data or documents from a variety of sources, and then activate the QuickSearch indexing utility. The indexing utility creates an alphabetical index of each word in the document that becomes accessible through the WordWheel, a small window that lets you quickly perform word-based searches and jump from search hit to search hit through the document contents. QuickSearch provides rapid full-text indexing and supports proximity searches, use of wildcards, phrases, embedded image references, as well as other techniques for locating information.

Support for image handling is extensive. QuickSearch can handle TIFF, PCX, GIF, JPEG, PhotoCD, TGA, BMP, WMF, CALS, WPG, DIB, DCX, and PICT. You could, for example, create an electronic document containing a series of PhotoCD images, and then display them by reference to text-based captions that can be displayed in an adjacent window. Figure 5.14 shows the image of the U.S. Constitution in one window and the text of the Constitution in another.

FIGURE 5.14.

An image of the U.S. Constitution can be examined beside the actual text.

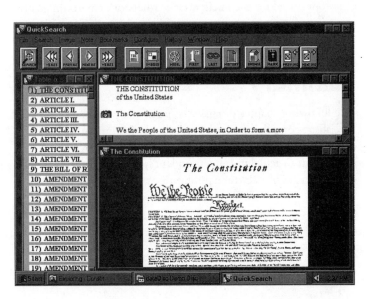

QuickSearch also provides support for two popular corporate and organizational approaches to data archiving and storage: COM and COLD. COM, Computer Output to Microfiche, lets you directly create microfiches from your computer-stored data. COLD, Computer Output to Laser Disc, lets you record records and data directly to recordable CD media. COLD promises to become one of the most important new technological uses for CD-ROM as a direct replacement for previous backup and archiving systems.

A companion product, DiscMaker, provides a simple way to transfer your QuickSearch files to recordable CD. The combination of these two software products, a suitable computer system, and a connected CD recorder could provide all the necessary tools to get started with full-fledged electronic publishing.

Other Tools

Other tools in this category include the following:

- **Guide Author by InfoAccess Inc.** creates hypertext documents in a Windows word processor-like environment. Includes a passive viewing tool that can be freely distributed.

- **HyperWriter for Windows by Ntergaid Inc.** provides a multitude of hypertext authoring features and support for interesting special effects, such as image fades that serve as transitions between sequences. A more elaborate product by the same company, HyperWriter Professional, supports branching links for more complex interactivity.

- **OracleBook by Oracle Corporation** provides tools to create hypertext documents optimized for use in client/server network environments that involve cross-platform use of documents. A variety of filters let you import documents from more than 80 different sources.

Summary

The following chapter discusses some of the potential career paths for electronic publishing specialists, completing Part I of this book. Beginning with Part II, "Organization and Design of Electronic Documents," you get the opportunity to see some of the tools introduced in this chapter put to actual use and abundant opportunities to try your own hand at creating several different types of electronic publications.

Career Prospects

6

by Lee Purcell

IN THIS CHAPTER

Electronic publishing and interactive multimedia call for skilled generalists rather than niche specialists. Successful practitioners of the various forms of new media come from every conceivable communications field: graphic arts, book publishing, cinema, music, technical writing, theatre, television production, radio, advertising, journalism. With a little searching you could probably even find a multimedia company executive who was formerly a dog-sled handler from a remote Alaskan village. The digital revolution rewards anyone who can learn to express ideas by manipulating the fundamental unit of exchange: bits.

Are there career opportunities for multimedia authors and electronic publishers? Yes, definitely, but the career paths are not as well-defined as are those for becoming a doctor or lawyer or electrician. One route to obtaining the necessary expertise is to attend a specialized educational facility. A growing number of schools are offering courses that teach the primary skills required for creating works in the electronic realm. For instance, the Georgia Tech Center for New Media in Atlanta offers a certificate program in Multimedia. Classes at The Art Institute of Pittsburgh promise to help you "Create your career in computer animation." The Vancouver Film School in British Columbia, Canada, offers full programs in Multimedia Production. As the importance of new media communication has become more evident, colleges and universities and private enterprises have responded to the challenge by designing coursework to provide the training and mastery of computer-based tools.

Another way to enter the field is to transfer your skills from a closely related communication medium, such as film. Paul Pallar and Peter Haklar of Palo Haklar Associates, a Los Angeles-area producer of educational CD-ROM titles, created a number of documentary films before becoming interested in the CD-ROM as a vehicle for interactive productions. They found working on CD-ROM titles a natural extension of their documentary production work. As Paul explained, "We approach creating a CD-ROM title in exactly the same way as making a film."

This includes writing a full script, creating an elaborate storyboard, and working with studio musicians to create the appropriate background music. The musicians hired to create background music for their titles, such as *Voyage through the Solar System*, are the same ones actively working in the Los Angeles area to write commercial jingles and musical soundtracks for television shows.

Although there is no single path to forging a career in electronic publishing, you can obtain job leads and learn about career possibilities in many places. Some fundamental changes are also arising in the way that people obtain jobs, such as an increasing reliance on electronic résumés and sophisticated search techniques to match employees with employers. The physical paperwork that has been the underpinning of job search and hiring activities is being replaced by speed-of-light information exchange through electronic channels. You can have your résumé in the hands of dozens of prospective employers faster than you could make a trip to the print shop to have some paper copies run. Chapter 26, "Publishing a Multimedia Résumé," describes techniques you can use to create your own electronic résumé.

This chapter looks at several areas related to careers in electronic publishing, including the types of jobs available, the effects of groupware and electronic résumés on the hiring process, and future employment opportunities and career possibilities in this rapidly evolving field.

Electronic Publishing and Groupware Change Hiring

Paper-based résumés and published job listings (usually appearing in newspapers or professional journals) have been the primary search tools for potential employees and employers. Job candidates scan the Sunday offerings in the employment section of the newspaper and mail out résumés to those companies that look interesting. The résumés get sorted by human resources professionals, dropped into file cabinets, and consulted as needed (assuming the hiring professional has a reasonable system of indexing and accessing specific résumés). Once you send out a batch of résumés, you can spend weeks waiting to receive a reply by phone or to receive one of those carefully neutral postcards that let you know the company has placed your résumé on file.

As a system woefully dependent on paper, traditional hiring practices are, by design, slow and inefficient. Lots of time gets invested in filling out pieces of paper, filing paper, sorting paper, and moving paper between desks and offices. Remove the element of paper, however, and substitute mobile, fast-moving electrons, and you have the basis of a system that can genuinely run rings around traditional systems. This fact has not escaped notice by some innovative companies and individuals who have adopted electronic versions of formerly paper-based information and embraced groupware as the solution to moving information among members of collaborative workgroups. Although particular organizations have accepted groupware for applications within their own walls, new applications are being devised to bring down the walls and extend the reach of groupware to participants outside the organization.

> **NOTE**
>
> You can find more information on this topic in Chapter 26.

Groupware refers to software applications designed for use among members of an organization with common goals, whether the goal is to write a marketing proposal, create an advertising campaign, launch a new product, or hire the best individuals to meet the needs of a company. Products such as Lotus Notes and Novell GroupWise are designed to break down the barriers of different computer platforms and provide a common medium for exchanging computer-based information. Groupware serves to transport and deliver business information, often across network channels, with speed, efficiency, and accessibility. If you think of all the paper information that is shuffled around within businesses—reports, schedules, résumés, spreadsheets, memoranda, databases, and similar information—all of this information can be gathered under a single umbrella and turned into electronically published documents. Once in electronic form, instead of lying dumbly in a file cabinet, documents become searchable using electronic methods. Stacks of résumés can be sorted by particular search requirements (collect all the graduates of Stanford and the Massachusetts Institute of Technology and place them in one big stack). Years of memos can be sorted on a timeline. Individuals can consult their personal schedules to see if they will be available for a critical product management meeting. Information can be more easily shared, assembled, assimilated, and directed towards solving problems. In many ways, groupware establishes a platform-independent method for distributing the reams of formerly paper-based information that feeds and nourishes an organization.

If you apply groupware tools to the hiring process, the improvements in the work flow can be enormous. One company, SkillSet Software, has done exactly that with their recruitment and hiring application, Desktop Recruiter. Constructed using Lotus Notes, Desktop Recruiter assists the hiring professional with each task required to fill a job position. After experimenting with other Microsoft Windows development tools to create the product, the staff of SkillSet Software (a group with a background in executive search techniques) finally decided on Lotus Notes as the most direct and flexible means for eliminating platform boundaries and providing flexibility and extensibility to Desktop Recruiter.

Like other forms of groupware, Lotus Notes relies on a client/server approach to shared information. The client portion of the program consists of an application that runs on each individual workstation. The server portion is a shared document database that resides in a central location and manages the use and modifications of the database contents. The client portion of the software makes queries to the server and receives data and requested information in return. For example, the client may initiate a query to search through the database and locate job candidates who recently graduated from mid-Western universities with degrees in Agriculture and who are willing to relocate to other countries. The server processes the query, searches through the stored data, and returns a set of matches to the client, who can then refine the original query and initiate a new one.

Employers at the client end of the program can custom-tailor it to suit an extremely wide variety of requirements. You can start out using any of the available Lotus Notes templates, or you can start from scratch using tools provided with the Notes: Forms, Views, and Macros. Hard-core programmers can also use collections of APIs (Application Programming Interfaces) to develop applications. With the availability of APIs, and the standardization provided by the data structures defined within the application, you can adapt Lotus Notes to extremely sophisticated types of applications much more rapidly than if you code an application from scratch.

Dan White, President of SkillSet Software, sees the shared database approach as unifying what used to be two completely separate aspects of the job recruiting process. "If you look at employment today, there are vendors who want to provide applicant tracking, résumé scanning, information management, and so on, from within the employer. Then there are those providers that want to gather information about people into databases and provide these databases to potential employers. There hasn't been the notion of the same system on both sides. We're trying to do that—to provide a single system that serves both needs."

SkillSet® Software uses the Lotus Notes database as a central repository to allow job seekers to directly input information and employers to search and directly output lists of prospective candidates. For example, the SkillNet Connect service of SkillSet Software links colleges with potential employers using Desktop Recruiter® as the common medium. Employers can post job openings directly to participating colleges; students can scan job listings and submit their résumés in electronic form to those employers who seem best suited to their aspirations. Job matches can be made in hours, rather than the weeks required by conventional job search techniques.

Applications such as Desktop Recruiter reduce the reliance on paper by creating electronic versions of familiar documents. Human Resources departments typically depend on an extensive array of paper forms used to initiate hiring: job descriptions, requisition forms, employment applications, interview notes, reference checks, employee evaluation forms, cost-per-hire listings, and so on. Each of these specific forms can be incorporated as an electronic form within Desktop Recruiter. Although the promise of the paperless office has hovered tantalizingly close for years, groupware products make this promise a reality.

Creating electronic résumés requires somewhat different skills than composing conventional print résumés, although in the case of adapting a print résumé to one of the portable document formats, such as Adobe Acrobat, the creation can be as simple as printing to the .PDF print driver. Other types of résumés that incorporate multimedia elements or use HTML as a creation tool require a bit more sophistication.

Dan White sees the nature of hiring changing as electronic techniques for exchanging job information become more prevalent. "Right now, as candidates compete for jobs, in terms of supply and demand, the job is the supply and the individual is the demand. Over the next several years, as online information exchange improves, jobs will become more like consumer products. The individual will be able to browse and select from available job options, as opposed to the way it is today (which is résumés being browsed through and selected from by employers). The way things are going—and part of the guiding philosophy behind our company—the person is a consumer of information. Companies will design persuasive presentations and online multimedia brochures to demonstrate to the individual: 'this is a good place to work.'" For more information about SkillSet, call 415-328-7858.

Groupware uses extend beyond recruiting to include any kind of collaborative efforts among individuals. Whether a workgroup is attempting to compose a marketing product description using network tools or write a script for a corporate training program, groupware can assist and coordinate electronic publishing efforts in a network environment.

Grooming Online Communicators

Like the swift and savvy "bicycle" messengers cruising future San Francisco streets in William Gibson's novel *Virtual Light*, online communicators must adapt to a new, fluid medium whose precedents are rooted in earlier, more static communication techniques. Online communication at its best includes more color, more dynamicism, and more inventiveness than prior print media and linear broadcast media. How does one acquire the design skills to participate in a largely undefined form of communication?

One way might be to log on to designOnline, a networked meeting place for new media design professionals and would-be professionals. designOnline sprang into being in 1990 with the intention of being an idea exchange for service bureaus, design firms, and graphic artists. The initial site consisted of a computer bulletin board enhanced with a graphical user interface. The BBS and FirstClass Client software still guide users through a mass of information relating to design conferences, font libraries, topical news coverage, and an ongoing forum; a recent added Web site provides another access channel for interested parties.

Staff member Jill Wohl, a self-described "editrix" for designOnline, sees the opportunity for providing information in two primary categories within this rapidly evolving framework. "We are looking to develop 'design on the edge', a section on our Web site into two main sections: 'how' and 'why'. Many people online are concerned with 'how' to do things: how to write HTML code, how to use Kai's Power Tools, how to wrap text on a curve in Illustrator. We would like to develop an even greater interest in the 'why' (design theory, systems design, and so on)."

"Why? Well, the world is undergoing a publishing revolution—sort of like Gutenberg to the nth power; online publishing and design tools are more accessible and easier to use than ever before. The byproduct of this democratization has glossed over providing equal access to design theory and systems. That is why we aim to be an information center for the "how" and the 'why', but especially the 'why'.

As designOnline continues to expand their coverage of techniques for presenting information electronically, they will be enlisting the services of contributors to provide topics in a form that can be easily accessed through online means. As Jill explains, "We do need contributors to our sites—however, we have realized that the format we provide this information in is limited by two factors: HTML constraints and our audience's attention span. But, while we are interested in manifestos and a new digital design order, we are not interested in esoterica and philosophies that cannot be communicated to the producers of next-generation design. As such, we would like to provide them with information and learning in 'chunklets.' The nature of hypertext makes the Web an ideal place to accomplish this goal—provide a taste of information along with links to more detailed stuff."

The boom in Web sites and the need for skilled online practitioners to present information in Web-digestible form has created many new job opportunities and this trend is bound to continue. To reach designOnline, point your Web browser at `http://www.dol.com.`, or access its BBS at 1-708-328-8723, `fcserver.dol.com`, Port 3000.

Virtual Campuses

Can educational coursework survive the transition to online delivery? If the number of online educational programs appearing in various media is any indication, online education is prospering. The advantages, of course, are the ability to sidestep geographic constraints and work around existing full-time jobs or other demands on your time. Ideally, online education can support career changes, allowing self-paced study, while still providing interaction with instructors and other students through interactive live forums, electronic mail, and other forms of online communication.

City University in Renton, Washington offers a program that they call INROADS (Information Resource and Online Academic Degree System), part of their Distance Learning approach to education. You need an Internet connection and a World Wide Web browser to gain entry to this virtual campus. You can obtain a bachelor's degree in a number of disciplines, train to take the exam for Microsoft Certified Professional status, or even complete a master's degree in business administration. For details, access `http://www.cityu.edu/inroads/welcome1.html`.

If you want to reach for an even higher degree, Walden University in Minneapolis, Minnesota offers doctoral programs tailored for mid-career professionals in their "university without walls." You can access Walden University through the Walden Information Network (WIN), which provides you access to faculty members, fellow students, the contents of a research university's graduate library, bulletin boards, and the Internet. A new Master's program in Educational Change and Technology Innovation has just been announced. You can obtain details by sending e-mail to `request@waldenu.edu`.

Obtaining Career Advice

The Web offers a considerable number of options for those seeking guidance and practical advice on beginning or continuing careers. Articles on establishing careers in high-tech areas and communication fields can help eliminate the uncertainty associated with entering into entirely new job areas.

Sources of online career information are increasing. *Career Magazine*, founded by a group of former executive recruiters and business managers, includes postings of current employment opportunities; a search engine that sorts listings by location, job titles, and skill requirements; and a news area that publishes articles on workplace issues, guidelines for obtaining the ideal job, job search strategies, and similar kinds of material. You can access *Career Magazine* at `http://www.careermag.com/careermag/`.

TechWeb, a production of CMP Publishing, presents 16 of its high-tech and communication-related publications online in a format expressly tailored for the Internet, with searchable article listings and a healthy sampling of perspective on the evolving job market in this area. Examples of its publications include *Communications Week*, *NetGuide*, and *Information Week*. You can reach their Web location at `http://www.TechWeb.cmp.com/net`.

A recent article from CMP's *NetGuide* entitled "Our Brilliant Careers" profiled a group of professionals who had successfully established new careers in niche areas involving the World Wide Web. The positions covered included Web designers, marketing and advertising professionals, interactive actors, small service providers, and skilled electronic librarians. These entertaining stories point out that jobs arising from the new media cauldron tap skills that require fresh definitions of conventional kinds of job experience. For example, the experiences of interactive actor Page Witte while she performed in Hyperbole Studios' "The Vortex" suggest that new theories of acting and stagecraft will be needed to support interactive drama. The Vortex, a CD-ROM title, weaves multiple plot lines throughout the story, each of which must be acted out by participants in the science fiction piece. Characters' reactions and manners change according to the viewer's responses as this interactive cinema work unfolds, leading to hundreds of different plot variations and sequences.

Another previously non-existent job category, the *cybrarian*, is also described in this article. Sue Feldman uses her background as a librarian, linguist, and researcher to help people find information in cyberspace. Sorting through masses of largely uncategorized information as well as carefully organized databases, Sue has turned her ability to ferret out needed information for clients into a successful business. She has founded the Association of Independent Information Professionals to further the goals of worldwide researchers who navigate networks in a never-ending quest for information.

Scanning the Job Market: Online Job Listings

For my own enlightenment, I searched a number of sites on the World Wide Web to see if anyone was actively soliciting people to work in electronic publishing-related careers. The good news is that there are numerous job openings and contract positions not only in the United States, but around the world. I noted that many of the companies attempting to fill positions mentioned telecommuting as a possibility; the chances of abandoning your daily commute and working remotely from your home computer are improving daily.

You also can find a number of places to post your personal résumé on the Web. With the soaring popularity of the Web, this might be the way to break into the field of electronic publishing, if you have acquired the skills to work effectively in this medium. By the time you have finished this book, you should have a solid start towards mastering the fundamental tools and understanding the steps required to create each of the primary types of electronically published works. We also devote Chapter 26 of this book to helping you prepare your own interactive résumé, which you could then distribute through network channels or on removable media.

Kinds of Positions

In my quick sampling of electronic publishing career opportunities on the Web, the kinds of positions available covered almost every conceivable aspect of the field. I've included the following list of employment possibilities and some important details for each one.

- World Wide Web developers are in demand in many places. In this capacity, you would design Web pages, create interactive response forms, establish links between individual pages, and generally create interactive documents using the tools of the trade. More experienced developers might get involved in setting up World Wide Web sites, a skill that requires significant network and computer hardware experience as well.

■ Technical writers with the ability to generate online help systems are in steady demand at many companies. Familiarity with help system development tools has replaced knowledge of specific desktop publishing packages as the most requested skill for technical writers. Once in a while (too rarely, unfortunately), companies are also interested in whether a technical writer understands the subject and can actually write. Windows help systems rank at the top of the desirability list; those who can develop Windows 95 help systems can probably write their own ticket at any company that is developing for this long-delayed platform.

■ Many publishers who have ventured into this field are seeking online editors for interactive journals. You'll find a wide assortment of companies and publications entering this domain: *Ziff-Davis Interactive, Utne Reader, Mother Jones magazine, Wired, Multimedia World,* and on and on. The role of the electronic journalist and online editor will become increasingly important in the years to come.

■ Graphic artists with the ability to design for electronic formats are in constant demand. Interactive catalogs, becoming common both on the Internet and on CD-ROM, require graphic artists and designers savvy to the latest generation of design tools. I also noticed many job offerings for computer animators; this specialty area seems to be gaining momentum as the interactive multimedia market heats up.

■ Fiction writers specializing in interactive works are represented in select areas on the Internet. Hypertext novels have become a quickly evolving artform, and the potential is enormous. One well-known electronic publisher, Eastgate, lets you sample hypertext works and order online. If you have a knack for fiction and can master the hypertext form, this could be an excellent way to showcase your talents.

■ Self-publishing opportunities abound on both the Internet and for CD-ROM distributed works. The software tools for developing electronic works are easier to learn, and hardware for mastering recordable CDs has dropped to within the range of anyone. You can distribute digital works in many ways inexpensively; self-publishing might be the best way to get your interactive reference, multimedia nature book, counter-culture fanzine, or jazz history CD-ROM into the hands of your audience.

■ Multimedia authors showed up quite often in the job postings on the Internet. Many organizations seemed to be looking for people with specific types of application knowledge, such as Macromedia Director, Authorware, Asymetrix Toolbook, or similar packages. If you can master one of these tools, you can gain a significant edge in the electronic publishing workplace. High-end multimedia authoring applications can usually perform well in a number of different development environments, from producing a simple interactive children's story to creating an extensive reference work with every known multimedia element. Your marketability rises sharply with your knowledge of these kinds of heavy-hitting, professional-grade applications.

FIGURE 6.1.

*Career Mosaic matches
employers with employees.*

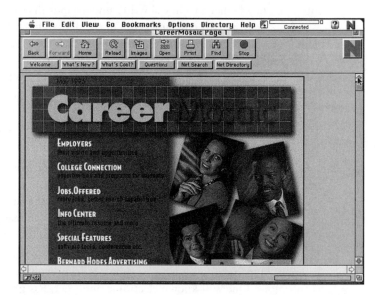

You can carry out searches of the extensive job offerings by filling in an on-screen form and launching the search (as shown in Figure 6.2). A list of jobs matching your requirements is returned at the end of the search.

Part of the excitement of the electronic publishing revolution is that opportunities and possibilities are arising every day as new tools are developed and creative minds devise new ways of presenting information within the digital framework offered by the computer.

#### Chapter 6

FIGURE 6.2.

Accessing the "Jobs Offered Database."

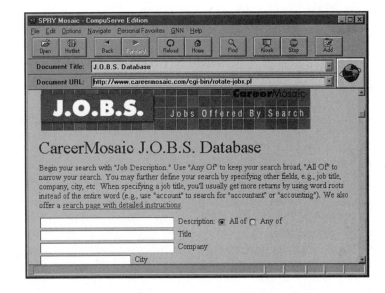

Summary

The goal of Part I of this book has been to introduce you to the concepts, tools, and possibilities of electronic publishing. With this background of knowledge you should feel comfortable as you begin Part II and move from the realm of theory into actual practice. The remainder of this book is devoted to giving you as much "hands-on" experience in the creation of electronic documents as possible. Those kinds of electronic documents that you've read about in Part I, you will be able to develop yourself in the chapters that follow.

PART

IN THIS PART

Organization and Design of Electronic Documents

Organizing Information

by

IN THIS CHAPTER

Blockbusters are not written, they are produced. Look at today's hit movies and TV shows. Behind the big scenes, you'll find a producer and often a collaborative team. Electronic mediums are no exception. Behind the big software titles, you'll find a team—producers, editors, writers, programmers, musicians, and artists. All these people help to organize ideas into a finely polished work. They do this by collaborating—organizing their ideas into a common structure through planning, revision, polishing, and evaluation.

Even when creative works are the result of a single person's efforts, the finished product is still a result of planning, revision, polishing, and fretting over the organization of the work. This is true even for creative people who claim never to use outlines. The simple fact is, finely polished works do not spring to the writer's pen, the painter's canvas, or the musician's note sheets. The best works are the result of effective strategies for thinking, planning, and composing. Helping you create the best electronic publications through effective strategies for thinking, planning, and composing is precisely what this chapter is all about.

You will learn the following in this chapter:

- Why organization is important
- The building blocks for creating effective electronic publications
- Improving ideas—techniques to better organize the electronic publication
- Effective strategies for planning and project organization
- Techniques to get the project started
- Techniques to organize the project for the audience
- The use of storyboards to help you organize and link the pages of the publication

Why Organization Is So Important

Electronic publishing is a new medium for your creativity. Spending a few hours thinking about something that you may spend years, or certainly months, working on makes sense. Getting organized is extremely important, more so when you are working in a new medium. Not only will it save you time, it will help you create a better project. This is true regardless of whether you plan to adapt existing projects or create entirely new projects for your electronic publishing ventures.

Too often, the tendency in electronic publishing is to produce an electronic version of the paper-based product. The result is a publication that does not work well and does not sell well. This is a major problem in electronic publishing today and nowhere is this more evident than on the Internet's World Wide Web. The Web is the ultimate form for electronic publications. It is an open-ended multimedia system that will let you seamlessly integrate sound, video, pictures, and text. Most of the electronic publications on the Web are organized like a book—complete with an index. The index is often the starting point for readers of the publication. Yet, an electronic extension of a traditional book is not what consumers want.

On the Web, you have only a few minutes to convince readers to stay. If you don't, they are going to go somewhere else for their information needs as quickly and effortlessly as you can remotely change the channel on your television. Yet, the key to success in Web publishing is not to attract one-time visitors, it is to attract repeat visitors to the publication. Publishers on the Web are discovering this the hard way.

The current trend in design on the Web is to create electronic publications primarily for repeat visitors while providing a means for the first-time visitor to learn about the publication. Publishers who have adapted this strategy have seen dramatic results, and all because a few innovative thinkers took the time to organize their thoughts before they created publications in the traditional manner.

These innovative thinkers applied some of the processes you'll learn in this chapter and came up with better ways to present information. You can apply these processes to any type of electronic publishing project. Creating electronic publications can either be a continuous struggle or a logically flowing process. Take the time to organize your thoughts. Not only will the pay-off be a better product, it will also mean time and resource savings.

Building Blocks for Creating Effective Publications

Think of the creative process as a building process. Try to build the roof of the house before you lay the foundation, and you are going to have serious problems. Pour the concrete for the foundation of the house before you put in the necessary plumbing for water and sewer access, and you are going to spend more money than you bargained for.

You build a house one step at a time. You ensure the house has a strong foundation. Buildings with strong foundations tend to weather the seasons and time. When you are almost done with the frame of the house, you build a roof. Although the roof of the house is the top of the structure, you don't stop there. It takes more than a covered frame to make a house. You hire an electrician to do the wiring and bring back the plumber to finish the plumbing. Afterward, you hang plaster board, add insulation, finish the exterior, add fixtures, and before you know it, you have a house that you can call home.

You build electronic publications in the same way, one step at a time following the activities covered in the previous section. Your start on the project is about as glamorous as the water and sewer pipes waiting for the foundation to be poured around them; for just when you are ready to roll back your sleeves and dive into the project with both feet, you may discover you need to conduct research, planning, or consider the requirements of the project. When you finally flesh out the foundation of the project, you start to build the framework. The basic components of any electronic publication are the pages that you link together. These pages help you create chapters, articles, and columns that can contain graphics and sound. Eventually, you finish composing the project, but find you still have to develop the software aspects of the project. Even when you have completed the composing and developing processes, the project still is not finished. You check the structure of the work for flaws. You make sure you have used the right mechanics and format. You examine the fixtures. Once all this is done, you finally have a project worthy of publishing.

Try to build the house all at once and you'll be overwhelmed. The same is true for any creative process. The way you organize your thoughts can make the difference between a successful project and a failed project. When you are building your electronic publication, you need to manage many things, both on a level of general organization and a more specific level of electronic publishing aspects including:

- Expectations
- Perceptions
- Strategies
- Goals
- Rules
- Behavior

Managing Expectations

If you mismanage expectations, your project will fail. Your expectations and the expectations of your superiors may be totally different. Before you begin any project, make sure your expectations and the expectations of your supervisors mesh. A good way to do this is to ensure that the communications channels are open and used. Discuss expectations from the beginning of the project. If you develop a rapid prototype of the project, your superiors should be the ones to verify that it meets their expectations. If the prototype does not meet their expectations, maybe the prototype was an example of what not to do for this project, or maybe the expectations were unrealistic.

You should also manage your personal expectations for the project. Your expectations play a major role in the success or failure of the project. The following is a list of do's and don't's to help you manage expectations:

- Don't expect the creation and development of the project to flow effortlessly.
- Don't expect first efforts to be perfect.
- Don't expect the completed project to be perfect.
- Do expect to make multiple drafts of the project.
- Do expect to revise, edit, and proof parts of the project.
- Do expect to say the project is "good enough" and that further time spent trying to perfect the project will not be cost effective.

Managing Perceptions

Your perceptions about the project play a decisive role in whether you'll ever finish the project. If you perceive the project as an impossibly large undertaking, you may cripple yourself mentally. If you perceive the project as a trivial undertaking, you won't produce your best work.

It is best to find a balance in your perceptions about the project. If you are working on an extremely large project, work on the project in manageable pieces. Do not try to combine the composition and development processes. Take them one at a time. Develop the textual part of the project a chapter, page, or word at a time—whatever it takes to pull you through the project.

As you begin to organize your project, keep in mind that electronic publishing is very often a team effort. Few electronic publishers will be able to handle all aspects of the publishing process on their own. For this reason, you should have an accurate perception of your abilities and know when it is in the best interest of the project to delegate tasks. For example, if the project requires extensive programming and you are not a programmer, you'll want to consider adding a programmer to the team. Not only will delegating tasks to other team members help ensure the success of the project, it will also take responsibilities off your shoulders and help you avoid feeling overwhelmed.

Managing Strategies

Could you imagine the task of writing 160,000 words, developing hundreds of graphic images, and creating two projects to fill over 425 pages in a little over two months? The thought of having to do this would overwhelm the best of writers. Yet, this is exactly what I had to do to complete my share of *Electronic Publishing Unleashed*. I managed the project by thinking of the work in terms that motivated me. It was not 159,000 words I had to write; it was 1,000 words completed. It was not 375 pages more to go; it was 50 pages down. It was not 16 chapters left to write; it was one chapter completed.

How you think about the project will materially affect the outcome. Manage the project in whatever way will motivate you. If one way of thinking about the project is not motivating you, change tactics. Break up difficult sections of the project. Tackle them one piece at a time. Rotate from section to section, working on each piece a little at a time. Whatever it takes to get the job done.

As an electronic publisher, you'll often wear many hats. You may have the role of the writer, graphic designer, composer, editor, and publisher. You may want to develop a strategy with these roles in mind. For example, if you are in the role of the writer and have been staring at a blank page for hours, you may want to change roles for a time. Why not create the preliminary artwork for a particular area of the publication? This will give you a chance to work on another area of the project, and you can return to writing at a later time with a fresh perspective.

Similarly, if you are working on a mundane but necessary part of the project, such as proofreading, think of a way to make the work more interesting or challenging. Bet yourself that you cannot proof portions of the project in certain amounts of time. And when you succeed, allow yourself a few moments of quiet celebration before you attack the project again.

Do not limit yourself to a few strategies or stick with one strategy when it obviously is not working. Make a list of strategies. If one strategy is not working, switch to a new one. If you don't have a new one, create a new one.

Managing Goals

When you start working on a project, one of the first things you should do is develop goals. Goals are usually developed in the requirements phase. Your goals should take into consideration the complexities and nuances of the project. Goals should be clear and relevant to the problem at hand. You should set major goals relevant to the purpose, scope, and audience of the project. You should also set minor goals or milestones for the stages of the project.

Goals and milestones help you define the project as a series of steps, processes or achievements. One major goal could be to complete the planning phase of the project. Another major goal could be to complete the design of the project. The series of steps or processes necessary to complete the major goals are the minor goals or milestones. Your first milestone will be to start work on the project. Another milestone may be to select and purchase an authoring tool.

Managing Rules

As publisher and project manager, you'll probably create or be provided rules that pertain specifically to the project, such as all programming aspects of the project will be written in the C++ programming language or the Web publication will be written entirely in the Hypertext Markup Language, HTML. As you start the project, these rules may seem perfectly acceptable. However, as you conduct planning for the project you may find that C++ isn't the best choice or that HTML is too restrictive for your needs. If these early rules cannot be modified to fit the project, you'll have problems. You may encounter delays due to loss of efficiency. The final product may not be what was expected. Or worse, the project could be a dismal failure.

No rule should ever be considered absolute. Even the best of rules should be interpreted as guidelines that can vary depending on the situation. Rules for a project should be flexible and make sense. A rule that conflicts with something you are trying to do in the project should be reexamined. The rule may be inappropriate for the situation you are trying to apply it to.

Managing Behavior

A project will never get finished if you avoid working on it. Putting off work until something is due is a poor practice. Quitting when things don't go your way or when you seem to have a block is another poor practice. Even if you are one of those people who thrives on deadlines, plan to work on a project regularly—every day if necessary and possible. You should also plan to work on the project during those times when your thoughts are not flowing. Everyone has bad days and good days. Some days you take more breaks. Some days you work straight through the day and into the night.

You may tend toward other destructive behavior besides avoiding or putting off work. Sometimes publishers go to the opposite extreme. They tear things apart impulsively before letting the work cool off so they can look at it objectively. Never edit, revise, or proof material immediately after it is drafted or put in near-final form.

For example, you have just completed the implementation phase of the project. You have been working on the project 16 hours a day for three weeks. You tell yourself if you do some minor tweaking now the project will be finished. You start correcting minor problems and before you know it, you are changing the master storyboard because things don't seem to fit right, or you are cutting Chapter 18. At this point, an alarm should go off in your mind. Take a break for a day or two before going back to the project. You'll be thankful you did.

> **NOTE**
>
> When working on a project, you should back it up regularly. I keep a master copy and at least one backup copy of all projects on floppy disk and on my hard drive. I also have my word processor set to make automatic saves of my work every five minutes. You'll be thankful for backups if you delete material in the heat of the moment and later regret it. Disk space is cheap compared to your time and ideas.

Improving Ideas: Techniques To Better Creativity

To improve your ideas, you must think in new ways. You must examine the ordinary through different eyes. You must look at the mundane in a new light. You must examine your ideas in fresh ways.

Tapping into your creativity is not a simple process. People have been trying to figure out how to tap into creativity throughout history. One of the great thinkers on the subject of creativity was Abraham Maslow. Maslow discussed creativity in terms of primary and secondary creativity. Secondary creativity is a restrictive creativity—the creativity of adults that is based on the creativity of others. Primary creativity is an innocent or original creativity—the creativity of children, which is blocked off by most adults and a part of our subconscious thoughts. Maslow further said that creativity is not necessarily the trait of those who are geniuses or talented, meaning that the fact that someone is a genius or has certain talents does not mean they are also creative.

Maslow's theories on creativity are very important to help people improve ideas. They suggest that you probably could tap into your creative processes by reaching into your subconscious mind. They suggest you should try to think freely without the inhibitions placed upon you by society or age. They suggest you should look at your ideas through innocent or unjudging eyes. Many modern techniques for aiding the creative process come out of this school of thinking, such as the following:

- Brainstorming
- Freethinking
- Storyboarding

> **NOTE**
>
> Although techniques to improve ideas are most often used at the beginning of projects, they can and should be used any time you want to try to improve your ideas. You may find these techniques especially useful at key stages in project development. For example, if you are considering what type of graphics or sound to include in the project, why not try brainstorming, freethinking, or storyboarding as a way of ensuring you make the best choices?

Brainstorming Techniques

Brainstorming was originally developed as a group problem-solving technique. The members of a brainstorming group were given a set of strict rules governing their behavior. These rules were designed to break down the barriers of communication. They did this by protecting the egos of the group members and promoting the need to be a productive member of the group.

The following are the basic rules of brainstorming:

- No evaluation of any ideas put forth is permitted.
- Realize that the ideas put forth are simply ideas and not solutions.
- Free your mind by first thinking of the wildest answers to the problem.
- Throw in as many ideas as you can—every idea that comes to your mind.
- Build on the ideas of other group members.
- When the ideas get more difficult to think of, don't stop. The best ideas are just ahead.

Similar concepts can be applied to single-person efforts. Brainstorming can boost your creativity tremendously. If you brainstorm, you'll tend to be less critical of your work. Eventually, you'll also tend to naturally think of more than one approach to solving a problem.

For one-person brainstorming efforts, the following are good techniques to follow:

- Identify the problem, purpose, audience, or subject you want to brainstorm.
- Write this down in the middle of a large piece of paper and circle it.
- Write down all the ideas that come to your mind concerning the topic and circle them.
- Do not stop until you have filled the page.
- Look for patterns or repeated ideas.
- Use these ideas to develop further ideas or to develop solutions.

Freethinking

Freethinking is another effective technique to boost your creativity. When you freethink, you begin by telling yourself, "I will think something!" You think about a topic for a set period, recording your thoughts. Another term for freethinking is freewriting. The latter term tends to be more restrictive than necessary because the form of your freethinking efforts does not have to be written.

When you freethink, you should record your thoughts in the way that makes you most comfortable—on paper, a tape recorder, or on a computer. You should also select a period for freethinking you are comfortable with. Ten minutes may be right for some people. Others may prefer longer or shorter periods. After a freethinking session, you review what you recorded and note the ideas you liked.

Often, several freethinking sessions are necessary to get the best ideas. For most people, two or three successive freethinking sessions may be enough to help generate their best material. Others may wish to try a series of freethinking sessions over a period of several days. The key is to find the freethinking method that works best for you and use it.

Storyboarding

Storyboards are a high-power approach to creative thinking. They are particularly useful for electronic publications because of the way they help you structure ideas visually. When you storyboard, you represent each page of the presentation in miniature form on a planning sheet and create a mockup of the project.

The storyboard not only serves as an outline for the presentation, it lets you visualize the project in a way you otherwise would not be able to. At a glance, you can see the publication from start to finish. This is extremely important in the way you conceptualize the project. The project is no longer a mysterious tangle of documents you have to string together. It has a logical order from beginning to end. Often, being able to see to the end of a complex project is 75 percent of the battle. Techniques used in storyboarding will be discussed in depth in later sections of this chapter.

Effective Strategies for Planning and Project Organization

Creating electronic publications is ideally a team effort, with each member of the team working in an area of the publication in which they specialize. In the real world, things don't always turn out ideally. Very often electronic publishers must wear many hats. They must be the writer, artist, musician, graphic designer, programmer, editor, and publisher.

The tasks involved in each of these roles can be broken down into three broad categories:

- Composition processes
- Development processes
- Publishing processes

Composition Processes

The processes involved in creating original material can be broadly defined as *composition processes*. In the role of the writer, artist, or musician, the electronic publisher creates new material or adapts existing material. This role for the publisher can be limited or extensive depending on the needs of the publication. The publisher will generally create new material only as necessary. Even if the publisher works directly with writers, artists, or musicians or purchases existing material, at some point the publisher should evaluate the work within the scope of the composition processes. (For more information on these techniques, see Chapter 12, "Writing Processes.")

Contrary to popular opinion, the creative process is not some mythical beast that you must hunt down. You may discover many ways to compose a work and many ways to get to the final product. This is true no matter the form of the creation, but generally composition processes include seven activities:

- Planning
- Researching
- Composing
- Evaluating
- Revising
- Editing
- Proofing

Before discussing these activities, let's dispel some myths about the creative process. Just because there are seven activities does not mean you have to perform them all. You'll use more of these activities when you are working in new mediums. When you are writing about a new subject area, you'll tend to use more of the activities than if you are writing about a subject with which you are very familiar. If you are writing for a brand new audience, you may want to follow the seven steps of the composing process carefully. The same holds true when you are creating a new type of work, such as switching from fiction to nonfiction titles.

You can perform the activities in any order you choose and you don't have to finish one activity before you start another. Sometimes you create an outline for the work. Sometimes you create the work first, pause to think about the structure, and then plan how to make the work better. Sometimes you tackle the work a section at a time, planning in spurts. Sometimes you are so familiar with your subject or the medium you are working in that planning is a natural part of your thought process.

Although planning is an important stage of the creative process, it is not the most important stage. This is contrary to the traditional school of thought that stressed planning and specifically advised writers to create an outline for everything they wrote. Whether you create an outline or do not create an outline is not going to materially influence the quality of your work. Research into the creative process has shown what matters most is how you organize your thoughts and the work.

Planning

When you plan, choose the way in which you are going to organize the work. You do this by drawing on experiences or thinking of new ways to create and organize material. Planning also means thinking about the strategies you are going to use to create the work. It involves analyzing the purpose, scope, and audience for the work. The purpose of the work is the reason you are creating the work or adding to the publication. Are you adding artwork to accent or clarify the story line? Are you adding music to heighten the mood?

The scope of the work defines what the work encompasses or the extent of the work. Scope can sometimes be defined in terms of focus and size. Is the work broadly or narrowly focused? Is the work large or small?

The audience is who you want the work to reach. Is the publication for children or adults? Have you identified a target audience such as males 16–24, or is the work designed for a general audience?

You have probably seen Broderbund's Living Books line on CD-ROM. A popular series in this line are the wonderful books by Mercer Mayer, such as *Just Grandma and Me, Just Me and My Dad,* and *Just For You.* Although children are the audience for the books, Broderbund did not forget that adults would be the ones purchasing the CD-ROMs. For this reason, the purpose of the books is to provide educational entertainment to children. Given this purpose, the CD-ROM editions of the print books are much larger in scope and were programmed with features to entertain and educate children. A key part of this is to allow children to interact with the publication or simply let the story be read to them.

Broderbund did not forget the potential for an international audience for the CD-ROM. Most Living Books allow you to select a language for the book to be read in such as English, Japanese, or Spanish. This gives the CD-ROMs international appeal and provides another educational outlet. Children in Japan could listen to the English version of the CD-ROM to help them learn English. Children in the United States could listen to the Spanish version to help them learn Spanish.

Researching

Researching involves gathering all the information you need to complete the work. This may mean gathering information about Eighteenth Century Europe from as many sources as you can to ensure your work has elements authentic from the period. Or it may mean driving to the ocean to photograph or video tape the seagulls and the spray of the waves, so you can later capture the moment in your work.

Composing

Composing is the act of putting your thoughts into a more permanent form. This means putting work on paper or using computer equipment to put work into an appropriate electronic form. The electronic publisher will most likely put words into a word processor, transcribe musical notes into a music program, and record brush strokes using a paint program.

The work as first put down on paper or recorded on a computer does not have to be the finished product. More than likely, it will simply be a start on a larger work. For the writer, a start on a project could be a few words, a list of thoughts, a paragraph, or pages of writing.

Evaluating

Evaluating involves looking at the work objectively to see if it meets your goals. Ask yourself if the work is right for the purpose and audience for which you are creating it. Often, the best way to be objective about a work you have created is to look at the work as if someone else had created it.

If you find that you cannot be objective about your own work or aren't as objective as you would like, perhaps you need to distance yourself from the work. Take a day off or put on one of your other hats and work on a different part of the project for a few days. This will help you return to the evaluation fresh and ready to think objectively.

Revising

When you revise, you change the structure of the work by adding, deleting, or rearranging. Often you'll revise after you have evaluated the work. Revisions can be cosmetic changes involving only a few minor areas of the work, but more often than not, revision means major reworking to keep the work focused on the purpose, scope, and audience for which it is intended.

Editing

Whereas revision looks at the structure of the work, editing looks at the style, mechanics, and format of the work. For writing, this means making sure you have used proper spelling, grammar, and punctuation. You would check word choice and format. Great tools to help you through editing are spelling and grammar checkers. These tools might catch 75 percent of your mistakes, but the other 25 percent you'll have to catch through careful reading.

During the editing stage, don't forget the non-written aspects of your electronic publication. You should also edit these aspects of the publication as necessary. Do the opening graphics match the tone and style of the graphics you selected in later sections of the publication? Do the sound clips have sections where nothing is audible for a few seconds? Is the video sequence for chapter four too long?

Proofing

When you proof something, you are checking the final copy to ensure it is error-free. In traditional publishing, proofing has been a critical area of the composing process. Typos are costly mistakes to correct when material has already gone to press. In electronic publishing, this may or may not be the case. Electronic mediums tend to be more liquid than traditional mediums. You can make changes very easily to a publication on floppy disk, but changes to a CD-ROM publication already in production are not easy to make.

You may be saying to yourself, wait a minute, I have seen typos in publications before. Although most publications have typos, they tend to make you look dumb. For this reason, you'll want to correct as many typos as you can, given the time constraints of the project.

Development Processes

The processes involved in developing the computer software aspects of the electronic publication can be broadly defined as *development processes*. In the role of the graphic designer and programmer, the publisher designs and develops the computer software aspects of the electronic publication. As you'll see from examples throughout this book, the electronic publisher should never have to resort to actual programming. There are many wonderful tools to aid the process of creating the computer software aspects of the electronic publication.

Therefore, the programming role of the publisher is more closely related to that of a software developer. The publisher will be responsible for the look and innerworkings of the publication. The publisher will also be responsible for selecting the appropriate electronic publishing software and tools for her level of expertise and a software process model under which the project will be developed. Fortunately for electronic publishers, the software process model of choice will normally be a rapid prototype model or a modified rapid prototype model. This is because toolsets exist to aid in the rapid creation of electronic publishing projects and because these tools are of sufficient quality to warrant their use. This section explains what these prototype models involve.

A major strength of the rapid prototype model is that you can develop the project in linear fashion. You proceed from the working model to the finished product. You can test the prototype in real-world situations or under the scrutiny of the boss. In doing so, you can ensure that what you are creating is what is actually needed. Applying this model to electronic publishing projects will also save you time.

This model also works well when you are familiar with traditional approaches to project development and are concerned about using new technologies. By developing a rapid prototype, you give yourself the chance to test the new technologies. Before making any further investments, you try out the tools to find out if they meet your needs. This will help you manage the risk of introducing a new technology while allowing you to assess new techniques.

A modified rapid prototype model for electronic publishing could include six stages:

- Requirements phase
- Rapid prototype phase
- Specification phase
- Planning phase
- Design phase
- Implementation phase

As you read about each of these phases, it is important to remember that the duration of each phase should be relevant to the size and complexity of the publishing project. The initial project you create using this or any other model will require more time. For a small project or for subsequent projects, you probably could perform all the phases through the design phase in a single eight-hour day.

The implementation phase for electronic projects tends to be the longest phase. Learning about the electronic publishing tools you have chosen will probably take up most of your time in your initial project, so the implementation phase may seem excessively long. It is important to remember that each subsequent time you use the tools should be easier than the last. The good news is that electronic publishing tools tend to be very user-friendly.

The wonderful thing about electronic publishing is that if you take the time to design a good product, you can reuse some of the same specifications and designs in subsequent projects. This will give your company's products a uniform look, and as an added bonus the payoff in time savings will be substantial.

Finally, remember the rapid prototype model as a linear part of your project's development life cycle. Unlike the composing processes, each phase of the development process should be conducted in order.

Requirements Phase

In the requirements phase you try to figure out what your needs are. You do this by first examining the purpose, scope, and audience of the project. Afterward, you examine your reasonable expectations for the project. You translate these needs, goals, and purposes into requirements for the project. Although the section on techniques to get the project started provides a sample schedule that lists goals and milestones, the basic needs for any electronic publication include the tools, such as those in the following list, that the publisher will need to complete the project:

- Acrobat or Corel Ventura Publisher.
- A drawing tool to create graphics, such as CorelDRAW!, Harvard Graphics, or PaintShop Pro.
- A sound tool to create or edit sound, such as SoundApp for the Mac, WHAM for Windows, or SOX for UNIX.
- A video tool to play or test video segments, such as an Apple QuickTime player, Video for Windows player, or MPEG player.

NOTE

Throughout this book, you'll find chapters about selecting and obtaining the tools necessary to create any type of electronic publication. You will find a preliminary discussion on authoring tools for CD-ROM publications in Chapter 15, "Hardware and Software Tools for CD-ROM Development." Drawing programs and graphics tools are the subject of Chapter 10, "Using Graphics." Web publishing tools are discussed in Part IV, "Online Publishing and the Internet."

You will also find tips on how to obtain these tools for free throughout the chapters covering the World Wide Web. For example, Chapter 22, "Incorporating Multimedia," tells you where to find freeware and shareware sound, video, and graphic tools.

You'll want to think beyond your basic tool needs. You should also consider time, budget, and personnel constraints. If you have only 10 weeks to complete the project, you may need to hire additional team members to get the project finished on time. In this case, hiring a specific number of additional team members would be one of your requirements. If you have a $2,500 budget, you'll have to scrutinize every aspect of the budget to keep costs down. In this case, you'll probably be extremely selective about the tools you purchase. You'll also hire outside help only as necessary. And if the budget constraints are so severe that they would materially affect the success of the project, you'll want to ensure your superiors are aware of the situation and possibly make a case for getting a larger budget.

Rapid Prototype Phase

In the rapid prototype stage, you roll back your sleeves and dive right into the project. Using the requirements for the project, you create a working model of the publication as quickly as possible. The prototype is far from a completed project. Its structure is rather skeletal in that not all the pieces work together, but limited interaction with the model is possible. You use this model to figure out your real needs and to find out whether you have selected the right tools to carry you through to the completion of the job.

The traditional school of thought on the rapid prototype model is that when you are done with this phase, you should discard the rapid prototype. If you don't discard the prototype, you may find yourself wasting time trying to continually build and fix the prototype. The purpose of creating the rapid prototype is to help you figure out real needs and save you time. Clinging to the prototype generally defeats the purpose of creating the prototype in the first place.

Your superiors must understand what this phase is all about. All too often, the prototype is mistaken for a start on the final product, when in fact, it is not. You should manage expectations by ensuring that your superiors understand this phase from day one and by recommunicating information about the purpose of the prototype periodically throughout the project.

This said, in electronic publishing in certain cases, you may want to keep parts of the prototype. You may want to reuse or refine for the finished product any creative work, such as graphic icons, art, or sounds, you developed for the rapid prototype. You may also want to keep portions of the interface you created with publishing tools.

Specification Phase

After you develop and verify the prototype, you go on to specify the complete innerworkings of the publication. You could do this in a traditional manner through specification diagrams such as data flow diagrams, state transition diagrams, or petri nets. But these types of diagrams are not really necessary unless you are writing actual programming code for the project. A good way to show how your publication will be linked is by developing a storyboard that graphically shows what the pieces of the project are and how they are linked together. Storyboards are discussed in depth later in this chapter.

In this phase, you'll want to select a target computer for the publication. Many types of computers are on the market. The IBM PC and PC compatibles have many generations of computer systems based on the different chip sets. Some PCs are based on the 80286, 80386, and 80486 chips. Other PCs are based on the Intel's Pentium chips. The same is true for Macintoshes—you might choose from a whole line of PowerMacs. There is even a PowerPC, a cross between a Mac and a PC. UNIX systems come in many configurations from Sun Microsystems' popular Sparc workstations to Silicon Graphics workstations.

The best system on which to publish your first project is the system you are most familiar with. If you use a PC, create your first project for use on PCs. If you use a Mac, create your first project for use on other Macs.

> **NOTE**
>
> When publishing on the World Wide Web, you can create platform-independent publications. This means you won't have to select a target computer for the publication and should use whatever system you are comfortable with to develop the Web publication. For more information on the Web, refer to Chapter 19, "The World Wide Web."

In this phase, you'll also want to consider the format (or medium) in which you wish to publish. There are many formats for the publication. You could publish solely on floppy disk, CD-ROM, or on the World Wide Web. You could plan to publish on any one of these formats or all three. Although the choice is ultimately yours to make, other chapters in the book will help you make the decision. Publishing on CD-ROM or floppy disk is the subject of Chapter 13, "When to Publish on CD-ROM or Disk." Web publishing is discussed in Part IV.

Planning Phase

After you verify the specification documents, you should plan the project. Using all the materials you have developed so far for the project, you determine how long the project is going to take and the steps necessary to carry you through the project. For this reason, the planning phase can also be a reality check for project constraints or requirements.

For example, after you plan each step of the project you discover that it will take a minimum of six months to complete the project, yet the deadline for project completion given to you by management is three months away. Here, something would have to give and you would have to work hard to manage perceptions and expectations concerning the project. You may have to renegotiate the deadline, hire additional team members, or eliminate certain time-intensive parts of the project.

The more complex the project, the more involved your planning will be. The plans for a small project could be very basic—a list of steps with deadlines for completion of each step written down on a single piece of paper. The plans for a large project could be rendered in detail on a project management tool such as Microsoft Project. Most projects have windows for project steps, such as eight days for planning or three weeks for preliminary design. There could be hundreds of project steps, with multiple steps being performed simultaneously or a handful of steps with each step being performed one after the other. Some steps would be dependent on other steps, meaning they could not be started until certain other aspects of the project are completed. Other steps would not be dependent on any other steps and could be performed at any time during the project's development.

Design Phase

After verifying your planning, you go on to the design phase. The design phase is one of the most critical phases of an electronic publishing project. During this phase you take the specification documents to another level of detail. You develop the look of the project. You design the layout for the publication and individual pages. By developing a master storyboard for the component parts of the publication, you can make the design phase easier and less time-consuming.

The master storyboard concept is a highly effective way to design. Instead of creating hundreds of individual storyboards, you create templates for the major divisions of the publishing project. These templates form the basis for the individual storyboards. In this way, you have to make only minor adjustments to the individual storyboards and you get a uniform look throughout major sections of the publication.

Implementation Phase

After you verify the designs you have created for the publication, you go on to the implementation phase. This tends to be the longest phase in electronic publishing projects because you'll actually create the electronic publication using the specification and designs you have created. You'll also integrate the creative materials from the composing processes in this stage.

Publishing Processes

The processes involved in producing the finished product can be broadly defined as *publishing processes*. In the role of the editor and publisher, the electronic publisher fine tunes the publication to make it a more commercially viable product. The publisher must take a hard look at the project through the eyes of an editor, and then take the project through the final five activities:

- Revision
- Editing
- Proofing
- Testing
- Publishing

These activities are very similar to the associated activities performed in the composition process. The primary difference is in the publisher's role. The publisher is no longer the creator of the work or a collaborator on the work. He or she should review the publishing project with as much objectivity as possible.

Revision

During the revision phase, the publisher is looking for major flaws in the project. The focus of revision is on structure. The publisher will reanalyze the individual parts of the project to ensure the work is focused and consistent throughout. To do this, the publisher might also have to reevaluate the purpose, scope, and audience for the project. Did the project turn out as intended? Is the project larger or more commercially viable than the original concept? Is the project still targeted toward the same audience?

When you revise the publication, you should scrutinize all its parts from start to finish. The soundness of an electronic document's structure is extremely important. You should test all links in the storyboard structure to ensure they work as you expect them to.

The depth of the revision often depends on your familiarity with the subject and type of publication. If this is your first project or you are publishing a new type of document, you'll want to use a very thorough revision process. A good technique to follow when doing a very thorough revision is the *rule of three*. Under the rule of three you follow all aspects of the publication from start to finish three times. Each time you revise, you are looking for different structure problems.

The first time through the process you check for clarity and content. Is everything in the publication clear and placed on-screen in a clear manner? Does the content of each individual part fit in with the publication as a whole? The first revision is the closest inspection of the publication during the revision process.

The second time, you look at the organization and layout of the publication. Is the publication organized in the best way possible? Is the layout of the document the best possible? Is there too much information? Does the screen look cluttered? Is the linking of the pages right? Are the navigation mechanisms easy to use?

The third time, analyze the publication to see if the overall message meets the proposed purpose and audience. Look at the big picture and ask yourself if the publication is right for the purpose for which it is intended. Is the reading level and style of the publication appropriate for the audience for which it is intended?

Editing

Editing should logically follow revision. There is no point in looking for mechanics and format problems in parts of the publication that might not be in the revised publication. Keeping this rule in mind when you start the publishing process will ultimately save you time.

Back in the editing mode, the publisher looks at the mechanics and format of the work. This is the point when the publisher should refer to a style manual to ensure punctuation, capitalization, and compounding of words are correct. Other good tools for the publisher at this point include grammar reference aids, bad speller dictionaries, and other types of dictionaries or reference materials to confirm facts.

In a publication such as an electronic novel, the tendency is to look at chapter text and not the text of titles and headings. Look at all text no matter where it appears in the publication. If graphics or video contain text, you should scrutinize this text as well. There should be smooth transitions between sections and topics. The capitalization in headings should be consistent throughout the publication.

For the textual portions of the publication, you should look at the following:

- Capitalization
- Grammar
- Punctuation
- Sentence structure
- Spelling
- Word choice and usage

Proofing

At this stage, the publisher proofs the entire project down to the most minor detail. The most common type of errors you'll be looking for are typos. Typos may not be as costly in electronic publishing, but they will cost you more time and money to fix after a project has been published.

The proofing stage differs from the revision stage and the editing stage in its scope. In revision, you are looking for major problems in structure. In editing, you are looking for problems in mechanics and format. In proofing, you are looking through a magnifying glass for minor problems. Although these three processes can be performed in any order, they work best when done in order. In this way, you are first looking at the big picture, then you gradually pan in. Otherwise, you'll spend too much time worrying needlessly about minor details before you look at the major problems.

When you proof something, you are checking the final copy to ensure it is as error-free as possible. You should recognize that given your time and budget constraints, you may have to compromise accuracy for timeliness. You should also recognize there is a definite point of diminishing returns and that finding 100% of the errors is costly and often not practical. For this reason, most publications contain typos and other types of minor errors. Therefore, the key to proofing is to reduce these errors and not to try to eliminate them.

Testing

Once the project is in its final form, the publisher may want to produce a limited number of samples. The purpose of creating samples based on the finished project is to test the publishing process and ensure the publication will work as advertised. Testing is not an absolute necessity; instead, it should be conducted when necessary. Whether you test the project will really depend on your publishing operation. If this is your first project, you may want to conduct extensive testing. You might also want to conduct extensive testing if you are publishing for the first time a Macintosh version of your product line.

The optimum number of samples that you should produce for testing really depends on the number of versions the project will have. For example, if you plan to publish a PC version on floppy disk and CD-ROM and a Macintosh version on floppy disk and CD-ROM you may want to test all four versions of the publication.

When you are testing, keep in mind that not all PCs are the same. The same is true for Amiga, Macintosh, UNIX, or any other type of system. Differently configured systems may have different system requirements.

Publishing

The final step in the publishing process is to publish the product for use on the computer systems and format you have chosen. The great thing about electronic publishing is that you don't have to run 5,000-copy print runs. A small publisher may only want to publish products when orders come in, which is the ideal situation when you are publishing on floppy. An order comes in, you spin up the computer, put the master disk in, and copy it. You attach a label to the disk, put the disk in packaging, and ship the finished product back to the customer. You have extremely low overhead and only have to maintain sufficient supplies in stock to meet the immediate demand.

This scenario might be true, even if you are publishing on CD-ROM. Technology is changing fast, as you'll see throughout this book. Not only is it possible today to master your own CD-ROMs, your costs will probably be significantly less than you would expect. See Part III, "Publishing on CD-ROMs," for more information of which medium to choose to publish your work.

Combining It All

Ideally, during the publication process you would follow the composing processes for the project first. When you finish, you would start the development phases. Finally, you would start the publishing processes. Although this is the ideal situation, life is never ideal. Often, you'll want to combine elements from each of the three categories and work on them simultaneously. This is fine.

You can conduct the composition process while you are developing the software aspects of the publication. This will work especially well when you are adapting existing material. It will also work well when you as the publisher are collaborating with writers, musicians, or artists to create a project.

The publishing processes are more difficult to integrate into the ongoing creation and development of the project. Yet, you could create or develop pieces of the project, and then examine those pieces from the viewpoint of the objective publisher. Exercise caution when trying to perform all three processes at once. The tendency is to gloss over the actual publishing process and not scrutinize the project as closely or objectively as you otherwise would have.

Techniques To Get the Project Started

To organize a project you must start the project. Getting the project started is often the hardest thing to do. If you get the project started, the odds are you'll probably finish the project. The key to starting the project and finishing the project is to develop good habits for working on the project immediately. Creative people often find themselves at a loss for one of two reasons. They either prefer to avoid work until a deadline is hanging over their head or they think of reasons why they cannot work.

Human tendency is to put off work until it absolutely has to be done or to think of excuses why the project cannot be started. Procrastination is a mind-set that you can overcome through positive thinking and good habits. If you find that you work on the publishing project only when absolutely necessary to meet a deadline or if you keep promising to start the project but don't, try giving yourself a publishing schedule.

The schedule should contain milestones, goals, and an allocation of time. Use the schedule as a flexible and realistic guideline to help you through to project completion. The purpose of the schedule is to help you start thinking about the project and to formalize the steps it will take you to complete the project. You should also use the schedule to help you set regular times to work on the project.

Milestones are generally smaller in scope than goals. A single week could contain many milestones; for example:

Week 1

- Select and purchase reference materials.
- Select and purchase authoring tools.
- Brainstorm.
- Develop weekly schedule overview.

Week 2

- Read introduction to authoring tool manual.
- Browse the reference materials to gather ideas.
- Freewrite.
- Develop weekly schedule.
- Start project, complete at least one page.

Goals are larger in scope than milestones. Goals for a typical project could be to complete activities or phases in the composition, development, or publishing processes. Goals are generally of longer duration. You would probably only have one goal per week during the project, such as the following:

- Week 1: Preliminary work on project
- Week 2: Planning
- Week 3: Research
- Week 4: Start project composition

More realistically, the duration of milestones and goals will depend on the time you allocate to the project. The milestones and goals from the previous examples could be rewritten to include the time you'll dedicate to the project each week and the duration of a task. Although it would be ideal to be able to work full-time on a single project, even full-time publishers don't have that luxury very often. Usually they are juggling several projects and can only dedicate a few hours a week to any specific project. If you are working part-time on the project, one of your first goals may be broken down as follows:

Goal: Preliminary work on project. Duration: 2 weeks.

Week 1: 10 hours

- Select and purchase reference materials. Duration: 2 hours.
- Select and purchase authoring tools. Duration: 2 hours.
- Brainstorm. Duration: 2 hours.
- Develop weekly schedule overview. Duration: 3 hours.
- Slack time: 1 hour.

Week 2: 20 hours

- Read introduction to authoring tool manual. Duration: 1 hour.
- Browse the reference materials to gather ideas. Duration: 5 hours.
- Freewrite. Duration: 1 hour.
- Develop weekly schedule. Duration: 8 hours.
- Start project, complete at least one page. Duration: 3 hours.
- Slack time: 2 hours.

There is no harm in building extra time into the schedule to ensure you meet goals. The above schedule contains 1 hour of slack time in the first week and 2 hours of slack time in the second week. By building slack time into the schedule, you help ensure the project can stay on track even if there are unexpected delays. Experienced project managers try to build in slack time whenever possible and practical. When you meet a goal, why not celebrate? Take a few hours off, go see the movie you have been wanting to see.

Techniques To Organize for the Audience

The way in which you organize a publication largely depends on who will be using the publication. The success of your publication relies on determining the audience for the publication and adapting the message to the audience. You will certainly organize the publication one way for adults and a different way for children. However, the audience for your publication is usually not in such simple terms. The problem of determining the audience is further complicated because most publications have more than one audience. Yet, correctly determining the target audience can have huge payoffs.

The target audience could be specific, males 16–24, or general, young adults. More often, a publication will have primary audiences and secondary audiences. The primary audience is the group of people for whom the publication is created. The focus and thrust of the publication should be directed toward the primary audience.

The secondary audience is the group of people who will read the publication incidental to its purpose. The secondary audience could include reviewers (people whose job it is to review electronic publications), consumer interest groups (people whose job it is to promote the interests of consumers), or anyone else who might read the book to determine its quality or to review its content. The secondary audience could also include parents if the book is directed toward children. Parents may be the ones ensuring the moral content of the electronic publication before purchasing it for their children.

Often, the primary audience for a publication seems straightforward but is not. Comic books are a good example of this. The reading level of the average comic book is at a sixth-grade level. The look of comic books with their graphically depicted pows, bangs, and booms seem to be directed entirely toward children. You may be surprised to learn that for many comic books, the largest percentage of readers is adults. Look at the price tag on comic books today and the phenomenal popularity of comic books with adult themes. What would have happened to comic books if the companies producing them had not realized that a large portion of their readers are adults?

You can figure out the audience for your publication by the following means:

- Using common sense
- Gathering statistics
- Evaluating trends

Using Common Sense

One of the best tools to analyze the audience for a product is common sense. Realize the audience probably will not have the same wants, needs, and desires as you. An electronic publication may or may not have the same audience as its traditional print counterpart. Try to put yourself in the position of consumers who will buy your product. Use what you know about people and what you know about the subject of your publication to predict likely responses to these questions, such as the following:

- What will the reader's initial reaction be?
- What will the reader's expectations be?
- What does the reader consider interesting?
- What features will the reader be looking for?
- What are the selling points for this type of product?
- How will the reader use your product?
- What reading level should you target?
- What level of violence or profanity is acceptable to this audience?
- What level of complexity in the linking and navigation mechanisms is acceptable?

Each of these questions should be answered with the publication's audience in mind. For example, the last question pertains to the complexity of the publication. Publications for adults tend to be more complex and serious. Publications for children tend to be less complex and include more entertainment features.

Gathering Statistics

One of the best ways to determine your audience is to use statistics. Sometimes you can simply ask consumers what they are looking for in a product. You could do this through a carefully designed survey. Other times, you might want to use existing statistics, such as demographic information, to determine the audience.

Surveys are often an inexpensive way to learn public opinion. Surveys could be provided with product samples passed out at the local shopping mall or given to your associates. Surveys are useful because they can be filled out by many people at the same time. A properly designed survey will be easy to answer and not time-consuming. This way, more people will fill out the survey.

Demographic information can also provide useful statistics. Demographic information includes age, sex, race, education level, income, and more. This data was probably gathered through surveys and made publicly available. Not all the demographic information available will be relevant to your needs, but some of the data will be extremely important. For instance, if the demographic information reveals most of the consumers buying your type of product are females age 40–45 or males over the age of 55, you would certainly adapt the message of your audience differently than if the information reveals the ages are 20–25 for females or 16–22 for males.

You can also look several places on the World Wide Web where you can find demographic data. This data covers a wide range of topics from many sources, ranging from the Census Bureau to public interest groups. You'll learn more about the World Wide Web in Part IV.

Evaluating Trends

Evaluating trends could also help you determine an audience for your product. To evaluate trends, you'll have to know something about the market for your product. You could begin by looking at similar products from other companies and asking yourself the following:

- What message do the products carry?
- Toward what target audience are these companies directing their products?
- Are the products being targeted toward secondary audiences as well?

In a new marketplace, trends often shift as companies try to figure out the audience for their products. You may want to look at what other companies are doing when you begin work on the project and again during the project. This way you can judge if the trend is more stable than fluid or more fluid than stable. For additional techniques on determining your audience, see Chapter 12, "Writing Processes."

Organizing the Publication Through Storyboarding

A *storyboard* can help you reduce complexity by structuring ideas in a less complicated manner. When you storyboard, you represent each page of the presentation in miniature form on a planning sheet. This enables you to visualize the publication from start to finish. Being able to see the component parts of the entire project makes the project more manageable and less mysterious. You don't have to wonder what is beyond the next page because when you use the storyboards you'll know what is beyond the next page.

You can represent a single project storyboard like the rectangle in Figure 7.1. The shape of an individual storyboard makes them look like little pieces of paper. The storyboard could represent a single page of the publication or a group of pages, like a chapter. Without information in the storyboards, the mockup of the project you create would have little meaning. Later examples in the chapter will detail how you add information to storyboards, such as chapter headings or titles, but the basic idea is to create a template or outline for pages or sections of the publication.

You can extend the idea of storyboards by using lines and arrows to show how the publication is linked. An arrow can show the flow of the publication from one page to the next. Arrows depict how the component parts of the publication link together. By examining the links you can see the logical structure of the publication and the level of interaction readers will have with the publication. Figure 7.2 shows how arrows can show the flow between two pages in a publication.

#### Chapter 7

FIGURE 7.1.

Use a rectangle to represent a storyboard.

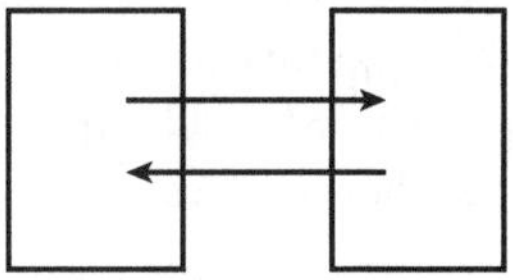

FIGURE 7.2.

Arrows show the flow of information or linking.

Developing storyboards for your publication is a critical part of the design process. Storyboards help ensure the publication is well-designed and that all the pieces of the project fit together. After you have developed the storyboard for your publication, you can immediately find flaws in the design. Finding flaws early in the development of the project will save you time and resources.

Having to rebuild the links on a complex project midway through the project could mean disaster. Often, you start a snowball effect. You change one link, and then discover you have to change an associated link. You change the associated link to make sure it leads to the correct page, and then find other links you have to change. Before you know it, you are reworking all the links in the project. At this point, the process may be so involved that you'll elect to start over rather than try to rework the links.

There are three phases in the storyboard design process:

- Developing the structure
- Developing the content
- Evaluating the logic

Each phase is progressively more detailed. When you are developing the structure of the project, you are looking at the project overview level. While keeping in mind that a single storyboard could represent any number of similar pages, you identify the number of storyboards for the project and the logical flow between them. When you are developing the content, you look very closely at the individual parts of the project. You develop the outline for individual storyboards or storyboard templates. When you examine the logic of the project, you scrutinize every detail of the project. You closely examine each storyboard and all links to ensure the project design and flow is correct.

Whether you perform each of the three phases will depend on the size and complexity of the project and your familiarity with the type of project you are publishing. However, each phase that you do perform should be performed in sequence. Even a small project of 5–10 storyboards can benefit from the structural development phase. This way, you'll have an easy way to see the following:

■ The structure of the project

■ The links of the project

■ The project as a whole

Although these phases should be performed in order, the important thing to remember is that the duration of each phase should be relevant to the size and complexity of the project. The initial project you create using this or any other model will require more time than subsequent projects. For a small project or for subsequent projects, you probably could create the entire storyboard process in two hours or less.

If you take the time to design a good storyboard, you may be able to reuse some of the same design concepts in subsequent projects. This way your publications will have a uniform structure. An added bonus to using reliable design techniques is substantial time-savings and a reduction in the amount of resources you'll need to complete the project.

Developing Project Structure Using Storyboards

Developing the structure of the project is the first phase in storyboarding. You can organize storyboards in many ways. The structure that is best for your publication depends on the complexity of the project. As complexity increases, you manage it by adopting a more advanced structuring method. Specific design models include the following:

■ Linear

■ Linear with alternative paths

■ Hierarchical

■ Combinations of linear and hierarchical

■ Integrated web

For a small project or project with limited complexity, a simple structure is often best. Simple structures include linear and linear with alternative paths. The simplest way to structure a publication is in a *linear* fashion. Using a pure linear structure, you can create a publication with a structure resembling a traditional print publication. Readers move forward and backward in sequence through the pages of the publication.

An *alternative path* structure gives readers more options or paths through the document. By providing alternative paths, you make the structure of the publication more flexible. Instead of being able to move only forward and backward through the publication, readers can follow a branch from the main path. In a linear structure the branches will rejoin the main path at some point.

The *hierarchical* structure is the most logical structure for a project of moderate complexity. In this structure, you organize the publication into a directory tree. Readers can navigate through the publication moving from one level of the publication to the next, more detailed, level of the publication. They can also go up the tree from the detailed level to a higher level and possibly jump to the top level.

The directory tree closely resembles the way you store files on your hard drive in a main directory with subdirectories leading to files. You could also think of the hierarchy as a representation of an actual tree. If you invert the tree, the trunk of the tree would be the top level of the publication. The trunk could be the overview of the publication. The large boughs leading from the trunk would be the next level of the document structure. The boughs could be the chapter overview pages. Branches leading from the boughs would be the next level. They could be pages within chapters.

The *combination linear and hierarchical* structure is one of the most-used forms for electronic publications. This is because it is an extremely flexible, but still highly structured method. Readers can move forward and backward through individual pages. They can navigate through the various levels of the publication by moving up a level or descending to the next level. They can also follow parallel paths through the document.

The most complex structuring method is the *integrated web*. This method lets the reader follow multiple paths from many options. This is a good method to use when you want the reader to be able to browse or wander many times through the publication you have created. Each time through the publication, readers will probably discover something new.

TIP

No matter the organizational style of the publication, you should remember to include a link to the first page of the publication. This feature is included in most electronic publications because it provides a way for readers to start reading the publication from the beginning at any time. Another key page to provide a link to is the table of contents page.

TIP

Just as the storyboard method can help you visualize the project, it could also help the reader. You may want to provide a graphical depiction of how the document is organized on a help page. This could be included as the first page of your help documentation and would certainly clarify how the publication's navigation mechanisms work.

Using the Linear Design Method

Sometimes you want to put together a publication quickly or you want the structure of the publication to closely resemble a traditional print publication. You can use a linear organization for the publication to do just that. You begin with an introduction and proceed through the publication a page at a time. The key to the linear structure is to provide a mechanism to enable readers to move forward and backward through the publication in sequence. The storyboard illustrated in Figure 7.3 shows this.

FIGURE 7.3.

A linear storyboard structure.

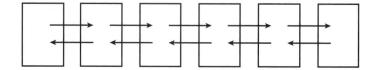

Linear organization works well for small projects and projects with limited complexity. It also works extremely well for any project in which you want readers to follow a strict path through the document. For example, if you want to depict the development processes as a series of storyboards, a linear organization will work best. This way, you would make sure readers could follow the six phases only in the proper sequence.

A good use of the linear organizational style would be in an e-pub containing a single short story because the project is small in size and can be best organized in a straightforward and logical fashion. The reader would generally want to access each page of the short story in sequence, and the publication would generally contain few graphics or multimedia sequences.

Using the Linear with Alternative-Paths Design Method

To increase flexibility, yet still maintain tight control on the path the reader follows through the publication, the alternative path method works well. This structure enables additional paths through the document. By providing alternative paths, you make the structure of the publication more flexible. Instead of having to progress through the publication in sequence, readers can follow a branch from the main path. This technique is illustrated in Figure 7.4.

FIGURE 7.4.

A storyboard with alternative paths offers simple flexibility.

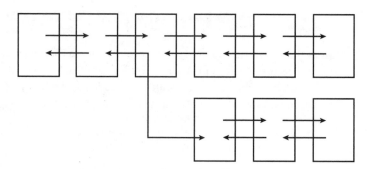

The alternative path gives the reader an easy way to jump to another linear path in the publication. Generally, the reader can follow the new path until it rejoins the main path or ends. You can use alternative paths to provide the following:

- Background information
- Supplemental information
- An orientation to the publication
- Online help documentation

Problems can arise if the alternative path does not rejoin the main path in a seamless fashion. The best way to ensure that readers don't have problems returning from the alternative path is to rejoin the last main path storyboard they read. The last storyboard they were reading is the point where the alternative path splits from the main path. This approach should be the least confusing to readers and the most useful.

A good use of the alternate path structure would be in an e-pub containing a collection of essays, short stories, prose, or poetry. Although such a project may be large in size, the best organization for the project is usually straightforward. The reader would generally want to read one complete essay, short story, or poem and then return to the table of contents to select another essay, short story or poem.

You could also use this structure for a choose-your-own-adventure novel. The reader would be able to deviate from the main path to follow alternate paths through the novel. Eventually, if they made the right choices, they would rejoin the main path and successfully complete the adventure.

Using the Hierarchical Design Method

A hierarchical structure is extremely logical. Using the branches of the inverted tree illustrated in Figure 7.5, readers can navigate through the document. The seamless and easy movement from one level of the publication to the next, more detailed, level is what makes the hierarchical structure so useful. Readers know precisely where they are in the publication. They know that if they descend through the structure, they will get more detailed information, and if they go back up the structure they will find less detailed information.

FIGURE 7.5.

A hierarchical storyboard offers levels of detail.

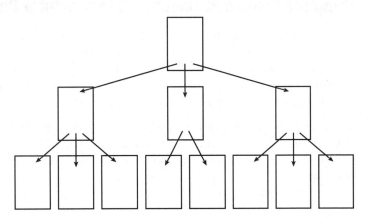

A good use of the hierarchical structure would be in a general work of non-fiction, such as a book on Web publishing. General non-fiction works are often broken down into parts that cover a specific theme, further into chapters that cover a specific topic and finally into subtopics within a specific chapter. Presenting information in a hierarchical fashion would allow the reader to easily select a theme of interest, then a topic of interest and finally a subtopic of interest.

This type of organization is commonly used with lists or menus. An upper-level storyboard containing a chapter index or a list of major topics would form the menu. The reader could select one of the menu items to read a chapter or a particular topic. If the publication is a collection of topics, the first menu could take the reader to an additional menu with subtopics.

To give readers an easy way to navigate the hierarchical structure, you can use three mechanisms:

- A feature to go down the structure
- A feature to go up the structure
- A feature to jump to a specific overview level of the publication

To keep the user interface consistent, you should provide these three basic navigation mechanisms throughout the publication. There are some exceptions to this rule. On the first storyboard, you would only provide a way for readers to go down the hierarchy. On a bottom-level storyboard you would only provide a way for readers to go up the hierarchy or to jump to a specific overview level.

Be careful not to provide too many levels in the document. This is particularly a problem when the publication contains topic and subtopic menus. If readers have to progress through six levels of menus before they get to any real information, they are going to get frustrated. To eliminate this problem, try to limit both the number of levels and the number of menu choices wherever possible. You may also want to start the readers on an index page.

Using the Combined Linear and Hierarchical Design Method

The combination linear and hierarchical storyboard method is the most used structure for electronic publications. This is because it is an extremely flexible, yet highly structured way of organizing the publication. Readers navigate through the publication using a variety of navigation mechanisms. As illustrated in Figure 7.6, this storyboard method enables readers to move forward and backward or to move up and down.

As you'll see, it is not always practical to provide both linear and hierarchical navigation mechanisms throughout the publication. Readers can get lost quickly when they are allowed to jump into the middle of topics. You also can lose continuity and logical flow by providing too much flexibility.

FIGURE 7.6.
Combining the linear and hierarchical storyboard method.

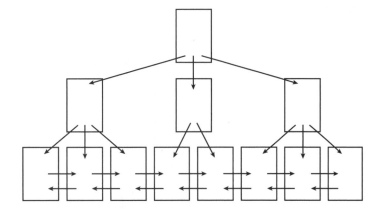

To reduce this problem, provide only the mechanisms that seem appropriate for the particular storyboard. In a few areas, you'll want to let the readers move in both linear and hierarchical directions. In some parts of the publication you'll want readers to move only up and down. In other parts, you'll want readers to move only forward and backward.

With this method you can easily provide access to many types of supplemental information throughout the publication. You could include access to an online help system on all pages and a mechanism to return to the point where the reader left off. Readers could be allowed to search through successive topics on overview or background storyboards in linear fashion. When they find a topic in which they are interested, they can progress down the hierarchy to more detailed information.

The freedom to follow alternate paths through links is a key difference between this style and the pure hierarchical style. Because this structure allows readers to jump from topic to topic or to instantly access related topics or subtopics via hypertext links, you could use it in any advanced electronic publication such as an electronic version of *Electronic Publishing Unleashed* or a mystery novel that contains background information and clues that readers could only access based on the page they were currently reading.

Using the Integrated Web Design Method

The integrated web is the most complex storyboard method because it lacks strict organization. If you are familiar with chaos theories, web storyboards, illustrated in Figure 7.7, are good examples of chaos in action. Readers can follow multiple paths, select from multiple options, and generally wander through the publication as they choose.

The Web is organized so that each storyboard will let you move in several different directions. The structure of the web is analogous to a labyrinth. The center of the labyrinth is the top-level page, but once you choose a path you never know where you'll end up. You often navigate through the publication seeing completely new material. Sometimes you wander back to a page you have already seen, but by choosing a different path you find more new material. Occasionally, you stumble through a series of pages you have already read, before you find new material.

FIGURE 7.7.

An integrated Web storyboard.

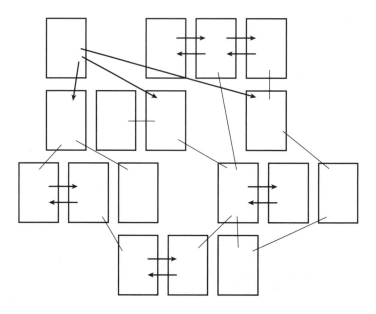

This is the nature of an integrated web structure. It is organized so that readers can browse or wander through the publication many times. If the publication is sufficiently complex, readers will always find new material.

This style works best with complex non-fiction works, especially reference works such as encyclopedias. You would use this style anytime the path the reader takes through the publication isn't as important as their ability or freedom to access information. The World Wide Web is structured in this manner. Web users are free to wander the Web in any way they choose. This method is the preferred way to wander the Web. Web users don't want to be restricted in the way they can search, wander, or browse. They want to do their own thing and find what interests them. Each time users browse the World Wide Web they discover something new.

For a massively complex structure like the World Wide Web, this type of organization is fine. However, if you use this method in an electronic publication that is not designed to be used on the Web, be careful. Readers will get lost quickly and wander aimlessly without structure. To reduce this problem, you can do several things:

- Put an appropriate title and subtitle on all pages of the publication. This way readers have an idea of where they are within the publication.
- On every page, provide a way to return to the first page of the publication or an overview page of a particular section.
- At the top or bottom of every overview page, provide a menu to enable readers to jump to other overview pages and not into the middle of topics if they so choose.

Developing Project Content Using Storyboards

Now that you have developed the structure of the storyboards, you'll want to look closer at the individual parts of the project. Developing the content of the storyboards will help you do this. The depth of the content development really depends on the size and complexity of the project.

A traditional way to develop a small project is to develop all content aspects of the storyboard, from the placement of graphics and menu buttons to the placement of text. Similarly, the traditional development method for a large storyboard is to outline each individual storyboard and then progressively work toward more detail as necessary. A better method is to use storyboard templates or master storyboards whenever possible and develop individual storyboards only as necessary.

Developing Master Storyboards

Master storyboards are a highly effective way to design. They make the design process considerably less complex and will save you countless hours of work. Instead of creating hundreds of individual storyboards, you create templates for the major divisions of the publishing project. These templates form the basis for the individual storyboards. In this way, you have to make only minor adjustments to the individual storyboards, and you ensure the look of the publication is consistent throughout.

The main idea behind master storyboards is that you identify repetitious or non-unique features of the publication and let a single master storyboard represent pages in the publication with like features. You do this by looking at the publication in progressive levels of detail. Most publications will have the following:

- Overview pages
- A table of contents
- Topic or chapter overview pages
- Pages within chapters or topics
- An index

Start by thinking about the publication as a whole. Are there component parts of the publication that will or should be uniform throughout? The answer is usually yes because the top of the page will contain a header consistent throughout the publication and the bottom of the page will contain a footer consistent throughout the publication.

Next, examine the sections of the publication. Multiple sections of the publication will usually have common parts. For example, all chapter pages will probably have the same menu options, such as the following:

- Previous chapter
- Next chapter

- Previous page
- Next page
- Go to chapter index
- Go to help index
- Go to start page or home page
- Search text
- Print text
- Quit or exit the publication

The last step is to examine individual sections of the publication for common material. Pages of an index will contain different features or organization from pages of a chapter. But all pages within a chapter or within an index should have similar elements.

After you have examined all aspects of the publication for common parts, you develop the master storyboards. You may have multiple levels of master storyboards:

- An overall master storyboard
- A master storyboard that can be used in multiple sections
- A master storyboard for individual sections

You may have only one or many master storyboards. The number of master storyboards you have really depends on the size and complexity of your project. Although some of the best authoring tools support multiple levels of master storyboards, most authoring tools support at least one level of master storyboards. Within the authoring tool, you can either turn on or off the features of the master storyboard for any pages of the publication.

One of the best values in authoring tools for DOS/Windows systems is NeoBook. The basic version of NeoBook costs $45. The professional version of NeoBook costs $99.95. NeoBook has most of the features of the high-priced authoring tools, and NeoBook Pro features multimedia support like stereo sound and animation.

Adobe makes some of the most popular authoring tools for Macintosh and Windows systems including Acrobat and PageMaker. Although the basic version of Adobe Acrobat costs $129.95, the professional version of Acrobat sells for around $400. Both versions of Acrobat are good buys. However, if you want to go all out, PageMaker is probably your best choice. PageMaker is one of the most feature-rich authoring tools on the market with a retail price of $599.95.

Developing Individual Storyboards

In the design stage, you'll rarely develop individual storyboards. This is especially true if you take the time to develop master storyboards. Whether you develop individual storyboards depends on the needs of the project. For a small project you may want to develop all the storyboards so you get a precise overview of the publication. For a large project you may make only simple additions to the individual storyboards, like adding the chapter title or page numbers for associated text.

Sometimes it is essential to develop the content for unique storyboards within the publication to see how they will fit in with the publication as a whole. You develop these storyboards because through them, you can get a better understanding of the publication. The following are examples of unique storyboards:

- Startup page (first page)
- Table of contents page
- Chapter index page
- Credits page
- Menu pages

Evaluating the Logic of the Storyboard

In the last phase of storyboarding, you evaluate the logic of the storyboard. This process is similar to the editing, revision, and proofing activities of the publishing process. You examine the links between storyboards. You ensure the publication has a logically flowing structure and that all storyboards are properly linked together. Then you examine the outlines the storyboards contain. Here, you are primarily making sure the key elements are placed on the storyboard in the most logical manner.

The storyboarding process is meant to save time, resources, and frustration. Do not spend too much time worrying needlessly about minor details. In this phase, look only for major problems in logic.

Summary

The best publications are the result of effective strategies for thinking, planning, and composing. Helping you create the best electronic publications using effective strategies is what this chapter was all about. Keep the following ideas in mind:

- You set yourself on the path to success by managing expectations, perceptions, strategies, goals, rules, and behavior.
- You improve your initial ideas through brainstorming, freethinking, and storyboarding.
- You convince yourself to stop procrastinating by setting a flexible and realistic schedule containing milestones, goals, and an allocation of time to help you through to project completion.
- You figure out who the audience for the publication is by using common sense, gathering statistics, and evaluating trends.

- You tackle the project and progress through the composition, development, and publishing processes.

- You reduce complexity in project design by visualizing the publication from start to finish using storyboards. Being able to see the component parts of the entire project makes the project more manageable and less mysterious.

Layout and Document Types

8

by William R. Stanek

Electronic publications are a new territory for publishers and readers. If you lay out the document poorly and make it impossible for the reader to coherently navigate through your publication, the reader's first trip into this powerful medium may be his or her last. Don't leave readers stranded in the publication without a road map. Help readers. Welcome them to this new medium with a layout that is inviting, friendly, and easy to follow.

This chapter explores layout concepts for electronic publications. Use the guidelines in this chapter to lay out a publication that will communicate your message to readers effectively. You will learn about the following:

■ Page layout:

    Text pages
    Graphic pages
    Combined text and graphic pages
    Multimedia access pages
    Title pages or overview pages
    Table of contents pages
    Topic or chapter overview pages
    Pages within chapters or topics
    Index or glossary pages

■ Layout styles:

    Traditional print-oriented layout
    Traditional software-oriented layout
    Combined print and software layout
    Modern freelance layout

What Is Layout?

Layout is a plan for the arrangement and relationship of the parts of the publication. Documents with poor layout are downright hostile to readers. No one wants a publication they have to fight with every time they try to read it. This problem can be solved through careful attention to three key factors: organization, layout, and page design. Although this chapter covers layout, the first of these factors is the subject of Chapter 7, "Organizing Information," and designing the pages of your publication is the subject of Chapter 9, "Page Design."

The layout of your publication depends on the type of publication you're creating. An electronic book will have a different layout from an electronic newsletter, for example. This is because the projects are of different sizes and complexity. They also have different components.

An electronic book is an involved project. The electronic book will have many component parts. It will have a cover page, a table of contents, chapters, tables, graphs, accompanying photos or other types of graphic images, an index, and more. The length of the project will be long. Most book projects run several hundred pages.

An electronic newsletter, on the other hand, has few component parts. It may or may not have a separate cover page and a table of contents. It will have articles and photos or other types of graphic images. The length of the project is short. Most newsletters have fewer than 20 pages.

Although chapters and articles are similar component parts, in an electronic book chapters are arranged differently from articles in an electronic newsletter. More than likely, parts of the newsletter's articles will appear on the first page of the publication. In the book, the chapters will be distinct parts of the book. In the newsletter, more than one article will probably be displayed on the same page of the newsletter.

> **NOTE**
>
> Although the issues discussed in this chapter can be applied to any type of publication no matter the medium, the discussion is focused on publications designed for floppy disk or CD-ROM. Please note, publications designed for the World Wide Web have design issues beyond issues you'll see in this chapter. The additional design issues for World Wide Web publications will be covered in Part IV, "Online Publishing and the Internet."

Types of Pages

Electronic publications can have many types of pages, the layout of which is more flexible than a traditional print publication. In a printed book, it is difficult and costly to incorporate text and graphic images on the same page. In an electronic book, you can incorporate high-resolution graphics easily and at no additional expense when the book is published.

Your pages may even include more than text and images. In an electronic book, you can add sound and video to any or all of your pages.

> **NOTE**
>
> Most electronic publications can be printed by the end-user for reading off-line or displayed on a computer screen. In the latter case, the screen is the reader's viewing area, and the word *page* really defines what a single screen of the publication will look like.

You can include any of the following basic types of pages in your publication:

    Text pages
    Graphic pages
    Combined text and graphic pages
    Multimedia access pages

Text Pages

In electronic publications designed specifically for viewing on a computer screen, there are no printed pages of clean white paper and typeset black print. You're free to place text on the screen as you wish. You can use a variety of colors and fonts. The font you use defines the way text looks on the screen.

Most text is placed on the screen in what is called a text window. As depicted in Figure 8.1, a text window is an area designated on the screen for text. The borders of the window are usually a different color from the background color of the text window. The background color of the window can be any color you want. The text within the window can be any color you want it to be.

FIGURE 8.1.

A text window should contain scrollbars.

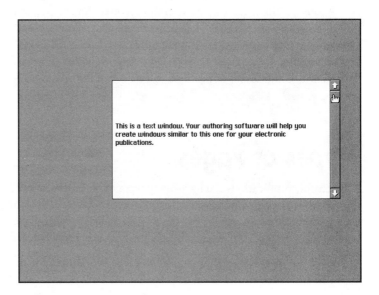

This is a text window. Your authoring software will help you create windows similar to this one for your electronic publications.

Look at the scrollbar on the right side of the text window in Figure 8.1. Readers of the publication can use scrollbars to move forward or backward through the contents of the window. This is useful if there is more text than will fit in the window. The little icon of the hand is pointing to the scrollbar and its scroll up mechanism. If a reader moves the mouse pointer to the up arrow and clicks the left mouse button, she would move backward through the contents of the window. Similarly, if a reader moves the mouse point to the scrollbar's down arrow and clicks the left mouse button, he would move forward through the contents of the window. Typically, the text scrolls up one line for each click on the up arrow and down one line for each click on the down arrow.

As Figure 8.2 shows, text windows can be of any size. You can also have several text windows on the screen at once. The text window readers are going to use to read your publication should occupy a large area of the screen. Yet the larger the text window, the more space it fills and the less space you have to add in graphics, navigation mechanisms, and other items.

FIGURE 8.2.

Two text windows of different sizes on one screen.

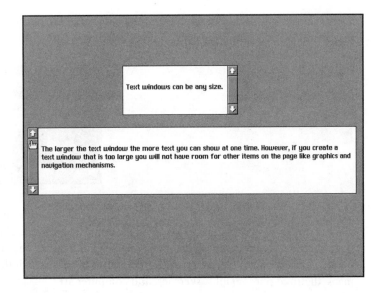

When you lay out the publication, you should carefully consider how much space you want text to occupy. Often you'll want heavily textual pages or pages that have a large text area. Heavily textual pages work well for the primary pages of the publication. The primary pages of the publication can include chapter or topic pages, table of content pages, overview pages, and index pages.

Graphic Pages

At times, you'll want other features of the page to command more attention than the text. Sometimes in an electronic publication, you'll want pages featuring only graphic images. These pages can contain one image or multiple images. You define what the images depict and how many images a page can contain.

Oversized images or images you want readers to be able to manipulate can be placed in a graphic window. As Figure 8.3 depicts, graphic windows are similar to text windows. Besides a vertical scrollbar, they usually have a horizontal scrollbar. This allows readers to move through portions of the image up or down and left or right.

Some authoring tools will let you manipulate images in other ways. For example, using a magnifying feature, you could zoom in on an area of the image. Using a minimize feature, you could shrink the image to the smallest allowable size. Using a maximize feature, you could open the image to its largest allowable size.

Small images or images that don't exceed the size of the screen are often simply placed on the page. These images are stationary images. You place them on the page where you want them to appear every time the reader reads the publication. Additionally, you'll want some graphics to appear on all key pages of the publication. These could include your company logo, the logo for the publication's imprint or small images used as a part of an on-screen menu.

FIGURE 8.3.

Graphic windows can also have scrollbars.

When you lay out the publication, you should carefully consider how much space you want graphic images to occupy. Sometimes you'll want heavily graphical pages or pages that have a large area for images. Heavily graphical pages work well for the supplemental pages of the publication. The supplemental pages of the publication can include pages for figures, charts, maps, digitized photographs, sketches, and computer art.

Combined Text and Graphic Pages

As you saw in Figures 8.1 and 8.2, pages with only text don't come alive before the reader's eyes. The same could be said about pages with only images. If the hero and heroine of your electronic novel ride off into the sunset, a photograph of a sunset may be a dazzling closing page. Yet, if you put the same page in the middle of the publication you may draw the reader's attention away from the story line. The hero and heroine don't ride off into the sunset on page 89.

Often there is a trade-off in the amount of text and graphics you want to place onto a single page. Most publications have pages featuring both text and graphics. Combined text and graphic pages often pack the most power. This is especially true when you design the graphics to accent the page. Images on primary pages that feature text, like chapter or topic pages, should not dominate the page. They should be smaller than the textual portion of the page and used to help make the page more visually appealing to the reader's eyes.

Multimedia Access Pages

Readers of electronic publications crave more than text and simple graphics. They want a work that comes to life and works better on the screen than it would in a traditional printed form. Therefore, most electronic publications contain more than text and graphic images. The best publications contain music, sounds, digitized video, or computer animation. If you provide these features, readers must be able to access them, and multimedia access pages are commonly used to do just this.

On multimedia access pages, you provide navigation features that allow readers to play digitized video, music or animation. Creating and incorporating multimedia into the publication can be tricky. This is why several chapters of the book are dedicated to using multimedia and incorporating multimedia. However, the access mechanisms you provide to readers don't have to be sophisticated. Often, you can provide access through a pull-down menu or on-screen buttons.

NOTE

A pull-down menu is a list of commands or actions that users can access by using the mouse or key combinations. The contents of the menu remain hidden until the user moves the mouse pointer to a keyword designating the menu and clicks on it. Prior to this, only a single summary command for the menu is visible on-screen. Once the contents of the menu are visible, the user can click a command to carry out the action, such as open an image file.

On-screen buttons are similar to menus in that they represent a command that will be carried out if the button is activated by clicking on it or using key combinations. Buttons are often represented by a small image called an icon or a small rectangular box labeled with a keyword. If you use Microsoft Windows, Macintosh, Amiga, or the X Window System, you're probably familiar with pull-down menus and on-screen buttons.

When you add a multimedia access page, you should carefully consider how this page will work into the overall layout of the publication. One way to add such a page to the publication is depicted in Figure 8.4. In this example, the page is dedicated specifically to the access of the publication's multimedia files. Using on-screen buttons enables readers to select from among the many files. This type of page would let readers explore the many features you have included in the publication separately from the publication and from one convenient page. This is good if you have included music, video, or animation that readers may wish to preview or play outside the main publication.

More often, creating such a page is a great starting point for you as you test multimedia features you'll want to add to specific pages within the publication. This is because most authoring software lets you run the publication while you're creating it for testing purposes. This way you can test the music, video, or animation sequences from a single page without having to roam through the publication. This is how real programmers test their multimedia sequences, too. You can sometimes find these test pages in the finished versions of computer software or video games.

FIGURE 8.4.

A multimedia access page for testing.

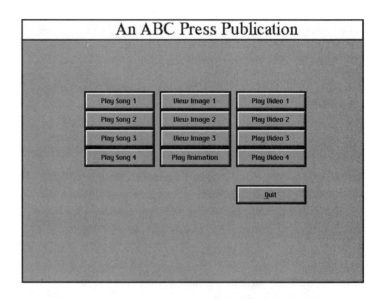

Your multimedia access page does not have to be a test page. Another way to provide multimedia access is to simply add access mechanisms to your text, graphics, or combined text and graphics pages. Again, these mechanisms could be on-screen buttons or commands listed in a pull-down menu. Your goal as you develop the overall layout of the publication would be to determine where in the publication you could add multimedia to enhance your message. Your goal as you develop the layout of specific pages would be to add specific access mechanisms for the individual multimedia sequences where they fit into the publication.

TIP

Any page of the publication could have both on-screen buttons and pull-down menus. You could also use pull-down menus on certain types of pages and on-screen buttons on other types of pages. However, for consistency, similar pages of your publication should contain similar navigation mechanisms. This means, if the pages of chapter 1 contain on-screen buttons, the pages of chapter 2 should not have a menu replacing the on-screen buttons. This will ensure a logical flow for the layout of your publication.

Using Traditional Document Components

Working in a new medium does not mean you should abandon layout techniques that work well. Your publication can and should include some traditional document components to make it flow coherently and logically. How you present and lay out these traditional components in an electronic publication is another matter. A table of contents page takes on a new meaning when you use on-screen buttons or a menu system to allow readers to not only read the table of contents, but also to quickly jump to a specific part of the publication.

This section presents the layout concerns for the following traditional components:

Cover pages
Title pages or overview pages
Table of contents pages
Topic or chapter overview pages
Pages within chapters or topics
Index or glossary pages

Cover Pages

The actual cover of your electronic publication will probably be the plastic case enshrouding a floppy disk. But when readers insert the disk into their disk drive and start the publication, they don't expect to see chapter 1, page 1 of the publication. They expect to see a startup page or pages.

The typical startup page includes artwork much like the cover of a real book. The artwork could be displayed while the publication is loading as a single image or series of images. It could also be displayed on a specific page that provides a way to start reading the publication. The artwork can be sophisticated and eye-catching, such as digitized photographs, high-resolution computer art, or computer animation, but it does not have to be. It could be simple line art or the company logo.

As you design the layout of the publication, create a storyboard for the cover page. Consider carefully the type of image or images you want to use to give readers the best first impression of your publication. If you plan to publish similar work, you may want to consider developing a cover page that is reusable.

Title Pages, Overview Pages, and Home Pages

Title pages in a traditional publication are one of the first pages in the publication. The title page displays the title of the publication, the author's name, and the publisher's information. Title pages are often followed by overview pages that give a brief explanation of the contents of the publication.

Title pages, overview pages, and home pages are often incorporated into electronic publications. Usually they are included as part of the startup sequence for the publication. As part of the startup sequence, segments of this information would be displayed briefly on the screen. One way to do this would be to create separate pages for each component of the publication you wish to display in this manner. Each page could be displayed on the screen for a few seconds before being erased and replaced with the next page. Although some of the best authoring software will let you do this in grand style, some basic authoring tools have add-ons that will let you do this. For example, if you use the $45 NeoBook for DOS/Windows, you can use NeoShow to create animated startup sequences and all for under $100.

Sometimes, you may want a simple title page that has as its main feature a way to start reading the publication. The title page may also serve as the cover page. This is something you should consider as you lay out the publication.

Table of Contents Pages

The table of contents page in a traditional publication is not interactive. It is a simple list of chapter titles, headings and subheadings. Its most useful features are the page numbers that correspond to the major components of the publication.

In an electronic publication, the table of contents page takes on a new meaning. Build the table of contents into a menu or a series of on-screen buttons, and readers can quickly navigate through the major components of the publication. Add in search features, and it will allow readers to quickly find topics of interest and move to them at the click of a button.

As you lay out the publication, keep in mind the table of contents page can be the primary link between the major components of the publication. The table of contents page can also be an alternative way to search through topics and a quick navigation aid. You'll find this technique useful in many types of publications. This will be especially true if you're using a hierarchical design. In this design model, the table of contents page could be the one top-level page you allow readers to jump up to. From this page they could move through the major sections of the publication as they want to.

Topic or Chapter Overview Pages

You can incorporate topic or chapter overview pages into electronic publications in several ways. In a traditional layout style, this page would be the first page readers would see when they start a new chapter. From the overview page, the reader would then be able to read the topic or chapter by advancing through the text.

Another way to lay out this type of page is to allow readers to navigate strictly through overview pages. In the layout of the publication, the overview pages would be sequential pages that the reader could easily navigate through until they find a topic or chapter they want to read. They would then be able to move to the text of the chapter they want to read. In this way, overview pages have an alternate path from the main path, and the reader only sees overview pages if they choose to.

Pages Within Chapters or Topics

The layout of the individual pages within chapters or topics is something you should consider carefully at an early stage in the design process. One school of thought for the layout of individual pages within chapters or topics is that each page should represent the equivalent of a physical page. A page in an electronic publication is often thought of in terms of a single computer screen. If the layout of your publication uses this school of thought, there would be one storyboard or computer screen for every page of the publication. For example, if a book in printed form had 379 pages, the book in electronic form would occupy 379 storyboards or computer screens.

Creating a book in electronic form with 379 individual definitions for a page can be tedious work. As you discovered in the previous chapter, you could create a master storyboard to define major components of the page. However, you would still need to split the text of your publication into 379 individual components. Usually this means creating 379 different text files.

By hand, splitting multiple files into even-length sections with a uniform look is difficult and time-consuming. On some systems, splitting a document up into this many pieces would be easy. For a UNIX system, one command string could do this for you. The problem is in the cleanup. Where were the files split, and how do they look when put together in the publication?

A solution is to use the text windows described earlier in the chapter. When you add navigation features to a page that includes scrollbars, you free the page from the limitation of being a single physical screen. The reader can scroll through hundreds of lines of text using the same text window.

To do this, you would place all the text you want the reader to be able to access through this window into a file and associate the file with the window. For example, if chapter 29 of your electronic book is 12,000 words in length and saved in a file called CH29.TXT, using your authoring software, you could create a text window and associate CH29.TXT with the window. When the readers use this window, they could read the entire chapter using the scrollbar to advance through the text. The disadvantage of this layout style is that the chapter is not broken down into distinct pages that may cause a conceptualization problem for readers; instead of being on page 28, they are now midway through Chapter 2 at a position relative to the location marker on the scrollbar.

Both layout approaches have additional advantages and disadvantages. By creating many individual pages, the reader does not have to scroll through text. You can provide navigation mechanisms that make it as easy as using the left and right cursor keys to move forward or backward through the pages of the publication. You're also less restricted in your freedom to include features in the publication. You can provide very specific information at more points throughout the publication. For example, every page could have a specific image that corresponds to the topic of the text.

Sometimes though, you just don't want to create hundreds of separate images or layouts for individual pages. By creating pages containing entire chapters or topics, you eliminate the problem. Yet, using a text window will mean the reader must scroll through text. The navigation mechanisms for this could be as easy as using the cursor-up and cursor-down keys to scroll up or down. You're more restricted in your freedom to include features in the publication. You'll usually provide only general or broad information on the chapter pages. For example, each chapter page could include an image that corresponds to a scene in the chapter or to the chapter as a whole.

In the end, it comes down to a design decision. You select the page layout that works best for the project given your time, resource, and budget constraints.

Index or Glossary Pages

In textbooks, reference books, and other nonfiction books, index and glossary pages are useful. An index helps you find specific topics quickly. A glossary gives you key definitions at a glance. In electronic publications, you can transform indexes and glossaries into the most useful and interactive resources in the publication.

You could build the index into a menu or a series of on-screen buttons for readers that is keyed to the glossary and to the text of the publication. This way the reader would either be able to quickly navigate to the page containing the key word or to its definition. The links could also work in the opposite direction. The reader could select a word in the text of a page or chapter and jump to its definition in the glossary. By adding in search features, you could allow readers to quickly find key words and their definitions.

If you want to use these techniques in your publication, you should consider several things. Currently, only high-end authoring tools support this level of sophisticated linking of ideas. Yet you can use more cost-effective alternatives to paying exorbitant rates for high-end tools. One option is to choose a new medium for the publication. On the World Wide Web, you could easily and cheaply create this advanced index and glossary link and search mechanisms using the standard, and often free, tools of the World Wide Web.

A better option is to develop a work-around. Most authoring tools, even the low-end ones, include menu and search mechanisms. An easy solution is to provide a go-to-glossary and a go-to-index button or menu option on the individual pages of your publication. Once on the glossary or index page, the reader could use a search option to find the key word they are looking for.

Because the real problem is the linking within the text of the page or chapter, another solution would be to only develop the index links to the text. You would build the index table into a menu or group of on-screen buttons and allow readers to jump to the pages of the book. Optimally, you would follow the individual page layout so the reader could see the entire text of the page without having to scroll. This way the key word would be in the visible portion of the text window.

The Layout of the Publication

Even in traditional print, the various types of publications have different layouts. Dictionaries have different layouts than textbooks. Magazines have different layouts from newsletters. The same often holds true for publications in the same broad category, such as books. Fiction books have different layouts from nonfiction books, and textbooks have another style of layout.

In electronic publications, some additional factors, beyond the type of publication you're creating, may influence your layout decisions:

- The resources you have available
- The features of the authoring software you have chosen
- The size of your publication
- The audience for the publication
- The end-user's computer

The resources you have available will play a key role in your layout choices. If you're working on an old computer, you may not have the means to add high-resolution graphics to the publication. If the publication is your first, it is often best to start with a basic approach. You can always work toward creating more advanced publications as you develop your publishing skills. Also, the basic approach will probably cost less to produce in both time and money.

The features of the authoring software you have chosen are another factor that may restrict the design of the publication. Not all authoring software is created equally. Although the best authoring software probably has more features than you'll ever use, low-end authoring tools have only the most basic features. This is another reason you should consider the features you plan to incorporate into your present and future publications before purchasing authoring software.

Size is another factor that will influence your design and layout decisions. A small publication, such as a 15-page electronic newsletter, may not need many advanced features. More than likely, the newsletter won't have a cover page or a title page. It will probably start on a combined text and graphics page that serves a secondary role as a title page. On the other hand, a large publication, such as an electronic book, may have many advanced features including a sequenced startup page.

The people who will buy or receive your publication are the audience for the publication. The way you lay out a trade journal for computer professionals may be entirely different from the layout of a trade journal for lawyers. As you lay out the publication, you'll want to design the layout with the needs of your audience firmly in mind.

When you design the layout, you should also consider that not all readers will read the publication using the screen size you're working in. On Windows systems, if you create the layout for the publication using a screen size of 1024×768, readers who view the publication in 640×480 won't be able to see the entire page you have created. Yet, if you lay out the publication using a screen size of 640×480, readers displaying the publication at 1024×768 could see the entire publication. Although to these readers the publication won't occupy the entire area of the screen unless they switch video modes, this is far better than using a screen size that will leave portions of the publication unviewable.

On Windows systems, common screen sizes are

640×480	The screen size in widest use, used by VGA monitors and associated video cards.
800×600	A widely supported screen size but not in wide use.
1024×768	A screen size in wide use on newer computers. Used by SVGA monitors and associated video cards.
1152×900	A screen size for use on newer computers.
1280×1024	A screen size for use on the newest computers.

If you are developing publications for viewing on the Macintosh, keep in mind Mac's display—72 pixels per inch, and the number of pixels viewable on the screen depends on the size of the screen. Monitor sizes vary from as small as 9-inch diagonal on older Macs to typical sizes of 13-inch and 14-inch diagonal and all the way up to 25 inches or more. To ensure the largest number of Mac users can display your publication, you should design the publication with the typical size of 13 inches in mind. Yet, no matter what size screen you design for, you should test the publication on other sizes. You may want to consider adding a mechanism to warn users with screens smaller than the one you designed for that the publication cannot be displayed.

Layout Styles for Electronic Publications

To communicate your message effectively, the publication must have an appropriate style. The styles currently in widest use reflect the roots of electronic publications in traditional print publications and in computer software. These traditional ways to lay out documents seemed logical to early electronic publishers. This way, the electronic versions of publications could be seen as extensions of the traditional medium. The next trend was to combine the styles.

A growing trend in electronic publishing is to adopt a more modern style and do away with the strong ties to traditional media. Although the best authoring software will let you create electronic publications in any style you choose, more restrictive authoring software will only let you create electronic publications in a single style. This is another reason you should choose your publishing tools very carefully.

When purchasing an authoring tool, you'll want to read the description on the packaging carefully. What you are looking for is very specific support of the features you would like to include in the publication. For example, if you want to include multimedia features, what multimedia features does the application claim to support? Will it play sound files and if so, what type of sound files is it capable of playing? Will it play video files, and if so, what video formats is it capable of playing? Will it display pictures, and if so, what graphic formats is it capable of displaying?

If the packaging description doesn't answer your questions clearly, you may want to take the time to call the company and ask them about their product. Because most companies have a toll free sales number, the call won't cost you anything. Table 8.1 presents a list of popular authoring tools and phone numbers for more information.

Table 8.1. Obtaining sales information on popular authoring tools.

Company	Authoring Tool(s)	Approximate Cost	Sales Phone Number in U.S.A.
Adobe	Acrobat	$129.95	1-800-833-6687
	Acrobat Pro	$399.95	
	PageMaker	$549.95	
Corel	Ventura Publisher	$429.95	1-800-836-3729
Frame Technology	FrameMaker	$629.95	1-408-433-3311
Macromedia	Director	$899.95	1-800-288-4797
	Director Multimedia Studio	$1,499.95	
NeoSoft	NeoBook	$45.00	1-800-545-1392
	NeoBookPro	$99.95	

Just because you adopt one style for a publication you produce, this does not mean you have to produce subsequent publications in this style. The style you adopt should be one that works best for you and for the type of publication. You may elect to use a traditional style for the newsletter you're creating and a modern style for the book you're creating.

You may also want to create a publication in several styles and let the reader select which one they like best. Electronic books I publish at The Virtual Press are published in two styles, a standard version and an enhanced version. One such book is *At Dream's End* which is published in both standard and enhanced versions. The Virtual Press Web site (`http://tvp.com/`) has screen shots of both versions of *At Dream's End*.

NOTE

If you don't recognize the universal resource locator for The Virtual Press Web site (`http://tvp.com/`), don't worry. URLs are explained in Chapter 19, "The World Wide Web," and in Chapter 20, "Using HTML."

As early authoring tools followed traditional methodology, they tended to be less demanding on the computer systems they ran on. This is true even for the most current versions of these types of programs. The standard versions of The Virtual Press' electronic books have a limited combined print and software style. They are developed for computer users with very basic systems. The enhanced versions of The Virtual Press' electronic books have a modern style. They are developed for computer users who can take advantage of audio and video enhancements.

The four layout styles presented in this chapter are

> Traditional print-oriented layout
> Traditional software-oriented layout
> Combined print and software layout
> Modern freelance layout

> **NOTE**
>
> A major factor in the model you'll use to design publications depends on the authoring software you plan to use. However, you should learn about each of the layout styles. In this way, you'll be able to make an informed choice in both the layout of the publication and the type of software you should purchase to create publications with this layout.

Traditional Print-Oriented Layout

The traditional print-oriented layout is a common way to arrange the components of an electronic publication. This is the most pure and basic style for electronic publications. The style mirrors that of traditional print publications, meaning the layout of your electronic publication closely resembles the layout of the traditional print version.

The style is largely text-based. The only graphic images in the publication would be images you include for display when the publication is first started. The reader sees the publication as one big file. The reader would start on the title page and progress through the publication a page at a time. This type of layout is linear.

Once the publication is started, the reader does not have to worry about menus, buttons or mouse controls. The primary controls the reader would have to navigate through the document would be forward and back cursor controls and possibly a top of document control. The advantage of this style is that it is unobtrusive.

Some shareware authoring tools will help you produce electronic publications in the print-oriented style. Developing electronic publications in this style is very easy because of the linear organization. If you want a quick and no frills way to lay out a self-running electronic book on disk, this is the style for you.

Traditional Software-Oriented Layout

The traditional software-oriented layout is a basic style for electronic publications. The style mirrors that of traditional software publications, meaning the layout of the electronic publication closely resembles the layout of your favorite computer software program. This style is in wide use in shareware and freeware publications on disk.

The style is largely text-based and menu-oriented. The readers would start on an overview page that would explain how they are to progress through the publication. The reader sees the publication as a series of files they can open through an open file menu option. Graphic images could be displayed when the publication is first started or accessed through an open image menu option.

The software style has many features from your favorite text editor or word processor. These features are included on a series of pull-down menus. The reader would use a mouse or key combinations to activate a particular menu. Some authoring tools will let you include links in the overview document that allow readers to quickly call up a file (chapter or topic) they want to read. Although this style is feature rich, it can be overpowering for readers who are not familiar with traditional text editors or word processors.

Many shareware authoring tools will help you produce electronic publications in this style. Developing electronic publications in this style is easy, but possibly confusing for readers. If you want a quick and no frills way to lay out a self-running electronic book on disk, this is also a good style.

Two shareware programs that will create publications exclusively in this style are Dart for MS-DOS and Waldo OpenBook for Mac. Dart and Waldo OpenBook will run on the most basic of systems and are no frills authoring tools that will let you display text that can include hypertext links and graphics using external programs to display the images. The shareware fees of $34 and $30 respectively for these programs are high when compared to some of the budget commercial options available that are more fully featured. However, if you want to ensure users with older systems have access to your publications, these may be good choices.

For more information on Dart, contact the following:

Ted Husted
4 Falcon Lane
Fairport, New York 14450-3312 USA

For more information on Waldo OpenBook, contact the following:

John Gaudreault
P.O. Box 3442
Omaha, Nebraska 68103 USA

Combined Print and Software Layout

The combined print and software layout is an advanced style for electronic publications. The method borrows the best features of the traditional styles and has a more modern look to it. Although only a few shareware authoring tools will help you develop publications in this style, most commercial authoring tools excel in this style.

Although you can incorporate text, graphics and possibly multimedia, such as music, computer animation, or video, usually the reader can only view one type of medium at a time or each type of medium is put into a separate window the reader can manipulate. Electronic publications developed with this style hide the pull-down menus from the user and allow simple keystroke combinations to perform many of the same advanced features as the software style.

The publication generally follows a hierarchical or a combined hierarchical and linear organization. Developing electronic publications in hierarchical organization is logical for you and the reader. The first page the readers see is usually a table of contents page organized as a list of component parts—chapters, images, and so on. The readers are allowed to scroll through the list using standard cursor controls or a mouse. They would select an item by pressing the return key, space key or an appropriate mouse button.

This style is great because the reader only has to worry about menus, buttons, or mouse controls if they want to. Using this style, you have great freedom and can include many different document components. Besides a table of contents menu, you could have other indexed menus like a keyword index, a table index, a graphic image index, or anything else you could think of.

Modern Freelance Layout

The modern freelance layout is the most advanced style for electronic publications. Using this style, you can create electronic publications in any organization method including the integrated web. Most commercial authoring tools, and primarily the high-end tools, will help you develop publications in this style.

This style will free your creativity. You can incorporate text, graphics, and multimedia, such as music, computer animation, or video. You can have multiple types of media on the screen at once, organized however you wish. Electronic publications developed with this style will be as simple or as complicated as you make them.

You determine what the reader sees when the program is first started. The reader is allowed to navigate through the publication in many different ways using the mechanisms you have provided. During project development, you can activate or deactivate standard navigation features like cursor, key combination and mouse controls. You'll also be able to create your own navigation mechanisms using pull-down menus or on-screen buttons.

Freelance is the best style to work in because you control all aspects of the publication. However, because you can do this, the freelance style is more demanding on time and resources. A project developed using this style will take longer, yet the result will also be a better product.

Summary

Layout is a plan for the arrangement and relationship of the parts of the publication. Although electronic publications can include traditional document components, these pages take on new meanings in electronic publications. Beyond traditional types of pages, electronic documents have text pages, graphics pages, and even multimedia pages. All these pages can be confusing to you and to the readers if you don't follow good layout techniques. Make sure your publication has a layout that is inviting, friendly, and easy to follow. Using one of the four layout techniques described in this chapter should start you on the right path.

Page Design

9

by William R. Stanek

Computer technology gives electronic publishers the freedom to provide information to readers in powerfully innovative ways. With this freedom comes opportunity, decisions, and options. The electronic publisher has to consider how to organize the publication, how to lay out the publication, and how to design the pages of the publication. You have already seen the many choices for organization and layout. With page design, you'll encounter many more choices.

Pages with high visual impact will leave a lasting impression on readers. High visual impact does not necessarily correlate to high resolution graphics. Some of the most visually stunning pages contain no graphics at all. They achieve their impact from simplicity of design. They use screen space, color, fonts, and headings to their advantage.

In this chapter, you will learn how to use screen space, color, fonts, headings, and more. The chapter explores the following:

- Using screen space
- Using color
- Using headings
- What fonts are and how to use them
- How graphic designers use grids
- Common page components
- Common page features
- Advanced page design

The best writing looks effortless. Words seem to flow straight from the writer's pen. The same is true about the best designed pages. Well-designed pages look effortless. They are organized in a way that is coherent and flowing.

The writer's secret to making words seem to flow effortlessly is simple. She knows that good work is the result of hard work—careful editing, revision, and proofreading. Creating a single polished page may take hours. Well-designed pages are also the result of hard work. Designs that seem simple and natural to the reader are often the result of intense efforts to make them seem this way.

> **NOTE**
>
> As you read through this chapter, keep in mind that the definition of a page is largely based on the medium you will be publishing in. For publications designed for viewing on the screen, the screen size determines page size. For publications that will be published on the Web, the screen size generally does not determine the page size. This is because of the availability of scrollbars in the applications used to display Web publications.

Applications used to display Web publications are called *browsers*. They have strict control over the displaying of your Web publications and because of this, some of the fundamental rules for page design are materially different. For this reason, specific design issues for Web publications are discussed in Part IV of this book. However, most of the page design concepts discussed in this chapter can be applied to any type of publication including Web publications.

Using Screen Space

Because electronic publications are designed primarily for viewing on computers, the computer screen is often the reader's viewing area. This means page design could also be called screen design. Sometimes it is not what you have on the screen that helps convey your message, rather what you do not have on the screen. Empty space on the screen makes the material easier to read by drawing the readers attention to the area of the screen that has material on it. It is the separation of the material that creates emphasis and draws the reader's attention.

Using space effectively is not a new idea. In traditional publications, graphic designers carefully balance the amount of empty space on the page to emphasize material. They do this by using wide margins whenever possible. Open your favorite textbook and you will probably find that the top margin is smaller than the bottom margin. Next compare the margins on two opposing pages. You might find that on the left-hand page the left margin is wide and the right margin near the binding is narrow. On the right-hand page, the left margin near the binding is narrow and the right margin is wide. Print publications are usually designed this way to make them more visually appealing.

Another common spacing technique is to vary the length of paragraphs. If you use the same paragraph length repeatedly, even the most lively material can seem monotonous. You should use short paragraphs more often and restrict the use of long paragraphs. A short paragraph has less than six lines. A long paragraph is more than 10 lines. If you are designing for the Web, it is difficult to count lines because the way you see the paragraph may not be the way the reader sees the paragraph. Yet by estimating that an average line may have 70 characters, you can also estimate the number of lines in a particular paragraph.

In the textual portion of your electronic publication, you can use these traditional design techniques, yet you do not want to stop your good design techniques at the publication's text window. The material you provide or do not provide on the screen is extremely important. A blank screen with a text window is dull and unimaginative.

NOTE

If you plan to publish on the Web, keep in mind that your publication will be displayed by an application called a browser. Browsers generally do not allow separate text and graphic windows to be displayed in the same viewing area. What most browsers do is combine text and graphics in a single window that can be manipulated by the reader. (For more information on Web browsers, see Chapter 19, "The World Wide Web.")

By adding a few graphics to the page, you will dramatically increase the page's impact. The images or features you add to the page do not have to be sophisticated or high-resolution. Simple is almost always best. The placement of images and features on the page should be such that they focus the reader's attention to the primary textual portion of the page.

HOW TO INCREASE THE IMPACT OF PAGE LAYOUT

Techniques for CD-ROM

For CD-ROM or floppy disk publications, you can achieve this effect using the following spacing techniques:

- Do not center the text window on the screen.
- Use a wide margin above the text window and a narrow margin below the text window.
- Combine this with a wide left margin and a narrow right margin.

When you add graphics:

- Add graphics on one or two sides of the text window but not on all sides of the text window.
- Instead of building a graphical border around the entire screen, try putting a border on only the top and left side of the screen and a plain border or no border on the other two sides.

Techniques for Web Pages

In Web publications, you generally cannot add graphical borders or easily manipulate the positioning of text on the page. The text is normally left-aligned and can sometimes be centered. However, here are some tricks to get around these limitations.

For Web publications, you can use these spacing techniques to get the reader's attention:

- Use the horizontal rule to set the text off from other text. This will effectively create a border above and/or below the text.
- Insert empty paragraphs or line breaks to create space above and below the text.

- Use the line break feature to keep the length of lines short, thus creating a wide right margin.

When you add graphics:

- Align a small eye-catching graphic on the left side of the paragraph you want to highlight.
- You could also replace the plain horizontal rule with a graphical line that would create a fancy border above and below the text.

You can vary these techniques to fit the needs of your publication. If you want to off-center text to the left, do so. Use a wide right margin and a narrow left margin. If you want to build a graphical border all around the screen, try using two wide borders and two narrow borders.

A page that is entirely graphical can also benefit from spacing techniques. If text is secondary to an image on the page, the center piece of the page should be the image. Then, you would design the page to enhance the value of the image. The key is to use space in a way that enhances the design and draws attention to what you want to emphasize.

Using Color

The use of color in publications has always caused problems. In the early days of desktop publishing, people were discovering color printers. Documents were printed in red, yellow, blue, purple, and combinations of any other colors you can think of. This was not done because it was a sound design technique, rather because the desktop publisher could.

Color also carries with it certain connotations. In the United States, red suggests danger, yellow suggests caution, and green suggests all is clear. Red could also represent hot. Blue could represent cold. To different groups of people, these colors carry entirely different connotations. On Wall Street, red means losing money. To doctors, blue means death.

Colors that mean certain things in one country carry completely different connotations in other countries. Red can suggest aristocracy or masculinity in France, blasphemy in some African countries, and in Korea, red can suggest death because red ink is used to record deaths. In the United States, black is the color of mourning, yet in Korea, white is the traditional color of mourning. Yellow suggests grace in Japan, prosperity in Egypt, and caution or cowardice in the United States. Therefore, the key to using color and ensuring international appeal for your publications is to make sure you are not using color to carry a hidden meaning to the reader.

Common computer graphic modes will allow you to use thousands of colors on the same screen. Some graphic modes will let you use 16.7 million colors. With this many choices, there are bound to be problems. This is especially true when you use color combinations with text and backgrounds. For example, lightly colored text against a white background is almost always a poor combination.

You can also create problems by using background colors with text colors. Readers with a monochrome screen might not be able to read some text and background color combinations. Despite advances in technology, monochrome screens are widely used on portable computers. Do you want to exclude a million portable computer owners who have monochrome screens just because you think pink text on a yellow background looks great?

The best rules to follow when using colorful text or backgrounds are

- Use basic colors for text, like black, gray, red, yellow, green, blue, and white.

- Use basic colors for background but contrast them with the text colors. For example, if you use a dark blue background, try using white, bright yellow, or black text.

- Do not use too many different color combinations with text and background colors on the same page. A text window with a blue background and yellow text and a text window with a green background and white text on the same page may clash. More than four different colors in a text window can also cause problems.

- Using color with graphic images can also cause problems. A photograph with 16.7 million colors may look fantastic, but only a few of the publication's readers will be able to view it. Most computers in use today are capable of displaying only 256 colors. This remains true despite advances in technology. The video cards and monitors used with many old computers simply cannot display more than 256 colors; the same goes for older Macintosh computers.

Common color capabilities are as follows:

Color	Capabilties
16	Displayable by all computers with standard color monitors and standard video cards (including all current Macintosh models) but not by some laptops.
256	Displayable by the majority of computers with standard color monitors and standard video cards and by almost all current Macintosh models. Often the best choice considering the trade-off between quality and number of computers that can display the colors.
32,768	Displayable by most computers capable of displaying color including most Macintosh models (may require additional video memory).
65,536	Displayable by most computers capable of displaying color including most Macintosh models (may require additional video memory).
16.7 million	Displayable by newer computers capable of displaying 24-bit color.

Using Headings

Headings are words or phrases that divide chapters or topics of the publication into sections or subtopics. In traditional publications, headings are often used to break up the page. A page broken into topics looks more manageable and interesting. Headings help the reader envision the organization of the publication at a glance by identifying the main points. They also help the reader quickly find topics of interest.

Normally, you will find that nonfiction works contain many headings and fiction works relatively few. Fiction works generally break down the publication by chapter or story. Nonfiction works generally break down the subject into topics and subtopics. Breaking down the subject into manageable pieces is critically important, especially for difficult material. Studies have shown that our short-term memories can handle only seven plus or minus two pieces of information.

The rule of seven plus or minus two pieces of information is known as Miller's Law. A piece of information does not necessarily correlate to a single word. Usually it represents concepts or ideas. A paragraph could represent a single idea. This is why the optimum grouping of paragraphs under headings is three to seven paragraphs.

One word headings are usually poor choices. Good headings explain what the topic is and convey information to the reader. Your headings could be a few words, a complete sentence or a question.

In your publication, headings can have many uses. You can use headings in text windows and on the page as a whole. In text windows, you can use headings to designate chapters, topics, or subtopics. You can use different heading sizes to create levels of headings. Therefore, the largest heading size would be your first level heading, and the smallest heading size would be your lowest level heading. Although you could create as many heading levels as you want, in general, you should only use three or four levels of headings. In Web publications, you can also use heading levels to clearly distinguish topics and subtopics. (For more information on using headings in Web publications, see Chapter 20, "Using HTML.")

You also should use headings outside text windows. Headings break up the screen space and add to the visual impact of the page. On the pages of the publication, you can use headings to designate publisher information, the title of the publication, and the title of the chapter or topic.

Typical headings in text windows include

> Title of chapter or story
> Title of topic
> Title of subtopics

Typical headings on a page include

> Publisher information
> Title of the publication
> Title of a chapter or topic

What Fonts Are and How To Use Them

The font you use defines the way text looks. When publications were typeset for a printing press, the number of fonts publishers used were limited. Each new font included in the publication cost the publisher money. Some companies specializing in creating fonts charged thousands of dollars for a single font and, because of this, even in the early days of computing, fonts were still expensive.

Thankfully, this is not true today. The power of type was unleashed in the early days of the desktop publishing revolution. Now, you can buy fonts for pennies, and there are thousands to choose from.

Fonts have many different characteristics. Some fonts, called screen or plotter fonts, look one way on the screen and print out another. Some fonts, called outline or scalable fonts, look the same on-screen and on paper. However, when your publication will be viewed on a computer screen, you probably do not care how text would look if it were printed out.

Beyond this there are other characteristics common to all font types. You can use normal type, bold type, italic type, and bold italic type. These different font types add emphasis and carry meanings. Italics can convey a sense of nostalgia. Bold type seems to be shouting at you.

NOTE

Normal, bold, and italic type form a basic font family. A font family is a group of related fonts. For most purposes; each font type in a font family is counted as a separate font. This means if you purchase a font pack that claims to have 500 fonts, you will not get 500 different type faces. What you will get is several hundred font families with each font family generally having three font types (normal, bold, and italic) or four font types (normal, bold, italic, and bold italic).

TIP

You may be wondering why underline is not included as a common characteristic of all font types. Underline is not included because it is a feature that can be added to any type of font and is not a characteristic of fonts.

There are decorative fonts, heading fonts, fancy fonts, symbol fonts, and standard fonts. The problem with this many fonts is deciding what font you should use in your publication. To answer this question, the following subsections explain some font basics:

Monospace versus proportional type
Font size
Font styles

Monospace versus Proportional Type

The kind of type that most typewriters use is monospace type. In monospace type, each letter, number, or symbol takes up the same space. A monospaced *l* takes as much space as a monospaced *w*. This is very easy to read and great for tired eyes. Monospaced type is still in wide use.

Another kind of type is proportional type. With proportional type, each letter, number, or symbol takes up only the space it needs. Today, most fonts are proportional. Using proportional type, you can create variety and thus get more visual impact.

> **NOTE**
>
> In Web publications using HyperText Markup Language, the publisher has no direct control over the type of font used. The type of font used depends on settings in the reader's browser. However, as you will see in later chapters and specifically in Chapter 20, "Using HTML," there are ways to specifically designate text to be displayed in monospace type. One way to do this is to use the HTML typewriter tag <TT>.

Font Sizes

Fonts come in many sizes. The larger the type size, the larger the type. Font size is specified in a unit called a *point*. A point is a printing unit that equals approximately 1/72 inch. However, the true size of the point really depends on how the font was designed. Words in 10-point type using one font might not be the same as words in 10-point type in another font. This ambiguity in font sizes is something computers and desktop publishing have brought to the art of printing.

The most common point size for material designed to be read on a computer is 12-point. This is a good size for the main textual portions of the publication. Other common sizes range from 9 to 12 for the main text.

When determining the size of the type to use in your CD-ROM or disk publication, use a size that is easy to read. Remember, the readers' eyes may get tired. Do not make the type size so small they have to squint to read. Do not make type size so large that they feel they have to sit across the room from the screen.

> **NOTE**
>
> If you are working with a Windows system, keep in mind that the font size is relative to your display mode. This means a 12-point font viewed in the 640×480 display mode will seem much larger than the same 12-point font viewed in the 1024×768 display mode. The display mode in widest use at this time is 640×480.

> **NOTE**
>
> Font size is another area Web publishers using the hypertext markup language have no direct control over. However, most Web browsers display headings in a font size relative to the level of the heading. This means the largest text on the screen will be in a level one heading. A level two heading will have slightly smaller text, and so on. Therefore, you could vary the size of text on the screen by designating the text as a heading.
>
> Additionally, one of the most popular HTML browsers, the Netscape browser, will let you specify a basefont size and offsets from the basefont size.

Font Styles

Fonts come in thousands of styles given names by their designers. Each font style, called a *font family*, will have different type sizes and should include normal, bold, italic, and bold italic fonts. Many font styles in use today are hundreds of years old. Fonts such as Baskerville have been around since 1766. Some types that are considered modern first appeared over 200 years ago. Others like Castellar, Contemporary Brush, and BriemScript have been around for only a few decades.

The name of a font sometimes conveys a message about the style of the font, but not always. Fonts such as Ransom, Futura, Century Gothic, and NuptialScript carry distinct messages about the style. Fonts like New Century School Book, Contemporary Brush, Courier New, and Times New Roman all have modern names. Thousands of other font styles simply have names that might or might not convey a meaning to you.

The font you choose for the main text does not have to be the font you choose to use in headings. Some fonts are meant to be used in headings. Some fonts are designed to be decorative. Other fonts are designed to be used in normal text. The key to selecting a good font style is to use a font that is easy to read under a variety of conditions and works well for the purpose for which you plan to use it.

> **TIP**
>
> A key concept in using fonts in your publications is to limit the number of font styles you use on any one page. For consistency, you should also limit the number of fonts you use throughout the publication. A good rule of thumb is to use no more than three different font styles on any page and, if possible and practical, use the same fonts throughout the publication.

NOTE

If you are designing for the Web using HyperText Markup Language (HTML), you have no control over font style. The style of font used depends on settings in the reader's browser. However, if you do want control over the font style, you will learn some alternatives in Chapter 21, "Inside SGML." In SGML, the publisher can adjust the font size, type, and style according to the availability of the font on the reader's computer system.

How Graphic Designers Use Grids

The grid system is a way of designing pages that will help you create a uniform and symmetrical look to the published page. Graphic designers have used the grid system to design pages for many years. Using the grid system, you would break the page into columns. Text, graphics, and other objects on the page are lined up within the columns.

A simple page could be broken into three grid columns. Complex pages could be divided into 10 or more grid columns. The number of imaginary grid columns depends on the type and number of objects you are placing on the page.

For example, a newsletter could be divided into three grid columns. Header and title information could go across the whole top of the page, meaning this text would be in all three grids. Pictures could be aligned in the first or leftmost grid, one under the other down the page. Text could be placed in columns two and three.

Although the grid system is used primarily in print publications, it also makes sense to use the grid system in electronic publications. Your publication should not look like an angry mess on the reader's computer screen. The pages of your publication should be pleasing to look at. Using the grid system will help you add symmetry to your pages.

Previous sections discussed moving your text window off center. A three-column grid could be used to align the text window on your page in this manner. As Figure 9.1 depicts, your text window would be placed in columns two and three on the page. Other objects such as navigation mechanisms and graphics could be placed primarily in column one. Headings could still be placed across the top of the page, and some objects could be aligned in columns one, two, or three.

FIGURE 9.1.
Using grids helps keep pages uniform.

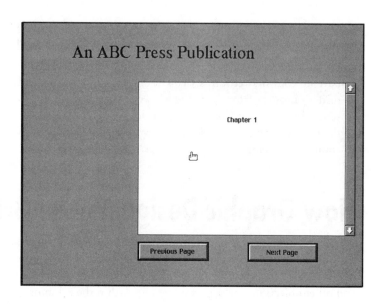

Common Page Components

As you saw in the previous chapter, your pages can include text, graphics, multimedia access, and navigation mechanisms. These broad categories of page components can be broken down into individual components to provide a clear picture of what goes into page design. Designing the pages of your publication is a highly creative process.

You control this creative process. As you design your first pages, keep in mind the techniques discussed in Chapter 7, "Organizing Information," for improving ideas and developing the publication. Often, your first design will not be the best design you are capable of creating. This is because you will probably spend most of your time learning about the new authoring tools you have purchased. Once you know the full potential of your tools and have worked on improving your ideas, you can create a better publication.

This section presents some common page components:

> Text
> Justified Text
> Graphics
> Menus
> Buttons

Text Components in Page Design

Text is the most basic page component. Almost every page you create will contain some text. This will be true even for pages that are highly graphical in nature. Most pages of your publication will include text in heading or title lines at the top or bottom of the page.

In page design, you need to carefully consider how you will place text on the page. Though headers are often placed directly on the page, the main text is normally placed in a text window. Windows usually provide the reader with control mechanisms. Often, your authoring software will put these control mechanisms in the text window automatically. However, sometimes, if the complete text of the page is viewable in the text window, you will want to remove control mechanisms from the text window. This way, mechanisms that serve no purpose are not in the publication.

NOTE

Usually, each window of text you bring into the publication will equal one text file. The text file will probably be saved in a plain text format, such as ASCII text, that has no special formatting. The entire contents of the file do not have to display on the screen. Using a scrollbar, the reader can scroll forward or backward through the text.

Justified Text in Page Design

Another concern when you are placing text on the screen is the type of margin you use within the text window. Some authoring software will allow you to justify margins, meaning text on the right side of the page will be evenly lined up. Justifying the text will allow you to cram more material on the page—up to 25 percent more text. It gives a uniform and professional look to the publication. If the authoring software does not directly support this feature, it might allow you to use special text files that save format information. Two such formats are the DOS text with layout format (.ASC) and the standard ANSI text with layout format (.ANS).

Although justified margins make the finished product look better, they mean more work for you as the publisher. This remains true even though most word processors will let you create justified text by simply selecting all text in a file and turning text justification on. Justified text will not work well with nonproportional text. If all your files are in a nonproportional font, you probably will have to convert them to a proportional font.

Justified text can leave gaping holes in your text. For lines of the file containing roughly half the character width of your justified text window, you will see large areas with no text where the short line was stretched to fill the window. You must fix each of these lines by hand or try to rework the paragraph.

If you choose to rework the paragraph, you have three options. You could rewrite the paragraph, changing words or word order, to make the paragraph work better with justification. You could try to break up large words using hyphenation. Or you could try both the rewriting and hyphenation techniques.

Graphic Components in Page Design

Graphics make up another basic page component. Almost every page you create will contain some graphics. This will be true even for pages that are highly textual in nature. Most pages of your publication will include graphical features that highlight or accent the main text.

Graphics on the page do not have to be dazzling images or photo-quality pictures. Often you will want to add small images called icons. Icons are used to represent complex ideas in a more comprehensible manner (for example, using a small picture of a camera on the page to denote that a picture is available for viewing if the reader wants to view it). Or, putting a small picture of musical notes could indicate music features are available on the page.

You could also add decorative features called *dingbats*. Dingbats are character-sized images like arrows, stars, and pointing fingers. Often your word processor will have a whole font dedicated to dingbats. Microsoft's TrueType font pack includes several dingbat fonts (called Wingdings 1, Wingdings 2, and Wingdings 3. On your Macintosh, look for a font called Zapf Dingbats.

> **NOTE**
>
> Before you use dingbats from a word processor font, ensure that your authoring software will allow you to import the font. Your authoring software may have its own dingbat font that you can use.

When adding icons, dingbats, and other graphic features to your pages, use moderation. A few extra features will make the page more lively and inviting. Too many features will make the page look busy and uninviting.

Menu Components in Page Design

Menus are combined text and graphic components for your pages. They are extremely useful and often used. Using menus, you can provide lists of commands and navigation mechanisms to readers in a quick and easy-to-use format.

Many pages you create will contain one or both of these types of menus:

On-screen menu
Pull-down menu

On-Screen Menus

As the name implies, an on-screen menu is displayed on the screen. The menu is a list of commands or actions that readers can access quickly and efficiently. Most authoring software will let you set up this type of menu. The software will also let you select the navigation mechanisms for the menu, such as allowing selection with the mouse, cursor controls, or key combinations. This type of menu works well if there are not many commands to list in the menu.

The menu depicted in Figure 9.2 is an on-screen menu. It consists of five menu options. The reader can select a menu item using the mouse or keyboard. The user would move the mouse pointer to the menu option she wants to select, and then push the left mouse button to perform the action. With the cursor keys, the user can scroll up or down through the menu options. Lastly, if the menu allowed quick keys, the user could use a key combination to access menu options.

FIGURE 9.2.

An on-screen menu offers quick access to commands.

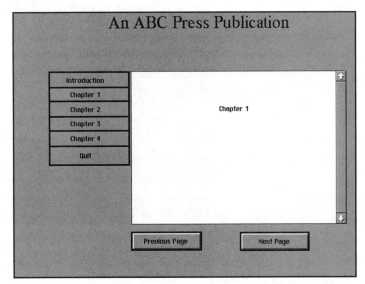

Common menu quick key combinations are

- Holding the Shift key while you press a letter or number key
- Holding the Ctrl key while you press a letter or number key
- Holding the Alt key while you press a letter or number key

Pull-Down Menus

A pull-down menu is a list of commands or actions that users can access with the mouse or key combinations. Until the menu is activated, the contents of the menu are represented by a single command or action visible on-screen. Once the contents of the menu can be seen, any command listed in the menu can be selected to carry out an action.

Most authoring software will let you create pull-down menus and navigation mechanisms for the menu, such as allowing selection with the mouse, cursor controls, or key combinations. This type of menu works well if you need to list many commands in the menu, and you do not want to take up screen space with a list of commands. This type of menu also works well when you simply do not want to list commands on-screen.

A single summary label called "Quick Menu" represents the pull-down menu in Figure 9.3. The user can activate the menu using the mouse or keyboard.

FIGURE 9.3.

Summary label representing a pull-down menu.

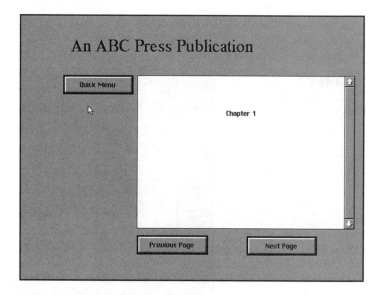

Once the menu has been activated, the menu options depicted in Figure 9.4 will be displayed. The menu consists of eight options. Once the menu is displayed on the screen, the menu options can be selected.

FIGURE 9.4.

An activated pull-down menu displays its commands.

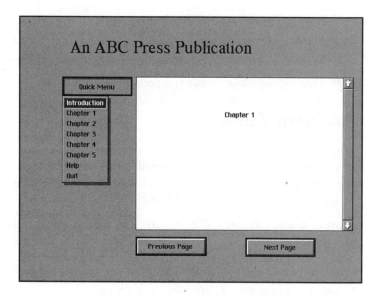

Buttons Used in Page Design

On-screen buttons represent commands that will be carried out if the button is activated. To activate a button, the user would use the mouse or key combinations. Buttons are often represented by a small image called an icon or a small rectangular box labeled with a keyword. Most authoring software will let you create on-screen buttons. The software will also let you select the navigation mechanisms for the buttons, such as allowing selection with the mouse or key combinations. On-screen buttons work well when you want control over the precise placement of individual commands or actions on the screen.

> **NOTE**
>
> Some software applications will call buttons, text windows with scrollbars, and menu icons "objects" because you have to specifically place them on the screen for them to be available for readers to use. As long as the functionality is the same, the name for the button, text window, or menu icon doesn't make a difference.

Examples of on-screen buttons are shown in Figure 9.5. The eight buttons shown in the figure are a representation of the pull-down menu from Figure 9.4. Each button on the page is an individual component. Using the mouse, the user would move the mouse pointer to the button she wants to select, then push the left mouse button to perform the action. The reader could also use a key combination to access the buttons.

FIGURE 9.5.

On-screen buttons with underlined quick keys.

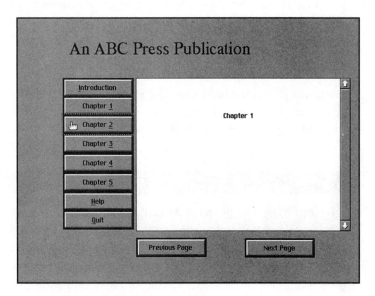

TIP

In this example, each button contains a character that is underlined. The underlined character represents the quick key that can be used to activate the particular button. This is a great way to let the user know which key can be used with the Shift, Ctrl, or Alt key to activate the button.

The first button has an underlined 1. The second, an underlined 1. If the Shift key was the key you designated as the first key for the quick key combination, the reader would press and hold the Shift key, and then press 1. This would let them quickly jump to Chapter one of the publication.

NOTE

The on-screen buttons depicted in Figure 9.5 are meant as an example only. The best place for an index of chapters or topics is in a pull-down menu or on a separate index page. The chapter buttons clutter the screen and take up space that could be used by more useful buttons or additional page features, such as a go-to-next-page button or a quit button.

Some authoring software will let you create additional navigation mechanisms for your menus and on-screen buttons beyond the mouse, quick key combinations, and cursor controls. One additional mechanism is the ability to use the Tab key to tab between all page components. Using Tab or Shift +Tab, the reader could move forward or backward through page components and use the enter or return key to select a page component. The active page component is usually highlighted with a dash line around it.

This is why you see a dashed white line around the third button of Figure 9.5. This button is active. Pressing the return key from the current position would allow the reader to move to the page for Chapter 2. Pressing the Tab key would allow the reader to move to the button for Chapter 3.

TIP

Internal navigation mechanisms are generally assigned when you are creating the publication. For example, you select that you want readers to be able to use the Tab key to navigate between options but not be able to use the Tab key to make a text window active for scrolling with the cursor keys.

Common Page Features

As you have seen, publications have many mechanisms to manipulate the components of the page. The publication also needs mechanisms to navigate to different parts of the publication and to manipulate the text itself. These features will be placed on the page using the menus and buttons discussed in the previous section.

These basic features should be included in your publications:

- Page-turning features
- Index access features
- Search features
- Multimedia features

Most authoring software currently available will let you add these basic features to your publication. The methods to add these features vary greatly. Some of the best authoring tools let you choose from a comprehensive list of objects you would like to place on the page. Once you choose an object, you can set the features you would like the object to perform.

Whether you use each of these features in a publication will depend on the type of publication you are creating. However, even the least complex publication will benefit from using most of these features.

Page-Turning Features

All publications use page-turning features. Without these features, the user cannot move to the various parts of the publication. Users will rely heavily on these features; therefore, they are often placed on the page as buttons. This enables the user to move quickly around the publication without having to access a menu to do so.

Table 9.1 shows common page-turning features. You do not need to use all these features in your publication. However, the reader will need a way to go from page to page or exit the publication. The way you use these features will depend on the layout of your publication.

If the publication is divided into chapters, meaning it contains a text window that readers can scroll through to view all the pages of a single chapter, you will use the previous chapter or next chapter features. This will allow the reader to move through the publication a chapter at a time.

If the publication is divided into individual pages, meaning it contains a text window that displays the full text available without scrolling, you will use the previous page or next page features. This will allow the reader to move through the publication one actual page at a time.

Most commercial authoring tools allow you to include the first page and last page in their list of basic features. The first page and last page features are very useful, but you need to label them carefully. First page allows the reader to jump to the start of the publication. This lets the reader start over instead of having to quit the publication to get back to the startup page. Last page allows the reader to jump to the end of the publication. Often the last page of the publication will be a credits page, but it could be a glossary or an index.

Table 9.1. Page-turning features.

Button/Menu Label	Type of Feature	Description
Previous	Previous chapter/topic	Enables readers to move to the beginning of the previous chapter or topic.
Next	Next chapter/topic	Enables readers to move to the beginning of the next chapter or topic.
Start	First Page	Enables readers to go to the start of the publication.
Previous	Previous page/subtopic	Enables readers to move to the beginning of the previous page or subtopic.
Next	Next page/subtopic	Enables readers to move to the beginning of the next page or subtopic.
End (Credits)	Last Page	Enables readers to go to the last page of the publication.
Return	Return to Page	Enables readers to go to the page they were on before the current page.
Quit	Exit the publication	Enables the reader to close the publication.

Index Access Features

Most publications will use the index features depicted in Table 9.2. Although table of contents access or general index access are usually included on a pull-down menu, help index access is usually an on-screen button. In a long publication, the reader will want a quick way to access the table of contents or the index page. A table of contents or index page will contain menus or on-screen buttons for each of the major subdivisions of the publication. When you provide access to these pages from any other page, the reader will have a quick and easy way to move around the publication.

Table 9.2. Index features.

Button/Menu Label	Type of Feature	Description
Index	Go to index	Enables readers to move to a page containing a chapter or topic index.
Table of Contents	Go to table of contents	Enables readers to go to a table of contents page.
Help Index	Go to help index	Enables readers to move to the beginning of the online help documentation.

An index to online help documentation is essential in all publications. Never assume the reader will know how to navigate or manipulate the features of the publication. Provide online help and an easy way for the reader to get to the help index. In the help documentation, you would provide basic instructions on the use of the publication. You would also explain how to use the buttons, menus, or other special mechanisms you have created.

Search Features

Search mechanisms are advanced features that readers love. In even the most basic publication, there will come a time when a reader wants to look for a key word or phrase in the text. Local text search and global text search are the two search mechanisms that are most widely supported by authoring software. Table 9.3 provides an overview of these mechanisms.

Table 9.3. Search features.

Button/Menu Label	Type of Feature	Description
Global Search	Global Text Search	Enables readers to search through main text on all pages.
Search	Text Search	Enables readers to search main text on the current page.

A local text search will let the reader search the contents of the main text on the current page. A global text search will let the reader search the main text of the entire publication. The main text includes text in windows and not text outside windows, such as page headings. If you allow text searching, it is best to provide both features as options on a pull-down menu. Although a local text search will be fast and efficient, a global text search is slow and thorough.

Multimedia Features

There will be times when you do not want to place an image on the page and times when you want readers to be able to access sound and video. Multimedia buttons and menus allow readers to access images, sound, and video. These features are described briefly in Table 9.4. Although most commercial authoring software support these advanced features, incorporating multimedia into the publication can be tricky.

Several chapters of the book are dedicated to multimedia. Chapter 11, "Using Multimedia," explores the uses of multimedia in publications. Chapter 21 provides the techniques for incorporating multimedia.

Table 9.4. Multimedia features.

Button/Menu Label	Type of Feature	Description
Sound*	Play sound	Enables readers to play a sound file.
Image*	View image	Enables readers to open a graphic window containing an image.
Video*	Play video	Enables readers to play a video file.

*Uses short description of actual sound, image, or video.

Advanced Page Design

All the basics have been covered. You have learned about graphic windows, text windows, icons, menus, and buttons. Now you are ready to explore advanced page design concepts.

The design of the individual pages of the publication will relate directly to the layout model you have chosen. Publications are created using one of the four layout models. In Chapter 8, "Layout and Document Types," you learned that the two basic layout styles are traditional print and traditional software. A publication with a traditional print layout will have a layout similar to its traditional counterpart in print. The style is largely text-based with few graphics. A publication with a traditional software layout will have a layout similar to your favorite computer software program. The style is largely text-based and menu-oriented.

The two advanced layout styles are combined print and software and modern freelance. The combined print and software layout borrows the best features of the traditional layouts. The reader can view images and text, but usually only one type of media at a time or each type of media is put into a separate window. With the modern freelance layout, you can use any organization method including the integrated web. This style can use text, graphics, sound, and video.

As you saw in the previous chapter, publications have many kinds of pages:

Startup page
Overview page
Table of contents page
Menu page
Topic or chapter overview pages
Pages within chapters
Index page
Credits page

Although these individual pages form the basis of your publication, a design concept that will save you time is the master page. Instead of designing many individual pages, you create a master page for the major divisions of the publishing project. The master page forms the basis for the individual pages. In this way, you only have to adjust the individual pages, and you ensure the look of the publication is consistent throughout.

The following subsections cover these two topics:

Page design using master pages
Individual page design

Page Design Using Master Pages

The master page can designate components and attributes that will be used on all, or most of, the pages of the publication. The page components you can place on the master page include headings, menus, buttons, graphic windows, and text windows. The page attributes you can define on the master page include default colors, background images called wallpaper, and special effects to use when the user moves to the previous or next page.

The master page is not a mystical design concept. Most commercial authoring tools support the master page concept. The best authoring tools will let you create multiple master pages. When you create individual pages of the publication, you can include the components and attributes you have defined for the master page. This will not only save you time, it will ensure a uniform and professional look for the publication.

NOTE

Some authoring tools refer to the master page concept as a document template. Concepts pertaining to document templates are very similar to concepts pertaining to master pages. The notion of a document template comes largely from word processors. Most word processors, such as Microsoft Word for DOS, Microsoft Word for Windows, or Microsoft Word for Macintosh, will let you create new documents based on a document template.

Templates are primarily used for formatting text. Therefore, you want to make sure an authoring tool that supports document templates also supports the embedding or defining of objects in templates. Including objects, such as images or on-screen buttons, as a part of the template is the key to creating templates that will save you time and effort.

Starting a master page in your authoring software can be as easy as selecting a Goto Master Page option from a pull-down menu, as depicted in Figure 9.6. Once you are on the master page, you can define the following:

Master page attributes
Master page components

FIGURE 9.6.

Direct support for master pages can be as easy as selecting Goto Master Page.

NOTE

The pictures in this section were taken from a popular authoring tool called NeoBook Professional. NeoBook and NeoBook Professional are two of the best values in authoring tools available.

Master Page Attributes

Although master page attributes are supported in various ways by authoring software, the basic idea of master attributes is to allow you to define attributes that you can apply to any or all pages of the publication. Usually the attributes you define can be applied separately from the master page components. In this way, you have more control over what features will be included on any individual page.

Figure 9.7 shows one technique for allowing master attributes in publications. The method used here is similar to ones used in other popular authoring tools.

FIGURE 9.7.

You can set master page attributes to create templates.

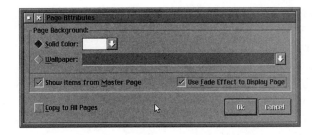

From the page attributes window in this example, you can select the following:

> Background color
> Wallpaper
> Show master page items
> Use fade effect to display page
> Copy to all pages

The background color in the example is white. This means any page that includes these master attributes will have a white background. Wallpaper is similar to the background color feature. This feature will let you put an image in the background. If the image is smaller than the screen size, duplicates of the image will be tiled across the background of the page to fill the screen. You can create great wallpaper backgrounds using very small images.

The page attribute's window will also let you show master page items on a particular page or copy the attributes to all of your pages. The latter attribute is very useful. After you have set up the master attributes, you can copy them out to all the pages of the publication with one click of the mouse.

NOTE

If your authoring software will let you create multiple master pages or multiple templates, it will generally prompt you to define what type of page you are creating or allow you to later select a page definition. If your authoring software does not directly support master pages or templates, you can still create pseudo-master pages. For example, you want a master page for chapter pages, a master page for the online help documentation, and a master page for index pages. First, you build three pages with the generic features for each of these pages. Then, you might be able to use cut-and-paste features to copy all the attributes of a your pseudo-master page to the page of a particular type that you are creating. Otherwise, you would have to copy page attributes to related pages one attribute at a time.

> **NOTE**
>
> Web publishers using HTML or SGML could also create pseudo-master pages. Here, you would create the necessary master pages and their attributes, and then copy the file containing the source code to a new filename. In this way, your Web publications could easily follow the layout of multiple types of master pages.

Some authoring tools will also let you create effects to use when the reader switches pages. In this example, the software lets you use a fade-in and fade-out effect between pages. This means the current page will fade out, the screen will turn black momentarily, and then the new page will fade in.

Master Page Components

When you are designing the master page, carefully consider the page components you will use. Your decision should be based largely on the components the readers will use the most. The most common components you will add to the master page are page-turning features. The reader will need a quick and easy way to move around the publication, and because these features are used heavily, you will probably want to use on-screen buttons for page-turning.

You may or may not want to include the return to start and exit publication features on the master page. Whether you do will depend on the number of components already on the master page. If the master page already has many on-screen components, you may want to add start and exit features to a pull-down menu. You may also only want to let the reader return to the start or exit the publication from certain pages of the publication. Then, you would put start and exit on these individual pages.

Most publications will benefit from index access features. The master page is an excellent place to create a quick access menu or buttons for the table of contents and the online help index. The same pull-down menu containing index access features could also contain options for search features. This way, commands that were used often, but not heavily, would be available from one primary page feature.

The master page is a good place to add the page number. Most authoring tools will let you add a page numbering feature to the master page that will update based on the actual page number of the publication. For example, if you placed this feature on the master page, and moved to page 29, the page would have the number "29" in the area you designated for the page number.

Other common features to include on the master page include headings and graphical elements such as ruling lines. Ruling lines are used to divide sections of the page and can be any color or thickness. Horizontal ruling lines that stretch from one side of the page to the other are the most common. You will often find a ruling line separating title information from the main body of the page. Thin black ruling lines on a gray page will give a shadow or 3D effect to the page.

Some master page components will not work on all pages. A goto index option will not work on the index page. A previous page option will not work on page one of the publication. A next page option will not work on the last page of the publication.

One way to get around this problem is to exclude the master page components on the problem page. However, this would mean recreating many of the master page components repeatedly. This defeats the purpose of creating the master page.

A better way to get around this problem is to create ghost components on the problem page. This means putting a blank or shadowed option over the option that serves no purpose. You would do this only on the problem page. Because the ghost option can have different functionality from the master page component, it could even play a warning tone to inform the user he or she has made an invalid selection. Usually you will only have to do this for a single component, such as the previous page option on page one of the publication.

Individual Page Design

Let's create a sample publication following the individual page design, without using master pages. After conducting the initial design phase, it is decided the publication will have nine pages. The first publication the ABC Press will produce will be a test publication. The ABC Press wants to familiarize itself with its new tools. The best way to do this is to create a sample publication.

Because this is only a test design, page one will be the first chapter of the publication. Figure 9.8 depicts the page layout of pages one through six after we have designed page one. The page one storyboard has page components. The storyboards for pages two through nine are blank. At this point, the publisher at the ABC Press would have to create the individual components for eight more pages.

FIGURE 9.8.

Page design without master pages means creating more storyboards.

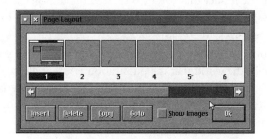

Designing pages without using master pages means you have to develop each individual page of the publication. For a large publication with dozens or hundreds of individual pages, design without using master pages would take weeks. Even for a small publication with less than 10

pages, many hours would be spent designing the individual pages. Introducing a master page into either design model would reduce the design time 50 percent or more.

A better way to develop the test publication for the ABC Press is to use a master page. The components created for page one of the test publication could be moved to the master page. The newly created master page is depicted in Figure 9.9. The text window shown in Figure 9.8 was not put on the master page because the contents of the text window will change from page to page.

FIGURE 9.9.

Using master page components save you time.

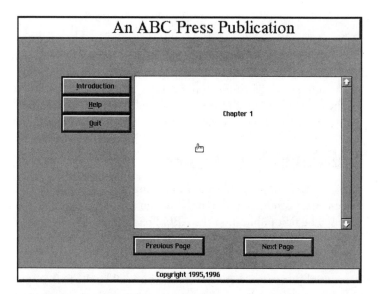

> **NOTE**
>
> Figure 9.9 shows an example of a permanent header and footer for the master page. Here, the header that will be displayed on all pages based on the master page is An ABC Press Publication. The footer that will be displayed on all pages based on the master page is Copyright 1995, 1996.
>
> Not only is adding a copyright notice to the pages of your publication a nice touch, it also tells the world that the publication is an intellectual property and as such, is protected under United States and international copyright laws. Although you may not want to display copyright information on every page of your publication, at the very least you should display it on the startup page.

Once these components are moved to the master page, they could be added to all the pages of the publication in one easy step. This could be accomplished using master page attributes called "Show Master Page Items" and "Copy to All Pages." Although your particular authoring software may have a different name for these attributes, the function remains the same. "Show master page items" will show the master page components you have defined on the current page. If you like the look of these components and want to copy them to all the pages of the publication in one easy step, you can select "Copy to all pages."

The ABC Press publication's new page layout with master pages is shown in Figure 9.10. All components of the master page have been copied to the other pages of the publication.

FIGURE 9.10.

Page layout with master pages.

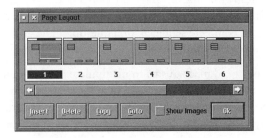

The text window containing the text for chapter one of the publication has been added to page one. This is shown in Figure 9.11. Instead of having to create many individual components for all subsequent pages, the next step is to add only the nonrepetitive components to each page. In this example, only one component, a text window containing text for each chapter, would be added to the pages.

FIGURE 9.11.

Two easy steps to a finished page by using a master page.

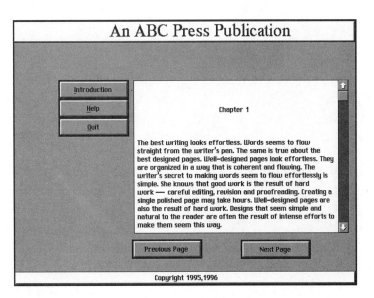

Summary

Using the techniques described in this chapter, you can design pages that have high visual impact. Empty space on the screen makes the material easier to read. It is the separation of the material that creates emphasis and draws the reader's attention. The use of color in publications has always caused problems. Use basic colors for text and backgrounds whenever possible.

The optimum grouping of paragraphs under headings is three to seven paragraphs. Good headings explain what the topic is and convey information to the reader. Your headings could be a few words, a complete sentence, or a question. The grid system is a way to design pages that will lend a uniform and symmetrical look to the published page.

Publications need mechanisms to manipulate the components of the page, to navigate to different parts of the publication, and to manipulate the text itself. Designing pages without using master pages means you have to add these mechanisms to each page of the publication. A better way to develop publications is to use a master page. A master page could reduce the design time 50 percent or more.

Using Graphics

10

*by Ewan
Grantham*

In this chapter, you learn a number of ways to use graphics in your electronic publication. Whether you will be using clip art or rendering a 3D image, you'll need to think about what images help to enhance your work and how best to use them.

Planning for Graphics

The first step in the process is to consider what things in your work you can enhance by including a graphic. Usually this will be a place in the publication where it is easier to show something than to explain it. As a fairly obvious example, rather than explaining that a butterfly has certain markings, you can simply show a picture or drawing of it. This works just as well if you are trying to explain a process or procedure to the user.

Of course, at times you will simply want to dress something up a bit. Using a graphic can be very effective for drawing a user's eye to an important topic or idea, or to relive the monotony if you have presented a large section of text.

As part of all this, you should also think about how you can use graphical elements to liven up your interface, and to make navigating within your title easier. This can be something as simple as having a custom arrow at the bottom of each logical page, to something as stunning as a 3D representation of a hallway with each door being a hot spot link to another area.

Once you have decided what graphics you need, it's time to decide things like what format they should be in (line art, picture, and so on), how you'll obtain them (clip art CD, freelance illustrator, or other means), and what tools you'll need to create, manipulate, and present them.

Once you make decisions in all these areas, you can then go through the next section to cover your design considerations.

Design Considerations

At this point, you have an idea of what you need in terms of graphical elements for your work. You now have to think about how those items will affect how your title is created and distributed. For example, if you decide to have your work set up as a historical brochure touring a castle with rooms to explore, a quick calculation might show you that the graphics to support this would make the overall size too large to fit on a single floppy disk—which would probably make it too long to download for many people as well. On the other hand, you might decide that because of your audience, or the way you will distribute the title, that file size isn't a problem.

Another consideration is the platform that you expect your title to be displayed on. This will affect the base resolution and number of colors your graphics can support. If your title targets Windows users, you will get the widest audience by doing graphics in 640×480×16. That's not to say that all Windows titles should use this format—going back to the castle example mentioned previously, you would have some pretty dingy looking rooms if you had to use a

16 color palette. On other platforms you will have different issues. As one example, on the Mac, you need to make sure that any graphics look just as good in grayscale as they do in color since there is still a sizable market of Mac users who don't have color. UNIX systems have similar restrictions.

This is also the time to start thinking about when your graphics should appear. In other words, should they always be visible, or should they just be displayed in response to certain actions. In addition, if they aren't always visible, how will you make them go away after they've been displayed? You will also need to consider whether you should compile your graphics into your work or whether you will have them in a separate file(s). Of course, some platforms (such as HTML which is used to create Web pages) require you to keep your graphics in separate files. In that case the decision has already been made for you.

So far, you've heard about design considerations for the final publication, but you also need to consider design elements for producing and/or incorporating graphics. To begin, you should have the capability to test your graphics at the most common resolutions that will be used—which is another way to say that you need to be able to display what you do both at a minimal resolution and at the maximum resolution your audience is likely to use. On most platforms this means you need to be able to test from 640×480×16- to 1024×768×24-bit color, and to also test the results in monochrome as well. By doing this, you can make sure that an image makes sense (even if it doesn't look the same) for all your readers.

Another consideration for the author is having plenty of hard drive space (1GB is good for starters) for storing multiple versions of images that you are working with. By having room to keep several versions of each image for experimentation you increase the likelihood of developing an image that's "just right," as well as having alternate versions available for use in the future.

Finally, you want to find a graphic program similar to the one in Figure 10.1 that has catalog capabilities so that you can view thumbnail versions of the various graphics you are working with.

FIGURE 10.1.

Choose a graphics program, such as ThumbsPlus, that has a cataloging option.

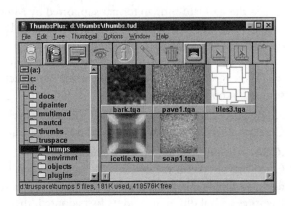

Without a program like this, it's very easy to get confused over which image is which. If you're developing for HTML, this can also give you a feel for what a thumbnail of your image will look like.

Types of File Formats

In working with graphics, it is useful to know what the two basic types of graphics are (raster and vector), as well as the various formats you might want to use, and their strengths and weaknesses.

To begin with, *raster* graphics (or bitmaps) are graphics images composed of small dots (called pixels). The pixels can be simple on-or-off bits, or represent various colors. Generally you will work with four levels of raster images: black and white (one bit per pixel), 16-colors (four bits per pixel), 256-colors (eight bits per pixel), or 16 million colors (24 bits per pixel, also called Truecolor mode). Raster graphics do not generally scale to larger sizes very well; the dots become squares or rectangles and the image appears grainy. Raster graphics also use large amounts of disk space and memory. However, they generally display faster than vector graphics and can show much more true-to-life detail than vector graphics. Examples of raster graphics are GIF files and BMP files.

Next are *vector* graphics which are graphic objects composed of the definition of drawn shapes and lines—rectangles, arcs, ellipses, curves, and other forms of line art. Because they are descriptions of shapes rather than a collection of individual dots (pixels), you may scale vector graphics more readily and more accurately than raster graphics. This also means that they tend to be smaller. However, they often are slower to display than raster graphics because of the need to "calculate" the picture each time. CGM and WPG files are examples of common vector graphics.

These are the file formats you are most likely to work with:

.BMP, .DIB, and .RLE—Windows Bitmap Files
This is the standard bitmap format supported by Microsoft Windows in programs such as Paintbrush. Unlike many other formats, BMPs and DIBs have no compression options, so even simple pictures can be quite large when they are stored on disk. Note that even though you can draw a line or a rectangle in Paintbrush, it's still a BMP (raster) image. The difference between raster and vector is based on how the image is stored, not on how it appears.

.CDR, .PAT, and .BMF—CorelDRAW and CorelGALLERY
Corel products use these formats, and they are a proprietary standard.

.CGM—Computer Graphics Metafile
CGM files are vector graphic files useful as clip art. They scale well, and have the distinction of being the only ANSI standard graphic format. CGM files come in many flavors as several different vendors first adopted, then "enhanced" the original format.

Although this is primarily a vector format, certain forms can also incorporate raster data.

.EPS—Encapsulated PostScript Files

EPS files are PostScript language files, created for PostScript printers. Many programs which understand PostScript (particularly from Adobe) will also use this format.

.GEM and .IMG—GEM Metafiles and GEM Image Format

GEM Metafiles are vector graphic files which include drawing commands for rendering pictures. They are similar to CGM files. GEM files originated on the Amiga, and have gone through several enhancement periods. The IMG format, on the other hand, was originally designed for the Atari computers, then migrated to PCs for several GEM-based products, such as Ventura Publisher. IMG files may also be embedded in GEM metafiles.

.GIF—CompuServe Graphics Interchange Format Files

CompuServe developed the GIF format to provide good file compression and relatively fast decompression speed—important criteria for pictures designed to be passed around electronically. GIF is a very popular format for online services, but is limited to a maximum of 256 colors. Two standards have been developed: 87a and 89a. The numbers are simply identifiers marking the version of the GIF standard used to create/store the image.

.JPG, .JFI, and .JIF—JPEG Compressed Files

The JPEG format was developed to provide a high degree of compression for images. It is a "lossy" compression method, meaning that some color and pattern information from the original is lost. JPEG is generally appropriate for photographed and scanned images, and works best if the images originate from 24-bit sources. JPEG is generally inappropriate for any type of line-drawn art because of its tendency to blur fine details.

.PCX—ZSoft Picture Files

PCX files are a fairly early PC graphic format, which has been extended over the years to support more and varied color depths. PCX files may or may not be compressed. PCX is the standard used for submission of graphic files to be incorporated in Sams books, as one example.

.TIF—Tagged Image Format Files

Several companies, including Aldus, developed the Tagged Image Format to be the be-all and end-all of image file formats. Because of its scope and extensibility, it is an extremely complex format. It also is an example of a standard that has as many exceptions as it does requirements, thus making it a clear example of the danger of design by committee.

.WPG—DrawPerfect Graphics Files

WPG files are a vector format that WordPerfect Corporation developed for use with its word processing products. Like other formats, WPG has evolved over the years.

The particular ones you use will depend on the tools you have available, what format any existing images you use come in, the platform you are developing on, and to a lesser extent, the audience you are trying to reach. One format that isn't listed above, but is expected to become a major player soon, is the new graphics format which CompuServe has developed to replace the GIF standard. This new, enhanced 24-bit lossless specification will offer the professional graphics community a significant enhancement to the earlier GIF 89a specification while also eliminating the proprietary LZW software, replacing it with compression technology compliant with the PNG (pronounced "ping") specification. At this time, it has not been announced if this graphics format will be called PNG or will simply be referred to as a new version of GIF.

Incorporating Existing Graphics

As often as not, you will be too busy putting together your publication, or promoting and distributing it, to spend a lot of time creating your own graphics (although you see how to do that a little later for those times when you need to). So, you need to know about the different ways to acquire graphics and how that affects their use.

Acquiring Graphics and Artwork

You can use several ways to get graphics and artwork to use in your electronic title. One of the easiest ways is to purchase a library on CD of clip art or images. Corel has an entire series of CDs that contain clip art, as well as a series of CDs with photo images of various types. Other companies also produce libraries of this sort, though usually not with as extensive a selection. The trick is to try to find the fewest number of libraries that carry the most images or graphics that you are interested in. Many of these collections offer a disk or CD with a thumbnail or text catalog of the images. Regardless of who you get your library from, it is important to check the licensing agreement for the material you've bought. If you are going to be charging for your publication, you will need to make sure that the images are redistributable for commercial use. Even if your title is free and contains no advertising, you need to make sure that you have the right to use the material for anything besides personal viewing. See Chapter 35, "General Laws and Copyright Information," for more information.

Many of the online services now have sections or forums that contain images that you can be download and purchase just like the CD and disk collections. Usually you can download all the images, and then pay for the ones you want to use in your work. This gives you the ability to see exactly what you are getting first.

Another, similar option is to check the artist forums or sections of the various services. Most artists in these forums have uploaded examples of their work that you can purchase directly from them. In addition, this gives you some contacts to use if you need something created specifically for your title.

If you don't use online services, or can't find someone who is creating the look you're trying to find, you can always check your local gallery or art supply store. Sometimes you'll see works exhibited there that you could then have scanned; you may also find contacts posted on the bulletin board, or get some suggestions from the sales staff.

Scanning

As mentioned above, one of the solutions for getting an artist's image into your computer is through the use of a scanner. Of course, this is also a way to take advantage of something you might have drawn, or taken a picture of yourself. Even a picture that is only somewhat related to the final image you have in mind can often be manipulated into what you want with a minimum amount of effort.

What you don't want to scan are images from magazines, books, or other sources without confirming that you have the legal right to do so. These are almost always copyrighted, and using them in your publication is not only wrong, but illegal.

EDITOR'S NOTE

In each case, the reader must assume responsibility to determine the availability of the work. For more information on legal issues, see Chapter 35. For more information on scanning techniques, see the section, "Republished and Prepublished Materials," in Chapter 3, "Terms and Concepts."

If you plan on using a lot of scanned images, you will want to have your own scanner. With service bureaus charging between $1–$3 per page, it doesn't take long to pay for a good flatbed scanner. You want to make sure that any scanner you buy can scan to at least 300 dpi directly, and should be able to use software interpolation to achieve results of 600 dpi or higher. Also, the scanner should allow you to scan images in Truecolor (24-bit) to give you the best beginning image. Finally, to make sure your scanner will work with the widest variety of software packages, it should have a TWAIN driver. This is a software driver that defines certain base functions that a scanner will support, and how the scanned data will be imported to the application.

Additional features that are nice, but not necessary for most uses, include a page feed mechanism to allow you to scan multiple pages automatically, and OCR software to allow you to translate scanned text into a format that your word processor can use.

Almost all scanners also include some form of image manipulation software to enable you to control the import of the scanned image, and to alter it to better suit your needs. Figure 10.2 shows one common program (Micrografx Picture Publisher) loaded with the File menu selected.

FIGURE 10.2.

Micrografx Picture Publisher loaded, and prepared to scan an image.

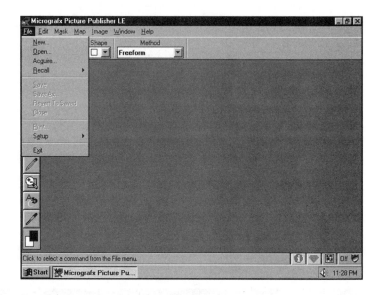

The choice you're interested in here is "Acquire", which is the standard way of specifying that you are going to scan in an image. After selecting this option, the TWAIN interface is activated. Although it will be somewhat different for each scanner, most of them have similar options even if they don't look exactly the same. In Figure 10.3, you see the TWAIN interface with options for doing a quick preview of an image (shown in the right window), adjusting the exposure and color balance, setting how the image will be configured, and so on.

FIGURE 10.3.

A TWAIN interface for the Epson scanner with a Preview scan.

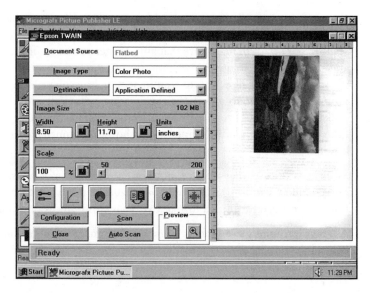

One thing you will notice is that the estimated Image Size of the scanned image is 102MB. You can do various things to make this more manageable. To begin with, you don't really need the whole page, only the portion that contains the picture. Figure 10.4 shows the picture "bounded" with a selection box, and shows the change that makes to the Image Size. The picture was bounded by clicking within the "preview" image and then stretching out a box around the part that actually should be scanned.

FIGURE 10.4.

Bounded picture and other changes to how the image will be scanned.

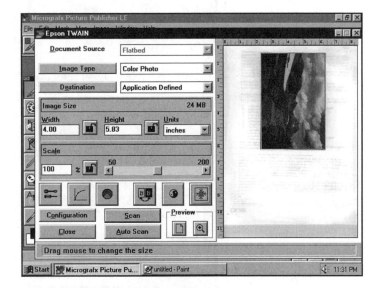

This would still produce a very large image, both in terms of disk space, and the size it would appear on the screen. To make it easier to work with, you can use the scaling control to change it to scanning in at 50 percent of its original size, which is shown in Figure 10.5 where you can see what the final size of the image will be. At this point, you've selected to have the picture automatically exposed—which means the software will adjust the brightness and contrast for the scanned picture.

You're finished working with the preview image and are ready to do the final scan of the image. Even on a Pentium with piles of RAM, Figure 10.6 shows that it can take a while (notice the time change between Figure 10.5 and 10.6 shown by the clock in the bottom right).

FIGURE 10.5.

Effect of the last changes to the previewed image before scanning.

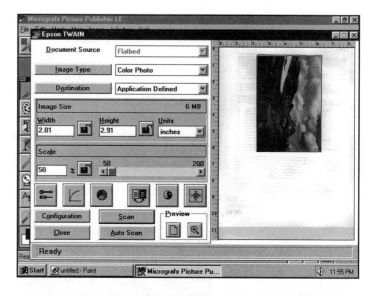

FIGURE 10.6.

Slowly(!) but surely the final scan proceeds.

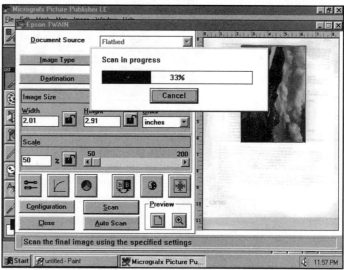

At this point, the image is returned to the original application as Figure 10.7. demonstrates. You'll notice that Picture Publisher automatically scales the picture to display on the screen. Here is another point where having a larger display is very helpful. If the screen resolution had been 1024×768 instead of 640×480, the picture could have been scaled less, and more detail would have been available.

FIGURE 10.7.

Scanned picture in Picture Publisher.

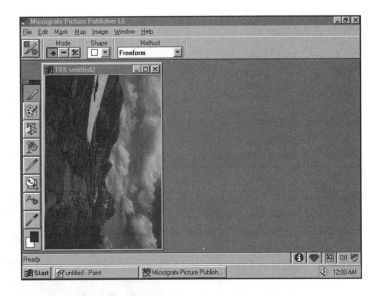

Before anything else, you'll want to make the picture easier to view and work with by rotating it into the final position. Figure 10.8 shows how to do this. Although in this case you're able to use one of the default choices (90 degrees counterclockwise), having the freeform percentage is important for correcting scans that were slightly skewed.

FIGURE 10.8.

Getting ready to rotate the image in Picture Publisher.

228

Now the image is larger (because it has been rotated, you can now show it at a larger scale on the screen) and easier to examine for the types of problems that come from scanning an image. If you look closely at Figure 10.9, you'll notice that the larger image makes it easy to see a slight pattern across the entire image.

FIGURE 10.9.

Rotated and larger (because of the different screen ratio).

Having a slight pattern is fairly common in high-resolution scans because of the tendency to pick up the texture of the paper the image was printed on. Picture Publisher has an Effect command for taking care of this called Remove Pattern. Figure 10.10 shows this option in action, with a close-up preview that shows you what the end result will look like. Removing the pattern also removes some of the image information. Because you can get away with just doing a "light" job of removing the pattern, select the Light Pattern option.

Finally, you have a good clean image you can use in a work. But you still have to save it, and Figure 10.11 shows all the different formats you can use to store the final image. What package you will be using to create your title and the amount of disk space you have available will help you to decide which of these to use.

FIGURE 10.10.

Using a photographic effect in Picture Publisher to remove the background "patterning" effect.

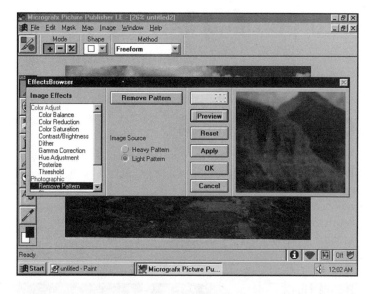

FIGURE 10.11.

Format choices for saving the final image.

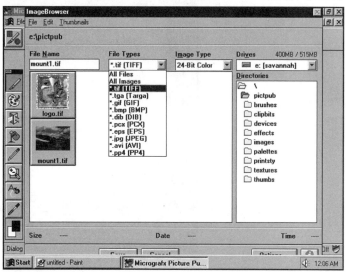

At this point, you're doing a fair amount of work to bring in an image. But it's still not quite as much as creating an original image. To see what is involved with that, you'll see how to create a custom graphic in the next section.

Incorporating Existing Graphics

In this section, you learn how to create 2D and 3D graphics for using in your publication. The emphasis here is in creating something attractive and useful without too much effort or time invested.

Creating a 2D Image

Many programs are available for creating various types of images, both raster and vector. Corel Draw and Adobe Illustrator are two of the better known ones. However, if you're in a hurry to get something done, or don't want to put a lot of money into creating something, there's a fairly powerful program already on your Windows-based computer—Windows Paint (or Paintbrush if you're using Windows 3.1—however, most of the same tools and options are available for both programs). If you haven't used Paint before, Figure 10.12 shows you the basic screen and tools available.

FIGURE 10.12.

Opening screen for Windows 95 Paint.

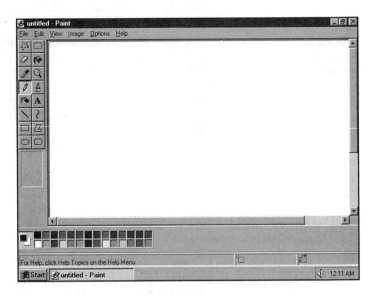

Figure 10.13 shows what many people think Paint is good for—drawing squiggly lines. Well, obviously you can do that, but at least you can draw them in several colors, as well as finding the starting place for using the other tools.

FIGURE 10.13.

Using Paint to draw a squiggly line.

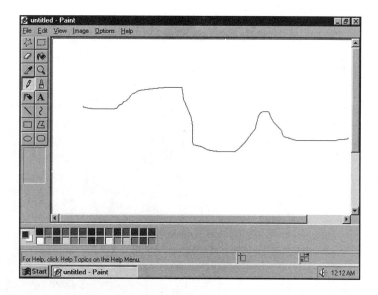

Starting with the same line, you can use a different tool to create a very different effect. Figure 10.14 shows how you can use the Airbrush tool to create a squiggly line that has quite a bit of character. Notice how selecting each of the three different options for the Airbrush tool, with varying amounts of space between the virtually sprayed dots, affects the look of the lines. From a design aspect, also notice how using multiple lines in different weights gives a feeling of texture to a simple graphic.

FIGURE 10.14.

Using the Airbrush tool in Paint.

Airbrush tool dispersal options

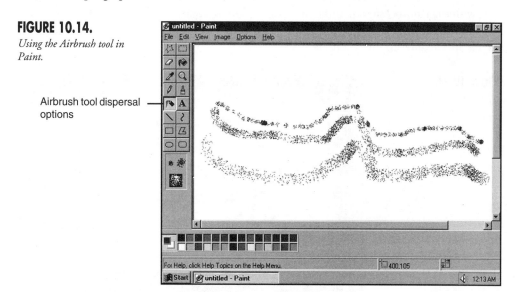

Another useful tool is the Fill tool (which looks like a paint can). Normally, you would think of using it to fill in a solid area like a square, but using the lines you had earlier, you can get an abstract, posterized effect by doing a fill of the background with a color. Looking at Figure 10.15, you'll notice how certain areas remain unaffected—adding to the overall feel.

FIGURE 10.15.

An unusual use for the Fill tool.

Fill tool —

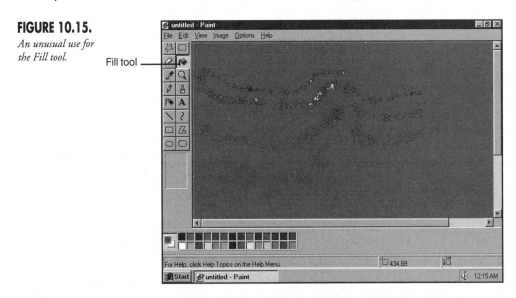

Although you drew a squiggly line earlier with the Pencil tool, going back and doing the same thing with the Paintbrush tool, using the various point options, can give us a number of interesting variations. Figure 10.16 shows how the various different strokes can give a variety of weights and textures to the end result.

FIGURE 10.16.

Different types of lines.

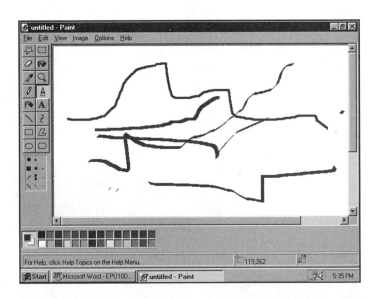

Finally, as an example of building something attractive, and quick, look at Figure 10.17 which is a sunset (sort of) that would be very acceptable to a reader, and still took under 10 minutes to create. In addition to the tools mentioned earlier, I used the Ellipse tool to create the sun and its companion.

FIGURE 10.17.

Stylized sunset using Paint.

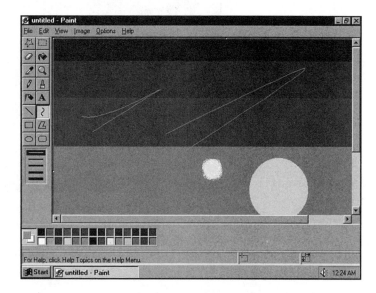

Now that you've seen some of what Paint can do, you should think about using it the next time you need a quick, custom 2D graphic. Of course, the need for 3D graphics is getting greater as the uses for them increase. You'll see how to create them in the next section.

Creating 3D Graphics

Unfortunately, none of the major operating systems currently comes with a free utility for creating 3D graphics. So, you'll have to purchase something, probably in the $200–$1000 range. On the positive side, almost all of the tools that enable you to create 3D graphics also are designed for creating 3D animations. Two of the main tools for the Windows market are Visual Software's Visual Reality 1.5, and Caligari's trueSpace2™. Having used both, I personally prefer trueSpace2, and will be using it in the examples below. The main reasons why are that it enables you to do everything from within one program, rather than working with a group of linked programs, and because it supports object animation.

If you're not sure why you should use 3D graphics, just think about a gear assembly like the one shown in Figure 10.18. Without a 3D graphic, you'd have a hard time displaying the various features without using several 2D shots, or a *lot* of verbiage.

FIGURE 10.18.

Example of a complex image done in 3D.

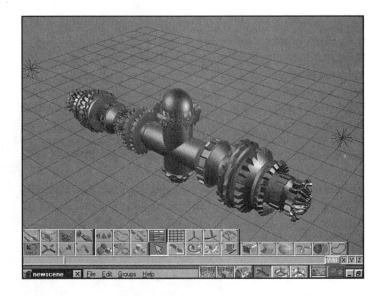

Additionally, you may find that 3D images get more attention from your readers, and make more of an impact on someone who is casually browsing through your title. Although you won't be creating anything quite as complex as the gear assembly, I'll show you some of the basics of building a 3D image as well as some considerations for building your own.

Figure 10.19 shows the default screen for new projects using trueSpace2. You'll notice that even the empty screen has a 3D grid with perspective to help you visualize what you will be creating.

FIGURE 10.19.

Opening screen for trueSpace2 showing the perspective grid.

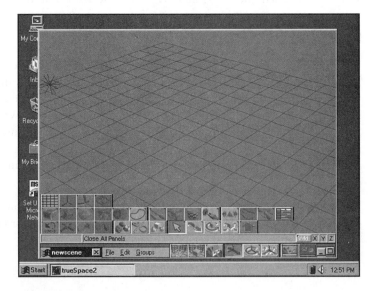

To begin with, you select the Primitives menu option to bring up the shapes and objects you can begin to create your graphic with. In trueSpace2 (and many other 3D programs), you want to think in terms of sculpting rather than drawing. Figure 10.20 shows this primitives panel so you can see what your starting options are.

FIGURE 10.20.

Primitives option for trueSpace2.

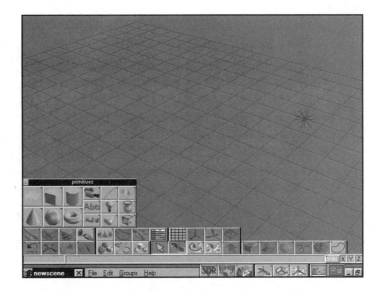

Start by selecting a sphere, and then select the deformation tool to create something besides a simple ball. In Figure 10.21, you see the default sphere, with the 3D arrow that is used to indicate this is the current object. The green grid around the object (or in this black and white figure, the white lines that are wrapped around the object) shows where it can be deformed.

FIGURE 10.21.

Beginning with a sphere.

In the next step (Figure 10.22), the object is deformed, and more primitives have been added to create a spaceship image with a default checkered background. Already we have a simple image that could be used to attract the reader's attention to a particular point. Or the beginning of a more complex space graphic.

FIGURE 10.22.
Start of a spaceship 3D graphic.

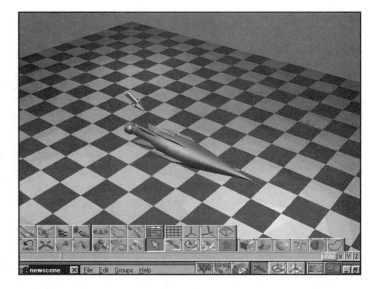

Just as with other graphics, you can use clip art libraries of objects to make it easier to create a particular scene. Currently, trueSpace2 ships with a CD full of objects and textures to make it easier to create a scene. Using some objects from the CD, it was possible to create the office scene shown in Figure 10.23 without spending much more than an hour.

FIGURE 10.23.
Office scene created using some objects and textures from the trueClips CD. Image courtesy of Caligari Corporation.

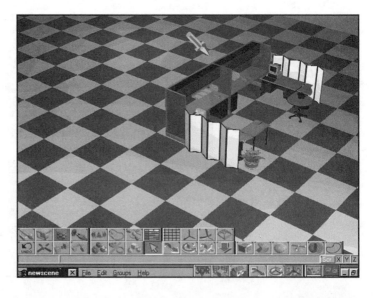

Just as with a 2D graphic, you have to be careful with your design. It is very common for beginning 3D users to put too many objects into an image. Not only does rendering the image take much longer, but it looks cluttered, and turns off the interest of the user.

The opposite can also be a problem. A chair or another object alone in a room is a nice minimalist statement, but rarely impresses the user.

Now that you have a feel for the possibilities, try to get hold of a 3D package, and see what you can create. It's fun, and the end results are stunning—which will help you to set your work apart from the rest.

Working Across Platforms

It is safe to say that an electronic publication will be read by users running different operating systems (particularly if it's a successful one). For this reason, it is a good idea to make sure your graphics will look okay on the various platforms.

One way to do this is to try to use standards for creating your graphics that run on most platforms—such as GIF or JPEG. These standards are designed to give a picture or graphic the same appearance no matter where they are used. If your graphics are separate from your main publication (in other words, they are in a separate file), this is essential. Even if your graphics are compiled into the file with your title, starting from the common heritage can help make sure that they are going to turn out okay.

A major reason why starting with GIF or JPEG can make things look better is that the palette that they use has been standardized. For 24-bit images, the palette is not a concern, but with 256 color images, certain formats (such as BMP) allow you to select your colors from a larger number of possibilities than is shown. The information about which colors you used is stored along with the image, and this is what is referred to as the palette. Different images can have different groups of colors selected as their palette, and so the images can look different on different machines. If you show multiple images at the same time with different palettes, one or the other of the images will be forced to use a different palette, and will look a bit strange.

Another cross-platform concern occurs if you are getting images from someone else. You need to make sure that images you order or have created are not only in a format that you can read, but on a disk or other media that you can read also. Having a JPEG image on a Mac disk is not helpful when you're running Windows. If nothing else, you can always ask to have the image sent to you via an online service—assuming the size is a megabyte or less.

Summary

In this chapter you've seen several ways to acquire and create graphics that can spice up your electronic publication. By improving the interface, and entertaining the user, the proper use of graphics and images can make your publication more successful.

Also, remember that your electronic publication is going to be used on multiple platforms. You've learned many of the issues raised by this in the chapter, but it is important to keep the idea of cross-platform standards in mind while you are developing your work.

Finally, remember that your graphics are designed to enhance your work, not the other way around (unless your work is an art title).

Using Multimedia

11

by William R. Stanek

Multimedia is a $25 billion business and growing. Multimedia software programs have been created for IBM, Macintosh, Amiga, UNIX, and many other computer systems. Many popular game systems, such as Sega Genesis and Sega Saturn, also feature support for multimedia. Some game systems were created to support multimedia directly, such as the 3DO interactive system.

At first glance, creating multimedia productions can seem daunting. Do not let this be the case. We will reduce its complexity by tackling the concept one step at a time. This chapter will explore the multimedia options available today, teaching the essential background necessary for success.

In this chapter, you learn the following:

■ What multimedia is

■ How readers can control multimedia aspects of publications

■ What types of publications can include multimedia

■ What the multimedia industry standards are

■ Multimedia tools and terminology

■ Three considerations to make before adding multimedia

■ How to use music and sound effects

■ How to use video

■ Critical questions to ask to determine multimedia needs

What Is Multimedia?

As you saw in Chapter 10, "Using Graphics," pictures are an essential element of an electronic publication—but multimedia is more than pictures. Books, journals, and magazines have pictures. Pictures are an important aspect of multimedia, but they are not the only aspect of multimedia. Multimedia productions come alive before the reader's eyes. The best electronic publications differentiate themselves from traditional paper-based publishing. They work better than traditional publications because they are multimedia productions that include graphics, music, sound effects, and video when necessary.

> **NOTE**
>
> This chapter discusses audio and video. Keep in mind that *audio* (sound) can include music, sound effects, digitized voice, or simple tones. *Video* refers to any digitally encoded motion video that includes full-motion video and animation.

Recent innovations in multimedia are making it easier than ever to incorporate sounds and video into your publications. Be aware that the same innovations making it easier to use multimedia in your publications are also driving changes in the marketplace.

Millions of people around the globe have seen what modern computers are capable of. We are buying faster, more powerful computers. We are installing sound cards, video cards, and CD-ROM drives. All in an effort to get the best and most powerful computer on the block. And we not only want multimedia in the products we purchase, we demand it.

If used properly, multimedia can be the living aspect of your publication. It is the spark that makes the work come alive. Instead of reading a book about Beethoven hunched over a chair, multimedia allows you to actually look over Beethoven's shoulder as he is rendering his latest masterpiece, listen to the symphony note for note as you watch his hands sweep through the air, and stare out past the orchestra to the captivated throng hanging on every note.

Some people use the terms *multimedia* and *interactive multimedia* interchangeably. Although they are very closely related, interactive multimedia is more often used to describe multimedia publications that enable the reader to actively participate. Active participation is the key to interactivity. The reader does not just sit idly and watch the production scroll by. He or she is offered the opportunity to control various functions of the publication and ultimately the way the publication performs.

CAUTION

Although electronic publications that include multimedia can allow readers to actively participate, they do not have to rival a popular CD-ROM game. The difference between an electronic publication that includes multimedia and a CD-ROM game is the focus on multimedia. In an electronic publication, the text of the publication is still the star of the show, and the multimedia features are added to enhance or highlight the publication's text. In a CD-ROM game, the multimedia is the star of the show, and the text is used to enhance or explain what the reader is seeing.

For this reason, do not try to include too much multimedia in your electronic publications. Before you create, purchase, or add multimedia, ask yourself this: Will the multimedia enhance, supplement, or highlight the text, and, if so, how?

How Can Readers Control Publications?

Think back to the storyboards discussed in previous chapters. The reader must be able to navigate from one storyboard to the next, but the controls available to the reader of your publication do not have to be elaborate. A simple facility to accomplish this would be to let the reader use keys on the keyboard, such as page up or page down, to get from one page to the next.

To extend this idea a bit, you could write a program that would allow the reader to select from two buttons on the screen. Figure 11.1 is an example of how this could look.

FIGURE 11.1.

Simple use of on-screen buttons.

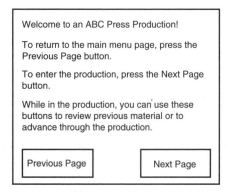

Just as the sample screen explains, the reader could then navigate through your publication using the two on-screen buttons. In the same way, we could use these buttons to advance or review previous pages, we could assign different functions to these buttons. Let's say we want the reader to be able to play music or video. We could rename the buttons to music and video as shown in Figure 11.2.

FIGURE 11.2.

Multimedia concepts.

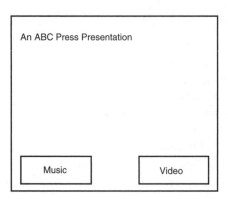

"Wait a minute; I'm not a programmer," you say—nor should you be. At no stage of the creation of your electronic publication should you ever have to resort to programming in a computer language, such as C or C++, to create a program to display text or view graphics. And just because you know how to program does not mean you should write your own programs. It could take days to create a relatively simple program to display your publication and advance through text. It could take months or years to create programs for playing sound and video.

When creating your electronic publication you will use the authoring tools discussed in Chapter 5, "Applications Tools." These tools will help you create the on-screen buttons I've just described. When adding multimedia to your publication, the same rule applies: Never resort to actual programming—do not try to reinvent the wheel. The tools described in later sections of this chapter will free you from the drudgery of programming. Use them! Direct your creative energies toward creating the publication and not toward creating programs that may someday allow you to make an electronic publication.

An important thing to keep in mind is that your use of multimedia in an electronic publication does not have to be sophisticated. As in the examples in Figures 11.1 and 11.2, you could use simple measures to allow readers to access multimedia. The electronic publications you produce are simply that, yours. Your electronic publications do not have to look like a multimedia software production from Westwood Studios, Broderbund, or New World Computing.

The level of technology you employ in the electronic publications you produce is up to you. The key is to use the right level of technology for the right reasons. Your use of multimedia will depend on the focus of your publication. In an electronic book featuring the latest mystery novel, the focus of the book should probably be on the textual portions of the book.

Types of Publications that Include Multimedia

Often, people associate multimedia with interactive computer games. Many companies make and sell interactive computer games. The software titles they produce not only include multimedia but have multimedia as their central theme. The entire mechanism for these games focuses on interactive multimedia. Some of these games have been explosive hits.

The 7th Guest and Myst sold millions of copies. The 7th Guest is a puzzle-solving game centered around a haunted mansion. Digitized video and computer animation scenes are the center pieces of the game, making it the phenomenal hit it has been. Myst is a fantasy adventure game centered around an island and mysterious circumstances. Myst has been so popular that it's been described as a new art form. The key to Myst's fame is a high-degree of interactivity coupled with high-power computer graphics.

Although interactive computer games are surely a focal point in the multimedia industry, multimedia can be used in many types of electronic publications:

> Books
> Consumer magazines
> Trade journals
> Technical journals
> Professional journals
> Company newsletters
> Special interest newsletters

244

    Newspapers
    Reference works
    Résumés
    Comic Books

Electronic books, magazines, newsletters, and newspapers can and should include audio, video, and graphic images. Electronic books are one of the biggest outlets for multimedia. Broderbund's Living Books series takes the use of multimedia and interactivity to the extreme. Every facet of these productions uses multimedia.

All types of electronic books can use multimedia. Multimedia can be used to great effect in fiction and nonfiction titles. Sound, video, and pictures can add depth to the publication. They allow you to draw the reader into the publication like no other medium can.

A few of the genres of fiction books that could include multimedia are as follows:

Adventure	Mystery
Fantasy	Romance
Horror	Science fiction
Humor	Suspense
Juvenile	Western
Literary	Young adult
Mainstream	

Some categories of nonfiction books that could include multimedia are as follows:

Architecture	History
Art	Hobby
Autobiography	How-To
Biography	Money/Finance
Business/Economics	New Age
Computers	Parenting
Cooking	Reference
Crafts	Science/Technology
Educational	Self-Help
Entertainment	Sports
Gardening	Travel
Health/Medicine	

Electronic magazines and journals are another great outlet for multimedia. If traditional magazines without pictures to accent the pages seem dull, try reading an electronic magazine without pictures. By adding sound, video, and pictures to an electronic magazine, you can capture the imaginations of your audience. Chapter 28, "Publishing a Magazine on a Floppy Disk," contains a detailed project that takes you through every step of the design and development of an electronic magazine.

The types of magazines and journals that can use multimedia include:

Alumni	Home/Garden
Architecture	Law
Art	Medical
Automotive	Military
Aviation	Motorcycle
Business/Finance	Music
Career	Nature/Conservation
Comic books	Personal Computers
Consumer service	Photography
Craft/Hobby	Religious
Entertainment	Science
Food and drink	Self-improvement
General interest	Sports
Health/fitness	Travel

The company newsletter is traditionally not a place for pictures. Most newsletters that use pictures or graphics use them only sparingly. This could be because the scope of the project is small or because of the expense of incorporating pictures into the newsletter. With electronic newsletters, the use of multimedia is more essential and central to the publication. Multimedia could significantly enhance the interactive nature of the publication. You could use graphics icons as menus to allow readers to maneuver through the newsletter. You could also use a digitized voice message from the CEO to introduce the issues of the newsletter, and much more.

Electronic newspapers will be able to broaden all aspects of their publications. Electronic newspapers could use digitized video clips to steal the spotlight from television news. They could use taped interviews and allow readers to play back the associated sound files. They will also be free from many of the cost constraints of traditional newspapers. Instead of pictures in black and white or poor quality color pictures, electronic newspapers can include full-color pictures at high resolution for virtually the same costs they would have incurred if the images were black and white. If you want to see firsthand how to design and develop an electronic newspaper, see Chapter 27, "Publishing a Newspaper on the Internet."

Reference works are another category of electronic publications with tremendous potential. Electronic dictionaries enable readers to quickly look up the definitions to words. Electronic fact books make it quick and easy to search for and find facts on hundreds of topics. Electronic encyclopedias bring history, culture, geography, and much more to life. *Compton's Interactive Encyclopedia* includes the complete contents of the 26-volume print version of *Compton's Encyclopedia*—more than 7,000 pictures and over 100 video sequences. In addition to the traditional style of encyclopedia, there are other types of encyclopedias that would work well in electronic form, such as a sports trivia encyclopedia. Chapter 29, "Publishing an Interactive Encyclopedia," takes you through the design and development of an electronic encyclopedia.

You may be surprised to find there is a growing outlet for multimedia résumés on CD-ROM and floppy disk. Providing a prospective employer with a multimedia résumé can distinguish you from all other applicants. Not only will employers be able to learn more about you, but if you provide video, they can see you in action. Chapter 26, "Publishing a Multimedia Résumé," takes you through the design and development of an interactive résumé.

The final category of electronic publications you may want to publish are comic books. Although interactive comic books are some of the most graphically intensive electronic publications, the text on the page is still the star of the show. The text contains the story line and outlines the action for the reader. If you want to see firsthand how you could put together an interactive comic book, see Chapter 30, "Publishing an Electronic Comic Book."

Using Multimedia

Several years ago it might have been difficult to find programs to help you add multimedia to your publication. This just is not the case today. Many wonderful tools are available to help you develop a multimedia publication. Tools like those explored in Chapter 5, help you integrate pictures, sound, and video into your productions. Some of those tools can also be used to create and view pictures, sound, and video, but this is not always the case.

Generally, the tools you use to create and play back sound will be different from the tools you use to create and play back video. Readers also need a way to play back the sound or video you've created. Generally, the tools the readers use to play back sound and video will be different from the tools you used to add the multimedia to your publication. Consider these two things before you add sound or video to your publication:

- What tools will you use to add sound or video?
- What tools will readers use to play sound or video?

If you talk about sound or video tools to initiates, they will bombard you with so many terms you will think they're talking a whole different language, for surely it is not English. Thankfully, there are concepts common to both the sound and video aspects of multimedia. By learning a few of these common concepts, you will have a better understanding of multimedia and multimedia tools. We will first take a look at the industry standard in multimedia. This standard is called MPEG. Afterward, we will look at common terms in multimedia.

What Is MPEG?

A more correct question to ask would really be: Who is MPEG and what is MPEG? This is because MPEG refers to a group of people and a standard. The Moving Picture Expert Group (MPEG) is a group of people that meet to develop and discuss standards for digital video and audio compression.

The group is a subcommittee of the International Standards Organization (ISO). They meet several times a year to discuss the technical aspects of digital video and audio compression, and thus the MPEG standard is an industry standard for compressing and decompressing digital video and audio.

How Does MPEG Differ from JPEG?

As Chapter 10, "Using Graphics," explained, JPEG is a standard for still image compression. MPEG is an emerging standard for moving images and audio.

The key difference here is still (non-moving) versus moving images. At first the notion of moving images versus still images may seem similar. After all, moving pictures are just sequences of pictures changing in time. In actuality, when you add motion—changes in time—you end up with a completely different problem.

Sound and moving video fall under the same standard because both can change with time and can be defined by sequences in time. Since this is true, similar techniques can be used to deal with them.

The MPEG Standard

MPEG seeks to define standards for multimedia that will enable multimedia objects to be used on any computer system. True standards workable on any system from the Amiga to Atari ST to Macintosh to IBM PC to UNIX are extremely important.

Although the Moving Pictures Expert Group is striving to improve standards, a number of forces are working against them. Different computer manufacturers, such as Macintosh and IBM, have different techniques for displaying video and playing sound. Further, these techniques have been in use for years, making it very difficult to adopt a universal standard. The good news is that, thanks to the MPEG subcommittee and other subcommittees in the International Standards Organization, there are a few universal standards for sound and video. The standards also make it easier for software developers to develop multimedia tools that handle compression and decompression.

The MPEG standard is seeking to define several progressive levels, where each advance in level represents a significant advance in the technology required to meet the successive level. This means that the first level in MPEG was designed to set the standard (in hardware and software) for its time; the second level was designed to set the standard for its time, and so on. In this way, the MPEG standard will continue to evolve as technology evolves and will be something for industry leaders to strive to achieve. You'll learn more about MPEG standard in Part III, "Publishing on CD-ROMs."

Currently, there are two world standards in MPEG—MPEG-1 and MPEG-2. If you've seen live video played on a computer, you've probably seen what MPEG level 1 video looks like.

The relatively small picture was played at roughly 30 frames per second with audio quality comparable to an audio CD. There were some tricks that could be used to make the image larger, but the effective resolution was still 352×240 pixels. In 1995, MPEG-2 became the high-quality standard in video. It offers true full-screen play capability at 720×480 pixels at 30 frames per second (U.S.).

What Is MPEG Compression All About?

Just as JPEG images and other graphic images can be compressed, so can digital audio and video. Although MPEG is a technical standard for compression, not a compression algorithm, manufacturers who follow the MPEG standard will develop or obtain a proprietary compression algorithm to achieve what the standard defines. A compression algorithm is a programmed mathematical formula for squeezing audio and video into smaller disk spaces. Sound and video that takes up less disk space will require less network bandwidth and will also download faster.

Some compression algorithms are superior to others because they are more efficient in the way they squeeze the audio and video. More efficiency normally translates to better quality when the audio or video is decompressed, or unsqueezed, during playback. The emphasis here is on the word normally.

> **TIP**
>
> MPEG-1 can be compressed using either software or hardware encoders. Software encoders offer the least expensive and easiest-to-use alternative. However, software encoders generally aren't as fast or efficient as their chip-based counterparts. This means it may take you longer to compress MPEG-1 video or audio using a software encoder.

When compressing multimedia files, you generally select a compression ratio and a quality setting. A compression ratio is the ratio at which audio or video is compressed. A general range that you can compress files in is from 2:1 to 100:1. The larger the compression ratio, the smaller the resulting file at a direct sacrifice to quality when later decompressed.

> **NOTE**
>
> A 20:1 (20-to-1) compression ratio means the file will be squeezed into a space approximately 1/20th of its original size. When you are squeezing that much space out of original material, something has to give, and normally it is the quality of the playback. An exception is MPEG-2 that can compress at 30:1 with no visible loss in image quality and can compress video up to 200:1.

TIP

In order to compress MPEG-2, you need an MPEG-2 video encoder chip. To decompress MPEG-2, you need an MPEG-2 video decoder chip. A few years ago, this type of video processing hardware would have cost as much as $50,000. Today, thanks to companies like IBM, which recently announced a low-cost video encoder chip, you can purchase MPEG-2 video production boards for under $2,500. The really good news for electronic publishers is the MPEG-2 decoder chip is priced right to become standard equipment on computer video boards. You will undoubtedly see MPEG-2 in action as TV-top interactive boxes become more widely available.

A quality setting is a largely arbitrary scale describing the tradeoff to make between the resulting size of the file and its quality during playback. A general range for quality setting is from 1 to 100. The higher the quality setting the larger the resulting file will be and the better its quality. Quality settings often confuse people because a quality setting of 75 does not mean keeping 75 percent of the information. The compression ratio describes how much information to squeeze out of the file.

The quality setting is more of a reality check. Let's say you'd like to compress at a ratio of 50:1 but want a quality factor of 100. The file created after you compress with these settings will not be significantly smaller. If you use a rational setting like compression 7:1 and a quality factor of 75, the result will be much smaller files and higher quality playback.

TIP

Use your software encoder or software interface to a hardware encoder to get the most out of MPEG compression. Most of the time, your goal should be to select the highest compression ratio and lowest quality setting that provides playback quality you feel is acceptable for your electronic publication. Try several combinations of compression ratios and quality settings. Also, you should never use a quality factor of 100. With a quality factor of 90–95, you probably will not notice any loss of quality and the resulting files will be many times smaller.

If the concept of compressing files seems confusing, do not get frustrated. Compression algorithms are complex beasts. Let the giants like Picture Tel of Massachusetts and Compression Labs of Silicon Valley worry about the innerworkings of compression algorithms. They've made a multibillion-dollar teleconferencing industry on the backs of their compression algorithms.

The bottom line about MPEG compression algorithms is: They are highly effective in squeezing the size of our audio and video files. They also enable us to create video productions playable on any computer system. In the next section, we will explore tools used to create, edit, and playback multimedia.

Multimedia Tools and Terminology

Tools used to create or edit multimedia files allow you to input the compression ratios and quality settings discussed in the previous section. In general, tools used for playback automatically decompress files for you. There are several key terms associated with these tools:

> Mods and clips
> Viewers and players
> Editors and trackers
> Authoring programs
> Converters
> Ripping

Mods and Clips

The words *mod* and *clip* are very closely related. Mod is short for *module.* Generally when people talk about mods, they are talking about segments of digital music files, where the segments are a set of samples containing playback information. Although this is true, video can also contain components called modules that refer to a particular segment of video or sound.

Clips are segments of video or sound. The word *clip* seems to imply that the work in question is only a part of a larger work, but this is not always the case. A clip can be a work in its entirety or only a part of the work. Video clips can and normally do include sound as well as moving pictures. Sound clips can contain music in full stereo that rivals the newest songs you listen to on the radio, or they can simply be computer generated tones or noises.

The word *clip* is also associated with artwork. Clip art disks are disks containing clips of artwork. Clip art was originally used to refer to line drawings but is now also being used to refer to all types of artwork collections on disk. This can include drawings, pictures, and digitized photographs.

Viewers and Players

People often use the terms viewer and player interchangeably. Viewers and players are helper applications used for playback of previously recorded sound or video. There is only a fine-line difference between the two. *Players* are programs used to play back sound or video that may include sound. *Viewers* are programs used to view video that may include sound. It could also be argued that because some players let you view the sound wave as it is played, they also could be called viewers. At any rate, the heart of these tools includes routines to decode or decompress the sound or video according to the format it is in.

The key idea to remember is that viewers and players are tools used for playback. If your multimedia production includes sound or video, readers need a way to play back the sound or view the video.

Authoring Programs

As you saw in Chapter 5, electronic publishers use many tools to create electronic publications. These tools are often called *authoring programs.* The best, also the most expensive, authoring programs have built-in features to support sound and video and can also create reader modules for your electronic publication that include provisions for playing back sound and video. The job of an authoring tool is to help you create electronic publications.

With the good, but less expensive, authoring tools this may or may not be the case. The good news is that you do have alternatives. From within most authoring tools you can run other programs like a viewer or player to run your multimedia clip. You can find a number of excellent shareware and freeware viewers and players. These options will be explored later in this chapter so you can select a sound player and video viewer that meet your needs. In Chapter 22, "Incorporating Multimedia," you will see a discussion on external viewers and helper applications of which viewers and players are subsets.

Editors and Trackers

Editors and trackers are very important in the creation and refinement of multimedia. An *editor* is a program that helps you revise a prerecorded segment of music or video. Normally, sound editors also include features that let you create sound or music within them, and this is why the term tracker is often used by people who create or adapt music. A *tracker,* as the name suggests, is a program that lets you put down a track of music.

Editors and trackers can save you hours of re-recording. The best of these tools include features that let you cut and paste segments of sound or video from existing sources into your creation. There are also ways to capture original audio or video from a CD-ROM playing on your computer. Most editors and trackers include viewers and players that can be provided to your customers for free. Some commercial vendors not only charge high prices for their editors, they also charge a licensing fee for each player or viewer you include in your publication.

The best editors are not necessarily the most expensive. Just as with freeware and shareware viewers, you can also find freeware and shareware editors. Most of these can compete head-to-head with commercial editors or are in fact, limited versions of the commercial tool. (For information on where you can obtain shareware and freeware viewers, editors, and trackers, see Chapter 22.)

Converters

Although it is true that universal sound and video formats exist, you will find it is often easiest to create system-specific sound and video formats. This may be because the system you are using includes basic tools for creating these multimedia files, like Microsoft's voice-annotation tool. It is also more economical to include in your publications multimedia from existing sources. You can obtain shareware and freeware multimedia files from a variety of sources including the

Internet. Most of the time these files were created with a specific system in mind, such as the Macintosh. Now what do you do if you'd like to include the file in the publication you are creating that will run on an IBM?

In the good-old days of computing, you would roll back your sleeves and write a 200-line program or script to convert file formats. However, that became tedious quickly, especially as the conversion process became increasingly complex. Most systems have multiple standard formats for sound and video. Today, the real solution is to use a converter.

A converter will let you change from one system's format to another, thus making it possible for you to create multimedia files on your IBM that will run on an Amiga, Macintosh, or UNIX system. For the most part, they are easy tools to use. In most instances, and especially when discussing video formats, converters were designed to convert one specific format to another specific format. The more recent converters will often convert to/from several formats. Likewise, newer editors may also include conversion features. Many converters are available online, and Chapter 22 tells you how to find them.

Ripping

Ripping is not a pleasant word. It is the multimedia equivalent of stealing. When you rip someone's multimedia clip, you are stealing it. With so much good shareware and freeware multimedia available on the Internet, no one should ever have to steal. Freeware multimedia authors only want acknowledgment if you use their files in your production. Shareware authors ask that if you use their hard work you acknowledge that fact and pay a small registration fee. More on finding shareware and freeware gems on the Internet is included in Chapter 22.

Three Considerations To Make Before Adding Multimedia

Understanding basic multimedia concepts is extremely important. Now that you know what multimedia is, what tools can be used to create, edit, and convert multimedia, you can make an informed decision before adding multimedia to your publication. Reaching the widest possible audience with your electronic publication should be a primary goal. If you are a small publisher it may be more than a goal, it may be what keeps you in business.

Millions of computer owners are craving multimedia—this is true. However, you need to carefully consider three things before adding multimedia to your publication:

- The hardware you will need
- The purpose of the sound or video
- The medium of the publication

Hardware Considerations

Multimedia will put more demands on your system and on the user's system. If you plan to publish your work on floppy disk, keep in mind sound and video files quickly eat up disk space. A few minutes of uncompressed sound can fill a floppy disk. A few minutes of uncompressed full-motion video can easily fill 10 megabytes of disk space. That is still three to four high-density disks, even if you compress the files.

Besides disk space considerations, there are other hardware considerations. Certain formats of multimedia may exclude groups of users. You may have the resources to record stereo sound on your computer, but not all users will. To play stereo sound, most computers require a special sound card. Other types of sound may or may not require a sound card. To display video, the user will need a video card. If the video is at a high resolution, such as SVGA (640×480 pixels or higher), the user will need a video card capable of displaying SVGA graphics. Carefully consider the multimedia formats you will use before applying them.

For a moment, do not think about the millions of computer users with CD-ROM drives. Think about the tens of millions of computer users who do not have CD-ROM drives (yet). Will they want to load 50 floppy disks onto their hard disk? Do they even own a hard disk?

It may seem that I'm trying to dissuade you from using multimedia in your publication. This could not be further from the truth. If used wisely, multimedia is one of the keys to success in your electronic publishing ventures. Something you may want to consider is developing several versions of your publications with each version targeted at a particular group of users: for example, producing a PC version targeted at the average computer user's system that includes a standard color monitor and a hard drive; then producing an enhanced PC version on CD-ROM targeted at the high-end computer user's system that includes the latest high resolution monitor, stereo sound card, and CD-ROM drive.

To create a high-end computer version of the publication, you will need the appropriate hardware. There is a hardware industry specification for multimedia called MPC, Multimedia Personal Computer. The standard has several progressive levels, where each advance in level represents an advance in the technology required to meet the level.

For example, in 1993, the hardware industry established the MPC Level 2 specification. To meet this specification, the personal computer must have a 25-MHz 486 SX central processing unit (CPU) or better with 4MB of RAM and a minimum hard drive storage capacity of 160MB. The computer must have a sound board capable of handling 16-bit digital sound with MIDI ports for input and output, a synthesizer and a MIDI player. A CD-ROM drive able to read multisession discs should be installed on the system. The CD-ROM drive must have a 300KB-per-second transfer rate and a maximum average seek time of 400 milliseconds. Lastly, the computer should have a video card and monitor capable of displaying Super VGA graphics at a screen resolution of at least 640×480 with 65,536 colors.

Although the specification is available to follow as a guideline, there is no need to get lost in the bits and bytes. Use common sense. Each level of the specification is stating minimum standards to meet the particular level. When you get past all the bits and bytes, the specification is really saying: to effectively use multimedia, and particularly multimedia on CD-ROM, you need a fairly new computer system that includes a sound card, a video card, and a CD-ROM drive.

When developing the CD-ROM version of the publication, keep the specification in mind. Currently, MPC Level 2 is a good standard to meet but not surpass. Remember, the more advanced and sophisticated the multimedia production, the more likely it is that the production is arbitrarily excluding a larger and larger group of computer users.

The good news is that computer prices are falling rapidly. Several years ago a computer system meeting MPC Level 2 would have cost $2,000 to $3,000. Today that same computer costs roughly $1,000. Tomorrow it will cost even less.

If you decide to upgrade your computer to meet your multimedia needs, you need to exercise caution. Multimedia technology is changing very rapidly. An outdated CD-ROM drive may look the same as the latest model, but internally it is not. The speed and efficiency with which CD-ROM drives can transfer information are increasing all the time. The first CD-ROM drives were very slow. The clunker in my system does not even meet the modest MPC Level 2 specification. Today that old clunker could be bought at the bargain price of $99, maybe less. But why buy hardware that is already outdated and soon to be obsolete?

SOMETHING OLD AND SOMETHING NEW: SHOULD YOU UPDATE AN EXISTING SYSTEM OR BUY NEW EQUIPMENT?

Some experts advise computer owners not to upgrade their systems, especially if they will mix old hardware with new hardware. Although in the increasingly complex information age this is often true, it is not always true. One specific exception to the rule of mixing old and new components I would make concerns CD-ROM drives. The primary reason for this is that CD-ROM drive vendors want computer owners to upgrade, and they are taking steps to make this task as easy as possible. For DOS/Windows systems, you can buy an all-in-one multimedia kit that includes a CD-ROM drive, sound card, and speakers to make the system work properly. Yet before you buy a multimedia kit, ensure your system is suitably expandable. Although you could add the CD-ROM as an internal or external device, you will need at least one expansion slot for the sound card.

For CD-ROM drive upgrades, Macintosh owners generally have the easiest systems to upgrade. However, many Macs don't have room for an internal CD-ROM drive. Although this will mean buying a slightly more expensive external drive, the good news is that the entire installation process will probably take only five minutes. If your Mac does not have a current operating system, you will also want to check with your computer dealer to see if you should upgrade your operating system to ensure you can run the latest CD-ROM programs.

Multimedia Should Serve a Purpose

Besides not wanting to arbitrarily exclude any group of computer users by adding multimedia, there are obviously times when including multimedia may not be appropriate. You should include multimedia to enhance the publication, not to distract the reader. Each and every bit of sound, whether music, speech, or simple tones, should serve a purpose. The same goes when you add video. The key to using multimedia in electronic publications is to minimize information overload while maximizing value.

Overwhelm the reader with gadgets, gizmos, and sound effects that do not serve a useful purpose, and your production will fail. Use multimedia in moderation. The most effective multimedia is simple in its design. The use of multimedia in a publication may be limited by the publication's:

> Audience
> Purpose
> Scope

Select multimedia that is appropriate for a particular project's audience and purpose. Limit the amount of multimedia in the project according to the scope of the project. The reasons for including multimedia do not have to be lofty; rather, they should tie-in with the purpose of the publication. Including a buzzer or bell to get the reader's attention or a sound effect to get a laugh are perfectly good reasons for adding sound. In both instances they serve a purpose.

The buzzer or bell can warn the reader something new is coming or that they've done something wrong. The laughter could be used for comic effect or as an ice breaker. If you are producing an action thriller, you may want to include sound effects like gunfire, explosions or screams. Your readers will be pleased. They may even be sitting on the edge of their computer chairs wondering what will happen next. But those same sounds may not be appropriate in an interactive children's story.

The Medium of the Publication that Includes Multimedia

The high storage capacity of CD-ROMs makes them a very attractive medium for electronic publishing. CD-ROMs can store the equivalent of hundreds of high-density floppy disks—the entire contents of a 26-volume encyclopedia including pictures and added sound and video.

The cost of buying 100 floppy disks would be $25–$50, depending on disk quality. The unit cost of mass-producing a product on CD-ROM would be between $7–$15, depending on the size of the production run. For small production runs, expect to pay more. The larger the production run, the lower the unit cost. Uncompressed 16-bit stereo sound at 44.1KHz can eat up 10MB of disk space per minute. Imagine how much disk space, uncompressed high quality video can take up?

TIP

A few years ago the price of a recordable CD-ROM system was exorbitant. That is not the case now. The price of recordable CD-ROM systems is falling fast. You can purchase a recordable CD-ROM system for DOS/Windows for as little as $1,500. Purchase recordable compact discs in bulk quantity (lots of 100) for $7–$10, and you can create your own CD-ROM productions without having to commit to production runs in the thousands of discs. (See Chapter 13, "When To Publish on CD-ROM," for more details.)

The many techniques available for squeezing sound and video into smaller spaces help to ensure publishing your multimedia project on floppy disk is still a viable alternative. Beyond MPEG compression or another type of compression, you can use other techniques to squeeze your publication onto fewer disks. You can drastically reduce the amount of space sound requires by transforming 16-bit sound to 8-bit sound or reducing stereo sound to mono sound. You can also drastically reduce the amount of space video requires by using fewer colors and smaller screen sizes.

Later chapters of this book will discuss CD-ROMs and the benefits of CD-ROM publishing in great detail. Part III of this book is devoted to the dynamics of publishing on CD-ROM. You may also be able to publish your multimedia publication directly on the Internet. Part IV, "Online Publishing and the Internet," is devoted to publishing on the Internet's World Wide Web. Chapter 22 specifically deals with incorporating multimedia into your publication and provides a full list of multimedia tools and where you can find them on the Internet. Some of the most powerful multimedia tools in use today are provided freely or as shareware on the Internet.

Let's Talk Sound

Earlier sections of this chapter explored the tools you could use to create, edit, and convert audio files. Sound can be a powerful medium to get your message across. Digitized voice can enhance the publication by making it seem more user-friendly. Simple tones can give unobtrusive warnings when the user does something wrong. Music can evoke a whole host of emotions. When incorporating sound into your production, you should always follow a few simple rules:

- Sound should never be distracting.

- Sound should serve a useful purpose, even if only to entertain.

- You should provide a way to turn the sound off and on, if possible.

- You should provide a way to adjust the volume, if possible and necessary.

- In the case of music, it should change, possibly in different sections.

As we progress through this section, keep in mind the ideas covered in previous sections of this chapter. To play sound, most computers require a special sound card. Different computer systems have different and very often incompatible sound formats. We will look at sound formats in a moment. For now, let's explore the types of sound and how they can be used in an electronic publication:

Music
Sound effects
Digitized voice
Simple tones

Music

Music is a great type of sound to include in your publication. It is also one of the hardest to create. At the high-end of multimedia publications that include lots of original music are interactive multimedia games. Most interactive games have several background musical compositions that play throughout the game. The type of music used in electronic publications can include:

Traditional compositions
The latest single from a compact disc
Original music scores composed on a computer

If you are a musician at heart, you could easily use software tools available today to create spectacular compositions. But not everyone (me for one) is musically inclined. Most musical compositions, especially original computer compositions and any commercially recorded music on CD-ROM, belong to the owner of the music. Before using this type of music you need to get written permission or pay a fee.

A good place to include music in your electronic publication is to allow it to be played in the background while the interactive production runs on. You could also include short music clips at key points in the publication. Another good place for a music clip is as an introduction to your publication. This introductory music should be brief as it will be played every time the publication is accessed, but it can add a nice touch.

Brevity in the music you include in an electronic publication is an important point, primarily because of the difficulty of simultaneously playing music and keeping the publication responsive enough to quickly respond to the reader's actions.

Sound Effects

Sound effects are fun because they are often easy types of sound to create. With a microphone and the plain-jane sound recording tool that came with your computer you can digitize your own sound effects. For example, PC sound boards normally include a microphone jack and a sound recording tool, so all you have to do is plug in the microphone, and you are ready to create sound effects of anything and everything from the dog barking, the kids screaming, or the wind in the palms.

The sound of a dog barking will not be appropriate for most publications, but could be used to tremendous effect in a children's story. The sound of a creaking door could be great in a murder mystery just before the *dénouement*. For a small-lively publication it could be fun to put in some teaser buttons that make noises.

Digitized Voice

Digitized voice is often useful. If you've used America Online before, you've seen a practical way to include brief digitized voice messages in an application. Basically, the America Online program says, "Welcome," when you start the program and has additional short greetings or sayings when you enter or leave other key places, such as, "You have mail." These verbal cues serve a useful purpose and primarily call your attention to something.

After a time though, verbal cues can become annoying, so it is important to make sure the user can turn them off. Remember, even the most pleasant things can become annoying if you have heard them too many times. The great thing about digitized voice is that it also can be recorded in the same manner as sound effects, making it not only useful but easy to produce as well.

Simple Tones

Most often, these little gems will be very useful in your publication. They are easy to generate and even more important, tones can be generated on a computer's existing internal speaker without the aid of a sound board. Using the computer's internal speaker is an important consideration, especially on a PC. You can use tones to warn the user they've made an incorrect choice or a soft tone to indicate the pushing of an on-screen button.

Through a series of these simple tones, you can also play music. Granted, it will not be the same as a music clip from a compact disc, but it can be enough to spruce up the low-end version of your electronic publication.

Sound Formats

Each computer platform has its own sound format. Most systems have more than one, which makes it very difficult to adapt sound for use on different systems. This is why the MPEG audio specification and similar industry standards are so important. Unfortunately, MPEG audio is also fairly new. Although it is experiencing tremendous growth in use, there are other more prevalent sound formats in use.

Concerning audio, there are other formats that are so popular they seem to be industry standards. Sun Microsystem's AU format was once very popular, but its popularity did not stem from the playback quality of AU recordings, which is very poor. It was so popular because it could be used on any computer system.

Things in the audio world are changing quickly. One very popular format with people who are serious about sound quality are MODs. MOD actually refers to a group of sound formats and is the origin of the term module (mod) that was discussed earlier in the chapter. The distinguishing factor for this group of sound formats is that MOD files contain sets of digital music samples and sequencing information for those samples. Most other sound formats are pure sample formats.

The multitude of MOD formats is a good case for industry standards. There are more than 100 MOD formats because just about every tracker that creates mods has a native format. The three most popular of these formats are MOD, S3M, and MTM. These three formats can also be played on any computer system when using a compatible tracker or player, and there are lots of compatible trackers and players to choose from.

Excellent pure sample formats are AIFF for Macintosh and WAV for Microsoft Windows. Although these two formats are very popular on their respective systems, they cannot be played on different computers systems without first being converted. AIFF and WAV are also becoming a defacto audio standard. Most Mac trackers/players will play, edit, or convert WAV files. Most DOS and Windows trackers/players will play, edit, or convert AIFF files. As an example, the basic waveform editor tool included with Microsoft Video for Windows can play and edit Macintosh AIFF files. This does not mean that the AIFF and WAV formats are interchangeable, but the likelihood that a Mac user can play a WAV file and a Windows user can play an AIFF file is increasing all the time. Table 11.1 is a review of popular sound formats; there are of course many other formats. Chapter 22 includes a review of popular trackers and players and where you can find them on the Internet.

Table 11.1. Audio formats and extensions.

Format	Extension
AIFF	`.aiff`
AIFF-C	`.aifc`
AU	`.au`
MOD	`.mod`, `.s3m`, and `.mtm`
MPEG (Audio)	`.mp2`
WAV	`.wav`

Let's Talk Video

Earlier sections of this chapter explored the tools you could use to create, edit, and convert video files. Video is another powerful medium to get your message across. Playing digitized video on your computer is a fairly recent actuality, which is good news and bad news, as you will see later.

As we progress through this section, keep in mind the ideas covered in previous sections. To display video, most computer users will need a video card or some type of special equipment. If the video is at a high resolution, such as SVGA (640×480 pixels or higher), the user will need a video card capable of displaying SVGA graphics.

When creating video, you should keep in mind the two key broadcast standards. NTSC is the broadcast standard in North America and Japan. PAL is the broadcast standard for most of Europe. Switching between these formats can cause problems. If possible, use hardware that supports both. Many shareware programs will let you display digitized PAL on an NTSC monitor and vice versa. What this means to you as a publisher is that if your authoring tool creates an electronic publication that is viewable only on an NTSC monitor and you want to distribute the publication in parts of Europe as well as the United States, you will want to consider obtaining a NTSC-PAL converter program and bundling it with your publication.

We will look at sound formats and how to create video in a moment. For now, let's explore the two basic types of video:

Animation
Motion Video

Animation

You have only to watch the latest Disney animation or watch the latest sci-fi TV show like *Babylon V* to see computerized animation is big business. Computer animation can also be a good technique for a small business. The idea of animation is conceptually very simple. You draw a number of individual still images and play them back in a series as if they were a film. For example, to bounce a ball inside a box, you could draw a consecutive series of images, moving the ball slightly in each new image. When played back, the slight variances in the location of the ball will make the ball seem to move around the inside the box.

To fit in with your publication, animation has to seem a part of the publication. This may sound redundant, but accept it at face value for a moment. If your publication is an interactive role-playing game where the main character or characters can be maneuvered around the screen, the animation of the character would seem a natural part of the publication. If your publication is an electronic magazine directed at young adults or children, a similarly animated character could turn the pages for the reader. This would also seem a natural part of the publication. On the other hand, if the publication is the electronic version of the *Communications of the ACM* (Association for Computing Machinery), this animated character would not have a natural place in the publication.

Motion Video

The digitizing of "live" video has great potential and will continue to be a growth area for years to come. The applications for live video in interactive multimedia are limited only by your imagination. Generally, live video works best as the featured component of the product and is often the selling point. Many multimedia publications are nothing more than someone's idea of a home video digitized and stuffed into an interactive front end. Although the quality of these productions has been poor, they sold, and they sold well.

Times are changing. The idea of digitized video on an interactive publication is not so new anymore. The same marketplace that accepted poor quality because it had no substitutes has evolved. Consumers have an ever-increasing number of titles to select from, and they are paying closer attention to the quality of the product.

Most video editors will convert to and from several types of video formats. They will also accept still graphic images in popular graphic formats, such as GIF, PICT, and JPEG. This is because the ways to create animation and video are closely related. *Animation* is a series of still images. *Video* is a series of moving images on film that must be broken down into frames before it can be processed.

TIP

When creating video, limit the width and height of the movie to save disk space. 160×120 (160 pixels wide by 120 pixels high) is a common size providing good playback speed with an acceptably sized playback window.

For the audio portion of the recording, eight-bit mono at 22.05 KHz offers a fair quality playback usable on most computers. Eight-bit mono sound will also save disk space.

For the video format, using an eight-bit bit depth will reduce space as well. Presently, the average user's computer will only display 256 colors anyway. You do not want to arbitrarily discriminate against large groups of computer users.

The steps for producing and editing video for multimedia could fill several books. Thankfully, many books are available on this subject. A good basic guide is *The Absolute Beginner's Guide to Multimedia,* and a source for video production is *Multimedia Madness,* both published by Sams.

Formats

There is good news and bad news with the "relative" newness of motion video. The good news is that there are not 100 different formats for video. There are only a few. The bad news is that the tools developed to edit and convert video have not evolved as far as their counterparts in audio.

The most widely used video format is MPEG, the industry standard. This is a pleasant change from the audio side of the house. As the standard, MPEG video can be played on any computer system. Since MPEG video players have been around for a long time, there are a number of old players that do not support audio tracks. This may seem a drawback for MPEG, but players are being rapidly updated. The newest versions of players will play the audio track as well, provided the file contains an audio track.

Apple's QuickTime format is not far behind MPEG in popularity. QuickTime is gaining popularity so rapidly in large part due to Apple's excellent support for the format and its promotion. A QuickTime 2.0 player is included in Apple's System 7.5. QuickTime has good audio track features, and players are available for Macintosh, Microsoft Windows, and the UNIX X Window System.

Microsoft's Video for Windows format, AVI, is another popular format. It is the dominating format for the Microsoft Windows environment. Video for Windows also features good audio track support.

Table 11.2. Video formats and extensions.

Format	Extension
Apple QuickTime	`.mov`
Autodesk Animation	`.fli` and `.flc`
Microsoft AVI	`.avi`
Microsoft DIB	`.dib`
MPEG	`.mpg` and `.mpeg`

Converters are available that will convert video files to and from any of these popular formats. Chapter 22 includes a review of popular editors, players, and converters and where they can be found on the Internet.

The Critical Question of Resources

If you plan to publish electronically, you need to understand what multimedia is and how it works. The best way to learn about multimedia is to try to create your own multimedia production using existing resources without investing a lot of money up front. Shareware sound clips, video clips, and tools are available. By paying small registration fees to the owners of the resources compatible with your existing system, you could have a very basic multimedia studio for under $300.

Although this basic multimedia studio includes no external facilities for creating audio or video, it is a good starter kit. The problem with multimedia is that you can quickly become caught up in the vortex of technology. With multimedia, for every level of technology you advance, the cost may increase by a factor of 10. For example, you could buy a video camera at the local video store, a video interface board, and editing software for $1,500. Or you could buy a semi-professional camera and multimedia setup for $15,000.

The cost of contracting individuals to create multimedia for your publication can be enormous. Be prepared to pay $200–$500 for key artwork and $500–$1,000 per finished minute of a professionally produced video segment. This is why learning to produce your own multimedia titles can offer tremendous savings over the long term. Sometimes it is not a question of money, but rather an issue in practicality. You may have the rights to a title you are sure will sell, but need to get the production in the stores while the issue is still in the headlines.

Every electronic publisher, whether a one-person operation or a large conglomerate, eventually has to make the decision to contract out or develop in-house resources. The decision does not have to be an all or nothing one. The following statements are designed to help you figure out short- and long-term multimedia needs:

- At present, we have the resources to create/edit music, sound effects, or video, and if we do not have the resource now, we can obtain the necessary resources at a cost within our budget.

- At present, our multimedia needs are at a level we feel comfortable with; we are willing to learn more about multimedia or already have started to learn more.

- Over the short-term, we have a reasonable and sufficient amount of time to devote to the project.

- Over the long-term it will be monetarily beneficial and to our advantage to develop in-house personnel and resources.

Read each statement carefully and answer the questions as they pertain to your multimedia needs. If each of the four statements seems true, you may do best developing all aspects of the organization's multimedia productions. If each of the four statements seems false, you may do best contracting your multimedia needs. If some statements are true and some are false, you may have conflicting goals and should carefully reevaluate your goals and needs.

Summary

Adding multimedia—graphics, sound, and video—to your publications is not only a possibility today, it is big business. Multimedia can significantly enhance the salability of your publications. The key to using multimedia in electronic publications is to minimize information overload while maximizing value. Many types of multimedia tools are available today. These tools help you create original sound and video. They help you edit sound and video. These tools help you convert between system formats, and they make the task of creating original video or editing existing material easier.

Although consumers crave multimedia, you should take into account many considerations before adding sound or video to your publication. You should carefully consider the purpose of the multimedia, audience, and hardware requirements for users and for your system. After you have decided on the multimedia needs for your publication, you should choose an appropriate format for the publication.

Writing Processes

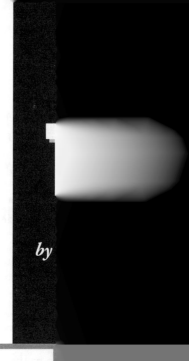

by

Many people have trouble getting a writing project started. They stare at a blank screen, sharpen pencils, play a computer game, reconfigure the screen saver—you name it. Many of these people don't realize that writing a major project is like taking a long and complicated journey. It needs planning, and it requires taking small steps in order to arrive at the destination.

Planning an Efficient Writing Process

Imagine starting a trip to California without having looked at a map. You've never been to California, but you say, "Well, I'll just head west." Eventually, you may arrive in California, but if you are in a hurry, you will experience disappointment with how long it took to get there. Yet, many people think they can embark on a major project and just see what turns up. They assume they'll figure out how to do what they need to do as they go, but many times these people have no sense of the overall route, so they get distracted by details. And when they run into a detour, they don't know what major roads to return to. Experienced travelers and writers know that a short time spent planning at the beginning (as well as replanning throughout the process as needed) can lead to a more efficient process later, especially when they are taking on major projects.

Many people believe that they can't write, that somehow the gods didn't give them the writing "gift" at birth and that they will never be "writers." But I believe that writing isn't all that mysterious. I also believe that there aren't shortcuts to good writing.

Writing for an electronic publication has much in common with other design or engineering processes. Basically, you are solving a problem for someone, and you can take several steps which make the process as efficient and effective as possible. Important tasks (not always in this order) that a writer/designer needs to do include:

- Analyzing the audience
- Observing examples of others' work
- Figuring out the problem that the product solves
- Exploring many options for solving the problem
- Creating a plan and a schedule
- Conducting subject matter research
- Creating templates and outlines
- Drafting and editing
- Reviewing and testing the publication
- Redrafting
- Editing/proofreading
- Publishing and distributing the finished product
- Maintaining the publication

I'll discuss each of these steps in the pages that follow, but first I want to re-emphasize that the more smart planning you do in the beginning, the less likely you are to run into problems in the later stages. You might run into detours on your trip, even with a plan, but at least you know what road you want to return to.

I also want to stress that these steps are recursive. In the middle of drafting, you might discover that you need to do additional research. Or, the marketing team may come in and say, "Why don't we expand the audience for this?" Figure 12.1 illustrates this recursiveness to an extent. As long as you plan for time for the unexpected, effective planning can help you manage large projects.

FIGURE 12.1.

Writing processes are usually recursive as illustrated in this Pert chart.

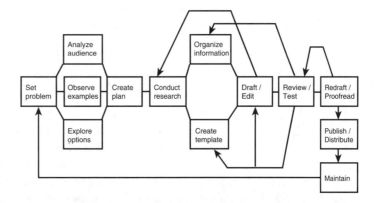

NOTE

In this chapter, I discuss these steps as if you are working alone. Although I'm aware that many electronic products are team-created, I'm assuming an individual author in this discussion just for simplicity. However, if you are writing in a team, it takes only slight adaptation to make these steps work for you.

I'm also assuming that you already know how to do the technical stuff involved with designing an electronic publication. If you don't, you need to master the technical how-to discussed throughout this book before or during the project.

Figuring Out the Problem That the Product Solves

Your publication is probably intended to meet a need for someone. Otherwise, you may enjoy creating it, but no one else will find it particularly useful. Sometimes you have the problem handed to you, whereas other times you observe it for yourself. Perhaps you have decided that teenagers need to know more about the Vietnam War, that maintenance personnel need training on how to maintain a complicated machine, or that music fans need more information on their favorite bands.

In some cases, writers try to solve too many problems or meet too many needs with one publication. They design something like an overgrown Swiss army knife, one with lots of gizmos that add extra weight in the pocket, when all the user needed was a bottle opener. (Naturally, some users need all the gizmos on a Swiss army knife, so that would be the best tool for them.) You need to aim your electronic publication at the users' needs. This may seem obvious, but it is more complex than it sounds.

Some problems have one correct answer. If someone wants to know what two plus two equals, most of us can give the answer of four. Problems with one right answer are called *well-defined* problems. However, designing a piece of writing for an audience is an *ill-defined* problem. There may be many ways to design it that work equally well. In fact, if you gave two writers the same problem, same audience, and so on, they would be likely to come up with two very different publications, both of which would get the job done. In defining your problem and your goals, look for a "good" solution rather than the "right" or "perfect" one. You get a lot more sleep if you don't try to pursue perfection.

At this phase, write out a set of goals for your publication. Discuss these goals with other members of your organization, but agree on the goals before the project begins. The goals should be clear and concrete, based on the user's needs. For instance, the user may have the goal of finding full information on the topic with which your publication deals. You, on the other hand, may have goals that are not necessarily the same as the user's. Your goal may be to make a huge profit on your publication, but obviously the user won't share that goal. In cases in which users' goals and developer's goals come into conflict, you can often achieve a compromise that takes both into account. However, if you ignore users' goals and concentrate only on yours, your publication will fail. This may seem obvious, but many people in the rush of development lose sight of users, much to the detriment of both the users and the project.

Knowing what needs you are meeting also helps you to know when you are finished. One can keep fiddling with a publication forever, but at some point, the writer has to call a halt and say, "This publication meets the audience's needs at this time." If the audience's needs change (or should I say, "When the audience's needs change"?), the publication can be redesigned later. Writing out the project goals in this phase can help clarify what the audience members will be able to do or know when they use your product. Later, you can test to see if your publication has reached these goals.

For example, one set of Web pages an acquaintance of mine (I'll call him Daniel) designed came about because he saw the need for more publicity about his organization. The organization, involved in teaching and research, wanted a way to publish information about its faculty and their credentials. After faculty in some of the more specialized research centers saw what could be done on the Web, they wanted pages for their programs. Then the admissions office wanted a way to attract undergraduate students with technical backgrounds to the graduate programs. After that, the placement office wanted to distribute electronic resumes of upcoming graduates so that prospective employers could find them easily. Over time, Daniel developed separate but linked Web pages to meet the needs of these varying audiences. He hopes in the future to develop pages for interaction with alumni.

Once you and your team have defined what problem you are solving, which can be very difficult and time-consuming, completing the tasks I outline below will help you decide upon and reach a realistic solution.

Analyzing the Audience

I place this task first after determining the problem because it is an important and complex task, closely linked to defining the problem. In making a product to distribute, you need to determine the intended audience. (Note that lots of products get used by other people who are not part of the intended audience, but that's out of your control.)

I recently participated in a meeting in which a group was trying to create a publication, but it wasn't clear who the audience for it was. Consequently, the group members debated fruitlessly about what should go into the publication. Had they settled on an audience, they could have worked toward selecting appropriate content for their publication. As it was, they wasted a great deal of time discussing many possible topics to include in the publication, with different individuals having fuzzy and differing conceptions of who the target audience might be.

If you have a small audience, analyzing the members and designing a publication is somewhat easier. Decisions get tougher with a big group, especially if the group is made of many types of people. Useful questions to ask about the audience include

- What use will my intended audience make of this publication? Entertainment? Education? Research? Decision-making? A combination? Other?
- How much background knowledge does my audience have about the topic?
- How much technical skill does my audience have in using the medium in which I'm creating?
- What are my audience's attitudes towards my subject matter? Toward the medium I am using?
- What conventions of visual and verbal design does my audience expect?
- What is the reading ability of my audience?
- What is the level of the hardware my audience will use to read my publication?

If you don't know the answers to these questions, you may need to conduct audience research. In doing so, you can talk to others who are familiar with the intended audience, or you can talk directly to typical members of the intended audience. Observing audience members as they work would also be helpful, if possible, in designing a highly interactive publication. (For more information on observing audience members, see Chapter 32, "User-Testing Your Material.") Even if you think you have a good picture of the audience, getting other perspectives helps you. The richer your picture of the audience, the more you can customize your publication to them. Many beginning writers assume that the audience is just like them. Although that may be true in some cases (and you *should* draw on your own experiences as a reader), the audience is frequently quite different from the writer, and the project may fail because the writer doesn't know the audience's needs and ways of working.

The most difficult type of audience to write for is a mixed audience, one with several levels of knowledge, several purposes for reading, several levels of skills, and several types of hardware. For instance, in Daniel's case mentioned earlier, his Web page had to appeal to scholars, prospective students, and prospective employers of graduates.

You might need to design separate products for each subgroup. If that's not possible, with the ability to create hypertext links in an electronic publication, you may also be able to create a *layered* document—one that allows differing groups to follow differing paths for the information they need. In this way, not everyone needs to move lockstep through your publication. If you do address a mixed audience, try to determine which part or parts of the mixed audience's needs should have priority. Cluster the subgroups of the audience into primary audiences and secondary audiences. Think about both groups as you design the publication, but the needs of the primary audience take precedence if there is a conflict between the needs of the two groups. Perhaps at a later date, you can create a publication more adapted to the secondary audience.

In some situations, you may have limited access to the audience and information about the audience. Find creative ways to build a mental image of that audience. You can talk to others who know the audience well and draw on your own experiences. For instance, if your organization has a phone support staff, they may know about questions users commonly ask. Sometimes the portion of a mixed audience that you know best unduly influences your image of the rest of the audience. Therefore, gaining as much information as you can, from as many sources as you can, provides you with a great deal of audience information useful throughout your entire project.

You also need to analyze the constraints that the audience faces. They may be limited by finances, time, technology, and so forth. Knowing these constraints well helps you evaluate options for solving your problem. In addition to knowing the audience's constraints, you also need to assess how highly the audience values these constraints. For instance, although nearly everyone is constrained by money, some people don't mind spending money if they can do work more efficiently, whereas others do mind.

You can never know everything about an audience, but you will be better off if you gather as much information and as many perspectives as you can while creating your publication. Working wisely involves being willing to enrich your image of the audience from time to time as the project continues.

Reading and Analyzing Others' Work

Imagine taking a class in which you want to learn to cook Chinese food. However, you have never tasted Chinese food. The instructor tells you to stir-fry your vegetables until they are crisp-tender. Because you have never eaten Chinese food, you have no idea what that crisp-tender feels like in your mouth. You would have to do a lot of trial and error before you reached what the instructor meant.

In the same way, when you write in a particular medium or genre (such as CD-ROM or the Web) and you have never sampled items in that genre, you aren't aware of the range of possibilities available to you, nor of the conventions that your audience may hold when using the medium. While designing your publication, take advantage of opportunities to sample what others have done in that genre. And as you sample, analyze, asking yourself questions such as: Who was the intended audience? How has the author designed this piece to reach the intended audience? What works well? What could be improved? What ideas could I employ in my design? This latter question is not intended to encourage plagiarism; naturally, you don't want to steal ideas. But observing and analyzing examples of the genre allows you to get a sense of what the audience may be expecting as they read. This knowledge makes designing formats for your product much easier.

Your audience's experience with these electronic genres affects their perceptions of your publication. If they usually see the link for the authors' e-mail address on a Web page, for instance, at the end of the first page, they may not expect to see it at the beginning of the page, or on one of the secondary pages. In fact, their expectations of where the address may be located may prevent them from finding it if you have placed it elsewhere.

If the audience has no experience with your genre, they bring with them analogies from other genres. For instance, if your audience is accustomed to reading paper documents, they may bring with them expectations about how information is formatted on paper documents. This can be both a blessing and a curse. It's a blessing because you, as designer, can draw on their experience with typical paper design. It's a curse, because they may ignore or be intimidated by the features which electronic publications have which are not found in paper documents. Many first time users of hypertext links, for instance, have no analogy for information presented in nonlinear ways. They may expect traditional logical connections and be confused when those connections aren't there. In addition, they may get lost quite easily. Fortunately, some new Web browsers and other well-designed software make getting lost more difficult, but novices can take amazing trips because of the analogies they bring from other media.

Analyzing examples of others' work can help you to understand the expectations of the audience about conventions of the genre in which you are publishing. Beware, however, of copying others' disasters or of mimicking features that would not be appropriate for your audience. (That's why audience analysis is so important.)

Exploring Many Options for Solving the Problem

Once you know what the problem is, who the audience is, and you are familiar with conventions of the genre, you can have fun with brainstorming many ways to solve a problem. Brainstorming involves writing down lots of options for solving the problem and not evaluating any of them—at least at first. In this stage, you don't reject any idea, no matter how silly it may seem. Silly ideas can lead to good ideas. I recommend writing down the options in some way, however, because writing makes the ideas more concrete than if you had only thought about them in your head. Again, I want to emphasize: Don't evaluate, don't critique in the early stages. Let your mind play and have fun. You can be more creative if you don't evaluate. Brainstorming in a group has been shown to generate even more creative ideas than brainstorming alone, as long as no one is rejecting ideas in the early stages. Don't just stop with your first idea, but explore many so that you can have the luxury of selecting the best one.

After you have brainstormed a list of options for solving your problem, then and only then should you evaluate them. Choose two or three of the options which seem most feasible. Evaluate those to find the best option for your publication. Base your evaluation on what you know of the audience's needs and constraints, as well as the constraints of time and energy that you face. In addition, you need to evaluate in light of the constraints of the technology, the publishing, and distributing processes that you use.

Creating a Plan and Schedule

The plan and the schedule you create may be for your benefit or for the benefit of others working with you. If the project is simple, familiar, and brief, you may not need to create a formal plan and schedule. Most people don't need to plan out a route for a trip for the local grocery store. You can keep that in your head, especially if you have done it many times. However, even if you don't have a written-out plan for simple routine projects, having a deadline helps you finish and prioritize.

Creating a plan and schedule for others you work with serves several purposes. For one, it shows that you know and want to help others understand what tasks go into creating the publication and how long these tasks take. If you are an experienced writer and have kept good track of projects in the past, you can estimate how many hours each task takes. If you have no experience of your own, it would be wise to consult with a more experienced writer for how long the planned tasks take. Either way, you can assume that a project always takes longer than estimated. Nonetheless, the estimate can be useful.

A plan can also let others working with you know when certain items are due. If they need to provide you with information, they need to know when you need it. If they review drafts of your work, they should see a copy of the schedule and agree to it early in the process so there will be no surprises later when you give them a draft to review.

A schedule and plan should include the required tasks and how long it will take to complete them. This can take various forms. You may want to try a Gantt chart or a Pert chart. Figure 12.1 gives an example of a simple Pert chart. Note that in a more complex Pert chart, one would also indicate on the links between the nodes approximately how long each task would take. Figure 12.2 gives an example of a Gantt chart. You can adapt these charts to fit your circumstances. Writers working in teams often also include a breakdown of who is responsible for which parts of each task.

FIGURE 12.2.

Gantt charts show relationships of writing tasks to each other.

Task	Month1	Month2	Month3	Month4	Month5	Future
Set Problem	X					
Analyze audience	XX					
Observe samples	XX					
Explore options	XX					
Create plan	XXX					
Conduct research		XXXXX				
Create templates		XX				
Draft / edit		XX	XXXXXXXXX			
Review / test				XXXXXXXXX		
Redraft					XX	
Edit / proofread					XX	
Publish / distribute					XX	XXXXXXXXX
Maintain						XXXXXXXXX
Keep project log	XXXXXXXXX	XXXXXXXXX	XXXXXXXXX	XXXXXXXXX	XXXXXXXXX	XXXXXXXXX

By looking at a Gantt chart, you can tell when several tasks need to be completed simultaneously and how long each takes. By looking at a Pert chart, you can see what task needs to be completed before another one starts.

In addition to a schedule, the plan should discuss all the following items:

- The problem you are solving
- The intended audience
- A sample format for the product
- A tentative outline of the contents
- A plan for producing and distributing the publication
- A plan for updating or revising the publication

A plan is not a contract signed in blood (well, not usually, anyway). If you fall behind schedule, the plan allows you to know what remains to be done. It can also help you decide where to cut corners and renegotiate deadlines, if you need to.

Conducting Subject Matter Research

If you know the subject matter of your publication well, you are fortunate because you have to do less research than someone unfamiliar with the topic. Even if you have the knowledge you plan to use, you may wish to see what others have said about the topic, just to be sure you're accurate and up-to-date. They may also have approaches that you hadn't thought of.

If you need to do research, you can use traditional methods such as conducting searches through a library, or you can use less traditional methods such as interviewing experts and conducting searches on the Internet. Make friends with a reference librarian who knows the secrets of searching the Internet and other electronic databases. (I admit it; I'm biased on this tip because I'm married to such a person.) Be cautious, however, with information you find on the Internet. Be sure your source is reliable and current, just as you would with a printed source.

If you are designing a Web page, look for other Web pages to which you may wish to create links for your users. Get a complete list now so that you can select only the most relevant and useful lists for your audience later. Remember, however, that because the Web is changing daily, a page you thought was perfect for your publication may disappear.

If you are designing a document that teaches users how to use a certain machine or tool, obtain a copy of the tool yourself and play with it. Learn all you can about the typical training processes that have been used in the past in the context.

In the example of Daniel, he was able to find some existing paper documents, such as the course catalog for master's degree students and the faculty handbook. He then adapted the documents for presentation on the Web. He hopes to develop an electronic archive of faculty research publications to make them available to other scholars.

Whichever methods you choose for finding out information, it's wise to have a list of questions prepared ahead of time so that you know what you are looking for and are less likely to get sidetracked. Naturally, you want to be open to serendipity, but having questions ready can allow you to search with a goal in mind. Preparing questions before an interview with an expert is especially important so that you get the information you need without wasting time.

Not all the information you include will be based on traditional formats. For instance, Daniel also needed to include material in his Web page about the Master's curriculum—material that was usually kept in a database. He was able to write a program which transferred the material from the database to his page. (When the data changes, Daniel updates it in the database and then transfers it to his page, freeing him from having to make all the changes twice.) Don't overlook unusual sources of information.

As you are researching, keep in mind that some of the material you gather may be copyrighted. If you wish to use it, you need to obtain permission from the original source. This permission may cost you some money, but in the long run is cheaper than a lawsuit.

Gather as much information as time allows so that you can move on to the next step: organizing and selecting your information. Remember, it's better to have more information than you will use than to come up short and have to go back for more.

Organizing and Selecting Information

Many times you collect about three times as much information as you actually use in the publication, which is better than not gathering enough information and having to return to your sources for more. In cases where you have more information than you need, you want to select only what's most relevant to the audience in order not to waste their time. This selection may be painful because you may have fallen in love with the information you worked so hard to find. Console yourself by telling yourself that you can save it for a sequel. Audiences appreciate information that is carefully selected and well-organized, but it's not as easy to produce as it looks.

The way in which you received the information is usually not the best way to present it to your audience. And if you have a mixed audience, there may be no one best order in which to present it. How you organize depends a great deal on your audience and purpose. If you are teaching people how to do something, organize your publication by the tasks they'll need to do. If you are informing people, you need to create meaningful categories for the information you have gathered. If you are creating an online journal, you need to organize several items in ways that allow the audience to select what is relevant to their interests. In addition, your audience's experience level should also affect how you organize. For instance, if you are teaching novices how to do a new task, what seems like one step to you may be a series of steps for them.

Because Web pages (and some other electronic publications) allow for links to other pages you have created, you also want to think about the size of the chunks of information included on a page. Too much information per page, and the audience scrolls through it forever. Too little, and the audience has to go through too many links and pages to arrive at the desired information, thereby increasing frustration and the chances of getting lost.

Also, because you can't always control the order in which your audience moves through the publication, consider each page or screen as a self-sufficient unit linked to other related units. Don't assume the audience has seen information from a previous screen or page. Even so, be sure to have a statement of the purpose of the publication readily accessible to audience members so they won't have to guess whether they might be able to use your publication for their needs.

In addition to how much information to include in a single page or screen, you need to decide what items to link to each other. Creating a map or a storyboard at this stage can be helpful, especially if you have a great deal of information. Also keep in mind that the more links you provide on a Web page, the more "costly" the resources used to maintain them.

When organizing, you also need to consider that with hypertext links, the audience may not read your document in the order in which you intended it. Although you can design a series of links that forces people to go only in a certain order, that may not be the best organization for your audience and purpose. You also want to design your series of links so that users won't get lost in hyperspace easily.

In paper documents, standard linear forms of organization have been used which may be useful in electronic documents as well. These include comparison/ contrast, chronological order, least to most (or most to least) important, spatial, and so on. But don't limit yourself to those patterns of organizing information in electronic publishing. Electronic documents allow (but don't require) you to organize information in nonlinear ways, allowing audience members to loop back to re-find information that they might need.

Having a good grasp of the audience's needs and style of processing information can make your job much easier at this point. There may be an almost infinite number of ways to organize, but you, as author/designer, need to select what you believe to be the most effective for your audience.

Creating Templates and Outlines

Before you begin drafting, you need to create a working outline of what to include. Many people think that an outline must have Roman numerals and letters in a specific order. That may be true for an outline that you show other people, but for your own purposes, you don't need to be that formal. In fact, you may want to draw charts and pictures to help you figure out how to organize the information, especially if you have a lot of it or if you are creating hypertext links. You need to use whatever method helps you shape the information. Experiment with different ways to organize the information so that you can select the best one for your audience rather than merely staying with the first one you select.

Once you have an idea of the overall structure of your information, create a template for how each screen will look. These templates allow you to create consistency from screen to screen so that your publication looks like a unit and not merely a collection of bits of information. As in the outline, think about the audience, but also about what types of information you include on the page. Then decide how each type of information should look on the page.

If you are creating a Web page, some of the conventions of design are determined by the browser, such as the color and format of a word that is a link. However, others are not fixed. For instance, you may decide that all of your major headings will be centered and in a certain size of font. In creating a Web page, keep in mind that different browsers provide the audience with different views of your information. In designing any electronic publication, also keep in mind that not all computer screens have equally sharp resolutions and so don't display all fonts equally clearly. Some of them show only 16 colors. Designing with an awareness of these constraints can help your publication be more successful with its audience.

If you are basing your work on existing paper documents, don't assume that you can simply transfer the format onto a screen. This may seem like obvious advice, but I have seen too many on-screen examples in which designers appeared not to consider the constraints of designing text and graphics for a screen, but rather merely transferred their paper document's format onto the online version. The result is usually a publication that is very hard for readers to process on screen. Such designers fail to take advantage of the features of electronic media, such as hypertext links, layout options, graphics, and color, which could make their work more attractive and appealing to the audience.

In addition to deciding where to place the content to send to your audience, you may want to decide on how you wish to solicit responses from them. Especially, if you are designing a Web page, in addition to the traditional link to the e-mail address of a developer, you may be able to design a comment page as Daniel did for people who wanted more information about enrolling on one of his organization's programs.

Also, when designing your screens, keep in mind the technical capabilities of the audience's hardware. Including too many graphics and sounds can slow the process down and frustrate the audience. Plan for enough to keep the publication interesting, but not so many that the publication alienates the audience. For more information see Chapter 10, "Using Graphics."

Experiment with various on-screen formats. Assume that visual design will take you just as much time as writing text for your publication. Choose the format you think will be most effective for your audience and purpose. Some formats can look attractive but are not appropriate for your audience and purpose. For example, if you are creating a Web page discussing alternative rock music, you would probably want a design which breaks with conventional layout so you can appeal to an unconventional audience.

A balance between attractiveness and usability serves most audiences well. An attractive appearance can be inviting, and a function that works well to communicate information satisfies the audience's needs.

Establishing Conventions for Styles

At some point before you start drafting, you want to establish what sort of style manual to follow, particularly if you are making a series of products that should have a consistent style. Many style manuals exist, so you probably don't have to write your own. Some style manuals are designed for use by journalists, others by academics, and others by other types of publishers. Whichever style manual you choose, be sure it's appropriate to the audience. For instance, if you design a publication for a British audience, be aware that double quotation marks and single quotation marks mean exactly the opposite of what they do in the United States.

Once you have workable templates and a style manual, you can finally move to crafting your words.

Drafting and Editing

Completing the previous steps makes the drafting phase much easier. You have broken down the topic into major categories, so you can then create what you have to say about each of the categories. Furthermore, because you've been working on the project for a while, thinking about the audience and their needs, conducting research, and organizing the information, you've solved many of the problems and have answered many of the questions that cause less savvy writers to chew many pencils.

While you are drafting, you may find two unexpected things happening. First, when you finally sit down and create words and sentences, you gain insight that you didn't have during your preliminary work. This is normal. Writing creates knowledge, not merely packages it. Enjoy this discovery. Second, you may discover that there are gaps in your information. This is also normal. Even though you have researched extensively, you may have overlooked something. Or, because of time pressures, you had to move into drafting. Feel free to return to the research step and get more information if you can. Your research while drafting will be more focused because you know exactly what you are looking for and do not need to look for general information.

While drafting, keep the audience in mind. Many writers find it helpful to imagine a typical member of the audience sitting nearby. One writer I knew imagined a tiny version of an audience member sitting on top of her computer, listening to all she wrote. At this point in the draft, don't worry too much about the finer points of style and grammar. You can always come back later to clean up. Rather, write as if you were speaking to the intended audience. Also, don't edit just yet. Even if you think you'll eventually need to cut out a portion of your text, leave it in for now. Too much editing while drafting inhibits drafting and thinking.

Work on the draft in small doses. Take breaks when you reach a stuck point, and go do something non-verbal. (My favorites are making quilts, walking, knitting, and playing computer games—not all at once!) This type of activity allows your subconscious to work on the problem. Come back to the work and continue drafting until you run out of energy for the topic. Then take a longer break, if possible. If you can, quit while you are still enjoying the work so that you won't dread returning to it. All these breaks are not wastes of time, but rather time for your mind to work on problems without conscious effort. (This also implies that you have planned well in advance and haven't put the writing off until the last minute.)

As you write and design information for your publication, keep in mind that you are setting up expectations for the audience, either through words or design. Be aware of how you set up those expectations and whether you deliver what you have promised.

When you have a draft with which you are satisfied, edit your words. Many people begin editing by reading the first sentence, making changes as needed, and then going on to the second sentence and so on. Unfortunately, this is not very efficient because you may find later that you didn't really need certain sentences and you have spent a lot of time cleaning them up.

Rather, as you reread your draft, try editing on three levels. (This usually requires three readings.)

1. Look at the large matters in the publication. Ask yourself if everything that is in the document needs to be there for your audience and purpose. Look to see if something is left out. On this first reading, also look to be sure that the organization is best for the audience and purpose.

2. Study the intermediate level matters. Ask yourself if each part holds together. Also, look at whether each part is organized in a way that would be most useful to the audience.

3. Look at style. Are sentences clear to the intended audience? Are they concise, getting your message across fully using as few words as possible? (This feature is especially important in text which appears on a screen because most people have a hard time processing great quantities of information without a paper publication.) Does each sentence fit with the sentences before and after it? Try reading your words aloud; doing so slows you down so that you can see how the words flow. Don't worry if your words don't sing like artistic prose; those writers spend hours (which you probably don't have) revising and playing with words. As long as the text is clear and easy to read, your audience will appreciate it. You can do some grammar checking and proofreading now, but you'll do the close work of it later.

After drafting and editing—sometimes you need to create four or five drafts—you have a publication ready for others to see. But don't release it to your intended audience just yet. First, put the publication through the quality checks described below.

Reviewing and Testing the Publication

After working on a publication for a long time, you may be so close to it that you no longer see what others may see in it. Therefore, you would be wise to have others read and use the publication before you release it to your intended audience. In addition, if you are writing for an organization, it usually requires that other eyes see it because the corporation is ultimately responsible for what is published in its name. Reviewers can look at three areas:

- Technical accuracy
- Forms of the presentation of information
- Ease of use

Some reviewers can do all three, but other reviewers may do only one. If, while creating your schedule and plan, you have asked the reviewers to look at your draft, they won't be surprised by your request and will usually be more likely to give you thoughtful responses. Let your reviewers know what you want them to look at in your publication; some writers create checklists to guide the reviewers.

It's wise to solicit several responses of several types. You should have at least one technical review for accuracy, one that tests usability with typical users (see Chapter 32), and one that looks at whether or not you have met with the conventions of the genre in which you are working. If two or more respondents agree on a certain suggestion, then it may be worth looking into. At this point, someone else may be able to help you determine whether or not you have followed the style manual chosen earlier in the process. Different reviewers will catch different problems before you release the project to the intended audience.

Allow enough time for the reviewers and testers to do an adequate job. Otherwise, you probably won't receive reliable feedback to guide the redrafting of the publication.

Redrafting

Once you have received your reviews and results from testing, you have to decide which comments you will attend to. Not all review comments are necessarily appropriate to your audience and purpose. Nevertheless, most review comments come in handy as you redraft. Sometimes reviewers recommend major structural changes within your document, so you need to decide whether these changes would fit your intentions and time limitations. Several approaches may meet the audience's needs, so don't assume that yours (or the reviewer's) is the only viable option.

Redrafting may involve only changing a few words and phrases or it may involve making major overhauls. Do what you need to in order to meet your audience's needs, given the time you have. You may find that you want or need to go through the review process again, depending on how much time you and your reviewers have before the release date.

Editing and Proofreading

Many people think that editing and proofreading are all there is to good writing, but having read this chapter so far, you now know better. Nevertheless, I don't want to give you the impression that you can skip editing and proofreading. These last two steps are like dressing for a job interview; clothes alone won't usually get you the job, but the *wrong* ones will make it difficult for you to get hired. So pay attention to this section, but keep editing and proofreading in perspective.

Grammar Shrammer

Don't let grammar intimidate you. Despite what you might believe, no one in the world has a total grasp of all the rules of English grammar and standard usage. People who have been teaching language skills for years still find usage rules they were unaware of. In addition, the rules of grammar and standard usage are constantly changing, albeit slowly. There may be times when you break the rules for a reason. Overall, it's best to think of usage as a convention, created and sustained by a group of people in power. You can learn enough about these conventions to use them, and then defy them when necessary.

Eventually, the publication is near completion. It's been planned, drafted, reviewed, and tested. Now is the time for detail work. After redrafting, edit on the three levels discussed previously, and then proofread. Again, if you can ask someone else to help you proofread, that person or persons can provide you with new perspectives. Proofreading differs from editing in that proofreading involves looking at grammar, spelling, punctuation, and conformance to other conventions depending on the style manual you are following. If you know you are not good at this, get help. Lack of proofreading ability is not equivalent to lack of intelligence. Even if you are good at proofreading, get help anyway. The best publications sometimes have four or five professional proofreaders.

If you don't edit and proofread carefully, two things may happen. One, your accuracy suffers. Your numbers may not add up, or you may make a statement that is not factual. If the intended audience members catch these errors, they may begin to wonder if they can trust other statements you make. Second, the audience will catch your spelling, grammar, and punctuation errors and think less of you and your work. They may find that these errors distract them from your message. It's not fair, but it happens. Try to prevent it as best you can. Usage conventions are like a windowpane. If it's dirty, people complain about the dirt because they can't see the view. If it's clean, people comment on the beauty of the view and not the cleanliness of the window.

Checking Spelling, Grammar, and Readability

Many electronic tools are available to help with checking your spelling and grammar. They have some usefulness, but they can't take the place of a good human proofreader. The spellchecker catches only words which are not in its dictionary. Consequently, if you use an unusual name or technical term, the spellcheck flags it, which slows you down if you have many unusual terms. Far more serious, spellcheckers can't detect context. So if I type "they" when I meant "then," the spellchecker won't call it to my attention. The error could only be caught by a person reading who is familiar with how words fit into contexts. Nevertheless, you should run a spellcheck if you can. It saves a human proofreader time with basic problems. But don't stop with running a spellcheck. Have an excellent speller look over the publication as well. In addition, as you are proofreading, read the document backward, word for word. This helps you break your usual pattern of reading and lets you see the words somewhat decontextualized.

Grammar checking and readability software can have some of the same limitations as the spellcheck. They have limited usefulness, and they should be used, but with caution. The grammar check and readability checks are usually designed for a general style and so may not fit the style in which you are writing. For instance, if you are writing a casual, conversational piece, the grammar check may flag terms that don't fit into "standard," somewhat formal writing.

Or, if you are writing for a specialized audience that expects lots of passive and complex sentences, the readability meter may register unacceptably high. Use these tools to help you, but don't let them become your masters. You are the final decision maker about the style of your words.

Publishing and Distributing the Finished Product

As mentioned, part of designing a publication is taking into account how it will be published and distributed. Some of this may be out of your hands, but you may also be involved in parts of the process. The more you know about publishing and distributing constraints early on, the better you will be able to design your publication to meet those constraints.

However, with distribution, your work is not necessarily finished, especially if you have designed a way for the audience to provide you with their responses and suggestions. Chapters 18 and 34 contain additional information on distributing your publication.

Maintaining the Publication

Electronic publications are seldom finished. They are merely released with the understanding that updates are forthcoming. This is especially true with Web pages. One frequently sees a note on a Web page that certain areas are under construction. As audiences change, as subject matter changes, as technology changes, and as new design ideas emerge, one may need to create a new version of the publication. Therefore, you begin the process over again—analyzing the new problem and audience needs, redesigning, conducting research again, updating the style manual, drafting, reviewing, and proofreading. Fortunately, this time you have some text to work with, so the process goes a bit more quickly. In addition, you may have audience feedback to guide your new directions. In fact, you'd be wise to solicit audience response to provide support for changes you plan to make. If your organization has telephone or e-mail help lines, find out what questions users frequently ask. (See Chapter 33 for more information.)

Unfortunately, some people grow bored or busy at this point and don't maintain the publication. Hence, a lot of Web sites serve more as archeological sites than as living, up-to-date resources. If no one can maintain the publication, it would probably be wise to remove it from circulation as much as possible.

Tasks Throughout the Project

Many writers find the two activities discussed below useful during a writing project. Each may seem a side track from writing, but they'll give you new and valuable perspectives. Try them and see how they work for you.

Incubating and Daydreaming

What seems like nonproductive downtime in a writing project can actually be a time during which your subconscious mind is working on a problem—a time for incubation. Sometimes you find yourself in a tangle of ideas, words, and seemingly insoluble problems, no matter how well you plan your process. At these times, it's wise to take a break. (This is not procrastinating, by the way.) When you reach a point where nothing seems to work, working harder may actually be counterproductive. Instead, take a break and do something else, preferably nonverbal. File papers, clean your desk, water the plants, climb stairs—whatever works for you. After daydreaming, come back to the writing when you feel rested and can look at it freshly.

If you are crunched for time and really can't afford to take time off from the writing, try working on a different part of the publication. You don't necessarily have to write the document in the order in which it will be presented to the audience. Many people start writing the body before they write the introduction. Or do something relatively mindless, like running a spellcheck.

Another tactic for dealing with problems which stop your work is to play with the problem. Draw cartoons of it, write it as snotty note, write that section badly—whatever you can do to rearrange the concept and get a grasp on it. You don't necessarily have to use this "play" material, but creating it can help you gain control over your final publication.

Record Keeping

In many organizations, you need to keep track of your hours when working on a project. This is valuable because it helps you to plan how long to allow for future projects. In addition, I'd like to suggest you keep records of the activities and ideas which have come up during the course of the project. A log in which you record what did not work as well as what did work well can be valuable for solving the problems for that project and for giving you ideas for future projects. This log can be the place to doodle, to experiment, to play. The more play you can incorporate into the work, the more creative you can be, finding options outside the usual ones. Especially if no one else sees your logs, think of them as a place to experiment with ideas to find the ones that work best.

Obstacles to Effective Writing

In any project, you will find obstacles to writing. An effective writer employs tactics to deal with these blocks. The following paragraphs, of course, don't cover all obstacles, but they should give you a sense of how to deal creatively with the problems you face as you create a publication.

Pursuing Perfection

Because many of us only see the final draft of someone else's writing, we may think that the first draft was pretty close to the final draft. And so, when our own first draft doesn't meet our high standards, we believe that we'll never get to those standards. In addition, some of us have standards which are impossibly high. The pursuit of perfection is an immeasurable waste of time. The pursuit of excellence, however, is not.

In order achieve "excellence" for your situation, trust the planning you have done. If you know the audience well, if you know the scope and purpose of your project, and if you know the subject matter well, you will probably produce a publication that does its job.

When I'm stuck because I want to produce a great publication, I often resolve to write a really "bad" draft first and then clean it up later. Surprisingly, when I go to clean it up, it needs far less work than I had thought it would. Decreasing your early expectations allows one to create, saving editing for the appropriate time.

Many people seem to have three "beings" in their heads: a child, an editor, and a pig. The child says, "Ooh! Let's play. Let's do this and this and this." The editor says, "Now, you have to think about commas and clarity and such." The pig says, "Humph! You are really stupid. Everything you write is stupid. Why don't you go back to third grade where you belong?" How can you deal with these three if they live in your head? First, butcher the pig. Take a big knife and stab it with glee. You don't need the pig. The pig has nothing you need to listen to. (Unfortunately, the pig has nine lives, so it may need to be butchered repeatedly. Keep at it.) Send the editor to Hawaii to soak up sun on the beach for a while. Let the child play while the editor's away. Then, bring the editor back to clean up after the child. You need both the child and the editor, but not at the same time, in order to produce an excellent publication.

Lack of Planning

Lack of planning often happens when people are short on time. It also happens when people think they know how to do a task and so don't need to plan. However, if you are short on time, you can't afford not to plan. Without a plan, you use lots of time producing a publication which doesn't fit the needs of the audience. You may complete your publication by its deadline, but if it doesn't meet the audience's needs, you have not been successful.

Naturally, one can have death through planning. Some people plan and plan and never implement. Even if your plan isn't perfect, you can still go ahead and produce something. Sometimes you don't realize where you need to go until you've done a little planning and then a little implementing. Planning at the beginning and then doing mini-plans throughout can help you complete the publication more efficiently and effectively.

People Around You with Differing Ideas

You've done all the needed research, you know the audience well, and you've designed a publication you think meets their needs. If you work within an organization however, there are bound to be people around you with different ideas about what would work best for the audience, or about who the primary audience should be, or about how much information to include, or about the design of the screens, or any other element of the project. This disagreement is normal. It can even be productive. These people can test your ideas in early stages so you may avoid disasters later.

Hear out their suggestions and involve them in the early stages of planning. In this way, you create the wisest course of action early, and you achieve "buy-in" from others who are in a position within the organization to support your publication.

Try to keep these conflicts from becoming personal. For example, assuming that Joe is questioning your plan not because there are holes in it, but only because you questioned his plan last week is not likely to lead to a useful solution.

If you do disagree with the ideas that others have and if you've done lots of audience research, you can use what you know about the audience to argue for another approach. For instance, you may say, "We considered using those colors on the screen, but have found that color-blind users can't tell the difference." The better your user information, the stronger your arguments.

In addition to arguing for your decisions, you also can suggest compromises which fit into the constraints you know about and the goals of the others in your organization. Therefore, in the scenario mentioned above, rather than stopping with the statement about why you can't use certain colors, you may then add, "But if you think the users need more variety on the screen, we could try different sizes of fonts and a different use of blank space."

Another misconception that others around you may have is that writing only involves putting words together. Even if there were no element of designing the text visually, a writer still needs time to do research to learn about the subject matter, and time to think. A truly understanding colleague knows that staring out the window or pacing the halls is writing.

Others may think you are wasting time. Keeping track of the time you have spent on various elements of the process can show them that writing involves more than putting words on paper or fixing commas. (However, some of them will never be fully persuaded.)

Lack of Time

This obstacle is tied in with the previous one. Usually lack of time is caused by people around you who don't know how long it takes to plan, research, write, and edit. So, they ask you to meet an impossible deadline. Or, in the middle of your project, they come up with a major change they'd like to see made. In addition, you as a writer are frequently working on several projects at once, and so can't dedicate the time to any one which you would like to. In an ideal world, you would have enough time to make the publication perfect. But because we don't live in that world, we have to do what we can with what we've got.

Knowing the goals of the publication helps you know where you can compromise. Sure, it might be nice to create 400 different links, but the audience probably only needs 20 of them most of the time. If you know the audience well, you can have a pretty good idea of which 20 they are likely to use and create your publication accordingly. Find a balance between your constraints and your goals; it's difficult, but experience in finding alternative ways helps.

In order to avoid time shortages, keep good records of how long tasks take you to do. Then when someone asks you to have something by next week, you can show the person that in the past, a similar task took three weeks.

At times, unexpected delays occur, usually out of your control, which also puts time pressure on you. Someone doesn't respond to the review draft on time. The computer on which you are working crashes. Your father-in-law has a heart attack, and you have to miss several days of work. Again, in an ideal world, these events don't happen. However, in the real world, having a schedule and a plan allows you to know approximately how much work remains to be done. So if you can't meet your stated deadline, you can renegotiate the deadline, letting the recipient know exactly where you are in the process and when you will complete the publication. Without a plan and a schedule, you have to guess and make lame excuses—not a pretty sight.

Not Knowing or Adapting to the Audience

You may find yourself in a situation with limited information about the audience. What many people do in such cases is imagine the audience is just like the writer. Well, sometimes it is, but often the audience has radically different characteristics from what the writer imagines. In response to writing in which the writer didn't take the audience into account, that audience may say, "That's way over my head" or "This writer treats us like second-graders."

A similar response comes from the audience when the writer assumes that a certain group is the primary audience and so designs the publication for them. Sometimes a second group comes along and complains how the publication doesn't meet their needs. Of course, the publication wasn't intended for them. These complaints don't necessarily indicate obstinacy on the part of the second group, but may reflect a real need for a publication adapted to their own needs.

If you can't get direct access to the audience, you can learn about them a number of indirect ways. I've already mentioned talking to the phone support people in your organization. You can also talk to Marketing because they are the ones who are responsible to deal with the audience regularly. Marketing departments usually keep extensive databases on your organization's clients, so if you can gain access to them, they may enrich your picture of features of the audience. As usual, creative tactics can help to make your publication successful.

Sometimes, even if writers know the audience's needs for information, they may not have taken into account the audience's style of processing information. Some audiences process information verbally, others visually, and others use a combination. In addition, some audiences read through a piece in a linear way, from start to finish. Other audiences read as they need to, skipping from one point to another as their interest is caught. Some want only basic information, whereas others want to understand all the background behind the basics.

Writers can't always accommodate these varying styles, but they can employ design tricks to adapt a publication to these varying audience styles, provided that they are aware that such styles exist. Creating alternative pathways through the electronic information may help. For instance, if you use an unfamiliar term which some audience members wouldn't know, you can create a link which provides a definition of or more information about that term. Attempting to make the audience conform their reading to the style of the document usually causes frustration on the audience's part. Rather, the document should try, as much as possible, to adapt to the audience's many needs and styles.

Lack of Access to Information

In some situations, you may not be able to find certain bits of information that you think your project requires. Perhaps an expert is unavailable for an interview, or a needed document has disappeared from the library, or the Web site to which you wished to link suddenly disappears.

You may need to offer to take the expert to lunch—even experts need to eat. You may find an alternate document or Web site with similar information. Think of yourself as a detective, hunting out all clues to the end.

If you have exhausted all the creative tactics you know for finding missing information, try to think of your publication as what you know at the time that it is released. If you have plans for maintaining the document, you can make information changes as they emerge. A statement to this effect is common in electronic publications, and many audience members are accustomed to this process of flux. Nevertheless, you want to do your work as well as possible for credibility's sake.

Trying To Say Too Much

If you have done extensive research, you may be tempted to include everything you have found. You may also be tempted to want to solve everyone's problems, to meet everyone's needs in one publication. Don't do it. Sticking to your clearly defined purpose statement helps you to know which details meet that purpose and which do not.

Others with whom you work may come up with different opinions of what is needed. However, someone has to decide finally what is necessary, or the publication sprawls and rambles, losing the audience you meant to reach. As I mentioned, you can always save the other material for another publication or a sequel. However, don't cut material too early in the process. Ramble during drafting and then tighten during editing.

Saying too much sometimes also involves repeating the same idea using different words. Sometimes you need to do this when explaining a new concept to the audience, but readers become impatient if you do this for simple, familiar concepts. Additionally, many people find it difficult to read great quantities of text in an electronic publication, so you need even more conciseness. Imagine you have to pay a dollar for each word you write, and then make sure each word is worth the money it might cost.

While aiming at lean prose, however, remember that because audiences don't have to read your publication in a set order, they may not have read the previous page or screen on which you explained a concept or term. Creating a link in this situation can help the audience and save you (and them) from needless repetition.

Too Many Audiences for One Publication

You may find that due to circumstances beyond your control, you have to try to reach many types of audiences with one publication. It can be done, but it's tricky. In a paper publication, such as a newspaper, the readers can just discard the sports section if they are not interested. But in electronic publications, allowing your readers to choose what they want or need to read involves careful design.

Having a clear sense of what your types of audiences are and who gets priority helps you make decisions about content and design. And when compromises are needed, you have guidelines in place as to whose needs take priority. Nevertheless, you may face difficult choices and may not be able to custom fit all your types of audiences. That is why presenting your purpose statement early in your publication lets the audience members know whether or not they will find your publication useful for their situations.

Summary

Completing the tasks discussed in the preceding paragraphs and dealing with obstacles can help you create a publication that is useful for your audience. You may need to adapt the tasks to your audience and your situation, but you should be aware of these writing tasks as options to take, especially if the project is not going well.

Even if the project is going well, the quality of the final product and the speed with which you created it can be improved with a better process. The more successful experiences you have with writing processes, the easier future ones will be. However, the most important point to remember is that you can learn the process—you don't need special innate gifts to create a publication which works well for your audience.

PART

Publishing on CD-ROMs

When To Publish on CD-ROM or Disk

13

by Lee Purcell

"Paper or plastic?" the grocery bagger asks as your purchases slide down the stainless steel ramp and await bundling. Even if your "green" intentions are unassailable, the question begs careful consideration. Paper bags are based on a renewable resource, but the process—from harvesting to manufacturing—crosses many lines that environmental purists might wish to avoid. On the other hand, plastic bags require less energy to produce, but they are also more difficult to turn into something else once you've finished toting broccoli and salsa to your home, and plastic doesn't degrade as well as paper.

"Paper or plastic?" may also be a key question when producing a document, such as a training manual, reference, or other work, whether the audience is your department coworkers or an international audience. Paper, the traditional medium for document exchange, is direct, simple to manage, and doesn't require any kind of viewer except for a hand to turn the pages and a pair of eyes to read them. Plastic, the substance composing the disc of a CD-ROM, supports inexpensive replication and high-capacity data exchange, but requires some kind of electronic playback device and takes more work—in many cases—to create.

One might also expand the question to include one more element: paper, plastic, or iron oxide. The hard disk—with its data surface fashioned from materials that can store magnetic pulses—can also serve as an efficient purveyor of on-demand documents, whether they are being passed around on a corporate local area network or are created as portable documents users can access on the Internet. Removable storage devices, such as magneto-optical cartridges, SyQuest cartridges, Bernoulli cartridges, and even diskettes can be a useful medium for distributing an electronic publication and in some situations may be ideal for certain types of applications.

This chapter explores the issues you should consider when creating electronic works for disc (as in CD-ROM) or disk (as in removable media). We'll discuss the trade-offs of various approaches and weigh the limitations of each medium.

Removable Storage Media

Removable storage media includes those kinds of data storage devices that can be physically removed from the computer: diskettes, tape and disk cartridges, and—for some applications—PCMCIA cards. Your potential audience as an electronic publisher depends greatly on who has the necessary equipment to read the data that you've placed on the media.

If you're planning on distributing electronic documents and network distribution doesn't suit your plans, early in your project you should select the form of removable storage media you'll use for distribution. Each different type of removable media has a finite capacity, a definable cost, and certain characteristics—such as durability and size. Some of these may be suitable for limited, small-scale uses (such as transferring the electronic version of a style guide to several company workgroups), and others are an economical means of performing large-scale distribution of data-intensive material—such as disseminating a quarterly corporate infobase to hundreds of different sites.

You'll no doubt base your choice of the ideal medium for your purpose on a combination of cost, the availability of required equipment, the ease of working with the selected medium, and the compatibility of the resulting electronic publication once it is replicated on disc or diskette.

The leading candidates in the removable storage arena are

- *Diskettes:* If your electronic publication is compact, the humble diskette may be perfectly suitable for distribution. The media itself is inexpensive (less than $.50 per diskette in bulk), and it's unusual to find a computer system that doesn't have a diskette drive. The diskette, however, limits your cross-platform options. While Macintosh computers can read IBM-formatted disks "right out of the box," you'll need additional software to read a Mac-formatted disk on an IBM-compatible machine. UNIX machines are a completely different story, as well. Some read many different formats; others are more selective. Diskettes work best if your target audience is using the same family of equipment—DOS, UNIX, or Mac— and your electronic publication is no larger than 3–4MB. Documents of this size can usually be compressed to fit the 1.4MB limit of a diskette. If you use compression, make sure that your audience has the necessary utility to decompress the document, or use the self-extracting archive option that is available with most compression programs.

- *Flopticals:* A hybrid of the floppy diskette and magneto-optical technology, a floptical disk can store from 40MB to a 100MB on what looks like a $3^1/_2$-inch diskette (but is actually a special, high-density medium). This form of storage can be effective for workgroups or environments where the necessary equipment to read and write the floptical disks can be installed on each workstation. For large-scale distribution, however, don't count on anyone in the population at large actually having one of these things. So far, their market penetration has been meager. As a specialized medium for creating and distributing moderately sized electronic publications, the floptical is worth consideration if you have some control over the acquisition of the playback equipment.

- *SyQuest cartridges:* The SyQuest cartridge has been the dominant form of removable media for many types of applications, such as delivering high-resolution graphics or desktop publishing documents to service bureaus for further processing or replication. The medium employs conventional Winchester disk drive technology, where the read/write head literally flies a fraction of an inch over the magnetic disk surface. A plastic enclosure—the cartridge itself—contains the disk, which is sputter-coated with a graphite material for durability. When you remove the cartridge, you separate the disk portion of the drive (in its cartridge) from the read/write head, which is mounted inside the drive.

  Cartridges come in different sizes (5.25-inch, 3.5-inch) and different capacities (44MB, 88MB, 105MB, 200MB, 270MB). The disk must be formatted for the host computer operating system, and depending on the software drivers you have available, may be readable on different platforms, though it's usually easier to read a DOS-formatted cartridge on a Macintosh than vice versa. SyQuest cartridges have been widely accepted and make a useful delivery medium for electronic publications if cross-platform compatibility is not your main concern. While a reasonably durable form of storage, a head crash (where the read/write head strikes the disk surface and damages both itself and the disk) can destroy data on the cartridge. If the read/write head is also scratched or damaged, inserting subsequent cartridges following a crash can precipitate additional data loss on each inserted cartridge.

■ *Bernoulli cartridges:* The Bernoulli cartridge uses a different technology than SyQuest cartridges to eliminate danger of data loss from head crashes. The data surface is similar to a pliable floppy diskette that actually rises up to meet the read/write head as the drive spins up to speed. A power loss—instead of causing a head crash—simply slows rotation and lets the disk droop away from the read/write head. Bernoulli cartridges have not been as widely accepted as SyQuest cartridges, but they are still commonly found at many service bureaus and CD-ROM replication facilities. Several different cartridge sizes and capacities are available, but the same formatting issues that limit cross-platform distribution of SyQuest cartridges prevails with Bernoulli media as well. Once formatted, the cartridge becomes associated with a single host operating system and requires special software to be readable on different platforms.

As with SyQuest cartridges, you can use Bernoulli cartridges to distribute electronic publications in situations where you can be sure your audience has the necessary equipment to be able to read the cartridge. This can be a very limited audience, so the Bernoulli may not be your first choice for wide-scale distribution.

■ *Magneto-optical cartridges:* Another hybrid technology, magneto-optical cartridges use a magnetic medium, but optical data writing techniques. The disk surface contains a layer of magnetic material; a laser beam strikes the disk and induces a phase change in the surface that the drive interprets as a data pulse during playback.

These cartridges have proven a popular and cost-effective form of data storage, but standardization of cartridges and drives has not been as consistent as for other media types. Consequently, your carefully prepared magneto-optical cartridge created on a Fujitsu drive connected to your IBM machine may not be seamlessly read by a Sony drive installed on your colleague's Compaq. Magneto-optical cartridges range from 128MB capacities up to more than a gigabyte using a couple of different cartridge sizes. The medium itself, unlike optical media such as recordable CD, can be rewritten, which can be a great advantage if you plan to reuse cartridges over a period of time. Costs of cartridges are fairly inexpensive: from $35 or so for 128MB cartridges to upwards of $100 for 1.3GB cartridges. While these may not be the way to distribute your interactive multimedia encyclopedia to the mass market, magneto-optical cartridges could be a good way to distribute an electronic version of your companies network documentation set to a more limited audience of in-house personnel.

■ *CD-Recordable:* Once an expensive, limited alternative to other data storage methods, recordable CD or *CD-R* has become a staple of corporate archiving and data distribution. Recordable CDs have a couple of great advantages over other forms of data storage. The recordable discs are relatively inexpensive—less than $10 in many locations—and each disc can store up to 680MB of information. A file system standard known as ISO 9660 can be used to allow data stored on a recordable CD to be read on a variety of platforms, including Macintosh, DOS, Windows, OS/2, and UNIX. In this sense, the CD-R provides a much more flexible distribution medium than any of the other data storage devices. Add to this the fact that most business machines today are being sold with installed CD-ROM drives, which ensures that your audience will have the necessary playback equipment, and you have the basis for a world-class electronic publishing tool.

You can create CD-ROMs either by bringing your source data to a replication service (on tape, removable cartridge, or other media) and having discs manufactured, or on the desktop using CD recorders. You can purchase relatively inexpensive CD recorders for less than $2,000, and the blanks (the recordable CDs) are widely available. Some compatibility problems still exist for discs that are written over more than one session (known as multi-session recording), but the industry is rapidly moving towards resolving these inconsistencies so that discs created on CD recorders can generally be read on any standard CD-ROM drive. In quantities, you can produce CD-ROMs for less than $1.00 each, and their light weight and relative durability make them easy to ship anywhere. Whether you might only need to produce a dozen CD-ROMs for in-house use or plan on replicating several thousand for large-scale distribution, the CD-ROM bears careful consideration for its combination of high-capacity and low cost media.

Issues When Publishing on Removable Media

One paramount goal of electronic publishing is to reduce the cost of creating, managing, and distributing information. As with most things in life, these advantages don't come without some upfront costs. When grappling with production issues for an electronic document, you should address each of the following questions:

■ **How many different computer platforms do you need to support? Does your audience use exclusively Macintoshes, or are you as likely to find Motorola Envoys as Sun SparcStations?** Determining the computer platforms your application should support will affect the tools you use to create the electronic publication, the media you choose to distribute it, and the degree of difficulty in adapting material for cross-platform use.

■ **How large is your electronic document or infobase?** If you can compress it to fit on a diskette, you may never need to consider additional storage media. If it exceeds 100MB, you need to decide whether CD-ROM replication is justifiable, or whether one of the other forms of removable media makes sense simply because it is easily available in your organization. However, if your electronic work is targeted for commercial distribution, diskette or CD-ROM are clearly the choices for playback on standard consumer devices. Bernoulli or SyQuest cartridges are simply too expensive for mass distribution.

■ **Is network distribution out of the question?** Clearly, if you can distribute your electronic document easily on the network, you'll have no need to replicate it on any form of removable media. However, if you are distributing to customers or to an outside audience who must dial up your server or a service to obtain network access, there exists a practical limit at which point downloading a document becomes excessively expensive when compared to the costs of replicating and distributing on CD-ROM. Depending on the speed of a network interconnecton, this point may be reached at 20 or 30 megabytes. As great as networks are for distributing information, no one wants to spend a couple of hours downloading a document, and then taking up a large chunk of his or her hard disk storage just to use it in electronic form. This is where the CD-ROM can make the most sense, because it enables you to ship several hundred megabytes of information without burdening your audience with storage demands or download time.

■ **Can the information on disk or CD-ROM be reasonably finalized without requiring frequent updates?** If you're planning on creating a corporate infobase that will be out of date in two weeks, the permanent nature of the CD-ROM limits its usefulness in this application. Unless a network infobase would be too large, you may want to use a more flexible solution and post an update form of the infobase every week or two where your audience can access it on the network. Of course, if the infobase is huge (above 200 or 300 megabytes), CD-ROM may still be the preferred method of distribution for limited quantities. The infobase may also exist on the network in a client-server framework, where the client doesn't need the entire database but can send queries to obtain needed information. Publishing electronic information in a client-server type structure may be the appropriate approach when neither CD-ROM nor full network distribution makes sense.

Recording to Disc

Electronic publishing on CD-ROM can eliminate many of the cross-platform compatibility problems and data capacity concerns that limit other forms of large-scale document distribution. The CD-ROM is unique, and with the advent of affordable CD recorders, this form of data distribution is available to anyone whose budget can include similarly priced add-on peripherals, such as laser printers or scanners. The CD recorder may become the "must-have" peripheral for the remainder of the 90s for anyone who must deal with large quantities of data.

For electronic publishers, the CD-ROM is the ideal delivery medium for many different types of applications—from electronic books to reference sets.

The Compact Disc Comes of Age

To understand how the compact disc has evolved from a medium designed for delivering high-quality, noise-free music to one of the most versatile, cost-effective data storage media, you need to trace the evolution of the disc, starting in the research labs of Sony and Philips in the 1970s. Sony's early experiments into digital sampling of sound waves were intended to help shape the design of a new type of tape recorder, referred to as Digital Audio Tape (DAT). During the course of these experiments, Sony confirmed that they could accurately recreate an analog (continuous) waveform by converting individual points along the wave into a series of levels, stored as binary values. If you stored enough of these digital values—each a discrete level in the sound wave—you could play the recorded values back and the result would be indistinguishable from the original sound.

Soundwaves have changes in frequency—which affect the pitch of the sound you hear—and amplitude—which indicates the volume. To adequately obtain a precise representation of a soundwave, the digital samples must take place at a rate which can capture even those frequencies at the upper range of human hearing (around 20kHz). Experiments (and a mathematical formula known as Nyquist's theorem) helped determine that, by sampling at a bit more than twice the frequency of the waveforms you want to capture, sound recordists could effectively replicate the waveform without losing any of the frequencies in the upper registers. A sampling rate of 44.1kHz was adopted, and this rate is used today for audio discs and has come to be known as *CD-quality* sound.

To record changes in the amplitude of the waveform, a 16-bit value is recorded each time a sample is taken—44,100 times a second. You can store 65,536 individual levels using the combinations available with 16 bits, and this number of levels proves effective in accurately recording amplitude changes in a waveform. However, this level of accuracy does not come without its cost. Recording stereo tracks to CD-ROM consumes 10.6 megabytes of storage space per minute. If you are creating an interactive multimedia work for CD-ROM, you can often use slower sampling rates (such as 22kHz) using eight-bit values for storage for less dynamic representation of sound, such as narrative voice-overs used in a production. If you want the highest quality, however, particularly for music recording, you will want to use 44.1kHz sampling with 16-bit values. In studio situations using professional gear, sampling rates of 48kHz are used for source recordings, and this data is downsampled to 44.1kHz levels for storage on disc.

The development of the DAT drive helped perfect digital recording techniques and set the stage for the compact disc. Philips, a Netherlands-based electronics firm, had been working on methods of optical storage in which they used a laser beam to read sound and video data embedded onto the first laser discs. Philips collaborated with Sony to develop a standard, known as the Red Book standard, that defined how audio information would be stored on a compact disc. Red Book established data-recording and formatting principles which were progressively adapted for use in non-audio applications and resulted in the first CD-ROM standard.

A Quick Look at Discs and Lasers

If you're planning to author productions for CD-ROM distribution, you might appreciate a bit of insight into what makes this medium unique. The design characteristics of the compact disc directly affect performance issues and the storage of different types of data.

A compact disc consists of a polycarbonate base overlaid with a layer of aluminum and protected with a lacquer coating. The disc contains data in the form of billions of microscopic pits that formed during the mastering process by beaming a laser at a layer of photo-sensitive material. Pits are arranged into a continuous spiral that begins in the innermost area of the disc (near the central hole) and extends to the outer edge. The spiral is subdivided into a number of tracks—99 tracks exist on a typical CD-ROM.

When you insert a disc into a CD-ROM drive, disc rotation begins and the rotation speed varies, depending on whether the drive is reading the inner or outer tracks. A laser read head, mounted on a servo-controlled sled that you can position over any of the individual tracks, accomplishes the reading. Laser light is highly focused (the individual beams are exactly parallel); a series of lenses allow the drive to direct the laser beam at the disc surface and aim the returning reflections at a photodiode. The read head electronics can detect minute phase shifts in the light as it strikes the pits. The areas surrounding the pits are called lands. Changes in the phase of the light waves as they move from pit to land and from land to pit are registered as transitions. Transitions on the disc surface are encoded in such a way that they represent the bit patterns composing the actual data, whether audio material or computer data.

Compared to data on a hard disk drive, which is arranged in concentric circles on independent, consistently spaced tracks, it requires more work to move the laser read head to locate data on a compact disc and to alter the disc rotation to the appropriate speed for retrieval. For this reason, data access times for CD-ROM are much slower than for hard disk. Modern hard disks can typically access data in around 10 milliseconds; the fastest 6× CD-ROM drives require about 145 milliseconds, and the average access time is about 200 milliseconds. Access time becomes an issue whenever you are trying to move a large amount of data, such as simultaneous audio and video data, to the computer for playback. When authoring for CD-ROM, you need to be acutely aware of how access time and data transfer rates affect the playback of your electronic work.

Evolving Standards

As they crafted the original Red Book standard, both Sony and Philips noted that the error rates of audio data recorded on CD-ROM were particularly low. While the Red Book standard included some basic error correction codes, sufficient to allow clean playback of audio—even if the disc surface became slightly scratched—when the two companies moved to the Yellow Book standard, the basis of CD-ROM storage, they expanded the error fields to ensure more rigorous detection and correction of data flaws.

A series of additional CD-ROM standards emerged, many of them drawn up in committee meetings attended by manufacturers in the CD-ROM industry who were attempting to solve practical problems of data storage and delivery. These industry representatives had the foresight to extend the original Red Book standard in such a way as to allow CD-ROM drives to read not only the newer standards, but also to be backward-compatible with the earlier standards. As Green Book and White Book and Orange Book added new capabilities and storage features to the CD-ROM (such as improved multimedia performance, storage of Photo CD data, and the definitions of recordable media), they always used earlier standards as the basis for these extensions. Consequently, CD-ROMs have matured in such a way that users can successfully play and transfer them to equipment on several different platforms. For example, virtually any CD-ROM drive you can lay your hands on has the capability of playing back Red Book audio tracks.

Cross-platform compatibility runs into a few serious glitches in some of the more recent standards, but generally CD-ROMs have succeeded where many other forms of storage media have suffered because of incompatible formats.

Universal File Systems

If you can remember the days when the first wave of personal computers were released, most of these relied on their own unique format for floppy disks, a situation that made easy interchange of data impossible. In the prime of the CP/M era, familiar $5^1/4$-inch disk might be formatted using Heath, KayPro, Osborne, Tandy, IBM, or DEC conventions, as well as many others. Most machines could only read disks created using their native format, so you had to devise some creative approaches to something as simple as moving a file from one computer to another. A similar problem limits the use of many removable storage media—such as SyQuest cartridges and magneto-optical cartridges—which are formatted with a specific operating system and computer platform in mind. In most circumstances, you need special software to read a cartridge formatted for another platform.

One of the strengths of the CD-ROM as a data exchange medium, and the reason it successfully fits the bill for many electronic publishing projects, is the adoption of a universal file system. Originally drafted as the High Sierra standard, the International Standards Organization later ratified this file system as ISO-9660. An ISO-9660 disc has files arranged in such a way that machines on a variety of platforms, such as DOS, Windows, Macintosh, and UNIX, can locate the files. ISO-9660 breaks down many of the barriers to widespread document distribution by creating a file system that lets most systems take advantage of the disc contents.

Computers with different processors can freely access certain types of files, such as graphics files (.EPS and .GIF, for example) or portable document formats (.PDF). However, the "readers" or the search engines used to access these files must still be processor specific; that is, they must be tailored for the instruction set of an individual processor, such as an Intel 80486 or a Motorola 68040. So, even when authoring an ISO-9660 disc, you generally must provide separate areas for those files that can be used in common—regardless of the processor type—

and those that must have their own specific applications for accessing the data. Another example of this involves popular authoring applications, such as Macromedia Director. Director can read files stored in its native format whether you created those files on a Macintosh or under Microsoft Windows. However, when accessing the files on the Macintosh, you need to use the Mac version of the Director player, and when on an IBM-compatible machine, you need to use the Windows player.

Most of the mastering applications that let you record CDs on the desktop provide full support for ISO 9660. In the large majority of cases where your interest is in creating a disc that users can read on many different platforms, you will want to use ISO 9660 for your file system. This creates some restrictions, such as Macintosh users having to adapt their more flexible file-naming conventions for the terse 8-plus-3 filenames permitted under DOS, but generally using ISO 9660 presents little inconvenience for authors aware of these constraints.

Desktop Recording for Publishers

This section would not be complete without mention of one of the more powerful technological marvels of recent times, the CD recorder. Using special blank discs, you can—from the desktop—create audio CDs or CD-ROMs that can contain any of the information commonly found on commercial discs with the same degree of data integrity and quality. You can use discs mastered in this manner on the desktop either for small-scale distribution of data, or as the masters for large-scale CD-ROM replication. Recordable discs offer considerable flexibility whether your goals are making your quality-assurance program available on CD-ROM to each of the departments in your company, or whether you plan to replicate 5,000 CD-ROMs containing business telephone directories for use at many different international sites.

The medium used for recordable CD applications is actually more durable than commercially replicated CD-ROMs. Instead of the aluminum layer that appears in a commercial CD-ROM, recordable CDs use a layer of gold overlaid by a layer of dye that reacts to the laser beam of the CD recorder. Aluminum-based CD-ROMs are more subject to corrosion, and thus have shorter lifespans than the gold-based recordable CDs.

Recorders are available to master at speeds equivalent to the most common CD-ROM drives: 1×, 2×, and 4×. With a 4× recorder, you can expect to spend about 20 minutes transferring the data to fill the disc. Single-speed recorders might take upwards of an hour to record the same information. Prices on this kind of equipment have been radically lowered over the past few months. At press time, you could purchase a CD recorder with software for $1,500. Projections have been published that lower the cost of recording to under $1,000 by the end of 1995. The CD recorder fulfills a critical corporate need for high-volume data storage and replication, and—despite the greater visibility of multimedia applications for CD-ROM—corporate usage is strongly driving this market at the moment.

A definition of the acceptable recording practices appears in the Orange Book standard, although extensions to this standard continue to develop as some problems with incremental writing are being debated and resolved. Problems that plagued the early recordable

CD equipment have been largely eliminated, but the technology has still not been simplified to the basic consumer level and recording still requires considerable expertise and knowledge of various formats and standards. The more recent generation of mastering software (products such as Corel's CD Creator, Incat Systems Easy CD Pro, and Moniker's Spira) have almost made it as easy as simply copying files to record to CD, but even these approaches can cause problems. Individual manufacturers persist in creating their own interpretations of multisession CD-R writing, which creates incompatibilities during playback on different systems.

If your electronic publishing plans adapt easily to CD-ROM, you will need to add more to your system than simply hooking up the CD recorder. Successful recording requires lots of hard disk space (1GB minimally; 2GB or more ideally), plenty of system throughput (a SCSI-2 adapter helps speeds the data flow), and a bug-free system configuration that can support uninterrupted, error-free data transfer for the 20 or 40 minutes that it takes to create a disk. Recordable CDs are also sometimes called "write-once" discs; if you get it wrong while recording, the disc becomes useless. Most CD recorder packages include a simulation feature to test the efficiency of the recording process before actually activating the laser beam to start burning pits into the disc. While the simulator actually moves the laser read head and goes through the process of transferring the data from hard disk to recorder, no data is actually recorded. Running a simulation of this sort lets you know if your system is properly tuned to create an error-free CD-ROM.

Guidelines for Choosing CD-ROM over Other Media

The selection of CD-ROM as the favored medium for distribution of an electronic publication should be based on several factors ranging from cost to cross-platform compatibility. CD-ROM makes a great deal of sense for low-volume applications, as well as high-volume replication. As an author or developer, you should choose your development applications and file formats early, with an eye toward the ultimate storage medium. If mastering for CD-ROM, certain applications lend themselves well to supporting multiple computer platforms. If your electronic document must be viewable on a UNIX machine, you will want to choose an authoring package other than Macromedia Director, which supports only the Windows and Macintosh framework.

Authoring for CD-ROM also doesn't require that you have an in-house CD recorder. Service bureaus and replication facilities can frequently provide cost-effective solutions even if you only need to create a dozen or so CD-ROMs. You can create your project on the computer and output the source files to any one of the storage media commonly accepted by service bureaus: Exabyte tape, SyQuest cartridges, Bernoulli cartridges, magneto-optical cartridges, or other sources. The service bureau can arrange the files for its replication equipment from your source data as long as you provide a thorough description of the ultimate disc contents and required organization.

> **TIP**
>
> One source of up-to-the-minute information about recordable CD practices and service bureaus is The CD Info Center. Serving as a clearinghouse for information on the subject, this company's Web site links developers with service bureaus, offers tips and guidelines on recordable CD, and includes links to home pages of many of the participants in this growing industry. Visit their Web site at this address:
>
> `http:///www.cd-info.com/cd-info/CDInfoCenter.html`
>
> For actual quotes on replication and additional services, The One-Off CD Shops, located in a growing number of metropolitan areas, offer guidance to anyone contemplating producing a CD-ROM title. The central number for The One-Off CD Shops headquarters is 1-800-340-1OFF (1633). Through CompuServe, you can view material by specifying `GO ONEOFF`.

Many times, however, producing what is called a one-off (single copy) CD lets you do real-world testing to confirm adequate performance of your CD-ROM project. It's more convenient, of course, to be able to create your own one-off on a desktop CD-R drive, but you can still obtain replication service from an outside facility. A one-off CD-ROM can be extremely useful for performance and error testing before beginning large-volume replication.

In what cases will a CD-ROM suit your requirements better than other forms of removable media (or network distribution)? Consider the following guidelines:

- Publishing electronically requires a commitment of time and energy, both to learn the tools and to adapt your source material to the development framework with which you are working. If the information that you intend to distribute does not justify this commitment, you might be better off sticking with the conventional publishing medium: paper. For example, if you're producing a set of twenty installation manuals to help a small group of field engineers install specialized hardware in the field, electronic publishing is very likely overkill, particularly when the engineers might not have access to a convenient playback device in the field. However, if you need to distribute the same installation procedures to hundreds of field engineers in branch offices, none of whom share a common network link and many of whom will be working on equipment onsite in a bench test area, then CD-ROM might fit the application perfectly.

- Is cross-platform compatibility essential to your strategy? If you need an electronic document to be available for users who may be running DOS, UNIX, or Macintosh equipment, CD-ROM provides the best distribution medium because of the widespread acceptance of the ISO-9660 file system.

- Is your electronic document larger than 200MB? If you are dealing with a complex electronic publication or infobase that contains numerous embedded graphics, audio material, and video, CD-ROM may be the only practical way to go. Although some magneto-optical cartridges can handle this quantity of data, the chances of finding a compatible MO drive in the general population is slim. The cost of the physical MO cartridges for the larger capacities is also considerable: from $50 to over $100 for a single cartridge. If you compare this with the cost of a recordable CD disc (about $10), the decision becomes obvious. Network distribution of data in these quantities is also generally impractical unless you have an extremely fast network connection (perhaps a T3 link) and an abundance of physical storage space on your system where you can place the downloaded monstrosity.

■ Is it important for the stored data to last for a number of years? All magnetic media have a gradual decline in the strength of the recorded impulses over time. Even magneto-optical discs rely on phase shifts recorded on a magnetic surface—though an optical laser performs the recording—making them subject to the same decline as other types of magnetic media, such as SyQuest cartridge drives and magnetic tape. You can maybe count on a lifespan of 5 to 15 years with most magnetic media. Recordable CDs last far longer—close to 100 years by some estimates. Commercially replicated CDs don't fare quite as well, however. Lifespan estimates for CD-ROM generally range between 10 to 25 years. Unfortunately, the aluminum layer on which the pits are embedded is subject to corrosion, and the resulting oxide can obliterate data. For long-term storage, however, both recordable CDs and commercial CDs surpass their magnetic brethren for durability and lasting data integrity.

■ Do you need the assurance of a large number of playback units available to your target audience, even if you will create the production with a single platform in mind? Another advantage of CD-ROM-based publications is the large and growing user base; some 80 percent of all shipping business machines are now equipped with CD-ROM drives and a significant percentage of consumer-level computers. Early developers were faced with a limited spectrum of users who actually had the equipment to play back their CD-ROM titles; this situation has improved dramatically to where there are more than 30 million CD-ROM drives installed, with the overall installed base continuing to rise sharply. Many software applications are even now distributed only on CD-ROM, a clear indication that manufacturers see this medium as the common denominator for large-scale data exchange in the future.

■ Can you cope with the marginal performance characteristics of CD-ROM? For all the good aspects of CD-ROMs, they are still not very quick at reading back data and developers rely on a host of performance tricks to keep data moving at a rapid rate, particularly when the production involves real-time responses, like interactive games, or multimedia epics. Electronic publications don't necessarily push the performance boundaries of the medium, but if your electronic work includes data-intensive transfers, you may want to carefully consider the limitations of performance. Copying the working parts of the CD-ROM production (the search engine, player, or custom application) to the hard disk drive can boost performance, but just remember to provide an un-install feature to remove all presence of installed material at the user's option. The zero-footprint approach to CD-ROM installation is one of the recommendations for Windows 95 developers. Clean up after yourself; your audience will appreciate the courtesy.

CD-ROM fits the bill for many different types of electronic publishing. Replication costs are low if you plan to produce thousands of units; the cost can drop as low as $.75 per disc. You can produce lesser quantities, perhaps up to 50 or 60 discs, using a fast CD recorder on your desktop. If you need to create quantities in excess of this, you might want to investigate some of the recorders that operate with a transporter that Kodak produces, allowing 75 or more discs to be sequentially recorded.

Summary

This chapter has presented some of the most important considerations when deciding to release an electronic publication on removable media. If you've detected the case is strongly biased in favor of distributing on CD-ROM or recordable CD, you've correctly interpreted this material. In a large majority of cases, compact discs outshine the competition in areas of cost, compatibility, and compactness.

The next chapter looks more closely at the kinds of material that can appear on CD-ROM (or removable media) and the issues that surround producing different types of specialized material. As you've probably discovered, the progression is leading towards your hands-on involvement in mastering a title for CD-ROM distribution.

What Goes onto CD-ROM (and How)

14

by Lee Purcell

IN THIS CHAPTER

You've just created a multimedia masterpiece, the *Scallion Eater's Gourmand Bible,* complete with animated segments of talking onions and a cartoon chase sequence where a Julia Childs caricature runs through a restaurant followed by the ghosts of all the four-legged creatures she has turned into meals in the last ten years. You borrowed money from your rich Uncle Cato in upstate New York and all of your generous friends who hold down real jobs while you are trying to launch an electronic publishing business. Your multimedia work occupies 376 megabytes of hard disk space, and you rented a CD recorder for the weekend to produce a one-off for test purposes and several demo copies. At this point, can you just slip a blank disc into the recorder and start copying files to the recordable medium?

Not exactly. You're not quite ready to fire up the laser and start burning pits yet. This chapter explains the formatting issues associated with CD-ROM mastering, the physical and logical formatting, and the different kinds of data that can be transferred to compact disc. Some formats are designed specifically to support certain data types.

The Effects of Format and Content

Disc format and media content influence each of the following factors:

- The relative size of the audience capable of playing back your title
- The types of data you can store on the media and the associated CD-ROM standards
- The development tools that best support your production work
- The kinds of viewers, readers, search engines, or playback applications you must supply to your audience before they can access your material

The choice of a disc format determines whether your potential audience will consist of the majority of CD-ROM drive owners on all computer platforms, or a more limited subset (such as Macintosh owners or Sun SPARCstation owners). The most universal CD-ROM format—ISO 9660—supports playback on all platforms, but also enforces some strong restrictions on file conventions and disc organization. Formats such as HFS (for Mactinosh computers) or UFS (for UNIX users) work well in environments where you can predict what the dominant computer will be, but will rule out DOS users. Most CD recording applications offer a choice of disc formats; before you start burning discs, you need to decide which one you want to use.

As discussed in the previous chapter, CD-ROM standards (specified as they are in the color books) have evolved to encompass more and more data types. If you go back to the original Red Book standard—pure audio data—all current CD-ROM drives and players can handle this form of data. With the proper software driver on your computer, you can slip the current Annie Lennox album into your CD-ROM drive and play back the music through headphones, or through a computer sound board connected to your computer's speakers. You can't, however, take the CD-ROM version of Marvin Minsky's book, the *Society of the Mind,* and play it on your audio CD player hooked to your component stereo system. The newer CD-ROM standards are downward compatible with the earlier ones, but the reverse is not true.

If the data on disc consists of photographic images presented in Kodak's Photo CD standard, CD-ROM XA capability is necessary to view the images. If the data consists of full-screen video material compressed in MPEG-1 or MPEG-2 format, you not only need a CD-ROM drive equipped for that standard, but additional decompression hardware installed in your computer. The CD-ROM standards have grown to accommodate new data types; once you decide what kind of data you want to present within a title, the appropriate disc format and development tools will become more clear.

The content of your CD-ROM material will lead you in certain directions as well. Certain types of data or information lend themselves to specific development tools. For example, if you're publishing a large infobase, infobase development kits, such as Folio VIEWS or dataDisc's Quick Search, offer many advantages for organizing and accessing information. If you're producing multimedia-rich content, Asymetrix Multimedia Toolbook or Macromedia Director become the tools of choice. If your primary goal is to present an electronic version of a documentation set without spending an enormous amount of time on the development, the portable document formats produced by Adobe Acrobat or Word Perfect Envoy become natural choices.

Each of these individual applications produces data in a form that also requires some type of reader or playback engine to allow your audience to access the data. Sometimes the reader is free, offered as an incentive by manufacturers to spread acceptance of their tools; other times you must pay a licensing fee to distribute the viewing utility on CD-ROM. Your choice of a development tool for the media content should take into account whatever costs are associated with the playback utility.

Once you've made all of these decisions, and produced your project in a form where it is ready to be transferred to CD-ROM, you need to decide whether it is critical to control the disc geography. Some CD recorder applications—not all—let you determine the placement of individual files on the disc. Files near the center can be more quickly accessed by the laser read mechanism. Playback performance suffers for data placed closer to the outer edges of the disc. If there are portions of the CD-ROM material that need to be played back at higher performance rates (audio/video data, application engines, and so on), use disc geography control to put these files close to the center.

CD-ROM Disc Formats

The data surface and physical formatting of a CD-ROM disc is unlike any other medium. As with hard disk drive data formats, there is a physical component to the disc format (the way the data is actually arranged and recorded on disc) and a logical component (consisting of the file system). Together, these components provide a bridge between the physical contents of the media and the techniques that the computer operating system uses to request and access files and information. To be able to read the information on a CD-ROM, each operating system needs a specific device driver that can interact with the data structure on a compact disc.

For MS-DOS, the appropriate driver is MSCDEX (or an equivalent). Other operating systems rely on other drivers. Newer operating systems, such as Windows 95, include built-in support for the CD-ROM file system. The Windows 95 CDFS (CD File System) is equivalent to MSCDEX running in protected mode.

> **NOTE**
>
> Formatting of a recordable disc is not performed separately from writing the data. You choose the disc format that you want to use while premastering (arranging the data files) and then record both the format information and the data at the same time.

The basic unit of data storage on a disc is the sector, also referred to sometimes as the block. A sector always contains 2,352 bytes, even though each of the CD-ROM standards specifies a somewhat different use of the data within the sector. Red Book, the audio standard, does not require much error detection and correction information mixed in with the data, so most of the data in a Red Book sector is just that: data. The correction codes under Red Book can handle small scratches and data imperfections so that you don't hear annoying pops, snaps, or dropouts when audio is playing back, but the method of error correction used is quite coarse and not suitable for handling computer data.

Yellow Book, the original CD-ROM standard designed for storing computer data requires more rigorous detection of read errors that occur during disc playback; after all, a couple of bits out of place in the program code directed to your computer's processor could crash the system. With more space given over to error detection and correction bytes, less bytes remain for actual data (2,048 bytes of data with the other 304 bytes devoted to catching and fixing read errors). The later CD-ROM standards further subdivide the data area versus the synchronization and error correction areas within the sector. This variance in the number of data bytes versus the number of error correction bytes is necessary to support data types that require more read and write precision (application and program data) and those that require less (audio, video, and photographic data).

> **NOTE**
>
> Technically, a sector contains 3,234 bytes. As originally specified in the Red Book standard, 882 bytes serve as control bytes and for error detection and correction. This applies to Red Book, Yellow Book, Green Book, White Book, and Orange Book. Most premastering/mastering applications and CD recordable references describe sectors as containing 2,352 bytes (ignoring the 882 bytes included for error correction). Some applications, however, include mention of the 882 error-correction bytes in the sector format and list the total as 3,234 bytes. If you run across this value in a reference, it is not a discrepancy—it's just another way, though less commonly used, of describing the sector format.

Although the term *tracks* is used to describe the circular data storage patterns on a hard disk surface, tracks have a different meaning on a compact disc. Data is arranged on a CD-ROM as a spiral originating at the center of the disc. The spiral pattern is subdivided into a number of physical tracks, from 1 to 99, within which audio data or computer data can be positioned. Individual tracks are subdivided further into sectors, which are addressable units used for storing data. Unlike hard disk sector addresses, CD-ROM sectors are addressed by means of minutes, seconds, and blocks. This is referenced in terms of the playback rates of the disc, which reads data at 75 blocks per second. The CD-ROM drive varies its speed when reading data from different radii on this disc; Starting at the inner tracks (close to the center) the CD-ROM rotates at 500 rpm. By the time it has reached the outer tracks, it has slowed to 200 rpm. This method of rotation is referred to as Constant Linear Velocity (CLV), and it explains why CD-ROM drives can access data more quickly from the center of the disc. Because the disc is rotating more quickly, the laser read head can position itself over the requested data and begin retrieving it more quickly.

The *minutes:seconds:blocks* addressing works like this. The number of minutes refers to elapsed time (starting playback at the center of the disc), up to the full 74 minutes of maximum time. As mentioned, this is based on a constant playback rate of 75 blocks per second. The seconds value refers to the number of elapsed seconds within the last minute (up to a maximum of 59). The blocks value is the number of blocks within the last second (up to a maximum of 75). An address of 22:30:10 indicates 22 minutes, 30 seconds, and 10 blocks into the disc. Many multimedia applications let you directly address the contents of a disc by specifying a script command containing the appropriate address. You can use this technique to access audio information when playing back sounds or music from a disc, even if the audio is stored in Red Book format on a mixed mode disc.

How do these disc formats and standards affect you as an electronic publisher? CD recorder applications all require a premastering step, which prepares files for transfer to compact disc. As a part of premastering, you select the disc format that you want to use. As a part of preparing either a virtual or a real image of the files for transfer, each application adds the necessary sync codes, headers, correction codes, and so on, and these get written to disc during recording. Keep in mind that the ROM in CD-ROM stands for *Read-Only Memory*; this is not a medium you can rewrite to correct your mistakes. If you record your multimedia files to Red Book audio format, you won't be able to play them back (but you could probably make your computer speakers howl as they try to interpret the data as music). The CD-ROM color book standards are each optimized for particular data types, as described in the following subsections.

Red Book

The Red Book standard encompasses only audio data. You cannot store computer data on a disc formatted for Red Book. A track on a Red Book disc usually contains a single musical selection, one song on an album or a single, uninterrupted succession of some kind of audio information, perhaps a seven-minute speech or a fifteen-minute sound recording of summertime night sounds from the Maine woods. The digital form in which the sound is recorded is called PCM (Pulse Code Modulation), and it has to undergo a conversion—digital-to-analog conversion or D/A—before it can be turned back into something resembling sound to the human ears.

The sector format for audio information under the Red Book standard is the simplest of all the standards, as shown in Figure 14.1.

FIGURE 14.1.

Red Book sector format with mixed-mode divisions.

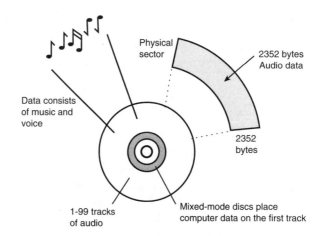

Two layers of error detection and correction codes (not shown in this illustration), each consisting of a 392-byte value, are used to trap readback errors resulting from vibration or damage to the media. Another set of 98 control bytes provides cue information to enable the CD player to locate individual selections, determine the actual running time of a selection, and display a running count of the elapsed time as the selection plays.

Because this book is about electronic publishing, and not about digital recording, you're probably not intending to produce musical CDs (if you are, try Jeff Bowen's book, *Becoming a Computer Musician*, also by Sams Publishing). Red Book becomes more important to the electronic publisher in a variation known as Mixed Mode, which combines the data handling capabilities of Yellow Book with the audio storage of Red Book. Put the two together and you have the simplest way to implement multimedia titles that involve sound as well computer information. The vast majority of the original multimedia titles were formatted as Mixed Mode discs, and this approach is still sometimes used in certain situations to ensure the greatest compatibility with playback equipment.

One example of an electronic publication involving effective use of a Mixed Mode disc could be a biography of a musician. Let's say you have produced an electronic book detailing the life of bottleneck blues guitarist Tampa Red. The first part of the book consists of background material, describing the early life of Hudson Woodbridge, brought up in Tampa, Florida by his grandmother in the early 1900s. He cut his first song, "It's Tight Like That," in the fall of 1928 as Tampa Red, and you have the audio track (and, through some additional magic, licensed rights to use it) ready to place on CD.

A mixed-mode disc contains an initial computer data track followed by a number of subsequent tracks of digital audio. The multimedia application you use to develop your work provides links to the sound using the *minute:second:block* format discussed earlier. In the example of the electronic biography, your interface could include a button labeled with the song title mentioned, "It's Tight Like That." When the viewer clicks the button, the multimedia program skips to the audio segment in the Red Book region of the disc and then back to the program when the song finishes. You could include buttons for additional Tampa Red songs: "Reckless Man Blues" or "Dead Cats on the Line."

This approach works very well for multimedia presentations where the viewer accesses the audio, sits back to listen to it, and then continues on to other interactive parts of the presentation. It doesn't work very well when the audio data needs to be synchronized with video or animation taking place at the same time. Typically, the CD-ROM drive is too slow to jump back and forth between the computer data region on the Mixed Mode disc and the audio data region (see Figure 14.1). This results in synchronization problems—either the sound skips or drops out, or plays at inappropriate times to what is being displayed on-screen. This poor synchronization was the key reason that the CD-ROM XA format was developed, as discussed in a later subsection.

Digital audio contained on a Mixed Mode disc has the advantage that it can be played back through all computers equipped with a CD-ROM drive, whether playback is through headphones or external speakers. This is not the case for some of the other CD-ROM formats, which may require particular features built into an installed sound card in order to access the audio data. As long as you do not have a lot of simultaneous events taking place in your multimedia work, the Mixed Mode disc can provide reliable, high-quality intermixing of sound and data.

A disadvantage of the Mixed Mode approach is the fact that storing audio information in Red Book format takes an enormous amount of disc space, perhaps too much to be justified in some kinds of multimedia where you just want sound effects or background music. Red Book audio requires more than 10MB of storage space for each minute of sound. Compressed sound storage formats were devised to be used with multimedia, and these commonly apply to CD-ROM XA applications (but require a sound card with ADPCM capabilities for playback).

Maybe as a developer you've decided to create an online historical book that combines numerous shorter histories of local regions in New England. Besides the electronic pages displayed (perhaps in Adobe Acrobat format), you would also like to include full audio narration for any of the individual histories at the click of a button. If you try to produce a Mixed Mode disc, you're limited to 74 minutes of maximum recording time minus whatever part of the disc is taken up by the Adobe Acrobat computer data files. If you have several hundred pages requiring audio narration, Mixed Mode probably doesn't allow sufficient storage space to meet your goal. This is where the compressed sound formats provided through CD-ROM XA (discussed in a later subsection) could allow you to record several hours worth of audio narration to accompany your electronic books. Being able to include lengthy audio sequences in this manner opens up many interesting possibilities, such as the ability to create multilingual tourist guides that can provide narration in French, Spanish, or Swedish, as selected by the viewer.

Many of the CD recorder applications use a tool known as the Cue Sheet to prepare digital material for inclusion in a Mixed Mode disc. The Cue Sheet gives you the ability to sequence tracks in a particular order, a factor that can be important if you are referencing individual tracks from your multimedia application. Audio files that are to be included in the Red Book region of the disc must be sampled at the standard audio rate of 44.1KHz. If you have WAV files or AIFF files that have been recorded at different sampling rates, there are a number of utilities that can convert these files to the format necessary for use in a digital audio framework.

Data in Yellow Book Format

The Yellow Book standard arose out of the realization that compact discs could be used for more than audio playback. The digital storage capabilities of the compact disc—as well as the techniques used to create the discs—were well adapted to data storage. The only thing lacking was an error correction and detection scheme elaborate enough to catch and recover errors in computer data at a much higher rate than required for audio data. With this incentive, Sony and Philips took the existing physical specifications for audio CD and adapted them for data storage. The result was the Yellow Book standard, which features two different modes. Mode 1 is used for computer data; Mode 2 can be used for audio and video data, but this format has not been applied to any real-world applications. Figure 14.2 shows the sector layout used for Yellow Book.

FIGURE 14.2.

The Yellow Book sector layout.

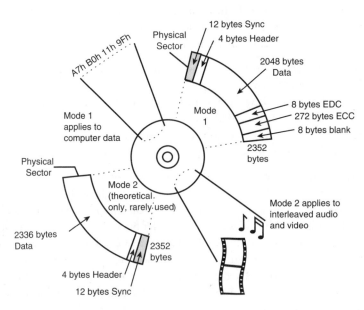

The 12 bytes of synchronization data (starting with a binary zero followed by a string of ones and terminated by a zero) let the CD-ROM drive precisely adjust rotation speed for data reading. Both Mode 1 and Mode 2 include these bytes. The additional four-byte header at the beginning of the physical sector contains the sector address in *minute:second:block* format. This provides for a crucial element of data storage—individual block addressability (something that was not possible given the sector approach used under Red Book). Simply put, the header address allows the computer to locate any data on the disc by means of a unique sector address. A byte also appears in the header to identify whether the sector appears in a Mode 1 or Mode 2 track.

Error detection and correction for Mode 1 is enhanced by the addition of 288 EDC/ECC bytes at the end of the sector. As with Red Book, Yellow Book sectors also include an additional 882 EDC/ECC and control bytes at the very end of the sector, a feature which is often undocumented in descriptions of CD-ROM sector layouts. Mode 2, which is designed for storage of less critical forms of information, such as audio and video, doesn't require the additional error correction information, although it also has the 882 EDC/ECC and control bytes as specified in Red Book. By the time all the sync, header, and correction bytes are tallied, Mode 1 leaves only 2048 bytes remaining for data storage. Mode 2 fares better with 2336 bytes, but as mentioned, Mode 2 exists only as a theoretical foundation for two other closely related standards that were to evolve from it: CD-I and CD-ROM XA.

If your development efforts consist of electronic books, references, infobases, and similar information-heavy material, you can transfer your files to discs formatted under Yellow Book, usually just called CD-ROM format. The files stored in this manner can include anything that can be read on the target computer platform, including sound files, video files, animation files, and so on. Depending on the configuration of the computer system and the speed of the CD-ROM drive on which playback takes place, performance may suffer for complex multimedia presentations. Yellow Book is best suited for judicious use of multimedia components; it can work effectively as long as the accessed sound or video files aren't too large and can be retrieved fairly quickly (it helps to position them near the center of the disc). Synchronization of audio and data is not a strong suit of Yellow Book either. Yellow Book makes sense for modest multimedia use only. However, for electronic publishing, this may be the format that you make the most use of.

For example, if you created an interactive guide to the San Diego Zoo, the CD-ROM could contain short sound files of the vocalizations of the animals and short video clips from different locations throughout the zoo. These could be effectively stored and played back from a standard Yellow Book CD-ROM (rather than a mixed-mode disc). Sound files stored in computer data formats, of course, require the equivalent to a sound card in the computer used for playback. If you want to broaden your audience to users who may not have a sound card (or equivalent), you can store the audio data on individual tracks in the Red Book region of a mixed-mode disc.

CD-ROM XA

The XA in CD-ROM XA stands for extended architecture; in this case, the extension consists of two additional track types referred to as CD-ROM Mode 2, Form 1 and CD-ROM Mode 2, Form 2, as shown in Figure 14.3.

FIGURE 14.3.

CD-ROM XA sector formats.

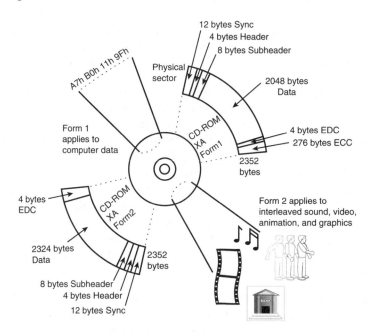

Form 1 of Mode 2 stores computer data, a fact that is duly recorded in the eight-byte Subheader at the beginning of the sector. The 12 bytes of Sync information and four bytes of Header information originally defined in Yellow book also appear at the beginning of the sector. Form 2 also features an eight-byte Subheader that indicates that the information contained in the sector consists of video, graphics, animation, or compressed audio. Because each of these sector forms can be identified by the subheader identification, they can be *interleaved* on the same track of a CD-ROM. Interleaved data can be accessed much more quickly than if the CD-ROM drive's laser read head has to seek radially between tracks to retrieve data.

The faster data access times permit improved synchronization of computer data and animated segments or video playback. For example, if you create an animated character whose lips move as the lines in a separate audio file are played back, you will have a difficult time syncing the lips with the words unless you use interleaving.

The drawback of CD-ROM XA is that it requires specialized hardware in the CD-ROM drive to separate the audio and data streams. The audio information, stored in a compressed format called Adaptive Delta Pulse Code Modulation (ADPCM), must be decompressed, and this requires a sound card installed in the playback computer with the proper built-in features. The necessity of having these two hardware features, one in the CD-ROM drive and the other in the sound-processing hardware of the computer, may limit your potential audience. However, if your multimedia projects require careful synchronization of elements, this format may be your only viable option.

> **NOTE**
>
> The Interactive Multimedia Association offers a version of ADPCM compression software that ensures compatibility and native support for Microsoft Video for Windows and Apple QuickTime 2.0. Given that many different versions of ADPCM exist, creating a multitude of compatibility problems, IMA ADPCM is a step towards establishing a common platform for ADPCM playback. The Interactive Multimedia Association can be reached by calling (410) 626-1380 or through their Web site at `http://www.ima.org`.

The use of compressed audio as a part of CD-ROM XA formatting presents some interesting possibilities to an electronic publisher. Electronic books are often accompanied by narrative, sometimes read in the manner of radio dramas from years past with each character being read by a different person, sometimes read by a single person as someone might tell a story. At the greatest level of compression, a CD-ROM XA disc can contain 20 hours of monaural narration with a quality that is roughly equivalent to AM radio. Imagine this medium as a computer-based substitute for the popular cassette-based audio books, and you have the potential for an entirely new product. Because the books on CD-ROM can also contain visual information, you could include biographical details about the author with photos, interviews with people associated with a book or the actual author, photographs from the time or place described in the book. All of which can be done on a medium that weighs about half-an-ounce, can be shipped for the cost of a first-class stamp, and can contain hours of audio along with tens of thousands of pages of text. Most CD-ROM drives being sold today feature XA-compatibility so the audience restrictions for using this format will diminish in time. As a high-power communication tool, the CD-ROM has potential uses that are only now being realized.

Another offshoot of the Yellow Book Mode 2 sector format was CD-I, also known as Green Book. Green Book defines a proprietary format designed by Sony and Philips that is targeted towards set-top playback units. Although it follows many of the conventions of CD-ROM XA,

CD-I specifies a unique file system—similar to ISO 9660 but with some of its own characteristics. You need to obtain a license to produce CD-I discs because this format is legally owned by Sony and Philips.

Orange Book

Orange Book defines the specifications that apply to writing to two forms of media: CD-MO (Compact Disc Magneto-Optical) and CD-WO (Compact Disc Write-Once). CD-WO includes recordable CD drives (as well as an earlier predecessor, the WORM drive, which stands for Write-Once Read-Many). A large part of this standard addresses those issues that make it possible for a CD-ROM mastered with a desktop CD recorder to be playable on CD-ROM drives everywhere. The effectiveness of this standard has led to the growth, popularity, and compatibility of CD-R systems with mainstream playback devices.

As an electronic publisher, you don't need to be intimately familiar with the contents of the Orange Book standard. Much of it consists of details that the manufacturers of CD recorders followed when designing their equipment. You'll see it referred to from time to time and when you do, now you'll know what it means.

White Book

Electronic books on CD-ROM with full audio narration is an exciting concept, but what about full-screen full-motion video? Clumsy, heavy video cassettes for movie distribution would disappear almost overnight—at least, so the theory goes. The problem has been that the laggard performance of CD-ROM drives made it difficult to play back video material fast enough at high enough quality to satisfy consumer demands. White Book addresses this problem by specifying a technique by which video information, compressed using a standard known as MPEG, can be embedded on a CD-ROM XA format disc. MPEG-1 has been superseded by MPEG-2, but even the original version of MPEG does a pretty effective job of delivering high quality video at thirty frames per second. The catch, in this case, is once again additional hardware is required for playback. MPEG-compatible playback boards are currently available, and an increasing number of movies and other features are appearing on disc in this format, but the standard has been slow to catch on in this country. Europe and Japan have embraced the format more readily, and some industry analysts feel that MPEG-1 has some utility and mileage left in it. For more information on MPEG standards, see Chapter 11, "Using Multimedia."

Currently in the United States, however, opposing factions are feuding over two competing standards for delivering larger amounts of data on compact disc; one of the goals is to provide sufficient capacity to support the distribution of feature films on CD-ROM. Sony and Philips on one side are presenting a double-layered CD-ROM format, while another camp led by Time-Warner is trying to introduce a double-sided CD-ROM.

To an electronic publisher, the setup expense to produce a title in MPEG format is much more significant than to produce other types of electronic books or multimedia works. MPEG workstations generally cost tens of thousands of dollars and require a higher level of expertise than other typical authoring tools. This is a fascinating technology with a good deal of promise, but perhaps one better left to the movie industry until the cost of development tools comes down and agreement on a prevailing standard is reached.

Deciding on a File System

The physical format of a disc determines how data is arranged upon the spiral tracks of the media, but it provides no clue as to where a particular file is located or how many directories are on the disc. To be able to rapidly locate data, a logical format is needed to present the necessary information in a form that can be easily used by the operating system. When the Yellow Book standard was first introduced, it was a file system free-for-all. Because there was no prevailing standard, every developer basically constructed their own file system. In the interests of encouraging widespread compatibility of CD-ROMs, industry representatives convened at a picturesque locale near Lake Tahoe in the mountains of California and drew up the standard that was to become ISO 9660, a file system designed expressly for CD-ROM. The beauty of ISO 9660 is that it permits any operating system with the necessary driver software to access the file contents of a disc.

During premastering and mastering of a CD-ROM, as a developer or electronic publisher, you must select from a variety of available file systems before you start "cutting" the disc. The CD recorder application then determines the appropriate volume descriptor and file system information to place on disc to prepare it for use by the selected operating system. In some cases, you may want to use a native file system, particularly if the users of the CD-ROM will all be using computers of a single type. For example, Macintosh users who feel comfortable with the folder and file approach used by the Mac OS usually don't appreciate having to deal with the shortened file names and directory structure of ISO 9660. The following subsections detail some of the pros and cons of the different file systems.

> **NOTE**
>
> If support for a native file system is an important consideration in your electronic publishing plans, check carefully before you purchase a CD recorder application to ensure the required support is available. Although many applications of this sort support the Macintosh file system (HFS) in native form, full support for the UNIX file system (UFS) is more rare.

ISO 9660

If your goal as an electronic publisher is to reach everyone with an installed CD-ROM drive, ISO 9660 is the file system of choice. ISO 9660 specifies a universal structure of filenames and directory organization so that files placed on a CD-ROM using this file system will be available to DOS, Windows, Macintosh, OS/2, and UNIX computer users.

Two additional requirements must be met if CD-ROMs are to be read by a particular type of computer:

- You need to provide an "engine" or reader of some kind specific to the processor of each target computer to provide access to files stored in the common area of the CD-ROM. For example, if the common files are in Acrobat format and they need to be available to Macintosh and Windows users, you need to provide a Mac and Windows version of the Acrobat reader.

- The operating system on the machine accessing the CD-ROM must have the necessary driver software installed to read the ISO 9660 file structure. On the Macintosh, this requires Apple Extensions. Under MS-DOS, MSCDEX is the necessary driver. These drivers make access to files on CD-ROM relatively transparent—files appear much as they do on floppy disk or hard disk drive.

The following diagram, Figure 14.4, shows how a common set of data files, `datafil1` and `datafil2`, can be placed on CD-ROM and then accessed from independent DOS, Macintosh, and UNIX applications also provided on the CD-ROM. Though the data files can be accessed from each of the three platforms, each computer requires a platform-specific application to access the data files.

> **NOTE**
>
> Readers and viewers take up varying amounts of compact disc real estate, ranging from about 500KB to 10MB. Macromedia Director, one of the most popular cross-platform development tools used for CD-ROM titles, uses a technique that stores an interactive movie in a "projector" file, that is, a self-contained playback engine that can link to other Macromedia movies. The size of the projector file varies depending on how you construct your interface to the multimedia material, but a typical projector file might be somewhere between 1.5MB and 5MB. To access a shared group of Macromedia files on a CD-ROM from both a Macintosh and a Windows machine, you would need to create a projector file under the Macintosh version of Director and another projector file under Windows. The projectors could then link to the shared files stored in a common directory.

FIGURE 14.4.

Developing cross-platform infobases using the ISO 9660 file system. Diagram courtesy of Optical Media, a wholly owned subsidiary of Microtest, Inc.

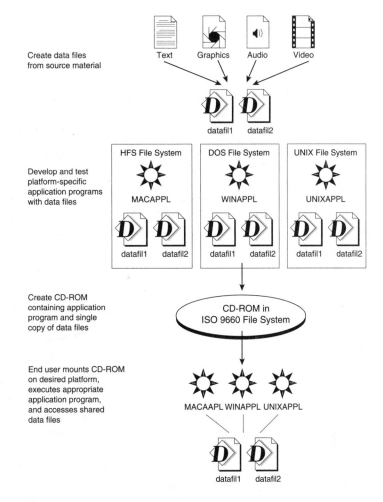

Diagram courtesy of Optical Media International.

Native File Systems

The situation is much simpler if your goal is to create a file system for use on a single computer platform, such as UNIX or the Macintosh. The CD-ROM can contain the conventional file structure used by the selected computer platform, as shown in Figure 14.5.

320

FIGURE 14.5.

Developing a native file system. Diagram courtesy of Optical Media, a wholly owned subsidiary of Microtest, Inc.

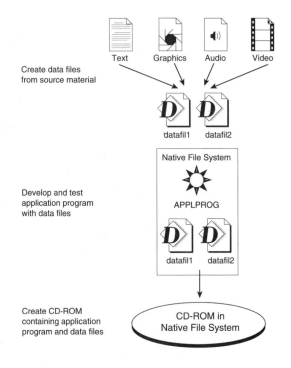

Create data files from source material

Develop and test application program with data files

Create CD-ROM containing application program and data files

Diagram courtesy of Optical Media International.

The use of native file systems on commercial CD-ROM titles is becoming much less common, however, because the advantages of cross-platform distribution are a significant incentive for developers and publishers to use ISO 9660 as the file system of choice. However, some major CD-ROM title producers, such as Voyager, still release Macintosh-only CD-ROM titles initially and then follow up with a platform-independent or Windows version of the same title.

ISO 9660 Restrictions

When you are organizing files under ISO 9660, you must contend with the following restrictions:

- The characters used as a part of filenames are limited to uppercase A through Z, numerals 0 through 9, the period (.), the semi-colon (;) when used as a separator, and the underline character (_).
- The depth of nested subdirectories cannot exceed eight levels deep.
- You cannot apply extensions to subdirectory names.

As you are using a CD recorder application that creates ISO 9660 structures, in most cases the program will dynamically rename files (usually prompting you first), if they don't meet the restrictions.

> **CAUTION**
>
> This automatic renaming of files could create problems if you have authored an electronic book or an infobase that relies on links to particular filenames. If the files are renamed during a conversion to ISO 9660 standards, the links will be broken. Plan for this by creating filenames and links that comply with ISO 9660 when you are authoring your electronic publication.

ISO 9660 employs a path table as a high-speed index to the file structure. The path table contains the address of each of the subdirectories located within the directory tree. This eliminates multiple seeks when data is being located, something that is essential when dealing with a slow performance storage medium such as CD-ROM.

For the large majority of applications, ISO 9660 will serve your purposes as an electronic publisher. At the very least, it can help you organize your electronic documents in a form that will make them widely available to everyone with a CD-ROM drive connected to their computer.

Hybrid Discs

ISO 9660 forces Macintosh users to give up many aspects of their operating environment that diminish its usefulness. ISO directories don't keep track of the creator application for Mac files, so you can't double-click an icon to launch the application. The icon itself loses its graphic identity. Long file and folder names are truncated to cryptic short forms, and deep nesting of folders is made impossible. With all of these restrictions, it's clear that most Mac users won't embrace ISO 9660 with enthusiasm.

One solution is to create a hybrid disc that contains characteristics of both ISO 9660 and Macintosh attributes as well. A disc created in this manner contains both the Mac's native HFS structure and the ISO 9660 directories. Some CD recorder applications handle hybrids by creating two separate data regions on the disc, which reduces the potential storage by half, because many files must be duplicated. Other approaches to hybrid discs can create a shared data region to work in combination with the two separate file systems. To do this, the disc also must contain additional data besides the shared data to support file system access by the individual platforms. One program that supports this approach is QuickTOPiX by Optical Media International.

The result is a disc that allows Mac users to view their files and folders in a manner identical to their normal operating environment. DOS and UNIX users see only the ISO 9660 portion of the disc, so this form of hybrid provides relatively transparent views to both platforms and eliminates the necessity of producing separate format discs to support the strengths of each platform.

UNIX users may also feel deprived by the restrictions of ISO 9660. A set of additions to ISO 9660, known as the Rock Ridge extensions, returns many of the file system features familiar to UNIX users to them. Mastering discs to include the Rock Ridge extensions is supported by some, though not all, of the mastering applications.

Virtual and Real Images

Once you've selected a disc format and file system, most CD recorder applications offer two choices for organizing the files in preparation to actually writing them to the recordable media. You can create a virtual image or a real image. A virtual image is similar to a set of pointers that indicates the files to be written to disc and their relative order. The recorder application supplies the headers, sync bytes, and error correction codes while the recording is taking place, or "on-the-fly" as this process is generally called. The file representing a virtual image is fairly compact, even if the actual files occupy hundreds of megabytes. Recording on-the-fly from a virtual image takes a little more time because files must be retrieved and transferred from scattered locations about the hard disk. Even if you defragment your hard disk drive before beginning (which is always recommended), retrieving files from a virtual image takes a little longer, and maintaining a consistent flow of data is crucial to successful CD recording.

A real image is a byte-for-byte representation of the data ready to be written to disc with all of the fields in place and all files in sequence. The recorder application only needs to direct the stream of data to the disc during recording. A real image occupies as much space as the actual final contents of the CD-ROM—if you're creating a CD-ROM with 400MB of content, the real image will occupy 400MB. A real image requires more storage space, but the data can be transferred more quickly because the processor doesn't need to do as much work to locate and move the files.

Once a recording is begun, the data must continue streaming to the CD recorder without interruption until the transfers have been completed. Otherwise, the medium can be ruined. For single speed recording, the transfer rate needs to be approximately 150KB per second (slightly faster for pure audio discs); because most hard disks can easily achieve average transfer rates of 1000KB per second or more, it doesn't seem like there would be a problem maintaining the flow of data, but many factors in a computer system can slow or interrupt the movement of data. If you have a fast hard disk drive with an average access time of 12 milliseconds or less and a fast hard disk recorder, you can probably record from a virtual image without problems. If your system is older and slower, a real image may be necessary to ensure a sufficient flow of data.

Almost all of the major CD recorder applications offer a test mode of operation where you can simulate the recording of the disc, actually transferring data and moving the laser read head of the recorder, without actually activating the laser. This allows you to see if your system can handle the recording at sufficient speeds to avoid ruining the disc. Most CD recorders include an internal buffer, ranging in size from 256KB to 2MB or more, that stores data en route to the recorder. The buffer supplies data when the transfer from hard disk is slowed or interrupted.

However, if the buffer runs out of data during recording, the medium is usually rendered useless. You generally can't go back and correct mistakes made during recording, but ruined discs make nice shiny coasters (though expensive). Chapter 15, "Hardware and Software Tools for CD-ROM Development," discusses recording options in more detail.

Publishing Within the Different Formats

To summarize the utility of the various physical and logical disc formats available to electronic publishers, consider the following guidelines:

- **Red Book:** As an audio data storage format, this standard makes the most sense to electronic publishers in mixed-mode applications where music or voice in the Red Book region is accessed through a multimedia application. Evolving formats, such as CD Plus, support the addition of electronic liner notes and biographical information to a music CD without risking squeals from playback devices when computer data is accidentally played back. Mixed-mode discs containing Red Book data could be used for: electronic books about musical instruments or musicians; history works that contain samples of speeches from famous figures; nature books that contain lengthy samples of whale songs or bird calls; children's books that contain extensive music selections.

- **Yellow Book:** As the mainstream storage format for computer data, Yellow Book can be used for almost everything that can be stored on disc. Performance limitations, however, prevent effective use of intensive multimedia playback of synchronized video or animation. Possible uses of Yellow Book include: infobases containing technical support data; encyclopedias with moderate multimedia content; phone number directories for residences or businesses; training applications that include short video clips and simple sound; company data to be distributed between different geographic sites; most types of electronic books. For the broadest compatibility with the full audience of CD-ROM drive owners, Yellow Book surpasses the other data storage formats.

- **CD-ROM XA:** This extended architecture offers compressed audio and interleaved video, sound, and data, making it ideal for intensive multimedia uses. The compressed audio feature supports extended narrative recording (up to 20 hours). Possible uses of CD-ROM XA discs include: narrated books on disc with accompanying text and supporting material; multimedia training materials with animated descriptions of procedures and extensive video; real-time simulators that teach driving, flying, or hurtling down a ramp on a luge; educational games that contain synchronized animation with voice-over commentary; electronic books with heavy multimedia content. When distributing CD-ROM XA format discs, however, you face a more limited audience: those with the required CD-ROM drive and sound card hardware that can read CD-ROM XA formats.

- **ISO 9660:** This logical file system allows the contents of CD-ROMs to be distributed to users on multiple computer platforms. Use of ISO 9660 is recommended for all applications where it is important to reach a wide audience of computer users.

■ **Hybrid Disc Formats:** These kinds of formats combine the universality of ISO 9660 with the preferred characteristics of native file systems, such as the Macintosh or UNIX.

■ **Native File Systems:** Discs created in native file formats will present the most familiar operating environment to users of particular computer platforms. This is recommended for situations where the target audience can be accurately determined, and where the native file system will be comfortable to users. For example, if you're creating a training package for a particular application, presenting that application in its native environment is very important.

Transparent Data Transfers

Although CD-ROM discs provide an economical and effective means for storing and distributing data, this chapter may have convinced you that the complex standards and disc formatting issues make this form of media far too difficult for the average computer user. If someone had to give this much thought to format issues when copying a few files to disk, no copies would ever be made. Clearly, it would solve a lot of problems if the CD recorder could just be connected to your computer like a hard disk drive and you could drag and drop files to it whenever necessary.

Fortunately, many of the more recent CD recorder applications—such as Corel's CD Creator and Moniker's Spira—have taken this route to eliminate confusion when using the medium. If playback performance and cross-platform support are not your highest priorities, you can easily distribute electronic publications on disc by just copying them to a CD recorder through one of these applications. This approach could be useful for making electronic documents available on a local area network. For example, you could copy the necessary files to a recordable disc and then place this disc on a CD-ROM drive connected to a network-accessible workstation or (for better performance) on a drive connected to a network-ready CD server. Network users could access and use your electronic documents by downloading them, or accessing portions of them when made available in a client-server environment, such as is supported by Lotus Notes. The point is this: You can effectively use CD-ROMs as the basis for electronic document distribution even if you don't want to go through the effort of learning the intricacies of the different formats and standards. If those workgroup members that you want to share documents with all use PCs, the quickest and most direct way to get large files to them could be by just copying those files to disc through an application that lets you do this.

Summary

This chapter has given you some perspective for understanding the use of the application tools discussed in the next chapter. Chapter 15 discusses both development tools that are useful for creating a CD-ROM title, and the programs that actually allow you to premaster and master discs. With the right tools and hardware, you can create CD-ROM titles from the desktop—this could be the greatest boon to electronic publishers since the invention of the floppy disk.

Hardware and Software Tools for CD-ROM Development

15

by Lee Purcell

IN THIS CHAPTER

The electronic printshop of the future does not come without a price tag. Fortunately, the price of admission is modest if you don't mind making some concessions to convenience. If you don't want to purchase a CD recorder immediately, you can still effectively submit the files for your CD-ROM title (on disk cartridge or tape) to a replication service so they can produce either a CD-ROM one-off or multiple discs. Even if you decide to set up a full CD recording station, the expense would be less than what it would have cost to construct a desktop publishing system back when PostScript laser printers were selling for $3,000 plus.

To get started on a shoestring you need nothing more than one of the premastering/mastering applications and some type of portable storage medium large enough to transfer files to a one-off CD service or a replicator. Premastering, you may remember, is the creation of a physical or virtual image of the contents of a CD-ROM. You can prepare an entire CD-ROM project, premaster the files to an image format, simulate playback for test purposes, and do 99 percent of your debugging without ever firing a laser at a disc. If you're working on a limited budget, you may want to complete a CD-ROM title or two before investing in the hardware equipment to record your own.

> **NOTE**
>
> The terms *premastering* and *mastering* have been used in a variety of ways by those in the industry. Premastering most accurately refers to the preparation of digital data for transfer to compact disc, including the steps required to specify the file and directory structure (for instance, if you're creating an ISO 9660 disc). If you're working with a desktop CD recorder, mastering generally refers to the physical act of writing the data to the recordable CD. If you're talking about a replication service, mastering applies to the operations involved in creating a glass master, which contains the CD-ROM data image in preparation for transferring this image to a series of stampers. Stampers are metal molds that carry the impressions of the pits and lands.

Acquiring a CD recorder of your own doesn't have to drag your budget into the dumpster. Current double-speed models range in price from $1,500 to $2,500 and include most of the features that you need to create CD-ROMs in the majority of formats. Most hardware packages come bundled with a premastering/mastering application, a blank disc or two, a SCSI cable, a SCSI terminator (usually passive), and some kind of instructions. Setup can be a bit more difficult than other hardware peripherals due to the demanding nature of recordable CD technology and the necessity of maintaining consistent data throughput at all costs. If you have any experience setting up hardware for PCs, the total setup time could range from a couple of hours to a day or two if you get into troubleshooting configuration problems.

This chapter describes the tools—both hardware and software—that you need to start mastering your own discs. Keep in mind that the suggested prices correspond with the publication date of this book, and if current trends continue, prices should become significantly lower for most items.

Starting Out on a Shoestring

What do you need at a very bare minimum to begin producing CD-ROM titles? Let's take a look at the simplest scenario and assume that you want to publish electronic books in one of the portable document formats without a lot of multimedia bells and whistles. We'll also assume that you have some kind of word-processing program; anything that will print to a Windows printer will do. The entry costs at this level are surprisingly inexpensive. One possible setup would include these items:

- **Common Ground for Windows version 2.0:** With a list price of $189 and a street price $30 or $40 less, Common Ground lets you create platform-independent portable documents that can be read with their free MiniViewer. The portable files are compact, font appearances can be captured without requiring that the actual font be embedded, and most of the common portable document features are supported. You can create a self-contained executable file that allows someone to read your electronic book without a viewer.

- **CDR Publisher 2.0:** If you don't have your own CD recorder, you need an application that can support external storage devices so that you can deliver a CD image to a replication facility. CDR Publisher 2.0, by Creative Digital Research, can output to two of the most common media used by replication services: 8mm Exabyte tape and 4mm Digital Audio Tape (DAT). Depending on the capacities, tape cartridges range in price from $8 to around $22 apiece. CDR Publisher also supports the creation of ISO images, which can simplify the replication process. For a list price of $495, it's not the most inexpensive premastering/mastering application, but it provides essential features that can help you ensure delivery of a premastered set of files for producing a trouble-free one-off. If you later decide to invest in a CD recorder, this software can be used with it as well.

- **Total Cost:** (full retail price for Common Ground and CD-R Publisher): $684.

Paying for One-Offs

If you've taken the shoestring route, you'll find that despite the low entry price, ongoing costs can escalate quickly if you have to make many trips to a replication service. Prices are all over the place since this is such a new market and small replication services are charging whatever they can get away with, in many cases. Costs to produce a one-off can range from around $90 to $300 or more, depending on whether you deliver a physical image file to the replicator or more work is required to prepare the files for transfer to disc. At these rates, you can see it doesn't take too many trips (or overnight FEDEX shipments) to justify the expense of a $1,500 CD recorder.

Starting Out with a Slightly Longer Shoestring

If you can afford a CD recorder, you'll save a lot of trips to the replication service, and the savings in replication costs might even pay for the unit in the first year. By choosing a less-expensive mastering application, you save some of the cost difference between this approach and the previous one. The following items get you started with your own CD-R and software:

- **Sony CDU920S/921S:** The new recording unit from Sony features third-generation performance, and it is widely supported by applications from other vendors. Sony provides a direct order line to obtain the internal or external versions of this drive; you can also purchase it in packages from other vendors. Prices have fluctuated recently on this unit—originally available for $1,499, it has risen to $1,675 due to international currency changes. With good fortune, it may have dropped again by the time you read this.

- **Corel CD Creator:** CD Creator provides a reasonable balance between full-featured premastering/mastering applications and simplicity of use. With a retail price of $249, CD Creator lets you create audio discs, CD-ROM Mixed Mode, CD-ROM XA, ISO 9660, and Photo CD. A utility included with the application handles Photo CD mastering in simple fashion. You can't do everything with CD Creator, but it should keep you out of trouble while you learn how to successfully master compact discs.

- **Total Cost:** (full retail for recorder and software): $1,924.

Selecting CD Recorder Hardware

The original first-generation versions of CD recorders were awesome in their primitive splendor. They were large, sized something like big, clunky, industrial-grade toaster ovens. They were expensive, with price tags rivaling products from the Bavarian Motor Works. They were sluggish and unreliable. No one had any inclination from these beginnings that this was a product that could become successful in the mainstream business and consumer marketplace.

We've now reached the third generation of recorders with vast improvements in all areas. Even the high-performance units, like Yamaha's internal quad-speed recorder, can fit in a typical 5 $1/4$-inch drive bay, and they consume no more power than a conventional hard-disk drive. Prices for entry level recorders are hovering between $1,500 to $2,000, with ongoing rumors of sub-$1,000 recorders being introduced any day now. Improvements in drive capabilities coupled with better software have reduced many of the problems associated with recording, including improved multisession recording, which allows discs to be recorded incrementally in several individual sessions (rather than being fully recorded at one time). In some configurations, CD recorders can be set up under a drive letter and written to in the same manner as you would write to a hard-disk drive.

On the negative side of the ledger, the present state of CD recording requires computer systems that have been carefully tuned to optimize throughput on the SCSI bus. Although internal buffers in CD recorders and software buffers associated with recorder applications have grown in size and effectiveness, some awareness of data transfer issues is essential for successful CD recording. Although software applications for handling CD recording have removed some of the concerns about various CD-ROM standards and formatting issues, you still need a basic grounding in the fundamentals and evolution of the standards to accomplish the creation of any kind of discs other than the simplest.

This section offers some insight as to the most desirable features to look for when you're shopping for a CD recorder. It also provides descriptions of several current CD recorders suitable for use in home or professional applications.

Certifying Your Host Computer

CD recorders are not stand-alone devices; they require a host computer. Although some audio CD recording units operate as stand-alone units, primarily designed for musicians interested in producing pristine demo CDs, in most cases you'll need a fairly recent model PC equipped with a SCSI host adapter. Some configurations work better than others. Consider the following questions to determine if your existing computer measures up:

■ **Do you meet the minimum hardware requirements?** To answer this question, you also need to look at the software you plan to use. Some recorder applications can operate efficiently with less powerful computers; some require heavier iron. For single-speed recording, on the PC side you can probably get by with a 25MHz 386 processor with 8MB of memory. Single-speed recording on a Macintosh can probably be handled by a 25MHz 68030 machine with 8MB of memory. Keep in mind, however, that different software applications may have their own requirements—double-speed, quad-speed, and six-speed recording requires progressively higher performance machines. On the Macintosh side, aim for a Centris, Quadra, or Power Macintosh. For PC multi-speed recorder connections, a 33MHz 486DX computer serves as a minimal platform. More memory and faster processors will simplify high-end configurations.

On PCs, you'll need to add a SCSI host adapter if your system doesn't already have one. Even if you have one, some software applications recommend attaching your recorder to a dedicated host adapter (not the same one as your hard-disk drive). Elektroson's GEAR user manual recommends a second host adapter, as does OptiImage's CD-It!All. Incat System's Easy CD-Pro user manual states that a second host adapter offers no advantages. Macintosh equipment, of course, has the SCSI interface built in.

■ **Is a special hard-disk drive required for mastering?** To reduce your risk of interrupting data throughput during recording, choose a hard-disk drive in the AV class. AV drives, originally designed for work in digital audio and video recording, are optimized for receiving long streams of data at one time—such as a 12-minute sequence of video frames. These drives defer thermal calibration cycles (which can briefly interrupt data flow and ruin a CD recording) until data transfers have ceased. Other non-AV drives, such as some of those manufactured by Conner, use separate control surfaces for calibration and can be used successfully for CD recording. With a large internal buffer in your CD recorder (1MB or above) and a fast system, you may be able to record successfully with a non-AV drive; you just run a higher risk of having an aborted session. In most cases, an aborted session results in ruined media; you can't rewrite the disc, but you can make a coaster out of it.

For manipulating files for CD recording, you also need a hard-disk drive with a capacity greater than 1GB. You can get by with less, especially if you recording entirely from virtual images (which consist of databases that link to files to be recorded on-the-fly). If you record from physical images, however, (which consist of bit-by-bit replicas of the data to be written to the CD—up to 650MB in size), you'll probably be more comfortable with a 2GB or larger drive. If you're doing multimedia development for transfer to CD-ROM, you may even want to shoot for a 4GB disk to handle the kinds of large video, audio, and graphics files that are a significant part of multimedia.

For best results, the hard-disk drive should have an average data access time of less than 12ms. Some software applications state that 19ms access rates are sufficient, but the majority lean more toward the sub-12ms performance region. Almost all modern hard-disk drives can accomplish this rate. If your drive is more than a year old, you may want to investigate the costs of updating to a model that is somewhat faster to improve recording.

■ **Is a SCSI-II adapter necessary?** CD recorders accept data at rates far below what the SCSI bus is capable of delivering. SCSI-1 busses can transfer data at 5MB per second; the fastest 6× recorders can only accept data at around 900KB per second. The recorder, not the bus, represents the data transfer bottleneck. Although SCSI-2 host adapters can manage data flow at 10MB per second, this generally is not required for single- or double-speed recording. If, however, you have a system with three or four SCSI devices sharing the chain with the recorder, a faster SCSI bus may be able to ensure that overall data throughput remains at levels sufficient to keep data in the internal buffer of the CD recorder during the entire write operation.

■ **Is any other hardware necessary to prepare for CD recording?** Although no other hardware is essential to CD recording, certain devices may make your life as an electronic publisher a lot easier. An uninterruptible power supply (UPS), large enough to power both your computer system and CD recorder during short power outages, provides additional insurance during the recording process, particularly if you're working in an area subject to power fluctuations. If you plan to transfer data to a replication service, some services actually prefer tape (most commonly in the Exabyte form factor), so an 8mm tape drive that handles these cartridges can be useful. If you have several SCSI devices linked within the same chain, I strongly recommend that you invest in active terminators (rather than the common passive terminators, which are just resistors) for both ends of the daisy chain. Active terminators electronically balance the signal levels on the SCSI bus and ensure more reliable device communication and data transfers.

Feature Summary

Discriminating between the various features of competing CD recorders is not unlike shopping for a new car. The vast majority of CD recorders all support a common feature set—those features that are required by the competitive pressures of the marketplace. Beyond the basic features, you can very quickly get into the subtleties of engineering design and technology that are often not quite so clear-cut. In the same way that you may need to do a little research to find out the differences between an inline 5-cylinder engine and a V-6 powerplant, it may help you select the best CD recorder for your purposes if you understand the significance of different product options. This section guides you through the most important features offered on CD recorders.

Recording Speed

Most CD recorders currently available are dual-speed models—capable of accepting data during write operations at 300KB per second. At this recording rate, you can generally complete the mastering of a 650MB disc in about 30 minutes. Most recorders in this class also include the option of stepping down to the slower single-speed rate if your system can't support the necessary transfer rates for double-speed recording operations. Most of these systems can also read standard CD-ROMs at the double-speed rates.

TIP

CD recorders function very effectively in the dual role as readers and writers. When you're not actually recording discs, you can comfortably use the recorder unit to play any of your commercial (or personally recorded) CD-ROM titles, or even slip an audio CD into the recorder unit to enjoy some music while you work. After paying $1,500 or more for a CD recorder, you'll want to find ways to get the maximum use from it.

Your options become much more limited when searching for faster recorders. Yamaha's quad-speed recorders, the internal CDR100 and external CDE100, have been available for some time, and these recorders are fully supported by most of the available mastering applications. Street prices for these units are around $3,500; like most CD recordable equipment, prices have dropped sharply (from a suggested list price of $5,000) over the last year. Other manufacturers are readying quad-speed recorders for the market, but at press time, these were not available for review. New units will also not be immediately supported by all of the mastering applications.

KODAK's PCD Writer 600 was the first six-speed recorder on the market; while it is considerably more expensive than other recorders, it can reduce the time to record a disc to under ten minutes. Some high-volume corporate applications may justify the extra initial expense. Once you get beyond generating a few discs a week and start producing hundreds, the capabilities and speed of the PCD Writer 600 become a necessity, rather than a luxury.

Dual-speed recorders should prove adequate in most situations where electronic publishers are not faced with high-volume, quick turnaround expectations. Since dual-speed recorders can also operate connected to more modest computer platforms, you not only save on the recorder purchase price, but on the cost of the computer host required for successful operation.

Cache Buffers

All CD recorders contain some form of internal cache buffering, consisting of a memory region within the recorder that holds data prior to writing it to the CD. During operation, the buffer compensates for data interruptions when the host computer fails to deliver data at a fast enough rate (due to events like thermal recalibration or contention for system resources). The larger the buffer, the less chance that data flow to the recordable medium will cease; consequently, there is less risk that the medium will be ruined.

Many of the original CD recorders had pitifully small internal buffers—some of them with as little as 64KB. Experience is a great teacher; as manufacturers grew tired of fielding complaints about ruined media, the size of the typical buffer was steadily increased. For dual-speed recording, a 1MB or larger buffer is recommended. Although you can get by with less (the Yamaha quad-speed recorder manages to accomplish on-the-fly recording with a relatively small 512KB buffer), a large buffer represents good insurance.

Also look for recorders that feature expandable buffers. Some of the newer models offer sockets or upgrades that allow you to expand the recorder's internal buffer to 24MB or more. Although you may not want to pay for a larger buffer initially, having the option to upgrade in the future is a useful asset.

Method for Firmware Upgrades

New technologies typically undergo a period of rapid changes during their inception. The CD recorder industry, in particular, has seen many shifts and turns as products have matured. Like computer systems, CD recorders contain firmware, usually in the form of a Read-Only Memory (ROM) chip that contains machine-level instructions which allow the device to communicate with host adapters and operating systems. During the early days of CD recorder evolution, firmware changes and upgrades were frequently required, and the burden fell on the customer to swap the internal ROM chip for a more current version supplied by the manufacturer. This is a minor annoyance if you are skilled in computer maintenance techniques, but a source of much frustration to anyone who prefers to leave chip-level tampering to technicians.

A better solution to firmware upgrades is through EEPROMs (Electrically Erasable Programmable Read-Only Memory). If your recorder contains an EEPROM, rather than having to swap out the ROM for a firmware upgrade, you can erase the contents of the EEPROM while writing the new firmware to this chip. This feature, common on many of the newer recorders, saves time and grief in accomplishing firmware upgrades. Some of the early implementations, however, require cumbersome command sequences from the DOS prompt (and therefore can't be upgraded on the Macintosh). Look for firmware upgrades that can be accomplished automatically from an inserted CD-ROM; these offer the greatest ease and fewest problems. Recorders from Plasmon, Pinnacle, JVC, and KODAK currently support this approach; you can expect more manufacturers to include this feature in upcoming models.

Both a Reader and a Writer

To fully support incremental write operations, allowing you to record to a disc over a number of sessions, a CD recorder must be equipped to read data while it is writing. Most of the newer recorders support this feature, but if you are considering investing in an earlier unit, you may not find this capability. The recorder should also be able to function as a CD reader when you are not burning discs; most can, but check this feature before you buy. This is especially important if you are purchasing an internal CD recorder and may not have drive bay space for both a recorder and a separate CD-ROM drive.

Compatibility with Mastering Applications

Software producers involved in the CD recording industry focus their support on the most popular hardware. If the recorder that you purchase is not a member of this popular elite group, you may find that your favorite mastering application does not work with it. Although some applications, such as Elektroson's Gear and Corel's CD Creator, include compatibility with most of the recorders that have been released, others, such as Moniker's Spira, only work with two or three recorders. If you have your heart set on using one particular mastering application, investigate the range of recorders supported by that application before you actually purchase a recorder. Fortunately, the compatibility situation is improving as hardware and software manufacturers are working closely to match applications with new release equipment. The sales volumes of CD recorders now justifies this level of commitment.

Calibrating Laser Power

The Orange Book recording standard specifies an area of each recordable disc to be used for calibrating the power applied to the laser during write operations. The combination of the correct laser power with particular media characteristics results in pits that are precisely the right size and shape—an important issue in disc compatibility with the large numbers of CD-ROM drives around the world. If the recorder you purchase does not include the capability of calibrating laser power before recording, you may end up generating discs that are marginally compatible or unreadable by standard CD-ROM drives. This becomes even more important if your goal is to use your one-off CD-ROM as the basis for performing large-scale replication. Poorly defined pits could be perpetuated through the replication process, resulting in disappointing data integrity in your CD-ROM title. The ability to perform laser power calibration should be considered an essential feature in any recorder that you purchase.

Software Bundles

CD recorder manufacturers typically bundle premastering/mastering applications with their products. The applications included in these bundles vary from the simplest to the top-of-the-line professional solutions. If you're considering the purchase of a CD recorder with bundled software, check to see if the bundled application will serve your needs (the next section in this chapter profiles some of the leading applications). If you have professional uses in mind that require full control of disc geography and access to all the CD-ROM standards, lower-end applications will fall short, and you'll need to invest another $500 to $1,000 to get suitable software. However, if the bundle includes a recorder application that fully suits your purposes, you'll save a significant amount of money in setting up your CD recording station.

Integrated Recorder Hardware and Software

You can gain a great deal of assurance by purchasing hardware and software that have been designed to work together. Many setup problems vanish given these kinds of controls, and the assurance of pretested configurations can eliminate much of the frustration in getting a recording system to work properly. Integrated systems such as Meridian Data's Personal SCRIBE 750 CD-R system include the SCSI host adapter, Personal SCRIBE software, a dual-speed CD recorder, all necessary accessories, and top-notch support. If you don't purchase an integrated system, you generally will spend some time getting the SCSI host adapter to communicate with the recorder and setting the mastering application options to properly communicate with the hardware. Young Minds, Inc. also offers integrated systems for CD recording; some of them also include the host computer, making the setup process even easier. If your computer configuration abilities are not strong, you may want to consider purchasing a fully integrated system.

Picks of the Litter: CD Recorder Choices

The following subsections profile a number of the currently available CD recorders. Often, these are bundled as packages with recorder applications, which saves you the trouble of having to purchase additional software.

JVC Personal Archiver Series

JVC offers bundled hardware and software solutions for CD recording in packages designed to accommodate DOS, Windows, Macintosh, and UNIX users. Their systems include the capability to create discs from a virtual image, eliminating the need to construct a physical CD image before initiating recording. JVC has also developed a technique for supporting incremental write operations that minimizes the amount of overhead required to support the individual sessions. At the conclusion of the last multisession write operation, the disc is finalized, and a single table of contents is produced that allows the disc to be read in any standard CD-ROM drive.

Both internal and external versions of the JVC Personal Archiver units are available, and JVC also produces a mini-tower model that includes its own 1GB SCSI hard-disk drive. If your needs run to multi-disc recording, there is also a multi-drive model that contains as many as five CD recorders along with a 1GB hard-disk drive.

The Personal Archiver software can match the file system and media formatting of a single platform—such as the Macintosh HFS or UNIX File System (UFS)—or produce discs within the ISO 9660 standard, for use an any platform. The UNIX version of the product runs on Sun SPARCstations and can support direct recording over a network link if the network has a sufficiently high bandwidth for this approach. Street prices for the entry level JVC Personal Archiver models run in the mid-$2,000 range.

> **JVC Information Products Company of America**
> 17811 Mitchell Avenue
> Irvine, CA 92714
> Phone: 714-261-1292
> Fax: 714-261-9890

KODAK PCD Writer 225

Kodak's interest and involvement in compact disc storage has resulted in the Photo CD standard, a widely accepted technique for storing photographic images on CD-ROM. Less widely known, Kodak has also produced a series of recorder products ranging from a double-speed unit to the current speed champion of the industry, the PCD Writer 600, which records at 6× speeds.

The PCD Writer 225, shown in Figure 15.1, includes a number of features designed to protect data integrity during writing and to reduce the chance of ruining media. These recorders include features for performing automatic error detection and correction during recording, maintaining active monitoring and control over the laser intensity during operation, and allowing read operations while writing to verify data and ensure integrity of the write operations.

FIGURE 15.1.

Kodak PCD Writer 225.
Reprinted courtesy of
Eastman Kodak Company.

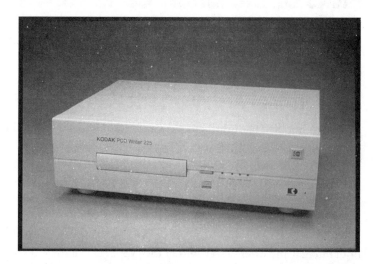

One unique feature of this recorder is the ability to be coupled with the Kodak Disc Transporter, a mechanical unit that alternately feeds blank discs to the recorder and unloads newly recorded discs onto a spindle. Using the Disc Transporter, you can record up to 75 CD-ROMs without any humans attending the process. An adapter kit is required to set the PCD Writer up for this use.

Another unique feature is a built-in bar code reader that, when used with KODAK Writable CD Media, enables you to identify and track disc usage, an extremely valuable asset if you need to juggle large numbers of recorded discs.

The PCD Writer 225 includes a 2MB cache buffer internally that can be expanded to as much as 32MB. The unit loads from a tray, rather than from a caddy, which can be more convenient if you prefer that approach to media handling. Like Sony's CDW-900E recorder, this KODAK unit supports the programming of P and Q subcodes, an important feature for professional audio applications.

The unit features a SCSI-2 interface and—with the proper software—can be moved freely between DOS, Windows, Macintosh, and UNIX environments. As might be expected, full support for the Photo CD standard is included, as well as all the other important standards: CD-ROM, CD-ROM XA, CD-I, CD-R, CD-DA, and CD Video. This unit also supports multisession write operations when used in conjunction with software applications that include this feature. Combined with Kodak's Arrange-It Photo CD Portfolio layout software and

Build-It Photo CD Portfolio disc production software, you can easily create a platform to develop and produce interactive presentations and training materials that include the high quality imagery supported by the Photo CD standard. Music, voice-over narrative, and interactive branching can be built into presentations using this software, and the final product mastered to disc.

Eastman Kodak Company
343 State Street
Rochester, NY 14650
Phone: 1-800-235-6325

Meridian Data Personal SCRIBE 750

Meridian Data entered the CD-ROM market in the mid-80s, and they have since developed a strong stable of personal and network CD recorders. Their CD recorder products combine all the necessary components for creating CDs from the desktop, including the SCSI host adapter, software driver, Windows and DOS application software, and the recorder unit itself.

The Personal SCRIBE 750 features a double-speed recorder with full support for multisession and audio CDs, as well as all other dominant CD-ROM standards. According to Meridian Data, the minimal requirements for the host computer specify a 33MHz 486 machine with 8MB of memory. The hard-disk drive and controller should be able to maintain a data transfer rate of 700KB per second.

Meridian Data now bundles WinSCRIBE software with its PC bundles. WinSCRIBE is a simplified approach to CD mastering that supports drag and drop file transfers from within Windows. The software includes a guided sequence that leads novices throughout the entire recording process. Meridian Data hopes that with this simplified approach, business users will adapt applications to CD-R where they formerly relied on other types of removable media. The Personal SCRIBE series is targeted at uses such as multimedia presentations, data distribution, backup operations, long-term archiving, interactive training, catalog production, and electronic references. A faster version in this product line, the Personal SCRIBE 1000, supports quad-speed recording.

Meridian Data also offers products for network recording and a wide selection of CD-ROM servers that allow 50 or more individual CD-ROM drives to be mounted on the network for workgroup member access. Through innovative software techniques—including high-performance caching, read-ahead schemes, and load-balancing—network access to CD-ROMs can often be as fast or faster than access from a personal machine.

Meridian Data's refined, well-integrated approaches to CD recording should find broad acceptance in both the business community and for individual uses of its products. The Personal SCRIBE 1000 has a suggested list price of $2,495. Their quad-speed product line starts at $6,195.

Meridian Data, Inc.
5615 Scotts Valley Drive
Scotts Valley, CA 95066
Phone: 408-438-3100
Fax: 408-438-6816

Young Minds CD Studio

Despite the fact that UNIX workstations and servers are still predominant in many business environments, the number of CD recording solutions for the UNIX platform has been far less than for the PC or Mac domains. One of the earliest contenders on the UNIX scene was Young Minds, Inc. This company, located in Redlands, California, specializes in producing bullet-proof, soup-to-nuts UNIX CD recording systems. CD Studio, their most well-established CD recording product, includes not only the recorder and mastering software, but something that Young Minds calls the CD Studio Intelligent Controller, a microcomputer dedicated to managing the recording tasks in a network environment.

Young Minds boasts (rightfully) of the range of support for this product, currently over 20 different UNIX platforms, including Silicon Graphics IRIS Indigo and INDY, SUN Microsystems SPARC10 and SUN series, Data General AViiON, and Hewlett Packard's 300/400 and 700/800 series. As might be expected in a UNIX implementation, CD Studio provides considerable flexibility for creating file systems under the various UNIX approaches, including support for UNIX File System (UFS), ISO 9660, ISO 9660 with Translation Tables, and ISO 9660/Rock Ridge. Developers formatting discs under UNIX can choose the degree of compatibility with the standard UNIX file system that they want to maintain and select an appropriate format accordingly.

Young Minds also has solutions for volume production, including the daisy-chaining of Sony recorders for simultaneous recording and the use of the 6× Kodak PCD 600 in conjunction with the Disc Transporter. There is currently no better range of options for an electronic publisher in the UNIX environment than those offered by Young Minds.

Young Minds, Inc.
1910 Orange Tree Lane
Redlands, CA 92375
Phone: 909-335-1350
Fax: 909-798-0488

Microboards PlayWrite Series

Microboards produces integrated CD recorder system solutions—hardware, software, and services—that effectively simplify the creation of CD-ROM titles. This Japanese company (with an office in Minnesota) has a long history and considerable experience in the emerging

CD-ROM industry, with a background in designing CD-I hardware and offering engineering services to many of the leading CD industry players, such as Sony, Philips, Ricoh, Yamaha, and Young Minds. The advantages of purchasing an integrated CD recorder package can be many: simplified setup, ease of use, and reliable support.

In their PlayWrite series, Microboards incorporates recorders from Ricoh and Yamaha to provide fully equipped single-speed (PlayWrite 1000), double-speed (PlayWrite 2000), and quad-speed (PlayWrite 4000) packages. Entry price for the PlayWrite 1000 is under $2,000, and you get everything you need, minus a host computer, to get started recording.

Ramp up to quad-speed levels, and the PlayWrite 4000 lets you record full 650MB discs in about 15 minutes.

> **Microboards, Inc. of America**
> 308 Broadway
> P.O. Box 130
> Carver, MN 55315
> Phone: 612-448-9800

Plasmon RF4102 CD Recorder

Plasmon Data Systems, with 10 years' experience in optical storage systems, has introduced a desktop CD recording system, the RF4102, to meet mainstream business requirements. The RF4102 both records and plays back compact discs at double-speed rates, and includes support for all standard CD-ROM formats: CD-ROM, CD-ROM XA, CD multisession, CD-I, CD-DA. Multisession recording capabilities fit within the parameters of Orange Book Part II to ensure maximum compatibility during playback.

The SCSI interface permits easy exchange of the unit between DOS, Macintosh, and UNIX systems. Plasmon also offers its own line of recordable media in 63-minute and 74-minute capacities.

Plasmon sees the CD-R expanding to include more banks, insurance firms, educational institutions, government organizations, and financial firms that use CD-ROMs to implement backup and archiving programs of vital data. The random access capabilities of the CD-ROM allow faster access to stored information than other backup systems, such as tape. Plasmon also offers a wide variety of support hardware and software, and subsystems optimized for specialized kinds of tasks.

> **Plasmon Data Inc.**
> 1654 Centre Pointe Drive
> Milpitas, CA 95035
> Phone: 408-956-9400
> Fax: 408-956-9444

Plasmon PD/CD Drive

Although not actually a CD recorder, this nifty device could serve admirably as support equipment in your CD recorder workstation. Plasmon's PD/CD drive, the PD2000e, incorporates a new form of optical technology that permits rewriting 650MB media more than 100,000 times. Although CD recorders can be used effectively as backup devices, the flexibility of being able to rewrite the medium is a major benefit to electronic publishers who may deal with hundreds of gigabytes on data during the course of a year. Recordable CDs are fairly inexpensive at $10 apiece, but if the data on them becomes outdated, they quickly become throwaway items. With Plasmon's PD650 media, available for under $60 for a 650MB cartridge, you can rewrite new data whenever needed. Data stored in this format is estimated as having a 10-year lifespan, making it better than tape for archiving, but not as long-lived as magneto-optical cartridges (10 to 15 years) or recordable CDs (about 100 years).

The Plasmon PD2000e also serves as a 4× CD-ROM drive; a unique tray-loading mechanism accommodates both the optical cartridges and CD-ROMs. The suggested price for this unit makes it particularly suitable for high-volume storage in the development environment—internal units list at $795 and external units at $925. Figure 15.2 shows the the PD2000e.

FIGURE 15.2.

Plasmon PD2000e PD/CD drive. Photo courtesy of Plasmon Data, Inc.

Phase-change technology permits a simpler approach to recording and reading data than magneto-optical techniques, which combine laser and magnetic approaches. Phase-change technology is a purely optical approach that uses a laser to create changes in the crystalline structure of the recordable medium. In its unwritten state, the medium exists in an amorphous condition (with no data indications of any sort). Data transitions are created by using the focused laser to heat a spot on the media, changing it to its crystalline state. This spot on the media can be returned to its original amorphous state by reheating it to a slightly higher temperature that actually melts the recording material. As it cools (or revitrifies, in technical terms), the media returns to the equivalent of an unrecorded state. This process requires less moving parts than magneto-optical systems that employ a three-pass approach to recording and erasing data.

Data access rates for the PD2000e range between 100 to 150 milliseconds. CD-ROMs can be read at 4× speeds. With a media cost of around $.09 per megabyte, PD/CD drives are less expensive for data distribution than Syquest or Bernoulli cartridges, which can cost between $.25 to $.58 cents per megabyte. This technology can provide an excellent supplementary means for data storage with a wide variety of uses for multimedia developers, electronic publishers, and anyone who handles large volumes of data.

> **Plasmon Data, Inc.**
> 1654 Centre Pointe Drive
> Milpitas, CA 95035
> Phone: 408-956-9400
> Fax: 408-956-9444

Ricoh RS-1060C

Ricoh Corporation has targeted the double-speed RS-1060C at what many consider the most rapidly growing area of recordable CD: the entry level corporate applications area. Businesses are expected to continue to migrate to CD-R for support of COLD, archiving, data distribution over networks and through media transmission, and similar applications. Like the Sony CDU-92X recorders, discussed in a later subsection, the RS-1060C has been a long time coming out of the chute, as firmware and production issues have been resolved.

Ricoh has designed its own recorder software—CD Print—to accompany the unit with an eye towards foolproof simplicity. Both Macintosh and Windows versions are available. As suggested by the title, the software attempts to make disc recording as simple as transferring files to a printer for output. Some of the high-end possibilities of the medium are hidden to encourage ease of use and to eliminate much of the confusion that has surrounded the creation of CD-ROMs.

Ricoh has also incorporated the dust-proof design principles that were originally included in Ricoh's magneto-optical cartridge drives, to seal the drive mechanism away from contaminants that might create data errors during recording. The company claims that the unit can be used to record even in environments with more dust and debris than the usual office setting.

You can expect to see this Ricoh unit as part of a number of VAR packages, as well as marketed internationally with Ricoh's own imprint. Prices for these drives are targeted for the $1,500 range, making them among the least expensive recorders currently available. Ricoh also produces its own recordable media for use in this drive or other CD recorders. Figure 15.3 shows the Ricoh unit.

FIGURE 15.3.
*Ricoh RS-1060C. Photo
courtesy of Richoh
Corporation.*

Ricoh Corporation
Peripheral Products Division
3001 Orchard Parkway
San Jose, CA 95134
Phone: 1-800-955-3453
Fax: 408-432-9266

Smart and Friendly CD-R 1002

Smart and Friendly adds value to CD recording components by assembling packages consisting of competitively priced hardware and software. Their CD-R 1002 package is based on the Sony CDU-921S, including versions for both PCs and Macintosh computers. The PC version includes Corel CD-Creator for Windows, as well as a SCSI host adapter (with support for bus mastering) and cable. List price is $1,729 for this version. The Macintosh bundle now includes AStarte's well-designed Toast CD-ROM Pro 2.5 recorder software and an external SCSI cable, with a list price of $1,999.

Smart and Friendly also offers bundles including software applications for multimedia development, quad-speed recorders, additional options for premastering/mastering applications, and UNIX configurations. Their packages are generally well-integrated and priced aggressively to offer substantial value in a crowded market.

Smart and Friendly
16539 Saticoy Street
Van Nuys, CA 91409
Phone: 818-994-8001
Fax: 819-998-6581

Sony CDW-900E

This Sony unit is one of the workhorse recorders that have helped open up the industry. It records at single- or double-speed rates and includes some standard features, such as a 4MB cache buffer, that separate it from other recorders in this class. The CDW-900E handles CD-ROM, CD-ROM XA, CD-I, and CD-DA formats with full compatibility for Red Book, Yellow Book, and Green Book. One unique feature is the ability to control subcode P and Q channels during audio recording, as well as R and W channels. Without getting too technical, the capability to control the information in these channels proves useful in professional recording environments. Sony units can also be daisy chained to perform simultaneous recording of up to 16 discs at a time.

The CDW-900E is not without weaknesses. It cannot handle multisession write operations, and it cannot perform audio reads (a feature which allows direct access to digital audio information without conversion through programs like OMI's Disc To Disk. Although accomplished, capable, and well supported, the CDW-900E appears expensive in comparison to some of the more recent CD recorders, including Sony's own CDU-920S, described in the next subsection. If you can find a discounted bargain price on one of these units, it should serve you in good stead. If the inability to write multisession discs creates problems for you, you should evaluate some of the other, more recent recorders on the market.

Sony CDU-920S and CDU-921S

As I was working on the material for this chapter, there were four- to six-week waiting periods to obtain these recorders, not unlike the situation that existed for Honda Accords some years back when they became so popular that dealers couldn't get enough of them—customers paid big deposits and got unceremoniously added to waiting lists until the car they wanted arrived. By this book's publication date, the situation should have improved, assuming that initial manufacturing setup and distribution issues have been solved.

These two double-speed recorders, the CDU-920S half-height internal and the CDU-921S external standalone, offer the right combination of features and price. They've been incorporated into many packages produced by value-added resellers, such as Smart and Friendly, Inc., whose CDR-1002 recorder bundle includes this Sony recorder at its heart. The recorders overcome one of the shortcomings of the Sony CDW-900E by offering full support for not only multisession recording, but for packet writing. Packet writing allows recording to discs in more precise increments and can facilitate useful functions, such as media recovery from partially recorded discs with data errors. It also lessens the likelihood of making a disc unreadable because of recording problems. This unit also supports Read Audio operations over the SCSI bus, allowing digital audio data to be extracted and manipulated directly by applications designed for this.

If you know what the most desired recorder features are, reading the Sony feature list carefully can make you nod with approval. The 1MB cache buffer represents a good, standard size for a low-cost recorder. The automatic lens cleaning mechanism should help avoid problems from bits of debris as the recorder accumulates hours of use. The caddy loading design with a double-shutter mechanism helps keep dust and grit out of the internal recording area. Support for the widest possible range of CD-ROM standards is included and the drive—even at this early stage of release—is widely supported by premastering/mastering applications. Sony has shown a good deal of perception in reading the needs of the marketplace and designing a unit to satisfy professional users as well as more casual entrants to the field. Pricing, depending on international currency rates, ranges between $1,500 to $1,675.

Sony Electronics, Inc.
Computer Peripheral Products Company
3300 Zanker Road
San Jose, CA 95134
Phone: 1-800-352-7669

Yamaha CDE100 and CDR100 Quad-Speed Recorders

As an indication of the rate that CD recorder prices are dropping, Yamaha reduced the cost of its internal quad-speed recorder, the CDR100, from $5,000 to $3,495 in April of 1995. This reliable and popular Yamaha unit has been incorporated into many different VAR packages—in fact, if you see a quad-speed recorder on the market and you peek beneath the cabinet skin, odds are you'll find the Yamaha recorder inside. Among the companies that are producing products based on the Yamaha recorder are: JVC, dataDisc, FWB, Meridian Data, Inc., Optical Media International, ProCom Technology, Inc., Rimage, CDROM Strategies, American Infoscience, Young Minds, Inc., Micronet, and Flore.

The compact internal unit fits neatly in a $5^1/4$-inch disk drive bay. The external version is a bit chunkier, but it still fits compactly on a desktop. The recorders share a common feature set, including the ability to perform multi-session write operations, and to modify recording speed from 4× to 2× to 1× to accommodate different recording situations. Full support for the leading CD-ROM standards is provided, including CD-ROM, CD-ROM XA, CD-I, and CD-DA. The SCSI-2 interface lets you quickly shift the focus of operations from your PC to your Mac, if your office is so equipped.

Recording at quad speed requires media that are optimized for higher speed uses. Whereas it used to be difficult to select recordable media that would reliably work in high-speed situations, the industry has moved closer to standards that support recording uses up to 6× speeds. Improved quality control during disc manufacturing and careful selection of materials is necessary to produce discs that can support higher speed applications. If you intend to record at 4× or 6× rates, be discriminating in the selection of your media. Yamaha has worked closely with a number of media manufacturers to establish minimal quality standards for recordable discs; those that meet the necessary requirements and are certified for quad-speed use bear a special logo that identifies them as 4×-compatible.

Quad-speed recording places higher demands on the host computer to maintain sufficient data throughput to avoid interrupting the recording process. The Yamaha quad-speed recorder features a 512KB buffer, which was considered large at the time the product was initially introduced, but is generally considered marginal (by current standards) to support quad-speed rates. Yamaha plans an increase in the capacity of the cache buffer for the next redesign of the product line. Most customers can perform quad-speed recording without difficulty, once they have optimized their systems for high-speed operation, but this technology currently places a greater burden on the customer to ensure a properly tuned system.

Yamaha Systems Technology Division
Yamaha Corporation of America
100 Century Center Court
San Jose, CA 95112
Phone: 408-467-2300
Fax: 408-437-8791

Selecting CD Recorder Software

The sophistication of CD recorder software has made giant bounds over just the last couple of years. More attention has been given to interface design, and many programs include some type of Wizard or Guide to lead a new user through the process of creating a CD-ROM. For example, Corel's CD Creator includes a Wizard sequence that appears the first time you use the program. You can follow a step-by-step sequence with instructions that answer many of the questions that a novice recordist is likely to pose. Similarly, CeQuadrat's WinOnCD ToGo! features a Guide sequence, accessible through the help system or the application window toolbar, that prompts you through the basic steps, letting you perform any necessary actions along the way. By the time you've finished the guided sequence, you're ready to burn your first compact disc.

Recorder applications can be grouped into two primary categories: those designed to hide details of standards and formats from the user, and those designed for professional-level use where more precise control needs to be enacted over operations. Some overlap exists between these two categories; even some of the simplified applications support some surprisingly sophisticated features. If your prospective CD-ROM applications are limited to archiving and storing files, producing ISO 9660 discs for cross-platform distribution, and creating audio CDs, almost any of the CD recorder applications can handle your requirements. Only when you venture into creating more complex discs—involving multimedia elements like video or synchronized sound and animation—do you need the additional flexibility afforded by the professional-level apps.

As a basic recommendation, when you start CD recording, try burning some discs using the basic formats. See if you can create a Red Book audio disc without any embellishments (most applications support this operation). Create a large group of test files and record them to disc in ISO 9660 format. Most beginners have no trouble with these fundamental standards, but quickly get lost when they start trying to produce Mixed Mode, CD-I, and interleaved CD-ROM XA formats. For some reason, there seems to be a tendency for people to jump in and start trying to produce complex discs before they fully understand the process. As the old adage goes, learn to walk before you run.

These are some of the features to look for in quality CD recorder applications:

- **CD recorder compatibility**: The package won't do you much good if it doesn't operate with your model CD recorder. Read the fine print to ensure compatibility— some applications have very short lists of compatible recorders.

- **CD-ROM standards supported**: Entry-level applications hide formatting details from the user and support fewer CD-ROM standard variations. High-end applications usually support all of the standards but require more knowledge on the part of the user to stay out of problems.

- **Multisession capabilities**: Individual applications have different ways of implementing the reading and writing of multisession discs. These ways are not always compatible. If you need to do a lot of multisession recording, make sure you understand how multisession operations are handled for your chosen application.

- **Incremental write operations and packet writing**: Some applications now support write operations in smaller increments (without incurring large overheads between sessions). Packet writing also reduces ruined media, but requires both software and hardware equipped for it.

- **Recording from virtual images**: Applications that can efficiently write from a virtual image save disc space and simplify your recording requirements.

- **Recording simulation**: Applications that can simulate the recording process without burning a disc can help you verify that your system is performing properly before you record.

- **Control of disc geography**: If you need to precisely place certain files in certain regions of a compact disc, some applications give you full control; others provide more limited, general control.

The following subsections describe a number of the current generation CD recorder applications.

Corel CD Creator

Designed for simplicity and ease of use, CD Creator also includes a number of features more common to high-end applications. Most activities can be accomplished from the Windows interface in drag-and-drop style. You can quickly transfer audio or data files into an image window in preparation for recording a disc. CD Creator also includes a special utility for preparing Photo CD discs and a test utility that can verify adequate performance of your hard disk and CD recorder before you start burning discs.

Throughout most areas of the program, prompts and hints appear at strategic locations to suggest a course of action. You can also follow the instructions provided by the Disc Wizard to painlessly ease your way into CD recording with an intelligent on-screen procedure. You simply respond to a series of dialog boxes and enter requested information into the appropriate boxes, and you're ready to go.

CD Creator differentiates between two main categories of data: data files and audio files. If you elect to create a data disc, you can navigate through the directories on your system and tag the resources to be added to the recordable media (as shown in Figure 15.4). CD Creator adds the selected files and directories to a window where you assemble the collection of material to transfer to disc. You can prioritize placement of files on the CD-ROM in one of three categories: Normal, Faster Access, or Fastest Access. Files to be accessed fastest get placed near the center of the CD-ROM.

FIGURE 15.4.

Adding files in Corel's CD Creator.

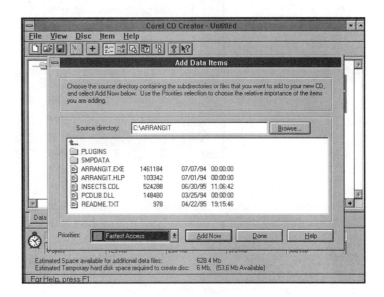

Before recording, you have the option of performing a sequence of tests to let CD Creator determine an appropriate recording speed for your system. Speeds up to 6× are supported, allowing you (in theory) to record to even the fastest KODAK 6× recorder. In practice, achieving the higher recording rates will test your skills at reconfiguring your system to obtain the right combination of memory resources, buffer availability, and hardware setup parameters to keep data streaming at the required rates. CD Creator includes a simulation function that lets you go through the steps to record a disc without actually activating the laser. You'll see lights flashing on your CD recorder, progress bars inching across the screen, and any resulting error messages splashed on your display. Simulating recording is highly recommended until you have your system behaving properly; otherwise, you'll probably waste a number of blank discs due to unexpected errors.

CD Creator includes a utility for converting WAV files into the necessary format to create a Red Book audio disc. If you are a musician creating a demo disc, you can even design an insert to slip into the CD jewel case to showcase your work (as shown in Figure 15.5). The jewel case editor, of course, can be used to produce professional-looking inserts for business or personal uses as well.

FIGURE 15.5.

Design a cover in jewel case editor.

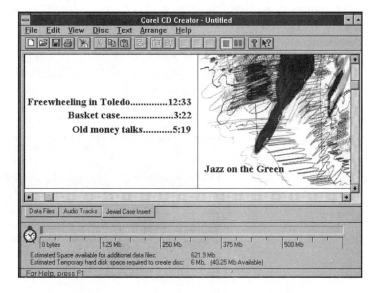

A program called PCD Creator provides a highly visual method for creating Photo CD discs. You can view a set of source thumbnails in one window and double-click those images that you want to transfer to a Photo CD format disc. Your disc layout—thumbnail images and data—appears in a window to the right. As you continue to add images, a moving bar indication at the bottom of the display shows how much of the blank disc space you have consumed (as shown in Figure 15.6). When you have completed the disc layout, you can click the icon to burn the disc, and the program goes to work.

With a list price of $249, CD Creator includes a surprising number of features and does a respectable job of simplifying the process of creating several different formats of CD-ROM (audio, data, and Photo CD). The software use is the easy part of the equation; the hard part (for this product and all the others I tested) is the hardware and software configuration issues, particularly to achieve the faster recording rates.

FIGURE 15.6.

Build a visual library with PhotoCD Creator. Clip art from CorelDRAW!™

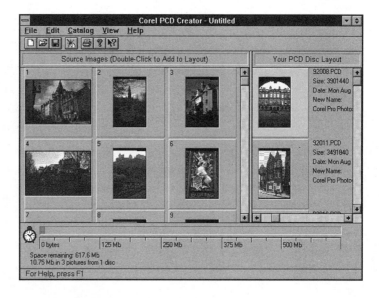

CeQuadrat WinOnCD ToGo!

Although CeQuardrat also offers professional-grade CD-R applications, WinOnCD ToGo! aims at the mainstream business market and individual personal computer users who want a direct, straight-forward means of recording the most common CD-ROM formats. The list price of $199 should prove appealing to users who want to gain some experience with the recording process before investing $1,000 or more in one of the high-end packages. For the price of entry, you gain the ability to create ISO 9660 discs, Red Book audio, Mixed Mode discs, and CD Plus formats. Support for most of the major CD recorders is provided at recording speeds as high as 6×. The combination of features and capabilities provided by this application is reasonable for the prospective primary users.

An increasingly popular feature in CD recorder applications is the guided approach to recording. Instead of having to spend an hour or two reading the user manual, you click an icon and let the program guide you through the process of setting options, selecting files, creating a disc image, and initiating a recording. WinOnCD ToGo! includes a help-system oriented guide that you can call up at any point in the program. As you're working through the guide, it can launch dialog boxes for specific functions—such as setting hardware options—and then return you to the guided sequence. Features such as this go a long way toward adapting previously inscrutable CD recorder interfaces to everyday use in the business and consumer marketplace. Figure 15.7 shows one of the popup guide dialog boxes.

FIGURE 15.7.

*Guide messages in
WinOnCD ToGo!*

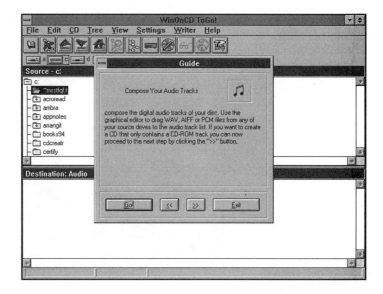

The program uses a pair of windows, one displaying your choices for source files and the other showing the current destination files (being prepared for writing to CD). By navigating through the upper window and dragging folders and files to the lower window, you prepare the contents of the CD image. The system is fast, highly visual, and well suited to beginning users. The main application window is shown in Figure 15.8. If you're selecting Audio files, you can use a browse-and-click approach to make your selections.

FIGURE 15.8.

*The main application
window for WinOnCD
ToGo!*

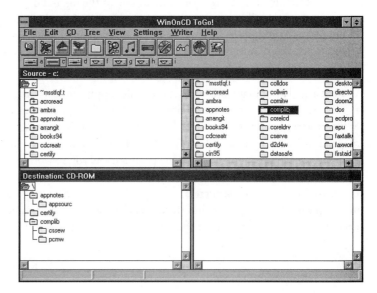

An Edit Placement function lets you choose from among three relative choices of file placement: Start of Session, Middle of Session, End of Session (as shown in Figure 15.9). You can reorder items individually within each of these lists just by selecting the item and dragging it to a new location. Although not as precise as some of the professional-level mastering applications, this approach provides a very workable solution for the majority of business and consumer applications. Search engines or runtime players can be placed at the Start of Session region, occasionally accessed data files can be shifted to the Middle of Session region, and those files that are rarely needed can be ostracized to the End of Session area.

FIGURE 15.9.

Edit Placement window lets you sequence files on the disc.

WinOnCD ToGo! automatically simulates the recording process before actually putting laser to polycarbonate and informs you if there are any performance problems with your system before it begins an actual recording. The program lets you create either permanent or temporary image files that replicate the contents of the CD before recording. A permanent image file can be used to quickly burn additional discs without having to perform any further file manipulation. You can also record on-the-fly from a selected group of files if your system is fast enough to assemble all the elements during the recording process.

Multimedia developers would want to choose the higher end WinOnCD for its additional options (commensurate with its $1,200 price tag), but for many electronic publishers, particularly those who will spend most of their time developing ISO 9660 discs, WinOnCD ToGo! offers a capable working environment and a healthy assortment of format support and options.

Incat Systems Easy CD Pro

Easy CD Pro is the middle range mastering application offered by Incat Systems. If you want primarily to do backups, you can use Easy CD Backup, a $249 package that creates ISO 9660 discs for data storage and distribution. On the high end, Easy CD Pro MM, gives multimedia developers an expansive set of tools to support more involved uses of the medium, for those who don't flinch at the $1,495 price. Easy CD Pro at $995 provides a middle-of-the-road approach, fulfilling many typical requirements of business and professional users, but stopping short of full multimedia support.

Easy CD Pro relies heavily on File Manager conventions to prepare a collection of files that can serve as a virtual image or can be copied to disk as a real ISO image. Figure 15.10 shows the typical working environment for the program with File Manager displayed on the bottom and the main application for Easy CD Pro on the top. You drag files and directories from File Manager and drop them into the virtual image window.

FIGURE 15.10.

Easy CD Pro main application window uses drag-and-drop file selection.

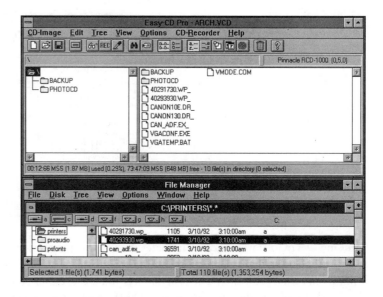

Once you've completed assembling the contents of the disc, you can click the Record icon, fill in some identification details for the disc, and then select the features to enable for the write operation, as shown in Figure 15.11.

FIGURE 15.11.

The Write dialog box gives you control over the details of a recording.

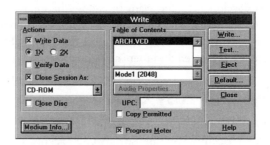

From the Write dialog box, you can either directly initiate a recording, or use the Test button to simulate the recording. The Test function goes through the steps of physically transferring files, controlling the CD recorder actions, and monitoring performance. However, the laser is not activated during the test pass. If the test fails at some point, the program displays a message indicating the nature of the failure.

The functions and options of Easy CD Pro have been arranged to appear in sequential form, as needed, so as you progress through the recording process, dialog boxes you must complete pop into position. Although the program does not include a guide or wizard, the help system menu offers quick access to procedures and the contents clearly explain most of the frequently required tasks.

Disc geography is controlled by the order in which the files are copied into the virtual CD image file. You can exercise precise control by simply choosing the order of files during the drag and drop operation. If you're creating new directories for file storage, to maintain the proper order of files on disc, you need to create a single directory, drag-and-drop the files to go into this directory, create the next directory, drag-and-drop its contents, and so on. The process is a bit cumbersome, particularly if hundreds of files are involved in building a CD image. In practical use, however, you would probably just be directing a limited number of files to the centermost position of the CD. Precise control of the contents of the middle or outer edge of the disc is not necessary in most cases. An option to Sort by CD Position lets you display each of the files and directories in relative order as they will appear on the CD. You can engage a Move operation by selecting a file or directory and then right-clicking on an item that you want to reposition. The Move dialog box lets you move the selected item before or after the highlighted line.

Instead of creating discs from a virtual CD image, you can create a real ISO image, consisting of a replica of the file-by-file contents of the final CD. From an ISO image, Easy CD Pro lets you simulate the performance of a program as it operates as run on a CD-ROM. This can be useful to test the prospective performance of your disc before you actually burn any media. The simulation results might suggest movement of particular files to a new position on the CD.

Easy CD Pro provides broad support for numerous CD recorders, an effective means for accomplishing multisession write operations, and many professional-level features that are embedded in the program as part of task sequences so as not to make the interface unnecessarily complicated. For anything less than full multimedia development, this program could support electronic publishing efforts of the most ambitious types.

Elektroson GEAR

GEAR provides an exceptional degree of power and control to both corporate users and multimedia developers. This feature-rich program has a very long list of supported CD recorders, as well as support for almost all of the CD-ROM standards, including those that are often excluded from other programs, such as 3DO, CDTV, CD-I, and VideoCD. The price tag of $799 places it as one of the least-expensive, professional-caliber mastering applications.

Full support for output media, such as 8mm Exabyte tape, 9-track tape, and Digital Audio Tape, offers an additional alternative for delivering a CD image to a replication service, if you decide to use that route. A verification process enables GEAR to check the contents of the recorded tape with the contents of the virtual image to ensure that the file transfer took place without errors.

The initial launch of the program gives you the opportunity to create a new imagefile (as shown in Figure 15.12). Imagefiles create what GEAR calls a Virtual Volume, a storage repository for the contents of your disc. You can then create tracks to be added to the Virtual Volume, allowing you to choose whether audio data, computer data, or ISO format files are to be contained within a track. GEAR also supports the creation of physical volumes that can be used to improve CD recording performance, if attempts to record from a virtual volume are unsuccessful.

FIGURE 15.12.

Starting a new imagefile is the first step in assembling disc contents.

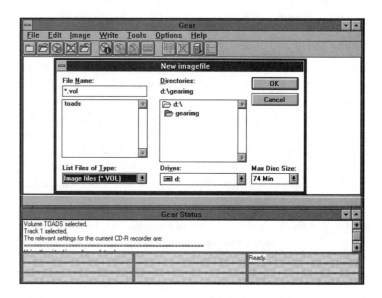

GEAR, as is typical for many of the programs of this type, uses File Manager as the means for selecting files to write to CD. You can drag-and-drop from the File Manager window to build a directory tree in the Virtual Volume window. GEAR uses a set of rules to prevent copying the wrong type of data to certain types of tracks or to control naming conventions within ISO 9660 formats. As you work on the contents of a track, the Status window, shown in Figure 15.13, shows the currently active track. The Status window is available through most functions of the program, and it provides valuable information during recording simulations and actual recording. The line-by-line comments that appear in the Status window can guide your troubleshooting efforts or help determine when it might be necessary to reconfigure your system for improved performance or reconsider your recording objectives.

FIGURE 15.13.

The Status window helps monitor various operations during file assembly and recording.

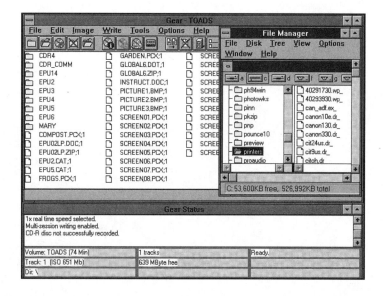

GEAR provides a good deal of flexibility in handling multisession recording. You can append new sessions to any session existing on a multisession disc. You can skip over a previous session if read errors occur within it. You can also use this function to create CD Extended or CD Plus discs.

GEAR's flexibility and support for multiple recording options and formats make it ideal for many different types of CD recording, from simple electronic publishing of portable document formats to multimedia training packages with embedded audio and video. Although the program is not completely intuitive in use, most of the features can be mastered with a minimum of difficulty. Program feedback during operation—such as is provided by the log options and status windows—can be helpful in eliminating problems and ensuring trouble-free recording.

Summary

Choosing hardware and software for CD recording forces you to balance the usual trade-offs of cost, functionality, and features. If you have the opportunity to test hardware and software, either through a computer dealer or within the office environment, this can help you get a sense for whether a program satisfies those intangible requirements that can only be discovered through use. An honest assessment of your present and future needs may also help determine which hardware and software can best serve as the platform for your electronic publishing efforts.

Incorporating Multimedia into CD-ROMs

16

by Lee Purcell

Creative writing instructors often return to a simple adage when explaining how to write compelling fiction: "Show the readers; don't tell them." Eight-hundred words of descriptive adjectives detailing Simon Nightshade's sly and sinister nature is not nearly as convincing as a short sequence where Simon calls another character on the phone, and speaking in a falsetto voice arranges a midnight meeting in an abandoned granite quarry. By the time Simon starts packing a bag full of sharp, stone-cutting implements, you're fairly sure he's not an out-of-work sculptor looking for employment.

Multimedia offers an electronic publisher the opportunity to *show* viewers, instead of just telling them. Several paragraphs about how an internal combustion engine works might make entertaining reading, but a 60-second animation with a voice-over explaining each of the engine cycles as pistons, valves, and cams move on-screen makes the point much more quickly. A short audio clip of a Charles Lindberg speech conveys more emotion than a text insert of the same speech. A video clip showing astronauts moving about inside an Apollo spacecraft carries more weight than a textual description of their "cramped quarters."

You don't need to be a games producer or creator of CD-ROM documentaries to take advantage of multimedia enhancements within your title. A variety of current-generation applications let you easily manipulate digital sound, video, graphics, and animation and include these elements within an electronic document. Most of the different types of electronic publications that we discuss in this book—help systems, infobases, HTML files, hypertext documents, and portable document files—include support for at least some multimedia elements.

A CD-ROM can store anything you can create digitally. Where you store data and what form you store it in, however, has considerable bearing when you are creating CD-ROMs. As you begin integrating more complex multimedia elements, you begin to run into some of the performance constraints of the medium. You also run into some capacity limitations. As immense as 650MB can seem to a developer, if you decide you want to include uncompressed audio files on disc, these can consume storage space at the rate of 10MB per minute of stereo sound. To overcome some of the storage and performance constraints, the original CD-ROM data storage standard, Yellow Book, was extended to include special methods of handling sound, video, photographic images, and other forms of multimedia. (For a refresher course on the color book standards, refer to Chapter 14, "What Goes onto CD-ROM (and How).") If you use these formats selectively, you can improve playback of CD-ROM titles that include multimedia and store multimedia elements more efficiently. You also create some obstacles that may limit your potential audience, as described in the following subsections.

This chapter explains the basic concepts of integrating multimedia material within a CD-ROM title and describes the techniques for doing so.

Incorporating Sound

Compact discs were invented to store sound—of all the multimedia elements, sound offers you the most options as an electronic publisher, from compressed ADPCM formats, to embedded WAV files, to full Red Book audio in all its pulse-code modulated (PCM) glory.

Your use of these different options for storing and playing back sound depends primarily on three considerations:

■ How much storage space is available for the sound files?

■ What type of playback equipment does your audience have?

■ Does the sound have to be synchronized with other on-screen events, such as video or animation?

There is one additional option open to you for storing and presenting musical information: MIDI. Although MIDI requires some form of synthesizer for playback, the playback device can be as simple as a single-chip FM synthesizer embedded on a standard sound card. Higher quality synthesizers sound better, but FM synthesizers work, and they are abundant—nearly everyone with a sound card (or equivalent IC capabilities) has this feature available. Game developers rely on this fact for providing background music during game play; because MIDI sequences can be dynamically manipulated under program control, this makes it easy for game developers to change the tone, tempo, or atmosphere of the music based on what is happening within the game. LucasArts uses this technique effectively in its Star Wars™ games, Dark Forces and TIE Fighter.

Types of Sound Files

Sound gets formatted in various ways for storage on CD-ROM; in working with this medium, you will often encounter audio data in each of the available formats:

■ Red Book audio data (PCM)

■ Adaptive Delta Pulse Code Modulation (ADPCM)

■ Windows WAV format files

■ VOC format files

■ Audio Interchange File Format (AIFF)

■ QuickTime for Windows

■ MIDI files

Red Book Audio Data

Red Book audio, the kind that you hear when you play a compact disc on your stereo system, uses a storage format known as linear pulse code modulation, commonly referred to as PCM. Sound waves are sampled at the rate of 44.1KHz to produce digital values indicating the amplitude at each sample point. This process, known as analog-to-digital conversion, converts the sound wave to the digital format. The reverse of that process, digital-to-analog conversion, turns the digital information back to waveforms, the signals that drive your computer (or stereo) speakers.

Audio information in Red Book format can exist on "pure" discs—those that contain only audio with no data—and in Yellow Book mixed mode—where a track of computer data coexists with several tracks of Red Book audio data. The new Blue Book format, sometimes called Enhanced CD or CD Plus, also uses a structure that combines Red Book audio and computer data, but places the data on the outside track of the disc (rather than the inside track).

Adaptive Delta Pulse Code Modulation

ADPCM, Adaptive Delta Pulse Code Modulation, is another variation on digitally storing waveforms, but in this case the sound information is compressed. ADPCM is specified as part of the CD-ROM XA standard, including the different levels of compression supported. This form of compression, however, requires that the user have a specific type of CD-ROM drive (with CD-ROM XA support) that is able to distinguish and decompress this form of sound information. Support is also required at the software level, with an appropriate software driver to handle the data. There are currently several variations on ADPCM (such as Microsoft's version, MS ADPCM, and another called IMA ADPCM); unfortunately, they are not directly compatible. Unless you supply an appropriate driver to accompany a CD-ROM containing ADPCM and the user has compatible hardware, the sound cannot be played back. Until there exists some common agreement on a single form of ADPCM, these compatibility problems will continue to exist.

> **NOTE**
>
> Although ADPCM represents a viable means of compressing hours of audio material onto disc, the playback complexities (requiring a compatible software driver and appropriate CD-ROM drive decoding equipment) have restricted its use. Windows 95 improves the situation significantly by providing several ADPCM drivers to accommodate different applications. Most new CD-ROM drives also include built-in support for ADPCM decoding; by these indications, we'll probably be seeing more extensive use of the approach to audio compression.

If you choose to create a CD-ROM using the CD-ROM XA standard, you have the option of interleaving the computer data with the audio and video data. This technique ensures more reliable playback of video sequence and better synchronization of sound with data being displayed on screen. CD recorder applications vary in their capability for creating discs based on CD-ROM XA format, but the more professional packages provide full support for this feature. Elektroson's Gear application lets you interleave data a sector at a time, giving the maximum control to developers who know what they are doing. Producing a disc within CD-ROM XA constraints requires considerable knowledge; this is not a feat to be attempted by novice CD-ROM developers.

Windows WAV Files

WAV files, one of the most common forms of storing audio waveforms for use with PC applications, are similar, though not identical, to PCM data. If you want to copy a group of WAV files to a recordable CD as Red Book audio data, can you just transfer them to disc? No, not directly. There is enough difference in the formats that a direct transfer will not work. However, many CD recorder applications support creation of Red Book audio data by converting a group of WAV files that you specify to PCM format on-the-fly (while the recording is taking place). This gives you the opportunity to use your favorite sound editing application to manipulate the audio material and then save it as a WAV file. A group of WAV files can then be transferred to individual tracks on a recordable CD by any application that supports this feature.

For example, Incat Systems' Easy CD Pro includes a utility called Waves that adapts WAV files to the 44.1KHz 16-bit storage format necessary to meet the Red Book standard. Corel's CD Creator lets you directly select WAV files for recording to a Red Book disc and performs any conversions that are necessary during premastering.

Sound files, including WAV files, can always be stored simply as files on any of the CD-ROM standards that support data storage (all but Red Book). Depending on how these are accessed by playback engine or viewer, the results may or may not be satisfactory. Large sound files stored in this manner and accessed in conjunction with a presentation taking place on-screen may cause synchronization problems (the sound plays at a different time than the corresponding display data or the sound breaks up during playback). Generally, if you are using very large sound files in a multimedia presentation, you can avoid problems by:

- Encapsulating the sound within a movie format, such as QuickTime for Windows or Video for Windows. When played back as a movie, the sound remains synchronized to the display data.
- Interleaving sound and data using the CD-ROM XA format for storage.
- Storing your sound data in smaller units. You can break down one large five-minute narration sound file into several shorter files that can than be sequentially accessed during playback.

Generally, WAV files on CD-ROM work best for sound effects, short narrative passages, and 10- to 30-second musical clips. For example, a typical CD-ROM encyclopedia contains a multitude of short sound files that usually range from the barks of the dingos of Australia to the spoken words of Winston Churchill. For longer audio sequences (where synchronization is not an issue), use a Mixed Mode disc format and access the sound data from the Red Book region. For example, if you were creating a documentary electronic book on the music of Pete Townsend, you could include buttons in your presentation to directly link to musical tracks stored in the Red Book portion of the disc. The viewer clicks the button, listens to the segment, and then goes to another page in the documentary. As long as there is not too much activity taking place on screen at the same time, this approach works very effectively.

Audio Interchange File Format

This format appears frequently in Macintosh applications and has evolved as a reasonable means for transferring data between different applications. It is supported by many of the leading multimedia development applications, such as Macromedia Director, and has a certain degree of cross-platform support. The large majority of sound editing applications can import and export sound files in AIFF format.

The same basic rules apply to use of files in this format as for WAV files, discussed in the previous section. Sound in this format works best for short passages, sound effects, and similar material. More demanding applications that require careful synchronization work better if the sound is encapsulated as a movie file or interleaved in CD-ROM XA format.

VOC File Format

Creative Labs' popular Sound Blaster sound board has its own digital audio file format, a format that became popular before WAV files became established in the Windows environment. For this reason, VOC files have wide support by many different manufacturers, and this format is supported by many applications. Although use of WAV files has become much more common, you will still find use of VOC files in different situations.

QuickTime for Windows

Although QuickTime for Windows primarily serves as a vehicle for presenting merged audio and video data, you can also use it for generating sound files that can then be accessed from multimedia applications. This has the advantage of giving the developer the freedom to use audio elements independently of video or graphic elements, a feature that can be useful for certain kinds of interactive presentations. Audio information in a QuickTime for Windows file can be accessed in the same manner as you would access a file containing audio and video. For example, you might be constructing an interactive CD-ROM title involving poetry that could display a Photo CD image of snow falling in the forest while a QuickTime audio clip of Robert Frost reading "Stopping by Woods on a Snowy Evening" plays. QuickTime file playback can generally be synchronized more effectively within authoring applications than other forms of sound playback.

MIDI

MIDI is a remarkably compact way to store musical information. MIDI does not represent a system for storing waveform information, like PCM, but a method of encoding the raw data of music—such as note, pitch, tempo, type of instrument, volume, attack, decay, and other characteristics—into a notational system. As a notational system, you can edit the musical data instrument by instrument and sound by sound. Sequencer software lets you manipulate the stream of musical data by moving notes, changing their volume, varying the tempo of a piece, and performing many other types of actions.

MIDI stands for Musical Instrument Digital Interface. The version that has been standardized for computer usage is called General MIDI; General MIDI defines a standard set of instruments and sounds that can be accessed by specific numbers—numbers that remain consistent throughout all compatible sound boards, synthesizers, and tone generators. This capability has led to MIDI becoming a convenient way for developers to add musical accompaniment to multimedia edutainment or game titles; tempo, volume, and pitch of musical sequences can be changed dynamically (and interactively) to support whatever is appearing on screen.

The quality of MIDI playback varies depending on the equipment available on the playback computer. Modest sound boards with FM synthesizers built in are adequate for games use and simple music instruction. The characteristic sounds of various instruments are simulated by shaping the output sound waves to approximate each instrument's pitch, tone, and timbre. More sophisticated onboard synthesizers that feature wavetable technology store accurate digital samples of real instruments for superior musical playback. MIDI playback on these devices can be a musical treat. External synthesizers can also be connected to a properly equipped sound board; models, such as the Yamaha W7 synthesizer, offer stunning sound from an elaborate, professional library of sound samples. External tone generators, such as the Yamaha MU80, can also be used to process the MIDI data.

To an electronic publisher, MIDI offers flexibility and more control over interactivity. MIDI makes sense in the following kinds of uses:

■ If you want to produce a musical instruction guide to teach young composers the effects of different musical elements, MIDI's ability to segregate instruments on individual channels lets you do this. For example, you could devise an interactive display to let a composer construct a melody line against a sequence of chords being played on guitar or piano. A click of a button could change the solo instrument from a violin to a vibraphone. Another click, and you could change the tempo from slow to quick. Another click and you could transpose the composition to a different key. MIDI gives very precise control over the playback of musical data, and because each instrument can be stored independently, you can include or mute instruments to hear the effect on the overall composition.

■ As a compact and adaptable means of storing musical information, MIDI sequences can be linked to electronic documents in a variety of ways. You could create a quiz module that plays a few notes of a tune and then lets the user guess the song. After each guess, a note or two could be added to the sequence until the right answer was provided. Although easy to do in MIDI, this would take more work and more resources using WAV files or Red Book audio.

■ For music that changes in response to the user actions, MIDI offers unsurpassed flexibility. For example, if you create an international tour guide that allows the user to follow paths while stepping through the guide toward their destination, you could add a sequence of MIDI music to match the local flavor at each node in the path sequence. Entering the United Kingdom, "God Save the Queen" could be played.

Stepping across to the Irish border, a fiddle tune could accompany the trip. A side trip to Scotland could be embellished with a solo bagpipe song. Executing MIDI files doesn't require long file loads; because the MIDI notation is compact, MIDI sequences can swiftly be accessed and directed to the output device.

At times multimedia producers have complained about the limited nature of General MIDI, which places limits on the number of simultaneous voices and the instruments that can be accessed. One of the leaders in the digital music revolution, Yamaha Corporation of America, has developed an extended version of General MIDI that caters to the needs of both musicians and multimedia developers. This new standard, known as the XG format, supports more than 600 individual instrument voices and 18 separate drum kits. Up to 32 different instruments can be played simultaneously. The XG format is downward compatible with General MIDI, but increases the range of expressiveness and complexity that can be incorporated into musical compositions by a musician or developer. Yamaha released a new tone generator, the MU80, as the first product including the XG format; given Yamaha's long history in digital music development and synthesizer design, there is a fairly good chance that the XG format will catch on in the industry and be embraced by sound board designers, software developers, and musical instrument companies.

Sound at the Application Level

To handle sound effectively within the CD-ROM development environment, you need a collection of tools that can successfully manage the different sound formats and provide sufficient flexibility to import and export sound data in any needed format. Many applications in this category are available, though many of the professional caliber applications are quite expensive; the following subsections list some tools that might be useful to an electronic publisher working with sound.

OMI's Disc-to-Disk

Digitally stored sound is by nature very clean and noise-free. Signal-to-noise levels are typically in the 90dB range compared with noise levels around 65dB for tape-based systems. However, if you are bringing in tracks of sound effects or royalty-free music from compact disc to use in an electronic publication, noise gets introduced in the process. Usually, you import music from CD by taking the stereo line out from your compact disc player or CD-ROM drive and bringing it into the stereo inputs of your sound board. The musical data gets converted from digital to analog format when outputted from the CD-ROM player and then the sound board converts it back again from analog to digital format. In the process, noise inevitably gets introduced. To make things worse, unless you own a very high-quality sound card, it is very likely that your card will contribute to the noise problems; system-induced noise on input and output lines can reduce the signal-to-noise ratio to 30dB or less. If you want to make use of music in its clean digital form, why not import it directly from disc as PCM data?

OMI responded to this challenge with a product called Disc-to-Disk, a means of transferring audio data from a disc in its digital form without going through a conversion. Figure 16.1 shows the difference in direct transfer of musical data compared to the D/A and A/D conversions that take place if you access music through a sound card.

FIGURE 16.1.
Transferring digital audio directly.

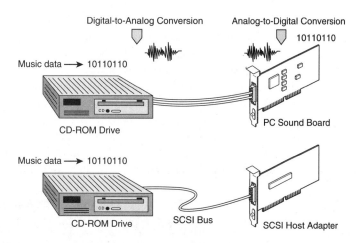

To use this program, you need a CD-ROM drive capable of responding to audio read commands. Audio data on CD-ROM was not designed to be precisely addressed by individual sectors; instead, addressing refers to a time-based system, and the precision is limited to 4/75ths of a second. Disc-to-Disk uses a number of techniques to overcome this somewhat sloppy addressing scheme to extract very specific pieces of audio from a CD track.

> **NOTE**
>
> CD-ROM drives that can respond to audio read commands include the Plextor 4PLEX family, Sony CDU 55S, NEC 3X family, Apple CD300 family, Sony CDU-561-7811, and the Toshiba 3401/4101/3501 models. Many newer drives also include this capability; check the manufacturer's specifications.

If you do have the necessary hardware, Disc-to-Disk can help you maintain the cleanest possible sound files by importing them without conversion. Disc-to-Disk also includes built-in editing tools, so you can continue to manipulate the sound waveforms after they are imported. Many compact discs containing sound effects and royalty free music use Red Book audio tracks for storage of the data; for capturing this kind of information for your multimedia use, Disc-to-Disk is ideal. Other discs containing sound effects and music use WAV files or other sound file formats for storage. In such an instance, you can copy the files directly from CD-ROM to your hard disk as you're preparing your electronic publication. Because there is no conversion, there is no loss in sound quality in copying the file in its original format. For a review of how sound files are incorporated into the different CD-ROM formats, refer to Chapter 14, "What Goes onto CD-ROM (and How)." The suggested retail price for Disc-to-Disk is $199.

Voyetra's Sound Suite

As you've seen by the descriptions in this chapter, audio information can be stored and manipulated in many different formats. To deal with the various formats, you need specific tools designed to handle data as it appears in the individual formatted files. Voyetra, a company with considerable experience in MIDI applications and synthesizer design, has released a collection of sound utilities in a package called Sound Suite for Windows. This tool collection includes two different MIDI sequencers, an AudioStation (shown in Figure 16.2) that controls a PC's sound hardware (modeled after a stereo component system), a simple presentation package for composing basic multimedia sequences called MIDI Orchestrator Plus, a waveform editing utility called AudioView, and a juke box that lets you create playlists composed of WAV, MIDI, or audio CD tracks and play them back through your computer.

FIGURE 16.2.

AudioStation control over sound hardware.

If your needs are not too demanding, the tools in this package could handle the majority of the tasks in your electronic publishing efforts. Serious sound professionals may want to seek out standalone packages that handle digital sound recording, production effects, and MIDI sequencing as independent tasks, but you can accomplish a great deal simply using Sound Suite, and the price is right ($199.95 suggested list). The interface design for the different utilities, particularly the two sequencer programs, is especially clean and understandable. Someone without a great deal of experience in sequencer operation could quickly adapt to these programs. Figure 16.3 shows the track view window for MIDI Orchestrator Plus.

FIGURE 16.3.

Track view in MIDI Orchestrator Plus.

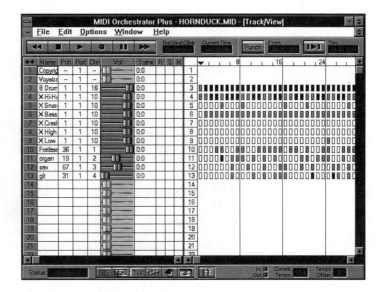

Digital sound editing capabilities have greatly improved the nature of the work performed by audio engineers. Editing on tape-based systems requires cueing up sections of sound and then physically cutting and pasting segments of tape to create a desired sound progression. Digital techniques allow you to view a representation of the sound wave and then make changes to the stored waveform, view the results, and listen to changes that you've made. Inappropriate changes can be erased with a simple Undo.

AudioView, a waveform editing utility, lets you manipulate sound by interacting with the physical waveform. Let's assume you have a taped interview with a leader of the women's movement for your electronic book about women in the twentieth century. You can import portions of the taped interview through your computer's sound card to convert the material to digital form. You can open this file in a program like AudioView, and cut and paste different portions to use in your electronic book. Snips of audio can be used as electronic versions of the "pull quotes" you often see in magazines (a brief quote highlighted within a tint block on the page, usually in a font larger than the normal text). Figure 16.4 shows the appearance of a soundwave consisting of human speech in AudioView.

AudioView includes a noise gate feature that you can use to digitally remove much of the tape hiss present on the original recording. A number of other features allow you to perform sophisticated editing tasks like creating smooth fade ins and fade outs, compressing the sound, creating cross fades with sound data stored in the clipboard, and adding echo effects to the sound. You can also save the resulting digital file at a different sample rate.

FIGURE 16.4.

You can cut and paste soundwaves in AudioView.

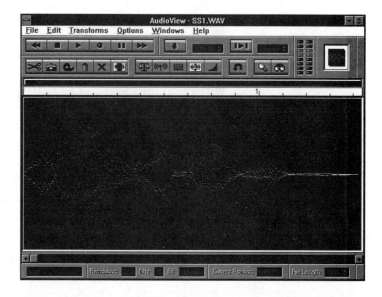

TIP

A common practice of many CD-ROM developers is to record sound initially at CD-quality rates (16-bit at 44.1kHz) and then to edit the sound by *downsampling*. For example, music downsampled to eight-bit values at 22kHz sounds fine for background or introductory music. Speech, because it doesn't require the dynamic range of music, can be effectively downsampled to eight-bit by 11kHz formats. Downsampling in this manner results in more compact sound files that can be more quickly loaded and played in a presentation.

Guidelines for Incorporating Sound into CD-ROMs

To summarize the material in this subsection, consider the following guidelines when you are using audio in a CD-ROM presentation:

- When the highest quality audio is required, use the original Red Book audio format for storing audio information. You can do this by creating a Yellow Book Mixed Mode disc where the computer data in Track 1 can be linked to audio tracks 2 through 99. Many of the recordable CD premastering/mastering applications support the creation of Mixed Mode discs.

- When using large WAV files, or files in other digital audio formats, check the playback performance through simulation of the CD-ROM operation and one-off testing. Large WAV files work best if they can be accessed and played while minimal display changes are taking place on-screen. When possible, break up large digital sound files into smaller units.

■ If your CD-ROM title includes animation or video where sounds must be carefully synchronized to the display, use the CD-ROM XA format so that computer data and audio/video information can be interleaved. Interleaved content can be accessed much more quickly than if the laser read head has to move around the disc seeking scattered information. CD-ROM XA requires a properly equipped CD-ROM drive for playback, possibly limiting your audience.

■ If you need to synchronize audio playback with animation or video without using CD-ROM XA format, embed the sound in QuickTime for Windows or Video for Windows format.

■ If you are creating digital audio files from imported analog material, always capture the sound at the highest available sampling rate: 16-bit at 44kHz. You can always downsample the audio data later to create more compact files for playback. If you sample at lower rates initially, your sound quality will suffer.

■ When it is necessary to use music in flexible and adaptable ways, consider MIDI as one alternative for including sound in your CD-ROM title. MIDI lets you isolate instruments, perform dynamic changes in a musical sequence (such as transposing keys on-the-fly), and it takes up little disc storage space.

■ If you need to use highly compressed sound files, the ADPCM formats can provide extended sound support to any viewers who have the necessary playback equipment and software drivers (ADPCM requires a CD-ROM XA-compatible and a corresponding software driver).

The creative use of sound can greatly enhance a CD-ROM production and the tools to master sound handling are within the range of any electronic publisher.

Incorporating Photographic Images into CD-ROMs

Kodak's Photo CD technology specifies a standardized method for storing scanned film images at various resolutions on CD-ROM. The technology has not yet quite caught on with the home photographer who wants to display photographs of Uncle Ernie barbecuing chicken in the backyard while the kids play badminton, primarily due to the expense of the set-top devices for viewing the images. The technology has caught on with multimedia developers, graphic artists, and others who need a convenient method of exchanging digital image information. PhotoCD images can be viewed on CD-ROM XA drives. The actual Photo CD disc standard, co-authored by Kodak and Philips and usually called Hybrid Disc, allows playback on a wide variety of set top devices, game players, as well as CD-ROM drives that meet the XA specifications.

Kodak recently opened the Photo CD standard to increase cross-platform appeal so that images can be created and distributed using Kodak's Image Pac format with the purchase of a royalty-free license. Kodak hopes the Image Pac format will become as common for image exchange as other formats, such as TIFF and JPEG. Kodak's new Photo CD Portfolio II disc format allows digital data, such as sound or script information, to be linked to Photo CD images, allowing the creation of interactive presentations. It also encompasses more types of image information than strictly scanned film, extending support to the output of digital cameras or images captured by scanners.

The Pro Photo CD Master disc standard supports image resolutions as high as 4096×6144, sufficient for demanding professional applications. The Portfolio II standard allows lower-resolution images to be used to tailor the technology more toward typical display uses; the highest required resolution under Portfolio II is 512×768.

Electronic books, training applications, interactive tour guides, and so on can be built around images in Photo CD formats. Because Photo CD data is stored at a number of resolutions, you can design the presentation to fit different display resolutions, allowing displays that fit the highest quality 24-bit color presentation for systems equipped with the necessary video adapter, and lesser resolutions for more modest equipment. Landmark CD-ROM titles such as Rick Smolan's *From Alice to Ocean* take advantage of the Photo CD's high-resolution storage for stunning display of photographs. Photo CD image storage offers significant advantages for certain types of electronic publications.

Some CD recorder applications include features or special utilities designed to support the creation of Photo CD discs. For example, Corel's CD Creator application includes a tool called PCD Creator (shown in Figure 16.5) that lets you incorporate images from a standard Photo CD disc (perhaps from your latest roll of 35mm film of your rafting trip down the American River) onto a recordable CD. The creation process is simple: you view thumbnail images from the source Photo CD in one window and double-click selected images to add to the recordable disc layout. When you've assembled the full disc layout, you can burn the recordable CD with the selected images.

FIGURE 16.5.

Corel's PCD Creator displays thumbnail images for transferring to recordable CD. Clip art from CorelDRAW!™ 5.

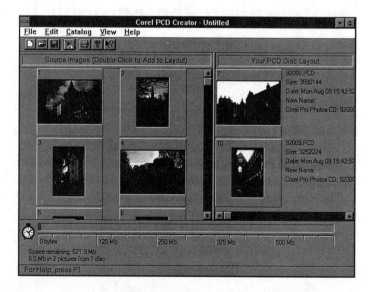

The Photo CD process makes it possible to match the image quality usually associated with coffee-table photographic books on a computer display. This is clearly a benefit in any kind of electronic publishing situation where image quality is paramount. Programs also exist, as discussed in the following section, that let you design interactive presentations from stored Photo CD images.

Kodak Arrange-It and Build-It

To work with Photo CD images from the desktop, Kodak has created two software applications that simplify the task. Arrange-It is a program that lets you combine audio files, Photo CD images, and other graphic files into an interactive presentation. The resulting script can than be used in Kodak's Build-It application to master a recordable CD from the contents of the script. Although they don't contain the high-end features and flexibility of a full multimedia development application, such as Macromedia Director, these two programs could help you quickly create kiosk displays, interactive training packages, and electronic books in which the images are the primary focus.

Arrange-It uses a simple drag-and-drop approach to creating presentations, as shown in Figure 16.6. You create a collection using images that you access from a variety of sources. You can then drag these images into a document window that allows you to control the sequence of display and design menus and interactive links. You can also attach audio files to provide narration to the presentation. Because the layout shows the links visually and lets you add and modify links as desired, the working environment lets you develop presentations and test them very quickly. Once the presentation has been completed, you can use a simulation feature to test playback and view the presentation in its final form. Once you have tested the presentation and compiled the script, you can either bring the files to a facility that offers Photo CD Portfolio service or (if you have a recordable CD drive) use the Build-It application to directly master a Photo CD containing your presentation.

FIGURE 16.6.

Arrange-It collection and document windows.

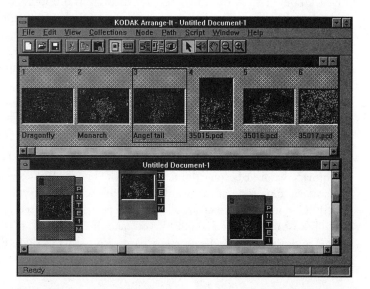

Arrange-It and Build-It offer two more tools in the electronic publishing arsenal, tools that could help you construct a high-quality presentation based on photographic imagery.

Incorporating Video into CD-ROMs

If your CD-ROM production requires embedded video sequences, you can easily add Video for Windows or QuickTime for Windows or QuickTime (Mac) files for playback on any system that has the necessary software drivers installed. These types of video files can be played back without requiring anything other than standard multimedia hardware: a CD-ROM drive, a sound card, and the necessary software drivers. For simple purposes, video files can be added to a CD-ROM as you would add any other interactive element. If you are controlling disc geography, you may want to place them near the center of the disc for improved access, but you don't need to treat them any differently than other files.

Playback of video from CD-ROM is among the most demanding tasks expected of this medium, and failure to maintain necessary performance rates during file access results in dropped frames, jerky images, and sound dropouts. Once you decide to include video on compact disc, you've entered a domain where only the highest performance equipment can seamlessly handle the output, and your potential audience may be frustrated when video sequences don't play smoothly. Because of the bandwidth limitations of the CD-ROM, you can't transfer data fast enough to handle video frames that occupy a full screen, so the video appears in a small box inset in the larger screen.

If you want full-screen, full-motion video as part of your CD-ROM title, this changes the situation considerably. The White Book standard described the MPEG-1 video format, opening up the CD-ROM to full screen video applications. The catch is that MPEG decompression hardware is required (usually as an add-on board to the PC) to be able to achieve the necessary playback rates. The cost of the necessary hardware is dropping, but it still presents a formidable obstacle to achieving widespread acceptance of this format. MPEG-1 has been technically superseded by MPEG-2, but some industry analysts think that MPEG-1 will still have a run in the marketplace before more-expensive MPEG-2 hardware is developed to the degree it can make inroads into the market. In addition, there are two opposing groups of manufacturers who are touting new high-density CD-ROM formats to allow motion pictures to be inexpensively distributed on disc. With Sony and Phillips in one camp, and Time-Warner and their allies in the other, this promises to be a long protracted battle. The outcome may determine the basic format that will be used to handle video materials on CD-ROM.

As an electronic publisher, you can easily add video sequences to CD-ROM using the standard file formats that have become dominant: QuickTime for Windows or Video for Windows. If, however, your interests range toward creating full-screen video epics, you will need to invest in an MPEG workstation to create files in the special compressed format. These workstations typically cost upwards of $10,000. If you take this approach, playback of your titles will be limited to those who have the necessary hardware. Sigma Design's RealMagic MPEG decoder board is one example of the decoding equipment that is required for playback.

Summary

By our original definition of electronic publishing, interactive media effects serve more as enhancements to the content rather than the primary focus. As you can see from this chapter, adding elements of sound, images, or video to a CD-ROM title requires some planning, but the process is not especially difficult. Always consider the performance and playback issues when selecting multimedia elements to include in your work; your audience will appreciate your foresight.

CD-ROMs and the Business Environment

17

by Lee Purcell

While the storm and tempest of multimedia games and video CD catches the headlines, business reliance on the CD-ROM for both archiving and data delivery continues to quietly increase. Business-oriented network hardware supports the mounting of arrays of CD-ROM drives that can contain everything from corporate procedures manuals to personal training packages to international telephone directories. Products such as Folio VIEWS enable businesses to convert print-oriented documents, such as word processor files, into fully indexed infobases that can be quickly navigated. The convenience of portable document applications allows any type of computer-generated information—including complex graphics, spreadsheets, and electronic memos and mail—to be distributed as soft platform-independent electronic bullets (packets of information that can be transported around the world in seconds).

This chapter looks at some of the current and developing applications for CD-ROMs in the business environment, including a perspective on the hardware required for serious business usage. In many ways, the business uses of recordable CD promise to eclipse and surpass other uses for this technology.

Archiving to CD-ROM

The characteristics of the compact disc as a long-term archival storage medium have slowly weaned businesses away from conventional tape-based backup systems and into CD recording. Here are some quick comparisons between the two forms of media that show the reasons why this trend is taking place so quickly:

- Tape is a magnetic-based medium with a lifespan of five to eight years. CD-ROM in its recordable form uses a gold-based reflective layer that ensures media lifespans of 100 years or more.

- Tape is a linear storage medium; accessing specific data requires long periods of tape streaming. The CD-ROM is a random access device; data can be retrieved from anywhere on the disc in seconds.

- Tape cartridges come in many different sizes and formats that are not readily interchangeable between different computer platforms. CD-ROMs can be formatted using the ISO 9660 file system for platform independence between DOS, Windows, Macintosh, and UNIX systems.

- Costs of tape drives for high-end high-volume systems, such as DAT drives, range from $650 upwards to $2,500. CD-ROM drives, on the other hand, can be purchased for less than $200 (for reading, but not writing data).

- Although some forms of tape have a slight price edge in terms of cost per megabyte of storage, blank CDs remain competitive with typical street prices of $8 to $10 apiece (in small quantities).

- Tape cartridges are relatively fragile, they can suffer data loss by stray magnetic fields, and they contain moving parts that can be damaged or misaligned. Compact discs are fairly durable, and they are totally immune from magnetic fields.

CDs do come with some disadvantages, however. The actual cost of the CD recorder is more than what you typically need to pay for a tape drive system, such as a DAT drive. DAT drives with capacities of 4GB per tape can be found for less than $800. Tapes, of course, are erasable and reusable, whereas recordable CDs can be used only once, making them impractical for any type of backup process that involves rotating the media. Recordable CD backup systems are also less forgiving of data throughput problems; with a tape backup system, if your data buffer runs out during writing, you can just back up the tape and try again. With a recordable CD system, if the data flow is interrupted, most often the media is rendered useless, and your only option is to insert another blank disc and try again. CD recording requires a much more finely tuned system, whereas a tape backup system can be successfully connected to any computer and generally used without difficulty.

All in all, the permanence of the medium, the random access to data, and platform-independent nature of CD-ROMs recorded under ISO 9660 make recordable CD systems competitive for use in a corporate backup and archiving environment.

> **TIP**
>
> Rather than having to decide between tape-based and CD-R-based backup and archive systems, a combination of these two approaches can successfully serve the needs of many businesses. Tape-based systems can be used for daily backups, using any of the media rotation schemes commonly employed by businesses. Information that needs to be stored in a more permanent form can be archived to recordable CD on a weekly, monthly, or quarterly basis. These two techniques complement each other very effectively.

Software for Corporate Use

One of the initial barriers to the penetration of CD-ROMs into the corporate environment was the difficulty in creating discs. The original premastering/mastering applications required considerable knowledge of the different CD-ROM formats, the ISO 9660 file system, sector and track organization, and other low-level details. The CD recordable process is also unforgiving. If you make a mistake writing to a disc, you can't erase or remove the mistake—the disc becomes unusable. This isn't as much of a tragedy today when blanks discs are selling for around $8 each, but back when the recordable discs cost $25 or more, ruining the media was a bigger concern.

The refinement of standards for multisession write operations makes it possible to record data to a compact disc over a series of sessions, rather than all at once. You don't have to wait until you have 650MB of data before you can archive it to CD. Discs can be written as needed; this took some fancy footwork to develop because compact discs rely on a table of contents and path tables for locating data. Once you write the table of contents, the disc is finalized (or another term that is frequently used is *fixated*) and no additional data can be added, even if you physically have room for another 300MB.

During multisession writing, data is bracketed on the disc by Lead-In and Lead-Out regions that contain important linking information to previous and subsequent sessions. Essentially, an ongoing interim table of contents is created and used to locate data on the disc as multisession write operations are continuing. In this stage, a disc is generally not readable by a standard CD-ROM drive, but can only be read by a CD recorder equipped to handle multisession writes. When all write operations have been completed, the disc can be finalized. The premastering/ mastering application compiles all of the data and creates the final table of contents, making the disc accessible to all CD-ROM drives without special software drivers.

TIP

In practical uses, multisession write operations to CD can be adapted to suit the flow of typical business activities. For example, an accounting department could perform weekly write operations to disc, recording the figures for each week's financial events to a session. At the end of the month (or quarter), the CD-ROM could be finalized, making the figures accessible to anyone with a CD-ROM drive. The single table of contents created during the writing of the final session would provide access to all previous sessions as well.

Some applications, such as Corel's CD-Creator, have utilities that enable you to read the contents of the individual sessions from a normal CD-ROM drive. This can be important if you need to access data on the disc before the disc is fixated.

In order to accommodate multisession writing, a large amount of information needs to be added to the recordable disc—this overhead substantially reduces the space available for actual data. The initial information for the first session requires about 30MB of disc space; subsequent sessions require 10 to 15MB of disc space. You can see that if you add data to the disc over 20 sessions or so, this overhead will consume close to half of your available storage space.

Some software manufacturers have devised methods for writing to disc without requiring the same overhead. There is also a very strong trend to remove the intricate formatting considerations from the attention of users and to make a CD recorder appear as just another drive attached to the system. As these trends continue, the popularity of recordable CD for everyday business use will probably skyrocket. Once you make that 650MB of data as easy to write as a file copy operation to a hard-disk drive, the largest barrier to practical business use has been removed.

Moniker's Spira

A small company in Scott's Valley, California, Moniker, has released a product to complement the latest generation of inexpensive CD recorders. Spira runs under Microsoft Windows, and it makes a connected CD recorder available as transparently as a hard-disk drive on the system. You can read and write to the CD recorder through Spira without consideration of CD-ROM formats, buffer underruns, and other perplexing CD-ROM issues.

Without adding new statements to AUTOEXEC.BAT and CONFIG.SYS, Spira brings up the installed CD recorder as a new drive letter on the computer. File sizes up to 10MB are supported through the default settings for the product, and this size can be expanded through an area of the program that allows advanced settings. Although the philosophy of the product is to install simply and unobtrusively, and hide the setup options from the user, Spira includes a CD-R Manager function that provides access to many of the advanced details of CD-R interconnection. CD-R Manager also serves as a control center for performing operations such as ejecting a disc.

Spira also includes features to prevent ruining recordable media, even if power failures occur in the middle of write operations. One of the greatest problems in common use of recordable CDs has been the necessity for maintaining stringent data flow conditions. Data write errors could not be corrected once written; in fact, sometimes the occurrence of even a simple data error can make previously recorded sessions on a disc unreadable. Under everyday operating situations this results in large numbers of wasted discs and also reduces the value of CD-R as an archiving or backup medium.

Spira overcomes this problem with automatic disc recovery processes that can detect problems that occurred in the latest session and write information to the disc that makes the remaining disc space available for new write operations. It also allows data stored in previous sessions to be read simply by switching to that session with the CD-R Manager. Moniker likens the process to what is called a rollback in transaction processing software, an important technique for avoiding data loss under real-world operating conditions.

Moniker has targeted Spira at the mainstream business user, the area where the company sees the greatest growth in recordable CD use. They foresee the following applications as being the most important to business use:

- **Archiving:** Financial data, software development project files, graphic images, databases, and similar files can be regularly archived to CD. Moniker also suggests that scanned images can be directly stored on CD by saving the file to the specified CD-R drive letter.

- **Backup:** Network or local backups can be performed from Window's File Manager or from a conventional backup utility. Backups from File Manager can be retrieved from any system because the data will be stored in standard CD-ROM format.

- **Presentations:** Training material, videos, multimedia presentations, and other data involving very large files can be conveniently stored and distributed on CD.

- **Distribution:** Certain types of files—such as financial data, sales information, graphic images, and so on—can be economically distributed on CD-ROM without the usual barriers of worrying about the playback equipment available at the destination site. CD-ROM drives are available almost everywhere.

- **Publishing:** As a method of producing test copies of CD-ROMs in preparation for larger scale replication, Spira simplifies the process. This technique works best for applications that do not require strict control of disc geography (the placement of files on the CD-ROM).

■ **Retail and Service:** Moniker suggests that another business application may be on-site delivery of custom CD-ROMs loaded with requested information by customers. For example, trade show systems could be set up to create a CD-ROM containing a specific collection of demonstrations, multimedia material, and infobases to match a customer's interests. The created CD-ROM could then be played back at the customer's home or office.

Making a recordable CD accessible through a simple drive letter has a great deal of appeal in the business marketplace, particularly when support can include modest systems without high-speed SCSI interfaces. Although the initial release of Spira is tailored to only the Yamaha CDR-100 and CDE-100 drives, the company is working on versions for other current generation CD recorders, such as the Sony CDU-920. Applications of this sort promise to make considerable inroads into corporate data storage domains previously dependent on tape and removable cartridges.

Spira has a suggested retail price of $249.

Hardware for Business Use

The slow performance of CD-ROMs in conventional systems can be improved by caches and other software accelerators. In the network environment, rapid retrieval of data becomes more critical because the network data retrieval overhead is added on top of the CD-ROM access rates. In many cases, the best solution is hardware based, configuring the shared CD-ROM drives in a way that permits free access to network users and improved access rates to counter the sluggish access times of the CD-ROM drives. Because network users may need access to several CD-ROMs at the same time, systems that make it possible to mount 10, 20, or 50 CD-ROMs on the network at the same time have become popular. This is typically done through disc arrays or CD-ROM servers—devices that make disc contents available by providing an independent drive for each disc. Jukeboxes are also sometimes used to provide access to CD-ROMs at the network level, but they have the disadvantage that each time a disc is requested, it must be physically loaded to the CD-ROM—this physical loading of the discs results in even slower access times to network users. It also limits network access to one disc at a time, whereas the CD-ROM server or disc array approach can provide access to 30GB or more information without disc changes.

Network use of recordable CD drives has also become popular since the hardware has become available to eliminate the data throughput problems that would otherwise make recording impossible under network conditions. The goal is to make CD recorders available to network users on the same basis that tape backup systems or other forms of archiving have been used in the past. Because data cannot be reliably transferred through the network to the CD recorder without the risk of network traffic interrupting the flow, many systems of this type rely on a hardware cache that may be as large as 1.45GB to store data for writing to the recorder. The better systems of this type make copying files to recordable CD as simple as a drag and drop operation. Files are first copied across the network to the cache buffer, which resides locally with the CD recorder, and then written in an uninterrupted stream to the recordable media. Network users are also able to read the contents of the disc as ongoing recording takes place, making this approach useful for workgroup collaboration where large files need to be both archived and made accessible to workgroup members.

The following subsections describe some of the hardware products tailored to network use of recordable CD technology.

Meridian NETSCRIBE 2000/3000

The headquarters for Meridian Data, Inc., are situated in the hills of Scotts Valley, California, separated from the high technology corridors of California's Silicon Valley by 25 miles of winding road north through the Santa Cruz Mountains. Since 1986, Meridian Data has been a key participant in the growth of CD-ROM industry, actively contributing to the standards development processes from which ISO 9660 and other CD-ROM standards originated. Meridian has focused a great deal of its efforts on providing business hardware and software solutions for network environments, and its products are widely regarded as stable, well thought out approaches to offering access to CD recorders and CD-ROM drives on the network.

The NETSCRIBE 2000 and 3000 products represent hardware/software solutions to the problems that Ethernet-based users have in accessing recordable CD drives. The software portion of the product is a client/server application that extends the network file system to include the CD-R unit. Several popular CD recorders are supported, and Meridian also offers its own recorder (repackaged from another manufacturer). The hardware portion of the product consists of a server unit with a built-in Ethernet interface loaded with the IPX/SPX protocol. Each of the server units contains its own built-in hardware cache: the NETSCRIBE 2000 includes an 83MB buffer region (with a file size limit equivalent to the size of the buffer) and the NETSCRIBE 3000 includes a 1.45GB buffer region (with a file size limit up to the maximum capacity of the CD-ROM).

The NETSCRIBE servers produce CD-ROMs in ISO 9660 format; recording can be accomplished in either single session or multisession operations. The resulting CD-ROMs can be distributed for reading on any typical CD-ROM drive.

Meridian's approach offers both a transparent view of the CD recorder to the network user and administrative controls over media access that are essential in the network environment. Although network users can read the contents of the recordable CD drive while it is mounted, access times across the network are somewhat slower than are typically experienced for users connected to a local CD-ROM drive. You can expect average access times of 1,000 milliseconds for a 2× recorder and 500 milliseconds for a 3× recorder. Local CD-ROMs typically have access rates of around 300 to 400 milliseconds. Slower access is one of the prices you pay for having access to CD recorders on the network.

Meridian CD Net Series CD-ROM Servers

Meridian Data offers several different products to make CD-ROMs available through a network at a departmental or organizational level. A stand-alone cabinet contains its own 486 or Pentium microprocessor, a set of CD-ROM drive bays (from 8 to 56), 16MB of main memory, and installed CD Net network server software. The CD Net cabinets can be integrated into a variety of local area networks as a peer network node, including networks offered by Novell, Banyan, Microsoft, and IBM. Once installed, MS-DOS users on the network have access to all of the fundamental CD-ROM formatted discs, including Red Book, Yellow Book, CD-ROM XA, Photo CD, and multisession-recorded discs. Data transfers take place at double-speed CD-ROM rates.

Meridian has designed the individual units in this series so that they can be expanded in modular increments, adding drives and additional cabinets as needed up to the limit of each model in the series. Security is provided by a locking cabinet door that keeps anyone from tampering with the CD-ROMs inserted into the drives. Because the cabinets operate as passive devices—without a keyboard or monitor directly attached—only the system administrator can control access and rights assignments within the parameters of the network software being used.

Small local area networks can economically take advantage of the CD Net 100/M, which is more closely scaled to the needs of workgroup situations or small departments. A maximum of eight CD-ROM drives can be installed in the bays within a single cabinet, offering up to 4.8GB of online storage. The CD Net 100/M contains an 80386 processor and 4MB of base memory. Support for workgroup-oriented types of network software, such as Microsoft LAN Manager and LANtastic, is included, as well as larger scale network operating systems, such as Novell 4 and Banyan Vines. Typical prices for the CD Net 100/M system range from $3,595 for a one-drive system to $6,995 for an eight-drive system.

At the other end of the spectrum, the CD Net 556/M provides access for up to 56 CD-ROM drives and a total online capacity of 950GB. This product includes Meridian Data's CD Net Plus Software, designed for simplified integration to Novell NetWare IPX environments. The CD Net 556/M cabinet includes a Pentium process and 16MB of main memory. Both Ethernet and Token Ring network configurations are supported. Prices range from $8,495 for a one-drive system to $14,845 for an eight-drive system. Current information about products from Meridian Data can be obtained by calling 1-800-767-2537.

Recording Multiple Discs for Business Use

Increased reliance on CD-ROMs to convey information in the business environment will produce a growing need for recording systems that can handle more than one disc at a time. Serious CD-ROM recording requires a dedicated host computer; don't expect to do multi-tasking on a system where recording is taking place. You don't want to do anything that has the potential for interrupting the data flow. Even if you're only attempting to record four or five discs, on a 2× recorder it takes approximately 30 minutes to complete a recording. Someone needs to be hovering by the system to change discs each time a recording is completed. You could easily spend half a day setting up and monitoring the process to produce a half dozen discs; unless this kind of activity is performed infrequently, if you produce a good number of discs per week, you probably want to investigate recording systems tailored to business uses.

In some cases where you want to limit your investment, an outside replication facility may be the answer. Using large-scale outside replication services, however, usually doesn't make sense unless you have a need for hundreds of CD-ROMs. Smaller replicators may be too slow or too expensive; they may also lack the quality control measures that make the difference between a professional replication job and a seriously flawed effort. If your business needs justify the expenditure, the purchase of a system to handle unattended multiple recording of discs will simplify your recording tasks. Two basic solutions exist:

- **Disc transporter:** This type of device works in conjunction with a CD recorder. You load a spindle of blank discs, and the device automatically transports a disc at a time to the recorder; when the recording is done, the completed disc is removed, and a new blank disc is inserted in the recorder. The process is serial, and unless you have a quad-speed or six-speed recorder, it can take a long time to record a group of fifty discs.

- **Parallel CD recorder:** This approach includes a network server acting as a master that handles the data being prepared for recording to CD. A number of slave units then complete the recording in parallel. This is a faster process, but—because a number of individual recorders are involved—the expense is significantly greater than the disc transporter approach.

The following subsections describe recording systems in each of these categories.

Kodak Disc Transporter

Kodak has had a strong presence in the recordable CD marketplace for a number of years, and their 6× recorder is—at press time—the fastest available solution for high-speed recording applications. The Kodak Disc Transporter, shown in Figure 17.1, provides a means for recording up to 75 CD-ROMs at a time for business environments that require this volume of recording. This machine is basically a mechanical solution that works with an existing recorder to load blank discs and transfer finished discs between spindles. Kodak offers Media Bulk Packs that can be used to quickly fill a spindle with blank discs.

The Disc Transporter can be mechanically coupled with the 6× Kodak PCD Writer 600, and can also be used with other recorders in the PCD Writer series, such as the 2× PCD Writer 225, with the addition of an accessory interface kit. A serial recording solution of this type makes sense in situations where you have time to spare while the recording is taking place. For example, you could load up the Disc Transporter with discs at the end of the work day, start the recording process and let it run all night, and return in the morning to a stack of completed CD-ROMs. If you need faster turnaround of recorded CDs, a parallel recording solution may be your best bet. An example of a system of this type appears in the next subsection. Information on Kodak products can be obtained by accessing the Kodak forum on CompuServe (GO KODAK) or by calling 1-800-CD KODAK.

FIGURE 17.1.
Kodak Disc Transporter.
Reprinted courtesy of
Eastman Kodak Company.

FIGURE 17.1.
Kodak Disc Transporter.
Reprinted courtesy of
Eastman Kodak Company.

Intaglio CD-R 2004 Recording System

Intaglio, a small company located in Santa Clara, California, provides parallel CD recording solutions for Ethernet and Token Ring networks. A master unit contains the network interface and acts as a server for a CD recorder. Additional slave units, consisting of two recorders, connect to the master. Anyone on the network with Network File System (NFS) capabilities can initiate a recording by creating an image file for the CD and transferring the file to the master unit. The master unit writes to the blank media in the requested format based on the contents of the image file. As the master unit is recording, all attached slave units also record in parallel.

Intaglio offers several different configurations, including cabinets that contain a master unit and four slaves, and rack units that can be combined and expanded in a variety of ways. The simplest configuration, designed for a single user, still requires a network interface card in the host computer. Either an Ethernet or Token Ring card can be used. Network File System software running on the individual PC is used to specify the contents of the CD image, which can then be transferred and mastered to the recordable media.

The expansion options offered by different Intaglio configurations support up to 75 simultaneous recordings. Quad-speed recorders can be specified in the master and slave units, which cuts the recording time for a 650MB disc down to 15 to 17 minutes. Pricing of the units is fairly steep, starting at $7,200 for an Ethernet master unit and $11,500 for a slave unit containing two recorders. Group configurations range from the low $20,000s to the mid $30,000s. If your business requirements include frequent CD recording activities, a parallel recording system of this type can shorten your overall recording times considerably.

Printing to Disc

In many office environments, the network printer gets the heaviest workout of any office equipment, in the process generating hundreds or thousands of pages a day. What if you could have a printer that would keep output in electronic form and had a paper tray that would hold 250,000 sheets of "virtual" paper. Young Minds, Inc., has come up with a network printer approach to creating documents on CD-ROM. Its AutoCDR product consists of hardware and software that installs on most NetWare, UNIX, and TCP/IP networks and mimics a network print server. Without needing to know any of the intricacies of ISO 9660 or other CD-ROM standards, AutoCDR captures document files sent across the network by workgroup members and transparently writes them to recordable media.

This system uses either the Kodak PCD 600 recorder (a 6× recorder) or PCD 225 (a 2× recorder), coupled to the Kodak Disc Transporter media loader. In actual use, workgroup members create files using whatever software application they typically use—word processor, spreadsheet program, or infobase application. When the files are saved, they "print" it, specifying the network printer designated as the AutoCDR print server and the number of copies needed. The AutoCDR server processes the job by queuing the data, using the media loader to set up a blank disc, recording a serialized disc bar code number and other identification on the disc, and writing the data. If additional discs are requested, the system unloads the first disc written and drops a new blank disc on the recorder spindle. Completed discs are stacked on another spindle. Single-session, multi-session, and multi-volume write operations are supported.

Young Minds, Inc., originated CD recording processes in the UNIX marketplace, where it is still the strongest presence. This new product provides one more tool for businesses interested in escaping the paper trap. Documents printed to CD-ROM using AutoCDR can be mounted on the network for access by all network users using any of the CD-ROM servers or disc arrays available for sharing CD-ROMs. More information about Young Minds products can be obtained through its Web site (`http://www.ymi.com`) or by calling 1-800-YMI-4YMI.

Computer Output to Laser Disc

Computer Output to Laser Disc (COLD) promises to be a technology that will ignite the business community as awareness of its benefits becomes more prevalent. In the course of everyday operation, businesses generate reams of data, much of it within the domain of MIS departments. Traditionally, computer-generated data gets printed to the familiar, fan-fold greenbar computer paper, or to microfiche, or to a tape backup system. None of these systems works very effectively for conducting searches or gleaning individual facts from a collection of data.

The concept of COLD has existed for some time, but early attempts at implementation floundered because of lack of standards, hardware setup difficulties, and overall expense. Magnetic-optical drives and WORM drives (Write Once, Read Many) were used in early implementations, but the results were not very satisfactory.

With the arrival of inexpensive CD recorders, COLD suddenly springs free of earlier obstacles. Compatibility and data interchange issues are solved: Outputting to CD-ROM in ISO 9660 format ensures data access across platforms. The expense issues have evaporated with CD recorders selling for $1,500, and the blank media available for $8 to $10. With compression utilities available, such as capaCD Pro by EWB, up to 4GB can be stored on a single recordable CD. The hardware necessary to access data stored on CD-ROM already exists in tremendous volume—CD-ROM drives sell for less than $200 and are widely bundled on both home and business systems.

The improvement in applications that can quickly index large quantities of data for CD-ROM access also provides an additional incentive for adopting this technology. Every word on a CD-ROM can be included in an index for search and retrieval, and proximity search techniques—which rank search hits in respect to how close the search terms are in proximity to each other in a document—make it much easier to target and locate specific information in a collection of documents. For harried MIS managers, the access to information that is afforded by new search and retrieval techniques can be a godsend.

Programs such as dataDisc's QuickSearch indexer and Folio VIEWS can work directly with raw text contained in unfielded files to produce elaborate, full-text indexes. Some products, such as IMR's Alchemy, are designed expressly for implementing COLD solutions using mainstream CD recorders. Other tools are quickly being developed by software companies who know that the potential of COLD is being realized. Many corporations are looking for software applications that allow the extension of search and retrieval abilities to up to 100 CD-ROMs that may be stored in a juke box unit or reside in a disc array. The sophistication to initiate searches of this sort has not yet been perfected.

Businesses thrive on readily accessible information; COLD is the technology that can provide them with the necessary information in quick and painless fashion.

Examples of Corporate Applications

The range of CD-ROM applications in the corporate setting continues to expand as imaginative new techniques are devised for presenting information within this framework. Many commercial CD-ROM titles aim directly at the business and institutional marketplace, with titles appearing with greater frequency in all of these areas:

- Legal infobases, including case histories, state and national statutes, and templates for specialized legal document preparation.
- Medical information, including research data, electronic versions of medical journals, educational material, and public information titles.
- Educational titles, including grade school through university-level instruction in science, art, music, literature, and engineering.
- Financial and tax resources, including specialized infobases, focused marketing data, tax law advisories, world market research, and similar kinds of material.

- Training, including instruction in employee and management relations, hiring practices, mastering software applications, learning specialized skills, and so on.

- Product support, including technical details about products, troubleshooting and repair information, software upgrades, product information infobases, and CD-ROM based reference sets.

Presenting Regulations in Electronic Form

Many corporations and organizations operate under a regulatory umbrella that requires compliance with many different federal and local laws. Given that these regulations are often contained in several different volumes, obtaining a single fact or piece of information usually requires an extensive search through hundreds of pages. Because this type of information can be critical to a company's operation, anything that makes it easier to navigate and interrogate the regulatory morass can be a major benefit to that company—and can also ensure compliance with the necessary regulations. Seeing a genuine need for electronically published versions of federal regulations, some companies have converted thousands of pages of Government Printing Office documents to more accessible electronic publications.

One example is a company called TEXT-Trieve, Inc., that has taken a collection of federal publications related to occupational safety and health and converted them into a Folio VIEWS infobase. Its product, FED-Trieve, includes documents from the Occupational Safety and Health Association, the Department of Transportation, and the Environmental Protection Agency, all neatly indexed on a single CD-ROM. Beyond the content of the basic regulations, this CD-ROM also contains material to help use and interpret the regulations. A collection of more than 1,600 letters from OSHA regional and national offices helps clarify the intent of the OSHA CFR's. Persons in an organizational position who need to stay abreast of the regulatory procedures that govern their operation can save countless hours in navigating and searching the many volumes that may apply to their situations. Having these volumes all contained on a single CD-ROM cuts search times down immeasurably.

Were you wondering what federal controls are associated with kyanite? It took about two seconds of search time to discover that kyanite is one of the minerals regulated by the Mine Safety and Health Administration. What considerations affect exposure to carbon monoxide in the workplace? Another four seconds of searching accessed material on carbon monoxide exposure. Try to imagine an equivalent search through thousands of pages in several different volumes, and you can get a sense of what a dramatic improvement in information access this is.

TEXT-Trieve, located in Bellevue, Washington, has been developing CD-ROM infobases since 1988 and has a number of different titles covering safety and health rules in the states of Washington, Oregon, and Alaska, as well as several dealing with federal health and safety rules.

For more information on using republished materials, see Chapter 3, "Terms and Concepts."

Information as a Business Commodity

Many of the electronic publishers who focus on the commercial and business markets have grappled with the problems of distributing copyrighted information through electronic channels. Digital information by its nature can be effortlessly reproduced and distributed around the world. How can electronic publishers and authors maintain some measure of control over their works to ensure that they are compensated for their efforts and the original copyrights are not violated?

A not-for-profit organization, the Copyright Clearance Center in Danvers, Massachusetts, has been collaborating with Folio Corporation to design a model by which these problems can be handled. Their strategy is to develop technical and contractual systems for accessing electronic books, journals, newsletters, and newspapers, while ensuring that authors receive royalty payments and that copyrights remain protected. As stated by the president and CEO of the Copyright Clearance Center, Joseph S. Alen, "In most cases, traditional print publishers and authors have been unwilling to release their copyrighted materials in digital form without adequate protection of their copyrights. By providing both technological and contractual controls, the Folio/CCC relationship promises to dramatically increase the flow of information from rightsholders to users."

The Folio/CCC proposals support access to digital materials on a metered, per-transaction basis. The framework initially provides coverage for CD-ROM uses and over local area networks, but they are also working to refine the usage strategy for the Internet. Folio Corporation's Information Marketplace plan has also elicited support from many digital information producers as a viable technique for handling information distribution through a variety of media.

The Information Marketplace model revolves around what the company calls an "InfoApp," which is a customized application geared to meet customer requirements in certain, focused business markets. Publishers can then sell their materials to customers through either a subscription approach or through a form of metering which assesses a fee for individual transactions. For example, if you download four articles about new discoveries in molecular chemistry from a service using the InfoApp approach, you might be billed $.55 per article. Similarly, the same information could be contained on CD-ROM and released through an encryption key approach. You purchase a CD-ROM containing a specialized database that might sell for $8,500 if all the information were presented in unrestricted form. You can then extract data as needed for a set fee that provides you with a certain number of transactions; perhaps $50 would let you access 200 individual items from the CD-ROM.

Henry Heilesen, Vice President of Commercial Publishing at Folio Corporation, likens one approach to postal metering: "Let's say someone buys a CD-ROM and from that CD-ROM they want to buy $500 worth of use. The metering software can tick off each time the person incurs a charge and deduct the amount from the $500 until they run out. You basically sell it much as you would postage for a postage meter. On a network, when you use time, the server could be interrogated remotely by modem—to download the amount of time that has been used on a particular infobase—and then a bill could be sent to the end user. There are several ways in which this can be implemented. I think, quite frankly, it will be implemented in many different ways, in one scenario or another, depending on how publishers want to sell their information and how they think people want to buy it."

The Copyright Clearance Center was created in response to requests by the U.S. Congress. They currently handle the licensing of reproduction rights to more than 1.7 million titles produced by more than 9,000 publishers. CCC is well positioned to serve as an information clearinghouse for publishing issues involving copyrights and payments associated with the use of copyrighted material.

> **NOTE**
>
> The development of techniques for effectively processing "micro-payments" (involving transactions of one cent or less) will serve as a significant incentive to the growth of information distribution channels. Information consumers will be more inclined to use these services as costs are scaled incrementally to allow inexpensive browsing and information retrieval. This technique could help spur a genuine information revolution.

Vertical Market Turnkey Solutions

Meridian Data and SilverPlatter Information have teamed up to introduce a fully integrated network information solution that includes both Meridian's CD Net 428 Enterprise network server and a set of CD-ROMs from one of SilverPlatter's databases. Although the initial offerings are targeted at the medical and educational establishments, this approach to providing integrated bundles of information for network users will probably become more important in mainstream business as well. As an example of the kind of material contained in these turnkey solutions, the following lists describe some of the contents:

- **CD Net Pharmaceutical SilverServer:** Includes MEDLINE Express (1984 to present), EMBASE Alert, International Pharmaceutical Abstracts, BIOETHICSLINE Plus, Inpharma, Reactions.
- **CD Net Academic SilverServer:** Includes ERIC Quarterly (1966 to present), GPO Statistical Abstract from A Matter of Fact database, Peterson's GRADLINE, PAIS International, EconLit, Sociofile, Choice, MDX Health Digest, Access: the Supplementary Index to Periodicals.

The pricing of these combination CD-ROM network servers and information sets—around $40,000—puts them beyond the reach of most individuals, but buyers in institutional settings actually experience significant cost savings compared to buying the network components and CD-ROM titles individually. This bundling approach lets an organization add the equivalent of an extensive, highly specialized library to its network with minimal setup difficulties as well as the advantages of high-speed search and retrieval of information. You can expect to see more extensive use of add-on CD-ROM libraries in government, education, and business.

CD-ROMs: The Recycling Issue

Businesses still represent one of the largest generators of refuse to worldwide landfills, and the use of paper in various forms has always been at the heart of the problem. Business consumption of paper products in the U.S. alone contributes hundreds of tons of debris to landfills— recycling helps, but there is clearly an enormous amount of paper products that are unsuitable for recycling or are not recycled because someone doesn't make the effort.

The promise of the paperless office has been an elusive one, and in many ways the use of computers has only generated new kinds of materials that are difficult to dispose of or to recycle. Floppy disks, tape cartridges, obsolete computer equipment, old monitors, and similar materials all present problems.

Until recently, the CD-ROM fit in the category of those materials that cannot easily be turned into anything useful during recycling. Despite the fact that the plastic contained in the disc consists of relatively high-grade optical polycarbonate, the other components of the disc—lacquer coating, aluminum, printing ink—resist being separated and removed from the plastic base.

A new process devised by a Pennsylvania inventor, August DeFazio, makes it possible for CD-ROMs to stay out of landfills. His invention strips ink and lacquer from the disc and extracts the aluminum from the disc substrate. More than 3,500 discs per hour can be processed without a human attendant, resulting in a plastic byproduct that can be sold for about $.40 per pound. The plastic generated during this recycling can be reborn in the form of automobile parts, protective headgear for bicyclists or football players, and handles for kitchen utensils, such as spatulas and sauce pans.

As promising as this recycling development is, the issue of CD-ROM packaging materials remains. Plastic jewel cases present a disposal problem. Other packaging solutions, such as fiber sleeves, require less material and can more easily be handled as part of a large-scale recycling effort. For the environmentally conscious company, when it comes to packaging, less is more. External packaging can be constructed of unbleached, recycled fibers; companies such as Apple Computer are already distributing many CD-ROM-based training materials and in-house corporate information using entirely recycled packaging materials.

Electronic Publishing and Business

Henry Heilesen, Vice President of Commercial Publishing at Folio Corporation, sees electronic publishing as attaining an increasingly important role in most businesses. His comments, from an interview conducted on June 16, 1995, follow.

"In observing the direction that we have seen electronic publishing take, we think it has a great future from the standpoint of becoming more and more useful and important in the field of professional work, as well as in consumer life. There are strong economic incentives that are going to drive this. Because of the inefficiencies of printing and distributing paper, and the associated costs, there will be a lot of pressure on businesses to go electronic (particularly as the infrastructure of PCs and modems and high-speed lines become more commonplace). We've seen a huge shift in the mix of printed publications and electronic publications from some of our publishers, going from where it had been—almost no electronic publications and all paper, to a very high percentage of electronic publications (and a much smaller percentage being paper).

"I think that paper versions are not going to disappear, printed publications are not going to disappear, CD-ROM will not disappear, and online will not totally dominate the market. They will all find their niche, and they will work very nicely together."

Folio Corporation has taken a leading role in developing techniques for distributing information electronically. A recent product, the Folio Infobase Web Server, accommodates online presentation and searching of very large infobases over the Internet. Heilesen sees each of the information delivery mechanisms as having its own role and purpose. "Networks will also play a very important role in this aspect of sharing information. We are excited about the Web servers on the Internet from the standpoint that it is another way for publishers to distribute their information. Not only will people read information printed on paper, but they'll also have it available—as we've noted—on hard disks, floppy disks, CD-ROMs, online services, and now over the Internet through Web servers. One of the advantages that we have built into the Folio product is once you've created an infobase with the functionality that we have in it today, it can be used on CD-ROM, on a network, on a hard disk, and on the Internet through the Folio Web server."

Some companies are adopting the hybrid approach to electronic distribution of information, where the CD-ROM provides the essential information content and the content can also be dynamically updated. As Heilesen explains, "The initial approach by a lot of our professional publishers—such as legal publishers and medical publishers—is to use the Web server as a method to update their information once they have put out a CD-ROM. The latest updates are available through the Web server, and then at an appropriate future point in time, they can send out another CD-ROM."

Summary

Used wisely, electronic publishing offers businesses an inexpensive and efficient way to distribute information, not only to employees, but also to customers and prospective customers. As the methods for presenting and searching information improve, and companies become more comfortable with the development tools and the methods for managing large volumes of electronic data, electronic publishing will continue to replace paper. Whether an employee needs an international telephone number, a procedure for filling out a requisition form, or details about a replacement part for a product, they will be able to display that information on-screen with just a few keystrokes. In a similar manner, companies will be able to creatively adapt and repurpose information about products, corporate identities, and applications and present this information through electronic channels to a readership that spans the globe. Best of all, this swift and pollution-free communication can be accomplished without chopping down a single tree.

Title Development, Production, and Distribution

18

by Lee Purcell

The corporate electronic publishing environment (as described in the previous chapter) lacks the glamour and panache of the interactive multimedia market, which is colored by the glow of fast-moving games, such as LucasArts' *Dark Forces*, and flashy references, such as the *Grolier Guinness Multimedia Disc of Records*. Nonetheless, the corporate applications—procedures manuals published on CD-ROM and tech support infobases circulated on LANs—represent the larger percentage of electronic publishing efforts today. If you are working towards gaining experience with new media, the corporate workplace is probably the logical place to acquire the necessary application skills and the knowledge to effectively publish works in electronic form. The interactive procedure manual you're working on today could lead you to the creation of your own multimedia guide to solar energy use sometime down the road.

Once you've gained the requisite skills, you may want to set your sights on creating and releasing your own CD-ROM title. As discussed in Chapter 15, "Hardware and Software Tools for CD-ROM Development," the hardware and software are not prohibitively expensive, and the learning curve for mastering the techniques is not any greater than for most current generation computer applications. Although the market for CD-ROM titles is going through one of those evolutionary bursts that Stephen Jay Gould discussed (within a biological framework), opportunities exist for fast-moving and innovative title producers. You may not be able to compete head-to-head with Microsoft to create a better multimedia encyclopedia, but you might be able to design a CD-ROM source book to material recycling resources in your county or state. Niche markets abound, and while the sales of CD-ROM players continue to accelerate, your potential audience grows as well.

This chapter covers the process of creating electronic publications on CD-ROM, from rights acquisitions to packaging and sales. This obviously covers a lot of ground in a limited amount of space, but the overview should provide you with enough information to get started.

Obtaining Source Materials

Materials for use on a CD-ROM title can originate from a variety of sources:

- Your personal written works, video clips, musical pieces, reference data, or artistic output (including novels, poems, short stories, and plays).
- Materials that exist in the public domain (free from copyright restrictions).
- Works for which you purchase a buy-out license, giving you the freedom to include the material with a CD-ROM title. This might include background and theme music, video sequences, photographic clip art, and similar kinds of material.
- Existing copyrighted works for which you negotiate a use agreement with the copyright holder. An agreement might require you to pay a single fee to produce an unlimited number of CD-ROMs using the material, or a small charge (essentially a royalty fee) per unit sold.

■ Depending on the nature of the material, a combination of these approaches may apply. Complex works, such as multimedia references that include hundreds of different clips and entries, may include original works, contracted works, public domain materials, and copyrighted materials. Licensing and rights negotiations could constitute a major portion of a project of this sort.

Do It Yourself

The best way to obtain source materials for a CD-ROM title is to create them yourself. With the do-it-yourself approach, you eliminate licensing concerns. You avoid paying royalties to a third-party source provider (which can be an excessive burden to a small-scale title producer). You gain the freedom to shape the content exactly the way you want it and express your point of view. Clearly, if you have a story to tell, useful information to relate, a skill to teach that is adaptable to the instructional methods of electronic media, a CD-ROM title can be an excellent way to communicate both artistic and practical ideas.

The act of creating and publishing a CD-ROM automatically bestows copyright protection to all original material contained upon it. Although you do not need to register the material with the government copyright office, a work must be registered before you can file an infringement suit. Filing early also entitles you to certain additional benefits if you win the law suit.

Bear in mind that if you contract someone to contribute music or photographs or written material to a CD-ROM title, unless your contract stipulates that they are forfeiting copyright ownership to their work, these contractors may be entitled to royalty payments when the work is distributed. Make sure any agreements for contracted work stipulate ultimate ownership of that work.

Public Domain Materials

You do not need to obtain any sort of license to use materials that exist in the public domain. By definition, these belong to no one—either the original copyright filing has expired, the works predate the copyright laws, or the creator has explicitly placed the works in the public domain. Early literary works are usually free of copyright restrictions: Edgar Allen Poe, Nathaniel Hawthorne, Samuel Clemens, Shakespeare, and so on. You can also tap a huge body of work available through certain federal agencies, which is public domain by reason of the fact that the work was created using public funds and released to public ownership. Voyage through the Solar System, by Palo Haklar is a CD-ROM title based heavily on the video materials accessed from NASA's extensive space archives.

The National Archives and Records Administration possesses a huge stock library of public domain materials covering every conceivable subject. Among their holdings are over four million photographs (some dating back to 1894), 35,000 sound recordings, 150,000 reels of motion picture films, and 20,000 videotapes. Within this collection you can find an incredible range of images and stock footage, including material focused on history, popular culture, the environment, space exploration, aviation, technology, agriculture, war, and international relations.

Samples of the holdings of the National Archives and Records Administration can be found on the Internet. For example, they list the following items as "self-service" film materials that can be freely viewed and copied:

- Eva Braun's Home Movies: Eva and Adolph at Berchtesgarden
- U.S. Space Program: Compilation from Project Mercury through Apollo-Soyuz
- The River: Pare Lorentz Ode to the Mississippi River
- The Plow That Broke the Plains: Pare Lorentz film about the Dust Bowl
- World War I Actions: World War I Trench Warfare

Some of the materials in the archives are subject to proprietary rights. Obtaining copies of those materials within the public domain varies depending on the type of material. You can obtain details by calling the National Archives and Records Administration at 301-713-6800 or sending e-mail to `mopix@nara.gov`.

Creative use of materials within the public domain can greatly enrich a CD-ROM title. You may need to perform some research to find the material that works most effectively, and you may need to do some work to determine that no copyrights prevail on the materials. For a limited-budget producer, however, obtaining your title content for free can be an enormous boost to the success of a project.

Purchasing Royalty-Free Materials

An electronic book can be greatly enhanced by multimedia elements such as music, short video clips, or sound effects. For example, Voyager's electronic book version of *Jurassic Park* included clips and sounds of dinosaurs (all approved by author Michael Crichton before release). One of the support industries that has sprung up in the multimedia world is content offered in "buy-out" packages where you purchase material, such as songs or video clips, and obtain the rights to use these materials in your productions.

Almost anything that can be captured in digital form is available in some type of royalty-free format. Many of these packages contain extremely high-quality content for very reasonable prices. For example, Corel Corporation offers high-quality Photo CD images on CD-ROM for a cost of around $15 to $20 per disc. Subjects include landscapes throughout the world, insects, technology, sports, and more. Most of these discs contain 100 individual photographs available in several different resolutions, so you can scale the image quality (and corresponding file size) to the requirements of your CD-ROM production. Royalty-free images are available from many other sources as well.

Music adds considerable atmosphere to many different kinds of electronic publications. However, unless you happen to be a practicing musician with your own home recording studio, where do you obtain music for use in a CD-ROM title? Buy-out music is the answer, royalty free music composed by professional musicians for use as theme music and background music. QCCS Productions (1350 Chambers Street, Eugene, Oregon 97402; phone: 503-345-0212) has a series entitled Pro-Background Theme Music (PBTM) that includes selections in varying lengths representing many different musical styles and moods. Music can be purchased on cassettes or compact discs. Each title contains about an hour of music for somewhere between $40 to $60. You can use these selections in a CD-ROM multimedia piece or electronic book without having to pay any additional royalties. During non-business hours, you can listen to demo selections from CDs in the buy-out library by calling the QCCS main business line, and demo cassettes containing samples of selections are also frequently available.

Sound effects can also enhance a CD-ROM title. These are available in sound libraries on compact disc from many sources. One of the most eclectic libraries of sounds comes from a San Francisco company, OSC. Their series, *A Poke in the Ear with a Sharp Stick,* Volumes 1 and 2, includes some of the strangest collections of industrial and techno-modern vibrations to ever travel through speakers. Sound samples can be directly embedded in CD-ROM titles or imported as MIDI samples that you further process. These sounds are better heard than described. OSC can be reached at 480 Potrero, San Francisco, California 94110; phone: 415-252-0460; e-mail: `OSC@applelink.apple.com`.

Video clip collections, animations, static clip art libraries, and many other kinds of multimedia resources can be purchased as royalty free materials for your title development use. Check your favorite computer software catalog or try a few searches on the Internet to discover additional resources.

Acquired Copyrighted Materials

A local musician has produced a compact disc of clawhammer banjo tunes, and one of them would be ideal to use as theme music for your electronic book about coal mining in the Appalachians. A photographer has produced a series of aerial shots of Point Lobos in Monterey County, California, and you'd like to include these images on a CD-ROM. Turner Broadcasting has the rights to a film including a little-known silent film actor; you'd like to include short clips of this actor in an interactive biography. In each of these cases, you need to obtain rights and permissions to use the copyrighted works of other individuals within an original work of your own. Acquisition of materials for multimedia and electronic publishing remains a quagmire for many small developers and producers because the ground rules are still being established. This entire area has become big business for many legal practitioners, and if your acquisition plans are complex, you are strongly encouraged to seek legal counsel.

If you intend to use copyrighted material in a production, you have two basic choices:

- Purchase the copyrighted material outright. If you own the material, you're generally free to use it as you see fit. There are, however, exceptions in some countries that include moral imperatives in association with copyright assignment; in other words, even if you purchase copyrighted material outright, you may not be able to use it in defamatory or questionable uses. The only way to overcome problems in this area is to ensure that the original copyright holder does not object to the intended use.

- Obtain licenses or permissions to use copyrighted material for an expressed purpose. The terms of such an agreement need to cover each of the following areas: the scope of the usage (can the material only be used for a single title or can it also be used in a future project?); the payment terms (does a one-time payment complete the license agreement, or will additional fees be required after a certain numbers of copies are sold?); and the presentation method (can the material be used both on CD-ROM and for Internet distribution, or only on a single medium?).

One final word of advice—don't leave the licensing and permissions process until last. This process can be time consuming, and it should be started as early as possible in the project development cycle.

> **CAUTION**
>
> Because of the differences in copyright laws in countries throughout the world, if you are using material covered by copyright laws outside the U.S., investigate the legal implications of international distribution and consult a legal professional skilled in international law if you have any doubts about potential uses of the material. Customs, laws, traditions, and possible enforcement actions can vary greatly from country to country.

Rights and Permissions

A CD-ROM title can contain material that encompasses a broad segment of rights and permissions issues. Obtaining the necessary legal clearance for use may be as simple as a one-page letter of agreement or as elaborate as a 20-page legal contract. If your CD-ROM title includes any of the following items, you generally need some type of agreement clearing the distribution of the finished work.

Software Engines, Readers, and Viewers

If your project consists of indexed data accessed through a search-and-retrieval engine, you typically need to pay a fee to the software producer to include the engine on a disc. This may be a one-time fee or a royalty based arrangement. Folio VIEWS (by Folio Corporation) and re:Search (by re:Search International) are products commonly used to distribute CD-ROM infobases. They both have different fee structures for different types of use.

If you produce works in Macromedia Director or Asymetrix Multimedia Toolbook, you can legally include the run-time engine on your CD-ROM to provide access to files created using these products. (Policies sometimes vary for different versions of these products; check the licensing agreement for a particular product version to ensure that the run-time engine is royalty free).

Portable document formats require a reader. If you're going to include files in these formats on a CD-ROM, can you legally include the reader? Most packages of this sort, such as Adobe Acrobat, Common Ground, and WordPerfect Envoy, let you freely distribute their basic reader, which can do simple searches, turn pages, and follow hypertext links. Often there is a tiered system where a higher-level reader is required for performing indexed searches, annotating the file contents, or using the product in a collaborative workgroup situation. The higher tier version usually has a higher one-time fee for use or, optionally, requires some type of royalty arrangement. Check the license carefully for use restrictions.

Personal Model Releases

Your interactive travel guide portraying sidewalk cafes of California includes video clips of diners eating outdoors. Do you need any specific release forms to include shots of individuals in your title? Technically, if you use the likeness of any individual in your commericial work, whether a still image or video clip, you need to obtain permission from that person before distribution. The common vehicle for this permission is the model release form, something that has been used by commercial photographers for years. Obviously, getting model releases from 20 people sitting around tables at an outdoor cafe requires a lot of work. You may need to plan your video shoots accordingly.

> **NOTE**
>
> Model release forms can be obtained from many retail and mail order photography stores, and from some video equipment dealers. You can investigate similar topics and receive information and advice related to image use through numerous Web sites. One good place to start is Keith Ostertag's index to photographic and art-related Web sites at the following address:
>
> ```
> http://www.lib/cortland.edu/photo.html
> ```

Interviews of individuals, whether in a corporate or government setting, usually require releases to ensure that the interview does not violate existing confidentiality agreements or other restrictions. If necessary, the release should be signed by a company officer. Recognizable individuals in interview sessions should also sign releases. Every face or likeness in a production requires a release; while not strictly followed in every instance (it would be pretty difficult if you were shooting pedestrian traffic on a New York sidewalk at 8 a.m.), being meticulous about this legal requirement can keep you out of trouble.

Trademark Agreements

Depending on the contents of your CD-ROM title, you may want to include trademarks or other indications of some of the included components on the packaging. For example, the use of a particular symbol for a type of video playback engine, or the logo of the company that produced the software engine used in an infobase both involve trademarks. You need either a release or permission form, or a trademark license, depending on the usage, from the original trademark owner.

Copyright Use Issues

For use of copyrighted material, you need at the very minimum a letter of agreement or permission form from the copyright holder stating the terms of use and declaring the compensation. For more intricate licensing arrangements, a formal contract may be required. In cases where a comprehensive license agreement needs to be formulated, legal advice can ensure that distribution and use disagreements won't arise in the future.

If In Doubt, Seek Counsel

Copyright laws, as they apply to multimedia works, such as CD-ROM titles, are complex and cannot be easily reduced to a simple set of guidelines. If you're producing a CD-ROM title based on source material for which the copyright is unclear or for which licensing will be necessary, you would probably be wise to consult a lawyer specializing in this field.

Many resources exist on the Internet for obtaining access to legal counsel or advice on copyright issues. Advice on copyright issues can be obtained from the not-for-profit Copyright Clearance Center at this address:

```
http://www.directory.net:80/copyright/
```

An online Web publication, "Intellectual Property," airs salient issues on this topic and includes articles by well-known authorities on the subject. You can access this publication at this address:

```
http://www.portal.com:80/~recorder/recorder.html
```

Links to additional topics can be found at the Information Law Web at this address:

```
http://seamless.com:80/rcl/infolaw.html
```

Assembling a Creative Team

If you consider yourself a renaissance man or woman, you may have the necessary skills to perform all of the tasks required to produce an electronic publication on CD-ROM, including the planning, hardware and software setup, writing, sound recording, graphic art and design work, marketing work, testing, and so on. If your skills are strong, this approach may be suitable for a small-scale project, such as the adaptation of a reference book for CD-ROM use or the creation of an online children's book. For larger projects, you'll probably require a support team, whether it is composed of staff members and coworkers or outside contractors that you hire.

Among the specialized talents required for creating a successful CD-ROM and marketing it, the following individuals could prove valuable as team members:

- **Legal professional:** For advice on intellectual property issues, contractual considerations, licensing questions, and similar issues.

- **Project manager:** For coordinating the different aspects of an electronic publishing project, keeping the project on time and on budget, and managing resources and workloads of team members.

- **Content specialist:** For providing essential information on particular topics and offering knowledge and insights as development progresses.

- **Writer:** For producing both the textual content of a CD-ROM title and producing scripts for interactive segments.

- **Researcher:** For ferreting out the necessary details to ensure factual accuracy of the CD-ROM content and investigating new material to expand the scope and coverage of a title.

- **Sound professional:** For handling the recording of narrative audio tracks, sound effects, background music, and the digital manipulation of all these elements (using compression, conversion, mixing, and special effects).

- **Animator:** For producing explanatory sequences or entertaining imagery for use with a title.

- **Graphic artist:** For creating and manipulating digital photographs and line art and preparing graphic files for use within a title.

- **Video professional:** For producing and editing video sequences, including interviews, outdoor scenes, training sequences, and product displays.

- **Marketing specialist:** For devising effective ways to promote, sell, and distribute your CD-ROM title, as well as analyzing audience needs and evaluating demographics.

- **Interface designer:** For planning and implementing the user interface for your title.

■ **Application specialist:** For providing specialized skills in the use of particular applications, such as multimedia development tools, SGML editors, HTML editors, infobase managers, or other development applications.

■ **Test coordinator:** For implementing a thorough testing and debugging procedure for the title on all of the specified playback platforms.

Obviously, a wide selection of skills come into play when producing and launching a CD-ROM title. Although you may want to combine these categories and merge specialties to assemble a much smaller creative team, consider each category carefully to ensure that you have the talent on-hand to perform the necessary tasks. If you're bold and talented, you still may want to attempt the entire project yourself—the digital realm encourages adventurous communication.

> **TIP**
>
> Development and production of CD-ROM titles can easily become an all-engrossing activity that can eclipse other parts of your life. My discussions with many different developers uncovered a recurrent theme: it inevitably takes more work to complete a CD-ROM project than you expect when you start out. If you embark on a CD-ROM project, keep some balance in your life, leave some time for friends and family, and— above all—try to have some fun along the way. If you're enjoying what you're doing, it will be reflected in your work, and the audience is sure to respond to it.

Prototyping a Project

Developing and releasing a CD-ROM title can involve many individuals and hundreds of hours of work. What if you reach the final stage of development and find out that the concept doesn't work—the interface is confusing or there are too many levels to navigate or the key ideas are not adequately expressed? Once you're well into development of a project, it can be extremely difficult to uproot components and start again. For this reason, prototyping is a popular method for devising and modeling the structure of a project. A prototype gives you the opportunity to collect feedback from fellow staff members, administrative personnel, clients, general users, or anyone else with an interest in the project.

A prototype is a working model of the structure of a title, usually with minimal content. If it's an infobase, it may contain only a very small sample of data. If it's a multimedia title, it may have only the general interface and one module operational. If it's an electronic book, it may include only the introduction, table of contents, and a chapter or two. The prototype should include enough information to give a clear picture of the method of presentation and a sense of the interrelationship of the different elements in a project. There should be enough material completed to encourage comments and suggestions—but not too much, since you want to minimize the time spent on any changes.

Ideally, the prototype lets you refine the rough edges of a project very early in the process. A clear and uncluttered interface will give users a feeling of confidence as they navigate through your title; you can successively improve the interface in stages as you collect and correlate comments obtained from circulating the prototype and soliciting opinions. Try to circulate the prototype to a diverse set of individuals: people familiar with the content and those who may not be, sophisticated computer users and utter novices, professional staff members and clerical workers. The most helpful comments often come from those who may be farthest from the development sphere.

The prototype can be constructed in the actual chosen development tool or a simpler tool that supports rapid construction of prototypes. If your CD-ROM title will be a complex photojournalistic work and include many branches and options from the main menu, you may want to use a simple slide show program to show the look and feel of the project before developing the more complex areas. Tools, such as Dan Bricklin's demo-it!, let you construct a working model of an interface in Windows in minimal time. You can then transfer the interface structure into another environment for the actual development work. The idea is to minimize your time investment while getting approval for the interface and structure of your presentation.

Skillful use of the prototyping process can strengthen and focus your work and maybe shave some hours from the required development time by eliminating false starts and misdirection. In large, high-stakes projects, prototyping is even more important to ensure that the project proceeds on course and satisfies its sponsors.

Developing the Title Contents

Once you've either obtained necessary rights to use certain materials on a CD-ROM title or produced the original content to include in a work, you can begin assembling the material. This typically involves two separate courses, depending on the nature of your source material:

- If you are repurposing existing works (such as a book or printed reference), you'll probably be spending a good deal of time converting source materials. You may be working intensively with a scanner and optical character reader. Depending on the nature of your content, you may also want to use specialized equipment, such as a slide scanner for 35mm slides or a digital camera to record three-dimensional objects. Sound on compact disc from a buyout collection can be incorporated in digital form by inputting it to your computer sound board line inputs (if you have a high-quality sound board that doesn't introduce excessive noise) or directly accessing the digital PCM data using a software utility, such as OMI's Disc-to-Disk.

- If you are prepublishing materials, your development efforts will typically require an entirely different set of computer applications. For infobases, you may be importing materials from word processors, spreadsheet files, or graphics programs, and then indexing them through the infobase manager. Portable document files can be initially created by outputting from a particular software application (such as WinWord, PageMaker, or WordPerfect) to the designated driver. You can then further process files by creating hypertext links, annotating material, providing a table of contents, or (for high-end products) creating a high-speed search index. Multimedia applications offer one other development environment that you can use to effectively create most of the types of electronic publications discussed in this book. Most multimedia development tools support importing and exporting to and from a wide range of file formats and types.

The tools and techniques employed in the creation of a CD-ROM title run the gamut of almost any application that can be used on a computer. Word processors rank close to the top of the list of useful programs. From text entered or imported into a word processor, you can produce output directed to infobase managers or databases, two common repositories for high-volume publishing on CD-ROMs. Through portable document utilities, you can capture the visual characteristics and layout of a word-processor formatted file and convert the file into one of the portable document formats, usable on any platform. Through output filters and editing macros, you can use a word processor to create SGML or HTML files, either in final form or in preparation for further processing in an appropriate editor. Word processor text can be imported into many multimedia development applications, such as Macromedia Director or Multimedia Toolbook, if your CD-ROM project involves the use of these types of programs. You may even have reason to include the actual word processor files, which can be accessed and used in a number of different ways if stored on CD-ROM. For text handling, a word processor that you're comfortable with provides the basic tool for everyday use—the Swiss Army knife of electronic publishing.

During development, you'll undoubtedly make use of additional tools and applications. You'll find many examples throughout this book of how to make maximum use of many different kinds of applications. Refer to the individual examples for details of various development procedures.

When the actual title contents and software engine have been completed and tested on hard disk, you still have some additional considerations to prepare the material for transfer to compact disc. In terms of actual guidelines for developing materials in preparation for transfer to CD-ROM, consider the following points:

- Double check all the material destined for the CD-ROM to ensure that you've obtained any necessary licenses or permissions. This includes contracted work (such as written material, graphics, or animations), photographs, musical recordings, software engines, and so on. Don't begin replication until you've obtained all clearances for material use (even if you think a signature or letter of agreement is forthcoming).

- If you're producing a CD-ROM title for multiple platform use, you'll have processor-specific files (such as search engines, players, readers, viewers, and similar playback utilities) and common files. Devise a storage system to organize and segregate the necessary platform-specific files for easy access by those viewing your title.

■ When producing ISO 9660 discs, use filenames that abide by the required naming conventions (8-plus-3 characters, all caps) *before* you write the files to disc. If you change filenames during CD recording and your application references certain filenames during operation, it may not function when transferred to CD-ROM.

■ If you plan to transfer your finished collection of files on tape or removable media to a compact disc replication facility, check well in advance for any special requirements of the replicator. Discuss the transfer media to ensure compatibility. It is generally safer and less trouble prone to transfer files that have already been premastered to a CD-ROM physical image. If you transfer a number of files independently on removable media, document each filename for the replicator, specify the structure and organization of the disc clearly, and insist on a one-off to test the CD-ROM before beginning high-volume replication. Confirm completion and shipment dates with the replicator the day you hand over the project materials.

■ If you have access to software that emulates the performance of disc-based material from a virtual image of the file, try some performance testing of your title before burning a disc or having a replicator create a run-off. If you experience performance problems, try managing the disc geography of your CD-ROM layout to improve file access (many premastering/mastering applications let you position files in specific locations on the disc). Your search engine or playback utility should either be copied to hard disk during CD-ROM installation or placed near the center of the compact disc for the fastest access. Any frequently accessed files should also be placed near the center of the disc.

■ If you're providing an installer utility to copy required playback files to the user's hard disk and set up the environment, make sure that you provide an uninstall utility that removes all files associated with the title from the user's disk. The uninstall should also clean up line entries in Windows .INI files to totally remove all traces of the product installation.

■ As you organize files for transfer to recordable CD, keep your directory structure simple—no more than three levels deep. More complex directory structures significantly slow access to files stored on CD-ROM. Try to arrange files so that there are no more than 30 to 40 files per directory.

■ Allow enough time in your planning to give a replication facility two to three weeks to complete the duplicates of your CD-ROMs (about the same amount of time you would allow for a conventional lithographic print job). Shorter turnaround times often require premium payments from the replicator and increase the chance of errors being injected into the process. Be sure that you understand the replicator's policy on the replacement of defective discs.

Premastering/Mastering

Premastering occurs at the stage where a collection of files has been assembled for transfer to a recordable CD, and you are ready to create a one-off for test purposes. Alternatively, you may want to produce an image of the disc contents to transfer to a replication service. Premastering typically produces output in two different forms:

- **Virtual Image:** A virtual image is the equivalent of a database that enumerates the contents of a CD-ROM without actually creating a physical image of the files. The virtual image details the format of CD-ROM, the order that files will be written to disc, and other information required for the CD recorder application to write to disc "on-the-fly" (as the recording is taking place). To successfully record from a virtual image requires a fast, defragmented hard disk drive (15-millisecond or better access times), a good-sized cache buffer in the CD recorder (512KB or above), and a computer system that can maintain uninterrupted data throughput for long periods (at 150 to 900KB per second, depending on the speed of recording). A virtual image saves hard disk space, since you don't have to create an exact replica of the CD-ROM contents before recording.

- **Physical Image**: A physical image is a bit-for-bit model of the data being prepared to write to recordable CD. The data includes formatting information and other details in a form that can be directly accessed from the storage medium and transferred to a CD recorder. On slower computer systems, you may not be able to record from a virtual image and will be required to produce a physical image to achieve the necessary performance. This requires sufficient disk storage space to accommodate as much data the final CD will hold. Some CD-ROM production systems incorporate their own internal hard drive for this purpose. Hard disk drives with available storage above the 1GB mark are strongly recommended for working from a physical image.

Most CD recorder applications (as discussed in Chapter 15) include both premastering and mastering capabilities. You can prepare files for writing to disc and then either directly output the files to the recorder or copy them to another medium (such as Exabyte tape cartridges or magneto-optical cartridges) for delivery to a replication facility. Check the requirements of the specific replication facility before producing an image for mastering.

As a part of creating a virtual or physical image, the CD-recorder application obtains information from you about the intended format for the CD-ROM data, the recording speed, whether the disc is to be recorded in multisession mode (allowing the possibility of additional recordings to the same disc), and additional options. Be sure you understand the implications of recording to particular formats before beginning. For example, if you record computer data to a disc formatted under the Red Book standard, you won't be able to access the computer data, but you will have a disc that makes some interesting screeches when placed in a CD player. CD-recorder applications often cross-check the file types to prevent you from doing things like this, but some of the format uses require a bit of thinking. If you want to assemble a collection of images using Photo CD storage techniques, you'll need to record in CD-ROM XA format. The modes applicable under these different formats also have important implications to the ultimate data uses. The chapters in Part III, "Publishing on CD-ROMs," delineate these differences and their importance to your recording efforts.

When the physical or virtual image has been prepared, you generally have the opportunity to perform a simulation of the recording. To do this, your CD recorder must be powered on and initialized by whatever application you're using to burn the disc. The simulation part of the application actually goes through the physical transfer of data from hard disk to compact disc, even moving the laser write head appropriately to instructions from the program. The only thing that keeps the disc from actually being written with data is that the laser is never activated.

If you have a 2× recorder and it fails the simulation test, note the error message that is returned. You may be able to correct the situation by reconfiguring your hardware, unloading some TSR programs from your system's memory, or some other simple action. If the problem persists, try running the simulation at 1× speeds. Even slow hard disk drives on older systems can generally maintain the data transfer rate to ensure error-free recording at single speed.

> **TIP**
>
> If the computer serving as the host for a CD recorder is connected to a network, you'll usually achieve better recording results by disabling the network software or disconnecting from the network before beginning to burn a disc. Network interactions could potentially disrupt the data flow from host computer to recorder, ruining the disc.

Recordable discs aren't incredibly expensive (about $10 apiece), but you don't want to unnecessarily waste them. Anything that interrupts recording can ruin the disc. Anything that interrupts the data flow (recorder buffer underrun, a power glitch, a thermal recalibration cycle on your hard disk, simultaneous use of the SCSI bus by other devices, a scanner creating noise on the SCSI bus) can defeat the recording process.

In preparation for successfully recording a compact disc, keep these guidelines in mind:

- Optimize and configure your system hardware for the recording process. Remove unnecessary devices from the SCSI bus (even powered down scanners can generate bus noise). Remove memory-resident utilities to free system memory. For insurance, add an uninterruptible power supply to your system to eliminate the risk of brief outages subverting the recording process. If you're adding additional equipment to your system, consider getting an AV-certified drive (which doesn't perform thermal calibration cycles while the drive is busy) or a drive with a separate dedicated control surface (some Conner drives have this feature).

- Make sure that your SCSI chain is correctly terminated. Active terminators, which contain electronics to balance the impedance of signals on the bus, are greatly preferred over passive terminators. SCSI bus problems represent a major source of recording difficulties, and improper termination is a very common source of problems.

- If your system has more than one hard disk drive, transfer your virtual or physical image files to the fastest drive (disk access times of 15 milliseconds or better are preferred).

- If you're recording from a virtual image, run a defragmenting utility on the disk drive before starting a recording. A defragmented disk accesses files more quickly and ensures more consistent data throughput during transfers.

- If your system repeatedly has problems when attempting to record from a virtual image, try creating a physical image for recording. Physical images typically transfer from hard disk to CD more readily and are less prone to problems during recording.

- Use approved media for recording. Most CD recorder manufacturers list the media types that have been certified for use with their equipment. Inferior discs can be a source of recording problems.

- Be alert to any error messages that occur during simulation. Even if the error doesn't cause the simulated recording to fail, it could create problems that generate an actual failure while you're burning the disc.

Testing

Testing for a CD-ROM title typically must be much more extensive than other types of software testing simply because so much data is involved. Although a software application may consist of 5MB to 10MB of program files, a CD-ROM project consists of hundreds of megabytes. To adequately test this much content, you need a systematic test plan. A stable of volunteers to run through the different areas of the title doesn't hurt, either. The goals for testing should be clearly stated. It is equally important to establish criteria for implementing changes to avoid endless cycles of adding new features or modifying existing ones. Some features may be fantastic additions to a title, but they can always be added for a future version. A released title might also be supplemented by downloading material from a network or service.

Testing of individual modules during product development, sometimes called unit testing, should be performed at several stages as the development efforts proceed. Individual units or modules must be able to work alone before they are combined into the large-scale project. Isolating problems that occur in units should make large-scale testing go much more smoothly.

Testing should be conducted in three separate categories:

- Functional testing
- Performance testing
- Platform compatibility testing

Functional Testing

Functional testing should ensure that every element of a CD-ROM title works as advertised. At a minimum, the following elements should be verified:

- Every file on the disc can be accessed and opened.
- All controls within the interface work flawlessly.
- The program loads and terminates without problems.
- Hypertext links contained within the title all jump to the correct locations.
- The help system (if applicable) works as intended.
- Display characteristics, including bit depths (whether the colors are stored as 8-bit, 12-bit, 16-bit, or 24-bit values), are appropriate for all supported monitor resolutions.
- Error handling for unexpected conditions works properly.
- Program flow can be interrupted when necessary, to terminate execution or return to the main menu.
- Interaction with any required peripheral devices, such as printers, works correctly.
- Font displays are appropriate (even if the requested font is not available on the user's system).

This is only a quick sampling of the areas you might want to test during functional testing. For test purposes, you might want to draw up an item-by-item checklist to guide members of the test team.

Performance Testing

Performance testing is particularly important for CD-ROM projects. Since the CD-ROM drive is inherently slow, you want to be constantly aware of performance issues. Run tests on a variety of systems, each with different performance characteristics, and try to test on a range of CD-ROM drives (from 1× to 6× models).

You can control some aspects of performance by disc file placement (frequently accessed files towards the center of the disc, related files located in close proximity). As you're performing tests, look for long delays in file accesses. How much delay is acceptable is a somewhat subjective consideration because both computer system and drive performance come into play, but file access and loading times should be as short as possible. Playback performance of multimedia segments should also be tested thoroughly. Look for skipped frames during video playback or breaks in the audio playback as signs of problems. Badly synchronized audio and display elements should be corrected before release. Jerky animation or any blockiness in the appearance of display elements should be fixed to ensure that your title maintains a professional appearance.

If key components of the title, such as the search engine or viewer, do not perform sufficiently when accessed from CD-ROM, you may have to copy these components to the user's hard disk as part of the installation process. Hard drive access times are faster by more than a factor of 10, so relocating critical components can often alleviate slow performance.

Platform Compatibility Testing

The ISO 9660 file system ensures cross-platform compatibility of CD-ROM titles at the file level. There are additional considerations to ensure that your title plays back properly on all intended platforms. Consider these guidelines:

- Make sure that you have isolated the playback engines for each platform where they can be easily located, typically in a directory or folder at the top of the directory tree.
- All the files stored in the common area of the disc should be in formats that are universally readable. Check file access from each of your target platforms.
- Perform functional tests (as described in the previous Functional Testing subsection) for each of the target platforms, testing each component of the interface and file access.
- Execute performance tests (as described in the previous Performance Testing subsection) for each of the target platforms. Performance may vary widely from low-end PCs to high-performance UNIX workstations; ideally, your cross-platform title should display correctly on a wide range of machines.
- Pay particular attention to the display characteristics of individual platforms. Do the fonts and graphic content of your title hold up on each of the different platforms? If not, you may have to modify your display environment to correct this type of problem.

Replication Considerations

How many copies of your title in CD-ROM form do you need? If the answer is half-a-dozen or so, primarily for department-wide use, you can probably get by with a single CD recorder. Plan on spending about an hour per disc for single speed recording; half that for dual speed.

Suppose you need more CD-ROMs, somewhere in the range of 20 to 100? This is a more difficult call. For in-house use, Kodak makes a disc transporter that coupled with a CD-R unit can progressively work through a stack of 50 blank discs, recording them one at a time. Even with a fast CD-recorder, such as the 4× Yamaha CD-R 100 or the 6× Kodak unit, you could still be looking at several hours worth of recording time.

Another company, Intaglio, makes a system that performs parallel recording of CDs from a single source. This may be an appropriate solution if you have company-wide needs that regularly require large numbers of CD-ROMs for distribution. The price tag of Intaglio's system, in the tens of thousands of dollars, rules it out for most small-scale developers.

What is the minimum volume that justifies commercial replication? Most large commercial concerns, such as JVC Disc America or DMI, are set up to favor large runs—quantities in the tens of thousands are often run, and hundreds of thousands for musical CDs are not uncommon. Unless you need at least a thousand copies of your title, using the large commercial replicators probably doesn't make sense. In many cases, the setup charge alone will be prohibitive.

Smaller services, usually located in metropolitan areas, are set up to produce one-offs or short runs of 100 to 200 discs. You typically pay a one-time setup charge for longer runs, perhaps $1000 or so. Disc prices can drop to under $5 for even fairly short runs. These services may provide a reasonable solution if your replication needs exceed the capabilities of your in-house equipment. If you need to use these services on a frequent basis, however, you may justify the purchase expense of the Kodak disc transporter or Intaglio parallel recording system.

Marketing and Distribution

CD-ROM titles suffer from the neither-fish-nor-fowl paradigm. Bookstores don't exactly know what to do with them yet, often confusing the contents with application software. Software outlets usually afford them some space, but the more serious titles often lose shelf space to brightly colored game packages showing reptilian mutants devouring spacecraft. Some mail order catalogs are now devoted to CD-ROM titles, but they are not yet in the mainstream. To a developer marketing a CD-ROM title, sometimes the best choices aren't immediately obvious.

Vertical and niche marketing is one possibility. If you have produced an elaborate infobase that has usefulness to the medical profession, advertise your product in journals and publications that focus on medicine. Word-of-mouth advertising becomes vitally important for independent publishers and title developers. If your title has interest to the educational marketplace and you have expertise in a certain area, see if you can arrange to give talks or lectures at schools or universities. Make up a one-page tri-fold brochure describing your title and distribute it freely. If you have created an instructional CD-ROM that gives tips for improving someone's golf game, see if retail outlets of sports equipment or golf gear will let you set up a rack with point-of-sale information in their store. Create a home page on the World Wide Web to describe the contents of your title, with appropriate enthusiasm, and include ordering information. You might also produce a short, downloadable demo that presents the essential contents and character of your title. If you've developed a title that includes historical information about the settling of your state, talk to historical societies throughout the state and offer to give a talk and presentation (a portable system with multimedia capabilities is helpful in this case). See if you can get on a local radio talk show to promote your title.

Many small developers of titles forge alliances with larger companies to ensure wide distribution of their products. HyperBole Studios, producers of the acclaimed Quantum Gate series incorporating Virtual Cinema, has worked out a distribution agreement with Warner Music Group. The producers of Myst, Cyan Software, distribute their best-selling title through

Broderbund. Eden Interactive, a small San Francisco based title developer, uses the distribution muscle of Creative Labs to get more exposure for their titles. If you have developed an electronic publication with the potential for national or international distribution, at least try to arrange for a discussion with a larger company with expertise in feeding distribution channels.

CD-ROMs are new enough that the marketing possibilities have not been fully explored. They are light-weight enough that you can mail them for the cost of a first-class letter, opening up many mail-order possibilities. They are by nature platform-independent, which makes them especially desirable in all the mainstream computer markets. They can store anything that can be converted to digital form, offering the potential for many new applications, such as the rush by movie companies to develop a format for distributing films on compact disc. Other possibilities, such as audio books on CD-ROM using ADPCM compression techniques, remain open for creative applications by entrepreneurial types. Use your imagination and see what you can come up with.

Packaging

Packaging for CD-ROMs comes in a bewilderingly large assortment of types, from simple vinyl sleeves to elaborate plastic enclosures embedded in book-sized cardboard boxes. A packaging product called the Compton Box, an $8^3/4 \times 5^1/2$-inch package with a right-reading edge title, slips neatly onto a bookstore shelf and—as it clearly was intended—resembles a book. This package type has become increasingly popular as CD-ROM title distributors seek ways to gain acceptance (and shelf space) in the market.

The ubiquitous plastic jewel box remains popular; as the most common packaging technique for audio CDs, it has carried that momentum into the CD-ROM marketplace. Other approaches have been introduced by a number of packaging manufacturers and given snappy names like the CD Pouch, Pop Pak, LokPak, RomGuard, CD Muffin, and Brilliant Box (no, I'm not making these up). Make a few calls to the packaging manufacturers, and within a few days you can have a room full of samples.

Packaging composed of recycled materials has become more widely available. Companies such as Apple Computer, Inc., bundle many of their corporate-produced CD-ROM titles in basic brown enviro-packaging. In this case, the package sends an unmistakable message that the company believes strongly in environmental responsibility. If the same message suits the character of your title, consider using packaging manufactured from recyclable products.

If you're creating a title intended for commercial distribution in retail outlets, packaging issues are paramount. Spend some time investigating the options and choose an approach that matches the character of your product (and remains within your budget).

New Markets

For the electronic publisher, emerging markets promise considerable opportunities in the near future. The educational marketplace for CD-ROM titles appears to be one of the high-growth areas at the moment. Some sources estimate this market, which exceeded $43 million in sales in 1993, as growing at the rate of 48 percent per year over the next five years. Many of the earlier offerings in this field are repurposed works, such as the adaptation of existing textbooks to CD-ROM formats. This medium will begin to flourish when educational materials are designed to take full advantage of the capabilities of interactive instruction. CD-ROM titles have the potential to become a major force in the educational marketplace in coming years.

The popularity of CD-ROMs within corporations has resulted in the addition of many networked CD-ROM drive installations. Disc arrays and juke boxes offer many gigabytes of data to network users. Certain types of directories, such as business telephone listings, have become extremely popular in the corporate environment. Similar kinds of source books, references, and directories offer many prospects for independent developers. Titles of this sort produced with the corporate market in mind could be extremely successful. Possible applications include:

- A CD-ROM directory listing places where different materials can be taken for recycling, indexed by geographic site and kind of material. Many corporations would recycle materials more frequently (such as paper, cardboard, batteries, sheet metal, outdated computers, circuit boards, old office equipment, tires, and so on) if they knew where to take these items.

- A sourcebook on where to obtain information about maintaining quality employee relations, including resources for psychological counseling, dispute management, state and federal regulations governing employee rights, published references, listings of agencies and organization involved in employee relations, and so on.

- A compendium of information about network products, including listing and reviews of major hardware and software solutions, electronic mail packages, distributors, networking consultants, test devices, and so on.

Summary

Electronic publishers equipped with a CD recorder, a few computer applications, and a good idea can now reach computer users anywhere in the world with self-published, professional-quality titles. The platform-independent nature of CD-ROMs makes this medium an ideal bridge for reaching beyond conventional computer barriers and presenting all types of information in fresh and novel ways. The best uses for CD-ROM are yet to come.

Online Publishing and the Internet

IV

PART

The World Wide Web

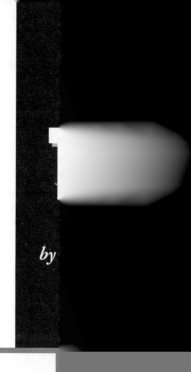

by

The World Wide Web is the explosive growth area in electronic publishing today. No area of electronic publishing is growing faster than the Web. The Web is the perfect symbol of the potential of electronic publishing in the Information Age. Its phenomenal popularity stems in a large part from the way in which it enables users to seamlessly navigate through complex webs of global resources. Even more amazing, the World Wide Web has been in common usage only since 1993, and already it is associated with all that is wonderful and wild about the Internet.

This chapter is a tour through the amazing "living" Web. It begins with a brief background of the following:

- The Internet
- Internet resource tools
- Internet information tools
- The World Wide Web

The chapter then propels you headlong into this highly visual arena, empowering you to play powerball in the majors. You will explore

- Web browsers
- How browsers use links
- Web features
- Popular Web browsers
- Home pages
- Bookmarks and hot lists
- Web retrieval tools
- Web searches
- Benefits of the Internet and the Web

A Brief History of the Internet

Five centuries ago the printing press with movable type brought society past an impasse with elitist control of knowledge and caused a revolution. It made possible the spread of knowledge to anyone with a passion to learn, and what is more important, it gave society an information base independent of a limited number of scholars. Today, the Internet is again causing a revolution in the way knowledge and information can be accessed.

The Internet began with the formation of the ARPANET (Advanced Research Projects Agency Network). In 1969, the four computers forming the original ARPANET were connected together over a long distance connection designed to prove such an outlandish concept could work. The ARPANET was first publicly demonstrated in 1972. Then fifty universities and research facilities with military projects had connections. By the end of the 1980s, over 80,000 computers were connected through a series of networks. Eventually, this collection of networks simply became the Internet, an international network spanning the globe.

The Internet has its own unique culture that stems in a large part from the Internet's past. Research, government, education, and defense-related activities have operated on the Internet for the entirety of its over 20-year history. From 1969 to 1991, the Internet was largely a private entity—the realm of researchers, scholars, and the military. Although commercial enterprises could connect to the Internet, the acceptable use policies pertaining to the use of the Internet prohibited them from conducting business. In 1991, this all changed. The ban on business activities was lifted largely because of the formation of the Commercial Internet Exchange (CIX). CIX provided a way for businesses to conduct commercial activities without using areas restricted to research and education.

The Internet has been growing at a phenomenal rate ever since; millions of computers are now connected to it. Figure 19.1 depicts the current activities on the Internet. Even though commercial activities have been permitted to operate only since 1991, they presently account for at least 53 percent of the Internet. The commercial sector is the fastest-growing sector of the Internet.

FIGURE 19.1.

Activities on the Internet.

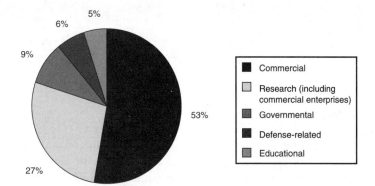

Legend:
- Commercial
- Research (including commercial enterprises)
- Governmental
- Defense-related
- Educational

Internet Resource Tools

Tools are an essential part of any operation. On the Internet, resource tools provide the basic means for the retrieval of information. The three basic tools of networking are

- Electronic mail (e-mail)
- FTP (file transfer protocol)
- Telnet (remote login)

E-Mail

Electronic mail is a great way to communicate within the global electronic community. Think of e-mail as a way to send letters to friends, associates, and colleagues "virtually" in an instant. Many e-mail programs enable delivery of mail to single users or groups of users. Some e-mail programs even provide ways to automate responses.

The value of e-mail is in its asynchronous nature—you can send e-mail whenever it is most convenient. Recipients of the mail message can read the message at their leisure and respond when it is convenient for them. Best of all, mail messages you send are normally saved so you can review them, and mail messages other people send you will be in your electronic mail box until you delete them or move them to another location for safekeeping.

FTP

File transfer protocol provides the basic means for delivering and retrieving files around the network. The files can be text, sound, or graphics. FTP provides a springboard for many information-based approaches to retrieving information. Many higher level tools that have friendlier interfaces use FTP or a protocol similar to FTP to transfer files. In Chapter 23, "Web Servers, Gateway Scripts, and Helper Applications," you will again learn about FTP as it relates to transferring files to Web servers.

TIP

A *protocol* is a set of rules for programs communicating on the network. It specifies how the programs talk to each other and the format of the data.

Telnet

Telnet lets you remotely log in to another system and browse files and directories on that remote system. Telnet is valuable because it is easy to use and basic to the network. When you telnet to another computer, you can issues commands as if you were typing on the other computer's keyboard.

Internet Information Tools

A potential customer must be able to learn about your company and its electronic publishing projects. You can use e-mail, FTP, and Telnet for this purpose, but they are very basic tools. They were designed as simple solutions to immediate problems. Researchers and scientists wanted an easy way to communicate with each other—e-mail was born. Data needed to be moved around the network—FTP was born. Sometimes, users who were away from their home site needed to log into it from a site they were visiting—FTP wasn't well suited to this task, and Telnet was born.

These basic tools are indispensable when used for the purpose for which they were designed. They even provide the fundamental basis for many high-level resource tools, but they simply weren't designed for the advanced manipulation of the wealth of information available on the Internet. This is why dozens of information resource tools have been designed to manipulate the Internet's data. These tools will help you reach customers and help customers find information about your company.

This section highlights the eight key information gathering tools. Later in this chapter you learn more about these tools and their benefits. After we discuss the Web and its characteristics, you will learn where you can go to use these tools on the Web. The following lists the eight key information resource tools:

Archie: A system to automatically gather, index, and serve information on the Internet. Archie is a great tool for searching file archives, especially the anonymous FTP archives on the Internet.

Gopher: A distributed information service that enables you to move easily through complex webs of network resources. Gopher uses a simple protocol that enables a Gopher client to access information on any accessible Gopher server. Public domain versions of the client and server applications are available.

LISTSERV: An automated mailing list distribution system. After you subscribe to a LISTSERV list you can read e-mail posted to the list or post e-mail to the list yourself.

Netfind: A basic Internet "white pages" facility that accesses several databases for you. Given the name of a person on the Internet and a rough description of where the person works, Netfind attempts to locate information about the person.

Netnews (Usenet): A great way to gain visibility and talk with people. There are thousands of Netnews discussion groups on just about every imaginable subject. These discussion groups are called *newsgroups*. To participate in a newsgroup you post messages to the group and read messages posted by other newsgroup members.

Whois: A utility that enables users to query a database of people, computers, domains, and more. It is a basic Internet "white pages" facility.

Wide Area Information Servers (WAIS): A distributed information service for searching databases located throughout the network. It offers indexed searching for fast retrieval and an excellent feedback mechanism that enables the results of initial searches to influence later searches.

World Wide Web (WWW): A hypertext-based, distributed information system created by researchers at CERN (European Particle Physics Laboratory). Users may create, edit, or browse hypertext documents. Public domain versions of the client and server applications are available.

What Is the World Wide Web?

The Web is an information system based on hypertext. The power of hypertext is in its simplicity and transparency. Users can navigate through a global network of resources with the touch of a button. Clicking one link can connect you to computers at NASA (North American Space Agency). Clicking another link can send you on a "virtual" trip to South Africa. Now that is true power!

Hypertext documents are linked together through keywords or specified hot areas within the document. These hot areas could be graphical icons or even parts of a world map. When a new word or idea is introduced, hypertext makes it possible to jump to another document containing complete information on the new topic. Readers see links as highlighted keywords or images displayed graphically. They can access additional documents or resources by selecting the keywords or images. Figure 19.2 shows how links can be used in a simple document.

FIGURE 19.2.

A document containing links.

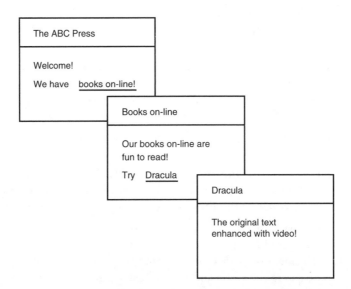

> **NOTE**
>
> The concept of hypertext may seem like a misnomer because we are really talking about links to both text and objects, where the objects could be image files, sound clips, or even full-motion video. Another word for hypertext could be hypermedia. The Web was really designed to be an open-ended multimedia system based on hypertext.

Text containing hidden links to other documents is underlined. The keywords in the first document are <u>books on-line</u>. Moving your mouse pointer to <u>books on-line</u> and selecting the link would take you to the document titled Books online. Similarly, selecting <u>Dracula</u> in the Books on-line document would take you to the third document titled Dracula. The neat thing about all this is that the book doesn't even have to be available at the current site. Dracula could be at a completely different site, and the reader could access this site simply by clicking on the link.

Figure 19.2 is a simple example of how hypertext links work. You could think of links as bookmarks. By activating the link, you are really jumping to a specific page in a book where each page of the book could be at a different site. The only thing keeping the book together are the links. Links anchor together the storyboards of a Web publication no matter where the parts of the publication are located.

If you want to create an entire online library—a "virtual" library—for The ABC Press, you would only need to add links to the existing documents and create new pages for the publication. As Figure 19.3 shows, you could easily do that using hypertext linking.

FIGURE 19.3.
An online library.

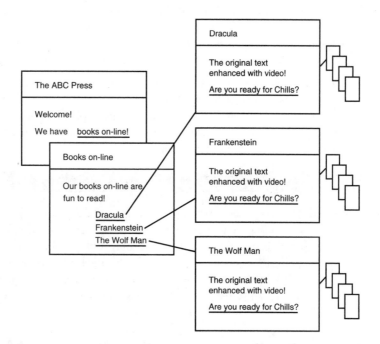

A Bit of History on the Web

The World Wide Web (WWW or the Web) originated at CERN, the European Laboratory for Particle Physics near Geneva, Switzerland. In 1989, Tim Berners Lee proposed the Web as a way for physicists around the world to collaborate. Originally, it was believed the Web would be the sole realm of physicists and a handful of academics. Until 1993, this was true.

Amazingly, in mid-1993 only about 50 Web sites existed worldwide. Then a wonderful thing happened. A tool enabling users to exploit the graphical capabilities of the World Wide Web was developed at the National Center for Supercomputing Applications. Color and images were precisely what the world wanted. The number of Web sites around the world grew explosively, seemingly overnight. The application that changed the shape of the Internet's Web forever was the Mosaic browser.

Browsers: Windows to the Web

A *browser* enables users to look through hypertext documents. Mosaic, which was developed at the National Center for Supercomputing Applications (NCSA) at the University of Illinois, was the first browser to use the colorful and graphical nature of the Web. Some people believe the Web is synonymous with Mosaic, and until recently this may have seemed true.

In reality, dozens of browsers are now available, and the most popular browser on the Web today isn't Mosaic; it is an upstart called Netscape. Oddly enough, Netscape was created by some of the same programmers who created Mosaic and its related applications.

Browsers are your windows to the Web. Browsers are also available for use on a variety of computer systems, including Amiga, Macintosh, DOS, Windows, and UNIX. A *browser* is a software application that enables you to access the World Wide Web. Accessing documents on the Web involves communications between two key elements: browsers and servers.

The browser's job is to help you—the Web client—access Web documents. Web servers process the requests made by clients. This client-server interaction makes the Web a very friendly place to visit because the server is blind to the type of platform on which the client is running. It only knows that when a request comes in, it is supposed to process it. In theory, a browser can be created for any computer system.

TIP

Using different browsers can change the shape and definition of your window to the Web. This is a key concept to remember when creating Web presentations. Some browsers, such as Lynx, which is still widely used, are text-only. Other browsers won't automatically display graphic images or enable users to disable the loading of images. Some browsers, such as Spry AIR, Mosaic, and Netscape Navigator, let users change fonts to any valid font or font size on their system. Other browsers have only default font types and sizes.

How Do Browsers Really Use Links?

To a browser, a hypertext link is like a postal address. The link contains a part the user cares about—the highlighted keyword or image—and a part the postman, your browser, cares about—the location of the resource. The address to a resource defined in the link is specified with a Universal Resource Locator (URL).

URLs are pointers to resources on the Web. Resources can be hypertext documents, sound clips, or even full-motion video. Often you will read or hear someone say "Point your browser to this site." What they mean is use an URL to access the site. The power of hypertext is that the site could be a local site or a site halfway around the world.

The part of the address the user sees in a hypertext document is defined by the hypertext markup language's anchor tag. The *anchor* is the text you see, and the URL is the part you don't see until you point your mouse at a particular link. HTML defines the structure of documents and not their appearance.

You will use the hypertext markup language to display your presentations on the Web. You will learn about URLs and HTML throughout this part of the book and in some detail in Chapter 20, "Using HTML," but go through a crash course now. This way, you will have a better idea of the Web addresses you will see throughout this and other chapters. A typical URL looks like this:

```
http://www.ncsa.uiuc.edu/SDG/Software/Mosaic
```

This address is the first place we will visit during our virtual tour of Web browser sites. At first glance, the address might seem strange, but that is okay. URLs are difficult to understand without actually breaking them down into parts. Hypertext URLs consist of four parts.

- A protocol. In the example: `http` (Hypertext Transfer Protocol)
- An address of a host. In the example: `www.ncsa.uiuc.edu`
- An optional port number. Sometimes a port number will follow the host address. The standard port number of 80 (for `http`) is assumed unless you specify otherwise.
- A directory path to a file. In the example: `/SDG/Software/Mosaic`

What the sample URL is really saying is to use the hypertext transfer protocol to access a document called Mosaic on NCSA's Web server.

TIP

Ports are rather like telephone jacks on the Web server. The server has certain ports allocated for certain things, like port 80 for your incoming requests for hypertext documents. The server listens on a particular port. When it hears something, it in essence picks up the phone and connects the particular port.

Web Features

People have told me that there is no true cross-platform solution. I look at them and smile because I know the Web is a true cross-platform solution. You can access the Web with your Amiga, Mac, PC, or UNIX workstation. In fact, if you can access the Internet, you can access the Web. Web servers are blind to the type of operating system you are using. They are only concerned about the requests coming from your browser, and requests look the same regardless of the type of computer you are using.

Another great thing about the Web is its distributed design. Information doesn't have to reside on your local computer or local server—you can access it remotely across the network. When people say the Web is distributed, they mean you can access data across the network without the data having to originate on your local computer. Could you imagine having to cram all the world's information onto the hard drive on your computer? You simply couldn't do it.

Instead of learning about the Web's cross-platform, dynamic, distributed, and interactive capabilities for a few dozen pages, you can plunge right in with a hands-on approach. After all, the Web is a highly visual medium, and the best to depict its capabilities is through pictures.

Virtual Tour of Web Browser Sites

Dozens of browsers are available today. Your computer system might have only one or two browsers available for it, or it might have 10 or more. Some browsers, such as Cello, offer basic features but are less taxing on your system. Others, like Netscape Navigator, are feature-rich and offer enhancements you won't find in other browsers. The good news is most browsers are freely available on the Web for non-commercial use and for trial periods for commercial use. This means that you can try all the browsers that are compatible with your system. This section looks at browsers available for the following systems: Amiga, Macintosh, Microsoft Windows, UNIX, and the UNIX X Window System.

Strap on your seat belt! It's time to take a virtual tour to get some first-hand information on the hottest browsers on the Web. You'll begin the tour with a visit to the browser that started it all, NCSA Mosaic.

NCSA Mosaic

Versions of NCSA Mosaic are available for Macintosh, Microsoft Windows, and UNIX systems running X Window System. This graphics-capable browser was the driving force behind the rapid expansion of the World Wide Web. There is no charge for non-commercial use of any versions of NCSA Mosaic. Most current versions of this browser support sending e-mail and fill-out forms. Although the X Window System version tends to get all the latest features first, MS Windows and Mac versions are well supported.

For the MS Windows environment, 16- and 32-bit versions of Mosaic are available. Both versions have their advantages and disadvantages. The 16-bit version features good documentation but will not work with Windows for Workgroups. The 32-bit version has a mode that gets rid of `winsock.dll`. This is a major improvement because many browser problems can be directly attributed to the winsock installed on your system. However, in order to use the 32-bit version under Windows 3.1 you need 32-bit extensions. The good news is that these extensions are freely available. Windows 95 users will want to watch for the Windows 95 version that should be released soon.

Figure 19.4 shows NCSA's Mosaic site on the Web. At this site you will find more information on this browser and be able to download the software. To visit NCSA's Mosaic site on the Web, use the URL

```
http://www.ncsa.uiuc.edu/SDG/Software/Mosaic
```

FIGURE 19.4.

NCSA Mosaic.

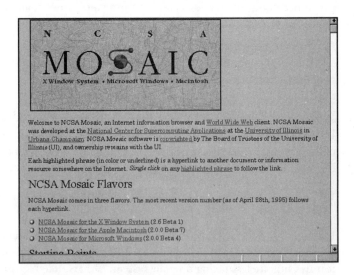

To download the software using FTP, visit NCSA's FTP site at the following address:

```
ftp://ftp.ncsa.uiuc.edu/Mosaic
```

Spry AIR Mosaic

Spry AIR Mosaic is one of the up and coming browsers. The current version will run only on MS Windows systems, but it may one day rival even top-dog Netscape Navigator. AIR Mosaic certainly has the features to do so, including direct support for incorporating system fonts into the browser at the touch of a button. This feature is powerful, especially when you compare AIR Mosaic to the many other browsers with fixed font types.

Early versions of AIR Mosaic had poor graphics support, but the latest release should correct this problem. AIR Mosaic is primarily available as a commercial product, but limited freeware versions of the browser are available. Interestingly enough, Spry Corporation is a division of CompuServe.

Spry Corporation has a number of products in its product line. Spry's newest product is Mosaic In A Box. Mosaic In A Box is a one-disk solution to obtaining access to the World Wide Web. You don't even have to find a local Internet service provider first. When you start the installation process, the software is loaded onto your system and a CompuServe account is set up for you. Because CompuServe now offers direct access to the World Wide Web, this is an easy way to get online fast. Figure 19.5 depicts Spry's product line.

FIGURE 19.5.

Spry Corporation's Internet products.

For more information on AIR Mosaic, visit Spry's Web site at the following address:

```
http://www.spry.com/sp_prod/index.html
```

Amiga Mosaic

As an Amiga fan, I was delighted to find this gem on the Web. Amiga Mosaic is available at no charge for personal use. If you have an Amiga, this is the browser for you. Figure 19.6 shows a screen shot from Amiga Mosaic available at the University of Stony Brook's Amiga site. You can find more information on Amiga Mosaic or download the software by visiting the Web site at the following address:

```
http://insti.physics.sunysb.edu/AMosaic/
```

FIGURE 19.6.

Amiga Mosaic screen shot from the University of Stony Brook Amiga site.

EINet Browsers

WinWeb and MacWeb are two browsers from Enterprise Integration Network. They are available for personal use at no charge. Both are fairly new browsers with a lot of potential for growth. Both need better documentation, but are easy to install and run well even on older computer systems.

Figure 19.7 shows EINet's MacWeb site. You can find more information about MacWeb:

```
http://www.einet.net/EINet/MacWeb/MacWebHome.html
```

To download MacWeb to use on your Mac, visit EINet's FTP site:

```
ftp://ftp.einet.net/einet/mac
```

Figure 19.8 shows EINet's WinWeb site. You can find more information about WinWeb at :

```
http://www.einet.net/EINet/WinWeb/WinWebHome.html
```

To download WinWeb to use on your PC, visit EINet's FTP site:

```
ftp://ftp.einet.net/einet/pc
```

FIGURE 19.7.

EINet Corporation's MacWeb.

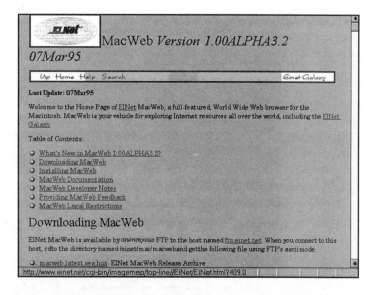

FIGURE 19.8.

EINet Corporation's WinWeb.

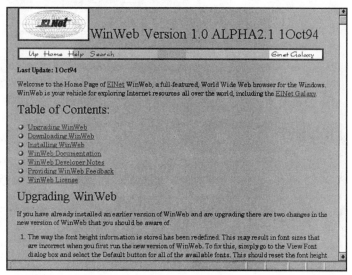

Netscape Navigator

Netscape Navigator is an extremely popular browser. Versions of it are available for Macintosh, MS Windows, and UNIX X Window System systems. Netscape has features that make it unique, and it already supports some advanced extensions to the HTML level-3 specification.

The most recent version of Netscape supports a secure data encryption mode, again putting the Netscape browser on the leading edge of Web technology. Netscape is freely available for use by students and employees of nonprofit companies. Others can use the browser for an evaluation period. If they continue to use the browser after this trial period, they are obligated to pay a registration fee. Figure 19.9 depicts the overview of Netscape Navigator at Netscape Corporation's Web site.

For more information on Netscape Navigator, visit Netscape corporation's Web site at:

```
http://home.mcom.com/comprod/netscape_nav.html
```

FIGURE 19.9.

Netscape Navigator overview.

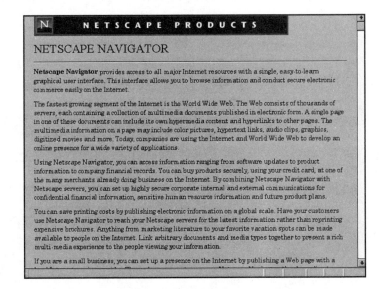

HotJava

The final stop on the Web browser tour is the site for the HotJava browser, because HotJava symbolizes the future of the Web. HotJava, developed by Sun Microsystems Incorporated, is written entirely in a language called Java. Using Java, you can create platform-independent interactive applications called *applets*. Applets are the most powerful and far-reaching extension to HTML to date. Not only can readers with a Java-capable application access the application you have created, they can play it directly in their browser. The applications you can create using Java are limitless. Already there are Java games, animations, simulations, and more.

Although the HotJava browser is currently in the testing stages, versions of the browser are already available for UNIX systems running Solaris, Windows 95, Windows NT, and Macintosh System 7.5. Figure 19.10 shows Sun Microsystem's Web site and explains more about the Java language. To download HotJava visit Sun at the following address:

```
http://java.sun.com/
```

FIGURE 19.10.
HotJava by Sun Microsystems.

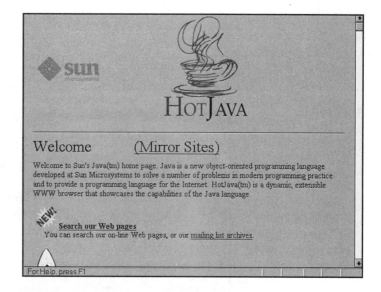

Other Web Browsers

Many other browsers, not discussed in this section, are also available. You can find a good list of available browsers on CERN's informational Web site:

```
http://info.cern.ch/hypertext/WWW/Clients.html
```

Home Pages

Home page. Whether you talk to someone who frequents the Web or publishes on the Web, or you simply listen to the sound bites on TV concerning the Internet, you will hear the term *home page* a lot. Often, the word is used in a confusing way because the word "home" carries with it certain connotations like saying, "Come over to the house," when you really mean, "Come over to my house," or even, "Come over to the house I'm at now."

When you start your browser, the "house you're at now" is the default home page. This page loads automatically and is often preset to the browser developer's site page. For example, when you first install and run NCSA Mosaic, the default home page is set to NCSA's home page.

You can change the default home page in your browser. The default should be a place you enjoy visiting or better, a page you created containing your favorite links. Unfortunately, each browser has a slightly different way to set the default page. This means the best place to find out how to change the default setting is to refer to the documentation that came with the browser.

A common misconception about the Web is that a single home page somewhere is the top-level index for all other home pages. Although many large databases contain links, the truth is that you can use any number of many starting points to reach any site on the Web; you are not restricted to a single starting point. Every house on the Web has its own door.

When I start my browser it takes me to the home page I created for The Virtual Press. Let's take a visit to my house on the Web, The Virtual Press Headquarters at the following address. Figure 19.11 shows this page.

```
http://www.aloha.com/~william/vphp.html
```

FIGURE 19.11.

My home page on the Web.

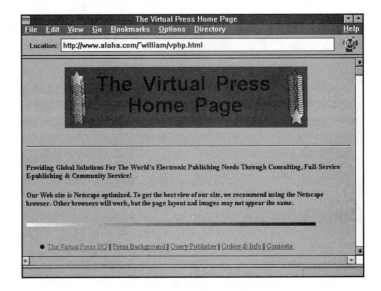

The screen shot in Figure 19.12 was taken from the Netscape browser. Most browsers place the document title at the top of the browser window. Other browsers place the title in a one-line window called "Document Title." The document in Figure 19.12 is titled The Virtual Press Home Page.

Almost all browsers place the URL in the browser window in a manner similar to the one shown here. The URL for this document is `http://www.aloha.com/~william/vphp.html`. This line means the document is a hypertext document located on the Web server at `www.aloha.com` with a path of `~william/vphp.html`.

Links on this page are underlined to distinguish them from ordinary text. The links presented at the bottom of the page form a basic menu for other documents at the Web site. Some browsers will expire links that you've visited, which means links you have previously visited will be depicted in a different color from links you have not visited.

On the Web, you choose the links you want to explore. Activating one of the links on this page will cause a new document to be displayed in the browser's window. Interactivity is a key concept of the Web, making it possible for anyone to publish electronically. And you can create links almost as easily as you can follow them.

FIGURE 19.12.

Notice the underlined links don't say "click here."

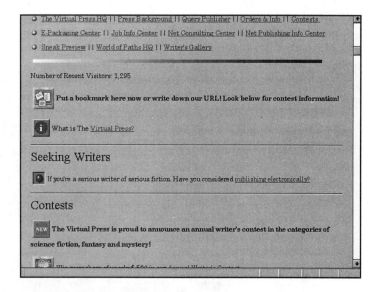

Figure 19.12 is another view of The Virtual Press home page depicted in the Kiosk mode of Spry AIR Mosaic. Kiosk mode is a pleasant way to surf the Web because it lets you hide the ugly toolbar until it is really needed. Notice how basic the entries on this top-level page are. Each entry has only a few words that highlight where a particular link will take you. Also notice the links don't say "click here." In hypertext you need only highlight the key idea from a passage that you will expand upon in a later document.

As you see, home pages can belong to individuals or companies. A home page can also refer to the default page on which your browser starts. In general, home pages are a basic or top-level entry point to information you or someone else has published on the World Wide Web.

Bookmarks and Hot Lists

There are literally millions of places to visit on the World Wide Web. Remembering where your favorite information is could be a nightmare. This is why most browsers support bookmarks or hot lists.

Bookmarks and *hot lists* enable you to revisit places you found interesting without having to tape dozens of notes around your computer monitor. Different browsers have different names for the mechanism to add a site to your preferred list of places to visit. In Mosaic, you add a site's URL to your hot list. In Netscape, you create a bookmark containing the URL to the location. No matter what the mechanism is called, the function is really the same. The location is saved to a file that you can access, generally from a pull-down menu. Figure 19.13 is a list of my favorite bookmarks. The list is from the Netscape browser.

Just as different browsers have different names for this annotation function, they also have different methods for making additions. Generally, to add a favorite place to your browser you first visit the Web site, and then select Add bookmark (or hot list) from a menu. Once a site is added to this list, you can revisit it quickly.

FIGURE 19.13.

Bookmarks are places you'd like to revisit.

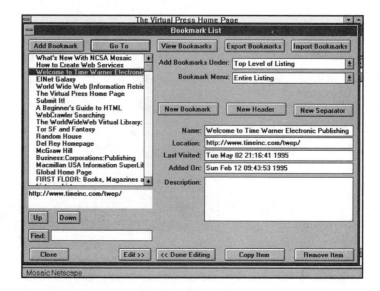

Web Retrieval Tools

Let's take another look at the eight key information tools you learned about earlier in this chapter. The World Wide Web is a dynamic information system; its versatility makes it the perfect tool to interface with the Internet's retrieval and indexing tools.

> **NOTE**
>
> If you visit the Web sites where gateways to these tools are found, during the visit place a bookmark or add the URL to your browser's hot list. This way you will have a list of locations for each of the various tools and you will be able to jump between them with the click of a button. And by all means, try using the tools to search for something. You'll be amazed at just how easy and fun searching really is.

> **TIP**
>
> An easy way to jump between completely new sites on the Web is to type the location into your browser's URL window and press Enter. Most user-friendly browsers will let you do this. Some less-friendly browsers make you open an URL window. In browsers this function is usually labeled Open URL and is accessible from a pull-down menu.

Archie on the World Wide Web

Archie is a great tool for searching file archives. The Archie database contains an indexed list of filenames and directory paths for millions of files located on thousands of FTP sites around the world. The files contain everything from public domain software to system-specific utilities and information files.

You can use Archie to easily search through those files, and Archie will provide a list of sites that store the file for which you're looking. You can then initiate an FTP session to transfer the file to your computer. One way to access Archie on the World Wide Web is to point your browser to the Archie request form at the following address:

```
http://bingen.cs.csbsju.edu/archie.html
```

Gopher on the World Wide Web

Gopher enables you to seamlessly search and retrieve information. Gopher presents information as a series of menus and submenus. This menu structure is a fairly intuitive way to search through directories for files, and just like Archie, those files can be anything from the latest Netscape browser to the PC utility you have been desperately searching for.

Gopher offers gateways to other services such as Archie, the World Wide Web, WAIS, and even WHOIS. This little rodent developed by the University of Minnesota is such a popular and powerful search engine that a number of utilities have been developed as extensions to it.

- Gopher Jewels enables you to search catalogs of Gopher resources indexed by category.
- JUGHEAD (Jonzy's Universal Gopher Hierarchy ExcavAtion and Display) enables you to search Gopher indexes according to specified information.
- VERONICA (Very Easy Rodent-Oriented Netwide Index to Computerized Archives) enables you to search Gopher menus by keyword.

One way to find information concerning Gopher on the Web is to visit the Gopher Jewel gateway at CERN's Web site:

```
http://www.mid.net/GJEWEL/
```

LISTSERV on the World Wide Web

Mailing lists are a great way for groups of people with common interests to communicate among themselves. The key to LISTSERV is its relative ease of use and wide accessibility. Virtually anyone with e-mail access to the Internet can participate in lists of their choosing. On the World Wide Web, you can find many directories to mailing lists. A good list is maintained at:

```
http://www.cis.hawaii.edu/MediaInfo/list.html
```

Direct marketing through e-mail, mailing lists, and newsgroups is frowned upon and will often generate hostile responses. There are acceptable practices on the Internet and a set of unwritten rules of etiquette often called Netiquette (Network etiquette). Acceptable ways to market on the Internet will be covered in Chapter 25, "Advertising and Protecting Your Documents."

Netfind on the World Wide Web

You can use Netfind to find Internet e-mail addresses. Netfind is a service similar to the white pages from your local phone company. You access Netfind primarily through a Telnet session, where you remotely log in to a Netfind server. However, there are several experimental gateways to Netfind servers on the Web. You can find an experimental Web gateway from Computing Services in Great Britain at the following address:

```
http://info.lut.ac.uk/dir/netfind.html
```

Once you have initiated a Telnet session to a Netfind server or accessed a Netfind gateway on the Web, using Netfind is easy. At the prompt or query window, you type in the name of a person and keywords indicating where that person works, and Netfind will attempt to locate information about the person. The keywords can be a partial or full name for an organization or the domain associated with the organization.

Netnews on the World Wide Web

Communicating with fellow Internet users through newsgroups is a great way to gain visibility for your electronic publishing ventures. Newsgroups are discussion groups similar to discussion areas or forums you might find on a bulletin board service or commercial online server. Thousands of newsgroups on just about every imaginable subject are available. To participate in a newsgroup, you post messages to the group and read messages posted by other newsgroup members.

Some browsers, such as Netscape, feature built-in support for newsgroups, making newsgroups extremely easy to access. Indexes to newsgroups are plentiful on the Web. A good index is at Colorado University's web site:

```
http://harvest.cs.colorado.edu/Harvest/brokers/Usenet/
```

WAIS on the World Wide Web

Wide Area Information Server (WAIS) is a useful database retrieval system that searches databases located around the world. The databases contain many types of files including text, sound, graphics, and even video. The WAIS interface is very easy to use, and you can easily perform a search on any topic simply by entering keywords and pressing Enter. Once you press the enter key, the WAIS search engine takes over. It will search WAIS databases around the world and return a list of files with brief descriptions matching your keywords in a few seconds. From this list you can select files to download to your computer.

The only drawback of WAIS is you need special software to use it. The good news is this software is freely available. If you take a virtual trip to France via your Web browser, you can visit a site where you can get the WAIS software:

```
http://discover.imag.fr/discover.html
```

Whois on the World Wide Web

Whois enables you to find people, host computers, and organizations on the Internet. Whois is similar to Netfind. You can perform a Whois search using keywords to find e-mail addresses, postal addresses, and telephone numbers for people and businesses.

The initial implementation of Whois was limited in use and scope because there was no real way to connect into a meaningful structure databases located at different sites. With the development of an extended protocol called Whois++, this has changed substantially. Using Whois++, users can now search among the many Whois databases located around the world. There is an experimental Whois++ gateway server at the following site:

```
http://www.wsnet.com/whoispp.html
```

W3 Search Engines

The last information search and retrieval tool discussed in this section is, fittingly, the World Wide Web's search engines. The Web offers the most powerful search engines available on the Internet today. The underlying concept that makes World Wide Web or W3 search engines so powerful is really quite simple. Everything you see is represented as a hypertext object. A WAIS database index, a Gopher menu, or plain text can all be described as a hypertext document.

W3 searches are easy to perform. As with WAIS searches, you simply enter keywords, press Enter, and the W3 search engine takes over. Although W3 databases primarily contain information pertaining to the thousands of Web sites around the world, the databases could also contain information on gopher and FTP sites as well. Figure 19.14 shows an index of W3 search engines. This index can be found on the Web at the following address:

```
http://home.mcom.com/home/internet-search.html
```

FIGURE 19.14.

W3 search engine index at Netscape Corporation.

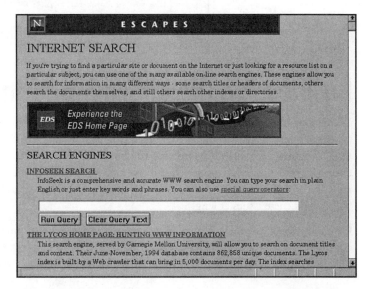

Web Search

Let's perform a search on the InfoSeek Web search engine depicted in Figure 19.15. This will demonstrate one of the most dynamic features of the World Wide Web: the ability to generate documents on demand. Type the keywords `Electronic Publishing` into the InfoSeek query window. A few seconds after you press Enter, the InfoSeek Web search engine will retain results similar to those depicted in Figure 19.15.

Creating Web documents when they are needed is an essential element in Web publishing. There may be many situations in which you will need to generate specific documents for a specific type of customer. This is especially true if you maintain a database customers can search. Traditional databases need users to learn the query language. With W3 searches there is no query language to learn.

FIGURE 19.15.

Using the Web search engine at InfoSeek.

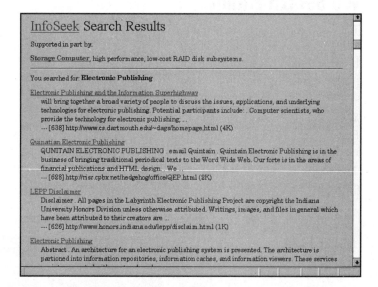

Business on the Internet and the WWW

If you want to do business on the Internet and the World Wide Web, you must know the potential benefits and associated risks. By knowing the benefits you can better exploit them to your advantage. Similarly, by knowing the potential risks you can safeguard the business and ensure maintenance of a competitive advantage. This section is an overview of the benefits and risks associated with doing business on the Internet and the World Wide Web. Chapter 25, will discuss these issues at length.

On the Internet, the most serious risk to your company and products pertains to security and copyright issues. Passwords can be stolen. Unprotected e-mail can be intercepted, read, or altered. Records on computers connected to the network are at risk. Customer credit card numbers can be stolen. The first step in safeguarding your products is to realize that security breaches, outright fraud, and pilfering of your products are possible no matter where you conduct business. Software manufacturers and traditional publishers have faced these problems for decades. They survived because they realized the risks were there and took precautions.

In general, Internet users do not like commercial marketing or direct advertising. Direct advertising on the Internet could have serious negative repercussions for the image of your business and may alienate you from the very customers you are trying to reach. You should be careful not to put an advertising message into inappropriate areas, especially mailing lists and newsgroups. Putting a message about your latest electronic publication into a discussion centered on Scottish culture will only gather anger, not customers. On the other hand, submitting material in a way that conforms to the network culture will mark you as a good net citizen and may attract customers.

Internet users' aversion to commercial activities relates strongly to the Internet's past and the culture that evolved over a period of two decades. It is important to remember that for more than 20 years commercial activities were prohibited on the Internet. This was true until 1991 when the ban on commercial activities was lifted. The culture of the Internet reflects this aversion to commercial activities in many areas, but there is good news. The Internet's dominant culture is changing dramatically. Some users have realized commercial activities are what will keep the Internet alive when government subsidies disappear. Others have realized the tremendous value of commercial information. Most Internet users also realize that businesses want to be good citizens.

A key benefit of the Internet is your ability to track the competition. Although tracking competitors is a benefit, remember that if you can track competitors, competitors can track you. For example, competitors could use discussion groups to track customer satisfaction with your newest product. To counter this, you could adopt a policy regarding the release of information. However, the real key to maintaining competitive advantage and enhancing customer connections is to keep customers happy by providing service and information to meet their needs. The World Wide Web is one of the best ways to provide service and information designed to meet customer's needs.

High-traffic areas of the Internet frequently experience connectivity problems. When too many people try to connect to the same location, traffic jams occur and traffic jams frustrate users. If one of the company's Internet areas is a high-traffic area, the best way to retain goodwill is to keep the users informed of the situation. Tell them they may experience delays or connection problems due to the high demand for information in this area. If the area continues to have heavy traffic over an extended period, you should be pleased and consider upgrading equipment or links as necessary.

Over 5,000 e-mail messages are sent each second of every day. Most commercial online services charge for connection time and for transactions. E-mail messages sent on a commercial service would incur connection time charges and per-message charges. E-mail on the Internet incurs no additional per-minute or per-message charges. In seconds a message can be sent to a user anywhere in the world.

This enables communication with customers in an effective and inexpensive manner. However, the Internet is not completely reliable. Messages and data can get lost. There is no guarantee a message or data will get to where it was sent quickly, and there are few ways to guarantee receipt. A counter to the reliability problem could be as simple as asking the recipient to confirm receipt in a reply message.

Users who want to access information databases on commercial services normally have to pay substantial fees. On the Internet and the Web, a large body of information is available for free. You have access to research and databases around the world, including these and many more:

> The Library of Congress
> Major universities
> Business-oriented databases, such as the Federal Register and
> > Government Accounting Office reports
> U.S. and Canadian Census Data
> Supreme Court decisions
> World health statistics
> Security and Exchange Commission corporate financial reports

Discussion groups on subjects related to a company's industry enable you to track trends, product introductions, and customer perceptions. Other benefits include enhanced customer service, low-cost marketing and advertising, and potential sales and distribution of products. These benefits are the primary arena for the World Wide Web and its friendly, all-encompassing interface. As you will see in later chapters, the Web is one of the most cost-effective ways to advertise your products. The Web also offers you the chance to provide advertising in a way that fits in with the culture of the Internet.

A House on the Web

Advertising on the Web in ways that fit in with the culture of the Internet is essential, and no one knows this better than Jordan Gold, the publisher of the Online Services Group. The Online Services Group is a division of Macmillan Digital that Jordan Gold helped start in January, 1995. Interviewing Jordan for *Electronic Publishing Unleashed* concerning Macmillan's "House on the Web" provides wonderful insight into what it takes to set up a world-class Web site. The text of the interview follows.

EPU: (William R. Stanek) Macmillan has a terrific site developing on the Web. As the hosts of the site, what is the role of the Online Services Group as a part of Macmillan Digital?

JG: (Jordan Gold) The job of the Online Services Group is to put Macmillan content online as appropriate. The Macmillan World Wide Web site is one vehicle for that, and there are other areas on commercial online services such as America Online and CompuServe. One of the most well-known areas is within ExpressNet, which is American Express' online area on America Online. At this site, users can access and the full text for 14 of our Frommer's travel guides in a searchable format, discussion groups, files to download, and a bookstore. On CompuServe there is a Macmillan Computer Publishing forum. At this time, the forum is exclusively for technical support. There are files to download, discussion areas, and, periodically, author conferences. The Internet site has a lot of things that are related primarily to Macmillan Computer Publishing, but that is changing as time goes on. By the time *Electronic Publishing Unleashed* is published we'll have all of Macmillan online at the Web site.

> **NOTE**
>
> The Macmillan FTP and Web sites can be accessed at `ftp://tvp.com/` and `http://tvp.com/`, respectively.
>
> To access the Macmillan CompuServe forum type `Go Macmillan`.
>
> The keyword to access Macmillan's area on America Online is `Frommers`.

EPU: The World Wide Web is growing explosively! In early 1993, only a few thousand users were on the Web; today, there are millions. The Information SuperLibrary (Macmillan's Web site) seems to be growing as explosively as the Web. Could you describe the underlying hardware and software architectures supporting your efforts and how they have grown with the site?

JG: That's an interesting question because our goal when we started the site was to continually build traffic, and the only way you can build traffic and keep up with it is to have hardware and software that can keep up with the increase. Our traffic is growing at 40 percent a month, which would drive MIS managers nuts unless they had the capability to handle it. So what we did was start small with a Sun Sparc 20 with one processor, 32MB RAM, and a 5GB hard disk. We picked the Sparc 20 because it was expandable. It can handle up to four processors, hundreds of megabytes of RAM, and many gigabytes of hard disk space.

We looked at the Sparc 20 and thought it would probably solve our problems for at least awhile. We didn't know what kind of traffic we were going to generate. There's no way to know that when you go online, but we knew we were going to build a good site with a lot of content and would market it effectively, so we thought we would do a good job managing the area and the growth. The Sparc 20 has already been upgraded to two processors, 128MB of RAM, and 9GB of hard disk space. So, we've doubled the number of processors, quadrupled the amount of RAM, and doubled the amount of hard disk space. Because the Sparc 20 can handle up to four processors, we think it can handle our growth for awhile, but we expect to have to buy a larger computer next year.

From a software standpoint, we continually upgrade the server software. We're using CERN 1.4 now, which is a public domain server. We're looking at some of the secure server solutions out there, but we're just not ready to purchase yet. We probably will do that next year.

EPU: What type of connection does the Macmillan Web site have to the Internet, and how is this growing with the site?

JG: We have a T1 and expect to add a second one next year. We're getting a lot of traffic. A month ago, our all-time high for hits per day was 50,000 in February just after the site went online. For five months, we didn't beat that record, and then suddenly, in the last six weeks, we've broken that record every day. In fact, the record was broken even on weekends, which are traditionally very low in traffic. Our all-time record is now 112,000 hits.

EPU: Publishing on the Web is constantly being redefined. A short time ago, HTML 2.0 was the standard, and even before the HTML 3.0 standard was ratified, radical new extensions to HTML were being introduced. To keep pace with the rapidly changing face of Web publishing, the average site is redesigned several times a year and is continually evolving. What are your comments on this continually evolving design process, and what advice would you give someone putting together their first Web publication or home page?

JG: That's interesting. The Web is similar to what desktop publishing was 10 years ago when we first got laser printers and had the ability to make fonts bigger and smaller. Everyone kind of went nuts, put as many fonts as they could on a page, and wound up with grotesque-looking images and unreadable text—just a total mess. The Web today is like that because people who've never done design before suddenly think they're designers.

The key is that you should always pay attention to people with modems. Think about those people with the 14,400 modems, and keep your graphics sizes accordingly small as well as keep an eye on how this really looks. Don't try to win a design award with your Web site. Try to create something that is usable and friendly.

EPU: What do you think about the growth of the HTML standard itself and the new extensions that are coming along? I noticed that the Macmillan site uses Netscape extensions. Could you comment on this?

JG: Yes, we do. In fact, we're going to support tables too. We're attending to what features are being embraced and supported, and are starting to support those as well. We test our system on a lot of browsers to make sure everything works, but Netscape at the moment is still about 80 percent of the market. I think that's going to change dramatically in the next six months as the third-party online services really take hold with Web access. Until that happens, though, Netscape is the *de facto* standard. Still, you have to keep those other browsers in mind and hope they'll continue to support the HTML standards.

EPU: Java and VRML are the latest rave on the Web. These extensions are radically different and powerful but aren't widely supported yet. Many new Web publishers may be considering adding these extensions to their sites, but often it is best to get the site up and working well using standard HTML features before trying to use advanced techniques.

JG: I think [getting the site up with the basics] is the first priority. I don't think you need to go out there and have something that can be viewed only by the few people with a VRML browser, for example. I think that is a major mistake.

EPU: Electronic commerce is in its infancy on the Internet. Companies from around the world are pouring millions of dollars into this area, and because of this, it's already possible to make secure money transfers on the Internet. Currently, hundreds of companies conduct business on the Internet, and Macmillan's bookstore is definitely an example of electronic commerce in action. Could you tell me more about "virtual" shopping and your "virtual" shopping bag?

JG: Those are currently being redesigned using Oracle to be friendlier and faster. For the shopping experience, we've tried to make the best use of available technology without adopting a secure standard that wasn't a standard yet. We've been waiting to find a solution that is a standard rather than embracing something that might not become one and wasting money on that. We try to make your purchases as secure as possible by allowing you to send your order in electronically and then call us with your credit card number. In return, we give you an account number you can use from then on. The account number process works very well because, if someone steals your account number, all they can do is order something that will be shipped to you and billed to your credit card. You could then void the order and send it back to us. This has never happened.

EPU: That's a terrific fail-safe for virtual shoppers. How exactly does the virtual shopping bag work, and how do you implement it?

JG: We have a search engine that enables you to search for any book on the site, which is every book we publish. You put one or more books in your shopping bag essentially by just clicking the Shopping Bag icon. You fill out an order form with your name, address, and other information, and then just click Send. If you have an account number, you put it at the top of the form and you're done. We even have an express-order capability that enables you to bypass the shopping-bag concept by just clicking the Express Order button to order the one book selected. If you don't want to shop that way, you can call the 800 number. If you're outside the United States, you can call our 317 number. You can also fax in the order. We've tried to make it as easy as possible for people to order whatever books they would like.

Our search engine enables you to find our books very easily either by category, title, author, or ISBN. The underlying mechanism for the shopping is a gateway script that was originally written in Perl, but everything is being changed to Oracle, which should make shopping even faster and easier.

EPU: Creating attractions to bring visitors to a site is a key part of Web publishing. A fairly recent addition to the Macmillan site is the SuperLibrary Newsletter, which is currently in its eighth edition. Running an electronic newsletter or any type of Web publication isn't easy. What lessons have you learned, and what are the future directions for the newsletter in light of the departure of the current editor?

JG: The newsletter was done by our marketing manager who left us to go to our parent company. At Paramount, he'll build Web sites for the movie studio. The newsletter has been with us since the beginning of the site, and it's a tremendous marketing tool because it enables our authors to communicate added-value information to our readers. It enables us to communicate news about our books to readers and readers to communicate with us. We have contests and surveys on the site and in the newsletter. It will be the new new marketing manager's job to do what he or she would like with the newsletter.

EPU: The Web site of the Week is a part of the newsletter. How exactly does that work, and how does it help the person trying to Web publish? Certainly it brings them increased visibility, but how does it help them beyond that?

JG: This is something where Web sites can nominate themselves, and if we like the site, we'll name it the Web site of the week. Selection as Web site of the week brings the sites visibility, credibility, and gives people one more reason to come visit. The reason why our traffic has increased exponentially is driven by so many factors that we can't point to just one, and I think that's the key. You can't do just one thing and expect a lot of people to come visit; you have to do a lot of things.

EPU: Wonderful insight on how to attract visitors to a site. Another key area at the Macmillan site is the software library. I understand there are just loads of software there that people can download from all the computer books Macmillan publishes.

JG: And other sources as well, because people are free to upload their own applications for other people to download. We have thousands of applications available on our site and hundreds of people downloading thousands of applications every day. The traffic level on that part of the site continues to increase; it's a very popular area.

EPU: Could you give me a brief description of some of the applications available that would help a Web publisher? Some of the gateway scripts, perhaps.

JG: We have a well-organized software library, and so it's easy for people to get information. Here are some examples from the Internet software section of the library. We have FTP navigation tools, Internet Works browser, Eudora, Mosaic, Internet Backbone, Win QVT, Win sockets such as Trumpet and Win32S, FTP servers—a ton of software that is downloadable from the FTP and Web site. In many cases, we not only have a list of products, but we also have descriptions. For example, in the games group, we have a Doom editor that says: "This is the latest version of the Renegade graphics Doom and Doom II editor for Windows." This program is featured in the "Totally Unauthorized Guide to Doom II" book. You can save levels up to 30 sectors, but you must register it to save large levels. To download, you just click on a link.

EPU: Web publishing is a continually evolving and developing process. What final word do you have for anyone wanting to publish on the Web?

JG: When it comes to the Internet, if you ever think you're finished, you're dead because you're never finished. It would be like a TV station that said, "Oh, we're done. We're done with all our programming." You need to have new programming every day.

Summary

The World Wide Web is growing every minute of every day. Its phenomenal popularity stems in a large part from the way in which it enables users to seamlessly navigate through complex webs of global resources. Another reason the Web is so popular is because it enables anyone to compete on the level of major corporations. By electronic publishing on the Web you can establish a global presence and reach thousands of potential customers.

The tools discussed in this chapter are the keys to navigating the Web, finding information, and reaching customers. Obtaining a browser is an essential step on the road to becoming a Web publisher. Navigating the Web and tracking essential information is another step. Reaching customers is the ultimate step.

Using HTML

by

446

The key to unleashing the power of the World Wide Web is HTML. The hypertext markup language defines the structure of documents in a way that is easy to learn and distribute. Using HTML, you can create dynamic documents for viewing by millions of Web users.

This chapter provides a look inside Web publishing with HTML. It explains the following topics:

- What markup languages are
- The HTML standard
- Non-standard extensions to HTML
- The home page—where it all begins
- Page basics
- Creating headings
- Creating paragraphs
- Breaking up the page
- Building highlights
- Creating lists
- Creating links
- The complete home page
- Publishing the home page

What Are Markup Languages?

A major predecessor of the Web was Gopher. Gopher defined a way of displaying information in plain ASCII text. ASCII text allows you to loosely format information with tabs, spaces, and line breaks. This was an easy way to widely distribute and display information. Yet the World Wide Web would not be as popular as it is today if documents could only be displayed as plain text. The simple fact is that plain text is not visually appealing, and this is where markup languages come in. Currently, three primary markup languages are in use on the Web:

SGML
VRML
HTML

SGML

The Standard Generalized Markup Language (SGML) forms the basis for most markup languages. SGML is an advanced language with few limitations. The limitations of your SGML documents are generally defined by you when you create your documents. In SGML, you can select the font size and type that will display on the user's browser. This allows you to use multiple font sizes and types for use with your documents. As long as the font is available on the user's system, the text will be displayed as you intended. If the font is not available on the user's system, you can define alternate or default font types.

In SGML, you have full control over the positioning of text and images. This means text and images will be displayed by the user's SGML browser in the precise location you designate. Although SGML is a powerful markup language, it is not widely used on the Web at the present time. However, this will change as more publishers become aware of the versatility of SGML and as more SGML browsers become available. SGML is the subject of Chapter 21, "Inside SGML."

VRML

Virtual Reality Markup Language (VRML) is an advanced markup language based on the standard markup language. To display VRML publications, you will need a VRML browser. VRML is definitely the wave of the future in Web publishing. If you have ever wanted to create virtual worlds that people can wander through, VRML is the ticket. VRML allows you to create multidimensional documents from virtual malls to virtual universes.

The depth and scope of your virtual reality publication is limited primarily by your imagination. However, VRML files tend to be large, and large publications require a lot of network bandwidth and CPU capacity. The key to the success of VRML will be compression algorithms that allow for faster downloading, less CPU capacity, and near real-time browsing. Currently the number of VRML sites on the Web is limited, but this number will grow steadily as the language and technology advances.

HTML

The HyperText Markup Language enables you to format information in ways that are visually appealing without sacrificing ease of use and the potential for wide distribution. HTML is a markup or page definition language based on the Standard Generalized Markup Language. SGML defines a way to share complex documents using a generalized markup that is described in terms of standard ASCII text.

Describing complex structures in terms of plain text serves a twofold purpose. It ensures the widest distribution to any type of computer and presents the formatting in a human-readable form called markup. Because the markup contains standard characters, this also means anyone can create documents in a markup language, such as HTML, without needing special software. In fact, you can create HTML documents using a standard text editor if you want to.

HTML differentiates between formatting and the text to be displayed using unique characters that identify markup codes. Markup codes that identify formatting or page elements are called tags. Tags define parts of the document and include an element name enclosed by angle brackets, such as <P>, which indicates the start of a paragraph. Markup codes can also define a type of special character to display. Special characters are described by an element name preceded by an ampersand and ending with a semicolon, such as < for the less than symbol < or > for the greater than symbol >. These special characters are called character entities and lists of them are available online.

The functionality of HTML is limited by markup defined by the HTML standard and a few extensions to the standard. One of the key limitations to HTML pertains to the handling of text. In HTML you can control many of the display aspects for text. You can control the relative size of headings and in some cases, the text. You can specify text styles that include bold, underline, and italics. However, the font type and size the user's browser will use to display your Web page is ultimately controlled by the user's browser. Some browsers allow the user to select a base font size and type. Other browsers use default settings for the base font size and type. HTML allows you to add images to your documents. If the user has a graphics-capable HTML browser, the image may be displayed with the document. However, your control over the positioning of the image is limited.

Although HTML has limitations, it is still the publishing language of choice on the vast majority of Web sites. Remember, the limitations were a way to drastically reduce the complexity of HTML. Each implementation of the standard steadily introduces more versatility and functionality. HTML 1.0 is very basic and only includes a few features. HTML 2.0 is more versatile and includes more features. HTML 3.0 is very versatile and includes many features.

The HTML Standard

HTML as a language is constantly evolving based on standards set forth by the Internet Standards Organization and the Internet Engineering Task Force. Currently three versions of HTML are in use:

> HTML Version 1 or HTML 1.0
> HTML Version 2 or HTML 2.0
> HTML Version 3 or HTML 3.0

HTML Version 1

As the first standard for HTML, HTML 1.0 was designed to be an easy to use and intuitive way of creating Web documents. HTML 1.0 documents have four primary features: multiple levels of page headings, paragraphs, links to other documents, and lists. Any HTML browser available can display documents written in HTML version 1.0.

HTML Version 2

HTML 2.0 was designed to solve many of the shortcomings of the original version of HTML and to take advantage of the Web's interactive multimedia capabilities. It includes provisions for images that could be displayed along side text, called inline images. It also includes provisions for interactive forms that users can fill out and submit online. Nearly all of the browsers available support inline images and interactive forms.

HTML Version 3

HTML 3.0 is an emerging standard in HTML that may be ratified by the time you read this. This version of HTML includes so many radical changes to HTML that it is often called HTML+. These improvements to HTML are in such wide demand that several browsers already support them and have supported them for some time.

HTML+ enhancements include support for the following:

- Tables, including nested tables
- Tables within forms
- Mathematical equations
- Aligning text in a column alongside any type of object such as an image

Non-Standard Extensions to HTML

Current versions of HTML including the emerging standard HTML+ have barely touched upon the true power of Web publishing. Web publishers know this and so do the users. Both want more, and the trend is to give everyone what they want.

Netscape Corporation was the first company to provide support for HTML+ extensions and to include support for unique extensions. These extensions include the following:

- The capability to center text
- The capability to make text blink on and off
- The capability to control relative font sizes
- The capability to specify image size
- Use of images or colors to form a page background instead of the standard gray background
- Defining the width, length and shading of horizontal rules

For more information about Netscape, you should visit its Web site at this address: `http://www.netscape.com/`.

Netscape isn't the only maverick creating extensions to HTML. The talented folks at Sun Microsystems Incorporated began developing applications for the consumer electronics market in 1990. One of the results of this effort is the most powerful and far-reaching extension to Web publishing to date, called Java. Java is the little dynamo that will one day make internal multimedia a reality for all Web users.

Although Chapter 22, "Incorporating Multimedia," contains a full discussion on the vast potential of internal multimedia, in short it provides this: a way to provide sound, video, animation and even video games to anyone—no matter what type of computer they are using to access the Web. Needless to say, Web users and publishers from around the world are clamoring for their morning cup of Java. To showcase Java, the team at Sun developed a Web browser called HotJava, written entirely in the Java language. If you are interested in learning more about Java or HotJava visit Sun at `http://java.sun.com/`.

The Home Page: Where It All Begins

Every new site begins with a single page called the home page. Your home page is the front door to your house on the Web, and it is very likely that it will be the first thing visitors to your site see. There are many front doors on the Web that I visit. Some sites I visit often because they are friendly and useful. Other sites I visit once and only once because they are unfriendly and do not respect my time or anyone else's. These are the sites with the 50,000-byte graphics doing the greeting instead of the Web publisher. Anyone can create monstrous graphics and pitch them at the world, but it takes practice and skill to obtain a working balance between efficacy and grandeur.

Consequently, home pages tend to evolve as the Web publisher seeks that balance. The typical home page goes through two or three evolutions a year. Let's take another visit to my house on the Web `tvp.com` to see how it has evolved. Figure 20.1 is the first thing visitors to the home page see. This section provides a brief overview of the site and is largely targeted at new visitors.

FIGURE 20.1.

The Virtual Press: A home page on the Web.

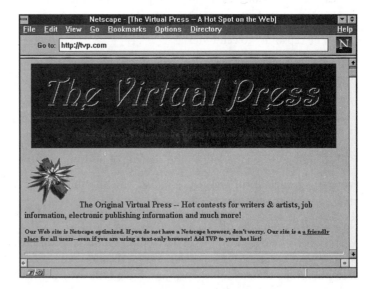

#### Chapter 20

Figure 20.2 shows a quick access menu for other sites and publications. The menu is organized by subject for easy browsing.

FIGURE 20.2.

TVP home page text menu.

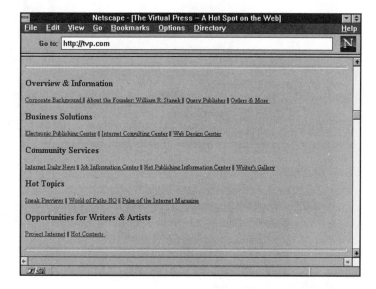

Figure 20.3 shows two of the site's coming attractions. This provides visitors with a clear idea of what they can expect to see at the site in the future.

FIGURE 20.3.

TVP home page upcoming attractions.

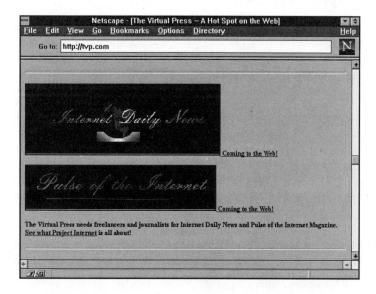

Figure 20.4 is the final section of the home page. This section of TVP's home page provides visitors with access to other places to visit and a copyright page.

FIGURE 20.4.

TVP home page copyright and more.

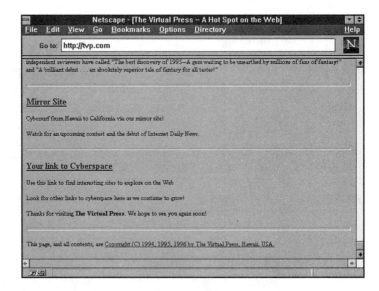

The next sections of the chapter discuss key concepts in HTML markup. By the end of this chapter, you will be well on your way to creating your own home page that is as good as or better than TVP's home page.

Page Basics

No matter what form professional writing takes, it is always structured. Books, magazines, and newspapers have titles, headings, and main components called chapters, articles, or columns. Similarly, HTML pages have titles, headings, and a main component called the body of the page. These parts of the publication are described using tags.

Tags are usually used in pairs. One tag, called the *begin tag,* tells the browser that a document element is beginning. Another tag, called the *end tag,* informs the browser that an element is ending. The only difference between a begin tag and an end tag is that the end tag contains a slash before the element name. For example, every HTML document begins with the markup tag <HTML> and ends with the markup tag </HTML>. The initial <HTML> tag tells the browser that the document is an HTML-formatted document and marks the beginning of the document. The end tag </HTML> marks the end of the document and is always the last item in any HTML document.

> **TIP**
>
> Because the formatting of HTML documents depends on tags, browsers normally ignore the ASCII formatting of text. This means tabs, extra spaces, paragraph breaks and page breaks are ignored. If your document contains these ASCII formatting

techniques, your readers will not see them, and therefore, the document will look wrong. Therefore, it is usually not a good idea to include ASCII text formatting in your HTML documents.

However, the authors of HTML realized there may be instances where you would want to retain ASCII formatting. Their solution was the <PRE> tag. In a later section, you will read about the <PRE> tag that allows preformatting of text.

Page Header

After the initial <HTML> tag, the next tag in your document is the <HEAD> tag. The <HEAD> tag identifies the beginning of the document header, and the </HEAD> tag identifies the ending of the document header. Every HTML document should have a header because the information contained in the header is treated specially by most Web software including browsers, servers, and indexers.

Presently, the primary tags reserved for the header pertain to the title of the document. The <TITLE> tag identifies the beginning of the document title, and the </TITLE> tag identifies the ending of the document title. Web browsers display the document title in a special location. Some browsers, such as Spry Mosaic, display the title in a clear window appropriately called "Document Title." Others, such as Netscape, display the title at the top of the browser's viewing area. The title of the document featured in Figure 20.4 is "The Virtual Press—A Hot Spot on the Web." The header and title information for the home page are as follows:

```
<HTML>
<HEAD>
<TITLE>The Virtual Press -- A Hot Spot on the Web</TITLE>
</HEAD>
. . .
</HTML>
```

NOTE

You would not actually type in the ellipses as shown in the example. The ellipses represent the rest of the document and are not an actual command. In later sections, the example will gradually be expanded. Also, keep in mind that an HTML page with only a header would display as a blank page.

Each document can only have one title. You should carefully think about the title for your document and the information it provides to readers. Although the title can contain no extra formatting or markup, it is the most referenced component of any page. The title of your document will appear on a user's bookmark or hot list, which contains a list of a user's favorite online

454

places, saved for future reference. The title will appear on the user's history list, which is a list of places visited during the current session. The title will also be referenced in the World Wide catalogs you will read about in Chapter 34, "Publishing and Marketing Tips."

Page Body

The main part of any HTML document is the body. All major components of the document will appear between the beginning and ending <BODY> tags. These components include section headings, paragraphs, links, lists, and graphics. When the BODY elements are added to our home page, they appear as follows:

```
<HTML>
<HEAD>
<TITLE>The Virtual Press -- A Hot Spot on the Web</TITLE>
</HEAD>
<BODY>
. . .
</BODY>
</HTML>
```

TIP

Most browsers display your text on a slate gray background. Netscape includes an extension for the <BODY> tag that enables you to add images and color to the background. Other extensions enable you to specify the color of text and links. If you plan to enhance your pages specifically for users with the Netscape browser, this can be a good extension to take advantage of.

Table 20.1 describes the attributes of Netscape's HTML extension, and the form of the redefined <BODY> tag is

```
<BODY BACKGROUND="image" BGCOLOR="#rrggbb" TEXT="#rrggbb"
LINK="#rrggbb" ALINK="#rrggbb" VLINK="#rrggbb">
```

Table 20.1. Netscape extensions to the <BODY> tag.

Attribute	Description
BACKGROUND="*image*"	Enables you to specify an image to be used as the background for the document. The image is tiled or repeated to fill the background area. You would type in the image name including the extension, such as .gif or .jpeg. You can also type in the relative or full path to the image. Specifying relative and full paths will be discussed later in the "Creating Links" section of this chapter.

Attribute	Description
BGCOLOR="#rrggbb"	Enables you to specify a background color for the document. The value "#rrggbb" is a hexadecimal value for the red, green, and blue contents of the color.
TEXT="#rrggbb"	Enables you to specify a color for document text to include headings. The value "#rrggbb" is a hexadecimal value for the red, green, and blue contents of the color.
LINK="#rrggbb"	Enables you to specify a color for links in a document that are unvisited. The value "#rrggbb" is a hexadecimal value.
ALINK="#rrggbb"	Enables you to specify a color for links in a document that are active (you have clicked on the link and are accessing the file or document associated with the link). The value "#rrggbb" is a hexadecimal value.
VLINK="#rrggbb"	Enables you to specify a color for links in a document that you have visited. The value "#rrggbb" is a hexadecimal value.

If you decide to use the extensions, you only have to specify the attributes you want changed. Any attributes you do not define will retain their defaults. The previous example could be modified to use the background extension as follows. The ➡ indicates that the line is a continuation of the previous line.

```
<HTML>
<HEAD>
<TITLE>The Virtual Press -- A Hot Spot on the Web</TITLE>
</HEAD>
<BODY BACKGROUND="waves.gif" TEXT="#FFFFFF" LINK="#FFFF00"
➡ALINK="#FF0000" VLINK="#00FF00">
. . .
</BODY>
</HTML>
```

TIP

You do not have to create separate documents especially for users with the Netscape browser. Typically, HTML browsers will ignore any tags or tag attributes that they cannot interpret. Therefore, if you specify a background extension and the user is not using the Netscape browser, your page will be displayed, but it will not have an enhanced background. This means you can use the background attribute for the <BODY> tag in a document intended for a general audience as well.

Table 20.2 shows some basic color combinations using hexadecimal values. Hexadecimal values are different from the decimal values you may be used to seeing. Although decimal values allow for 256 colors using the values 0 to 255, hexadecimal values allow for 256 colors using the base 16 numbering system from 00 to FF. The decimal value 255 in hexadecimal is FF. You can create a rainbow of colors by combining values or slightly altering values to create darker or lighter shades.

Table 20.2. Hexadecimal values for basic colors.

Color	Hexadecimal Values
Black	00 00 00
Red	FF 00 00
Green	00 FF 00
Blue	00 00 FF
Yellow	00 FF FF
Purple	FF 00 FF
White	FF FF FF

Creating Section Headings

HTML headings work just like the headings you are familiar with from outlines or works of nonfiction. Each chapter of a nonfiction book will contain headings pertaining to each major topic and subheadings pertaining to subtopics. Headings are usually in bold type and larger than the text on the page, similar to the bold print section heading above this paragraph.

In HTML, you can create up to six levels of headings. Each begin tag <H1> through <H6> has an associated end tag </H1> through </H6>. Headings are displayed in bold type and usually in a larger font size than the normal text on the page. In general, a level-one heading uses the largest font of heading sizes, and a level-six heading uses the smallest font of heading sizes.

> **NOTE**
>
> Keep in mind, the font size and style used with each heading changes according to configurations set up in the browser that is displaying the document. Although you have no direct control over these in HTML, they will be consistent relative to each other and the main text.

Although it is a good idea to organize information under headings, you do not want to use so many levels of headings that the work becomes incoherent. You should divide your ideas into manageable chunks of information but not divide topics so far that they become meaningless.

So, normally you should use only three or four levels of headings. Additionally, most browsers will display only visible differences in the first four heading levels. This means that heading levels four, five, and six will often be indistinguishable.

The text menu from Figure 20.2 uses a level-two heading to separate topics and text. The HTML code for the menu headings is as follows:

```
<H2>Overview &amp; Information</H2>
<H2>Business Solutions</H2>
<H2>Community Services</H2>
<H2>Community Services</H2>
<H2>Hot Topics</H2>
<H2>Opportunities for Writers &amp; Artists</H2>
```

> **NOTE**
>
> The HTML code contains a character entity similar to those discussed earlier in the chapter. The & is a character entity for the ampersand symbol. In HTML, there are actually two types of entities: character and numeric. When a browser reads the character or numeric entity value, the browser displays the corresponding character if possible.

If this HTML code is incorporated into our homepage, here's how it would look:

```
<HTML>
<HEAD>
<TITLE>The Virtual Press -- A Hot Spot on the Web</TITLE>
</HEAD>
<BODY>
<H2>Overview &amp; Information</H2>
<H2>Business Solutions</H2>
<H2>Community Services</H2>
<H2>Community Services</H2>
<H2>Hot Topics</H2>
<H2>Opportunities for Writers &amp; Artists</H2>
. . .
</BODY>
</HTML>
```

Creating Paragraphs

Many formatting mechanisms in word processors are so automatic that you probably don't even think about them. You press the Tab key to indent. You press the Enter key to insert blank lines or start a new paragraph. Indentation and blank lines serve to visually separate paragraphs of your document. Word processors will even insert blank lines between paragraphs and indent the first line of each paragraph for you automatically. In this way, the Enter key became the general-purpose formatting tool.

The original version of HTML thought of paragraph markings in this way. Under HTML 1.0, the <P> tag was just a way to insert blank lines into the document to separate paragraphs, and initially the <P> tag was put at the end of paragraphs. However, Web publishers soon discovered this wasn't a clear or distinctive way to identify paragraphs. To correct this shortcoming, the end paragraph tag became optional under HTML 2.0 and may be mandatory under HTML 3.0. The end paragraph tag ensures paragraph markings are used in pairs just like other tags and clearly defines the beginning and ending of paragraphs. A mandatory end paragraph tag may open the door for adding attributes to the paragraph tag in future revisions of HTML.

Using paragraph markings, you could complete and enter the textual portion of the menu from the home page example into the document as:

```
<H2>Overview &amp; Information</H2>
<P>Corporate Background ¦¦ About the Founder: William R. Stanek ¦¦
Query Publisher ¦¦ Orders &amp; More</P>
<H2>Business Solutions</H2>
<P>Electronic Publishing Center ¦¦
Internet Consulting Center ¦¦ Web Design Center </P>
<H2>Community Services</H2>
<P>Internet Daily News ¦¦ Job Information Center ¦¦
Net Publishing Information Center ¦¦ Writer's Gallery</P>
<H2>Hot Topics</H2>
<P>Sneak Previews ¦¦ World of Paths HQ ¦¦
Pulse of the Internet Magazine</P>
<H2>Opportunities for Writers &amp; Artists</H2>
<P>Project Internet ¦¦ Hot Contests </P>
```

> **NOTE**
>
> The double vertical bars are simply the pipe symbol (¦) typed twice and are a basic way to visually break up the menu. You will find the double vertical bars in use on many text menus. Most browsers will recognize and properly display the vertical bar. However, if you find that a specific browser cannot display the vertical bar properly, you may want to use the following numeric entity code:
>
> ```
> &#124;
> ```

Creating Links

Most Web documents contain hypertext links. Links are like postal addresses. They tell the browser where to send a request for a particular file. At this point the browser does not care what type of file it is supposed to retrieve, it just tries to retrieve the file based on the address it is given. The file could contain any type of information, such as another HTML document, image, sound file, or video file. If the file is addressed properly, the browser will retrieve the file and display it.

Do you hate it when receive a letter marked "address unknown" returns to your mailbox? I know I do, and so do users who are trying to access your Web pages. The real trick to creating links in your documents is in providing the correct address for a particular file. To get to a file, browsers need to know the location of the resource. The location of the resource is specified as a Universal Resource Locator, commonly called a URL.

Simply stated, URLs are the addresses we have been talking about. The part of the address the user sees in a hypertext document is defined by the Hypertext Markup Language's anchor tag. The anchor is the text you see, and the address is the part you don't see until you point your mouse at a particular link. A typical URL looks like this:

```
http://tvp.com/vphp.html
```

This URL tells the browser to use the hypertext transfer protocol to access a document called vphp.html on the tvp.com Web server. URLs with complete address information will enable you to link your documents to documents on other Web servers. These URLs contain everything your server needs to contact another server and retrieve the file you have requested from it. In the Web document referencing the URL, the URL would be a part of an anchor tag such as:

```
<A HREF="http://tvp.com/vphp.html">The Virtual Press Home Page</A>
```

The three key elements in this type of anchor tag include:

Address	The opening <A> tag contains the address of the files you are linking to. The address is not visible in a document unless the mouse pointer is over the anchor. You specify the file to link to using a URL in the following format:
	`<A HREF="URL">`
Anchor	The anchor is the text portion of the link that is visible when a browser displays the document. The anchor is positioned between the begin and end anchor tags. In the previous example, the anchor text was:
	`The Virtual Press Home Page`
End anchor tag	The </A> tag specifies the end of the anchor text.

You can find as many ways to use links in HTML documents as there are ways to send letters through the postal system. A letter mailed without a ZIP code might get to where its going if you are mailing the letter to a local address. Otherwise, you will probably get it back stamped "Cannot mail without ZIP code." The ZIP code is necessary to indicate a specific destination within a larger area. A large city such as New York has dozens of applicable ZIP codes, and West 52nd Street is only relative or meaningful to you if you know where it is. When your local postmaster—your browser—accesses files, the browser can determine the location of files on a particular Web server in relation to other files you accessed previously. Files accessed in this manner use relative paths to locate a file in relation to other files. However, for files not on the local Web server, you must specify a complete path to the file. Files accessed in this manner use the full paths to access the file directly.

URLs with relative file paths generally do not name a protocol or a Web server in the link. A relative file path is a location relative to the current position or directory. For example, if you have already accessed a particular Web server such as tvp.com in the previous example and now want to access another page at the same site, you could specify a relative path such as:

```
<A HREF="page2.html">Next Page</A>
```

The Web browser servicing a request for this link would expect to find the file page2.html in the current directory. You could also specify a file in a directory relative to the current directory, such as:

```
<A HREF="../new_pub.html">New Publication</A>
```

In this example, the file is located in the directory above the current directory. You could also specify a file in a subdirectory of the current directory:

```
<A HREF="docs/new_pub2.html">Another Publication</A>
```

TIP

You can think of the directory and subdirectory structure as an inverted tree. The base of the tree is the root directory. All other directories build off the root directory and form branches. Each branch can have smaller branches and so on. The way you traverse the directory tree is to specify the full path from the root directory or a relative path from your current position.

If you were actually logged on to the Web server you could move around the directory tree using the CD or change directory command. If you typed the following line:

```
cd /usr/local/cgi-bin
```

you would be in the cgi-bin directory. From the directory structure you can see that cgi-bin is a subdirectory of the local directory, and the local directory is a subdirectory of the usr directory. If you typed the following relative path using the change directory command

```
cd ..
```

You would move up the directory tree to the parent directory of cgi-bin, meaning you would now be in the local directory and your full path would be /usr/local.

Links Within Documents

You can also link to a location within a document using links. Links to locations within long documents enable you to provide ways to quickly jump to key sections. This is done by labeling the link with a keyword in the form:

```
<A HREF="#keyword">
```

The pound sign (#) preceding the keyword identifies the link as an internal page link. When a user activates an internal link, the key section of the document will be displayed. If the internal link is in the current document, the browser will jump to the section specified using the <A NAME> tag. If the internal link is within a different document, the browser will load the document and then jump to the section specified using the <A NAME> tag.

The key word used with the link and anchor name must match exactly. You can specify internal links within the current document as follows:

1. You create a special link as follows:

    ```
    <A HREF="#keyword">Anchor text for the current document</A>
    ```

2. Label the section of the document you want the user to be able to jump to using the <A NAME> tag:

    ```
    <A NAME="keyword">Text to jump to</A>
    ```

The format for specifying internal page links within a different document is to precede *#keyword* with the document's URL. This URL can be the relative or full path to the document. This example uses a relative path:

```
<A HREF="home_page.html#keyword">Anchor text for the specified document</A>
```

Combining the Link Examples

Using the linking techniques you have learned about in this section, the menu on your home page can finally be completed. The menu for TVP's home page was completed as follows:

```
<H2>Overview &amp; Information</H2>
<P><A HREF="vpbg.html">Corporate Background </A> ¦¦
<A HREF="vpfound.html">About the Founder: William R. Stanek </A> ¦¦
<A HREF="vpqry.html">Query Publisher</A> ¦¦
<A HREF="vpdord.html">Orders &amp; More </A></P>
<H2>Business Solutions</H2>
<P><A HREF="vpepc.html"> Electronic Publishing Center</A> ¦¦
<A HREF="vpicc.html">Internet Consulting Center</A> ¦¦
<A HREF="vpwdc.html"> Web Design Center</A></P>
<H2>Community Services</H2>
<P><A HREF="#IDN"> Internet Daily News</A> ¦¦
<A HREF="vpjic.html">Job Information Center</A> ¦¦
<A HREF="vpipc.html">Net Publishing Information Center</A> ¦¦
```

```
<A HREF="vpwg.html">Writer's Gallery</A></P>
<H2>Hot Topics</H2>
<P><A HREF="vpdream1.html"> Sneak Previews</A> ¦¦
<A HREF="vpdest1.html">World of Paths HQ</A> ¦¦
<A HREF="#PULSE">Pulse of the Internet Magazine</A></P>
<H2>Opportunities for Writers &amp; Artists</H2>
<P><A HREF="projint.html">Project Internet</A> ¦¦
<A HREF="vpcon.html">Hot Contests </A></P>
```

The example contains two links to locations within the current document. The first internal link is identified by the reference to #IDN. Here, IDN is the keyword the browser will look for. When the browser finds an <A NAME> tag containing the keyword, IDN, it will display the corresponding section of the document. This link is referenced at the location the user will jump to as follows:

```
<H3> <A NAME="IDN"><IMG SRC="idnttl4.gif" ALT="">
Coming to the Web!</A></H3>
```

The second internal link is identified by the reference to #PULSE. Here, PULSE is the keyword the browser will look for. When the browser finds an <A NAME> tag containing the keyword, PULSE, it will display the corresponding section of the document. This link is referenced at the location the user will jump to as follows:

```
<H3> <A NAME="PULSE"><IMG SRC="pinttl3.gif" ALT="">
Coming to the Web!</A></H3>
```

> **NOTE**
>
> The <IMG SRC> tag enables you to reference an image to be displayed along with the text of the currently displayed document. The <IMG SRC> tag is covered in depth in Chapter 22, "Incorporating Multimedia." To see what these images look like, you can refer back to Figure 20.3.

Breaking Up the Page

Browsers won't display text as you see it in your word processor. They will wrap text according to the size of the font and viewing area as selected by the user. Browsers also ignore tabs, line breaks, page breaks, and multiple spaces. In fact, multiple tabs, spaces, and line breaks are displayed as a single space. To overcome this problem, you can use several techniques to break up the page:

- Line breaks
- Horizontal Rules
- Preformatted text

Line Breaks

Often, you want a line to break at a certain point without double-spacing. Using the line-break tag, you could do just that. The <BR> tag enables you to break a line without adding a space between the lines. Because an end break tag would serve no useful purpose, the <BR> tag is one of the few tags that has only a begin tag.

A key thing to note about the <BR> tag is that you can use it inside other tags without affecting the font or style of the previously declared tag. If you insert <BR> into a level-one heading, the text before and after the break will be formatted in the style and font of a level-one heading. All <BR> does is start a new line, like the carriage return on a typewriter.

Horizontal Rules

Horizontal rules are a great way to identify distinct sections of a page. Using the <HR> tag, you can insert a shaded line across the width of the page. The shaded line is drawn in with a nice effect that makes it appear to be engraved into the page. Because the horizontal rule carries out a predefined action, it is another tag that doesn't have an end tag.

The Netscape browser includes four very useful extensions to the horizontal rule. These extensions allow you to define the alignment, width, size and shading of the rule. Table 20.3 describes the attributes, and the form of the redefined <HR> tag is

```
<HR ALIGN="alignment" NOSHADE SIZE=number WIDTH=number >
```

Table 20.3. Netscape extensions to the horizontal rule.

Attribute	Description
ALIGN="alignment"	Specifies the alignment of the horizontal rule. You could type in any of the three values for the ALIGN attribute: LEFT, RIGHT, or CENTER.
NOSHADE	Specifies the rule should be solid instead of shaded.
SIZE=number	Specifies the thickness of the rule in pixels or as a percentage width relative to the width of the document.
WIDTH=number	Specifies the width of the rule in pixels or as a percentage width relative to the width of the document.

Preformatted Text

Web browsers ignore extra spaces, tabs, and blank lines. However, sometimes you will want portions of your document to be formatted precisely as you typed it in. You can declare text as preformatted with the <PRE> tag. Any text between the beginning and ending </PRE> tag will be formatted according to the text formatting you have provided.

However, the <PRE> tag is a mixed blessing. Usually, the font type used to display preformatted text is different from the default font used to display other text on the page. Although the font used for preformatted text is dependent on configurations set up in the browser reading the document, the font is often a monospaced typewriter font such as Courier.

CAUTION

You need to be especially careful when using the <PRE> tag. Monospaced fonts will appear much wider than proportional fonts because each letter of a monospaced font uses the same amount of screen space. Proportional fonts use the amount of screen space proportional to their size, which means that an *i* uses less screen space than a *w*. When preparing preformatted text, you should try to keep the line length to 60 characters or less.

NOTE

Another rule is to preview the text in your browser or a collection of browsers with the standard 640×480 video mode (PC) or a 9-inch screen (Mac). You will also want to test all links and check the appearance of each of your pages.

The <PRE> tag can be a time-saver and a quick solution to a presentation problem you face. You will find the <PRE> tag is most useful for any material that was originally formatted as plain text, such as e-mail messages or newsgroup postings. Using the <PRE> tag, you won't have to reformat, and you will save time. Until recently, the <PRE> tag was also widely used to format text into columns for tables. The feature that is replacing preformatted text tables is the <TABLE> tag defined under the HTML 3.0 specification.

Breaking Up the Page with Basic Formatting Techniques

The following examples are a comparison and contrast using the basic page formatting techniques previously discussed. The first example shows how you could use standard formatting techniques to format text using headings, paragraphs, and line breaks. The second example shows how you could format the material into a table using the <PRE> tag.

The HTML markup for the first example follows:

```
<HTML>
<HEAD>
<TITLE>HTML Versions: Support and Features</TITLE>
</HEAD>
<BODY>
<H1>The HTML Standard, Features &amp; Support</H1>
<H2>HTML 1.0</H2>
<H3>Features</H3>
<P>Multiple level headings<BR>
```

```
Paragraphs<BR>
Links to other documents<BR>
Lists</P>
<H3>Support</H3>
<P>Any HTML browser</P>
<H2>HTML 2.0</H2>
<H3>Features</H3>
<P>Inline images<BR>
Interactive forms<P>
<H3>Support</H3>
<P>Nearly all browsers available<P>
<H2>HTML 3.0</H2>
<H3>Features</H3>
<P>Tables<BR>
Tables within forms<BR>
Mathematical Equations<BR>
Aligning text alongside objects</P>
<H3>Support</H3>
<P>A growing number of browsers support</P>
<H1>HTML Non-Standard Features &amp; Support</H1>
<H2>Netscape Extensions</H2>
<H3>Features</H3>
<P>Center/Blink<BR>
Control over relative font/image sizes<BR>
Background images and color<BR>
Horizontal Rule length, width and shading</P>
<H3>Support</H3>
<P>Netscape Browser</P>
</BODY>
</HTML>
```

The previous HTML markup is shown in two parts. Figure 20.5 shows the first section of the example, and Figure 20.6 shows the second part of the example. For some purposes, such a long display would not be practical. This would be especially true if the information is meant to be a part of a longer document accompanied by a detailed explanation.

FIGURE 20.5.

Basic formatting techniques establish heading levels in a long list.

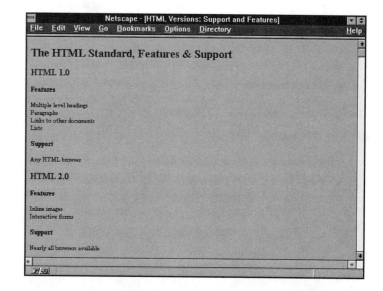

FIGURE 20.6.

This is the second page of the example.

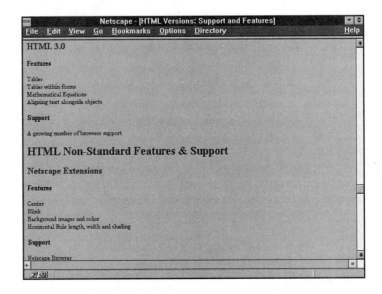

In some instances, the two-screen example shown previously could be hard to work into a longer more detailed document. An easy work-around for the problem would be to use the <PRE> tag. Using the <PRE> tag, you could create a simple table as follows:

```
<HTML>
<HEAD>
<TITLE>HTML Versions: Support and Features</TITLE>
</HEAD>
<BODY>
<PRE>
The HTML Standard, Features & Support

HTML 1.0                  HTML 2.0            HTML 3.0
Multiple level headings   Inline images       Tables
Paragraphs                Interactive forms   Tables within forms
Links to other documents                      Mathematical equations
Lists                                         Aligning text & objects

Support
Any HTML browser          Most browsers       Some browsers

HTML Non-Standard Features & Support

Netscape Extensions                           Java Extensions
Center/Blink                                  Apps - self-running
Control over relative font/image sizes
Background images and color
Horizontal Rule length, width and shading

Support
Netscape Browser                              HotJava, (Netscape)
</PRE>
</BODY>
</HTML>
```

The preformatted text example is shown in Figure 20.7. As you can see, by presenting the information as a table, the space required for the information can be dramatically reduced.

FIGURE 20.7.

Using preformatted text enables you to condense a long list into a table.

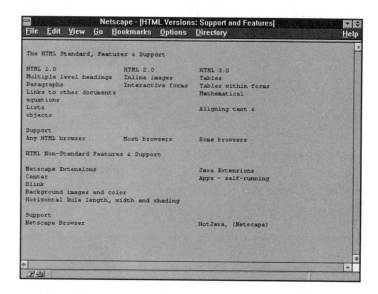

Building Highlights

Documents that contain only paragraphs and headings offer little variety. Everything between the open and end tags of a paragraph or heading is the same font size and style. When you insert a new paragraph, the browser knows to insert a space between the previous paragraph and the next. When you insert a new heading, the browser knows to insert a space above and below the heading. This works just fine for basic documents, but often you will want to highlight or emphasize keywords, sentences or portions of paragraphs. To do this, you can use a special set of tags called character style tags.

All character style tags have a begin tag and an end tag. The job of character style tags is to highlight the text using techniques such as boldface, italics, and underline. Character style tags do not insert spacing. They are designed to be used within other tags, such as paragraphs and headings. Consequently, you can highlight a single word or a group of words.

In HTML, there are two subsets of character style tags:

- Physical style tags
- Logical style tags

Physical Styles

Physical styles tell the browser the precise format to display. Four physical styles correspond to bold, italics, underline, and monospaced type. Each style has a begin tag and an end tag, and could be used in an HTML document as follows:

```
<H1>Using Physical Styles</H1>
<P>A <B>bold</B> style creates great <B>highlights</B>.</P>
<P><I>Italics</I> can be used to <I>emphasize</I>.</P>
<P>Inserting a <TT>monospaced typewriter font</TT>
can create <TT>subtle</TT> differences in the text.</P>
<P><U>Underline</U> will be a useful addition to HTML if
readers <U>don't</U> confuse it with a link reference.</P>
```

As spaces are not inserted before or after these tags, they can be used with other tags including other physical style tags. An example of combining tags would be to combine the bold and underline tags so that text will appear as both boldface and underlined:

```
<P>Combining <B><U>bold and underline</U></B> is often useful.</P>
```

> **NOTE**
>
> Underline is a tag that will be defined under HTML 3.0, which means many browsers do not support the underline tag. Although browsers typically ignore tags they cannot interpret, you may want to use italics instead of underline. In professional writing, underlined text is often converted to italics for publishing in the finished document.

> **TIP**
>
> Note the order of the bold and underline style tags in the previous example. The order of tags is often extremely important in your HTML code. When you combine styles, you should keep them in parallel order.

In Figure 20.8, the previous examples using physical styles are combined into a single document titled "Physical Styles." A browser accessing documents containing physical styles will try to display the text using the strict format you have specified. If it is unable to, it may substitute another style for the one you are using or it may ignore the tag and display the text in the standard style. For this reason, logical styles are the preferred style to use.

FIGURE 20.8.

Using physical styles creates highlights in your text.

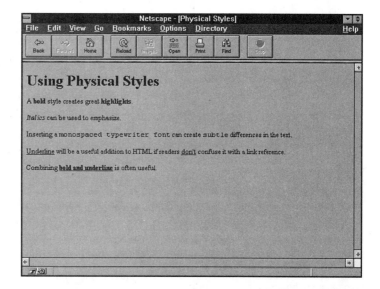

Logical Styles

Logical styles tell the browser how the text is to be used and let the browser display the text according to a set of configurations specific to the browser. This gives control of the style handling to the browser and is a more intelligent way to handle styles that mirror the handling of other tags such as <P>. There are eight logical styles, and each style has a begin tag and an end tag. Because spaces are not inserted before or after these tags, you can use them with other tags including other logical style tags.

Two styles are used more than any of the others. The <EM> tag and the <STRONG> tag are close equivalents of the italics and bold physical styles. The <EM> tag is used to emphasize the text enclosed by the begin and end <EM> tags. Most browsers display emphasized text in italics. The <STRONG> tag is used to strongly emphasize the text enclosed by the begin and end <STRONG> tags. Most browsers display strongly emphasized text in bold.

The other six style tags are falling out of common usage, primarily because they duplicate styles easily created by other means. These six tags are

<CITE> Indicates that text is a citation. Most browsers display CITE text in italics. This tag is the most frequently used tag in this list.

<CODE> Indicates computer code or a program sample. Most browsers display CODE text in a monospaced font such as Courier.

<DFN> Indicates that text is a definition. Most browsers display DFN text in italics.

<KBD> Indicates text that a user would type in on the keyboard. Most browsers display KDB text in a monospaced font such as Courier.

<SAMP> Indicates a sample of literal characters. Most browsers display SAMP text in a monospaced font such as Courier.

<VAR>   Indicates that text is a variable name such as those used in computer pro-
         grams. Most browsers display VAR text in italics.

You can use logical style tags in many ways in your HTML documents. Like physical style
tags, they can be combined with other tags, such as headings, paragraphs, and even preformatted
text. Figure 20.9 shows how the <STRONG> and <EM> tags could be combined with these elements and it is based on the following HTML code:

```
<HTML>
<HEAD>
<TITLE>Logical Styles</TITLE>
</HEAD>
<BODY>
<H1>Logical Style Tags</H1>
<P>To create a <STRONG>STRONG</STRONG> emphasis, use the
➥<STRONG>STRONG</STRONG> tag.</P>
<P>To <EM>emphasize</EM>, use the <EM>EM</EM> tag.</P>
<PRE>
Using Logical Style tags in preformatted text is easy.

To create a <STRONG>STRONG</STRONG> emphasis, use the
➥<STRONG>STRONG</STRONG> tag.

To <EM>emphasize</EM>, use the <EM>EM</EM> tag.
</PRE>
</BODY>
</HTML>
```

FIGURE 20.9.

Using logical styles to highlight text.

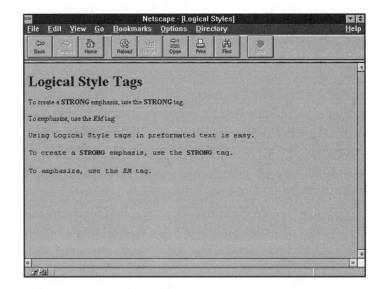

Creating Lists

Lists are used widely in any type of writing. A glossary contains a list of keywords and their
definitions. In HTML, a list of glossary terms is called a *definition list*. Bulleted lists are often

used to outline goals, objectives, or tasks that have no specific order; and they're called *unordered lists*. Numbered lists are used when tasks must be performed in a specific order, and they're called *ordered lists*.

The authors of the original HTML standard recognized the need for these three fundamental types of lists, and because they were programmers, they added two other types of lists related to programs. *Menu lists* were meant for lists of the contents of program menus. *Directory lists* were meant for lists of the contents of directories. Menu lists and directory lists were rarely used, and when they were used, browsers typically followed the rules for another list type to display the list. Consequently, the current specification for HTML 3.0 only supports them as deprecated elements, and only for historical compatibility.

Although the latter two of the five types of lists have fallen into disuse, ordered lists, unordered lists, and definition lists are increasing in popularity. This is because most Web users are simply browsing or Web surfing. They are looking for an interesting site to visit and don't want to wade through pages of information at every intermediary site. To see how you can grab the attention of those Web surfers, the following subsections describe these kinds of lists:

Bulleted lists
Numbered lists
Glossary lists

Bulleted Lists

Bulleted lists are called unordered lists in HTML, and the <UL> tag is used to mark the beginning of the list. Each item in the list is preceded by the list item tag <LI>. Although the end list tag </LI> is not required under current implementations of HTML, it is a good idea to use it for the sake of consistency in your HTML markup. It will also save you from having to revise your documents later should the end list tag </LI> become mandatory.

When a browser sees the begin list tag <LI>, it inserts a new line but does not separate the list items by spacing. Therefore, the begin and end paragraph tags are often used with the begin and end list tags to create spacing before and after list items. The browser also inserts a bullet character before the text following the begin list item tag. Most browsers display the bullet as a large solid dot. Text browsers, such as Lynx, display the bullet as an asterisk. Other browsers, such as the Netscape browser, enable you to assign attributes pertaining to the shape of the bullet. Some browsers also use a different symbol for the bullets at each level of nested lists.

The following code shows how the menu at The Virtual Press home page could be made into a bulleted list. Figure 20.10 shows how the bulleted list would look in a browser.

```
<H2>Business Solutions</H2>
<UL>
<LI>Electronic Publishing Center</LI>
<LI>Internet Consulting Center</LI>
<LI>Web Design Center</LI>
</UL>
<H2>Community Services</H2>
<UL>
```

```
<LI>Internet Daily News</LI>
<LI>Job Information Center</LI>
<LI>Net Publishing Information Center</LI>
<LI>Writer's Gallery</LI>
</UL>
<H2>Hot Topics</H2>
<UL>
<LI>Sneak Previews</LI>
<LI>World of Paths HQ</LI>
<LI>Pulse of the Internet Magazine</LI>
</UL>
<H2>Opportunities for Writers &amp; Artists</H2>
<UL>
<LI>Project Internet</LI>
<LI>Hot Contests</LI>
</UL>
```

FIGURE 20.10.

A bulleted list.

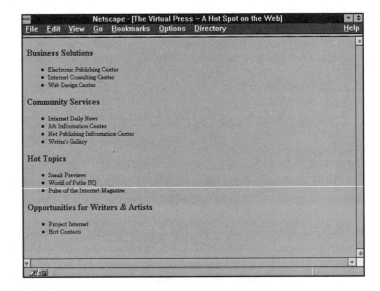

Numbered Lists

Numbered lists are called ordered lists in HTML. The begin ordered list tag <OL> is used to mark the beginning of the list, each item in the list is preceded by the list item tag <LI>.

Each item in an ordered list is consecutively numbered or lettered. When a browser sees a begin list tag <LI> it does several things. First, it inserts a new line. Second, it indents the text of the list item. Third, it puts an appropriate number or letter in front of the list item. Letters are used only in nested lists. With minor modification, the bulleted menu from the previous example could be made into a numbered list:

```
<H1>12 Reasons To Browse Our Site</H1>
<OL>
<H2>Business Solutions</H2>
<LI>Electronic Publishing Center</LI>
<LI>Internet Consulting Center</LI>
<LI>Web Design Center</LI>
<H2>Community Services</H2>
<LI>Internet Daily News</LI>
<LI>Job Information Center</LI>
<LI>Net Publishing Information Center</LI>
<LI>Writer's Gallery</LI>
<H2>Hot Topics</H2>
<LI>Sneak Previews</LI>
<LI>World of Paths HQ</LI>
<LI>Pulse of the Internet Magazine</LI>
<H2>Opportunities for Writers &amp; Artists</H2>
<LI>Project Internet</LI>
<LI>Hot Contests</LI>
</OL>
```

Figure 20.11 shows how the numbered list would look in a browser.

FIGURE 20.11.

A numbered list auto-matically numbers each list item.

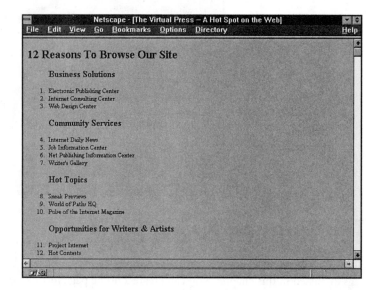

Definition Lists

Definition lists can be used to create glossaries. The <DL> tag is used to specify the beginning of the list. Each item in the definition list contains two elements: the definition title and the definition data. The definition title tag <DT> is used to specify the glossary term that is being defined. The definition data tag <DD> is used to specify the definition. Just as terms in Webster's dictionary can have multiple definitions associated with them, so can terms in your glossary list. For each unique definition, you could insert a corresponding <DD> entry. Although the <DL> tag has a begin and an end tag, only the begin <DT> and <DD> tags are normally used.

To define the list shown in Figure 20.12, you could use this glossary list:

```
<DL>
<P><DT>Electronic mail</P>
<DD>Also called e-mail.
<DD>Provides the basic means to send letters electronically to friends,
➥associates and colleagues "virtually" in an instant.
<P><DT>File Transfer Protocol</P>
<DD>Also called FTP.
<DD>Provides the basic means for delivering and retrieving files
➥around the global network.
<P><DT>Telnet</P>
<DD>Provides a way to remotely log in to another system.
</DL>
```

FIGURE 20.12.

A glossary list showing multiple definitions for each term.

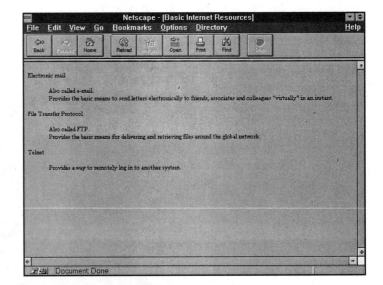

The Finished Home Page

The following is the source code for The Virtual Press home page. Using the HTML markup tags discussed in this chapter, you can create a home page just like this one.

```
<HTML>
<HEAD>
<TITLE>The Virtual Press — A Hot Spot on the Web</TITLE>
</HEAD>
<BODY>
<P> <A HREF="http://tvp.com/vpbg.html"><IMG SRC="vpttl11.gif" ALT=""></A></P>
<H2><IMG SRC="bboard.gif" ALIGN="BOTTOM" ALT="* ATTN *">
➥The Original Virtual Press — Hot contests for writers &amp; artists,
➥job information, electronic publishing information and much more!</H2>
<P><EM>Our Web site is Netscape optimized. If you do not have a Netscape
➥browser, don't worry. Our site is a <A HREF="vpintro.html">a friendly place</A>
➥for all users—even if you are using a text-only browser! Add TVP to your
➥hot list!</P></EM>
```

```
<HR SIZE=4>
<H2>Overview &amp; Information</H2>
<P><A HREF="vpbg.html">Corporate Background </A> ||
<A HREF="vpfound.html">About the Founder: William R. Stanek </A> ||
<A HREF="vpqry.html">Query Publisher</A> ||
<A HREF="vpdord.html">Orders &amp; More </A></P>
<H2>Business Solutions</H2>
<P><A HREF="vpepc.html" > Electronic Publishing Center</A> ||
<A HREF="vpicc.html">Internet Consulting Center</A> ||
<A HREF="vpwdc.html"> Web Design Center</A></P>
<H2>Community Services</H2>
<P><A HREF="#IDN"> Internet Daily News</A> ||
<A HREF="vpjic.html">Job Information Center</A> ||
<A HREF="vpipc.html">Net Publishing Information Center</A> ||
<A HREF="vpwg.html">Writer's Gallery</A></P>
<H2>Hot Topics</H2>
<P><A HREF="vpdream1.html"> Sneak Previews</A> ||
<A HREF="vpdest1.html">World of Paths HQ</A> ||
<A HREF="#PULSE">Pulse of the Internet Magazine</A></P>
<H2>Opportunities for Writers &amp; Artists</H2>
<P><A HREF="projint.html">Project Internet</A> ||
<A HREF="vpcon.html">Hot Contests </A></P>
<HR SIZE=4>
<H3> <A NAME="IDN"><IMG SRC="idnttl4.gif" ALT="">
Coming to the Web!</A></H3>
<H3> <A NAME="PULSE"><IMG SRC="pinttl3.gif" ALT="">
Coming to the Web!</A></H3>
<H3>The Virtual Press needs freelancers and journalists for
Internet Daily News and Pulse of the Internet Magazine.
<A HREF="projint.html">See what Project Internet</A> is all about!</H3>
<HR SIZE=4>
<H2><A HREF="http://www.tvpress.com/">Mirror Site</A></LI></H2>
<P>Cybersurf from Hawaii to California via our mirror site!</P>
<P>Watch for an upcoming contest and the debut of Internet Daily News.</P>
<HR>
<H2><A HREF="vplink.html">Your link to Cyberspace</A></H2>
<P>Use this link to find interesting sites to explore on the Web<P>
<P> Look for other links to cyberspace here as we continue to grow!</P>
<P> Thanks for visiting <EM>The Virtual Press</EM>.
We hope to see you again soon!</P>
<HR SIZE=4>
<P>This page, and all contents, are <A HREF="vpcopy.html">
Copyright (c) 1994, 1995, 1996 by The Virtual Press, Hawaii, USA.</A></P>
</BODY>
</HTML>
```

Many of the design concepts used in this home page are critical to the success of your Web publishing operation. One of the keys to success is to provide an easy way for return visitors to browse their favorite sections of the site, such as a menu. Menus have been set up at Web sites in a variety of ways. The normal convention is to place menus at the top of a page or at the very bottom of the page. The latest craze is to make these menus graphic images that can be clicked on. Although these icon menus are eye-dazzling, they are not entirely practical because of the number of users who presently cannot view graphics or simply prefer not to view graphics. If you include a graphic menu, be kind and include a text-based menu as well. The friendlier your pages are, the better. Visitors to your Web site will appreciate every effort you have made to save them time.

As more Web users start to use graphics-capable browsers and the bandwidth with which they access the Web increases, it will become more practical to use graphical menus. Do not worry, the Web and computer technology are changing rapidly. It will not be long before 28.8 modems and graphics-based browsers are in the hands of all Internet users.

The key is to provide features for all users and remember the three categories of users: those with text-based browsers, those with graphics-capable browsers, and those with browsers able to use the advanced features of HTML. The structure of your document hierarchy does not have to be rigid. You can and should link keywords and ideas across your Web site. By linking keywords, you can provide parallel ways for users to access parts of the site.

Good Web sites feature community service pages as well as business pages. It is fine to sell your products on the Web, but you will build tremendous good will by simply providing information for free. Share a bit of your area of expertise with the world and give visitors a reason to return to your site. Your investment in time will be paid back exponentially.

Publishing the Home Page

Normally I create Web pages in the Microsoft Windows environment using a standard word processor. The finished documents are saved as ASCII text with an extension of `.htm`. Although the extension `.htm` is used on DOS/Windows systems, the extension `.html` is commonly used on Macintosh and UNIX systems.

The next step in the publishing process is to test the documents. I test documents by viewing the home page locally on three different browsers. The browsers used are a text-only browser, a graphics-capable browser, and an advanced browser that takes advantage of extensions to HTML.

> **NOTE**
>
> Testing with several browsers is something that some electronic publishers completely ignore. You can notice this immediately if you visit their site with a browser other than the one they used to test their pages on. Sometimes these pages are completely unreadable or unusable. When this happens, users simply do not return to the site. Making sure aspects of your pages are optimized correctly for all types of users is a small price to pay to attract readers to your site.

After testing, the documents are downloaded to a server running under the UNIX operating system. Once on the server the documents are renamed with the HTML extension, .html, and put in a mode accessible by other Web users.

Summary

HTML enables you to publish on the World Wide Web. A Web browser differentiates between the formatting and the text to be displayed using unique characters that identify markup codes. The most common markup codes you will use are called tags. Using the markup tags you have learned about in this chapter, you can create your own home page. So, what are you waiting for?

Inside SGML

by William R. Stanek

21

IN THIS CHAPTER

Look at the snappy graphics and fancy texts in modern magazines and you might understand why some page designers have nightmares that revolve around their PCs or lack thereof. Modern designers depend on their tools. A day without Interleaf 5 <SGML> or Author/Editor would be unbearable, unthinkable, and possibly impossible. At the heart of these and other page design tools are page definition languages such as SGML.

Standard Generalized Markup Language, commonly called SGML, represents the past and the future of publishing. Before SGML, the page design process was time-consuming and largely the domain of page designers. Today, the lengthy and specialized process is reduced to keystrokes on a keyboard, and this has changed the face of publishing forever. Nowhere is the influence of page definition languages more prevalent than in electronic publishing. In fact, without SGML the World Wide Web as we know it would not exist.

Yet SGML's power is not in what is does. It is in what it defines, which is a way to produce and distribute complex documents. This chapter provides the keys to using aspects of SGML in your electronic publishing ventures. You will learn about

- Designing pages with SGML
- Advantages of SGML
- How SGML relates to HTML
- SGML basics
- SGML helper applications
- Page layout tools

Designing Pages with SGML

Standard Generalized Markup Language defines how pages should look on paper and on-screen. Before SGML, the page design process was left to specialized designers. These designers marked up each page of the publication with instructions. The instructions told the typesetter where to place every component on the page, the style of the component, the font to use, and much more.

The placement of a standard header was carried out through a series of instructions such as the header should be centered, bold, and in 16-point Helvetica font. To make the job easier, designers reduced the structured sentence to a series of cryptic notations called a markup language. This meant every page crossing the typesetter's desk had dozens of instructions that needed to be entered into a typesetting machine. The machine would translate the instructions and create the typeset pages.

For text-only publications, page design was more tedious than problematic. Designers spent a considerable amount of time doing repetitive work. For publications such as magazines, page design was tedious and problematic. Designers labored over the details of every page from the fit of text and advertising to the placement of sidebars and figures. Serious problems occurred when what was scrawled on paper did not turn out as planned and had to be reworked. These errors cost publishers time and money.

Changing the format of a document was extremely difficult and meant editing thousands of instructions in every file associated with the publication. Another problem designers and type-setters faced was a lack of standards. Codes meaningful to one typesetting machine were meaningless to another typesetting machine. This was often true for different models of typesetting machines from the same manufacturer.

Computer technology changes rapidly and advancements in typesetting technology were no exception. Replacing the old typesetting machine created many problems. Buying a new machine with the latest features meant learning a new coding system. It also meant files in the old format were obsolete and would require updating to republish—a process just as labor- and resource-intensive as publishing a new manuscript.

As typesetting technology continued to advance, the necessity for a standardized markup language became clear. Not only was there a tremendous need for backward compatibility in document formats, there was also a genuine need to exchange documents between different types of systems. SGML was designed to solve compatibility issues and does so by providing a machine-independent format for documents. This meant computer systems could exchange documents without regard to the type of receiving system.

Advantages of SGML

Using SGML or an associated markup language, the receiving computer could display or print the document in the precise format and style of the original document. SGML defines the formatting of documents in terms of the standard ASCII character set. This makes SGML easy to read and distribute.

In addressing compatibility issues, the authors of SGML solved other problems concerning document design as well. They recognized that formatting generally changes according to the component parts of the publication. This recognition became the basis for a language that replaced the cryptic notations of early markup languages with a logically structured language. For example, page headers are defined as a distinct part of the page because the type face, pitch, and style of the header is generally different from the rest of the text on the page.

SGML differentiates between component parts and the text to be printed using unique characters that identify tags and entities. *Tags* define parts of the document and include an element name enclosed by brackets, such as `<H1>`, which indicates a first-level heading. *Entities* are generally special components of the document, such as graphic images or special characters. Entities are described by an entity name preceded by an ampersand and ending with a semicolon, such as `&lsquo;` for a left single quotation mark or `&ldquo;` for a left double quotation mark.

To ensure 100 percent portability and maximize functionality, SGML uses constructs similar to many computer languages. You can define a library of terms to carry out basic operations and make assignments just like you can in any computer language. For example, you could define a term called THE_BOOK in the header of the SGML document and assign the term a value of Electronic Publishing Unleashed: A Look Inside Internet and Electronic Publishing. In this way, every occurrence of the term THE_BOOK would be replaced by its value, Electronic Publishing Unleashed: A Look Inside Internet and Electronic Publishing.

If you later changed the title of the book, you would not have to change every occurrence of the title throughout the book. You would simply update the term assignment in the document header. For example, if the new value for THE_BOOK was Electronic Publishing Unleashed, a single change in the document header would change the title throughout the book. Not only does this save time, it also minimizes the possibility of error. Although this is a simple example of the use of assignments, you can see how a global search and replace mechanism could be extremely useful.

SGML documents are viewed with an application called an SGML browser. As you will discover in later sections of this chapter, SGML browsers can be used just such as HTML browsers. In fact, you can use an SGML browser to view SGML-formatted documents found on the World Wide Web.

How Does SGML Relate to HTML?

SGML is the enabling technology that makes the hypertext markup language possible. It does this by defining a way to produce documents that are interchangeable regardless of the end user's computer system. HTML takes these definitions and applies them to publishing on the World Wide Web.

In the process of ensuring the interchangeability of documents, SGML developed into a complex language with many nuances. A goal of the authors of HTML was to drastically reduce this complexity and make HTML the tool for every would-be Web publisher. Therefore, the basic premise of HTML was to create a clear and uncomplicated way to produce generic documents. The level one standard of HTML with its straightforward and easy-to-use syntax accomplished this goal. However, it did so at great expense to functionality.

The loss of functionality became a central issue in the HTML standard. The authors of HTML decided to overcome this issue in the long-term. To do so, they would continue to develop HTML and introduce new versions with increasing levels of complexity. HTML has come a long way. By the time you read this, HTML level three will be the world standard. HTML level three includes support for mathematical formulas, tables, forms within tables, and extended support for images and lists.

There was such a tremendous demand for these enhancements that several Web browsers, such as the Netscape Navigator, supported many of these enhancements long before HTML level three became the world standard. Although these enhancements to HTML are significant steps forward, SGML has always supported these features. In fact, what HTML is slowly working toward is a level of functionality equivalent to what SGML already supports.

SGML Basics

SGML is a language similar in style and complexity to an actual computer language. In the first part of the program programmers declare parameters that will be used throughout a particular program. These global parameters then form the basis of many operations throughout the program. In SGML, global parameters are defined in a similar manner. Documents are created by declaring a document type and defining all assignments and entities associated with the document type. The document type is formally called a *document type definition* (DTD) and can apply to a single document or a group of related documents. Assignments are defined by declaring them in the basic form:

The open and close brackets declare the beginning and end of the assignment. The keyword following the exclamation point names the type of assignment being defined, which is followed by its parameters. Assignments can declare any of the following types for the document type definition of your document:

```
DOCTYPE
ELEMENT
ATTLIST
ENTITY
NOTATION
```

NOTE

The key to learning SGML is not in memorizing the constructs. Later sections of this chapter will give you a complete list of tools that dramatically reduce the complexity of producing SGML documents. Therefore, the key to learning SGML is to be familiar with the constructs in order to understand your options. Providing this familiarity is what the declaration sections that follow are all about.

As you read the examples in this chapter, keep in mind what you learned about tags in Chapter 20, "Using HTML." Everything you learned about HTML and HTML tags can help make learning SGML easier. Unlike HTML where tags such as the paragraph tag <P> are defined by the standard, in SGML you define the tags and how they will be used in your documents. In fact, you define everything about the document and how it will look when read by the end-user.

Using the *DOCTYPE* Declaration

To assign a name to a set of declarations used throughout the document, you will use the DOCTYPE declaration. DOCTYPE is the first declaration made in any SGML document. The basic form of this keyword is

```
<!DOCTYPE document_type_name [parameters associated_parameters ]>
```

SGML uses a naming scheme that is not case-sensitive. Parameter names can be up to eight characters in length. The first letter of the name must be an alphabetic character, but the remaining characters can include combinations of alphabetic and numeric characters. SGML further enables you to use periods and hyphens in names, for example:

```
<!DOCTYPE my.e-bks [parameters associated_parameters ]>
```

> **NOTE**
>
> Although SGML is not case sensitive, a general rule of good SGML programming is to type keywords in capital letters. For this reason, DOCTYPE is entered in the above statement in all capital letters. Using capital letters will allow you or anyone reading your SGML code to quickly and easily differentiate between keywords and parameters.

There is generally a large group of parameters associated with the doctype. Therefore, the parameters and associated parameters are normally on separate lines following the document type declaration. One important note is that the last entry in the document type declaration is always the closing brackets for the DOCTYPE keyword. An example of this is

```
<!DOCTYPE my_book

[<!KEYWORD_A parameter associated_parameter(s)>
<!KEYWORD_B parameter associated_parameter(s)>
<!KEYWORD_C parameter associated_parameter(s)>
<!KEYWORD_D parameter associated_parameter(s)>
<!KEYWORD_E parameter associated_parameter(s)>
<!KEYWORD_F parameter associated_parameter(s)>

]>
```

Keep in mind that the names of parameters are arbitrary and that each associated parameter identified should have its own declaration statement to describe it. SGML is also versatile enough to enable some or all of the document declarations to be in another file. In this case, you would declare the location of the file in a parameter following the name of the document type.

Using the *ELEMENT* Declaration

To declare the main objects of the document, use the ELEMENT declaration. The ELEMENT declaration consists of two parts: a name and a description of the contents of the element. The basic form of this declaration is

```
<!ELEMENT element_name (subelement1¦subelement2¦...¦subelementX)>
```

The naming convention for element names follows the eight-character rule outlined earlier. The subelements between parentheses describe the contents of the element. The pipe character (¦) is a logical OR statement, meaning the element would occur with one of the subelements that could include *subelement1* through *subelementX*.

The previous example is too restrictive for practical use in your documents. Thankfully, SGML gives you many ways to describe how often and in what context parameters will occur. For example, the asterisk is one of the many symbols you can use to increase functionality.

```
<!ELEMENT chapter (chptitle¦heading1¦heading2¦heading3¦paragr)*>
```

The asterisk says the subelements can occur zero or more times. As you will see in later examples, you can place further restrictions on the subelements. However, the asterisk by itself means the subelements can occur in any order and frequency. The subelements could even be interspersed. Table 21.1 lists the context descriptors and their uses.

Table 21.1. ELEMENT **context descriptors.**

Descriptor	Concept	Explanation
?	Optional	A parameter that appears once or not at all.
*	Optional and repeatable	A parameter that appears zero or more times.
+	Required and repeatable	A parameter that must appear one or more times.
&	Logical AND	The parameters on either side of the ampersand must occur but can appear in any order.
¦	Logical OR	Only one of the parameters on either side of the pipe symbol can occur unless another context descriptor is used as a qualifier. For example, (A¦B¦C)* says the OR is not mutually exclusive and the parameters A, B, and C can occur zero or more times in any order.
,	Sequential	Used to define a parameter that must follow another parameter unless another context descriptor is used as a qualifier. For example, A,B?,C says the sequence A-B-C is not fixed for B, meaning if B is not present A must be followed by C.

To better explain the SGML's context descriptors, let's expand the previous example. The following chapter element declaration is fairly complex but can be broken down easily if examined one step at a time. The breakdown is shown in Table 21.2.

```
<!ELEMENT chapter (chptitle, heading1+ (heading2¦heading3)* paragr+)>
```

Table 21.2. Breakdown of an advanced ELEMENT declaration.

Parameters	Description
chapter (chptitle, heading1+ (heading2¦heading3)* paragr+)	The element named chapter will include a chapter title, headings, and paragraphs.
chptitle,	The comma indicates that each chapter must include a single chapter title that must be followed by a level-1 heading.
heading1+	The plus indicates that each chapter must have at least one level-1 heading and possibly more.
(heading2¦heading3)*	The asterisk indicates that each chapter can include multiple occurrences of what is included between the parenthesis. The pipe indicates this could be multiple occurrences of the level-2 or level-3 headings.
paragr+	The plus indicates that each chapter must include at least one paragraph but could include more.

Keep in mind that parameter names are arbitrary and are further defined in separate ELEMENT declarations down to the most basic element declarations. The basic elements of the document could contain a declaration stating they are parsed characters or raw data without any subelements.

Raw data means the element contains the actual ASCII characters that form the text of the document. This includes letters, numbers, punctuation, and special characters. In SGML, PCDATA is a reserved name that describes these elements. The following element declaration means elements of type paragr contain raw data and as such are the most basic elements of the document structure:

```
<!ELEMENT paragr    (#PCDATA)>
```

Another basic element is one with no defined parameters, such as

```
<!ELEMENT text    EMPTY>
```

The keyword EMPTY identifies the element as having no defined parameters. Generally, empty elements are assigned an attribute list that further describes them.

In your SGML document, element declarations are used the same way you use HTML tags. The only difference is that in SGML you can define your tags. For example, if you made the following declarations:

```
<!ELEMENT chapter (chptitle|heading|paragr)*>
<!ELEMENT (chptitle|heading|paragr) #PCDATA>
```

You could use the declarations in an SGML document as follows:

```
<CHAPTER>
<CHPTITLE>Inside SGML</CHPTITLE>
<HEADING>Designing Pages with SGML</HEADING>
<PARAGR>Insert the first paragraph here</PARAGR>
</CHAPTER>
```

Using the *ATTLIST* Declaration

ATTLIST is used to declare a list of attributes associated with a previously defined element. You can use ELEMENT and ATTLIST declarations to create the structure for a complete information system. The information system could range in complexity from an automated forms database to turnkey publishing solutions for a particular type of publisher. Are you beginning to see the power of SGML?

The basic form of an ATTLIST is

```
<!ATTLIST element_describing attribute_name attribute_value
(associated_attribute1|associated_attribute2|...|associated_attributeX) default>
```

The first parameter names the element to which the attribute list pertains. This is followed by the name of the attribute, its value, and associated attributes. The final parameter is an optional default value. The following is an example of an attribute list used with an element:

```
<!ELEMENT e-pub (book|zine|n-paper|n-letter)>
<!ELEMENT (book|zine|n-paper|n-letter)     EMPTY>
<!ATTLIST book type (fiction|nonfict)>
<!ATTLIST zine type (quartly|monthly) monthly>
<!ATTLIST n-paper type (daily|weekly) weekly>
<!ATTLIST n-letter type (quartly|monthly) quartly>
```

The preceding example defines elements and attributes for a fictional electronic publisher. The publisher produces four types of publications: books, magazines, newspapers, and newsletters that are defined respectively as book, zine, n-paper, and n-letter. Although there are no associated elements with the publications, there are lists of valid attributes.

The books element can have a type of fiction or nonfiction. The zines element can have a type of quarterly or monthly. If no type is specified for the zine, the default type is monthly. The n-papers element can have a type of daily or weekly with a default type of weekly. The n-letters element can have a type of quarterly or monthly with a default type of quarterly.

By making further assignments to cover each valid option, the electronic publisher could have turnkey solutions for her electronic publishing needs. When publishing an electronic magazine, the publisher would set the zine attribute. With the zine attribute set, the document type descriptor defined in the header of the document would format the zine's articles accordingly for viewing or printing and the end user would see only the formatting rules for a magazine.

The publisher could incorporate the same material as a part of a book she was producing without reformatting. She would simply set the book attribute. This means one change instead of hundreds would enable the end user to see the material in the publisher's book format.

As shown in Table 21.3, attributes can have many values. These values are used to define complex structures that can be associated with ELEMENT declarations.

Table 21.3. ATTLIST value descriptors.

Descriptor	Explanation
CDATA	Character data and can contain zero or more valid characters that can be letters, numbers, punctuation, spaces, and special characters.
ENTITY	Specifies a declared entity name.
ID	A unique identifier such as an account number.
IDREF	A reference value to a unique ID.
IDREFS	A list of references values to unique IDs.
NAME	A string of up to eight characters. The first letter of the name must be an alphabetic character. The remaining characters can be combinations of alphabetic characters, periods, and hyphens.
NAMES	A list of NAME strings; each NAME string must be separated by one or more tabs, returns, or spaces.
NMTOKEN	A name token that is a string of up to eight characters that can include and begin with letters, numbers, periods, or hyphens.
NMTOKENS	A list of NMTOKEN strings; each NMTOKEN string must be separated by one or more tabs, returns, or spaces.
NOTATION	Provides a way to process special information in your SGML documents.
NUMBER	A string of up to eight numeric characters.
NUMBERS	A list of NUMBER strings; each NUMBER string must be separated by one or more tabs, returns, or spaces.
NUTOKEN	A string of up to eight characters that begin with a number and can include letters, numbers, periods, or hyphens.
NUTOKENS	A list of NUTOKEN strings; each NUTOKEN string must be separated by one or more tabs, returns, or spaces.

Attribute lists can also have special default values as shown in Table 21.4. These values give you additional flexibility when you declare attributes.

Table 21.4. ATTLIST **default values.**

Default Value	Explanation
#IMPLIED	A value is optional for this attribute.
#CURRENT	The value must be specified the first time it occurs and will apply to all future occurrences of the attribute unless otherwise specified.
#FIXED	The value is fixed and cannot be changed.
#REQUIRED	A value is mandatory for this attribute.

An example of using ATTLIST descriptors and default values follows. Table 21.5 provides a complete breakdown of the element declarations.

```
<!ELEMENT s.record (customer?,sale)>
<!ELEMENT customer (custname & custacct)>
<!ELEMENT (custname & custacct) #PCDATA>
<!ATTLIST custname name NAME #IMPLIED>
<!ATTLIST custacct account ID #IMPLIED>
<!ELEMENT sale (charge¦cash) >
<!ELEMENT (charge¦cash) EMPTY>
<!ATTLIST charge credit ID #REQUIRED>
<!ATTLIST cash number NUMBER #REQUIRED>
```

Table 21.5. Breakdown of an advanced declaration using ATTLIST.

Parameters	Description
s.record (customer?,sale)	The element type s.record is declared with two parameters: customer and sale. The question mark indicates the customer information is not mandatory. However, the comma indicates that if customer information is present, it must be followed by sales information.
customer (custname & custacct)	The element type customer is declared as parsed character data with two parameters: custname and custacct. The ampersand puts two conditions on the information in parenthesis. If the customer element is used, both the customer name and customer account attributes must be used. However, they can appear in any order.

continues

Table 21.5. continued

Parameters	Description
(custname & custacct) #PCDATA	The keyword PCDATA indicates the element types custname and custacct are raw data containing no subelements. (However, they do have associated attributes.)
custname name NAME #IMPLIED	This declaration describes the custname element through an attribute called name. This attribute is of type NAME and as indicated by the keyword IMPLIED is optional.
custacct account ID #IMPLIED	This declaration describes the custacct element through an attribute called account. This optional attribute is of type ID.
sale (charge¦cash)	The element type sale is declared with two parameters: charge and cash. However as indicated by the pipe symbol, if the sale element is used, either the charge attribute or the cash attribute must be used.
(charge¦cash) EMPTY	The keyword EMPTY indicates there are no defined parameters associated with these elements. Generally, empty elements are assigned an attribute list that further describes them.
charge credit ID #REQUIRED	This declaration describes the charge element through an attribute called credit. The keyword REQUIRED indicates the attribute is mandatory. This mandatory attribute is of type ID.
cash number NUMBER #REQUIRED	This declaration describes the cash element through an attribute called number. The keyword REQUIRED indicates the attribute is mandatory. This mandatory attribute is of type NUMBER.

After the previous example, you can probably understand why a key concept in SGML is never build complex structures on the fly. These structures can be extremely confusing and time-consuming if you try to build them without careful thought. The best way to create structures using attribute lists is to write down the project requirements on paper before applying them in SGML markup.

In your SGML document, attribute declarations are used to assign values to the declarations. This assignment of values is similar to the way you can assign values to HTML tags, such as <HR SIZE=4>. Using the <HR> tag in an HTML, you can insert a shaded line across the width of the page. The SIZE attribute for the <HR> tag specifies the thickness of the rule in pixels. Here, the horizontal rule would be four pixels wide. The primary difference between HTML attributes and SGML attributes is that in SGML you define the acceptable values. For example, if you made the following declarations:

```
<!ATTLIST book type (fiction¦nonfict)>
```

you could use these declarations in an SGML document as follows:

```
<BOOK TYPE="fiction">
```

or

```
<BOOK TYPE="nonfict">
```

Using the *ENTITY* Declaration

Entities can be powerful components in SGML. In its basic form, an *entity* is an object that can be substituted into an SGML document based on a declaration. The object can be a text string or any type of file. Because entities allow objects to be substituted into the document, they can be used to automate global search-and-replace facilities in SGML documents. The object to be substituted could be text that occurs between quotation marks after the declaration, as shown in the following code:

```
<!ENTITY entity_name "The text to substitute">
```

The object could also be instructions for loading a file to place into the document, as shown in the following code:

```
<!ENTITY entity_name KEYWORD "path/to/file">
```

The entity declaration provides a placeholder for files that will be included when the document is printed or viewed. You can insert a picture or a multimedia file. You can even insert another SGML document with its own declaration rules into the current document, such as

```
<!ENTITY file2 SYSTEM "/docs/sgml/file2.sgm" SUBDOC>
```

The entity named file2 contains two important directives. The first directive, SYSTEM, is a reserved keyword that means the referenced external entity is a file. The second directive, SUBDOC, is a reserved keyword that means the file contains formatted SGML text with its own document declarations. The formatting declarations in the subdocument will be used instead of declarations in the current document.

SUBDOC is an extremely useful keyword. It enables you to retain the formatting of SGML documents you are incorporating without making declarations in the current document. If you omit the SUBDOC keyword, the entity will be formatted according to the rules of the current document. Omitting the SUBDOC keyword is an easy way to reuse old material without having to reformat it according to new rules.

In your SGML document you describe entities by typing an entity name preceded by an ampersand and ending with a semicolon. For example, the following declarations describe a book:

```
<!ELEMENT e-book (part¦chapter)>
<!ELEMENT (part¦chapter) #PCDATA>
<!ATTLIST part (ptitle¦header¦paragr)>
<!ATTLIST (header¦paragr)  #PCDATA>
<!ENTITY ptitle "Using SGML in Web Publications">
<!ATTLIST chapter (ctitle¦header¦paragr)>
<!ATTLIST (header¦paragr)>
<!ENTITY ctitle "Having Fun With SGML">
```

The markup in your SGML document would appear as follows:

```
<E-BOOK>
<PART>&ptitle;</PART>
<CHAPTER>&ctitle;</CHAPTER>
<HEADER>Insert Header</HEADER>
<PARAGR>Insert Paragraph</PARAGR>
</E-BOOK>
```

When your SGML document is printed or viewed, text would be substituted for the entity declarations. The first declaration &ptitle; would become

```
Using SGML in Web Publications
```

The second declaration &ctitle; would become

```
Having Fun With SGML
```

> **NOTE**
>
> The search and replace mechanism from SGML described in this section is used in HTML to display special characters. In HTML, special characters are described by an element name preceded by an ampersand and ending with a semicolon, such as < for the less than symbol "<" or > for the greater than symbol ">". When an HTML browser sees a special character declaration such as & it replaces the declaration with the special symbol.

Using the *NOTATION* Declaration

The NOTATION declaration provides a way to process special information in your SGML documents. Using notations, you can process mathematical equations through a program that will display it in a formatted output. You can create pointers to graphic files that are displayed via a drawing application.

The basic form of a notation is

```
<!NOTATION notation_name reserved_word "Identifier">
```

Notation names follow the eight-character naming conventions used with other SGML declarations. The reserved word is usually the keyword SYSTEM, which implies you are identifying a system file. The identifier is the name of the application that can include the full path to the application.

You can also use notations with entity declarations. The entity declaration can include a pointer to the data contained in the notation. The keyword NDATA, or notation data, is used to identify a pointer to a previously declared notation. A pointer could be used as follows:

```
<!NOTATION jpeg SYSTEM "ImageMagick">
<!ENTITY waves SYSTEM "/usr/bin/images/waves.jpeg" NDATA "jpeg">
```

The jpeg notation declares that a program called ImageMagick can be used on the system. ImageMagick is an X Window System image viewer. The second declaration names an entity called waves. The keyword SYSTEM means the external entity waves is contained in a system file. The parameter between quotation marks gives the location and name of the file containing the data. The keyword NDATA creates a pointer to the notation name that follows. Through the NDATA pointer, the system knows there is a link between the notation jpeg and the entity waves. The presence of the link informs the system that in order to display the waves.jpeg image, it must be displayed via ImageMagick.

SGML Helper Applications

As you have seen in this chapter, SGML is a complex language with many structures. SGML helper applications can make the task of creating and viewing SGML documents easier. There are four basic types of SGML helper applications.

- SGML parsers
- SGML editors
- SGML browsers/viewers
- SGML converters

SGML Parsers

The process of reading and interpreting SGML data is called *parsing*. SGML parsers read and interpret the SGML code in your SGML documents. After reading and interpreting the code you have defined, the parser passes the information to another application. For this reason, another name for an SGML parser is an *SGML engine*. There are two types of SGML parsers: non-validating and validating.

A *nonvalidating parser* is the most basic type of parser. This parser reads and interprets the data literally, meaning it expects the data to be error-free and reads it as such. A nonvalidating parser will not report errors. On the other hand, a *validating parser* will find and report errors. Based on the error report from the validating parser, you will be able to find and fix format and syntax errors in your SGML documents. As you might imagine, if you are creating SGML documents you want to ensure you are using a validating SGML parser or that your helper application uses one.

Another reason SGML parsers are often called SGML engines is that they are the basic components of most other types of SGML helper applications such as SGML editors, browsers, viewers and converters. Although SGML parsers are freely available, the SGML parser you use will probably be a key component of one of these tools. However, sometimes you may want a parser that is not a part of another program. For example, if you want to create your own SGML browser, one of your first steps would be to select a parser. You may also want to use a validating parser if you are conducting extensive testing on your SGML documents. Some people, myself included, find it easier to check the accuracy of SGML documents with a validating parser. I use a validating parser for this purpose primarily because I create SGML documents in my word processor, and if the document will not display in my SGML browser, I need a way to check the validity of the SGML code. The alternative to testing SGML documents in this way is to buy a rule-checking SGML editor, such as Author/Editor, which will be discussed in the next section.

One of the first publicly available SGML parsers was ARC-SGML. This shareware parser was the model of many parsers that followed it. Versions of the Almaden Research Center SGML parser are available for UNIX, DOS, and Macintosh systems.

SGMLS is a popular parser written by James Clark. It is available as shareware for DOS, UNIX, and Macintosh systems. Clark has written another parser called SP. SP has many extra validation mechanisms that SGMLS doesn't and is available for DOS and UNIX systems. A Macintosh version of the parser should be available soon.

One of the newest shareware parsers is YASP. This parser is growing in popularity because of its flexibility and speed. A great place to find SGML parsers is the FTP site shown in Figure 21.1. In this directory, you will find YASP and other parsers covered in this section.

SGML Editors

When you create any type of SGML document you will find SGML editors are especially useful. Most SGML editors are rich in features. Although they are often more sophisticated than your average word processing application, most SGML editors have excellent documentation. Dozens of editors are available for MS Windows, Mac, and UNIX systems. This section highlights the top editors.

FIGURE 21.1.

SGML parsers and more.

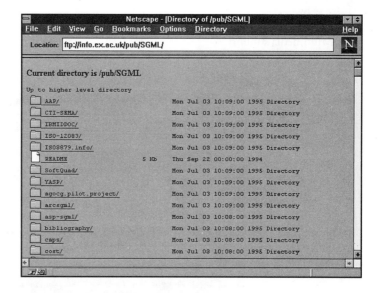

Currently, two types of SGML editors are available: basic editors and full-featured high-end editors. Although basic editors are not rich in features, they are good for beginners. They will let you create and publish many types of SGML documents without a large initial investment. In this section you will find information on a freeware editor called Panorama and its commercial counterpart, Panorama Pro, which is available for $139. High-end editors are complete SGML publishing solutions that include support for multimedia. However, high-end editors generally require a large initial investment. For example, Author/Editor from SoftQuad is $995 for Microsoft Windows and Macintosh versions and $1,995 for UNIX versions.

Author/Editor

SoftQuad, Incorporated produces a powerful SGML authoring system called Author/Editor. The popularity of this complete SGML publishing solution stems from a user-friendly environment and great technical support. Author/Editor is organized like your favorite word processor and comes complete with spell checking and online help.

As shown in Figure 21.2, the place to find detailed information on Author/Editor is at SoftQuad's Web site. SoftQuad touts Author/Editor as "The authoring tool of choice." The editor has an excellent track record through three major upgrades in the past five years. Some of Author/Editor's features include the following:

- Automatic rules checking
- Built-in templates and style charts
- Built-in SGML parsing and validation
- Document previewing

- Table and mathematical equation support
- Multimedia support
- Macro support

FIGURE 21.2.

SoftQuad's Author/Editor.

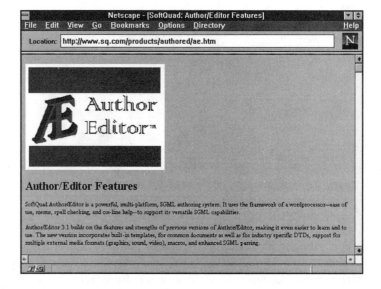

Grif SGML Editor

The Grif Company of France produces several SGML publishing solutions. At the heart of its product line is the Grif SGML Editor. This high-end editor can be customized for multiple user environments and features WYSIWYG (What You See Is What You Get) formatting. WYSIWYG is an important feature for conceptualizing the finished document markup; the formatting you see as you produce the document will be the same as the formatting produced in the final product. Some of Grif SGML Editor's key features are shown in Figure 21.3. At Grif's Web site, you can find information on its complete line of SGML products.

Versions of the Grif SGML Editor are available for the Macintosh, MS Windows, and UNIX systems. UNIX versions have an open architecture, which means the editor can be easily integrated with external applications such as databases. Grif also produces a low-cost version of the editor called Grif SGML Notes. Grif SGML Notes is identical to the high-end version except that it does not enable printing or the displaying of images. Currently, Grif Notes is available only for MS Windows systems.

FIGURE 21.3.

Grif SGML Editor.

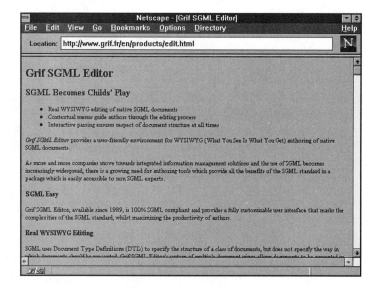

Interleaf 5 <SGML>

Interleaf 5 <SGML> is a high-end editor that enables you to migrate to SGML at your own pace. The slow transition to full SGML compliance is made possible through a merger of Interleaf's proprietary page definition language and SGML. A page definition language is a type of markup language that is generally based on SGML.

Interleaf 5 <SGML> is extremely user-friendly, well-supported, and will let you create documents in SGML and Interleaf formats. As Figure 21.4 shows, Interleaf features advanced support for analyzing the content and structure of your documents. The figure also shows one of Interleaf 5's unique features, the capability to graphically display the structure of a document using diagrams. Interleaf 5 also has built-in support for creating and editing raster and vector graphics.

For a complete SGML publishing solution, you will also want the Interleaf 5 <SGML> Toolkit. The toolkit includes document templates, advanced tools necessary to create complex documents, and other essentials that most SGML authors will find helpful and useful. Interleaf 5 <SGML> and Interleaf 5 <SGML> Toolkit are packaged in a combined set called SGML Express. To get more information on Interleaf 5 or related products visit Interleaf on the Web at the following address:

```
http://www.ileaf.com/sgml.html
```

FIGURE 21.4.

Interleaf 5 <SGML>.

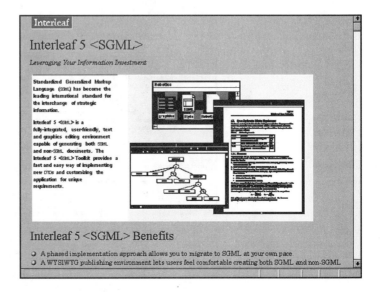

Panorama Pro

Dollar for dollar, SoftQuad's Panorama Pro is the best bargain in SGML editors. The editor is based on SoftQuad's popular freeware SGML browser, Panorama. If you are interested in creating SGML documents for the World Wide Web, Panorama Pro might be your editor of choice.

Although Panorama Pro is currently available only for MS Windows, a Macintosh version will be available soon. From the Web page shown in Figure 21.5, you can go on a virtual walk through of the editor, access online ordering, or download the freeware version.

FIGURE 21.5.

Panorama Pro.

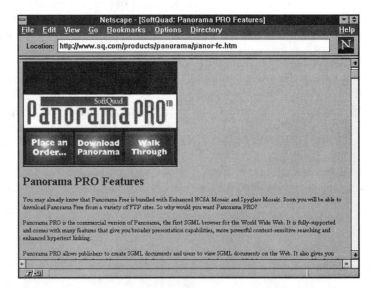

SGML Browsers

The purpose of an SGML browser is to help you view SGML documents. Therefore, browsers are often called viewers. However, the name for the application displaying the document isn't as important as its function. An SGML browser reads the formatted text and associated files and creates a document for your viewing on-screen. If an SGML document contains an inline image, the image will be displayed along with the text.

SGML documents can also contain links to other documents and multimedia files that could include sound, graphics, and video. Hypertext linking in SGML documents works the same as hypertext linking in HTML documents. In fact, SGML browsers are very similar to the HTML browsers that you might be more familiar with.

DynaText SGML Browser

The DynaText SGML browser is produced by Electronic Book Technologies, Incorporated. This good all-around SGML browser is available for Macintosh, MS Windows, and UNIX systems. DynaText features built-in support for raster and vector graphics, advanced search capabilities, and will display mathematical equations. Figure 21.6 shows the overview page EBT has put together to showcase DynaText.

FIGURE 21.6.

The DynaText browser.

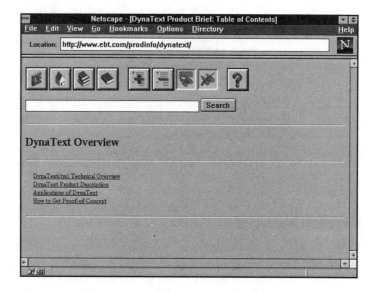

Grif SGML ActiveViews

Grif SGML ActiveViews is a full-featured SGML browser from the Grif Company of France. Although most browsers will let you place bookmarks within documents for easy reference, ActiveViews goes a step further. The browser will let you add dynamic annotations to SGML documents. The annotations are saved separately from the main file and can contain formatted text, tables, graphics, and mathematical equations. These changes or notes are linked to the original document and can be displayed. If you want the changes to be permanent you can merge the annotations into the original SGML document using the Grif SGML Editor.

FIGURE 21.7.

Grif SGML ActiveViews.

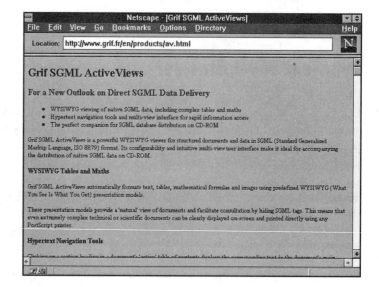

ActiveViews can be customized. Using Grif's toolkit, you can add menus and new functions. The browser is available for MS Windows, UNIX, and soon the Macintosh. Figure 21.7 highlights more of the features of ActiveViews and shows you where you can find the English version of the product notes.

Panorama

Panorama is the freeware version of SoftQuad's commercial SGML browser and is the first browser specifically designed for viewing SGML documents on the Web. The Web page shown in Figure 21.8 touts Panorama's selling points as a Web dynamo and lets you download the browser for free. Currently, Panorama is available only for MS Windows.

FIGURE 21.8.

The Panorama browser.

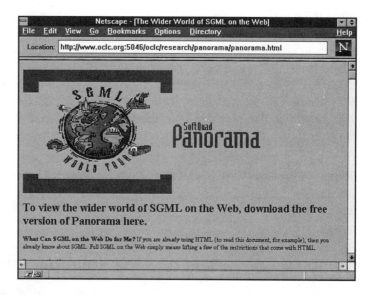

WorldView Browser

WorldView, produced by Interleaf, Incorporated, is the browser of choice for the Interleaf family of SGML applications. The browser is fast, sleek, and its menus are intuitively organized. It will display documents in SGML and Interleaf's proprietary format. Figure 21.9 shows screen shots of WorldView in use. The following page on Interleaf's Web site contains an abundance of information on WorldView:

```
http://www.ileaf.com/wvds.html
```

FIGURE 21.9.

WorldView from Interleaf.

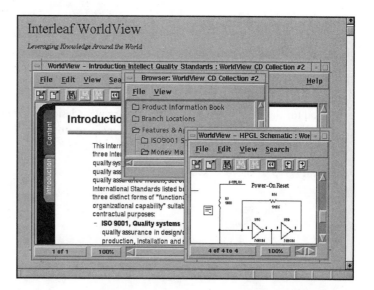

SGML Converters

If you want to convert a word processor or file format to SGML, a converter is the tool of choice. A *converter* interprets one type of document formatting to produce another type of document formatting. Because SGML has a complex structure, converting document formats to and from SGML is difficult. Consequently, there aren't as many SGML converters as there are HTML converters. Still, there are SGML converters for most major document formats. If you find that a converter isn't available for your favorite document format, keep in mind most high-end editors will also convert popular document formats.

The good news about the lack of SGML converters is the issue is being addressed by the SGML industry. Several initiatives are underway to promote SGML and produce tools that will make it easier to convert other document formats to SGML. One of these initiatives is the Rainbow Initiative outlined below.

Rainbow Converters and the Rainbow Initiative

Electronic Book Technology, Incorporated is leading a major initiative to create conversion tools for SGML. The purpose of the Rainbow Initiative is to create tools for translating proprietary word processor formats to SGML. The emphasis of the initiative was on creating documents with useful SGML markup that retained as much of the original formatting as possible.

Because of this initiative, several rainbow converters are available to convert Microsoft RTF, FrameMaker MIF, Interleaf, and WordPerfect formats to SGML. Figure 21.10 shows an FTP site that contains these converters, as well as terrific information on the Rainbow Initiative. The Rainbow mailing list can help you keep track of new developments pertaining to the initiative. For subscription information to the mailing list, send e-mail to

```
rainbow@ebt.com
```

ICA

Integrated Chameleon Architecture, or ICA, is a toolkit for generating converters. ICA has been used to create converters for LaTeX, BibTeX, and troff. However, the converters generated are only good for the specific type of document they were designed to convert. ICA is available for the UNIX X Window System environment. One place to obtain ICA and find additional information is

```
ftp://ftp.archive.cis.ohio-state.edu/pub/chameleon/
```

FIGURE 21.10.

The Rainbow Initiative documents.

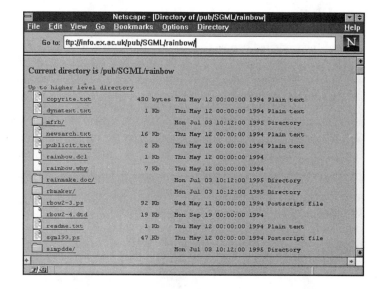

DynaTag

DynaTag is an excellent converter from Electronic Book Technology, Incorporated. This user-friendly converter has direct support for the conversion of MS Word, FrameMaker, and Interleaf file formats. DynaTag will convert some international language formats and has extensions that will enable future Rainbow conversion formats to be incorporated easily.

EBT's DynaTag information page on the Web is featured in Figure 21.11. From this page you can find detailed information on DynaTag and the Dyna family of products for EBT. Versions of DynaTag are available for MS Windows and UNIX systems.

FIGURE 21.11.

DynaTag SGML converter.

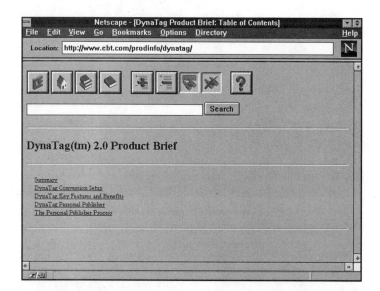

WorldView and WorldView Press

Interleaf Incorporated's conversion solution is called WorldView Press. Electronic publishers in the international marketplace will find WorldView to be especially useful. WorldView supports international user interfaces in English, French, German, and Japanese.

WorldView is part of Interleaf's family of products. The full version of WorldView is a development system for electronic publications. WorldView is designed to facilitate the distribution of electronic publications over networks, on floppy disk, and on CD-ROM. The complete package comes with a browser, editor, and conversion tools.

As Figure 21.12 shows, WorldView Press converts many text and graphic formats to the Interleaf proprietary markup format. The formats it supports include PostScript, Microsoft RTF, WordPerfect, SGML, FrameMaker MIF, PICT, CGM, TIFF, and HPGL. WorldView Press is available in UNIX and MS Windows versions. To learn more about this converter visit Interleaf at

```
http://www.ileaf.com/wvpds.html
```

FIGURE 21.12.

WorldView Press.

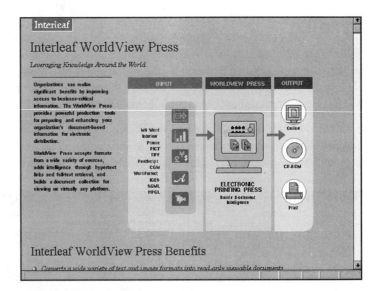

Page Layout Tools

Page layout tools are advanced applications for creating both electronic and print publications. These high-grade commercial tools often have the friendliest interfaces for creating documents and are usually good choices for beginners. Because SGML defines how to create the formatting or layout of the published page, many page layout applications are based on the standards set forth by the developers of SGML. However, most page layout tools use a proprietary format. Proprietary formats that are usable only with a certain company's products break the spirit of generalizing markup for easy interchange of documents. However, recently the trend has been to allow for easier exchange between proprietary formats.

This section highlights the most popular page layout tools, including

- Adobe Acrobat
- Adobe PageMaker
- Ventura Publisher

Adobe Acrobat

Adobe Acrobat is an all-in-one publishing solution for producing and distributing electronic documents. Basic and professional versions are available for Macintosh, MS Windows, and UNIX systems. The basic software package is a complete toolkit that includes an editor, converter, browser, and analysis tools. The professional version includes a postscript converter, an indexer for creating catalogs, and a 10-user workgroup license.

Adobe Acrobat's popularity is due in large part to its reputation for excellent technical support. Some of Acrobat's features are highlighted in Figure 21.13, which shows Acrobat's product information page.

FIGURE 21.13.

Adobe Acrobat.

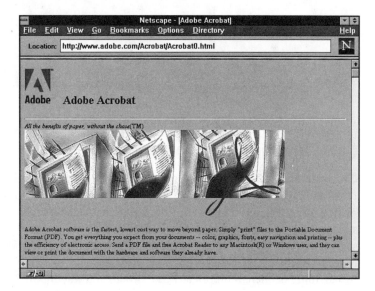

Adobe PageMaker

Adobe PageMaker is a cross-platform publishing solution for designing electronic and print publications. PageMaker has been on the market for over a decade. Its features include the Kodak Precision Color Management System, a built-in word processor with spelling checker and search-and-replace features, and an advanced plug-in technology that lets you easily customize aspects of PageMaker for individual projects.

Figure 21.14 shows Adobe's PageMaker site on the Web. The site contains a wealth of information on PageMaker and related products. Versions of PageMaker are available for Macintosh and MS Windows systems.

FIGURE 21.14.

Adobe PageMaker.

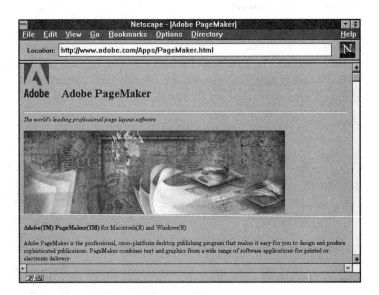

Corel Ventura Publisher

Corel Ventura Publisher is an integrated package for publishing electronic and print publications. As one of the most flexible page layout systems on the market, Ventura Publisher has many advanced features, including support for dynamic linking to other applications for easy sharing of data; direct spreadsheet, database, and table support, and a word processor with spelling checker and thesaurus. Versions of the application are available for Windows and Macintosh systems. Although Ventura Publisher has a proprietary format, it will also convert to and from 36 different proprietary text formats and will import 23 different graphic formats.

A great source for information on Ventura Publisher is CorelNet. At CorelNet, you will find archives of the Ventura Publisher Newsgroup shown in Figure 21.15.

FIGURE 21.15.

The CorelNet Ventura Publisher newsgroup.

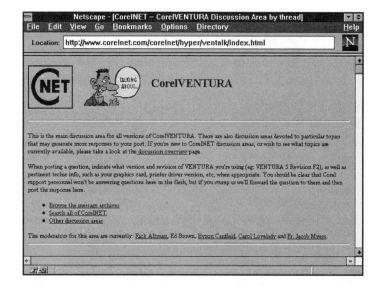

Summary

SGML is an advanced markup language with tremendous potential. Even the popular HTML format in wide use on the Web includes only a fraction of SGML's capabilities. With SGML you can design powerful documents that can be distributed without regard to the type of computer on which they will be used.

Thanks to helper applications, SGML's complexities can be dramatically reduced. An SGML parser is the most basic part of your SGML toolkit, and it does the actual translation of the SGML markup. You might want to obtain your own parser, but it is incorporated into SGML editors and browsers.

SGML editors help you create SGML documents. The documents you create with an SGML editor can be viewed by the end user with an SGML browser. SGML converters are another helper application you might want to add to your toolkit. Converters will translate proprietary formats such as Microsoft's RTF format to SGML.

Incorporating Multimedia

22

by William R. Stanek

The World Wide Web has powerful facilities for handling multimedia. The linkage behind the Web's power is the hypertext transfer protocol and the hypertext markup language that enable the Web to be an open-ended multimedia system. Incorporating multimedia into your Web publications can be easy if you learn the basics and know the proper tools to use.

In this chapter, you learn the following:

- What internal and external media are
- How to find multimedia sources
- How to add sound to Web pages
- Where to find sound tools on the Web
- How to add internal and external images to Web pages
- Where to find image tools on the Web
- How to add video to Web pages
- Where to find video tools on the Web
- Putting sound, graphics, and video together on Web pages

Internal and External Media

Internal and external media are the two basic categories of media that can be used in any Web presentation. Internal media is media directly supported by browsers. Graphics-capable browsers can automatically load internal media with a presentation. External media is media indirectly supported by browsers. Text-based and graphics-capable browsers use applications called helper applications to load external media.

> **NOTE**
>
> The key distinction between internal and external media pertains to whether the media is directly supported by the browser or not. If the browser can display or play the media without using a helper application, it is internal media. For example, something I am considering for The Virtual Press site is a virtual Hawaii tour featuring sites from Sunset Beach on the north shore of Oahu to Kilauea Crater on the island of Hawaii. When you access the "Hang Ten" page, a picture of the popular surfing area called the Pipeline will be displayed along with information on surfing in Hawaii. The picture of the Pipeline is displayed automatically by the browser and is internal media.
>
> The "Hang Ten" page will also contain links to more pictures of popular surfing areas. When a user clicks on one of these links, they will either be able to download the picture or display the image using an image viewer. Pictures that require an external image viewer are examples of external media.

At present, inline images are the only form of internal media available on all graphics-capable browsers. Inline images will appear directly on the Web document when it is accessed, as long as the automatic image-loading feature of the browser is turned on. If properly used, inline images can accent a Web page and make it more visually appealing. As you will see later, the only image format you should use with inline images is GIF. This is because all graphics-capable browsers feature support for inline images in GIF format.

The future of internal media is promising, especially with the recent introduction of the Java language. As audio and video become more prevalent on the Web, the tools to preview them are becoming more standardized. Soon browsers may start to directly support many types of multimedia. The MPEG specification and other standards will surely spur this along, but the implications of the internalization of multimedia would be far-reaching. Soon it will be possible to include sound, animation, and full-motion video that will automatically play when your web document is accessed. Now that is an exciting idea!

With external media, you don't have to wait to see what the future will bring. Right now, all Web users can indirectly access external media. Helper applications, such as the players, trackers and viewers discussed in Chapter 11, "Using Multimedia," make it possible to preview audio, external graphics and video. All browsers feature some type of support for helper applications.

Browsers know which helper application to launch based on the file type extension (`.jpeg`, `.mov`, `.wav`, and so forth) of the external media in question. For example, when you access a local link to a WAV sound file, the browser looks in its helper application table to see which helper application should play the file. These files are linked in the Web document so they can be accessed via a helper application. This is why all your Web files should be named with the appropriate extension. If the file is in GIF format, name it with a `.gif` extension. If the file is in WAV format, name it with a `.wav` extension.

Sometimes you have to tell your Web browser which helper application to launch for a particular file format. You do this by setting preferences from an options menu. Figure 22.1 shows the Netscape Navigator's option menu for helper applications. The helper application configurations shown are the default settings. If you visit a Web site using the Netscape browser with the example helper application configuration and select a link to an image file in TIFF format, the browser would ask what helper application you want to use to display the file. If you select a page link to an image file in JPEG or GIF format, the browser would display the file because it features direct support for JPEG and GIF images. If you select a page link to an audio file in AIFF format, the browser would launch the NAPLAYER helper application to play the file.

FIGURE 22.1.

Setting Helper Application Preferences in Netscape.

There are types of external media beyond audio, external graphics, and video. Most of these deal with the format or compression of text files. Within your browser, you can configure helper applications to deal with virtually any type of file. The browser will simply match the file type to the necessary helper application based on the file type extension. If you do not want the browser to automatically launch a helper application, you could configure the browser to prompt you as shown in the figure. This option is useful because sometimes you want to test a new helper application or want to select one from several available on your system.

Sources of Multimedia

Many sources of commercial, shareware, and freeware multimedia clips are available.

Clips are simply segments or pieces of a larger work. Sound clip discs usually feature a particular type of sound such as animal sounds or sound effects. Video clip discs feature video on particular themes, such as animals in the wild or animation. Graphic clip art discs feature the widest array of clip discs. You can find everything from photo-quality pictures to simple line art.

Generally, commercial audio and video sources, such as music on CD-ROM or prerecorded video, require the payment of royalties and permission before use. Although this is true in most cases, a growing number of commercial vendors are creating royalty-free clip discs. Royalty-free multimedia collections offer significant advantages and cost savings over strictly commercial multimedia. Not only do they provide collections of sound, video or pictures that are in the public domain at extremely affordable prices. The only fee you will ever have to pay is the purchase price of the floppy disk or the CD-ROM disc. Look into royalty-free multimedia before purchasing multimedia you may have to pay fees for every time you use it in a publication.

Shareware clips are another great source for multimedia. Shareware authors ask that if you like or use their products, you pay them a registration fee before using their creations. The registration fee is usually only a few dollars and when you pay the fee, you are generally granted unlimited permission to use the multimedia you are registering in your publications. Shareware and royalty-free multimedia can be purchased from shareware vendors. These vendors normally charge a nominal fee for distribution, copying, and the disc the multimedia is distributed on.

Some authors offer their creations freely but ask that if you use them, you give the author credit. Putting the author's name on your Web page is a small price to pay for original work.

Often the best place to find multimedia is the Internet. On the Internet, you can search hundreds of multimedia archives. These archives are generally organized by the platform the media was designed for and the media type. Although thousands of files are readily available, keep in mind that just because you found the file on the Internet does not mean it is free for the taking.

For files you find on the Internet and would like to use, contact the person who posted the file. If they created the file, get their permission before using the file. If they did not create the file, get the permission of the file's creator before using the file. This is a good rule to follow even if the files are supposedly free for the taking. Better to be safe than face legal hassles later. For more information on using copyrighted material, see Chapter 35, "General Laws and Copyright Information."

ONLINE MULTIMEDIA HOTSPOTS

No section on sources of multimedia would be complete without listings of the Internet's multimedia hotspots. Most of the hotspots on the Internet for multimedia are archives or large collections of works that can be downloaded directly from the site. A few of the hotspots are indexes containing links to dozens and often hundreds of multimedia clips that are available from other sources. Here's a look at sound, image, and video sources.

Sound Sources on the Internet

The Internet is the best place to find shareware and freeware sounds in popular formats. One great place to find sounds is Rutgers University. You can visit Rutgers' sound archive at:

```
http://ns2.rutgers.edu/sounds/
```

A good collection of sound effects and music are located at this site:

```
http://www.wavenet.com/~axgrindr/quimby.html
```

Another great source for sounds is

```
ftp://sounds.sdsu.edu/sounds/
```

Sunsite's sound collection is located at this site:

```
http://sunsite.sut.ac.jp/multimed/sounds/
```

Image sources on the Internet

Image collections are plentiful on the Internet. You can find large image collections in popular formats, such as GIF and JPEG, at the following sites:

```
http://www.maths.tcd.ie/pub/images/images.html
http://www.comlab.ox.ac.uk/archive/images.html
http://white.nosc.mil/images.html
http://wuarchive.wustl.edu/multimedia/images
http://sunsite.unc.edu/pub/multimedia/pictures
```

You can access the National Aeronautics and Space Aministration's digital image collection here:

```
http://images.jsc.nasa.gov/html/home.htm
```

You can access the Smithsonian Institute's image archives at:

```
http://sunsite.unc.edu/pub/multimedia/pictures/smithsonian
```

Video Sources on the Internet

Although Internet video collections are sometimes hard to find, a few excellent video collections are available. Popular formats such as QuickTime, Video For Windows (AVI), and MPEG are widely supported. Cornell University has a good collection of MPEG, QuickTime, and AVI movies. You can access this collection on the Web using this URL:

```
http://tausq.resnet.cornell.edu/mmedia.htm
```

A good place to find some neat MPEG movies is

```
http://ice.ucdavis.edu/whimsy/fun_stuff/fun_stuff_movies.html
```

Animation and movies in MPEG and QuickTime formats can be found at

```
http://www.acm.uiuc.edu/rml/Mpeg/
```

Another good source for QuickTime movies is

```
http://www.sigma.unb.ca/optimus/movie.htm
```

Adding Sound to Web Pages

Sound is a powerful medium to get your message across. Imagine a music store on the Web. The store could feature clips of the latest recording stars, segments of hits from the billboard charts or classic oldies. After listening to a segment of a song, the user could be offered the opportunity to purchase the song or the record the clip was featured in.

Adding sound to your Web pages can add style and a touch of sophistication. You could use a digitized voice message to welcome visitors to your Web space. Voice messages can add sincerity and a personal touch. Or you could feature original music or a music archive, either of which would attract visitors to your Web site. Many types of sound can be included in your Web pages:

- Digitized voice
- Original music scores composed on a computer
- Sound effects
- Traditional compositions

Sound Basics

Possible uses for each type of sound were examined in Chapter 11. When you are applying those concepts to Web pages, the best advice is to use moderation. Add sound to the Web publication where it makes sense and serves a purpose. Often the best place for sound is on an archive page that includes links to sound files.

A link to an external sound file in an HTML document would look like:

```
<A HREF="sound_file.format">Description and format information</A>
```

A basic example of how sound links could be used in your Web page would be to simply group the sound files together and list them under a common heading. Figure 22.2 is an example how you could do this.

FIGURE 22.2.

Links to sound.

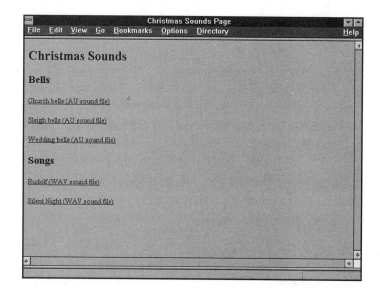

To create the HTML document displayed in the figure, you would include the following header information and links:

```
<HTML>
<HEAD>
<TITLE>Christmas Sounds Page</TITLE>
</HEAD>
<BODY>
<H1>Christmas Sounds</H1>
<H2>Bells</H2>
<P><A HREF="cbells.au">Church bells  (AU sound file)</A></P>
<P><A HREF="sbells.au">Sleigh bells  (AU sound file)</A></P>
<P><A HREF="wbells.au">Wedding bells  (AU sound file)</A></P>
<H2>Songs</H2>
<P><A HREF="rudolf.wav">Rudolf  (WAV sound file)</A></P>
<P><A HREF="snight.wav">Silent Night  (WAV sound file)</A></P>
</BODY>
</HTML>
```

The larger the file size, the longer it takes to download. Visitors to your Web site may get frustrated waiting for large sound files to download, especially if they do not know how long they may have to wait and at what point the download will finish. For this reason, a better way to link sound files to Web pages is to provide information about the length of the file. The file size is useful for many reasons. Users will know how much disk space the file will require. Based on their experience with their modem setup and speed, users may be able to approximate the amount of time it will take to download your sound file. Lastly, when a browser downloads a file, it generally displays a continuously updated count of the current number of bytes, kilobytes, or megabytes downloaded. Based on the download count and the file size you provided on your Web page, users will know when the download is almost finished.

> **CAUTION**
>
> Some electronic publishers make the mistake of putting an approximate time the file download will require, such as stating "This file will require approximately 25 minutes to download." You should NEVER put hard times on your Web pages unless you know specifically that all users of your Web pages are using a specific modem or connection speed. The amount of time a file download takes is largely dependent on the speed of the connection, meaning a user with a 14,400 bps modem will be able to download a file faster than a user with a 9600 bps modem.

Figure 22.3 shows how you could provide file size information on Web pages. The new HTML code would look like this:

```
<HTML>
<HEAD>
<TITLE>Christmas Sounds Page</TITLE>
</HEAD>
<BODY>
```

```
<H1>Christmas Sounds</H1>
<H2>Bells</H2>
<UL>
<LI><A HREF="cbells.au">Church bells  (65K AU)</A>
<LI><A HREF="sbells.au">Sleigh bells  (79K AU)</A>
<LI><A HREF="wbells.au">Wedding bells  (128K AU)</A>
</UL>
<H2>Songs</H2>
<UL>
<LI><A HREF="rudolf.wav">Rudolf  (800K WAV)</A>
<LI><A HREF="snight.wav">Silent Night  (752K WAV)</A>
</UL>
</BODY>
</HTML>
```

FIGURE 22.3.

A better way to show sound links.

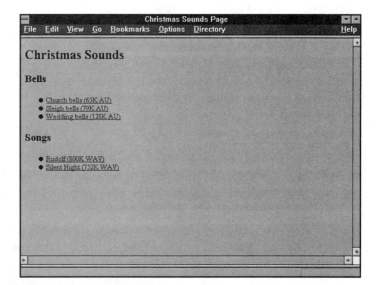

Concepts To Consider When Using Sound

When adding links to sound, you should always tell the reader what format the file is in and the length of the file. Beyond this, you should provide a brief, but good descriptive of what the file contains. Although it is true that on most browsers the reader could move the mouse pointer to the link to see the path and the file extension, and thus discover the filename and format, this rule is more of a courtesy. It always pays to be courteous, especially if you feature multiple sound files or multiple sound formats on your Web pages. This can also save the reader time and reader's value their time.

Just because a reader can see the link to a sound file and download the file does not mean they will be able to play the file. Each computer platform has its own sound format. Most systems have more than one, which makes it difficult to adapt sound for use on different systems. Two of the most popular sound formats are Apple's AIFF format and the WAV format for Microsoft

Windows. These formats provide quality playback with options for stereo sound, including eight-bit and 16-bit sound samples. Sun Microsystem's AU is a popular format, but not a quality format. Its popularity stems from the fact it was one of the original cross-platform sound solutions. Digital music fans love module formats such as MOD, S3M, and MTM. The many types of digital music formats are often lumped into a single category of formats called *mod*, which is short for module.

As Table 22.1 shows, these popular sound formats are playable on other platforms. However, the user must have a compatible tracker or player to play the file. To ensure the widest use for a sound file, use one of these popular sound formats. If you want to ensure most users of a particular platform can use the sound file without needing a special player, choose a sound format that originated on the platform.

Table 22.1. Popular audio formats.

Format	Extension	Original Platform	Systems that Format Will Play On
AIFF	.aiff	Apple	Amiga, Apple, Microsoft Windows, UNIX
AIFF-C	.aifc	Apple	Amiga, Apple, Microsoft Windows, UNIX
AU	.au	Sun UNIX	Amiga, Apple, Microsoft Windows, UNIX
MOD	.mod, .s3m, and .mtm	Amiga	Amiga, Apple, Microsoft Windows, UNIX
MPEG Audio	.mp2	(UNIX)	Any system, Industry standard
WAV	.wav	Microsoft Windows	Amiga, Apple, Microsoft Windows, UNIX

Thousands of sound files are available in Internet archives. Even some discussion groups are devoted solely to sound. The wonderful thing about sound, though, is that if you cannot find the sound clip you are looking for on the Internet, you probably can easily create it or copy it from an existing audio source. Most computers allow you to easily create sound files. PC sound boards normally include a microphone jack and a sound recording tool. Many other computers include features to record or create sound. With a microphone and the sound recording tool that came with your computer, you can record voice, sound effects, and more. If your computer did not come with a sound tool, don't worry. The next section will show you where you can find sound tools on the Internet.

Sound Players, Trackers, and Where To Find Them

Hundreds of sound tools are available on the Internet. This section will highlight a few of the best available as freeware or shareware. Most of these tools are updated frequently and faithfully by their creators, and their version numbers are ever changing. These applications are often named with a suffix that denotes the version, such as zgv2.5 for version 2.5 of ZGV or winjp265 for version 2.65 of WinJPEG. In general, always look for the most current version—the highest suffix.

The best way to ensure you get the most current version of these tools is to provide a directory path instead of an absolute path to the file. If you access an FTP site with an absolute path to a file, the FTP site will only try to access the specific file you named. Although this may be well and good in a few cases, nothing is more frustrating than discovering the particular file is no longer available. The second most frustrating thing is downloading an outdated version of a tool—especially when you later discover there are several more current versions of the tool you were looking for readily available.

TIP

The directories where these applications can be found are treasure-troves. You will find dozens of multimedia programs for your particular system. Anonymous FTP sites are directly accessible through your Web browser. All browser packages include support for FTP using an FTP URL:

```
ftp://ftp_server/directory
```

Your browser will log in to the anonymous FTP site using the login ID of anonymous and a password that is your e-mail address. By giving you a directory path instead of a full path to a specific file, you will get a directory listing of all files and subdirectories in the directory. This allows you to search the treasure troves available at these sites. Later examples will provide you with lists of specific FTP sites and directories to search at the sites.

Two basic types of sound tools are used to play sound files. A *player* is a general purpose sound tool that allows you to play sound files. Although sound files must be in a format readable by the player, most players will read and play several types of sound formats. Players are great for the average sound file. A *tracker* is a sound tool specifically designed to play digital music modules (mods). Trackers usually have much wider support for sound formats and advanced features.

The following subsections present the top players and trackers available for these systems:

- Amiga
- Macintosh
- MS-DOS

■ OS/2

■ Windows

■ UNIX

Amiga

For the Amiga, two popular players are DeliTracker and EaglePlayer. DeliTracker is a good player if you have Amiga OS 2.0 or higher. It plays more than 80 different mod (digital music) formats, including the popular MTM and S3M formats. The shareware price for the current version is $20.

EaglePlayer is another good player for the Amiga. It plays more than 100 different mod formats and supports DOS/Windows sound formats. There is also a PC version of the program. Two versions of EaglePlayer are available: a commercial version and a limited shareware version. The cost of the shareware version is $20.

One of the hottest trackers around is Protracker. It is based on the original Soundtracker interface and has been greatly improved over the years. As the name implies, Protracker isn't for the novice. It expects you to know a lot about creating sound. The best thing about Protracker is that it is freeware.

Amiga sound tools are available from the many `aminet` FTP sites around the world, but these sites are often busy. Not to worry, one of the fastest `aminet` FTP sites in the United States also has a Web site. You should search the following `aminet` directory for popular Amiga sound tools:

```
http://www.netnet.net/aminet/dirs/tree_mus.html
```

Macintosh

For the Macintosh, the two most popular players are Player Pro and Sound Trecker. Player Pro and Sound Trecker are hot players that support mods and Macintosh formats. Player Pro and Sound Trecker are the most popular for good reason. They are continually upgraded and have good interfaces.

Player Pro is fully PowerMac-native. The shareware version of Player Pro requires you to pay a $20 shareware fee before you can unlock its best features.

Sound Trecker is comparable to Player Pro. It has a shareware fee of $40. Sound Trecker has many advanced features, good menus, and upgrade modules that should enable full PowerMac capabilities.

A good all-around player and converter for the Macintosh is SoundApp. The great thing about SoundApp is its wide support for other popular sound formats. It will handle AU, AIFF, SND, WAV, and many popular mod formats. SoundApp can also use the advanced features of PowerMac, and it is freeware.

The following utility archive is a great place to find Macintosh sound tools:

```
ftp://wuarchive.wustl.edu/systems/mac/info-mac/snd/util
```

MS-DOS

Dual Module Player plays the three most popular mod formats as well as Sound Blaster and WAV formats. The quality of this player is getting better and better with each new version. Dual Module Player is cardware, so be sure to send the author a card if you try out this software!

NOTE

Cardware is similar to freeware in that authors of cardware applications are basically giving away their creations for free. However, cardware authors ask that if you use their products, you send them a card as sole compensation for your use of the work. Sending a card to the author of a product you value enough to use is a great way to say thank you.

Two other good DOS players are Cubic Player and Omni Player. Both have a lot of potential and are sure to be excellent players as new versions are released. Cubic Player will play many mod, Sound Blaster, and DOS formats and has some nice features. Omni Player is another good DOS player that supports many mod and Sound Blaster formats.

Scream Tracker is one of the best digital music players available for DOS. It supports numerous mod and Sound Blaster formats. This tracker has many advanced features. Best of all, Scream Tracker is freeware.

Another popular DOS tracker is Fast Tracker II. It supports mod and Sound Blaster formats as well. The shareware fee for Fast Tracker II is $20.

To find these and others DOS players, trackers, and converters look in these directories at `eng.ufl.edu`:

```
ftp://ftp.eng.ufl.edu/pub/msdos/demos/music/programs/converters
ftp://ftp.eng.ufl.edu/pub/msdos/demos/music/programs/players
ftp://ftp.eng.ufl.edu/pub/msdos/demos/music/programs/trackers
```

OS/2

For OS/2, the Digital Music Player is a good choice. It will play the popular mod formats as well as MIDI and WAV. To use this player you need to have the multimedia support module for OS/2 loaded (MMPM OS/2). A good place to find OS/2 multimedia tools is this FTP directory:

```
ftp://hobbes.nmsu.edu/os2/mmedia
```

Windows

MIDAS is a good player for Microsoft Windows. It plays some popular mod formats including S3M and will also play WAV files. MIDAS also supports 16-bit stereo sound at common mixing rates. Best of all, MIDAS is freeware.

WHAM is another good all-around sound tool for Microsoft Windows. Not only can it play sound files, it will also let you edit sound files and convert sound files from one format to another. WHAM also features support for many popular sound formats.

A good place to find Windows sound tools is

```
ftp://ftp.eng.ufl.edu/pub/msdos/demos/music/programs/players
```

UNIX

For UNIX systems, one of the best digital music players is Tracker. It supports the very popular Protracker player formats and has player modules that will run on other types of UNIX systems such as Silicon Graphics, Sun Sparc, and Linux.

SOX is a great all-purpose sound tool for UNIX systems. It is a basic editor and converter. SOX can convert many popular sound formats including AIFF, AU, and WAV. A good place to find UNIX sound tools is:

```
ftp://sunsite.unc.edu/pub/Linux/apps/sound/players
```

Adding Graphics to Web Presentations

Images are great for catching people's attention. The best Web pages use images to accent and highlight and not to replace text. This is important to remember because millions of users still use text-based browsers to explore the World Wide Web. Two basic types of images can be included in your Web pages:

- External Images
- Inline Images

External Image Basics

Adding an external image to your Web page is easy. Using the anchor tag discussed in Chapter 20, "Using HTML," you can create a link to the external image. When the user activates the link by clicking on it, the user's browser will call a helper application to display the image. For example, if the user clicked on a link that said "Waikiki Beach at Sunset (360KB GIF)," the user's browser would start the appropriate helper application (if available) and a picture of palm trees and sandy beaches could appear on-screen. Here is an example of how you could use an external link in your Web publications:

```
<A HREF="/home/william/waikiki.gif" >Waikiki Beach at Sunset (360KB GIF)</A>
```

In this example, the full path to the image is specified. When displayed, the text portion of the anchor tag `Waikiki Beach at Sunset` will be highlighted. This is the text the reader will click on to activate the link. Specifying the full path isn't necessary when the image is located in the same directory as the Web document. Although the implications of this will be discussed later, here's an example of not using the full path to the image file:

```
<A HREF="pipeline.gif" >See the awesome waves at Pipeline (490KB GIF)</A>
```

Although adding an external image to a Web document can be as easy as providing a link, it does require some forethought. To display the image, the user must have a helper application configured for viewing. The format of the image will determine what image viewer the browser selects. This is why it is very important to use formats displayable by the majority of users.

Inline Image Basics

Web pages without inline images to break up the text can be downright ugly. Inline images should supplement text, enhance the page, but should never replace text. If you use inline images in GIF format, you don't have to worry about what type of system the reader is using. This is because inline images in GIF format can be loaded automatically by the reader's browser. However, this automatic image-loading feature can be turned on or off by the reader, which is another reason not to rely solely on images to convey your message.

The way to specify an inline image using HTML is with the `<IMG>` tag. The `<IMG>` tag has three basic attributes and no closing element. The only attribute of the `<IMG>` tag you must use is `SRC`, which specifies the source, or path to the image including the name.

A basic link to an inline image in an HTML document would look like this:

```
<IMG SRC="/home/william/waimea_bay.gif">
```

Very often the image is located in the same directory as the HTML document or in a directory that can be addressed relative to the location of the HTML document. By removing the full path information, a relative path to the image can be specified. Using a relative path serves a threefold purpose:

- It makes using the image in the Web document easier.
- It makes maintaining the document easier in the event the paths change.
- It will eliminate a problem with some browsers that reload the image every time a full path is specified.

Here is an example of a relative path to an inline image file located one directory up from the directory of the HTML document:

```
<IMG SRC="../surfs_up.gif">
```

Here's an example of an inline image file located in the same directory as the HTML document:

```
<IMG SRC="volcano.gif">
```

NOTE

Some browsers can automatically load other image formats. However, GIF images can be loaded by all graphics-capable browsers. Again, do not arbitrarily exclude groups of readers. Provide features that everyone who visits your Web pages can enjoy.

Concepts To Consider When Adding Images

When adding images, there are many concepts to consider. The best Web pages are very user-friendly and provide features for all users. Remember, not all users have graphics-capable browsers. Millions of Web users rely on text-based browsers to explore the Web. Many millions more, discouraged by Web pages that weren't user-friendly, switched off the automatic image-loading feature of their Web browser.

Making your Web pages user-friendly should be a top priority. The concepts covered in this section will help you do this.

THE 14-SECOND RULE

Image formats and general information on how to use images in electronic publications were discussed in Chapter 11. When applying those ideas to Web pages, use moderation. Every inline image you include must be loaded when the page is accessed. Some viewers will not display anything on the page until the entire page is loaded. Web pages with large or many inline images frustrate users. A good rule to follow when adding images to your Web pages is my 14-second rule.

Let's explore this rule for a moment as it can also help you select an optimum textual length for individual Web pages. The 14-second rule has the average user in mind. Currently, the average user accessing the Web has a 14,400 bps modem.

Make sure the automatic image-loading feature of your Web browser is turned on, then try loading one of your Web pages. Use a modem speed of 14,400 bps. If under the best of conditions it takes more than 14 seconds to fully load all text and graphics—assuming no other time delaying features are adversely affecting the page loading—look at the page and see what is slowing the load time. Consider modifying the offending element. Keep in mind that your Web pages will load faster for you because of your proximity to the site. If it takes you 14 seconds to load the page, it will probably take users located at disparate sites a lot longer.

Fourteen seconds is really the average (median) value in a frustration window that weighs poor performance and slow access speeds at one end and the top performance and quick access speeds at the other end. Don't use the rule as an absolute. Use it as a reality check to help you develop user-friendly pages. This is the basic precept of the rule—make sure your pages are user-friendly by valuing the user's time. After you have browsed the Web for a while, you will discover there is nothing more frustrating than waiting for thousands of bytes of graphics to load, and undoubtedly, you will wish more Web publishers followed this rule.

NOTE

If you analyze this loading time statistically, use the median so that extremes won't have a large affect on the outcome. The current trend is toward 14,400 bps, with many Web users accessing at 9,600 bps and an increasing number accessing at 28,800 bps.

Thumbnail Images

One of the best ways to avoid putting slow-loading graphics on a page is through thumbnail images. A thumbnail is a scaled down representation of a larger image that users can load if they so choose, by activating a link you have provided. Slow-loading graphics aren't necessarily large graphics, they are high resolution graphics or graphics with many colors. A very large two-color image at low resolution will load faster than a small 256-color image at high resolution.

Thumbnail images are a great way to link to large images and other resources. The notion of a thumbnail describes how these resources are pinned together. You use a small image, the pin, to lead to something bigger, the larger image or another resource. The small image is pinned, or linked, by putting the image tag inside an anchor tag.

Here is the general format for a thumbnail:

```
<A HREF="action_or_file_to_load" ><IMG SRC="image_name.format"></A>
```

Here is an example of using a thumbnail:

```
<A HREF="http://tvp.com/william/waikiki.html" ><IMG SRC="waikiki2.gif"></A>
```

In the thumbnail example, the small image of Waikiki would be surrounded by a border showing that the image is a clickable hotspot on the Web page. When you clicked on the image, your browser would use the hypertext transfer protocol HTTP to access the `tvp.com` Web site and retrieve the HTML document called `waikiki`. The `waikiki` page could contain information about Waikiki, such as a list of hotels, restaurant, and clubs.

The following line is a way to link a thumbnail to an external image:

```
<A HREF="pipeline_large.jpeg" ><IMG SRC="pipeline_small.gif"></A>
```

> **TIP**
>
> Using a thumbnail to link to a larger image does not mean you have to be referencing an external image. Remember, an external image, no matter the format, requires the user to have a viewer configured for use. To avoid using an external viewer, link the thumbnail to another HTML document containing the larger image.

Using the concept explained in the tip, the previous example could be re-written as follows:

```
<A HREF="pipeline.html" ><IMG SRC="pipeline_small.gif"></A>
```

The small image of Hawaii's popular surfing area, the Pipeline, would be surrounded by a border showing that the image is a clickable hotspot on the Web page. When you clicked on the image, your browser would access the HTML document called `pipeline` which could contain a larger image. The HTML code for this page could look like this:

```
<HTML>
<HEAD>
<TITLE>The Pipeline in Hawaii</TITLE>
</HEAD>
<BODY>
<P><IMG SRC="pipeline.gif"></P>
<P><STRONG>Catch a virtual wave!</STRONG></P>
</BODY>
</HTML>
```

Practical Use of Images

Let's build a home page for the ABC Press using the ideas discussed in the previous sections. To do this, you create some simple GIF images, and then write the following HTML code:

```
<HTML>
<HEAD>
<TITLE>Welcome to the ABC Press Home Page</TITLE>
</HEAD>
<BODY>
<H1>The ABC Press</H1>
<ADDRESS>
123 Sunnybrook Lane
Anywhere, NY 12345 USA
</ADDRESS>
<P><A HREF="mailto:your_user_id@anywhere.com"><IMG
```

```
SRC="mail.gif"></A></P>
<IMG SRC="gradline.gif">
<P><IMG SRC="new.gif">
This type of icon is a good way to introduce new items on the page.</P>
<P><A HREF="info.html">   <IMG SRC="help.gif"></A>Do you have a question
about features on our home page?  We've set up a page to provide you with
background information that will make your visit to the ABC Press a more
pleasant one.</P>
<P><A HREF="books.html">   <IMG SRC="books.gif">Our selection of
electronic books is great!</A></P>
<P><A HREF="order.html"><IMG SRC="order.gif"></A></P>
<HR>
<P> (C) 1995 by The ABC Press</P>
</BODY>
</HTML>
```

Although inline images can be of any size, Figure 22.4 contains a number of small images for demonstration purposes. Take a close look at the figure. It depicts the various ways inline images can be used. The first example shows how an inline image can be linked to an action. Note the border around the mail image.

FIGURE 22.4.

Inline images.

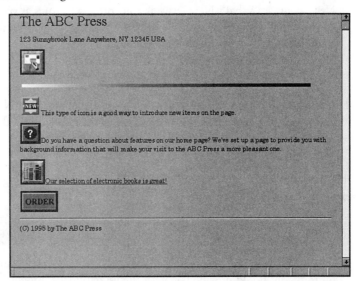

The second example shows an alternate way to break up major parts of the page. Although the `<HR>` tag puts a clean horizontal rule across the page, a line you create yourself can be of different colors and lengths. The line here is a gradient fill from gray to black.

The third example shows a way to put an inline image onto the page to direct the reader's attention to information on the page. Images announcing new items are great additions to your Web pages. If you have a large Web space and links to multiple pages, you should also have a link to a "What's New" document.

TIP

A newspaper or magazine whose readers read the publication once and never again would not be in print very long. For this reason, a key concept in newspaper or magazine publishing is to continually change the content in an effort to build readership by attracting new readers and keeping the current readers. Web publishers can learn an important lesson from these traditional publishers, and that is, to ensure your Web publications continually grow or change. Web publications that grow or change will help you build a following of new and old readers.

One way to show readers that your site is growing or changing is to feature a "What's New" page. A "What's New" page is a list of new features at your site. The list could contain links to pages or sections you have added to the publication. It could contain a list of updates to pages, such as links you have added to interesting places on the Web. It could also contain a list of graphics or multimedia that you have added to the site.

The fourth example is an image with a link to another document. Notice the text is not aligned in a column next to the image. As you will see in the next section, this is important to remember when using advanced techniques to align text and inline images.

The next example shows how to link both an inline image and text. The user can click on either the text or the image. This is a good technique to use. Relying only on a linked image to explain what a link does is poor form.

CAUTION

Even if the image link seems self-explanatory as in the final example of the order button, you should provide text with the linked image. By failing to provide text with the linked image, you may be excluding many visitors to your page. For users using a text-based browser the link will be unusable. For users who have turned off the automatic image-loading feature of their browser, the contents of the image will be unreadable.

In Figure 22.5 the automatic-image loading feature of the browser was turned off. This graphically depicts the importance of ensuring your page is friendly for all users.

FIGURE 22.5

Inline images disappear with graphics loading disabled

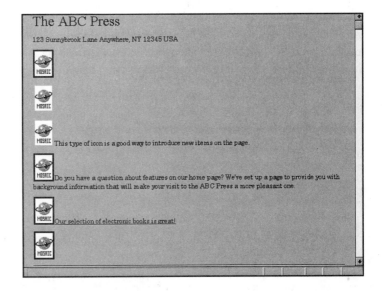

Advanced Image Techniques

Advanced techniques for putting inline images on Web pages can help you create friendlier pages. One in particular will help make visits to your Web page more enjoyable for users with text-only browsers. This is the ALT attribute of the IMG tag. ALT lets you specify text to place on the page when readers cannot or do not want to view images. Here is the general format for using the IMG tag's ALT attribute:

```
<IMG SRC="image_name.gif" ALT="*The alternative text goes here*">
```

An example of using ALT is:

```
<IMG SRC="order.gif" ALT="*Place Order*">
```

To help all readers enjoy the page, use ALT with inline images. The text between the quotation marks is interpreted as a literal string of characters. A common technique is to enclose the text string in brackets or asterisks as in the example. This will ensure the text is set off from other text that may appear on the same line. A good rule to follow is to keep the string short—no more than a few descriptive words.

Another useful attribute of the IMG tag is ALIGN. This attribute controls how text is aligned with an inline image. Text can be aligned with the top, middle or bottom of the image. Here are the three values for the ALIGN attribute:

```
<IMG SRC="image_name.gif" ALIGN=TOP>
```

```
<IMG SRC="image_name.gif" ALIGN=MIDDLE>
```

```
<IMG SRC="image_name.gif" ALIGN=BOTTOM>
```

The ALIGN attributes you will use most often are TOP and MIDDLE. This is because by default, text is aligned with the bottom of the image. Remember from Figure 22.4 that text is not aligned in a column next to the image. Therefore, the ALIGN attribute is most useful to align a single line of text in a specific manner. The ALT and ALIGN attributes can be added easily to the IMG tag in an HTML document:

```
<HTML>
<HEAD>
<TITLE>Welcome to the ABC Press Home Page</TITLE>
</HEAD>
<BODY>
<H1>The ABC Press</H1>
<ADDRESS>
123 Sunnybrook Lane
Anywhere, NY 12345 USA
</ADDRESS>
<P>Send <A HREF="mailto:your_user_id@anywhere.com">
<IMG SRC="mail.gif" ALIGN=MIDDLE ALT="[your_user_id@anywhere.com]">
</A> to our publisher.</P>
<IMG SRC="gradline.gif" ALT="[line]">
<P><IMG SRC="new.gif" ALIGN=TOP ALT="[New]">   This type of icon is a
good way to introduce new items on the page.</P>
<P><A HREF="info.html">   <IMG SRC="help.gif" ALIGN=MIDDLE
ALT="*Information*"></A>Do you have a question about features on our home
page?  We've set up a page to provide you with background information that will
make your visit to the ABC Press a more pleasant one.</P>
<P><A HREF="info.html">   <IMG SRC="help.gif" ALIGN=BOTTOM
ALT="*Information*"></A>Do you have a question about features on our home
page?  We've set up a page to provide you with background information that will
make your visit to the ABC Press a more pleasant one.</P>
<P><A HREF="books.html"><IMG SRC="books.gif" ALIGN=MIDDLE
 ALT="[Books]">Our selection is great!</A></P>
<P>Place an on-line <A HREF="order.html"><IMG SRC="order.gif"
ALIGN=BOTTOM ALT="*Order*"></A> today!</P>
<HR>
<P> (C) 1995 by The ABC Press</P>
</BODY>
</HTML>
```

Figure 22.6 shows how the HTML code using ALT and ALIGN would be seen in a text-only browser. The ALT attribute made the Web page more friendly for these users. Figure 22.7 shows how images can be aligned with text.

Two of the entries are identical except for the use of the ALIGN attribute. In the first use of the information button, text is aligned with the middle of the image. This leaves an ugly blank space. In the second use of the information button, text is aligned with the bottom of the image, and the second line of text wraps around the image.

> **NOTE**
>
> Notice how the improper use of the ALIGN attribute can affect multiple lines of text following an image. When multiple lines of text follow or surround an image, aligning the text with the bottom of the image will not leave empty spaces.

FIGURE 22.6.

Using the ALT attribute for text-only browsers.

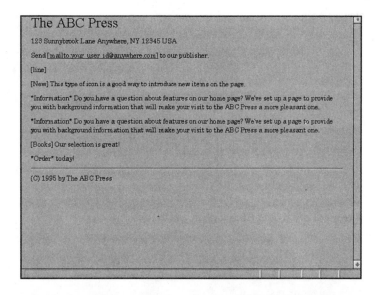

FIGURE 22.7.

Aligning text with images.

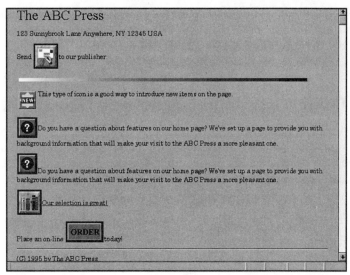

An actual example of the use of inline GIF images from The Virtual Press Home Page is shown in Figure 22.8. The figure depicts good use of inline GIF images. The featured inline image and the accompanying text can both be selected. The links take the reader to a page featuring the product, in this case, a series of electronic novels.

FIGURE 22.8.

Inline images in use on the Web.

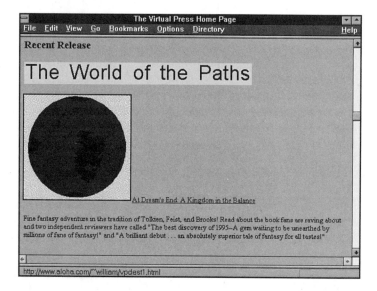

On the product information page there are other inline images. One inline image leads to a virtual tour of places in the book. The virtual tour uses a series of inline images. These images could have been external images, but that would have been an intervening step requiring readers to have an image viewer configured.

Image Viewers and Where To Find Them

Image tools are widely available on the Internet as freeware or shareware. Most of these tools are updated frequently and faithfully by their creators and their version numbers are ever changing. The directories where these applications can be found are treasure-troves. You will find dozens of tools for your particular system. The best way to find these applications is to browse the directories using your favorite Web browser.

The best image tools available for the following systems are presented in the next several subsections:

- Amiga
- Macintosh
- MS-DOS
- Windows
- UNIX

Amiga

FastView is a great all-around viewer for JPEG and GIF files. It requires Amiga OS 2.0 or higher. FastView is shareware and has a registration fee of $15.

Another good Amiga viewer is FastJPEG. FastJPEG will work on a system running Amiga OS 1.3 or higher. This freeware viewer is very user-friendly. To find these and other Amiga viewers use the following aminet directory:

    http://www.netnet.net/aminet/dirs/tree_gfx.html

Macintosh

One of the best viewers on the Macintosh is JPEGView. With JPEGView, you can view most popular image formats including JPEG and GIF. JPEGView is fast and has low overhead, meaning it isn't a memory hog and will run efficiently on older systems.

GraphicConverter is a great all-around editor, converter and viewer for the Mac. It will edit, display and convert many popular image formats. GraphicConverter requires System 7 and QuickTime to be installed, so if you have an older system, try GIFConverter. GIFConverter will display fewer image formats but is still a good choice. The following FTP directory is a good place to find Macintosh image tools:

    ftp://sumex-aim.stanford.edu/info-mac/grf/util

MS-DOS

QPEG is a great viewer for JPEG, GIF, TGA, BMP, and PCX files. The shareware fee of $20 is a bargain. QPEG loads images fast and has some nice features, such as a preview window for quick browsing of multiple images.

The newest versions of the handy GIF to JPEG converter, called GIF2JPEG, and a JPEG to GIF converter, called JPEG2GIF are available as freeware. These two programs produced by Handmade Software Incorporated are gems for free. If you need to convert GIF and JPEG images, GIF2JPEG and JPEG2GIF are good choices. To find MS-DOS image tools, look here:

    ftp://oak.oakland.edu/SimTel/msdos/graphics

Windows

LView Pro is an excellent all-around image viewer for most popular PC formats, as well as JPEG and GIF. It will also let you edit and convert file formats. In addition to a 16-bit Windows version, LView Pro has a version that takes advantage of 32-bit extensions for Windows, and a version optimized for the Pentium. A shareware fee of $30 applies in most instances.

Another good combined editor, viewer, and converter for Microsoft Windows is WinJPEG. WinJPEG will display and edit many popular formats including GIF and JPEG. It even includes a screen capture utility. The shareware fee for WinJPEG is $25. Windows image tools can be found at

    ftp://oak.oakland.edu/SimTel/win3/graphics

UNIX

UNIX viewers primarily run under the X Window System environment. One of the best all-around viewers for X Window System is ImageMagick. It handles JPEG, GIF, and other image formats quite nicely. ImageMagick will also let you convert image formats. The following directory has several good X Window System viewers:

```
ftp://ftp.x.org/contrib/applications
```

For Linux, a good viewer is zgv. This Linux viewer works with VGA and SVGA monitors. You can find the most current version of zgv at

```
ftp://sunsite.unc.edu/pub/Linux/apps/graphics/viewers
```

Adding Video to Web Presentations

Video is the ultimate form of multimedia. With MPEG-2 as the new world standard in video compression, the multimedia market is poised for rapid expansion. Prices for professional quality video production boards and equipment are plunging. Leading-edge electronic publishers will display video clips of their products on the Web for the world to see.

The two primary types of video that can be included in your Web pages are

Digitized motion video
Computer animation

Digitized video is becoming increasingly popular. More people are purchasing computers capable of playing video. As computers become more powerful, their ability to handle video grows. The Web's versatility and the relative ease with which video can be incorporated into HTML documents can help you take the all-important first step to becoming a video producer.

Computer-generated animation can be just as powerful as digitized video. Animation is extremely effective in communicating new ideas to viewers. Many of today's popular science fiction television shows use computer animation. On the Web, the electronic publisher could use animation in the same way. If you are dealing with a unique or fantastical idea, animation can draw the viewer in and ultimately help sell your product.

Video Basics

The best way to learn how to use video in your Web pages is to start with the basics. Begin by working with royalty-free clips or shareware clips that you can purchase at bargain prices. Finished video on disc does not require special hardware. You will not need a video camera or specialized video equipment to port the video to a computer.

Many rules that apply to sound also apply to video. Inform the reader about the content and format of the files you feature. If you offer many videos in different formats, the best place to put these clips is on an archive page that includes links to video files.

A link to an external video file in an HTML document would look like this:

```
<A HREF="video_file.format">Description and format information</A>
```

A basic example of how video you could use links in your Web page would be to simply group the videos together and list them under a common heading. Figure 22.9 shows how this could be done. The HTML code for the document would include the following header information and links:

```
<HTML>
<HEAD>
<TITLE>Welcome to the ABC Press Video Page</TITLE>
</HEAD>
<BODY>
<H1>The ABC Press</H1>
<ADDRESS>
123 Sunnybrook Lane
Anywhere, NY 12345 USA
</ADDRESS>
<H2>Christmas Videos</H2>
<P><A HREF="tree-light.AVI">Tree lighting ceremony
(2.8MB AVI)</A></P>
<P><A HREF="carolers.AVI">Carolers passing by the Window
(2.5MB AVI)</A></P>
<P><A HREF="first.snow.AVI">First Snow Fall  (1.1MB
MPEG)</A></P>
<H2>Other Holiday Videos</H2>
<P><A HREF="newyear.MOV"> New Year's Eve in the Big Apple
(3.8MB MOV)</A></P>
<P><A HREF="fourjuly.MOV">Fireworks (2.9MB MOV)</A></P>
<HR>
<P> (C) 1995 by The ABC Press</P>
</BODY>
</HTML>
```

FIGURE 22.9.

Using links to video files.

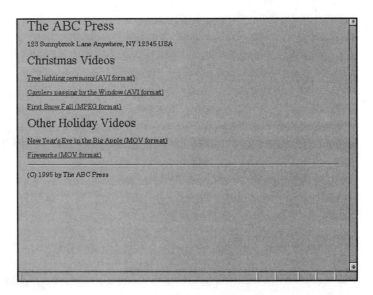

A better way to link video files to Web pages is to provide information on the length of the file. This way readers can better determine if they want to download the file. Figure 22.10 shows an example of this.

FIGURE 22.10.

A better way to use link video files.

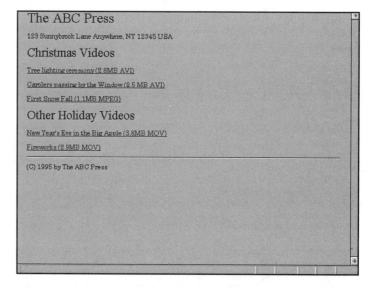

Christmas Videos content shown:

The ABC Press
123 Sunnybrook Lane Anywhere, NY 12345 USA
Christmas Videos
Tree lighting ceremony (2.8MB AVI)
Carolers passing by the Window (2.5 MB AVI)
First Snow Fall (1.1MB MPEG)
Other Holiday Videos
New Year's Eve in the Big Apple (3.8MB MOV)
Fireworks (2.9MB MOV)

(C) 1995 by The ABC Press

Concepts To Consider When Using Video

Although there are many uses for video in your Web presentations, it is often difficult to integrate video. The primary reason for this is video clips will seem out of place if they don't relate to the subject matter on the page. For business operations, this may mean creating a video production for the Web publication.

Although creating an original digitized video can be expensive, the growing availability of royalty-free and shareware clips is making it easier to find video clips on a wide range of topics. With royalty free clips, you can edit them as you see fit or integrate them into other clips to make a video production.

Here are some practical and fun uses for video on your Web page:

- Use original video to show visitors to your virtual store what the actual store looks like.
- Use video to show off your product line.
- Create a live product tutorial.
- Provide live installation instructions.
- Create a live introduction to the Web site.
- Create an author or editor's introduction to an electronic publication.
- Create a live video clip on subjects relating to the feature publication.

A collection of video clips featuring animals in the wild to go along with a virtual zoo collection would be a great way to use live video clips. Think seriously about using video in your Web pages. If pictures are worth a thousand words, a video must be worth millions of words.

Video Editors, Players, Converters, and Where To Find Them

Video is more proprietary than other types of multimedia. There are fewer video tools available. Although this may seem like a bad thing, this is actually a good thing. Fewer tools help reduce complexity in an already complex problem. For the most part, video tools write files in their native formats and include the capability to convert other formats to the native format.

For animation, the most popular formats are Autodesk's FLI and FLC formats. The tools for creating animation are primarily system specific and commercial. The best place to find animation software is the local computer store. Although high-end animation programs are costly, you can find quality animation software for under $100.

For video, there are three main formats: AVI, MOV, and MPEG. All three are excellent formats that offer the ability to include stereo sound tracks with the video. Because of this, your format of choice will most likely depend on the type of system you prefer to work with. Video tools and concepts are rapidly changing. Keeping your video tools current with the times is extremely important, more so than any other form of multimedia. The best way to find current tools and information on a particular format is the Web. Web sites are dedicated to each of these formats.

As Table 22.2 shows, some popular video formats are playable on other platforms. However, the user must have a compatible player. If you want to ensure most users of a particular platform can use the video without needing a special player, choose a video format that originated on the platform.

Table 22.2. Video formats and extensions.

Format	Extension	Original Platform	Systems Will Play On
Apple QuickTime	.mov	Apple	Apple, Microsoft Windows, UNIX X Window System
Microsoft AVI	.avi	Microsoft Windows	Microsoft Windows (if converted Apple, UNIX)
MPEG	.mpg and .mpeg	(UNIX)	Any system, Industry Standard

MPEG Format

The MPEG format is the industry standard for video. MPEG players for MPEG level 1 are available for all computer systems, making MPEG a true cross-platform video solution. In the past MPEG lagged behind other formats simply because early MPEG players did not support audio tracks. This is no longer true. Most current MPEG players support CD-quality audio.

The best place on the Web to find tools and information on MPEG is the Moving Pictures Expert Group Frequently Asked Questions page. At the MPEG FAQ page, you can find tools, detailed information on the MPEG standard, and information on making MPEG videos. The URL for the MPEG FAQ is

```
http://www.crs4.it/HTML/LUIGI/MPEG/mpegfaq.html
```

Another great site for technical information on MPEG is the MPEG resource list. The list contains detailed examples of how MPEG video can be created and then converted to and from popular formats. You can find the MPEG resource list on the Web at

```
http://www.arc.umn.edu/GVL/Software/mpeg.html
```

Video For Windows Format

Microsoft's Video for Windows format, AVI, is popular, and well it should be, considering Windows-based systems have an extremely large share of the world's PC-base. Video for Windows includes a suite of tools for editing audio, animation, images and video. Microsoft distributes a QuickTime to AVI converter for use on the Macintosh. Video for Windows players are widely available for use on Windows systems. These players are runtime players, meaning they were designed for playback purposes only and are generally freeware.

You will find AVI converters at the Apple and MPEG sites listed in this section. A good site to get a runtime AVI player is at MediaShare Corporation's Web site:

```
http://www.mediashare.com/mshare/vidview.htm
```

MediaShare has many videos available in AVI format. This site is less busy than Microsoft's Web site. However, Microsoft's TechNet directory service is the place to find information on Microsoft Corporation.

Microsoft has done an excellent job to ensure product information is readily available. The TechNet directory will let you search Microsoft's Web site using key words. A search on the TechNet page for "Video for Windows" will return dozens of places where you can find information on the AVI format. These are indexed TechNet pages, so it is best to take a virtual stroll over to Microsoft and see what the latest search reveals:

```
http://www.microsoft.com/pages/services/technet/technet.htm
```

QuickTime Format

Apple's proprietary set of video tools feature QuickTime and the MOV format. Apple has worked hard to ensure their format is portable and playable on other systems. Apple includes QuickTime players with System 7, and some QuickTime players are freely available for Macintosh, Windows, and UNIX X Window System systems. A key idea in this portability to non-Macintosh systems is a process called flattening.

Macintosh systems have better than average facilities for handling video. Some data necessary to play the video is stored separately from the main data. This helps with smoother playback. To play QuickTime videos on other systems, this data must be moved back in with the main data. This process of moving the extracted data back in with the primary data is called *flattening*. If the process sounds confusing, do not worry. There are several easy-to-use tools to flatten QuickTime videos.

Apple's QuickTime site is the place to find information on QuickTime:

```
http://quicktime.apple.com/
```

At the site, you will find the latest players for the various systems QuickTime supports, lists of useful utilities and even QuickTime videos. One of the utilities you will find at the QuickTime site is a conversion gem called Sparkle. Sparkle runs on the Macintosh and will play or convert to a playable form any video format.

For information on converting to and from QuickTime, the cross-platform QuickTime resource page is an excellent choice. The resource page lists dozens of QuickTime conversion tools for Macintosh, Microsoft Windows, and UNIX X Window System:

```
http://www.astro.nwu.edu/lentz/mac/qt/home-qt.html
```

Putting Sound, Graphics, and Video Together

In this chapter you have seen how sound, graphics and video can be used on Web pages. Let's put together a multimedia archive using the ideas covered in previous sections. Adding a few simple inline GIF images to the Web page can have a dramatic effect. Using your favorite image editor, you could create the following GIF images:

abcpress.gif	A GIF image introducing the Web page
soundlib.gif	A GIF image introducing the sound library
videolib.gif	A GIF image introducing the video library

These inline images do not need to be fancy. Very often, header, title and menu images will only contain text set against a colorful background. This is also true in the following example.

After creating the three title GIFs, you may also want to create thumbnail GIFs to highlight the sound and video titles available at the archive. Using your image editor, you could create the following images:

`sndclip.gif`	A thumbnail GIF highlighting sound titles
`vidclip.gif`	A thumbnail GIF highlighting video titles

Once these images are created, they could be incorporated in the code for the multimedia archive. Figures 22.11 and 22.12 show how the multimedia archive would look using the GIF images and this HTML code:

```
<HTML>
<HEAD>
<TITLE>ABC Press Multimedia</TITLE>
</HEAD>
<BODY>
<P><IMG SRC="abcpress.gif"></P>
<P><IMG SRC="soundlib.gif"></P>
<H3>Bells</H3>
<P><A HREF="cbells.au"><IMG SRC="sndclip.gif" ALIGN=MIDDLE
ALT="*Sound Clip*">Church bells  (65K AU)</A></P>
<P><A HREF="sbells.au"><IMG SRC="sndclip.gif" ALIGN=MIDDLE
ALT="*Sound Clip*">Sleigh bells  (79K AU)</A></P>
<P><A HREF="wbells.au"><IMG SRC="sndclip.gif" ALIGN=MIDDLE
ALT="*Sound Clip*">Wedding bells  (128K AU)</A></P>
<HR>
<H3>Songs</H3>
<P><A HREF="rudolf.wav"><IMG SRC="sndclip.gif" ALIGN=MIDDLE
ALT="*Sound Clip*">Rudolf  (800K WAV)</A></P>
<P><A HREF="snight.wav"><IMG SRC="sndclip.gif" ALIGN=MIDDLE
ALT="*Sound Clip*">Silent Night  (752K WAV)</A></P>
<HR>
<P><IMG SRC="videolib.gif"></P>
<H3>Christmas Videos</H3>
<P><A HREF="tree-light.AVI"><IMG SRC="vidclip.gif" ALIGN=MIDDLE
ALT="*Video Clip*">Tree lighting ceremony (2.8MB AVI)</A></P>
<P><A HREF="carolers.AVI"><IMG SRC="vidclip.gif" ALIGN=MIDDLE
ALT="*Video Clip*">Carolers passing by the Window (2.5 MB AVI)
</A></P>
<P><A HREF="first.snow.AVI"><IMG SRC="vidclip.gif" ALIGN=MIDDLE
ALT="*Video Clip*">First Snow Fall  (1.1MB MPEG)</A></P>
<H3>Other Holiday Videos</H3>
<P><A HREF="newyear.MOV"><IMG SRC="vidclip.gif" ALIGN=MIDDLE
ALT="*Video Clip*">New Year's Eve in the Big Apple (3.8MB MOV)
</A></P>
<P><A HREF="fourjuly.MOV"><IMG SRC="vidclip.gif" ALIGN=MIDDLE
ALT="*Video Clip*">Fireworks (2.9MB MOV)</A></P>
<HR>
<P> (C) 1995 by The ABC Press</P>
</BODY>
</HTML>
```

#### Chapter 22

FIGURE 22.11.

A multimedia archive at the ABC Press.

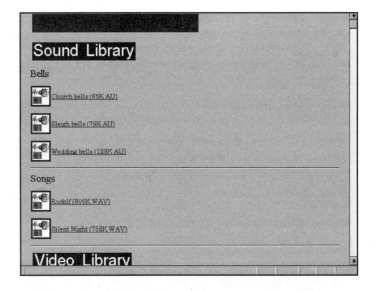

FIGURE 22.12.

Video library collection in the ABC Press multimedia archive.

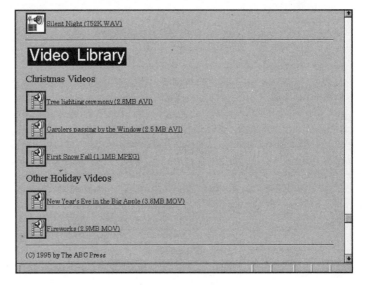

Summary

Sound, video, and graphics are powerful mediums for your message. On the Web, you can find hundreds of tools for creating, editing and converting multimedia. There are also multimedia archives on the Web where you can find thousands of multimedia files.

Web pages can contain inline images or links to external media. Inline images can accent the page and make it more visually appealing. With thumbnail images, you can link to large images on other Web pages or external media that require the user to have a helper application configured. Multimedia, such as sound, computer animation, and full-motion video, will attract visitors to your site.

Web Servers, Gateway Scripts, and Helper Applications

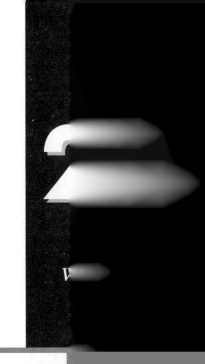

To set up your Web pages, you've taken into account the principles of graphic design, storyboarding, and more. However, unleashing your finely crafted HTML documents on the free world is what you really want to do, and that is exactly what this chapter is all about.

In the first part of this chapter, you learn everything you need to get started publishing your work:

- How to publish on the Web
- What a Web server is
- How to install, support, and maintain your documents on the server
- What connection options are available
- When to rent space on a Web server
- When to buy your own Web server

Publishing on the Web

The World Wide Web (WWW or W3) is an information system based on hypertext. The hypertext transfer protocol (HTTP) offers a means of moving from document to document or of indexing within documents. A *protocol* is a set of rules for programs communicating on the network. It specifies how the programs talk to each other and what meaning to give to the data they receive. Accessing documents on the Web involves communications between two key elements: browsers and servers.

Browser Communications

In a browser, such as Netscape, the HTTP processes are "virtually" transparent to the user. All the user really has to do is activate links to move through your Web presentation. The browser takes care of interpreting the hypertext transfer commands and communicating requests.

Server Communications

The mechanism on the receiving end, which is processing the requests, is a program called the Hypertext Transfer Protocol Daemon (HTTPD). That's *daemon* with a long "a," not *demon* as I've heard these programs called before—because they lurk in the background and handle tasks rather transparently once running. Daemon is a UNIX term for a program that runs in the background and handles requests. If you've used a UNIX system, you have probably unknowingly sent requests to the line-printer daemon (LPD) to print material to a printer using the commands lp or lpr. The HTTP daemon resides on the Web server, which is at the heart of your connection to the World Wide Web. Your documents will "live" on a Web server.

What Is a Web Server?

Understanding how a Web server works is essential to your decision either to purchase your own server or to rent time on an out-of-house server. Web servers present information to browser programs based on requests made via the HTTP daemon. Requests are usually in the form of Universal Resource Locators (URLs), which specify the path to your resource. A typical URL, or path to a resource, would be as follows:

```
http://www.anywhere.com/yourdocument.html
```

> **NOTE**
>
> If a request is for a resource located on the local server, the machine where your Web documents live, the server handles the request.
>
> If the request is for a resource located on another server, the local server redirects the request to the server that should process the request.

URLs can also specify programs that return information to your document, launch other documents or provide input to create dynamic documents on demand. Programs launched by the Web server are called *gateway scripts*. The specification that describes how gateways pass information to the server is called the Common Gateway Interface (CGI). CGI provides the basis for creating interactive forms, image maps, and much more. It's a powerful tool for creating interactive documents on demand.

Web Server Fundamentals

There are four things to consider regardless of whether you want to rent space through an Internet service provider or purchase your own Web server:

- How to organize your documents into directories
- How to install your documents
- How to maintain your documents
- How to support your documents

Organizing Documents into Directories

Data organization is the most important design issue in setting up a Web site. Whether you're thinking on a grand scale or a small scale, you should consider how you will organize your documents. All businesses large and small must understand the implications of the information infrastructure they are creating. The power of Web publishing is that you can seamlessly integrate complex presentations. Behind those complex presentations are dozens, possibly hundreds, of individual documents, images, and more. The result can either be a tangled mess to maintain or, if organized properly, a pleasant task. But the implications of the information infrastructure you are breathing life into are even more extensive.

Once you set up a directory structure, thousands of users (potentially millions) around the world may create links to your documents. If you delete, rename, or move documents, all those links become invalid. You not only will frustrate users, but they may decide to look elsewhere for their information needs—especially if you change page location links frequently.

CAUTION

Directory structures should not be created without careful thought. Linking all the departmental documents into your organization's hierarchy once the infrastructure is in place could result in a horrible mess.

Suppose one department within a large organization decided to put all its documents into the main directory thinking that other departments could use subdirectories. This department's material is now at the top of your directory hierarchy, and, to the outside world looking in, everything this department does seems representative of the entire organization.

For example, suppose that this department posted a directory of departmental personnel in a file called `http://www.yourcompany.com/personnel.html`. How do you now post a personnel directory for another department or for the organization as a whole? What happens when two departments choose the same directory name? Does one department go back and change references in hundreds of documents? To keep that from happening, here are some rules to follow when organizing documents into directories:

- Documents at the top level of the directory hierarchy should pertain to the overall organization.

  For example, the document `http://www.yourcompany.com/index.html` would be an index containing links to the organization's resources on the Web.

- Each department or division within an organization should have a separate subdirectory for its overview documents and projects.

  For example, the document `http://www.yourcompany.com/HR/index.html` could be the overview document for the human resources department.

- Each project should be organized into its own logically named subdirectory.

  For example, your book on the Internet could be in a subdirectory called `I-book` or `Internet.book`.

- Each document within a particular presentation should be named logically.

  For example, the documents `ibook.overview.html`, `ibook.pg1.html`, and `ibook.pg2.html` would be links to the title page and subsequent pages of your Web book on the Internet.

■ Graphic images, sound clips, or full-motion video should reside in a common directory if possible.

For example, company GIFs could be in the directory `http://www.yourcompany.com/extras/gifs`.

Installing Documents

A common and mistaken myth about renting space on an Internet service provider's Web server is that it will be difficult to install and update documents once you put them on the server. This simply is not true and depends entirely on how the service provider set up the server. Your documents could reside in your account in a public directory such as `public_html`. Within this public directory, you could create a directory hierarchy suitable for multiple complex projects.

Regardless of whether you rent space or buy your own Web server, you can install documents on the server as soon as you've decided on a directory structure. Here are a few rules to follow for file installation:

■ Make the subdirectories either in the appropriate location on the Web server or under the `public_html` directory in your account.

■ Copy the documents to the appropriate location.

■ Change the name of HTML documents and files, giving them the proper file extension (`.html`, `.gif`, `.jpeg`, `.mpeg`, `.mov`, `.wav`, and so on) if necessary.

■ Change the mode of the documents to ensure they are in the appropriate mode for Web access.

■ Always proofread and test your documents after installation.

NOTE

It's easy to set up the Web server to map requests to a subdirectory in a user's home directory. Typically, all the service provider or system administrator must do to enable this feature is to set a variable called `UserDir` to the subdirectory that will be mapped to users' home directories, such as:

```
UserDir        public_html
```

If the above variable is set, local users can publish their own pages directly on the Web without going through the service provider or system administrator. For example, requests to `http://www.provider.com/~yourcompany` would be mapped to the subdirectory called `public_html` in your company's account. This issue and the associated security concerns are discussed in later chapters.

Making Directories

It's important to set up your directory structure in the proper location either on the Web server or within a public_html directory. On UNIX systems, the permissions set for the directories are very important. The permissions should be set so that only you have write permission for the directory. For security reasons, outsiders should only be able to read and execute the files in these directories.

Help with Copying Files

There are several ways to copy your documents to the Web server or to an appropriate subdirectory within your public_html directory. The two most common methods to transfer the files are File Transfer Protocol (FTP) or Zmodem transfer.

Using FTP to Move Files

There are pitfalls associated with moving files using FTP. The safest way to transfer files using FTP is to always initiate binary transfers. That way you won't have to worry about which files are binary and which files aren't. When moving files from a Macintosh to a different computer platform such as UNIX, you should transfer the files as regular binary files and not Macintosh binary files. Other computer platforms cannot read Macintosh binary files.

FTP commands are fairly straightforward and thankfully few. The two most useful FTP commands to learn are

```
?
help
```

Initiate an FTP session by typing **FTP** then pressing Enter. This will put in FTP's command mode. Now type in **?** (or **help**) on a line by itself, followed by Enter; a list of commands will scroll onto the screen. If you type **help** *command*, you'll get a brief description of the command's function. For example, typing the following will provide a brief summary of the get command:

help get

The FTP commands you'll use the most are these:

Command	Description
ftp *hostname*	Initiate an FTP session where *hostname* is the name of the machine you want to transfer files to or receive files from.
bye	End an FTP session.
cd	Change directories.
dir	Print the current directory to the screen.
get	Transfer a file to your machine.

help	Get helpful information or a list of commands.
mget	Transfer multiple files to your machine.
mput	Transfer multiple files to another machine.
put	Transfer a file to another machine.

Moving Files by Modem

There are many modem transfer protocols that could be used to transfer files. The Zmodem transfer protocol is increasing in popularity because of its ease of use and reliability. You would initiate a Zmodem transfer within your communications program while connected to the Internet. There are only two commands you'll ever have to learn:

Command	Description
rz	Receive via Zmodem transfer protocol.
sz	Send via Zmodem transfer protocol.

Typing sz or rz and then pressing Enter from the Internet host will give you a brief summary of the commands. The most basic format is as follows, where *filename* is the name of the file to transfer:

```
rz filename
```

The great thing about transferring via modem is that current modem software is making it easier to transfer files this way. On recent versions of communication software, the transfer process is largely automated.

Naming Conventions for Documents

When moving files between different types of platforms, you must observe the filename restrictions. On a DOS-based machine, filenames must be only eight characters long with a three-character extension. When moving files from a DOS machine, you should give them a proper extension, such as .html, .jpeg, .mpeg, and so on. Some UNIX systems do not recognize files with an .htm extension as an HTML document. Before moving files to a DOS-based machine, the files must be renamed to conform to DOS naming conventions.

Other things to watch out for are wildcard characters in filenames. On a Macintosh system, it's perfectly acceptable to use wildcards when naming files. However, other systems may not recognize these special characters.

CAUTION

When moving files to or from a UNIX system, it's important to remember that UNIX is case sensitive. A file with a name in uppercase letters becomes a different file if saved in lowercase letters. UNIX also lets you use filenames containing a mixture of upper-

and lowercase letters. Filenames on your DOS machine are shown in all uppercase or all lowercase letters. When you move DOS files to a UNIX system, the filenames will be in all lowercase letters and must be referenced as such in any document links.

Change the Mode of the Documents

The mode of the documents refers to the permissions allowed to users of the document. The permissions that can be granted or denied are read, write, and execute. The mode of documents is particularly problematic on UNIX systems. Just as you must set the mode of the directory in which your files are stored, you must also set the mode of the files you put into the directory. Make sure that files have the appropriately restricted mode for Web access, such as 705 on a UNIX system, which means that the file is readable, writable, and executable by you, but only readable and executable by others.

Check Your Documents After Installation

Always test your documents after installation to double-check their appearance, accessibility, and correct interworkings. Use a browser, like visitors to the Web space will use, to check format and appearance. Sometimes during transfer, data will get garbled. Also, different platforms have different methods for specifying the end of a line. Usually, this is not a problem because in HTML tags are used to specify the format of text: <P> and </P> specify new paragraphs. However, HTML text that has been preformatted using the <PRE> tag may not display on the reader's browser the way you expect it to.

Testing Your Documents After Installation

Testing your documents goes hand in hand with checking your documents. As a rule of thumb, try using different browsers. Documents viewed using the popular Netscape browser will not look the same when viewed in a browser such as Air Mosaic. You may have to tweak your documents for optimal appearance on different types of browsers.

If your documents contain forms, e-mail, or other special types of links, you should test them with a browser such as Netscape that is capable of dealing with forms.

NOTE

Testing with several browsers is something that some electronic publishers completely ignore. You can notice this immediately if you visit such a site with a browser other than the one the publisher used to test the pages on. Sometimes these pages are completely unreadable or unusable. When this happens, users simply do not return to the site. Making sure aspects of your pages are optimized correctly for many types of users is a small price to pay to attract many types of readers to your site.

Document Maintenance

Now that you've properly organized and installed the Web documents, maintaining them will be an easier task. Obviously, there will be situations when the documents have to be updated, deleted, and possibly renamed. When making these changes, it's important to remember those thousands of users around the world who may have links to your documents on their home pages, in bookmarks, or in other annotations.

The cardinal rule of document maintenance is: Inform users when changes occur. A little common courtesy to those who visit your Web space goes a long way. This can be as simple as telling users that you've added something to your pages by inserting an inline graphic image into a document that says "New!"

For large or complex Web spaces, having a "What's New" page is a great way to inform users of recent changes. Again, common courtesy goes a long way. Repeat visitors to your Web space will appreciate the effort because a "What's New" page makes it easier for them to use your Web space efficiently. You will save them time, help them find new information faster, and ultimately, they'll return the favor by revisiting your friendly Web site again.

When deleting, moving, or renaming documents, exercise prudence. Do not shuffle documents around haphazardly! Delete, move, or rename documents only when it serves a useful purpose or when a main resource link is no longer valid. Whenever possible, substitute a placeholder document for the old document. The placeholder should contain either a link to the new document or a message stating the document was deleted. After a sufficient time, you can retire the placeholder document.

You should also consider the other side of document maintenance. Links posted in your pages to other resources on the Web can also get changed, deleted, or moved. Someone should be assigned the task of periodically checking the validity of links posted in your pages.

NOTE

If dozens or hundreds of documents are involved, it may not be possible or practical to substitute placeholder documents. In this case, substitute a placeholder document in place of the main link to the old resources whenever possible.

Document Support

Building and maintaining an information infrastructure simply is not enough. The new infrastructure must also be supported and promoted within the organization and outside the organization. This includes training personnel as necessary and communicating an organization-wide policy concerning the Internet resources you've created.

Every site has a *webmaster*, an electronic mail alias that provides a point of contact at the site. Web users can direct queries or comments to the webmaster. A mail alias is a generic mail address that can be assigned to a single user or group of users. On UNIX systems, common administrative mail aliases are `root` and `postmaster`. By assigning the `root` mail alias to your system administrator, she can receive feedback concerning system problems. By assigning the `postmaster` alias to your e-mail administrator, he can receive feedback for e-mail problems.

Similarly, the `webmaster` alias can be a single person, your system administrator, or many people who answer specific types of questions. The mail address for the webmaster is typically `webmaster@yourcompany.com`.

> **TIP**
>
> If you are obtaining service via an Internet service provider, webmaster queries normally go to the service provider. However, a mail alias with a similar function can be used in your Web space. The service provider can assign a generic mail alias to the person or persons you wish to handle general queries and comments about your Web space.

Things To Consider Before Making Buy-versus-Rent Decisions

Before determining whether it is best for the enterprise to rent space on a Web server or purchase a Web server there are many things to consider. Factors that will influence the decision are

- The size of the presentations that will be posted to the Web
- The volume of use of the site
- The nature and purpose of the use
- The size and type of the company
- Whether your company is already connected to the Internet
- Whether your company already runs an internal network
- The cost of connecting to the Internet
- What your company hopes to gain from its Web presence

The Size of the Presentations Posted to the Web

Before making any decision to buy or rent space on a Web server, you should estimate the actual storage space you'll need based on the type and length of documents you plan to publish on the Web. The average HTML document may only require between 2 and 8KB of storage space for its textual component, but even the smallest button GIF can add 1KB to your storage needs. Large GIFs may eat up 10–100KB each. Full-motion video or sound clips can eat up megabytes (1,000,000 bytes).

> **TIP**
>
> Internet service providers normally provide the first .5–2MB of storage space free. Additional storage space usually can be obtained at a cost of $1–5 per megabyte. Provisions for and costs of additional storage space should be detailed in the contract between you and the service provider.

The Volume of Use of the Site

The projected number of visitors to the Web space will influence your buy-versus-rent decision. An Internet service provider may have the line capacity to handle the load of a few hundred additional visitors to the Web site each day, but if the hundreds turn into thousands, the service provider's system could quickly become overloaded.

> **TIP**
>
> Read the fine print of your agreement with the service provider carefully. Some service providers charge fees based on the number of times that pages at your site are accessed. Typically, the first 25–50,000 accesses are included as part of your monthly premium. Accesses over the stated limit may have a per-access fee attached, which can range from affordable to outrageous.

The Nature and Purpose of the Use

The projected number of visitors to the Web space may be small, but the type of resources they'll be accessing determines the nature and purpose of the use of your Web space. For example, will users be accessing simple text documents with inline graphics, fill-out forms that have to be processed and that require access to programs in the `cgi-bin` directory, full-motion video that requires a great deal of bandwidth during retrieval, or databases that are maintained by company personnel?

The Size and Type of Your Company

Large organizations may have different concerns from smaller organizations, but their large size does not exclude them from taking the simple alternative of renting space on a Web server. In some situations this is a very practical decision. Similarly, just because an organization is small does not mean it shouldn't consider setting up a Web server.

Is the Company Already Connected to the Internet?

If the company is connected to the Internet, a communications infrastructure of some type is already in place. The company has either chosen to set up Internet services in-house or go through an outside source. If the services were set up in-house, there may be a workstation available for use as a Web server. This would of course depend on the workstation's current load and purpose.

Does the Company Already Run an Internal Network?

The company may have workstations suitable to serve as a Web server, but the private nature of the internal network may conflict with the open nature of the Internet. Many potential hazards are associated with doing business on the Internet. Security is the biggest risk area for private companies connecting to the Internet. One security solution is to set up a firewall or intermediary between the internal network and the workstation connecting to the Internet.

The safest security solution is to set up a stand-alone workstation that is not connected to the internal network. The *Internet Business Guide: Riding the Information Superhighway for Profit* discusses connecting to the Internet and the risks and realities of connecting to the Internet in some depth. Security concepts for documents are discussed further in this book in Chapter 25, "Advertising and Protecting Your Document."

The real question is not whether the benefits outweigh the risks. The benefits far outweigh the risks as long as the risks are put in perspective and precautions are taken to safeguard the company's interests. The real question that would-be Web publishers should ask is: What are the potential risks of not establishing a Web presence?

The Cost of Connecting to the Internet

The cost of an Internet connection is largely determined by the area in which the service is obtained and the type of connection. There are two basic connection options available for Web services:

> Dedicated connections
> Dial-up connections

Both types of connections give you full access to the Web. With dedicated connections, you either can connect directly to the Internet, which is the most costly method, or you can connect via a service provider. Either way, you must have a workstation that is configured and dedicated for a network connection. Depending on the speed and reliability you want for the connection, you may also need leased lines. A typical leased line is a dedicated 56Kbps line that connects your Web server to the Internet. With a leased line, you get the certainty that the line is always available and is relatively free of noise. A noise-free line will allow for efficient transmission at or near the speed the line is rated for. Internet service providers are becoming very competitive when it comes to dedicated connections. Basically, service providers are leasing you their excess capacity. With a dedicated connection, you'll be able to provide 24-hour Web services to users worldwide, but the cost will be hundreds to thousands of dollars depending on the speed of the connection.

Dial-up connections require a workstation with networking software and a modem, whereas the workstation does not have to be dedicated to networking. You can also use standard phone lines to connect to the Internet. With a dial-up connection, you can operate your own Web server or publish your documents on the service provider's Web server. If you choose to operate your own Web server, the public will have access to your documents only when the server is online. A dial-up connection to the Internet is the least expensive option, costing from $20–100.

NOTE

A local Internet service provider here in Hawaii, Flex Information Network (`http://www.aloha.com`), charges $24.95 per month for a full SLIP/PPP account with unlimited access to the Internet at speeds of up to 28.8Kbps. Flex provides 2MB of storage space with each account, and additional storage space is charged at a rate of $1 per megabyte per month. Flex users can publish their documents on the Flex Web server free of charge. Flex also offers the bargain rate of $14.95 per month to students and senior citizens. These bargain prices are the result of tough competition in a highly populated area. The good news is that as competition increases between service providers and as the number of Internet users grows, the price of Internet accounts should start to fall.

What Does the Company Hope To Gain from Its Web Presence?

This is the bottom-line question that all Web publishers must ask themselves. Fitting Web publishing in with the company's mission and goals as well as setting a company-wide Internet policy are the keys to the success of your e-publishing ventures. The Web is an unparalleled medium for world-wide advertising and marketing that can help any business (regardless of its size) reach a global audience. The Web levels the playing field, allowing a one-person operation to compete head-to-head with corporate conglomerates that employ thousands of people.

Competing in the global marketplace requires planning from day one because, without direction, your Web operation will flounder. You must establish objectives and define what you hope to gain from your Web ventures. You must establish an identity for yourself and your company. To do this you must use your skills, ideas, and company name to sell yourself and your company to the world.

The face of the Web is changing rapidly. Early Web publishers were primarily individual entrepreneurs who created small sites with one or two interesting items. This changed dramatically as large corporations flexed their muscles and vied for the attention of the millions of Web users. For a time, the entrepreneurs prevailed, yet the big fish bought what they couldn't create, and many of the hot sites are getting gobbled up.

To establish a presence on tomorrow's Web, you must adopt a vision for success focused on global outreach. Remember, it will not be the size of your site that sells your ideas and products. It will be your vision and ability to find a niche in the world community.

When To Rent Space on a Web Server

The factors discussed in the previous sections should help you make the decision to buy a Web server or to rent space on a commercial Web server. Ultimately, if most of the following circumstances are true for your company, renting space would be a good idea:

- You have insufficient in-house resources to support and maintain the Web server.
- Budget constraints limit the amount of funds that can be allocated to the electronic publishing project.
- Your goals are primarily for the short term, or you wish to experiment.
- The total size of your planned or actual publishing projects is small, and you can obtain sufficient storage space at a reasonable cost from a local service provider.
- The projected usage of the site is less than 10,000 page accesses per week.
- The type of documents that will be accessed do not involve databases or require excessive bandwidth.
- You want to publish your documents in a hurry.

When To Buy Your Own Web Server

The decision to buy a Web server should be made only after careful consideration is given to the costs associated with the installation, maintenance, and support of the information infrastructure you wish to build. Purchasing a Web server could be the first step to great success in electronic publishing if the decision to buy-versus-rent was made for the right reasons.

Ultimately, if most of the following circumstances are true for your company, purchasing a Web server would be a good idea:

- You have sufficient in-house resources to support and maintain the Web server, or you could obtain these resources in a way that agrees with the company's mission and goals.

- Budget constraints won't severely limit the amount of funds that can be allocated to the electronic publishing project.

- You have long-term goals for electronic publishing and an interest in establishing a major online presence.

- The total size of your planned or actual publishing projects is substantial.

- The projected usage of the site is more than 10,000 page accesses per week.

- The type of documents that will be accessed involve databases or require excessive bandwidth.

> **NOTE**
>
> The location of CGI programs and CGI utilities may also influence a decision to rent space on or buy a Web server. CGI programs are usually located in a directory called `cgi-bin` in the usr file system. CGI utilities are usually located in a directory called `cgi-src` in the usr file system.
>
> If you rent space on a commercial Web server, you may not have control over what happens to programs or utilities located in these directories. You may have to rely on your Internet service provider to manage these directories. The bottom line is this: If you decide to rent space through an Internet service provider, make sure the wording of your contract is very clear as to your rights on the system and the service provider's obligations to you.

Gateway Scripts, Editors, and Converters

Links in HTML documents can call programs that return information to a Web document or launch other programs. You can even create customized documents on-the-fly based on a user's inputs. The specification that describes how gateways pass information to the server is called Common Gateway Interface (CGI). It allows HTML documents to call external programs. By calling external programs, you can make your Web publications highly interactive and extremely dynamic. CGI provides the basis for creating interactive forms, image maps, and much more.

Fill-out forms and image maps are the most advanced features of the hypertext markup language, and the CGI specification is the enabling structure behind these advanced features. This part of the chapter provides an overview of these advanced HTML features. It also shows how to practically apply the concepts using editors, converters, and ready-to-use scripts—tools that dramatically reduce the complexity of CGI and HTML. Here's what you'll learn:

- What the Common Gateway Interface is
- What gateway scripts are
- Why to use gateway scripts

- How gateway scripts work
- How to write gateway scripts
- How to use fill-out forms
- How to use image maps
- What helper applications are available
- Where to find helper applications on the Web

What the Common Gateway Interface Is

You've seen references to the Common Gateway Interface specification in previous chapters. CGI is a most remarkable and powerful addition to the hypertext markup language and all because the specification defines the process of interfacing with external programs. *Interface* seems such a portentous word, but it's something computer users do every day. When you write a letter using your favorite word processor, you are interfacing with the computer. However, most of the time you aren't concerned about how the word processor works, only that it does work. The word processor reduces the complex process of creating, storing, editing, and printing documents to a few basic procedures. In today's computer environment, these steps usually require activating a pull-down menu, a few keystroke combinations, and occasionally textual input.

For the reader of your Web pages, the CGI specification works in a similar manner. CGI reduces the complex process of interfacing with external programs to a few basic procedures. The reader must only click on an area of an image map or submit their fill-out form after completing it. Everything after the click of the mouse button happens automatically. What is more important, processing takes place behind the scenes so the reader doesn't have to worry about the how or why, only that it works.

Behind the scenes, the server is directing the input to the external program for processing. These external programs are called *CGI scripts*. Once the external program finishes processing the input, it normally directs output back to the user. This output can be anything from the results of a database search to a completely new document generated based on the user's input.

These background processes are what electronic publishers care most about. Thankfully, the CGI specification defines for you how these processes are directed to external programs. This enables the electronic publisher to concentrate on the external programs and their required input and output.

What CGI Scripts Are

CGI scripts are programs on the Web server that can be called by HTML documents. CGI scripts are also called *gateway scripts*. As with many computer terms, the word *script* as it is associated with CGI is somewhat of a misnomer. The term *script* came from the UNIX environment where shell scripts abound, but gateway scripts don't have to be in the format of a script. You can write them in almost any computer language that produces an executable file. The most common languages scripts are written in are

C/C++
C Shell
Bourne Shell
Korn Shell
Perl

Just because Perl, C/C++, and UNIX shells are the most popular languages for scripts doesn't mean you should write your scripts in these languages. The best computer language for you to write scripts in is the one you're most proficient in. If you're in a Windows environment, you might prefer using batch files to an actual programming language. This is fine as long as the file is executable.

On UNIX systems, CGI scripts usually are located in a directory called `cgi-bin` in the usr file system and CGI utilities usually are located in a directory called `cgi-src` in the usr file system. On other systems, your Web server documentation will explain what directories CGI scripts and utilities should be placed in. One common use for CGI programs is to track visitors to Web pages and post continually updated numbers to the Web page as it is accessed. Another common use for CGI programs is to process inputs, typically database search strings, and output a document containing the results of the database search.

Why Use CGI Scripts?

At this point, you may be worried about having to program and be wondering why you would want to use gateway scripts at all. This is a valid concern. Learning a programming language isn't easy, but as you'll see in later sections of this chapter, you may never have to program at all. Typically, you'll be able to use existing programs, thus reducing the complexity of the problem another level.

There are many reasons to use gateway scripts, but the primary reason is to automate what would otherwise be a manual—and probably time-consuming—process. Using gateway scripts benefits the reader and you. The reader gets simplicity—automated responses to input, easy ways to make submissions, or fast ways to conduct searches. By making things easier for the reader—the customer—you benefit directly. Gateway scripts also let you automatically process orders, queries, and much more.

How CGI Scripts Work

The basic requirement for a gateway script is an input. Input is usually in the form of environment variables passed to the gateway script by the Web server. Environment variables describe operating parameters and the information being passed. These variables define the version of CGI used on the server, the type of data, the size of the data, and much more.

Readers of your Web pages initiate this process by activating a link containing a reference to a gateway script. The gateway script processes the input and formats the results as output the Web server can use. The Web server takes the results and passes them back to the reader's browser. The browser displays the output for the reader.

Again, all this processing is hidden from the reader. The only real part of the process you have to worry about is providing input to the gateway script and ensuring the output is in a form usable by a browser. Usually, the output is in the form of an HTML document, but it also can be instructions to the server for retrieving a document.

Input to CGI Scripts

Although input to gateway scripts is usually in the form of environment variables, gateway scripts also receive input as command-line arguments and standard input. As you read through this section, keep in mind that in order to execute a script, the script must exist on the server you are referencing. You must also have a server that is both capable of executing gateway scripts and configured to handle the type of scripts you plan to use.

Environment Variables

The Web server passes environment variables to gateway scripts. These variables are associated with the browser requesting information from the server, the server processing the request, and the data passed in the request. This section includes basic descriptions of environment variables. Familiarize yourself with the variables and values, but don't try to memorize them. As you'll see from later examples, these variables are set automatically by passing a gateway script to the server in the correct format.

AUTH_TYPE	The authentication method used to validate a user. Used only on servers that support user authentication and only if the script is protected.
CONTENT_LENGTH	Used to provide a way of tracking the length of the data string as a numeric value—the number of characters in the data passed to the gateway script.
CONTENT_TYPE	Indicates the MIME type of data. The variable is set when passing attached data to the standard input stream. The format is *type/subtype*.
GATEWAY_INTERFACE	Indicates the version of the CGI specification the server is using. The value is *name/version*. For example, CGI/1.1.
HTTP_ACCEPT	The MIME content types the browser will accept, as passed by the server from HTTP header information. The format is *type/subtype*.

HTTP_USER_AGENT	The type of browser used to send the request, as passed by the server from HTTP header information. The format is *software type/version* or *library/version*.
PATH_INFO	The extra information included in the URL, after the identification of the gateway script. The format is */path/to/gateway/script/extra/path/information*.
PATH_TRANSLATED	The server translates the PATH_INFO variable into this variable. It does this by inserting the default Web document's directory path in front of the extra path information as in the following example: */path/to/web/documents/extra/path/information*.
QUERY_STRING	If the URL contains a query string, this variable is set to the query string. The information following a ? in the URL is the query information.
REMOTE_ADDR	The numerical address (Internet IP address) of the remote computer making the request.
REMOTE_HOST	The name of the machine making the request. This will be set only if the server can determine this information.
REMOTE_IDENT	The identification of the machine making the request. This variable will be set only if the server and the remote machine making the request support the identification protocol.
REMOTE_USER	The user name as authenticated by the user. As with other types of user authentication, this variable will be set only if the server supports user authentication and the gateway script is protected.
REQUEST_METHOD	The method by which the request was made. For HTTP, the methods could be any of the following: GET, HEAD, POST, or PUT.
SCRIPT_NAME	The virtual path to the script being executed. This is useful if the script generates an HTML document that references the script.
SERVER_NAME	Identifies the server by its hostname, alias, or IP address.
SERVER_PORT	The port number the server received the request on.
SERVER_PROTOCOL	Indicates the protocol of the request sent to the server. The format is *name/version*, such as HTTP/1.0.
SERVER_SOFTWARE	Identifies the server's software. This format is *name/version*, such as NCSA/1.3.

The HTTP_ACCEPT and CONTENT_TYPE variables can have a number of values. These variables are important because they describe the types of data the browser will accept and the actual type of data. If the gateway script returns an invalid data type to the browser, the browser won't know how to handle it. The data in these variables is expressed as *type/subtype*. Each *type/subtype* pair is separated by commas, as in *type/subtype, type/subtype*. The first part of the pair is the basic type of data—is the data text, audio, video, or an application-specific type of data? The second part of the pair specifies a format for the data. Some common *type/subtype* pairs are shown in Table 23.1.

Table 23.1. Common MIME types.

type/subtype	*Description*
Text/plain	Plain text with no HTML formatting included
Text/html	HTML-formatted text
Text/richtext	RTF-formatted text
Application/postscript	PostScript-formatted data
Audio/basic	Audio in a nondescript format
Audio/x-aiff	Audio in AIFF format
Image/gif	An image in GIF format
Image/jpeg	An image in JPEG format
Image/tiff	An image in TIFF format
Video/mpeg	Video in the MPEG format

Command-Line Arguments

The term *command line* is used by programmers in many ways. The use discussed in this section comes from UNIX X Window System environments where users can pass information or execute shell scripts from an area known as the command line. Information typed on the command line is normally passed as input to an interpreter that uses the input to carry out an action.

The command line is usually used to perform an ISINDEX query. An ISINDEX query is a way to pass a search string to a gateway script. To activate an ISINDEX query, the user must first access a gateway script that generates an HTML document containing the ISINDEX tag. When the user enters information requested by the query, a special URL containing the path to the original script and the information the user typed in is sent to the server as a single input. A question mark is used to separate the script's path information from the user's query. For example, if the path to the script is

```
http://www.mcp.com/cgi-bin/squery
```

and the user enters the following command at the command line:

```
books
```

the resulting input sent back to the server would be

```
http://www.mcp.com/cgi-bin/squery?books
```

The server receiving the input splits the data into two variables based on the location of the question mark. The script URL is assigned to the environment variable SCRIPT_NAME. The form data is assigned to the environment variable QUERRY_STRING. The way an ISINDEX search works is very similar to the GET submission method for forms that will be discussed later in this chapter.

Command-line arguments can also be a neat way to directly execute a gateway script that will return a value or perform an action. The following HTML code contains a command-line argument that executes the named script, access_history:

```
<P>
Total Number of Visitors:
<!--#exec cmd="/usr/local/src/httpd/cgi-bin/access_history" -->
</P>
```

The access_history script is a simple counter program that adds one to the count of visitors every time a reader accesses a page. Using a similar technique, you could write a gateway script for use on your own Web server. Although the line of code to be executed is hidden within an HTML comment tag, the command still executes and returns a value that will be substituted in place of the comment. In this example, the reader sees only the outcome, the output that would be

```
Total Number of Visitors: 530
```

The number 530 is a cumulative total of visitors to your Web page.

NOTE

The interesting thing about using a command-line argument in the manner shown in the example is that even if readers view the HTML source code, they would see only the output value. This remains true even if they download the source to their computer and view it in their word processor. The reason for this is that the command is executed explicitly whenever it is encountered. Your server must be configured to process this type of command.

The part of the code that tells the software to execute the script is exec cmd, which is followed by the argument to execute enclosed in double quotation marks. In this case, the argument to execute is /usr/local/src/httpd/cgi-bin/access_history.

TIP

Remember that CGI programs usually are located in a directory called cgi-bin in the usr file system. If you are renting space on a commercial Web server, you may not have control over what happens to programs placed in this directory.

A simple work-around for this problem is to mail the contents of the form to your account using the "post" method:

```
<form method="POST"> <FORM ACTION="mailto:you@anywhere.com">
```

Once the information is posted in an e-mail message to your account, you can process it as you wish. The contents of the message will be URL encoded, but routines can be set up to translate this to a more readable form.

Standard Input

Forms send data to gateway scripts in two primary methods as a query string or directly as standard input for processing. To send data as standard input, you would use the HTTP POST method, which will be described in the section about fill-out forms. Sending data as standard input is the preferred way to pass data from fill-out forms because the direct method of passing data is also the less troublesome method.

Output to CGI Scripts

The output of gateway scripts must begin with a header containing a directive to the server. Currently there are three valid server directives: Content-type, Location, and Status. The header can consist of a directive in the format of an HTTP header followed by a blank line. The blank link separates the header from the data you are passing back to the browser. Output containing Location and Status directives usually are a single line. This is because the directive contained on the Location or Status line is all that is needed by the server and when there is no subsequent data you do not need to insert a blank line.

The three valid server directives are

Content-type	The MIME type of the document being passed back to the browser. For example: `Content-type:  text/html`
Location	Used to reference a specified document with a URL. If the document referenced by the URL is on the server, the server will pass the document to the browser. For example: `Location:  http://www.tvp.com/`
Status	Passes a status line to the server for forwarding to the browser. The format is a three-digit code and a string explaining what has happened. For example: `Status:  403 Forbidden`

A Gateway Script From Your Browser to the Server and Back

The best way to clarify input and output to gateway scripts is through an example that applies these concepts practically. This section contains a step-by-step explanation of the trip from your browser to the server and back to you. Figure 23.1 shows the Web page that the example begins with.

FIGURE 23.1.

Times Around the World Web page.

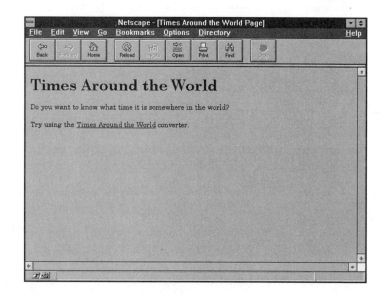

Here is the HTML code for the Times Around the World Web page:

```
<HTML>
<HEAD>
<TITLE>Times Around the World Page</TITLE>
</HEAD>
<BODY>
<H1>Times Around the World</H1>
<P>Do you want to know what time it is somewhere in the world?</P>
<P>Try using the
<A HREF="http://www.your_company.com/cgi-bin/times_around_world">
Times Around the World</A> converter.</P>
</BODY>
</HTML>
```

By activating the link, `Times Around the World`, you would be starting the gateway script embedded in the link. Your browser would contact the server at the site www.your_company.com. The value of the input coming into the server would be as follows:

```
argc is 0.
argv is .
```

566

```
PATH=/bin:/usr/bin:/usr/etc:/usr/ucb
SERVER_SOFTWARE = NCSA/1.3
SERVER_NAME = www.your_company.com
GATEWAY_INTERFACE = CGI/1.1
SERVER_PROTOCOL = HTTP/1.0
SERVER_PORT=80
REQUEST_METHOD = GET
HTTP_ACCEPT = text/plain, text/html, text/richtext, application/postscript,
audio/basic, audio/x-aiff, image/gif, image/jpeg, image/tiff, video/mpeg
PATH_INFO =
PATH_TRANSLATED =
SCRIPT_NAME = /cgi-bin/times_around_world
QUERRY_STRING =
REMOTE_HOST =
REMOTE_ADDR =
REMOTE_USER =
AUTH_TYPE =
CONTENT_TYPE =
CONTENT_LENGTH =
```

Because this example doesn't pass any data to the server, most of the environment variables are not set. You can see this immediately by the values of argc and argv. These variables have values when you pass data to the server. For example, if you passed a query to the server containing two values, the value of argc would be 2, and argv would know that the type is a query.

> **NOTE**
>
> argc is the traditional name for the first argument passed to a C program and is understood to be a count of the parameters being passed. argv is the traditional name for the second argument passed to a C program and is understood to point to the actual parameters being passed.

By examining the value of the environment variables that were set, you can determine the following:

- The default path set up for scripts is /bin:/usr/bin:/usr/etc:/usr/ucb.
- The type of server software is NCSA version 1.3.
- The name of the sever is www.your_company.com.
- The gateway interface is CGI version 1.1.
- The protocol of the server is HTTP version 1.0.
- The port the request came in on is 80.
- The method of the request is GET.
- The browser will accept responses in the form of text/plain, text/html, text/richtext, application/postscript, audio/basic, audio/x-aiff, image/gif, image/jpeg, image/tiff, and video/mpeg.
- The name of the script that the server is executing is times_around_world.

The script can make use of these environment variables if it needs to. If you programmed the `times_around_world` script in Bourne shell for an NCSA UNIX server, the script would look like this:

```
#!/bin/sh

echo "Content-type:  text/html"
echo
echo "<HTML>"
echo "<HEAD><TITLE>Times Around The World</TITLE></HEAD>"
echo "<BODY>"
echo "<H1>Times Around The World</H1>"

date_converter

echo "</BODY>"
echo "<HTML>"
```

The format of the script's output is defined in the header. Here, the output is in the form of an HTML document. Notice the `echo` statement separating the header from the body of the output. The `echo` statement inserts the blank line necessary to separate header information from the data. To keep the example simple, this script calls a UNIX program called `date_converter`, which does the actual work in creating a list of times for places around the world.

When the server runs `date_converter`, the current system time will be used to calculate the times around the world. The program will generate HTML code based on these calculations. The code will then be inserted into the Web document passed back to the reader's browser. The output from `date_converter` will look similar to this:

```
<H3>Time Zones & Cities</H3>
<P>2:05 AM  Los Angeles  <STRONG>Pacific Time Zone</STRONG></P>
<P></P>
<P>3:05 AM  Denver   <STRONG>Mountain Time Zone</STRONG></P>
<P></P>
<P>4:05 AM  Chicago   <STRONG>Central Time Zone</STRONG></P>
<P></P>
<P>5:05 AM  New York  <STRONG>Eastern Time Zone</STRONG></P>
<P></P>
<P>6:05 AM  Saint John  <STRONG>Atlantic Time Zone</STRONG></P>
```

The server sees the final output of the script as

```
Content-type:  text/html

<HTML>
<HEAD><TITLE>Times Around The World</TITLE></HEAD>
<BODY>
<H1>Times Around The World</H1>

<H3>Time Zones & Cities</H3>
<P>2:05 AM  Los Angeles  <STRONG>Pacific Time Zone</STRONG></P>
<P></P>
<P>3:05 AM  Denver   <STRONG>Mountain Time Zone</STRONG></P>
<P></P>
<P>4:05 AM  Chicago   <STRONG>Central Time Zone</STRONG></P>
<P></P>
```

```
<P>5:05 AM  New York  <STRONG>Eastern Time Zone</STRONG></P>
<P></P>
<P>6:05 AM  Saint John  <STRONG>Atlantic Time Zone</STRONG></P>

</BODY>
</HTML>
```

The server in turn passes this output to the browser. The part of the output displayed on the browser is the HTML document, as depicted in Figure 23.2.

FIGURE 23.2.

*The output of Times
Around the World.*

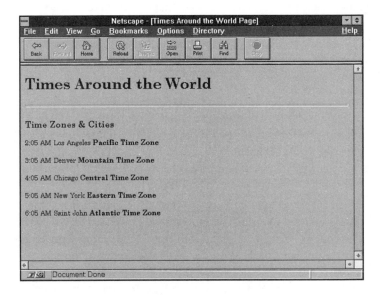

Broken down in order, the trip from your browser to the server and back may seem long, but all the processing takes place in a few hundred microseconds. This example shows that many environment variables are created automatically even if no real data is passed to the script. Just remember that these environment variables are available for use in scripts if you need them.

Consider a more complex example of how to use the environment variables passed to gateway scripts. In this example, I've chosen to program the script in the Perl language. Perl combines elements of C and UNIX shell features like awk, sed, and grep to create a powerful language for processing text strings. The Perl routine is called FormParse and has two main parts. The first subroutine determines the form submission method. Because all form input is URL encoded, the second subroutine decodes the URL encoding so the data can be used normally.

```
# Forms submit inputs to scripts using either the POST or GET method
# This simple script uses the environment variable REQUEST_METHOD
# to determine what method is being used to input data to the script.

  $METHOD = $ENV{'REQUEST_METHOD'};

# With the POST method, encoded form data is passed directly to the
# script as standard input.  Therefore, if we read the standard input for the
# number of characters determined by the CONTENT_LENGTH variable
```

```
# the standard input will be correctly read in.
# The input is stored in the variable SINPUT.

if  ( $METHOD eq 'POST' )
{
read(stdin, $SINPUT, $ENV{'CONTENT_LENGTH'});
}

# With the GET method, the form data is encoded into the URL.
# This encoded data is then assigned to the environment variable:
# QUERY_STRING.
# The input is stored in the variable SINPUT.
# Note:  The information following a ? in the URL is the query information.

else
if  ( $METHOD eq 'GET' )
{
$SINPUT = $ENV{'QUERY_STRING'};
}

# This last subroutine handles the situation of an invalid method type
# In the case of an invalid method, the script will simply exit.

else
{
exit( 1 );
}
# When data is passed to the script it is URL encoded
# URL encoded variable name and value pairs are separated by the &
# The first part of this routine divides the input back into distinct variable
# name and values.
#
# Note that the foreach structure is a loop that will be executed once for
# every occurrence of the &—or once for every value/pair of the input.

foreach $SINPUT (split(/&/))
{

# Encoded spaces are represented by +, the next line substitutes spaces
# The next step in URL decoding is to turn encoded spaces back to spaces

$SARRAY[$i] =~ s/\+/ /g;

# The input values are still represented in the form: input_name=value
# The next step is to split them back into distinct names and values so the
# data can be used as necessary.

($input_name, $value) = split(/=/,$SARRAY[$i],2);

# Special characters are represented as %hexadecimal value
# The next step is to convert hexadecimal to the standard character set
# so the data can be read normally.

$input_name =~ s/%(..)/pack("c",hex($1))/ge;
$value =~ s/%(..)/pack("c",hex($1))/ge;

# The final step is to assign the input_name to the value it should have
# This is done via the array
```

```
$SARRAY{$input_name} = $value;

}

# The input values can now be used according to the variable name and value
# from the fill-out form.
```

After executing `FormParse`, you would be able to manipulate the data stored in the array. Ideally, this data would be written to a file, passed to another script for further processing, or checked against a database.

Hopefully, you will never have to resort to programming routines to parse the output of forms. The software tools distributed with the server software probably will include a form-parsing tool. The key thing to remember is that all input to the gateway script, including the environment variables, can be used if the script is set up to manipulate the environment variables. If the parser script included with your server software doesn't meet your needs, you may want to consider creating your own parser to serve a specific purpose.

Keep in mind that dozens of ready-to-use gateway scripts are available on the Web. You'll often find that someone already has created a solution to a problem you're trying to solve. A great place to find gateway scripts is at NCSA's FTP site:

```
ftp://ftp.ncsa.uiuc.edu/Web/httpd/Unix/ncsa_httpd/cgi/
```

Another place to find useful CGI scripts is University of California at Berkeley:

```
http://violet.berkeley.edu/cgi.html
```

Now that you've seen how gateway scripts work, you're ready to learn about two advanced features you can include in your Web pages:

> Fill-out Forms
> Image maps

Using Fill-Out Forms

Although fill-out forms are widely used and a feature common to Web pages, support for forms was not included in the original HTML specification. This, unfortunately, means that older browser and server software does not support forms, but this is changing rapidly because browser and server creators just couldn't ignore one of the most advanced and versatile features of HTML. Presently, nearly all browsers support forms, and most servers not only support forms but often have tools that make parsing the output of forms easy. So, if you use a browser that doesn't support forms, check to see if an updated version that supports forms is available.

The *FORM* Tag

The FORM tag is used to define forms. The form is enclosed by the beginning-of-form tag, `<FORM>`, and closed with the end-of-form tag, `</FORM>`. Although multiple forms can be built in to a single Web page, you can't have subforms within other forms. The beginning-of-form tag can have three attributes:

ACTION="*action*"	The action to be performed when the form is submitted.
ENCTYPE="*type*"	The optional type of encoding to be performed on the form.
METHOD="*method*"	The method by which the form is to be submitted.

A FORM tag in an HTML document would look like either of the following:

```
<FORM METHOD="POST" ACTION="mailto:your_id@your_company.com">
```

```
<FORM METHOD="POST" ACTION="/path/to/cgi/script/to/be/executed">
```

The *ACTION* Attribute

The ACTION attribute specifies the action to be performed when a form is submitted. The ACTION attribute is mandatory for the form to get processed in some way and has more than one purpose. It either can specify the URL of the gateway script to be executed, or it can specify an actual action. An interesting fallout of being able to specify the URL path to the script is that the script doesn't have to be on the same server that the Web page containing the form is. The script can be on any server as long as the full path to the script is specified. If the script exists on your server, you can also specify the relative path to the script:

```
ACTION="../cgi-bin/script_name"
```

This ACTION could be inserted in the FORM tag as follows:

```
<FORM METHOD="POST" ACTION="../cgi-bin/FormParse">
```

Using the relative path to the script is useful primarily when the script and the Web page are located in subdirectories of a parent directory. Otherwise, it's just as easy to specify the full URL path to the script:

```
ACTION="/www.your_company.com/usr/cgi-bin/script_name"
```

This ACTION could be inserted in the FORM tag as follows:

```
<FORM METHOD="POST" ACTION="/www.mcp.com/usr/cgi-bin/FormParse">
```

The ACTION attribute can also refer to an actual action to be performed. Currently, the only action supported is mailto. This fairly new value for the ACTION attribute filled a large need to simply be able to mail the contents of the form to an intended recipient. Most current browser and server software supports the mailto value. You could use the mailto value in the FORM tag as follows:

```
<FORM METHOD="POST" ACTION="mailto:william@tvp.com">
```

Although form data from the example would be sent to william@tvp.com, you can specify any valid mail address as a recipient. From the perspectives of security and simplicity, the mailto value is one of the best options for forms. Because the contents of the form are mailed directly to an intended recipient, the data can be processed off-line as necessary. Making this an off-line process precludes many forms of code cracking. Keep the `mailto` value in mind if data from fill-out forms doesn't need immediate processing.

The *ENCTYPE* Attribute

The `ENCTYPE` attribute specifies how the server will encode the data output from the form. This attribute is optional. However, the general form for the attribute is

```
ENCTYPE="type"
```

You could use `ENCTYPE` in the `FORM` tag as follows:

```
<FORM METHOD="POST" ACTION="/www.mcp.com/usr/cgi-bin/FormParse"
ENCTYPE="x-www-form-encoded">
```

By default, form data will be `x-www-form-encoded`. This encoding is also called URL encoding. If you do not specify `ENCTYPE`, the default value is used automatically. Although there are other possible types of encoding, most forms you'll find on the Internet use the default, `x-www-form-encoded`, because other types of encoding are not widely available. Also, if you use other types of encoding, you'll need server software that supports it—and a whole new tool set to decode it.

The *METHOD* Attribute

The `METHOD` attribute specifies the method by which the form is to be submitted. The value can be either `GET` or `POST`. The preferred method is `POST`. I use the `POST` submission method in most of the examples in this chapter. With `POST` the form data is sent as a separate stream to the standard input, meaning the server passes the information directly to the gateway script without assigning variables or arguments. Using this method, there is no limit on the amount of data that can be passed to the gateway script. If you use the `POST` method with the `mailto` `ACTION`, the form data will be sent in the body of a mail message to the recipient you specify.

If you do not specify a method of submission, your form data will be sent to the server using the `GET` submission method. The `GET` method is restrictive and practical only for small amounts of data. Form data sent to the server using `GET` is appended to the script URL. The script URL and the form data are passed to the server as a single input. The server receiving the input assigns the data being passed to two variables. The script URL is assigned to the environment variable `SCRIPT_NAME`. The form data is assigned to the environment variable `QUERRY_STRING`.

Assigning the data to variables on a UNIX system means passing the data through the UNIX shell. There are limitations on the number of characters you can send to the UNIX shell in a single input, which means only a limited amount of data can be appended to the URL before truncation occurs. If truncation occurs you will lose some of the information. Because `GET` has limitations, it has fallen into disuse.

Elements Within Forms

Many elements are designed specifically to be used within forms. Within a form, you can use any of the HTML tags discussed in previous chapters of this book. The horizontal rule tag, <HR>, is useful to indicate the beginning and end of a form. Tags such as the paragraph tag, <P>, are useful to separate textual information for the reader. However, the elements designed specifically for use within forms are what make fill-out forms useful and highly interactive.

There are three key elements for use within forms:

INPUT	Used to define input fields.
SELECT	Used to create selection menus.
TEXTAREA	Used to define a multiple-line text input window.

Input Fields

The INPUT element is the most versatile form element. It is used to define input fields. This element has a number of values that determine how input fields will look on the screen. Using the INPUT element, you can create checkboxes, hidden elements, menu buttons, and more.

A basic INPUT element inside an HTML form would look like this:

```
<INPUT  TYPE="type of field"  NAME="input field name">
```

All input fields should have a NAME attribute and a TYPE attribute. The NAME attribute will be the variable name passed to the gateway script. The type of input fields are specified by the value of the TYPE attribute. There are eight values for the TYPE attribute:

CHECKBOX	Creates one or more boxes that can be checked by a user.
HIDDEN	A field that is not displayed to the user but is visible in the source.
IMAGE	An image that can be clicked on to submit the form.
PASSWORD	A text field where all data entered is seen as the * character.
RADIO	Creates one or more radio buttons that can be enabled by a user.
RESET	Creates a button that clears the form when clicked.
SUBMIT	Creates a button that submits the form when clicked.
TEXT	A one-line text field of a width defined in the form.

These types have many attributes that can be associated with them. Forms will let you try to associate just about any attribute with any type. However, certain attributes should be used with certain types. Knowing this will save you a lot of time when you create forms.

Checkboxes in Forms

Checkboxes are useful items to include in forms. CHECKBOX has four attributes that can be used with it:

CHECKED   The checkbox is automatically checked when viewed. It can provide users with a default option that can be unchecked if necessary.

DISABLED   The user can neither check nor uncheck a disabled checkbox. This is used primarily for testing forms to see if a certain condition exists. However, it can be useful for a mandatory input field that is checked, and the user acknowledges acceptance of a condition by submitting the form.

NAME   The variable name associated with the input field.

VALUE   The value of the input field if it is checked.

Checkboxes with the same NAME attribute allow groups of options to be listed together. Any or all these options can be checked. Here is a sample checkbox input field:

```
<INPUT  TYPE="checkbox" NAME="checkbox1"  VALUE="first-input"  >
```

Figure 23.3 depicts how checkboxes would be used in a form. The HTML code for the form would be as follows:

```
<FORM METHOD="POST" ACTION="mailto:your_id@your_company.com">
<H1>Checkbox</H1>
<P>What type of fruit do you prefer?
<P><INPUT  TYPE="checkbox" NAME="checkbox1"  VALUE="Apples"   CHECKED>Apples</P>
<P><INPUT  TYPE="checkbox" NAME="checkbox1"  VALUE="Bananas"  >Bananas</P>
<P><INPUT  TYPE="checkbox" NAME="checkbox1"  VALUE="Cherries" >Cherries</P>
<P><INPUT  TYPE="checkbox" NAME="checkbox1"  VALUE="None"  >None</P>
</FORM>
```

FIGURE 23.3.

Using checkboxes in forms.

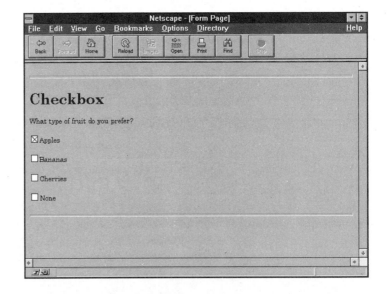

Hidden Elements in Forms

Hidden elements are input fields that are not displayed to the user. This element is useful to provide essential input to your script. For instance, you may want the same script to serve more than one purpose, or you may have several forms that are similar but you want to track the source. Hidden elements have two mandatory attributes:

NAME   The variable name associated with the input field.

VALUE   The initial value of the field.

Here is a sample hidden-form element:

```
<INPUT  TYPE="hidden" NAME="name"  VALUE="information_to_track">
```

Image Elements in Forms

Image elements are input fields used to submit the form and, as such, should be placed as one of the last elements on the form. Readers submit the form by clicking on the image. Image elements have three attributes:

ALIGN   The alignment·of the image with text in the same line. Valid values are TOP, MIDDLE, and BOTTOM.

NAME   The variable name associated with the input field.

SRC   The relative or full path to the image to be displayed.

Here is a sample image element:

```
<INPUT  TYPE="image" NAME="form1"  SRC="submission.gif" ALIGN="MIDDLE">
```

PASSWORD Elements in Forms

The PASSWORD element is a text field where all data entered is seen as asterisks. This does not affect how the form output is passed, only how it is displayed on the user's screen. This is useful if users must log in to places at your site. You could send a login ID and password via a form to a script that would validate the user's access. You should use this field if there is a chance users may be providing private information from a public computer screen, such as a computer at a university, library, or office.

This element has four attributes that could be used with it:

MAXLENGTH   The maximum allowable length of the field. If this is not specified, there is no limit.

NAME   The variable name associated with the input field.

SIZE   The width of the input field, expressed as the number of characters for the text field.

VALUE   The initial value of the field.

Here is a sample password element:

```
<INPUT  TYPE="password" NAME="name"  VALUE="123" SIZE=25 MAXLENGTH=25 >
```

Radio Buttons in Forms

Radio buttons are similar to checkboxes and are also useful in forms. The RADIO element has four attributes that could be used with it:

CHECKED	The button is automatically selected when viewed. It can provide users with a default option that can be unselected if necessary.
DISABLED	The user can neither check nor uncheck a disabled checkbox. This is used primarily for testing forms, but it is useful only for a mandatory input field that is checked, and the user acknowledges acceptance of a condition by submitting the form.
NAME	The variable name associated with the input field.
VALUE	The value of the input field if it is checked.

Here is a sample RADIO element:

```
<INPUT  TYPE="radio" NAME="radio-input1"  VALUE="first-input"  >
```

Figure 23.4 depicts how radio buttons would be used in a form. The HTML code for the form would be as follows:

```
<FORM METHOD="GET" ACTION="mailto:your_id@your_company.com">
<H1>Radio Buttons</H1>
<P>What is your favorite color?
<P><INPUT  TYPE="radio" NAME="radio1"  VALUE="blue" >Blue</P>
<P><INPUT  TYPE="radio" NAME="radio1"  VALUE="green" >Green</P>
<P><INPUT  TYPE="radio" NAME="radio1"  VALUE="orange" >Orange</P>
<P><INPUT  TYPE="radio" NAME="radio1"  VALUE="purple" >Purple</P>
<P><INPUT  TYPE="radio" NAME="radio1"  VALUE="red" >Red</P>
<P><INPUT  TYPE="radio" NAME="radio1"  VALUE="yellow" >Yellow</P>
<P><INPUT  TYPE="radio" NAME="radio1"  VALUE="nofavorite" >No Favorite Color</P>
</FORM>
```

RESET and *SUBMIT* Buttons in Forms

RESET and SUBMIT buttons have similar features. Both should be used at the very bottom of the form and usually are found next to one another. RESET buttons clear the form when selected and have a default value of reset. SUBMIT buttons submit the form when selected and have a default value of submit. The value of the button is the name as it will appear on the screen. You can set this using the VALUE attribute or accept the defaults. The NAME attribute is useful for a SUBMIT button and could be used to track which SUBMIT button a user pressed if your form used multiple SUBMIT buttons as in the menu example you will find below.

Here is a sample RESET button:

```
<INPUT TYPE="reset" VALUE="Reset Form">
```

Here is a sample SUBMIT button:

```
<INPUT TYPE="submit" NAME="button1" VALUE="Submit Form">
```

Figure 23.5 merges the previous two examples and adds SUBMIT and RESET buttons.

FIGURE 23.4.

Using radio buttons in forms.

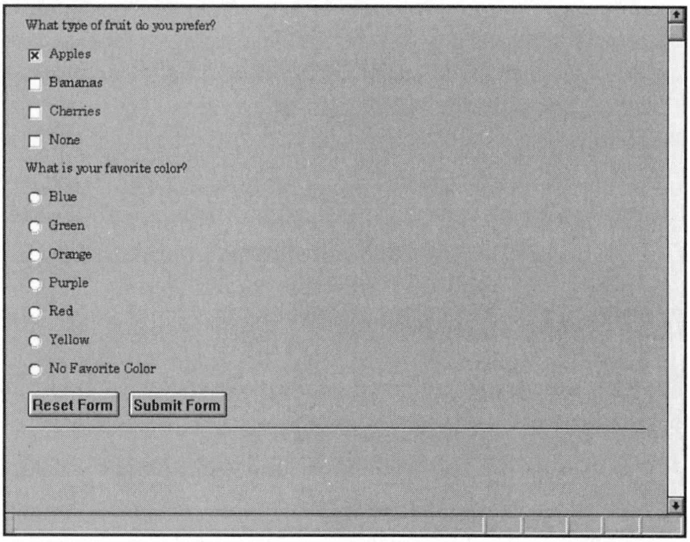

FIGURE 23.5.

Fill-out forms with SUBMIT and RESET buttons.

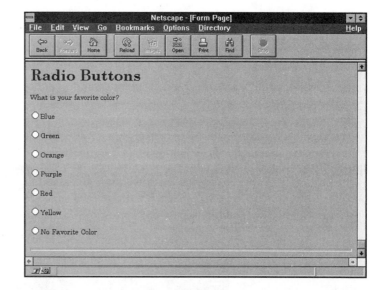

The SUBMIT button has an interesting extended use because you can set the value and thus the name of the button as it will appear on the screen. Multiple SUBMIT buttons could be used as a menu system. The key to the menu system would be assigning a unique NAME attribute to each SUBMIT button, which would enable you to track the button the user had pressed. The gateway script receiving these values as input could use a simple if-then or case-in structure to output an URL location. Figure 23.6 shows how this type of menu would look.

Here's the HTML code for the menu form:

```
<FORM METHOD="GET"  ACTION="../cgi-bin/quick-menu">
<INPUT  TYPE="SUBMIT"  NAME="BUTTON1"  VALUE="ABC Press Home Page">
<INPUT  TYPE="SUBMIT"  NAME="BUTTON2"  VALUE="BackGround"
<INPUT  TYPE="SUBMIT"  NAME="BUTTON3"  VALUE="What's New">
<INPUT  TYPE="SUBMIT"  NAME="BUTTON4"  VALUE="Book Info">
<INPUT  TYPE="SUBMIT"  NAME="BUTTON5"  VALUE="Orders">
<INPUT  TYPE="SUBMIT"  NAME="BUTTON6"  VALUE="User Help Center">
<INPUT  TYPE="SUBMIT"  NAME="BUTTON7"  VALUE="WWW Info">
<INPUT  TYPE="SUBMIT"  NAME="BUTTON8"  VALUE="WWW Resources">
<INPUT  TYPE="HIDDEN"  NAME="MENU"  VALUE="MENU1">
</Form>
```

FIGURE 23.6.

Menu created using form techniques.

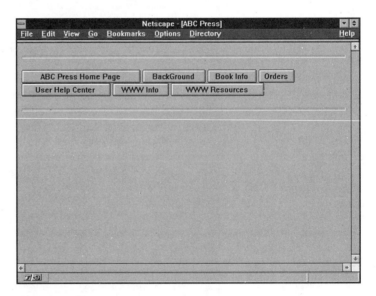

TEXT Elements in Forms

The TEXT element is a basic text input field that encompasses one line. There are four attributes that can be used with TEXT:

MAXLENGTH   The maximum allowable length of the field. If this is not specified, there is no limit.

NAME   The variable name associated with the input field.

SIZE	The width of the input field, expressed as the number of characters for the text field.
VALUE	The initial value of the field.

Here's how you could use the TEXT element in your forms:

```
<INPUT TYPE="TEXT" NAME="text_input1" SIZE="25">
```

In the example, the SIZE attribute defines the visible area for the TEXT element on the screen to be 25 characters wide. However, it does not specify the maximum length of the field. If more than 25 characters are entered, the text will scroll. To limit the input to a specific value, you should use the MAXLENGTH attribute, such as:

```
<INPUT TYPE="TEXT" NAME="text_input1" SIZE="25" MAXLENGTH="50">
```

SELECTION and *OPTION* Elements

The SELECTION element has an opening and closing tag. It doesn't have as many attributes as the INPUT element but is just as useful. With this element, you can create lists of items from which users can select. By using the SIZE attribute, you can create a menu window with a scrollbar. The element has three basic format elements that look like this:

```
<SELECT SIZE=1 NAME="Menu Name">
<SELECT SIZE=5 NAME="Menu Name">
<SELECT SIZE=5 NAME="Menu Name" MULTIPLE>
```

The first line of code creates a one-line window with a hidden menu. The second line creates an on-screen menu with five displayed items and a scrollbar. The last line enables the user to select multiple options from the list.

The SELECTION element is associated with the OPTION element. The OPTION element is how you specify options for the list. This element has two basic formats:

```
<OPTION>listed item
<OPTION SELECTED>listed item
```

The first option is a normal option that can be selected by the user. The second option shows an option that is selected by default. Users can unselect the default option by clicking on it if they want to.

The following is a simple SELECTION menu:

```
<SELECT NAME="Favorite_Sport" SIZE=1>
<OPTION>Baseball
<OPTION>Basketball
<OPTION>Football
<OPTION>Hockey
<OPTION>Swimming
<OPTION>Skiing
<OPTION>Soccer
<OPTION>Surfing
</SELECT>
```

This simple example, as depicted in Figure 23.7, would display the first option, and the other seven options would be hidden until the user clicked on the SELECTION menu. Once the menu is activated, the user can make a selection. The value of the option selected would be the output for this field. To make a menu window, the SIZE option could be increased as follows:

```
<SELECT SIZE=5 NAME="Most_Watched_Sport">
<OPTION>Baseball
<OPTION>Basketball
<OPTION SELECTED>Football
<OPTION>Hockey
<OPTION>Swimming
<OPTION>Skiing
<OPTION>Soccer
<OPTION>Surfing
</SELECT>
```

FIGURE 23.7.

Using a hidden SELECTION menu.

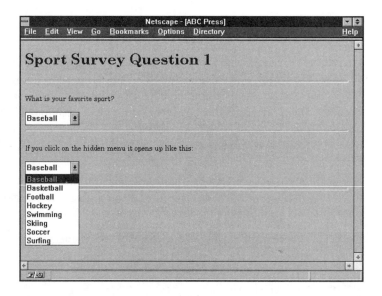

This example as depicted in Figure 23.8 would display a SELECTION menu of five lines.

The other three options could be accessed via the scrollbar. This example also has a default option, Football, which would be selected unless the user unselected it. When using default options, ensure that the default is either the first option in a default SELECTION menu or in the viewable portion of other SELECTION menus.

Another nice feature you can add to a SELECTION menu is to allow the user to make multiple selections. In Figure 23.9, three selections have been made. To make a SELECTION menu that would accept multiple options, the MULTIPLE attribute could be inserted as follows:

```
<SELECT SIZE=7 NAME="Top_Three" MULTIPLE>
<OPTION>Baseball
<OPTION>Basketball
<OPTION>Football
```

```
<OPTION>Hockey
<OPTION>Swimming
<OPTION>Skiing
<OPTION>Soccer
<OPTION>Surfing
</SELECT>
```

FIGURE 23.8.

Menu with default selection.

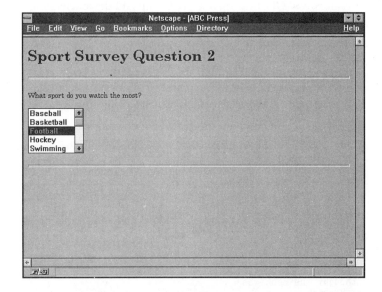

FIGURE 23.9.

Allowing multiple selections.

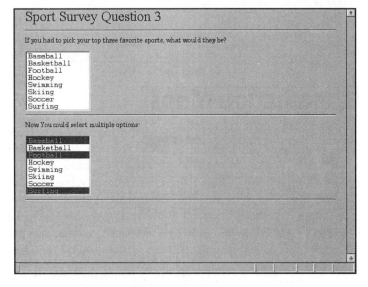

The *TEXTAREA* Element

The TEXTAREA element enables you to define text input windows on the screen. It has more functionality than the text field used with the INPUT element. However, TEXTAREA has no MAXLENGTH element. The text window is displayed with horizontal and vertical scrollbars. The window will scroll left to right as well as up and down, enabling users to enter as much data into the text window as they want.

TEXTAREA has an opening and closing tag. Any text between the opening and closing tags is used as the initial input to the text window. The user can erase any default input if necessary. TEXTAREA has three basic attributes:

NAME	The variable name associated with the input field.
ROWS	The length of the text window in number of lines.
COLS	The width of the text window in number of characters.

The following is how the TEXTAREA tag could be used:

```
<TEXTAREA NAME="Publisher_Query" ROWS=5 COLS=70></TEXTAREA>
```

To include default text for the text windows and a line explaining the window, you could use the following:

```
<P>Did you like the preview of our book?</P>
<TEXTAREA NAME="Book_Review" ROWS=5 COLS=70>
I thought the book was
</TEXTAREA>
```

Any default text provided for the text window will be displayed exactly as entered. Some browsers also let you use HTML tags in the text window to format text in a specific manner. Figure 23.10 depicts how text windows with default text would look in a browser.

Using Image Maps

Image maps are another powerful feature to include in Web pages and are commonly used to create graphical menus. Image maps enable you to create a graphic image that has several hot areas. A *hot area* is a part of the image that the user can click on. Each hot area can have a specific action tied to it. This enables you to create easy, graphic-based ways for users to browse information at your Web site. You could create an image map showing company products, and each specific product depicted in the image could be defined as a hot area that the user could click on to bring up information about the product. The process of creating an image map with defined hot areas sounds complex, but it isn't, as you'll soon see.

Image maps are defined with the IMG tag by adding the ISMAP element. Image maps are used in conjunction with the anchor tag <A>, which defines the gateway script to call when the user clicks on the image, as follows:

```
<A HREF="/path/to/image/map/script"> <IMG SRC="image_map.gif" ISMAP></A>
```

FIGURE 23.10.

Textarea windows using default text.

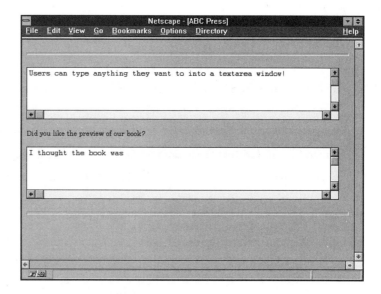

Image maps are made possible by gateway scripts included with most server software. If the software to enable image maps on the system wasn't included with your server software, you might be able to find a suitable script on the Internet. The mapping script is the key to image maps—without it, you won't be able to use image maps at your site because when you define an image map, all you're really creating is a script containing a set of coordinates that define the hot areas. The coordinates are the horizontal and vertical locations within the image.

Hot areas are defined in terms of three geometric shapes:

circle   Either a center point and radius or a center point and a point on the circumference of the circle.

rectangle A four-sided object defined by the coordinates of two opposing coordinates.

polygon   An object with three or more sides defined by specifying the end points.

There are many ways image maps could be applied to graphic images. Almost any graphic image can be turned into an image map, but the best images to use for image mapping have sections that include these three geometric shapes. Because the polygon shape allows for an object with three or more sides and is defined by end points, almost any shape could be defined. This includes stars, octagons, or even a hundred-sided object.

CERN Web servers use a program called htimap to define image maps. NCSA servers use a program called imagemap. Most image map programs follow either the NCSA or the CERN method for defining image maps, or a derivative of these methods. This is true even in the Microsoft Windows and Macintosh environments.

If you are using the CERN's image map script, you might reference the script in your Web documents as

```
<A HREF="/usr/cgi-bin/htimap"><IMG SRC="imenu.gif" ISMAP></A>
```

If you are using the NCSA's image map script, you might reference the script in your Web documents as

```
<A HREF="/usr/local/src/httpd/cgi-bin/imagemap"><IMG SRC="imenu.gif" ISMAP></A>
```

Image map files for CERN `htimap` can include the following shapes and values:

`default URL`	The default is used when a point not specified is selected.
`circle (x,y) radius x URL`	The center point of the circle and the radius.
`rectangle (x1,y1) (x2,y2) URL`	The two opposing coordinates.
`polygon (x1,y1) (x2,y2) ... (xn, yn) URL`	The end points on the polygon.

Your map file for use with CERN `htimap` could look like this:

```
circle (10,20) radius 15          /samples/books.html
rectangle (10,40) (30,20)         /samples/orders.html
polygon (20,30) (40,10) (20, 50)  features.html
default                           http://mcp.com/index.html
```

Image map files for NCSA `imagemap` can include the following shapes and values:

`default URL`	The default is used when a point not specified is selected.
`circle URL x1,y1 x2,y2`	The center point of the circle and a point on the circumference.
`rectangle URL x1,y1 x2,y2`	The two opposing coordinates.
`polygon URL x1,y1 x2,y2 ... xn,yn`	The end points on the polygon (limit 100).

Your map file for use with NCSA `imagemap` could look like this:

```
circle /wg/index.html        10,20 25,20
rectangle orders.html        10,40 30,20
polygon /samples/books.html  20,30 40,10 20, 50
default http://tvp.com/
```

A sample image map is shown in Figure 23.11. The sample depicts the NCSA image map method. The points on the sample are meant only to demonstrate the points you would have to put into your NCSA image map file. Although the example shows a rectangle, polygon, and circle, any image using basic geometric shapes could be used. An image map can contain any type of picture.

FIGURE 23.11.

Sample image map.

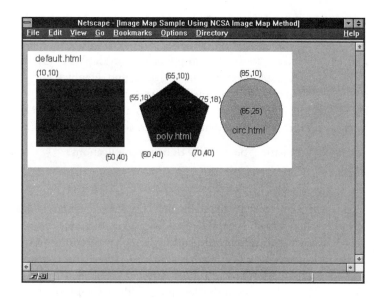

If this were a picture of a house with a garage and swimming pool:

- The rectangle could be the defined area for the garage.
- The polygon could be the defined area for the house.
- The circle could be the defined area for the pool.

If a user clicked on one of the defined areas of this example, it would take them to the appropriate corresponding file:

Area Clicked On	Corresponding File
Any area not defined	default.html
The area defined by the rectangle	rect.html
The area defined by the polygon	poly.html
The area defined by the circle	circ.html

You can find imagemap version 1.5 at NCSA:

http://hoohoo.ncsa.uiuc.edu/docs/setup/admin/imagemap.txt

You can find htimap installation and configuration instructions at CERN:

http://www.w3.org/hypertext/WWW/Daemon/User/CGI/HTImageDoc.html

HTML Helper Applications

Helper applications are the key to publishing on the Web. Other chapters discussed helper applications for graphics, sound, and video. Sound, graphics, and video tools were designed to make the task of creating multimedia easier. Similarly, there are tools to make the job of creating HTML documents easier. HTML helper applications will help you apply the fundamentals of electronic publishing that you've read about in this and other chapters of the book.

There are three basic types of HTML helper applications:

- HTML editors
- HTML templates for word processors
- HTML converters

HTML editors have features similar to your favorite word processor and enable you to easily create documents in HTML format. Typically, these editors enable you to select tags from a pull-down menu. The menu has brief descriptions of elements you can add to the document. The editor places the tags in the document in the proper format, which frees you from having to memorize the format. When creating complex forms, you'll find HTML editors especially useful.

HTML templates enable you to add the functionality of an HTML editor to your favorite word processor. The great thing about templates is that you can use all the word processor's features, which could include checking grammar and spelling. More importantly, you'll be using the familiar features of your word processor to add HTML formatting to your documents.

Although the task of creating HTML code is fairly complex, some helper applications called *converters* try to automate the task. HTML converters convert your favorite document formats into HTML code and vice versa. At the touch of a button, you could transform a Word for Windows file into an HTML document. Converters are especially useful if you're converting simple documents and are less useful when you're converting documents with complex layouts.

HTML is closely related to the form definition languages used in large databases, and it has some of the complexity of an actual computer language. Computer languages tend to evolve slowly over a period of many years. Currently, only a few computer languages support automatic creation tools and rapid prototyping. These are fourth-generation languages, which enable users to create code without in-depth programming skills. Fourth-generation languages such as Informix, Natural, and Powerhouse simply wouldn't be possible without the stepping-stone connections to third-, second-, and first-generation languages.

The same things are true concerning HTML. HTML is evolving. Level-three HTML features have been incorporated into a few advanced browsers such as Netscape. The tools that support HTML are evolving with the language but not quite as quickly. The first generation of helper tools were very basic and not at all intuitive. The current generation of HTML helper tools have come a long way but are not entirely effective in automatically generating HTML documents for you.

A general problem with programs generated by fourth-generation computer languages is that they tend to have much more code than is actually needed. This is because fourth-generation languages reduce multiple, complex processes to a single generalized process. Many fourth-generation languages put together modules of code, the result of which are workable solutions but not optimal solutions. A good programmer would go back in and optimize the sections of the code that are flabby.

Although HTML helper applications definitely are not at the level of fourth-generation language tools, some concepts and problems are similar. The purpose of helper applications is to reduce complex processes to simpler processes. These tools generally will output workable solutions but not optimal solutions. More often than not, you'll have to go back into the HTML code to fix problem areas or to optimize the code.

Despite the problems you may experience while using HTML helper applications, they are the best way to learn HTML. Experiment with the HTML helper applications you'll read about in the next sections of this chapter. Find one or two you prefer to work with, and start creating and learning. Having to fix problems or to optimize code will seem a blessing after you've tried to create HTML documents on your own. The key to HTML helper applications is to manage your expectations. By learning about the thorns in the rose garden, you know there is no simple way to create HTML code, but there are alternatives to programming HTML code straight into a text editor.

HTML Editors

HTML editors are available for many different operating systems. Dozens of editors are available for Microsoft Windows, Macintosh, and UNIX environments. Some editors check the syntax of your HTML. These are called *rule-based* editors and are good for novices to use. Some editors offer many of the features from your favorite word processor and create HTML in *WYSIWYG* (What You See Is What You Get) fashion. WYSIWYG as it pertains to HTML tools really means that the formatting you see on your screen is the formatting that will appear in the code of your finished document. The best HTML editors are both rule-based and WYSIWYG. This section presents three editors that meet both these criteria.

HoTMetaL Pro

HoTMetaL Pro created by SoftQuad Incorporated is possibly the best HTML editor available. Not only is it WYSIWYG and rule-based, it is also a commercial-quality word processor with spellchecking and a thesaurus. HoTMetaL Pro is available for Macintosh, Microsoft Windows, HP9000/700, DEC Alpha, Sun OS, Solaris, Silicon Graphics, and the IBM RS6000.

HoTMetaL Pro is loaded with features that make it easy to use. It is the only editor that comes close to breaking the rule about the quality of the current generation of HTML helper applications. The only real drawback of HoTMetaL Pro is the price of the commercial version—$195. For more information on HoTMetaL Pro, visit the SoftQuad Web site at the following address:

```
http://www.sq.com/hmpro.html
```

HoTMetaL for Windows

HotMetaL is a limited freeware version of HoTMetaL Pro. HoTMetaL is available for Microsoft Windows and the X Window system. It is rule-based and WYSIWYG. HoTMetaL offers many of the great features of its commercial counterpart, including support for forms, images, and document templates.

You can download the software from the following FTP site:

```
ftp://ftp.uoknor.edu/mirrors/networking/info-service/www/ncsa/html/hotmetal/
```

HTML Web Weaver for Macintosh

HTML Web Weaver is one of the best HTML editors for Macintosh, and it is shareware. It has basic text-editing features, pull-down menus, and full support for forms and images. This editor is near-WYSIWYG and has great help features that will provide rules and information on tags. HTML Web Weaver is an upgrade to the popular HTML SuperText Editor that was a development version of the Web Weaver.

The shareware fee for Web Weaver is $25 ($14 for education use). You can find more information about Web Weaver at the following informational site on the Web:

```
http://www.potsdam.edu/Web.Weaver/About.html
```

HTML Templates

HTML templates for word processors and text editors are starting to come into widespread use. This is especially true for Microsoft Word for Windows. HTML document templates for MS Word 2.0 and MS Word 6.0 are available from a variety of sources. A great document template for MS Word 2.0 is CU_HTML, which you can find on the Web at CERN's Web site:

```
http://info.cern.ch/hypertext/WWW/Tools/cu_html.html
```

Two of the best document templates available for MS Word 6.0 are Internet Assistant and HTML author. Both templates are freeware. Created by the powerhouse Microsoft, the Internet Assistant has many excellent features. The Internet Assistant can be found at Microsoft's Web site at

```
http://www.microsoft.com/pages/deskapps/word/ia/default.htm
```

HTML Author also has excellent features. It is available from the following Web site:

```
http://www.salford.ac.uk/docs/depts/iti/staff/gsc/htmlauth/summary.html
```

For the Macintosh, HTML extensions are available for the popular text editor BBEdit. These macro extension packages will work with BBEdit and BBEdit Lite. The HTML extensions are free. For more information about them, visit this Web site:

```
http://www.uji.es/bbedit-html-extensions.html
```

HTML Converters

An amazing number of converters are available for HTML. There are converters from just about format you can think of to HTML. In addition to templates for word processors, there are macros for word processors that convert word processor documents to HTML. Macros and converters are available for programs such as the following:

Microsoft Word	QuarkXPress
WordPerfect	DECwrite
FrameMaker	Interleaf
PowerPoint	LaTeX
PageMaker	BibTeX
Scribe	

Converters are available to convert specific formats such as these:

PostScript
MS RTF
MIF
UNIX MAN pages

There are converters to convert programming languages to HTML. You can convert your favorite programs to HTML if they are in these languages:

C
C++
FORTRAN
Pascal
Lisp

There also are a number of converters from HTML to popular formats such as the following:

FrameMaker/MIF
PostScript
LaTeX
Standard ASCII Text

CERN is the best place on the World Wide Web to find information on converting to and from HTML. CERN has set up a wonderful information site. Its section on HTML converters is top-notch. CERN maintains an updated list of sites where these converters can be downloaded to your system. The top-level page for these converters is

```
http://www.w3.org/hypertext/WWW/Tools/Filters.html
```

Summary

Publishing on the World Wide Web involves browsers and servers. You can publish your project on a commercial server or your own server. Never make a hasty decision about buying or renting. The key to buy-versus-rent decisions for Web servers is to ensure that you make the right decision for the right reasons. Rent space on a commercial server when it is to your advantage, financially or otherwise. Purchase your own server when it is to your advantage, financially or otherwise.

Regardless of the choice of server, there are many choices you'll have to make pertaining to your documents. The organization of your documents is critically important. You must decide on a structure for the site you're creating. You have to create your documents and move them to the site, and then publish them for all the world to see. After you install the documents, you have to maintain them as necessary. To do this, you may need a webmaster, a person who maintains your Web pages.

Part of your decision to buy versus rent may be based on the availability of advanced HTML features which use gateway scripts. The Common Gateway Interface is a powerful tool to use in your HTML documents. Gateway scripts can serve many purposes. You can set up scripts to handle the output of fill-out forms. Using the output of forms, you can generate documents on demand or create a quick-menu system. Users could use forms to answer surveys, provide feedback, or perform database searches. Using scripts, you also can create image maps. Image maps enable you to define hot areas in any image. Users are then able to click on these hot areas to access other documents.

HTML helper applications are widely available on the Internet. If ever a set of tools could help reduce the learning curve, HTML helper applications are the ones. These tools will help you create HTML documents and even convert existing documents to or from HTML.

LAN and WAN Publishing

by

Publishing on the Local Area Network (LAN) or even a Wide Area Network (WAN) is really the practical application of Web publishing to a real-world business problem. A LAN is a network situated in a small geographic area, such as an office building. A typical LAN may have 100 computers attached to it. A WAN spreads across large geographic areas, such as states and countries. Although a typical WAN may be a network of hundreds of computers and composed of any number of LAN segments or nodes, the key distinction between a LAN and a WAN is not size but geographic area. WANs generally span geographic boundaries and are connected together using phone lines, satellite links, or cables. When it comes to network publishing, however, the size of the network and the area it spans do not matter as long as the computers are linked together in some form of network. The network could be 10 computers or 10,000. The network could span the globe. The type of computer doesn't matter either. The computers on the network can be a mix of Sun Sparcs, Macintoshes, IBM compatibles, or any other system you can think of.

Although many types of network publishing operations are possible with today's technology, the focus of this chapter is on using the hypermedia capabilities of the World Wide Web to set up a network publishing operation. As you've seen in previous chapters, the power of the Web is in its diversity. Its handling of hypertext objects enables cross-platform solutions. With network publishing you easily can set up a mini-Internet within your company. Your mini-Internet can be accessible by the outside world or be exclusive to the company. The choice is absolutely yours.

This chapter will give you the inside scoop on

- What LAN/WAN publishing is
- Why you don't have to be on the Internet to take advantage of Web facilities
- LAN/WAN publishing versus paper publishing
- Choosing a platform
- Web server software
- Installing server software
- Configuring the server
- Web server Administration
- LAN/WAN publishing on the new server

What Is LAN and WAN Publishing?

A reality in the business world is that company-wide databases tax resources in both labor costs and real-money terms. Even the best conventional database tools have high learning curves. Another reality is that sometimes you just don't have two to four weeks to train new personnel on the use of the database. And, company-wide databases are growing in size and complexity.

Databases aren't the only part of the company that grows as the company grows. The paper trail of documents—brochures, information packets, policies—also grows with the company. Maintaining an ever-growing paper trail is costly and personnel-intensive. Every time there is a product release, product update, or a press release, documents must be distributed to support personnel and other key personnel within the company. This costs money. Other problems stem from this paper trail. The customer support department may be misinforming customers based on data that is days or weeks old.

To better serve customers, employees need access to the most current information. What employees really need to do this is a meta-index of company resources and documents in a searchable form so information can be retrieved in an instant. A company-wide meta-index of resources and documents would be astronomically expensive using conventional means. Publishing these documents electronically on the Local Area Network or a company-wide Wide Area Network is a nonconventional solution to this problem that will drastically reduce costs and save countless hours.

Extending the functionality of the World Wide Web to the Local Area Network or a Wide Area Network is a cost- and time-effective business solution. The facilities of the World Wide Web don't have high learning curves. In fact, there isn't much of a learning curve at all if the facilities and tools are a part of the company's infrastructure.

The only thing network publishing requires is that you install and configure two things:

> Web server communications
> Web browser communications

Through network publishing, you can provide a meta-index of documents, access to company databases, and much more. Using tools discussed in previous chapters, you can automatically convert most existing document formats to the HTML format. The great thing about HTML documents is they are dynamic. Personnel don't have to rummage through a paper trail or learn the commands to interface with the company database. To find a related reference with HTML, all they have to do is click on links. To perform a database search, all they have to do is enter a word or two at a prompt. Some of the types of documents you can network publish include:

> Policies
> Standards
> On-the-job training documentation
> Online help manuals
> User manuals
> Department/company-wide memos
> Project descriptions, goals, and contacts
> News releases
> Trip reports
> Employee recognition awards
> Company mission, goals, and objectives
> Company background and history

Company forms
Company product and sales information
Company telephone directory
Office and key personnel rosters

Why You Don't Have To Be on the Internet

A common misconception about the Web is that to set up a Web server you must be on the Internet. This simply is not true. The company does not have to be connected to the Internet to take advantage of Web tools. The Web server doesn't have to be linked to the Internet, and company personnel don't have to be able to access the Internet to make network publishing a reality within the company.

Several books concerning the Web and the Internet specifically—and mistakenly—state that a TCP/IP connection to the Internet is an absolute requirement for setting up a Web server. It's true that an Internet connection would help in obtaining Web server software because server software is widely available on the Internet. However, this software, the installation instructions, and manuals can be downloaded from any Internet account and subsequently loaded onto the company network.

The more correct statement is that if the company wants to use the Internet and take advantage of the World Wide Web that is a part of the Internet, there must be some kind of connection to the Internet. But the company does not have to be connected to the Internet or any part of the Internet to set up a Web server for use within the company.

The Federal government has "private" internets. Some large corporations have "private" internets. You could call these mini-internets or simply internets. The internet with the little "i" is simply a network of networked computers. What these private internets allow on their networks is their business. What you provide on your network is your business.

When you set up a Web server, you tell it the domain—structure—you want it to operate within. You can include or exclude links to the outside world as you see fit. You can even include or exclude divisions within the company. It all depends on how you set up the Web server and the permissions you grant or deny.

LAN/WAN Publishing versus Paper Publishing

No doubt, you've heard the term *paperless office* before. Don't cringe. Although this eventuality isn't outside the realm of possibility, this isn't a lecture on how Web publishing can help make the office paperless. The truth is that Web publishing company documents won't eliminate the paper trail, but it can help to dramatically reduce the paper trail. It can help to streamline the update and correction process. It can also help to distribute large amounts of up-to-date information throughout the organization. The decision to Web publish or not to Web publish ultimately comes down to simple economics:

- Is network publishing affordable?
- Is network publishing cost saving?
- Is network publishing cost effective?

Network Publishing Is Affordable

Costs for incorporating Web publishing into an existing network are negligible. Often a network will already have a workstation capable of carrying the additional load as the Web server. The Web server doesn't have to be a dedicated machine. This is especially true for small networks or networks where a limited number of personnel have access to the Web server.

Usually, you won't need a full-time Web server administrator. Existing networks already have, or should have, a system administrator who can handle the additional duties as the Web server administrator. Web servers are very easy to administer once they are set up and running.

Although using an existing workstation is not always a possibility, the good news is that the Web server doesn't have to be a power machine. Web servers serving hundreds of users are running on network-configured 486DX 66MHz computers.

Network Publishing Saves Money

Network publishing the company documents can reduce print costs and other associated costs dramatically. Printed documents quickly become outdated. Technical manuals, company policies, and other important documents are expensive to maintain and reprint. With network publishing, there aren't any print costs, and you'll find that maintaining Web documents is easier than maintaining printed documents.

There simply aren't high-learning curves in a point-and-click interface environment. There are even ways to automate the updating of documents. Time savings for easy maintenance and use adds up to big money savings over traditional alternatives. The savings also extends to personnel savings. Your company can realize these personnel savings in fewer hours spent building, searching, and maintaining company documents. Ease of use means that finding information is less frustrating for workers, and a less stressful environment is good for the company as well as its workers.

Ease of use may also mean that new employees can become productive company assets sooner. Using a Web browser, such as Mosaic, a new employee with little training could make retrievals from the company's Oracle database on the first day on the job. To do this, the employee would access a Web page with a fill-out form or query box such as those discussed in Chapter 23, "Web Servers, Gateway Scripts, Helper Applications." After typing in the information to retrieve, the employee would simply click on the submit button, and soon afterward, the retrieval would display on the screen.

Network Publishing Is Cost Effective

Network publishing is a highly efficient way to ensure that company information is distributed throughout the organization. Putting a document on the company Web can provide instant access for all personnel, several departments, or an individual department. You'll discover that Web documents are easier to maintain, produce, index, and use—which translates directly to cost efficiency.

If cost efficiency is a big consideration for the company (and it should be), consider the case of the company with global offices. These offices are probably already connected via a Wide Area Network or have some kind of dial-up access to the Internet. Despite the ease of use of electronic mail, company documents flow back and forth through conventional mail every day. This is because some types of documents aren't suited for posting to e-mail. Posting a 500-page policy manual via e-mail to all company personnel would probably bring the network to a screeching halt. Even if it didn't, the people who should be reading the policy manual wouldn't because of the form of the message.

With network publishing, the policy manual would be an interactive, indexed document that personnel could easily search for references important to the operations of their respective departments. More importantly, the entire huge manual wouldn't have to be mailed and re-mailed to a dozen global or regional offices.

Platforms for Web Servers

Before setting up or installing software, you must determine what platform the Web server will run on. Until recently, your choices were limited, but this changed rapidly as the World Wide Web grew in popularity. Today, Web server software and server management tools are available for almost every platform. And, like other software developed for use on the Internet, this software is available as freeware, shareware, and commercial server software.

The best server software for you is most likely the software that will run on the workstation you plan to use as the network's Web server, but several factors come into play that could change your mind. The four primary factors are

- Expertise of the installation team
- Reliability of the Web server
- Necessity of support
- Security

The Expertise of the Installation Team

The level of expertise of the installation team will be a major determining factor in your choice of server. To configure for specific types of platforms, and primarily UNIX platforms, some Web server software must be compiled from source code. This is a good thing if you have an experienced team capable of setting parameters within the code to optimize for the intended system. Having the source code also means you can easily trace down and correct bugs and create enhancements to the existing code.

However, having the source code will do you no good if you cannot optimize and compile it. Therefore, if you do not have an experienced team or are looking for an easy solution for your network publishing operation, you will want to look at server software that does not need to be compiled or optimized. Often the easiest server software to install is for Amiga, Macintosh, and Microsoft Windows systems.

Reliability of the Web Server

The necessary reliability of the Web server is the second major determining factor in choosing a server. Examine carefully how the company plans to use the Web server. The projected nature of the use will help drive your decision. Some server software is being continually updated and improved. Some platforms have a variety of support tools. Both are especially true for UNIX platforms, but not necessarily true for other platforms.

UNIX systems are the lifeblood of the Internet, and, naturally, some of the best server software is for UNIX systems. Because UNIX server software has been around longer, most of the bugs have been worked out, and it is generally being continually improved.

The Necessity of Support

The type of support needed to maintain the Web server is the third major determining factor in choosing your server. The primary reason for opting to use commercial Web server software is software support. If you believe the organization will need software support to keep the operation alive, commercial software is the best choice. Freeware software is generally provided on an "as is" basis. The creators ask only that if you improve the software or fix bugs, you send them the updates.

> **NOTE**
>
> Because software support can play a major role in your decision to purchase Web server software, you should also know about other options such as hiring a software support firm to provide your company with technical support. Software support firms are a $100-million-a-year niche of the computer industry and are growing in number. Software support firms specialize in providing technical support for a wide range of products and are positioned well to replace many traditional help-desk centers. Several of the early software support companies have been tremendously successful because of the strong need in the business community for prompt, reliable, and accurate technical support. As the Internet and the World Wide Web grow, these companies will undoubtedly start to support key Internet and Web software applications.

Security Concerns

Security is the fourth major determining factor in choosing your server. Web server software that lacks adequate security constraints can put the company's network in jeopardy. This is critically important when the company plans to connect to the Internet.

All Web server software has some security features. Permissions granted or denied to users when the server software is being configured play an important role in security. Some of the most secure server software is available for UNIX. Again, this is primarily because Web server software for UNIX platforms has been around longer and has had more developers working on it.

Web Server Software

This section examines server software for specific platforms and their major features. For UNIX platforms, there are dozens of possibilities, but only the most popular server software will be described here. Until recently, there was only one good choice for the Windows NT environment, but this has changed. There are now many excellent commercial and freeware choices for Windows NT.

For other platforms, there is generally only one choice in server software. Having only one choice of server software for your Amiga, Macintosh, or Windows system doesn't mean the quality of the server software is poor. Quite the contrary, the quality of the software is often quite good.

> **NOTE**
>
> The central process running on a Web server is the Hypertext Transfer Protocol Daemon (HTTPD). A *daemon* is a program that runs in the background and handles requests. Similarly the HTTP daemon, or HTTPD, is the process that handles requests for a Web server. Although the daemon is only a part of server software, the term *HTTPD* is often used to refer to the server itself. For example, the Web server from CERN is referred to as CERN HTTPD, and when people refer to CERN HTTPD, they are generally referring to the entire Web server software package from CERN.

This section covers the following platforms and server software:

Platform	Server Software
Amiga	AWS
Macintosh	MacHTTP
UNIX	CERN HTTPD
	NCSA HTTPD
	Netscape Servers
	WN

Platform	Server Software
Windows	Windows HTTPD
Windows NT	EMWAC HTTPS
	Netscape Servers
	Purveyor

Amiga Web Server

Amiga Web Server is a newcomer and is available as freeware. The software was written specifically for the Amiga. It makes great use of the Amiga's power and includes limited security mechanisms. AWS just finished beta testing, and version 1.0 of the server is now available.

AWS was written by the same team of programmers that developed AMosaic, the Amiga Web browser. The developers of AWS and AMosaic recently formed Omnipresence International. Omnipresence International will develop freeware and commercial Internet products for the Amiga.

A commercial version of AWS called AServer will also be available soon. The commercial version will feature add-on modules that enhance the capabilities of the server. The add-on modules can also be purchased separately, which means you'll be able to enhance the capabilities of the freeware server to meet your needs. Figure 24.1 shows where you can find information about the Omnipresence Amiga server on the Web.

FIGURE 24.1.

Amiga server software on the Web.

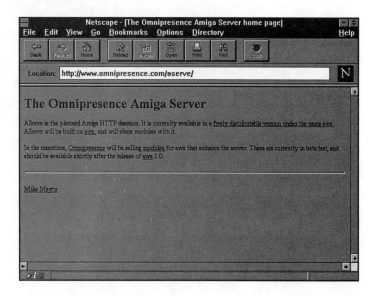

Macintosh Server

MacHTTP is one of the easiest Web server software packages to install. It is great for use on small networks and has one of the lowest fees of any commercial server. The most recent version includes support for CGI scripts.

You can purchase this software from StarNine Technologies Incorporated, and it has a 30-day evaluation period. After the evaluation period, you're obligated to register the server or cease using the software. Most educational organizations can purchase MacHTTP for $65, and other organizations can purchase MacHTTP for $95. Figure 24.2 shows where you can find information about MacHTTP on the Web.

> **NOTE**
>
> CGI scripts are programs on the Web server that can be called by HTML documents. These scripts enable you to take advantage of some of the most advanced features of HTML, including fill-out forms, image maps, and indexed searching. Gateway scripts were discussed in Chapter 23.

FIGURE 24.2.

MacHTTP server software on the Web.

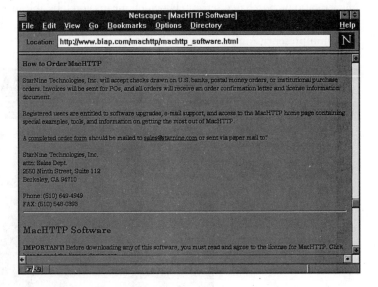

If you have a Macintosh running A/UX, there is a version of CERN's HTTP server that will run on your system. The CERN HTTP server is featured in the section on UNIX Web servers later in this chapter.

UNIX Servers

For UNIX platforms, there are many great server software packages. Most of the software have pre-compiled versions available. Some UNIX platforms offer the capability to proxy serve documents. This means company personnel could access the Internet's World Wide Web past an existing firewall, and the outside world could get Web documents on the firewall but should not be able to get past the firewall.

A *firewall* is a workstation that shields the internal network from the outside network—the Internet. It is the only machine that is directly connected to the Internet. This a great way to minimize unauthorized access to the company network.

CERN HTTPD

CERN HTTPD runs on UNIX platforms. This server software is one of the most popular. It is well-maintained freeware with excellent documentation. One of CERN HTTP server's greatest selling points is that it can also be run as a caching proxy server. The server will cache recently or frequently retrieved documents to improve response time.

This server's features include:

- Directory indexing
- The capability to process CGI scripts
- Access authorization mechanisms

The source code and numerous pre-compiled versions of the software are available. Pre-compiled versions are available for the following: Dec-Alpha, Decstation, Dec OSF, Hewlett-Packard, Linux, NeXT, RS6000, Solaris, SunOS, Ultrix, VM, and VMS. The CERN HTTPD technical guide is shown in Figure 24.3. At this site, you can find complete documentation for CERN HTTPD.

FIGURE 24.3.

CERN HTTPD documentation.

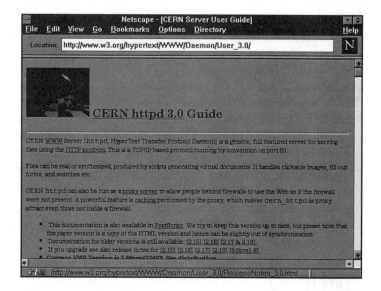

NCSA HTTPD

NCSA HTTPD runs on UNIX platforms. NCSA's server was designed to be fast and have a low-overhead, meaning not taxing on the system. It is freeware and feature rich.

This server's features include the following:

- Directory indexing
- Access authorization mechanisms
- The capability to process CGI scripts
- The capability to include the output of commands or other files in HTML documents

With NCSA HTTPD, you can make the server more secure by limiting access to server directories. The source code is available to optimize, but you can probably obtain a pre-compiled version for your system. Pre-compiled versions of the software are available for the following: Dec Alpha, Hewlett-Packard, Linux, Pentium, RS6000, SGI Indy, Solaris, and SunOS. A visit to the NCSA HTTPD document site depicted in Figure 24.4 will immediately answer the question of why you should use NCSA HTTPD.

FIGURE 24.4.

NCSA HTTPD overview.

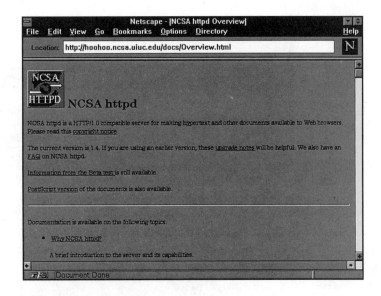

Netscape Servers

Netscape offers four commercial server software packages for UNIX and Windows NT systems:

Netscape Commerce Server	Designed to enable secure commerce on the Internet.
Netscape Communications Server	Designed to handle heavy loads and multimedia.
Netscape Proxy Server	Designed to provide secure Internet access and document caching, much like CERN's HTTP server.
Netscape News Server	Designed to help companies create their own newsgroups, and using Netscape's security protocols, these newsgroups can be either public or private.

Each of these software packages is directed toward specific needs and toward companies planning to connect to the Internet. The price of the server software is considerable. Netscape makes up for this by ensuring that their server products are easy to install, easy to maintain, and backed by good product support.

Netscape claims that their server software offers increased performance over the competition and can easily be integrated with commercial or custom applications. The software tends to have higher overhead than other HTTP servers, but it definitely makes up for this by reducing response times and making better use of the communications bandwidth.

The Netscape server FAQ depicted in Figure 24.5 is the place on the Web to find answers concerning the installation of Netscape server software.

FIGURE 24.5.

Netscape server software FAQ.

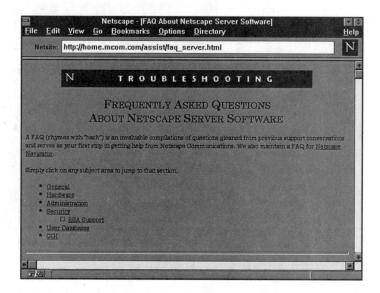

WN

WN is another good Web server for UNIX. It has great built-in document-indexing facilities and was designed with security and flexibility in mind. The two terms may seem conflicting, but WN manages to create both a very flexible and a very secure Web environment.

WN's security design and mechanisms are very different from other UNIX servers. Some servers may, by default, serve a file to someone simply because they know the name of the document. With WN, users can access documents only when they have been explicitly granted permission to do so. Another great security aspect of WN is that it can also restrict access to CGI scripts based on file ownership.

The only bad thing about WN is that pre-compiled versions aren't available. The source code must be optimized and compiled for your UNIX platform. Still, WN is one of the best UNIX servers available. For more information on WN server software visit the site depicted in Figure 24.6.

FIGURE 24.6.

WN server software overview.

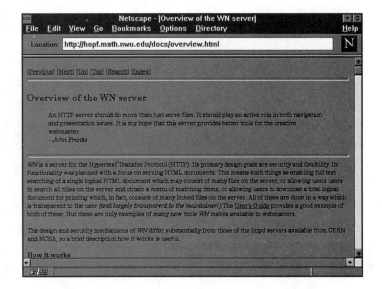

Windows Server

For Microsoft Windows, there is one primary choice, Windows HTTPD. Windows HTTPD installs easily and has low overhead. Just like MacHTTP, Windows HTTPD is a good choice for use on small networks and has a low fee. The server software was ported from NCSA's server and has many features including:

- Directory indexing
- Access authorization mechanisms
- The capability to process CGI scripts
- The capability to include the output of commands or other files in HTML documents

You can purchase Windows HTTPD from City Net Express, and it has a 30-day evaluation period. After the evaluation period, you are obligated to register the server or cease using the software. You can purchase the software for $99. City Net Express' site depicted in Figure 24.7 is where Windows HTTPD can be found on the Web.

FIGURE 24.7.

Windows HTTPD at City Net Express.

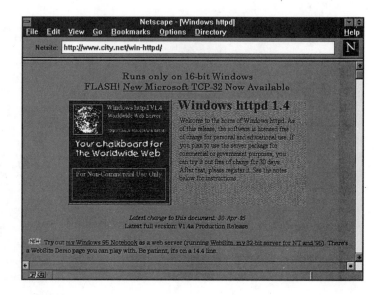

Windows NT Servers

There is a growing number of Windows NT server software packages. Because Windows NT servers are installed primarily on company networks, most of these software packages are commercial.

EMWAC HTTPS

HTTPS is for computers running Microsoft Windows NT. HTTPS is freeware and was created at part of the European Microsoft Windows NT Academic Center (EMWAC) project by Edinburgh University Computing Service. Once configured, the Web server runs as an available Windows NT service, similar to the FTP server facilities included with Windows NT.

Although EMWAC HTTPS is a quality server for the Windows NT environment, the installation of HTTPS is not for the novice. The installation instructions and the manuals assume you already know a lot about the Windows NT environment and HTTP. Figure 24.8 depicts where you can find the EMWAC HTTPS software manual on the Web.

FIGURE 24.8.

EMWAC HTTPS software manual.

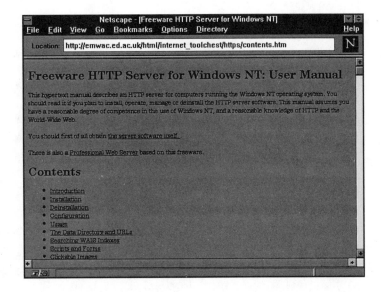

Netscape Servers

Refer to the UNIX section for details on Netscape's Windows NT servers. Netscape offers four advanced packages designed for both UNIX and Windows NT systems.

Purveyor

Purveyor is hot commercial server software for the Windows NT environment with a hefty price tag—$1,995.00. Purveyor was created by some of the same people that created HTTPS at Edinburgh University Computing Service. Purveyor is an extension of HTTPS and includes all the features of HTTPS with significantly improved functionality and security.

With Purveyor, you can maintain a list of authorized users and groups of users. Access to the server can be restricted according to individual files and directories. Like CERN's HTTP server, Purveyor can be used as a proxy server. The proxy can be used on the firewall to allow company personnel to access the Internet but not allow outsiders into the company network. The server will also cache documents to improve response time. Figure 24.9 depicts the Purveyor informational site on the Web.

FIGURE 24.9.

*Purveyor Windows NT
server solutions.*

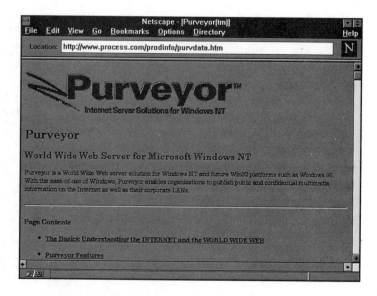

Selecting a Domain Name

After you've selected a platform and Web software, you should decide on a domain name for the Web server. During the installation process, you'll have to enter a domain name for the Web server. Common domain names for Web servers begin with www, such as:

www.*yourhostname*.com

If the company has decided to connect the server to the Internet, the network must have a unique identifier and domain name. You must register with the Internet Address Naming Authority (IANA). Your company can select any domain name as long as it is unique.

TIP

As *Electronic Publishing Unleashed* was going to press, the InterNIC announced that it will begin charging for domain name registration. Thousands of domains are submitted for registration every day, and this major change in policy caused a ripple that businesses around the world felt. Most businesses in the Internet community were surprised by the move. Some knew it was coming because they saw how the free system was being exploited by individuals trying to make a profit at the InterNIC's expense. If you plan to register a domain, check with the InterNIC for the current price for registration.

Each computer connecting to the Internet must have a unique IP address. The necessity of a unique IP address may mean changing the IP address on computers you plan to connect to the Internet. Obtaining IP addresses from the InterNIC is a three-step process:

1. Obtain the InterNIC Internet number registration form from:

   ```
   ftp://rs.internic.net/templates/internet-number-template.txt
   ```

2. Following the comprehensive instructions included with the form you retrieved using the FTP address above, fill out the form.

3. E-mail the completed form to:

   ```
   hostmaster@internic.net
   ```

Domain-name registration for ROOT, EDU, GOV, COM, NET, and ORG domains is also a three-step process:

1. Obtain the InterNIC domain name registration form from:

   ```
   ftp://rs.internic.net/templates/domain-template.txt
   ```

2. Following the comprehensive instructions included with the form you retrieved, fill out the form.

3. E-mail the completed form to:

   ```
   hostmaster@internic.net
   ```

CAUTION

Beware of persons trying to sell registration services. Ultimately, these individuals must go through the InterNIC to register your doman. On the Internet, I've seen individuals selling registration services. These individuals provide easy-to-use fill-out forms for processing your registration and charge fees ranging from $50–$500. As you've seen, the submission process is not difficult and is certainly not worth $500.

NOTE

The InterNIC is a very busy organization. Not only do they provide detailed explanations with registration forms, they include multiple sources with each of their forms that you can use to find additional information. Refer to these sources of additional information before sending inquiries to the InterNIC. If you have a unique situation that is not covered in either the IP or domain registration forms, such as registering as an Internet Service Provider, you can find a list of registration forms provided by the InterNIC here:

```
http://rs0.internic.net/templates.html
```

The Basics of Installing Server Software

Now that you've selected your platform and software, you're ready to begin the installation process. After following the tips you'll find throughout the rest of this chapter, you should have your server up and running before the day is out.

You may be amazed at how easy it is to get the server up and running now that the major decisions as to the platform and software are behind you. Although commercial server software is nearly trouble-free and includes automatic installation processes, freeware server software is not a bad way to go either. As you have seen, for most freeware server software there are pre-compiled versions of the software available. This makes installation very easy.

The six basic steps of the server installation process are as follows. Each of these steps is described in more detail in the following sections.

1. Purchase or download the software.
2. Begin the installation process by compiling the software or selecting installation options after initiating the automatic installation process.
3. Configure the server, or select automatic configuration options.
4. Ensure that all the files are in the locations specified in the documentation and that permissions are set correctly. This is usually an automatic process for commercial and freeware software, but it doesn't hurt to be safe.
5. Start the server.
6. Test the server.

Purchasing or Downloading the Server Software

Most server software packages are available for downloading on the Internet. If you have access to the World Wide Web, visit the site that has the software you would like to obtain. There, you will find information about the most current version of the software and instructions on downloading the software. Many of these sites have installation instructions available at the Web site and complete operating manuals that also may be viewed as HTML documents or downloaded.

Some commercial server software packages must be purchased directly from the creators and are not available for downloading. These are primarily the Netscape servers and the Windows NT server, Purveyor. Before paying big money for a product you are unsure of, visit the site and check the available documentation carefully to ensure that the software will meet the needs of your organization. It may also be possible to obtain a test version (Alpha/Beta versions) of the software for trial and evaluation.

Beginning the Installation Process

Most of the server software packages you'll find on the Internet are compressed. Although the type of compression really depends on the platform for which the software was designed, the installation instructions will usually explain how to uncompress the software. Before uncompressing the software, you should create a new directory and move the file to that directory for unpacking. Uncompress the software, if necessary, and then start the installation process. You may be prompted to enter the domain name you selected earlier or be directed to add the domain name to a system file.

Configuring the Server

Each type of server software has different configuration steps. This section outlines the key ideas and potential problem areas you may encounter. The best source for configuration information is the server documentation. Read the documentation thoroughly. If the documentation isn't clear on an area that involves security, you should follow the strictest security option.

Configuring commercial server software is a simple process. After starting the installation process, you either select configuration options or make simple adjustments to your system. At some point during this process, you'll be asked to input the domain name you have selected.

For CERN HTTPD, NCSA HTTPD, HTTPS, and WN there are some special considerations. After you've unpacked the files and compiled the software, if necessary, you will need to edit configuration files and create logs as necessary. Configuring these servers is an involved process that could fill a chapter for each software package. This is primarily because of the numerous options and features available. Read the manuals and go through the configuration files line by line. After carefully considering the options, enable or disable (turn on or off) the server parameters.

For MacHTTP and Windows HTTPD, the installation process can be made clearer and easier by providing a series of steps outlining the process. Here's a closer look at the setup and configuration process for these two systems.

MacHTTP

For Macintosh, after you unpack the file archive, all you need to do are these three steps.

1. Put an alias to MacHTTP in your system's Startup Items folder.
2. Put your HTML documents in the MacHTTP folder or subfolders.
3. Create a file named default.html according to the MacHTTP instructions.

Windows HTTPD

Windows HTTPD is easy to configure. Just follow these steps.

1. Exit Windows if you are running Windows. You must set up and configure the Web server from DOS. (DOS running from within Windows will not work; you must exit Windows completely.)

2. Set the time zone in your AUTOEXEC.BAT file as specified in the instructions. After putting this information in AUTOEXEC.BAT, you can type the same command at the DOS prompt so you don't have to restart the computer:

```
SET TZ=TTT#SSS
```

In this command, *TTT* equals your time zone, such as EST; # equals the offset from Greenwich Mean Time—the number of hours; and *SSS* is the optional daylight-savings time zone.

3. If you plan to allow CGI scripts, edit the SYSTEM.INI file. Make sure the following line is in the [NonWindowsApp] section:

```
CommandEnvSize=8192
```

4. Create a new group and/or select icon for WinHTTP. To do this, access the desktop file menu, and select the New command (Alt+F followed by Alt+W). Select the group to which you want to add WinHTTP, and enter the path information and description.

Double-Checking for Security

This is a last check for security. Always make sure that all the server files are where they are supposed to be and that file permissions are set as appropriate. This is normally done for you during the installation process. However, if you updated files or moved files around the system, you may have changed file permissions.

Server and network security is critically important. Even if you don't plan to connect to the Internet, it is best to test the server internally for a trial period before opening the floodgates. Let your Tiger Team discover the possible security problems, and not hackers that may be after company secrets.

> **NOTE**
>
> A *Tiger Team* is a group of people assigned to find security problems. They try to break into the system to find its weaknesses. If you don't have a special team assigned, or you are a one-person operation, test the server's security yourself. You probably will be glad you did.

Start the Server

After setup, configuration, and final checks for security, you're ready to begin. Start the server and enter the world of network publishing! If you haven't already created your documents and moved them into place, follow the procedures in this book. In particular, Chapter 23 discusses installing, supporting, and maintaining your published documents.

Test the Server

Now that the server is up and running, you should test it out. If the server isn't running, check the next section for some helpful troubleshooting tips. The best way to test the server's operational status is with a Web browser. Load your favorite browser software and access the Web server with either of the following URLs:

```
http://www.yourcompany.com/
http://www.yourcompany.com:portnumber/
```

The name between the slashes is the name you gave to the server—its domain name—during the setup process. If you set up the Web server's ports in a location other than the default port, you must enter the port number parameter. If all went well, this should be the last step in the setup and configuration process. Congratulations!

Trouble-Shooting Problems

Even the best of plans can go awry. If you know the type of problems you may experience and their symptoms, there is a better chance that you'll be able to correct the problem quickly. In this early stage of trying to get the server running and testing your document, the main types of problems you may experience are

- Problems with server processes—the server simply won't run the HTTPD.
- Problems accessing documents—you can't load a page into the browser or you're denied permission to do so.
- Problems within documents—the pages just don't look right.

Problems with Server Processes

Don't fret if something goes wrong and the server software doesn't start. If this happens, review the server documentation step by step. Ensure that you've performed every step and that things on the server are as they should be. Chances are you skipped an important step or forgot to change the mode on a file. Some good indicators of problems with setup are

- Server processes start and then die.
- Server processes start, and many errors are written to the screen.

■ Server processes start but won't execute properly.

■ Other erratic behavior occurs, such as the server freezing up.

As you reexamine the installation procedures, pay close attention to syntax. Syntax is critically important, particularly on UNIX systems. Syntax includes punctuation marks such as periods or dashes that are included in filenames. Syntax problems could also come from files being in the wrong case. UNIX is case sensitive, meaning that WSERVER, WServer, and wserver are three different filenames. Additionally, on a UNIX system, type in the lines exactly as they are shown, including all spaces between assignment operators.

Problems Accessing HTML Documents

Sometimes the server processes and other associated processes may seem to be running fine, but you just can't access your documents. The first thing you should do is to make sure all files are where they should be. Most of the time, HTML documents and associated files must be in very specific directories in order for the files to be accessed. If they are, there are several key things on the server you should check next. Problems accessing HTML documents stem from three main sources:

■ Incorrect file or directory permissions

■ Incorrect file extensions

■ Lack of an index file

Incorrect File or Directory Permissions

Restrictions on files and directories are another key area to examine when you are having problems accessing files. During setup and configuration, you may have restricted access to files or directories inadvertently or purposefully but forgot the parameters you set. Check the configuration files to see what features you turned on or off, and then check permissions.

The permissions on the HTML documents and directories are very important. This is especially true on UNIX systems where the default file permissions are set according to an involved permission set. All operating systems flag documents with permissions, such as these flags on DOS/Windows systems:

Is this a system file?
Is this a hidden file?
Is this file read-only?
Is this file executable?

UNIX systems add to this simple set of permissions by an order of magnitude. Files and directories have owners and group membership. Additionally, these files and directories have associated privileges: read, write, and execute permissions for the owner, the group, and others with access to the system. On UNIX systems, a directory must be executable to be accessible.

Incorrect File Extensions

The file extension of HTML documents and other file formats is also critically important. Web servers may use the extension to determine what type of file you are trying to access. Web browsers may use the extension to determine what type of file you are retrieving and the action to take on the file. The proper extension for HTML documents is .html or .htm.

Without additional server configuration steps, most software will not recognize the extension of .htm as being a valid HTML document. The primary exception to this rule is on Windows systems where file extensions are limited to three characters.

Lack of An Index File

This is another place you should check if you are having problems accessing documents. Most Web server software wants directories with HTML documents to have an index file. If you don't include these index files, you may experience problems. The server will generally display this default document when a user specifies a directory name instead of a filename. This file is sometimes called index.html but not always. For example, MacHTTP, NCSA HTTPD, and CERN HTTPD each have different conventions for this index file:

MacHTTP	Each folder should have a filename: default.html.
NCSA HTTPD	Although an index.html file isn't required for each directory, srm.conf should be set up properly to deal with this.
CERN HTTPD	Although this server will let you use alternate filenames for index.html (Welcome.html, welcome.html, index.html) these files should exist in the appropriate directories.

Problems Within HTML Documents

If you are having problems displaying documents, the appearance of objects and text in documents, or with hypertext links, the first place to check for problems should be the HTML structure in the documents. Syntax is critically important in HTML. Two of the most common syntax problem areas revolve around two sets of characters:

The tag enclosure set	< >
The double-quotation mark set	" "

These two sets of characters will cause more problems than you can imagine. If the HTML document has an <, the closing > must be present. Consider the following example:

```
<STRONG>This is standard text./STRONG>
<STRONG>This is standard text.</STRONG>
```

The first line has a syntax problem that will cause problems in the HTML document. The missing closure on the STRONG tag will cause all text in the document up to the next properly closed STRONG tag to be in bold or emphasized type.

If the HTML document has a " inside a tag, the closing " must be present. Consider this example:

```
<A HREF="the_linked_document.html>Visit the new link.</A>
<A HREF="the_linked_document.html">Visit the new link.</A>
```

The syntax problem in the first line will cause problems in the HTML document. Not only will the missing quotation mark cause the link to fail, the browser will think that everything up to the next quotation mark is a part of the link. This means that part of your document will not be displayed. The quotes must also be the standard ASCII double quotes. Some word processors have so-called *smart* quotes, where the opening quotes look different from closing quotes. If your word processor has this feature, disable it. Smart quotes are not standard ASCII and will not work in your HTML documents.

Web Server Administration

Someone should be assigned to administer the new server. Although the network administrator or system administrator could easily take over the additional responsibilities, administrative duties don't have to be the responsibility of one person. As you'll see, it is sometimes a good idea to share these responsibilities.

There are four general administrative duties:

- Answering technical questions
- Checking logs
- Keeping the server running
- Adding updates to the server

Answering Technical Questions

The server should have a point of contact for technical questions. This is normally the webmaster, an electronic mail alias providing a point of contact for the site. Web users can direct queries or comments to the webmaster. A mail alias is a generic mail address that can be assigned to a single user or group of users.

On UNIX systems, common administrative mail aliases are `root` and `postmaster`. By assigning the `root` mail alias to your system administrator, she can receive feedback concerning system problems. By assigning the `postmaster` alias to your e-mail administrator, she can receive feedback for e-mail problems.

Similarly, the webmaster can be a single person, your system administrator, or many people who answer specific types of questions. The mail address for the Webmaster is typically `webmaster@yourcompany.com`.

Checking Logs

Checking system logs should be the responsibility of one person. There are different types of logs. The most important log is the server's error log. The error log keeps track of system problems. The access log is another important log. It tracks who accessed what documents.

If the system seems sluggish or is experiencing problems, the first place the administrator should look is in the error log. The error log will tell the administrator what has been going wrong, and repeated entries will provide an excellent time-picture of the problem. The error log also tracks bad links and bad HTML documents. If you search through the log for these problems, you will be able to identify problem documents and erroneous links.

The access log is another good log for the administrator to check periodically. This log tracks who accessed what documents. The accesses to documents can be critically important in tracking down security violators and suspicious system activity. The access log will come in handy also when you want to count the number of accesses to your site or accesses to particular pages at your site. For example, you may want to count all accesses to the site for the first week of the month.

A single access is usually referred to as a *hit*. A hit count is completely different from a visitor count, which is especially true for large sites that may have hundreds of pages. For example, one visitor to your site accesses 25 pages. If you look only at the number of hits, it looks like 25 visitors came to the site. Keep this example in mind when you try to determine the number of visitors to your site.

Server logs tend to grow rapidly, and the contents of these files are erased on a periodic basis. A better method is to periodically copy the old logs to backup files and save old files for as long a time as seems practical. The logs may be your only proof someone has been violating system security.

Keeping the Server Running

The most critical administrative duty is keeping the server running. Just as someone is responsible for the operational status of other networked workstations, someone must be responsible for the operational status of the Web server. The best choice for this duty is at the system administrative level. Let your system administrators tack a new title onto their old one as the Web server administrator.

Updating the Server

The Web server administrator should ensure that the server software and tools are kept up to date. Most server software is under constant development. The most recent version will probably run more efficiently and include new features.

The responsibility of publishing, maintaining, and ensuring the accuracy of Web documents should not rest on the shoulders of the Web server administrator. Although network publishing is understandably a cooperative process between the administrator and department personnel, the administrator should be *responsible* for technical problems and not content. The administrator is there to answer questions, help with the general network publishing process if need be, and not to create documents for every department within the organization.

Large organizations should assign the additional duty of creating and maintaining Web documents to appropriate personnel in each major department that will network publish. Often, the logical choice for this additional duty will be the person who was responsible for creating and disseminating these documents under the old mechanism for distribution.

Network Publishing on Your New Server

Network publishing on your new server may at times be frustrating. This is especially true when you are first trying to install and configure the server. The important thing to remember is that network publishing can pay off in huge dividends. The time and money savings for network publishing company user and technical manuals alone make network publishing worthwhile. Not only can the documentation be maintained so it was always up to date at a cost less than the original publishing and distribution of the manuals, but employees will be able to search the entire text of manuals in an instant and at the touch of a button.

Although network publishing can bring dramatic improvements in the accessibility of information within the company, part of the problem with any project is that people often have unrealistic expectations or mismatched perceptions. The process of setting up your network publishing operation is no exception. The best thing you can do is to remember the following:

- Network publishing is a learning process.
- Take it one step at a time.
- Set realistic goals.
- Adopt a company-wide policy for use and publishing of information on the company Web.

A Learning Process

This is your first network publishing operation. It should be a learning process. Do not expect all the pieces to fall into place in a day. It simply will not happen. Give yourself and the project a fighting chance. Manage your expectations to help the project become a success. Remember, your expectations may not match the expectations of your superiors.

Before you start to set up the Web server, do the following:

- Make sure that your expectations and the expectations of your supervisors mesh.
- Make sure that the communications channels between you and your supervisors are open.
- Discuss expectations at the start and manage them properly.

One Step at a Time

Never let your thoughts about the complexity of the project overwhelm you. Your perceptions about the project play a decisive role in whether you will ever finish the project. Convince yourself you can do this.

Often, people forget that sometimes you need to take a breather. You cannot possibly try to do everything all at once. Set up your network publishing operation one step at a time. Begin by planning your course of action, and slowly progress from platform selection to server installation.

Set Realistic Goals

One of the first things you should do is make sure that your goals are realistic. Your goals should take into account both the complexities of the project and the possible setbacks. Your goals should be clear and relevant to the problem at hand—setting up the Web server and a networking publishing operation. As you set goals and milestones for each stage of the project, remember to provide flexibility. Never give yourself deadlines you cannot meet. If possible, give yourself a window for project completion.

Adopt a Company-Wide Policy

When you complete the project, remember to adopt a company-wide policy pertaining to the use and publishing of information on the network. The key is to not only adopt a policy, but to communicate it throughout the organization. Be sure that company personnel know the following information:

- Who to contact for technical problems
- Who to contact for setup
- Who to contact for training
- What documents or services are available
- How to access Web documents
- The responsibilities of departments and individuals
- The acceptable uses of the company's network publishing operations

Summary

Network publishing is an extremely cost-effective and time-saving way to publishing company documents. To set up a network publishing operation, you need to install and configure a Web server. Although you must be on the Internet to take advantage of the information resources of the World Wide Web, you do not have to be on the Internet to take advantage of the features offered by Web servers and browsers.

The Web server could be one of your existing network workstations or a new workstation you purchase specifically for the task. Once you have selected a platform for the server, you need to select server software. Server software is often freely available or available for a reasonable fee. After the server is set up, you are free to publish the company's documents.

Advertising and Protecting Your Document

25

by William R. Stanek

At present, an estimated 30,000,000 consumers around the world have access to the Internet. The year 1995 has been a growth year for the Internet and especially for the World Wide Web. During the late spring and early summer months, 5,000,000 users around the world gained full access to the Internet and the Web. In May 1995, CompuServe was one of the first major online services to bring a complete Internet package including access to the Web to its 2,000,000 subscribers. During the same month, America Online followed, providing full Internet and Web access to its 1,000,000 subscribers. Other major services, not to be outdone, scrambled to get their Internet projects completed.

Entrepreneurs, small companies and corporate conglomerates have discovered that the Internet is a gold mine. It is not uncommon for businesses to substantially increase their total annual sales simply by establishing an online presence. They have discovered the tremendous potential in advertising to 30,000,000 consumers. A single advertisement published on the Internet or the Web could be seen by millions of users. The cost of such advertising is negligible—often the cost of your time and the cost of an Internet account. When compared to traditional advertising costs, this probably makes the Internet and the Web the two most cost-effective advertising mediums.

Companies worldwide are scrambling to get online and reach consumers. Very often these enterprising companies are blinded by the numbers and overlook the risks to their own peril. On the Internet, security breaches, outright fraud and pilfering of your products are complete possibilities. The laws governing the electronic world simply do not yet exist to protect your intellectual rights. In this respect, the Internet may seem a wild free-for-all where anything goes. But even a place as wild and free as the Internet is not without some rules. These rules are defined by the dominant culture online: rules defined by standards of network etiquette; rules defined by the segment of the Internet you are in; rules defined by the type of activity you represent. If you wish to advertise on the Internet, you should follow the rules. Break the rules, and suffer the possible consequences.

On the Internet and the Web you can find many ways to spread the word about your products. This chapter explains the fundamentals of safe and effective advertising on the Internet and the Web. These fundamentals will help you become a good citizen of the Internet and protect your products. This chapter covers the following:

- Defining advertising
- Traditional advertising versus interactive information
- Inside Internet advertising
- Forces at work on the Internet
- Acceptable use policies
- Cultural aversion to advertising
- Tips for being a good citizen on the Internet
- The commercialization of the Internet

■ Adjusting strategies
■ Protecting your products
■ Establishing sound policies

Defining Advertising

Advertising is more than simply distributing information about your products to consumers. It is a way to call public attention to a product or service. The best advertising is done with a strategy in mind. Companies first determine the audience for a product. This can be done by surveying the public, evaluating trends or looking at the target audience for similar products. The result is that the company determines an audience for its product.

The target audience could be specific, males 16–24, or general, young adults. Sometimes the audience for a product seems evident by the type of product. An interactive children's book is seldom designed for adults. Although this is true, adults will probably be the primary purchasers of the product. Here, you would want to target advertisements at children as well as the adult buyers. Eventually, the advertising strategy develops into an advertising campaign or a series of strategies to capture the attention of specific audiences. Creating advertising campaigns is a billion-dollar business.

Traditional Advertising

Traditional advertisements are paid announcements in magazines and newspapers, over the radio or television, and on billboards. You can advertise through in-store brochures or mass-mailings of direct advertising. Each method of advertising has advantages and disadvantages.

Magazines and newspapers tend to be good low-cost means of advertising. A typical single-issue advertisement for the average small business probably costs $300–$500. This said, you probably could find bargain advertising, $50 for five lines in the back of a magazine or newspaper, or you could run full-page ads for $10,000 in a leading trade magazine. This is because the size of the ad and the circulation numbers of the magazine or newspaper greatly affect the cost of the ad. An ad that may be seen by millions will cost considerably more than an ad that may be seen by a few thousand readers. Large ads make statements about the companies placing the ads. If you have to turn past a two-page advertisement, chances are you will read something on those pages. Take a look at large ads in magazines or newspapers, you usually will not find much content, but you will find a highly effective way to sell products.

The problem with magazine advertising is that most magazines have very specific audiences. Your product may fit this audience and sell wonderfully. Then again, it may not fit the audience at all. If you select the wrong type of magazine to run your ads, the advertising will be a dismal failure.

Newspapers are great places to advertise business services, but not the best place for narrowly focused commercial advertising. Pick up the local newspaper and you will see the commercial advertising in newspapers is for specific types of products that generally appeal to the masses.

Radio and TV advertising are very effective means of advertising if the ads are targeted at the right audience and played at appropriate times. However, radio and TV are high-cost means of advertising. This is because the larger the potential audience, the higher the cost of the advertising. Usually radio advertising costs are substantially less than television advertising costs. A 30-second spot on the local radio station may cost $500. A 30-second spot on a syndicated radio show broadcast by many stations will cost thousands of dollars. Television advertising costs have a scale from thousands of dollars to millions of dollars.

Mass-mailings of direct advertising seem appealing. You are guaranteed that at least consumers will receive the advertising in the mail. The problem is that they may not read the advertisement at all. Most unwanted mail ends up in the trash. A more effective method of advertising is to use in-store advertising, such as brochures. This way if consumers are interested in learning more about the product, they will probably read the brochure.

The real problem with traditional advertising is that it comes with no guarantee of sales. Large companies generate sales through brand name recognition. Small businesses simply cannot afford to run costly ads that may generate limited sales. This is where hands-on advertising comes in. You sell a product through phone sales or personal sales visits.

Unfortunately, this hands-on approach has problems similar to those of traditional advertising. Telemarketing or advertising using the telephone is big business. Phone sales are slightly more effective than mass-mail advertising. This increase in effectiveness can be directly attributed to the increase in interaction with the potential customer. However, you still need to reach the appropriate target audience.

Personal sales visits work extremely well, especially if you have a product of interest to other businesses. With personal sales visits you have the highest degree of interaction with customers. This tremendously increases your chances of selling them your idea. The interactivity is the key to the sale.

Traditional Advertising versus Interactive Information

The difference between traditional advertising and interactive information-based advertising is very distinct. Television and radio ads are broadcast to consumers. Magazine and newspaper ads can only be read. Conversely, phone sales are highly interactive. But how much information can the sales representative really give a consumer in five minutes or less? For example, you probably hang up on the telemarketer that calls during dinner or any other inappropriate time. This is where Internet advertising comes in. Internet ads can be fully interactive. You can read Internet ads at your leisure and at a pace of your choosing after you put the kids to bed. If done well, Internet ads contain more information than advertising. For this reason, you will usually spend much more time browsing the advertiser's Web site than you would have spent listening to the telemarketer.

Traditional ads are inflexible and of narrow content. Internet ads can contain many depths of information from major topics to subtopics. These topics can be accompanied by dazzling graphics that can display automatically with the page or by multimedia segments that can be played using a helper application. Consumers can progress quickly through topics and subtopics in search of specific information they are interested in. Consumers want interactivity. They want to actively communicate, to exchange ideas and information with others. This type of exchange is fundamental to discussion groups that attract millions of Internet users.

Traditional advertising is low in information content and in interaction with consumers. The idea is to come up with a catchy slogan or eye-catching displays and not necessarily to provide information to consumers. An extension of traditional media advertising are infomercials— the long, documentary-style television commercials. The idea behind infomercials is to provide consumers with information about a product in a way that seems interactive.

The guise of interactivity is a key concept in infomercials. Although a 30-minute television spot is extraordinarily expensive, a surprising number of companies are trying to sell products in this manner, partly because infomercials are extremely effective ways to generate sales. You bring the product to the consumer's living room and draw them in by involving them with the product. Seeing the product in use and hearing the testimonials of satisfied customers sells the product.

Currently, it is impractical for the majority of consumers to interact with the television. Cable companies and technology companies are working to change this. TV-top interactive sets have already been tested in Miami and in Canada. The primary segment of television programming to feature interactivity is commercial advertising. Corporate giants were delighted to create interactive commercials for the testing because interactivity is going to have a payoff hundreds of times greater than the New York lottery.

These TV-top interactive sets offer many wonderful things to consumers. Imagine an interactive commercial produced by Ford Motor Company. No longer do you have to suffer through the same five Ford truck commercials in a few hours of television. When the first Ford ad airs, you can select from any car in Ford's line up. When the second Ford ad airs, you can elect to play more information about the previous car or preview a different car.

The initial sets were expensive, but recent advances in technology have made TV-top sets affordable for the masses. The next step is to bring interactive TV into your living room. "Why?" you might ask. The answer is that most consumers want interactivity. They want to be participants and not observers. They want the television to be something other than a dumb box.

These TV-top boxes will bring more than interactive commercials; they will also bring the best of the Internet and the World Wide Web because the Web is an enabling technology behind

TV-top boxes. The Web was designed to be an open-ended multimedia system. Any object, whether sound, graphics, video, or something yet to be defined, can be expressed in terms of a hypertext object. This is the power of the World Wide Web.

TV-top boxes may one day be the greatest thing to happen to advertising, but why wait 5-10 years to take advantage of a technology already in wide use? The World Wide Web and the Internet are tools you can use right now to advertise interactively with consumers. Interactivity is what makes Internet and Web advertising extremely powerful and highly effective.

Advertising on the Internet

Advertising by electronic means, such as the Web and discussion groups, rates on a level with a personal sales visits for information content and interaction. Information advertising works extremely well in a network environment. The following list includes a few of the many ways you can advertise to consumers on the Internet:

- Direct e-mail
- Press release postings
- Relationship marketing
- Display advertising on the World Wide Web
- Sponsorship

These advertising methods and more are the primary subject of Chapter 33, "Advertising Your Document." On the Internet, you can participate in any of over 6,000 discussion groups that you choose. You can post responses to specific questions about your company or simply join in the conversations. If you have information that is particularly useful, you can share it with a relevant discussion group or make it available in a FAQs (Frequently Asked Questions) posting for automated retrieval. You could set up a specially designed Web site to attract consumers, or you could sponsor other Web sites.

The interactive component of network advertising is equally as important as the information content component. Tools, such as Gopher, allow customers to locate the precise information they need and at the level of detail they are looking for. As far as the customers are concerned, the information is tailored to their needs, interests, and is available whenever they need it. Timing and availability are the key differences between synchronous and asynchronous communications.

Synchronous communications require that both a sender and a receiver are available at the same time to communicate the message. For example, a telemarketer that calls when you are away from home is not going to make a sale because she needs to talk to you to make the sale. However, asynchronous communications do not require both a sender and a receiver to be available at the same time. For example, you can send someone interested in your products an e-mail message containing complete product information on Thursday, and he can read it the following Monday. Or better yet, you can Web publish the company product information on your

Web site and consumers can access it whenever they want. As you can see, there is significant advantage in asynchronous communications. Information is available 24-hours a day, seven days a week. In the eyes of the customer, the company's operations are always open.

Information that would be prohibitively expensive to produce and distribute can be provided online at very little cost. Errors, typos or corrections to material can be fixed virtually cost free. This is not so when print material has already gone to press. Large numbers of customers can access the material at once, and companies that participate in relevant discussion groups can track customer reactions to products.

Company representatives can quickly step in to answer questions and even avert or resolve complaints. Beyond providing customer service, the company can also track customer interests. The companies will know what information customers are finding the most valuable by tracking the type and frequency of access. The bottom line result—interactive advertising on the Internet and the World Wide Web can lead to increased market share, lower cost margins, and enhanced customer satisfaction.

The Internet and the Web are not places to advertise haphazardly. Direct advertising on the Internet is frowned upon and can generate serious negative publicity. As you will see in the next section, providing value as perceived by the reader is a key to success in Internet and Web advertising.

Successful Internet Advertising

The Internet can be one of the most hostile places you have ever been if you attempt to advertise directly in total disregard for what the dominant culture deems acceptable. This section will help you navigate past the pitfalls and provide you with the keys to success in your Internet and Web advertising ventures. It will do this by discussing the following areas:

- Forces at work on the Internet
- Acceptable use policies
- Cultural aversion to advertising
- Tips for being a good citizen on the Internet
- The commercialization of the Internet
- Adjusting strategies

Forces at Work on the Internet

Many forces are at work on the Internet. Veteran users want to protect it. Governments want to control it. Some want to exploit its freedoms. Others want to make it a safe and useful place for children. Journey into the dark corners of the Internet, and you may understand the interests of each of these groups.

Users who have been on the Internet the longest feel they have certain rights and obligations. They remember the Internet as a place where commercial activities were prohibited and kept out of sight. They do not want the Internet to change and feel they not only have the right to defend it from commercialization, they feel it is their obligation to defend the Internet from commercialization.

Another force at work are governments who want to control the Internet. This should come as no surprise. Governments have always wanted to control the aspects of commerce, and electronic commerce is no exception. Yet, the issue goes way beyond commerce. People are lawlessly exploiting the freedoms of the Internet. Criminal activities are widespread. These activities range from copyright infringement to fraud to child pornography.

Given the situation on the Internet, it is understandable some legal standards must be established. The question is who should establish these standards. Government control tends to be expensive and not especially effective. Internet users probably could police themselves to avoid government involvement. A deciding factor may be public opinion. Concerned parents and teachers are getting involved in this issue. They want the Internet to be a place where the youth of the world can come and learn. And why can't it be? Providing information that is acceptable to as wide an audience as possible should be a key part of your electronic publishing and Internet advertising strategy. Another part of your strategy should be to follow the guidelines set forth in acceptable use policies that apply to your company and the Internet area you are operating in.

Acceptable Use Policies

Acceptable use policies play a major role on the Internet. Governments, corporations, schools and many other organizations have policies that specify what constitutes acceptable use of computer resources. If you have an Internet account through a non-commercial or corporate source, carefully read the acceptable use policy. The policy should state very specifically the types of activities that are considered acceptable.

Governmental and educational organizations have the most restrictive acceptable use policies. These policies usually preclude users from using their gratis accounts for commercial activities. To conduct commercial for-profit activities on the Internet or the Web you should have a commercial account. However, you generally can use government and educational accounts for non-profit activities or other activities that further the interests of research and education.

The National Science Foundation Network (NSFNet) retains an acceptable use policy that restricts commercial activities for all computers connecting to the Internet through the NSFNet. For-profit activities conducted on the NSFNet must relate to specifically acceptable uses of the Internet as stated in the NSFNet Acceptable Use Policy. Thankfully for the betterment of business, other less restrictive networks exist, such as the Commercial Internet Exchange (CIX) backbone. The CIX backbone is a parallel backbone to the NSFNet. It was established in 1991 by a group of commercial Internet service providers. Its purpose is to promote commerce on the Internet. Today, most Internet service providers are a part of the CIX.

Cultural Aversion to Advertising

Societies throughout history have been distinguished by their various cultures. Cultures provide patterns of acceptable behavior, values, and beliefs. In free societies, behavior, values, and beliefs have generally been determined by the majority and adopted by the whole. Communities around the world have cultures, yet culture is not limited to societies or communities. Culture is also not limited by size. Any group of people can have a culture that drives their patterns of what is and what is not acceptable. Corporations have subcultures separate from society as a whole because the rules of what is and is not acceptable are different within the corporation. The Internet also has a culture.

The dominant culture of the Internet has evolved over a period of 20 years. The people who initially formed the culture of the Internet were scholars, scientists, researchers, and government employees. Their beliefs about the Internet are very strong. They believe the Internet is not a place to conduct business. Advertising is unwelcome and unproductive chitchat that wastes network bandwidth.

The issue of conserving network bandwidth is a major one, especially in discussion groups. If you do not have something productive to add to a conversation, Internet users do not want to hear from you. Nothing will mark you as an outsider more quickly than sending a "me too" or "I agree" message. The opinion is that if all you have to say is "me too" or "I agree" save the network bandwidth and keep your comments to yourself.

Providing value as perceived by the recipients is an absolute necessity. Direct advertising on the Internet is frowned upon and can generate serious negative publicity. Any company that directly advertises on the Internet faces a barrage of negative publicity, thousands of e-mail messages generated by angry users and in extreme cases loss of access. This said, there are individuals selling lists of thousands of e-mail addresses targeted at specific groups of users. Other individuals are offering to distribute your direct advertising message for you. Both groups promise instant response and sales. What they neglect to tell you is that most of the responses may be hostile.

Companies familiar with the culture of the Internet have already adopted information-based approaches for reaching customers. They go out of their way to avoid any appearance of unwanted advertising.

Being a Good Citizen of the Internet

To fit in with the Internet's culture you need to know the rules of conduct. The rules of conduct on the Internet are called netiquette or network etiquette. Unfortunately, rules of etiquette are rarely written down. Although the etiquette of the Internet is also not written down, these guidelines can help you become a good citizen:

- Etiquette basics
- Read the FAQs

630

■ "Lurk" for a while

■ Participate responsibly

Netiquette Basics

Netiquette is more than the etiquette rules for the network. Following the rules of netiquette will help you and your company fit in. Most of the rules of etiquette are common sense rules. For example, you should always ensure you are sending mail to the correct address. Or when you post messages to discussion groups or any other public area of the Internet or the Web, do not send anything you would not actually write down in a letter or tell someone to his or her face. Sometimes when people correspond on the Internet, they forget there are real people on the receiving end.

Some rules of netiquette are simple, such as never type in all caps. Not only are messages typed in all caps hard to read, they show you have a poor understanding of Internet etiquette. If you type in all caps, you are shouting. Never shout unless you have a reason to.

Another basic rule is never post a private message to a public discussion group unless you have permission. Private messages are just that—private. They are a conversation solely between you and someone else. The sender may not want you to make the message publicly available.

In your electronic publishing ventures, you should keep the rules of netiquette in the back of your mind whenever your communicate on the Internet. When you advertise, advertise with a global perspective for a global audience with a diverse background. You should also ensure the advertisement contains more information than actual advertising. For example, several newsgroups discuss parenting issues and education. If you created a series of interactive children's stories designed to help children learn to read and decided to distribute the first story as freeware, there are several approaches you could take to distribute advertising in a non-intrusive manner.

You could start by posting a press release to newsgroups and mailing lists related to parenting issues and education that details the value and benefits of your free product. The message should state briefly that the first story is one in a series of stories that will be sold as commercial products. Although you generally should not provide ordering or price information for the commercial products in the message, you should tell readers where they can obtain the free story. Ideally, the free story would be available via FTP or as a Web publication. The FTP file the reader downloads could contain a brief commercial message at the end of the file with ordering instructions for the commercial product. The Web site could contain detailed information for ordering the commercial product. However, you would generally want to provide this as a separate Web page that readers of the free story can access if they want to learn more about your product.

Read the FAQs

FAQs are list answers to frequently asked questions. Most areas of the Internet have an associated FAQ or a place where you can go to learn about the area. FAQs were created because newcomers to areas focused on a particular subject often have the same questions. Instead of answering these questions repeatedly, the participants of a group simply tell newcomers to read the FAQ.

FAQs help everyone. If you ask a question that is covered in a FAQ, the group members will probably tell you to read the FAQ. They are not sending you away from the group. Rather, they are asking that you be courteous and spend some time learning about the group before asking questions that have already been covered by the group many times. FAQs can be marketing tools to help you determine the audience for a particular discussion group. FAQs may also provide posting rules and general guidelines for the group.

Lurk for Awhile

Lurking may sound like a bad thing, but actually it is a good thing. When you lurk in an area of the Internet, you are simply being an observer. You follow postings to discussion groups. You follow the chat sessions on the Internet Relay Channels. You browse an interactive conference room on the World Wide Web. Although you are observing, you learn how the group works. You learn what the acceptable practices are. You learn about the participants and their interests.

Spend a few days or a week learning about an area of the Internet before you become actively involved. As an electronic publisher wanting to further your business, this is especially important because first impressions are often lasting impressions. While you are lurking, you can make observations about the group that may help you plan your advertising strategy. You may decide that one group is a good audience for your publication and that another group is not a good audience.

Participate Responsibly

As a business person, you should always try to be on your best behavior. Responsible participation encompasses many things, from common courtesy to common sense. It involves keeping your messages brief and to the point when possible and furthering the discussion in the area by discussing subjects of interest to the group. It means that when you respond to a message you quote the original message only as necessary. This is important because most message systems allow you to easily include the original message in its entirety in a follow-up message. When you quote the original message, you should manually delete the irrelevant parts.

Being on your best behavior also means remembering to be courteous even when the other participants are not. Some discussion areas are downright hostile places to be, but that does not mean you have to contribute to the hostilities. No matter how careful you are in posting an advertisement to a discussion area on the Internet, you will probably offend someone. This is not always related to the actual content of your message. Sometimes it is a function of who you are and what you represent.

To support this theory, I tested out some advertisements on the Internet. I sent identical messages to similar discussion groups on the Internet. The wording of the message was very careful and primarily an introduction to free services my company offers on the World Wide Web. I posted a message from an account I maintain with a commercial online service. A short time later, I posted the same message to a similar discussion area from an account I have with an Internet service provider.

At the time of this posting, two major online services had just opened access to Internet newsgroups for their subscribers. Prior to this, no commercial online services had access to the Internet. As you might imagine, Internet users were in an uproar because the culture of commercial online services and the culture of the Internet were extremely different.

Commercial services have always been exposed to some type of commercial advertising. On the Internet, this was still mostly taboo, but this was not the only issue. The etiquette of commercial online services also differed greatly from the etiquette of the Internet. This created additional hostilities, and it was these hostilities that prompted users to respond angrily to the advertisement I posted from the commercial account.

The posting from the commercial account received two hostile messages, called flames, and no messages of inquiry. It was clear the responders had not even read the message and simply reacted spontaneously. Interestingly enough, these flames seemed to be form messages these particular users were sending out to any commercial entity that sent a message they did not like. A form message is a standard message that the writer sends out over and over again.

In contrast, the message I sent out from the other account received no hostile messages and hundreds of inquiries. Those responding were eager to learn more about the free services. Most thanked me for sending the message.

This disparity is not fair, but it happens. Some users will simply not like you for who you are or for what you represent. The key thing to remember is when you receive a hostile message, do not respond in kind. If the flame is posted to you privately, the best course of action may be to simply not respond to the sender. If the hostile message is posted publicly to the discussion area, you may feel obligated to answer. If you answer a hostile message, answer intelligently.

Changing Paradigm: The Commercialization of the Internet

Although cultures tend to resist change, the fact is that cultures evolve over time largely because opinions change as the majority changes. What was an acceptable practice a few years ago might be now unacceptable. What was unacceptable a few years ago may now be acceptable.

Previously dominant cultures are extremely resistant to change. This can be true even if the holders of those opinions are no longer the majority. This causes problems, and the result is a cultural lag. This is what is happening on the Internet today. Some Internet users are willing to accept the commercialization of the Internet; other users are not.

The truth is that the Internet is being commercialized and the anti-commercial Internet users are no longer the majority. According to a recent study released by the Internet Society, an international organization promoting cooperation among networks within the Internet community, commercial users presently account for at least 53 percent of all Internet users. Government, defense-related and educational activities currently account for approximately 20 percent of Internet users. Researchers, including commercial enterprises conducting research, account for approximately 27 percent of Internet users. Figures released in similar studies show similar trends. If the figures remain accurate, the number of non-commercial users will remain steady or grow less than one percent per year, while the number of commercial users will increase by 5–7 percent per year.

Evidence of the commercialization of the Internet is everywhere. Practices that would have caused flame wars just a few years ago are now common occurrences. Most users are tolerant of commercial activities, and the tolerance is growing. This does not mean it is time to seize the moment and start pumping out advertising. The growing tolerance shows users generally recognize businesses have information to offer that may be just as valuable as information other users have to offer.

Commercialization is spreading to traditional Internet stomping grounds as well. In the early days of the Internet, services were provided freely by such major participants as universities, research institutes and government agencies. Funding for the activities of these organizations came largely from the government and your tax dollars. Today, the issue of where funds are coming from is moving into the spotlight. The government is no longer footing the entire bill, and the amount of government subsidies are projected to decrease. This means some of these organizations are looking at ways of generating funds to support their Internet activities.

Recently, Internet users had two major wake-up calls that commercialization had arrived on the Internet. In March 1995, InfoSeek Corporation, owner of one of the largest information databases on the Web started charging for their services. An excerpt of the announcement of this change in service is depicted in Figure 25.1. Because InfoSeek services roughly 500,000 queries every day, to say the announcement shocked Internet users who had not anticipated this change would be an understatement.

FIGURE 25.1.

Commercialization of the Internet.

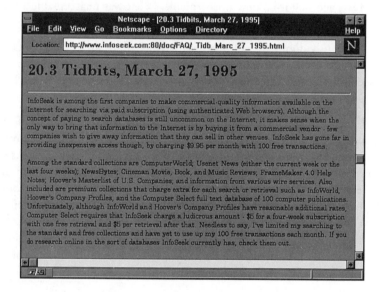

InfoSeek still allows Internet users to search the database for free, but the database will only give them a few of the top matches to each query. If they want to see more matches, users have to pay a fee. The fees for InfoSeek's standard pricing plan are depicted in Figure 25.2. The costs for searches are modest, from 10 to 20 cents. InfoSeek also has a premium pricing plan for specialty databases, as depicted in Figure 25.3.

Another change fueling the fires of those who warned of the impending commercialization of the Internet was when the Yahoo information database moved from its home at Stanford University (http://akebono.stanford.edu/yahoo/) to a commercial server. Yahoo is the brain-child of two Stanford doctoral candidates, Jerry Yang and David Filo. Yahoo's phenomenal popularity has put the academic careers of Yang and Filo on hold and launched their business careers into orbit. The Yahoo database was started in 1994. A year later, 200,000 visitors were performing an average of 2,000,000 searches a day.

The new home of Yahoo's database is at yahoo.com. Figure 25.4 depicts Yahoo's FAQ page where you can find everything you ever wanted to know about Yahoo. Yahoo Corporation plans to follow a sponsorship model to generate revenues to maintain its database. Interestingly enough, InfoSeek had a sponsorship model to help generate revenues for its database prior to adopting a fee-charging model and there continues to be sponsorship for the limited free searches.

#### Chapter 25

FIGURE 25.2.

InfoSeek standard pricing plan.

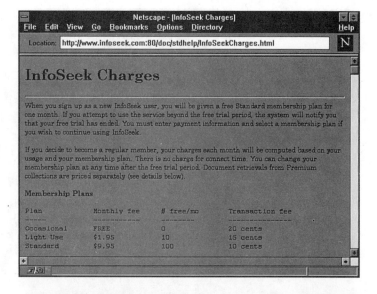

FIGURE 25.3.

InfoSeek premium pricing plan.

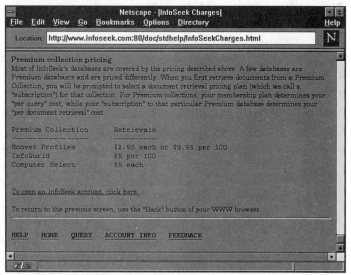

Although InfoSeek and Yahoo are some of the first major services to go commercial, they are not the only services to go commercial. Internet and Web technologies are rapidly evolving. Secure protocols, such as SHTTP (secure hypertext transfer protocol), are making it easier to set up Internet commerce. SHTTP removes a major obstacle to users who provide credit card information. With SHTTP, users can provide credit card numbers and other private information without worrying if a code cracker somewhere is going to steal the information.

FIGURE 25.4.

Yahoo Corporation FAQ.

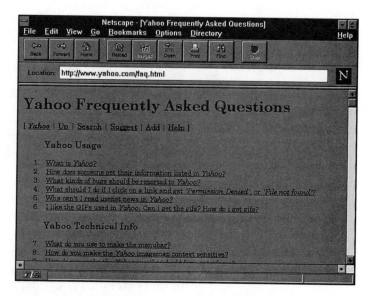

Adjusting Advertising Strategies

Just because an advertising campaign was successful elsewhere does not mean it will be successful on the Internet. Quite the contrary, what worked elsewhere will probably not work on the Internet. Internet users do not want to see electronic versions of print advertising. They do not want to see ads you posted to a commercial online service either.

Subscribers to commercial online services see some form of advertising every time they log in. Most of these services display highlights of new services or offers after users log in. Most of these services feature online shopping malls that are blatant advertising. Some services, such as Prodigy, even scroll commercial advertising along the bottom of the subscribers' screens. In the commercial online environment, advertising is deemed acceptable because it is the norm.

These users may not always like the advertising, but often see it as a necessary evil. Without advertising, the commercial service's monthly fees would be considerably more. The same is true in other mediums as well. A magazine without advertising would have a newsstand price that would make you think twice before reaching into your wallet. We do not have to wonder what television would cost us without advertising, just look at the rates for premium cable channels.

Before you attempt to advertise on the Internet remember these guidelines:

- Follow the rules of good citizenship.
- Be an observer for a time.
- See what other businesses are doing.
- Learn from their mistakes.
- Benefit from their successes.

Remember, this chapter provides only the fundamental background for advertising on the Internet. Chapter 33 explores specific and effective ways to advertise on the Internet. Chapter 34, "Publishing and Marketing Tips," provides you with specific tips for publishing and marketing your electronic publications that will save you hours of frustration.

Information and Protection

Releasing a creative work on the Internet without protecting the information is like putting a guppy in a tank full of piranha. You know the piranha are going to eat the guppy, you just do not know how soon. The Internet is unlike any other medium you have worked in. Before you release any creative work, even if it is just advertising, you should know the potential risks and take precautions as necessary.

On the Internet, as far as data is concerned, it is open season. Warnings that the information is copyrighted is only a step in the protection process. Copyright notices will not dissuade anyone from copying the information and using the information as they see fit. It is the electronic format of the information that makes it easy to steal. This is true anywhere on the Internet, but no place is it more clear than on the World Wide Web. On the Web, stealing your Web publications is as easy as saving the source code to a local file—a feature almost every browser in use has.

Some Web publishers have learned the hard way just how easily months of work can be stolen. There has been a rash of cases where software pirates have saved the HTML source code for hundreds of files at a World Wide Web site, changed the headers at the top of the pages and published the pages as their own. Maybe the pirates thought the Web was so vast no one would notice, but people did notice and more quickly than the pirates had anticipated.

One Web publisher knew right away the Web publications had originated from his site because the software pirates copied the entire site in tact, including the typos. The only item on the pages the pirates changed was the company logo. The files that were stolen represented six months of work and countless hours of research.

The Web publisher definitely had recourse to take action against the software pirates but to do this, he needed to prove the files originated from his site and were stolen from his site. Unfortunately, the publisher was ill-prepared to take action. He did not have a security policy or an information release policy. He had taken no steps to safeguard the information or to protect his intellectual property rights in case of infringement. After consulting an attorney, the publisher decided to accept the loss.

The steps the Web publisher should have taken to help protect the publications are not all that complicated. If he had spent a few hours in an effort to protect six months worth of work, the theft of his intellectual property may never have happened.

This section will provide you with the fundamentals to create sound information release and security policies. You should be able to develop these policies by examining the following:

- What you are trying to protect
- What the vulnerabilities, threats, and risks are
- Lessons learned from others
- Guidelines for establishing policies

What Are You Trying to Protect?

Determining what you are protecting is an all-important first step. This step is often skipped because it seems obvious that you are trying to protect your products. Although protecting your products should be a primary goal, your products are not the only resources at risk. As an electronic publisher, your resources are any creative works you produce and probably even your thoughts. If you have set up your own Web server, another one of your resources is the server. Any hardware attached to the server are also resources at risk. This includes computers connected to the Web server via the company network.

The information you have published is not the only information at risk. Any information that you leave in your account on the Internet Service Provider's server or on your own Web server is also at risk. Data coming to your Internet account and leaving your Internet account are also at risk. All these resources are things you should protect.

Not only do you need to know what things you are trying to protect, you also need to know what you are protecting them from. The average user may not understand that saving your publications and later using them for their own purposes infringes on your copyright. Most users do not have malicious intent when they download information that may or may not be copyrighted. After all, the Internet is a general free-for-all. Users search the Net for new and wonderful data to read and download to their computers.

How Do You Protect Your Document?

You need to be very explicit about the purposes for which information you provide can be used. You do this by prominently displaying copyright notices and inserting a brief "acceptable use" message into the text of any publication you wish to retain rights to. Obviously, this will not fend off those with criminal intent, but taking the proper precautions can help you avoid problems later.

You can also do many other things to help protect your publications. For starters, never make the entire publication publicly available if you are not comfortable with the thought of someone using the publication without paying for it. When you create Web publications, never put all your eggs in one basket. Remember, the Web publisher that put six months of work into creating a hot Web site only to have it stolen by a hacker. Part of the blame could rest on the publisher's shoulders because he made it too easy for the hacker to steal from him.

There was no real complexity to the publisher's site. The pages at the site were self-contained units that linked only to the top-level page. The pages themselves were lengthy, roughly 1,000 lines of wonderfully complete information that could stand all on its own outside the context of the publication. With a dozen pages containing 100 percent of the site's information, the hacker probably got away with everything the site had to offer in about five minutes.

> **TIP**
>
> One way to deter software pirates is to add complexity to the site. Create more levels in the document hierarchy. Make it more difficult for them to steal everything at your site by sharing the wealth of the site among many documents. As an added benefit, this will decrease the time it takes for the page to load and will actually make it easier for legitimate users to navigate the site because visitors will not have to read 900 lines of information before they find specific information they are interested in.

What Are the Vulnerabilities, Threats, and Risks?

Vulnerabilities, threats, and risks to your electronic publications may or may not be obvious. This is true for publications on the World Wide Web, floppy disk, CD-ROM, or whatever other medium you have chosen to electronically publish in. Electronic publications suffer from some of the same vulnerabilities, threats, and risks as their traditional counter parts.

Software publishers have always faced the problem of illegal copying—pirating of their publications. They have tried time and time again to protect their products. Software copy protection began as simple deterrents. Some manufacturers wrote codes to a certain sector of the disk. Some manufacturers formatted their disks in a certain way and checked to see if the current disk was formatted in this manner before loading the software.

Eventually software copyright protection evolved into elaborate schemes costing companies hundreds of thousands of dollars to develop. Yet no matter how advanced the schemes became, hackers found ways around the copy protection. The simple fact was people wanted to be able to copy products they had purchased. The elaborate nature of these schemes helped give birth to a segment of the software industry that specializes in producing software programs that could copy protected disks. Today dozens of these programs are on the market.

After pouring millions of dollars into research for copy protection, a growing number of software publishers are abandoning copy protection schemes. To their chagrin software companies are discovering the cost of trying to protect their products simply is not worth it. Sure the cost of protecting the software was passed on to consumers as mark up, but consumers were not always willing to reach into their pockets for a few more dollars. Because of this, these companies are actually able to lower prices, sell more product and make more money.

Many software publishers saw the CD-ROM as the Holy Grail of copy protection. CD-ROM mastering used to be extraordinarily expensive. CD-ROMs are read-only and can store massive amounts of data. To copy a single CD-ROM, users would have to store the data to their hard drives or dozens of floppies. However, even CD-ROMs are not safe from software pirates.

The price of CD-ROM products has made them very attractive to pirates. If a profit can be made in an illegal activity, you can be sure someone is going to seize the opportunity. The illicit copying of CD-ROMs is big business, especially in the Far East. One way to combat this, as software publishers have discovered, is to simply produce more product and lower prices. In this way, they are decreasing the software pirates' profit margins and making the illegal copying of CD-ROMs less attractive.

Although modern technology makes it easy to pirate publications no matter the form, the illegal copying of publications is not the only problem. Book publishers have had problems with copyright violators even before the coming of the copy machine. Books that were reported to the publisher as destroyed often show up on sale at bargain prices.

Book Publishing

In paperback publishing, fraud is a huge problem. Mass market publishers generally only require book sellers to return the cover of the book and not the book itself because the publishers want to cut their losses. They published the book and shipped it to a book seller. The expense of returning and storing paperbacks in a warehouse that may never be resold will only increase their potential losses.

In overseas markets, books and software are often illegally reproduced and packaged for resale. This is especially true in the Far East and in Eastern European countries. Sure some countries have intellectual property agreements, but if we cannot stop illegal copying in our own country, how can we realistically expect other countries to be able to stop it?

A major problem is that the reproductions are often either identical to the original product or very similar. To distinguish their products from the reproductions, companies, such as Microsoft, created elaborate packaging with special foil seals. The foil seals were specially produced and embedded with holographic images or writing that was revealed when held to the light in a certain way. They were supposed to be unreproducible or nearly so—an idea that did not deter the software pirates. Within a few months, these foil seals were being successfully reproduced, and the pirates were back in the business of creating and selling clones.

Protecting Your Documents by Giving Them Away

One way to protect your rights may be to give the publication away as shareware. When you distribute a publication as shareware, you ask the users who use the publication to pay a registration fee. In return for paying the registration fee, publishers generally give the user a license to use the publication and a means to obtain free or low-cost upgrades to the product. The best publications to distribute as shareware are reference works or works that will be updated annually, such as annual directories.

Another way to distribute your publication is to offer it to readers on a free trial basis. In this way, you freely distribute one or more issues of the publication to readers on a temporary basis. If readers like the publication and want to continue to receive the publication, they are asked to pay a subscription fee. The best publications to offer to readers on a free trial basis are periodicals, such as electronic magazines, newspapers, or newsletters.

You may also want to offer your publication as limited capability shareware, which is also called crippled shareware. In this way, you freely distribute the publication to anyone who wants to read it. However, the publication is not complete. For example, you freely distribute the first short story in a collection of short stories, hoping to hook the reader and sell them the collection.

The possible negative connotation for crippled shareware can be interpreted as a warning for publishers who wish to try this method. Some shareware software publishers created products that were too limited in their capabilities to be useful in any way. The lesson here for electronic publishers is to ensure your limited capability publication has enough substance to make it useful or enjoyable. The best publications to distribute as shareware are collective works or works with sections that can stand on their own.

Lessons Learned

Although the previous section showed one lesson you can learn from shareware publishers, you can learn other important lessons by examining the past as well. In particular, electronic publishers can take away lessons from the problems that book publishers and software producers have endured. These are some of the major lessons:

- All products deserve some type of protection.
- Protect your products in a way that makes sound financial sense.
- Determine very carefully the threats to the product and the potential losses from illegal copying.
- Look realistically at the problem of illegal copying or selling of the product.
- Determine very carefully the level of protection the product really needs.
- Do not price yourself out of sales by using increasingly elaborate protection schemes.
- The cost of protecting the product should be less than the total cost of the actual lost sales.

People often view the costs of protecting products as a cost of doing business. Although this is true, the costs of protecting products from software pirates or hackers are ultimately passed on to consumers in the form of higher prices. Higher prices may drive down your sales by forcing consumers to choose alternative products or simply not purchase your product.

As you have seen from previous examples in this section, it will not always make sense to try to protect products in an extreme manner. Protect your products in a way that makes sound financial sense. Focus on actual lost sales and real threats to your commercial viability.

The illicit copying of your product in Eastern Europe is undoubtedly a crime, but does the company currently have or will it have in the future, a means to profitably distribute the product in Eastern Europe? If the answer is no, trying to protect your product from reproduction in Eastern Europe is probably not worth the expense, the time, or the effort.

Yet, anything you produce deserves some protection, even if you plan to give it away freely. If you took the time to produce something, spending time and resources, why not protect it? On the Internet, it's a common practice of authors or programmers who create freeware products to provide a copyright notice. Some authors take this a step further by putting a clear disclaimer stating they reserve exclusive rights over the program and further reserve the right to start charging for use of the program.

Recently, a major corporation started charging fees for the commercial use of its extremely popular image compression algorithms. The image compression algorithm is GIF and all its associated formats. Saying the general image format that began on CompuServe is extremely popular is an understatement. The GIF format is the most widely used image format in the world. It has been in use for years and is one of the most efficient image compression algorithms. Millions and millions of images are in GIF format.

The company that retained the right to charge fees for use of GIF compression algorithms is Unisys Corporation. What this means to businesses is that a small percentage of royalties from any commercial product containing images in GIF format goes to Unisys. As you might imagine, Unisys Corporation's announcement to start charging fees caused an uproar.

Some commercial companies who create paint programs, authoring tools, and other programs using images have removed support for the GIF format in the latest release of their products. These companies are banding together to fight what they see as an injustice. Unisys maintains that it provided the format freely for many years, informed the public that it reserved the right to charge fees in the future, and has now exercised that right.

Establishing Policies for Documents

When corporate America thinks of policies, they often think in terms of unwieldy documents that make *Webster's Unabridged Dictionary* look scrawny. The word policy does not have to be an ugly word. For a small company or a one-person operation, the policies you adopt may only be a few pages.

The key idea is to write down your thoughts and turn those thoughts into a general guideline that you or someone else can follow. Remember, your Web documents will only be as safe as you make them. Two key policies will help you protect your Web documents:

- An information release policy
- A security policy

Information Release Policy

The key to protecting your publications is to have a plan before you release products or information about products. On the Internet and the Web, where a single message posted to a discussion area could be seen by thousands of people, this is critically important. The information release policy you adopt should help you determine the level of product information you feel comfortable distributing. The policy should also help you determine the degree of protection you feel your products deserve.

Some companies adopt information release policies only when problems arise, but by this time it is already too late. The only thing the company can do is try to minimize the damage or cut the losses. As you create your information release policy, consider the topics discussed in the previous sections. Think carefully about each of these:

- How do you plan to release products or information about your products?
- Who is authorized to release products or information about your products?
- How much and what type of information do you feel comfortable releasing?

Detailed information about a product released prematurely can be damaging to the company's reputation if the products do not go to market on time or worse—if the product does not go to market at all because of development problems.

Security Policy

A security policy pertaining to your Web publications is not the same thing as a Web site security policy or a company security policy. Yet, they have many common elements. In each case, you determine:

- What you are trying to protect
- What you are trying to protect it from
- What the likely threats, risks, and vulnerabilities are

After you determine these items, you should implement measures to protect the assets. The measures you implement depend on the degree of risk and the level of protection you feel a particular asset needs. For Web documents, you may feel all the protection your documents need is a copyright notice. You may want to restrict access to the information. One way to restrict access is to require all users to have an account at the site.

The choices are yours, but you should take the time to make those choices before you are forced to. It is too late to adopt a security policy when someone has stolen your ideas. Months of hard work can be protected with a few hours of planning. Think about the ideas discussed in this chapter and adopt a document security policy you feel comfortable with.

Here are a few guidelines on establishing a security policy:

- Choose controls to protect documents in a cost-effective way.
- Choose the right set of controls for the right circumstances and reasons.
- Use common sense.
- Use multiple strategies.
- Monitor access as necessary.
- Define actions to take when illegal activity is suspected.
- Communicate the security policy throughout the company.

Summary

Products are sold through advertising. You can potentially reach millions of consumers on the Internet and the World Wide Web. Not only can you reach consumers, but the online world is one of the best mediums to use to do so because, by nature, the Internet and the Web are highly interactive, and interactivity is the key to sales.

The way you reach consumers online is extremely important. You should follow the rules of netiquette and be a good citizen of the Internet. Before you advertise, you should understand the risks, threats, and vulnerabilities to your products and take measures to protect your products. One of the best ways to do this is to establish a sound security policy and an information release policy.

V

Projects

Publishing a Multimedia Résumé

26

by William
Montemer

IN THIS CHAPTER

Résumé—a short account of one's career and qualifications prepared typically by an applicant for a position.

Technology has changed the face of publishing in the 90s. Just as desktop publishing made high-quality, high-resolution typography easily accessible for almost any writer and editor in the 1980s, desktop multimedia—video, animation, high-resolution color imaging, and CD-quality sound—promises to bring professional multimedia capabilities to any would-be producer and media mogul. The time is right for any talented and enterprising media author or artist to "get the word out" and let employers and corporate sponsors know they are able and available for work.

However, in this age of "information superhighway" light-speed delivery and electronic distribution, our method and medium for getting that project or landing that "dream job" remains a hangover from the "information dirt road"—the paper résumé. You might upgrade the résumé's look with classy fontography, clever clip-art and expensive paper, but the end product will still be earth-bound and limited. Surely there must be a more suitable vehicle to speed new media proponents down the infobahn.

In this project you'll learn how to create a multimedia résumé that truly breaks new ground and opens up a world of possibilities. Like any of the new media forms, our résumé project is based on the tried-and-true principles of clear communication and solid visual design. The résumé also introduces design concepts that are particular to multimedia production—in fact, by approaching your résumé as a microcosmic mini-multimedia project, you'll be exposed to most of the basics of real-world multimedia production.

In the 90s job marketplace, a multimedia résumé will truly separate you from the crowd. But even more importantly, a multimedia résumé can effectively communicate more information about you and what you can do—using non-verbal audiovisual communication and computer interactivity—than a conventional paper-based product.

If you already know the fundamentals of good writing in general—and résumé writing in particular—extending your skills to a new medium should prove to be very valuable, and hopefully fun, too.

Before you go any further, you might want to load the sample résumé on the accompanying CD and try it out. You'll find a file called MYRESUME.EXE under the Chapter 26 directory on the CD. Figure 26.1 shows the résumé app in action. This résumé application demonstrates several critical factors about your presentation. Remember that everything about your résumé—what it says, how it looks, and how easy it is to install—creates a first impression. As you build this application and explore some of the other samples included on the CD you'll learn how to create sophisticated mini-applications. As a bonus, you'll learn how to create a first-class installation setup program that lets prospective employers know that your work is thoroughly professional.

FIGURE 26.1.

The résumé application in action. The design of the résumé demostrates several principles of interactive design.

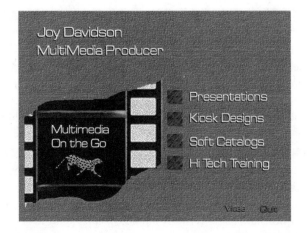

Right now, however, consider one very important question about the multimedia résumé—is a multimedia résumé right for me?

Is a Multimedia Résumé Right for Me?

How you answer this question can determine whether you skip this chapter and save yourself some time or get your hands dirty and work along with the chapter. Even if you're not sure you could use one, or only wondered "how would they do that?" when you flipped through the table of contents, a résumé is a good starting point to begin your multimedia explorations. First, consider who might benefit most from using a multimedia résumé to present themselves to prospective employers.

Obviously, multimedia producers could use a good multimedia résumé. Other than having an armload of best-selling CD-ROM titles and games to your credit, there is no better way to present your credentials as a true multimedia creator than to use your own creative medium. (In fact, the basic format of this project is derived from my own working résumé, which has done its job to get me interviews and opportunities as a multimedia producer.)

In general, professionals and people from other creative trades—graphic artists, animators, video producers, trainers, public relations people, advertising and marketing consultants, even print authors, composers, and musicians—might benefit from presenting themselves and their abilities in multimedia form. The key element of multimedia production is visualization: can you show your work and your ability using a visual—and to a lesser extent audio—medium?

> **NOTE**
>
> Although electronic and CD-based résumés might be in keeping with the spirit of the information age, paper-based résumés are definitely not dead. As one professional recruiter stated recently, "Make sure you send a paper copy. Busy recruiters like to walk around with stacks of résumés. They can't do that with a CD." Besides being easy to handle, a paper version is much easier to distribute to fellow workers and team members—something that happens quite often in the larger team-oriented multimedia ventures.
>
> Finally, remember that a multimedia résumé is a great opener, especially if the position for which you're applying involves multimedia production and graphics. An interested employer can then study, and possibly notate, the paper copy. For obvious reasons, the electronic and paper versions should complement each other in both style and content. Although an identical match might not be necessary or desired, some synergy will help and is best accomplished in the preliminary design and first-draft production stages.

Even the more adventurous practitioners of more "standard" occupations might use a multimedia format to make an impression. Be aware, however, that in some job situations a multimedia presentation is simply an added distraction that might actually do more damage than good. With that warning, look at some multimedia basics and how they apply to your résumé project.

A Multimedia Development Primer

A multimedia production is really a collegial activity involving a variety of creative disciplines. Even in a small team, it is unlikely that one individual will possess all the skills necessary to create and produce a multimedia product. But it is often the case that a few individuals will wear many hats as the production makes its way from a sketchpad drawing to a fully realized multimedia implementation.

As in any team activity, a unified vision and good communication will make or break the end product. The following section briefly summarizes the activities found in a typical multimedia production.

Specification

This phase involves creating the initial concept and developing a strategy for implementing it. Several practical decisions made at this point will affect how the project is developed, for what hardware platform—IBM, Mac, or both—it will be developed, and how the end product will be used and delivered. At this phase, a budget and timeline for the development are also drafted.

A written specification produced in this phase can be used as a guideline throughout the development process. As a practical matter, the written specification lets both the developer and the client know when a project is completed and keeps the project from entering an endless loop of requested changes and client demands.

Design

The design phase determines what the end product will look like and how the user will interact with it. In this phase you can generate a written script or a storyboard or both. Also, the structure of the interaction, which determines the format of the multimedia project—how options are presented and how individual branches are connected—is determined in the design phase.

Prototype

The prototype might be as simple as a series of crude sketches or as complex as a working model developed with a visual drag and drop environment. Usually, however, the prototype phase consists of a storyboard and a few screens placed together in a slide show. The prototype enables the developer to visualize the final product and also describe it to clients, employers, and users.

Multimedia Element Production

The body of any multimedia production will be the individual multimedia elements. These might include scanned and composed stills, motion graphics, two-dimensional (2D) and three-dimensional (3D) animation, digital video, digital audio music and voice-over, and synthesized Musical Instrument Device Interface (MIDI) music. Each of these elements could require an individual specialist or at least a small production team. However, for some in-house or corporate presentations, using professional stock footage, animation, and clip art can significantly improve the production quality of an otherwise limited project.

Programming and Integration

Up to now, all the elements of the multimedia product have been developed almost independently. In this phase of the development, you finally see how the individual pieces "play together" as a whole. This is also the time when you see if your original design is appropriate, especially if there are hardware problems to resolve. For instance, if you are working with a more-common 256 color palette instead of a more generous but less-universal 64,000 color one, you might find it difficult to combine animation, still graphics, and digital video without unsightly palette flashes. In this case, you can attempt several "palette management tricks" in production and code, redeeming an otherwise unacceptable production flaw.

Final Delivery

The final delivery involves giving the customer a product that is bullet-proof, easy-to-install and easy-to-use. It is also where any design misunderstandings, programming faux-pas, and conceptual misjudgments usually appear. Often it is only at the final delivery that the customer finally gets a sense of what the production will be. Hopefully, you have successfully kept the customer advised and gotten sign-offs and approvals all the way through.

As you prepare a final "gold master" to send to a duplicator/manufacturer or develop installers and multi-floppy disk sets for distribution by a client, all your previous groundwork and preparation—or lack of it—will be exposed. On the other hand, if you do all your preparation and design work right, your final application can be ready to distribute with only a few minor tweaks. As you and your team get more experience in multimedia, you will hopefully experience more of the latter exhilaration and less of the former anxiety.

The Résumé Multimedia Project

As stated earlier, your multimedia résumé is a microcosmic multimedia project, with most of the components of any real-world multimedia production. To demonstrate this—and force yourself to follow some structured development scheme—you'll progress through and discuss every step of a full-blown multimedia production. As shown in Figure 26.2, your multimedia résumé production can be divided into phases.

FIGURE 26.2.

The production phases of your multimedia résumé project.

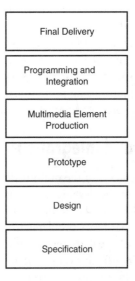

Final Delivery

Programming and Integration

Multimedia Element Production

Prototype

Design

Specification

The Multimedia Résumé Specification

As far as specifications go, creating one for a multimedia résumé is straightforward, especially if you already have a working résumé. For simplicity, you can consider the specification in two parts: the content of the résumé and the résumé as a software end product.

The content of the résumé will be standard résumé fare: short and crisp, active tense résumé language, results-oriented job descriptions, accurate and inclusive dates.

The résumé end product specification is similar. You will put the résumé together in Visual Basic because it is fairly common, reasonably priced, and provides more than enough room for interactivity. It is also supported by a number of very "cool" third-party tools like the Motion Tools animation engine from Motion Works, a demo of which is included on the accompanying CD. These tools enable even beginning Visual Basic programmers and users to quickly create great-looking applications. In particular, by using a stand-alone animation tool to develop your multimedia opening, you take the opening design out of the programming realm and make it a completely visual drag-and-drop activity—something almost any resourceful and creative person could master.

In its simplest form, the résumé application will consist of a menu of category buttons, icons, and simple "graphic hot-spots" that are linked to additional information. The basic operation is trivial: each time a user clicks a button, the program brings up a defined set of graphics and text.

The graphics will be 256 color Windows bitmaps running on a standard 640×480 pixel screen. You will also add a tiny bit of sound—enough to tell users that this is a real multimedia application, but not enough to inflate the size of the application. Most of the multimedia activity in your résumé takes place in your opening sequence. You'll be surprised to find out how easy it is to assemble the opening so that, hopefully, you can create your own animation, place it into your template, and have a working distributable résumé by the time you finish this chapter.

To make your project more usable, you'll design your résumé to be easy to change and update. In particular, the design enables information to be "dynamically" loaded or pulled off the hard disk as it runs. This makes it possible to adapt the résumé application on the fly.

Although the design of your project is not the most creative approach to building a multimedia résumé—you might be able to create a game-like interactive piece complete with motion graphic "sprites" and animated buttons—its effectiveness comes in its understated elegance and simplicity. If you can create a multimedia résumé with all these attributes, you will definitely be ready to speed down the infobahn in style.

Designing the Multimedia Résumé

Because your project is so simple you could easily combine the design and prototyping steps. As a matter of fact, if you take the time to develop a functional prototype you'll find that your work will be already done.

As stated earlier, creating your résumé project really involves crafting two components: the résumé content and a piece of software. Because this chapter is not trying to show you how to write a résumé, but how to implement one in a multimedia format, look at the content part only as it pertains to multimedia.

The Résumé Content

As you might already know, there are three basic styles of résumés: chronological, functional, and a combination of the two. The most common type, the chronological style, is often simply a historical documentation of what jobs you have held and what you did in them. On the plus side, it usually contains the type of substance employers like to see in a résumé. On the minus side, it can be dull and sometimes restricts how you'd like to present yourself, especially if you are trying to negotiate a career shift or change.

A QUESTION OF STYLE

The dictionary defines a résumé as a short account of one's career and qualifications that is prepared typically by an applicant for a position. This is an effective description that will fit this project quite easily.

Rather than throwing out every copy of your résumé and any résumé books you might own, I suggest you use them as a starting point and rework them. Even for a seasoned writer, multimedia is a new medium that should be approached with freshness and new vision. Just as writing a novel differs from writing a screenplay, writing a résumé for multimedia requires a different emphasis than writing one for print.

Because a résumé is often your first and only chance to make a good impression on a busy employer, you want your résumé to stand out and yet not appear too contrived or gimmicky. As a multimedia presentation your résumé will definitely stand out, but there is a very real danger that recruiters might not appreciate this approach. Obviously, if your résumé is badly organized and sloppy the multimedia element will simply look like a cheap trick used to cover an obviously thin piece of work. For that reason, if you choose to create and use a multimedia version take time to do it right, and make sure you have an equally good paper copy.

If done elegantly and well, a multimedia résumé can be the perfect opener for a solid creative professional, giving you a chance to prove your worth to a prospective employer right away. Therefore, you should put a lot of thought and time into the design, the text copy, and the preparation of all the various multimedia elements used in your résumé.

Professional résumé writers suggest that you spend an inordinate amount of time developing an effective paper résumé. It should be short—preferably one page—and detail your strengths in a way that invites employers to predict how you will succeed in their environment. Developing a multimedia version should take as much time as it takes to write a paper version, and then some, depending on the availability of other graphics, sound, and animation source material.

A multimedia résumé gives you more avenues in which to demonstrate your style and capabilities than the paper-based version. For instance, the selection of graphics, music, text style, and placement can be used to non-verbally illustrate your sense of style and how you approach projects. The individual job descriptions—the core content of the multimedia résumé—combined with effective graphics and sound give you ample opportunity to show your versatility in writing, and in the audio-visual realms.

The chronological style is not well-suited for the project in this chapter because it is basically a linear way to present information. The functional résumé style, on the other hand, emphasizes capabilities and accomplishments over chronology. It gives you the chance to present yourself anyway you'd like, but sometimes disappoints employers by not including enough substance.

For the purposes of this chapter, you can start with a functional style and choose three or four definite categories of accomplishments or capabilities. If you group your work experience around these categories, a structure will begin to suggest itself. As a bonus, if you include samples and clips from a working portfolio your extended format can also present additional substance and satisfy employers who want to see more.

Structuring the Interaction

The idea of structuring how you present information is a very powerful concept, especially in multimedia. Anyone who has ever written a good letter or essay knows that organizing the material is a necessary and difficult first step. In multimedia, organizing your content is the key to structuring how a user will interact with it.

For instance, if you present the information in a very tight linear form (see the left image in Figure 26.3)—you must always read paragraph A before paragraph B and so on—an interactive user will begin to feel constrained. At the same time, as shown in the right image in Figure 26.3, if all options are available at all times and a user can go from one section to another, even if there is no logical connection between the two, the user will get confused.

FIGURE 26.3.

The two extremes in poor interactive design—no choices and too much linearity and too many choices with no linearity.

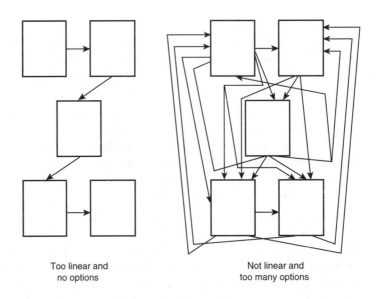

Too linear and
no options

Not linear and
too many options

As shown in Figure 26.4, a reasonable compromise to either extreme is a simple, single-level tree. Here, each selection on the main menu branches to reveal more text and graphic information. The format is simple, clean, and easy to implement. It is in some ways very similar to the old résumé adage recommended by résumé books and writers: make it fit on one page. It gives the user a very clear, easy-to-understand path for moving around in your application and this style is much easier to implement in a program.

FIGURE 26.4.

A single-level tree structure lets the user explore the many details of the résumé while maintaining a simple look.

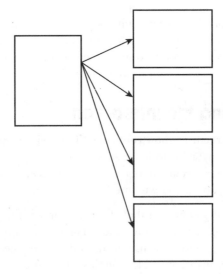

Making sure that users always know where they are and where they are going is crucial to creating a good interactive product. Along those same lines, giving users a clear way to safely exit the program and any of its processes is another necessary characteristic of good interactive design. In this project you'll include a system menu—not a standard Windows one but a much simpler, graphically pleasing version. Besides including a Quit button to provide a clean way to exit the application and close any open files, you'll use a Back control to return to the main menu from the various branch selections. Finally, you'll add another system menu selection that you'll use to display your educational background and your chronological employment history.

Figure 26.5 shows a flowchart of your final interactive résumé design, which you can dub the multimedia portfolio styled résumé. Your version of the résumé will and should differ, but if you divide your résumé information in the same way, the project model should work for you. In fact, if you wish to try out a simple interactive résumé you can simply rewrite the résumé text files, rework the static and animated graphics, and use the application directly.

FIGURE 26.5.

A flowchart of your final interactive résumé design.

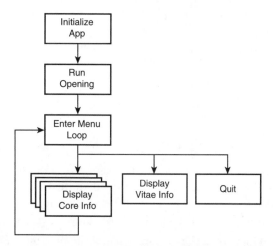

HOW TO USE THE RÉSUMÉ APPLICATION ENGINE DIRECTLY

The résumé application developed here is designed to be reusable and easily maintained. If you wish, you can simply change graphics, edit the content text file, and use the application engine directly. Be sure to rename the files correctly so that the application can find them. To personalize the résumé application:

1. Edit the MAINFORM.BMP bitmap file in a paint program. Of course, the better the paint program, the better the edited image will look. A blank copy of this background bitmap—one without any text—is provided on the CD as BLNKFORM.BMP. Edit this blank file and save it as MAINFORM.BMP. Use a text tool in the paint program with a medium-sized font to add your name and other information to the blank bitmap. Also add four category headings—which we'll call heading #1, heading #2, heading #3, heading #4—to the right of the four square buttons. The words will be the same words used in the RESUME.TXT file.

2. Edit the RESUME.TXT file in an ASCII text editor such as Notepad. The editor should not add any formatting to the text. It should produce a pure, simple text file. The RESUME.TXT format is very simple. It contains four headings inside double quotes (for instance, "ThisHeading"), with each heading followed by a few descriptive paragraphs also in double quotes (for instance, "This is descriptive text that can include carriage returns."). The double quotes separate the text file into sections as follows:

```
"heading #1"
"description #1"
"heading #2"
"description #2"
"heading #3"
"description #3"
"heading #4"
"description #4"
```

3. Edit the HISTREF.BMP file in a paint program. Once again, a blank version of this 478×258 pixel bitmap is provided on the CD. Clicking on the system menu Vitae button brings up the HISTREF.BMP image. The HISTREF.BMP image displays your education, work history, or almost anything else you consider vital statistics.

4. Acquire or create four small sample graphic bitmaps called SAMPLE1.BMP, SAMPLE2.BMP, SAMPLE3.BMP, and SAMPLE4.BMP. These bitmaps should be resized to 195×146 pixels. Again, using a good paint program will make these small samples look better.

5. Make sure all graphics use the same 256-color palette (the one used by the original MAINFORM.BMP) then place the files in the same directory as the RESUME.EXE file. You probably also will want to modify the opening animation in the MYOPEN.MWF file. See the section "Producing the Animation" later in this chapter for details.

6. Now running the RESUME.EXE application from Windows should display your own personalized multimedia résumé.

The Prototype

Now that you have a starting point for our résumé, consider what you want the résumé to look like. Begin by visualizing and sketching it. Sketching is important because, in multimedia, you are constantly revealing and hiding images. In fact, the technical part of multimedia involves knowing how to show a graphic image and how to string together a sequence of images. The artistic part of the process involves knowing when to show the images. Using a sketchpad enables you to focus on the artistic issues without complicating the multimedia creative process with hardware or software concerns.

Begin by considering a standard functional résumé with three or four categories. As Figure 26.6 shows, even a basic single page résumé has too much information to display on a single computer screen. What you want is to display a single item on-screen at one time. Also, use a lot of "white space"—blank border areas without text or graphics—to give the text screens room so they don't look cramped or sloppy. Obviously, to give the finished page enough space to look less cluttered you need a lot less text. For your design, try using half of the screen for text. You can use the other half for a graphic that supports the text.

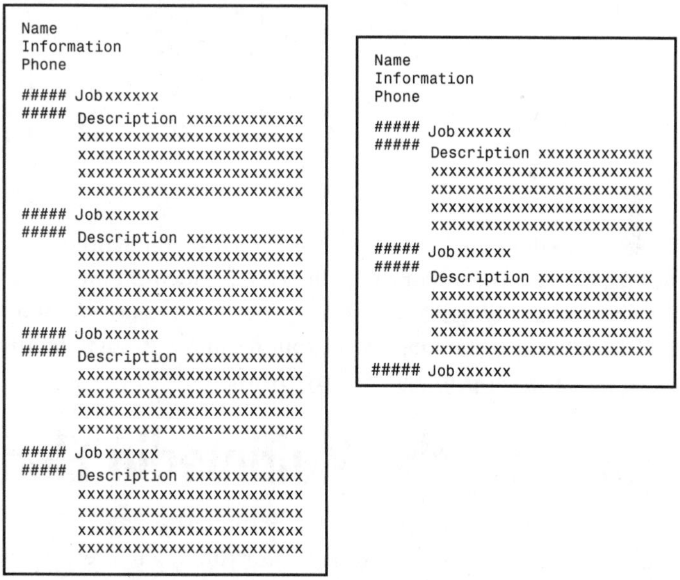

FIGURE 26.6.

Even a single page résumé has too much information to display on a screen at one time.

As you saw before, the functional résumé (a résumé style that highlights capabilities and accomplishments) is sometimes a little light on substance, but it suits our presentation style. Try writing text on a half sheet of paper and see if you can break or embellish each section to fill the half page. By carefully selecting your words and restructuring your ideas, you should be able to create four tight and well-written paragraphs about your various functional areas.

At this point, you might try to write out a first draft using the RESUME.TXT file found on the accompanying CD as a template. Don't worry about writing too much or too little. Because you plan to load the text information dynamically, you can change and edit the wording as necessary later.

Working backward, list the functional categories as a menu, and organize the sketchpad sheets as shown in Figure 26.7. You can already see how the images are starting to suggest some kind of organization. If you added the system menu Quit and Vitae buttons, you'd already begin to see what the application will look like.

FIGURE 26.7.

As you can see, the sketchpad images begin to suggest some kind of organization.

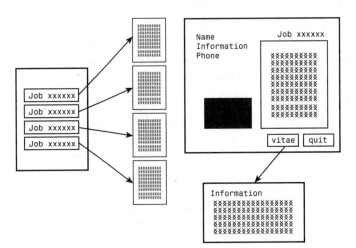

While you're thinking in broad strokes, visualize some sort of opening for your piece. In multimedia, you can control or direct the viewer's focus in much the same way as a film director influences what a filmgoer sees and experiences. Because you show static graphics once you're inside your main menu loop, begin your résumé with some motion. For now, you can simply sketch an image on your pad and say "Move it."

Producing the Multimedia Elements

This part of your résumé project is very subjective. You are in the best position to visualize your work. If you are an artist or animator you might already produce visual multimedia elements for the computer. If you are a video person, try getting some video captures of a few choice moments from a demo reel. Photographers can select some choice photographic moments and have them scanned and prepared for computer use. An author might take another route, such as scanning a book or magazine cover featuring his or her work, or even recording a reading. Obviously, if you added more sound than the little bit used in this project, your application will get much larger. You can, however, trigger any additional sounds by sending Media Control Interface (MCI) command strings directly to the multimedia engine inside

Windows. These command strings use the same technique as the code that produces sound throughout this project. (See the XTRASNDS.TXT file included on the CD for more information.)

However you get your images (scan, create, or digitize) you'll need at least one image for each résumé category page. If you choose to add images to the animation opening, you will also need images for that.

> **NOTE**
>
> The demo version of Motion Tool included on the CD supports a limited number of graphics: four static "prop" graphics and four animated "actor" graphics. By using single-frame animation actors, you can conceivably stretch the limit; however, this version is best suited as a teaching rather than a production tool. The retail version of the MediaShop animation system can be used to create some very impressive animations, as shown in some of the samples on the CD.

You can always use clip art; just be sure to personalize it some way. (Most clip art is created to be multipurpose and generic, whereas your résumé should be unique and focused.) If you adapt preexisting material, use a high-quality paint program that enables you to change the palette or colors used in your graphics.

Graphics Tools

Multimedia developers can pick and choose between many forms of media—digital video, audio waves, computer-generated imagery and animation—but they must always use static graphics or standalone, non-animated images. These images maybe photorealistic scans and renderings, more impressionistic and fanciful computer art, or even scratchy, handmade doodles and cartoons. Whatever form they take, multiple graphics almost always present special challenges to a multimedia creator. The most overriding problem in Windows-based multimedia is working with color depth or how to handle an almost infinite number of colors on a machine that displays a lot less.

In computer graphics, it's been determined that there are about 16 million shades of color detectable by the human eye. Most Windows PCs are capable of displaying 256 colors (called *indexed color*) out of these 16 million at any one time. Of course, PCs that support 16 million colors (called *true color*) are getting more and more common; in a year or two the industry baseline PC should support true color.

However, if there are 16 million possible colors, why work with only 256? That's a reasonable question, but the answer is somewhat convoluted. Because almost all PCs support 256 colors, even though some support more, targeting 256 colors means that more people can run your application today. Running in 256 colors can be very tricky, especially if you combine images made up of very different colors. To work with images with high color depth a developer must generally use very sophisticated and expensive paint programs.

One standard in multimedia production circles is Adobe Photoshop. Photoshop lets you edit and manipulate images in true color and then convert them down to 256 colors. Of course, converting a true color graphic to an indexed color version is relatively easy. What's difficult is coverting several different images down to the same set of 256 colors. This single set of colors, called a palette, is necessary to avoid an annoying artifact of 256 color graphics systems called *palette flash*. Palette flash occurs in the Windows 256 color mode when two consecutive images use more than 256 colors between them. At some point during the transition from one image to the next, a few colors from the first image will be sitting in color "slots" used by the secong images. During that brief moment, the two color sets play an electronic version of "musical chairs" where there are not enough places to go around. Eventually everything is set back in order, but not before a brief color-mixup—known as a palette flash. By using a single palette for all your graphics, you can make sure there are no unsightly palette flashes.

With a program like Photoshop, you can save the palette from one graphic and apply it to another one. The only problem this presents is choosing which palette to use for all your graphics. In the project in this chapter it's rather easy. If you use the animation engine, you must also use its internal palette. The current version of Motion Tool will not accept another palette. It uses its own and converts any loaded graphic to match it. Luckily, its internal palette is a fairly good universal one.

USING IMAGE ALCHEMY TO CREATE A UNIFORM PALETTE

Even though Windows programs look better and are easier to use than plain old DOS programs, there are some DOS programs that do what they do so well that it's hard to find a good Windows replacement. Image Alchemy from Handmade Software fits in this category and a demo version is included on the CD. Image Alchemy is a graphics conversion utility that converts one graphic format to almost any other format. During the conversion you use various command-line options to make Image Alchemy perform any number of additional functions. For instance, the `-f` option takes the palette from one file and applies it to another.

You use Image Alchemy like any pure DOS command-line driven program; type the executable's name followed by options and the source filename. For instance, to apply the standard palette of your résumé program (this palette is used in the image file on the CD called `BLNKFORM.BMP`) to a file called `SAMPLE1.BMP`, you first convert the `SAMPLE1.BMP` to an intermediate format such as PCX or GIF. Then you convert the file back to the Windows BMP format, this time using the palette from `BLNKFORM.BMP`. The steps are

1. At the DOS prompt, convert the original BMP file to a GIF file (using the `-g` option) by typing

   ```
   alchemy -g SAMPLE1.BMP
   ```

2. `SAMPLE1.GIF` will be created. Now convert the GIF back to a BMP (using the `-w` option) and use the palette from `BLNKFORM.BMP`. (You must use the `-o` overwrite option to overwrite the original `SAMPLE1.BMP` file.)

   ```
   alchemy -w SAMPLE.GIF -f BLNKFORM.BMP -o
   ```

3. The `SAMPLE1.BMP` file will now contain a "palettized" graphic that uses the same palette as your animation engine.

By now, you might still be wondering why you must use the same palette for everything. Figure 26.8 shows two 256 color images, `ABC01.BMP` and `ABC02.BMP`. If you open both ample files with Paintbrush and place the two copies side-by-side, you'll notice something strange; you cannot show both at the same time without the colors shifting. The images are basically identical except that each image uses a different palette. As you click one image and then the other, you'll notice a momentary color flash. When clicked, a window becomes active and its 256 color palette becomes dominant. The flash is caused by drawing the the other non-dominant image with the wrong set of colors. This behavior is caused by the Windows Palette Manager matching an image's desired 256 colors to the closest available colors currently used by the system.

FIGURE 26.8.

Two 256-color images with different palettes. Due to a palette flash in the Windows 256 color mode only one appears correctly at a time.

When Windows operates in 256-color mode, it enables a program to change any of the middle 236 colors. It reserves the first ten and last ten to draw Windows resources (menus, toolbars, scroll bars, icons, and frames). As far as Windows is concerned, the inside 236 colors are used to paint using a "color by numbers" technique. Windows considers the inside colors to be color number 11, color number 12, and so on, up to color number 246. If one image uses red for color number 11 and another image uses yellow for color number 11, when you display both images at the same time either the reds in one image will turn yellow, or vice versa. Of course, the Palette Manager inside Windows works very hard to match each color to it nearest match, but the end result is this: mixing two different palattes creates an unpredictable mess.

This explains the two image experiment. Although the images are the same, the palettes clash, producing a miscolored image. Also, as you display one image after the other there will be an annoying "flash" between the two. This occurs because the Windows palette manager tries its best to renumber or remap the colors from one image palette to the other.

These types of color-shift artifacts happen only in lower color modes—256 colors or 16 colors. In the high color (64 thousand) and true color (16 million) modes, color-shift is not a problem because there are more than enough colors to go around and Windows can easily match any color to a close neighboring color. Once again, multimedia is currently developed for 256-color mode because the higher modes are still not universally supported.

Producing the Animation

To get back to the résumé project, you've added animation to the opening to give it a special look. Most animation is difficult and requires many specialized tools, but the Motion Tool animation system demo from Motion Works on the companion CD contains everything you need. Motion Tool is sophisticated, easy to use, and easy to integrate into Visual Basic, which makes it perfect for your project.

The Motion Tool animation package is a stand-alone animation editor with three modules: a timeline/motion editor for designing two dimensional (2D) motion, a paint program, and a sound recorder. These modules are to create a proprietary multimedia animation file (similar to a WAV sound or AVI video file but with an .MWF extension). After you create the file you play it back in Visual Basic with the Interactive Animation VBX control.

By creating the animation separately, a graphics person or animator can develop the animation independently from a programmer. The programmer simply adds the Animation VBX control to the Visual Basic application and writes some code to open the animation, play it, and then close it. What's even better is that the same code could run any Motion Tool Animation—provided you renamed the file correctly.

To use your own animation in this project, create your own animation and name it MYOPEN.MWF. It you place it in the same directory as the MYRESUME.EXE application, the résumé will begin with your own personal animation, before launching into your résumé!

In a nutshell, the process of creating a Motion Tool animation involves the following steps:

1. Create a new animation container file and new animation within the container.
2. Import the graphics content into the new file.
3. Place static images called "props" on the view screen.
4. Place motion cels or "actors" on the view screen.
5. Move the props and actors along the timeline.
6. Add and synchronize sound.

USING MOTION TOOL FOR A SIMPLE ANIMATION

Using Motion Tool, you can easily create 2D animation, including making graphic objects appear on cue, moving objects across the screen along designated paths, and showing sequences (something like a flipbook) that appear to move in sync with other sounds and images. The Motion Works demo package on the CD contains an online tutorial that explains the Motion Tool animation process in more detail than you will learn to do here.

Begin by creating an opening sequence. For fun, place a text graphic and a small cartoon actor inside your film strip fragment. By using some premade animation clips, you'll get a sense of how an animation is made. Finally, add a little intro music to create a complete stand-alone animation.

CREATE A NEW ANIMATION

First, create a new animation. If you open the Interactive Animation Editor, you should see the Motion Tool main menu. From the File menu item, select New File and then type MYOPEN.MWF in the prompt field of the New Animation File dialog box, as shown in Figure 26.9. Click the OK button to get to the New Animation prompt box. Type firstOne in the Name field prompt and 180 in the Frames prompt to indicate 180 frames. Click the OK button to create a container file in which you'll place other multimedia elements or objects. Now you're ready to import these other elements.

FIGURE 26.9.

Motion Tool uses dialog boxes to prompt the user for information needed to create new animations.

The other objects include background and foreground images called *props* and any special animation cel sequences called *actors*. For now, you'll import your actors and props from an existing animation—a supplied library called UNLEASH.MWF. As you see in Motion Tool, it's possible to build your own library of motion actors, props, and sounds that you can use to easily populate any of your animations.

IMPORTING AND PLACING A PROP

To import a prop, select the Import Object item, found under the File option on the Motion Tool main menu. From the cascading menu, select the Prop item to bring up the Select Library File To Import dialog box. Browse through the Directory and Filename list boxes until you find UNLEASH.MWF in the \MYRES project directory. Select that file to bring up a Select a Prop to Import dialog box, which shows the props available in that library. Select the prop name Titles and click the Done button. The prop is now imported into the MYOPEN.MWF animation file, but it's not used yet.

To use the Titles prop, select the Place Prop item under the Objects option on the main menu. Select the item called Title from the displayed dialog box and then click the Place button. The prop should now appear in the middle of the Motion Tool work area.

There are two ways to place a graphic object which in Motion Tool is a prop or an actor: you can click on the object and drag it visually, or you can select the object in the timeline and place it by entering exact X and Y coordinates using the keyboard. Because this image will be the background of your little animation, use the keyboard entry method to be precise.

First, make sure the Timeline window is displayed by clicking the fourth button on the toolbar or selecting Timelines from the Media main menu option. Bring up the Prop Information dialog box for the Titles prop by clicking the prop icon next to the word Titles in the Timeline Window. In this dialog box, shown in Figure 26.10, click the box next to Horizontal in the Start Position area and enter 0, and then click the box next to Vertical and enter another 0. Finally, click the Locked check box to lock in this position, and press OK.

Import and place actors exactly as you would props. Import the "cheetah" actor from the UNLEASH.MWF file and place it in the animation. For final placement however, drag the running cheetah image and place it as shown in Figure 26.11. Drag the left edge of the cheetah's timeline to the right (approximately 30 frames). Now lock the position by clicking the lock icon to the left of the cheetah timeline.

Figures 26.10 and 26.11 show two ways to position objects on the Motion Tool screen.

FIGURE 26.10.

Use the Prop Information box to enter precise X and Y coordinates for placing a background prop object in the Motion Tool work area.

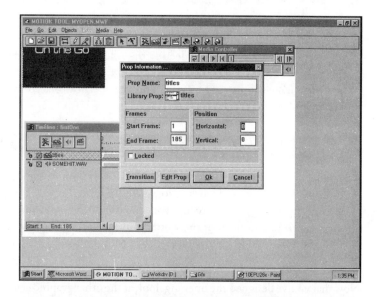

FIGURE 26.11.

Use the "click and drag" method to visually position a graphic object in the Motion Tool work area.

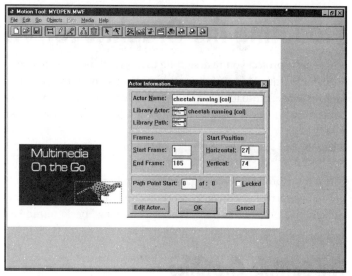

By moving props and actors along the timeline you can set the frame at which each one appears or disappears. The length of the individual timeline controls the duration, or how long each object appears.

ADDING AND SYNCHRONIZING SOUND

As a final bit of animation work, add a sound—the SOMEHIT file—to your animation. Import a sound from the UNLEASH.MWF using the same steps as just shown. Place the sound into the animation by selecting the Add Sound item under the Objects option on the main menu. Select the Somehit object displayed in the Select a Sound dialog box and then click the Add button. The sound is now placed in the animation.

PLAY THE ANIMATION

To play the animation, click the forward arrow button of the Motion Tools Media Controller. (It looks and works a lot like a VCR controller.) If your sound card and speakers are hooked up correctly, you should hear an electronic synthesizer and see the cheetah running in front of the words Multimedia On the Go. As you can see, creating animation files can be easy with tools like Motion Tool.

Now that you've designed the opening, look at the other graphic elements used in your résumé.

Producing the Graphics for Visual Basic

The résumé project you're designing uses several bitmaps that are embedded or loaded into the Visual basic form. Most of the graphics that you might want to change, besides the main background image, are loaded into Visual Basic image controls when the application starts up. The background image is loaded into the main Visual Basic form at start up.

The Background Graphic

The résumé project uses a single background image for the main Visual Basic form. The background pattern of the image is random enough that you can seamlessly overlay one part of the background on another part. With a "forgiving" background such as this one, you can type words on it, clip it out, and seamlessly paste the words back into the main graphic.

The Sample Graphics

Our résumé project uses four smaller sample graphics, one for each of the four functional areas that we defined in writing our the text that contains our content. All the sample graphics are hidden until the user clicks a button. At each button click, the appropriate graphic is made visible and appears within the single filmstrip as shown in Figure 26.12.

FIGURE 26.12.

For every menu selection, the résumé application displays a sample graphic in the filmstrip.

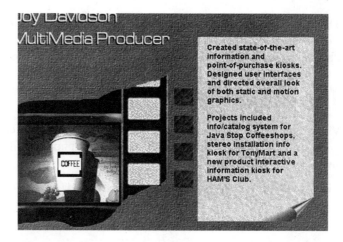

The Page Content Graphics

The actual content of the résumé—the functional category descriptions and education/work history—is displayed when the user makes certain choices. When the résumé application detects a mouse click on one of the menu buttons, it loads the appropriate text into a transparent Visual Basic label that sits on top of the half-sheet page image. Then both the label and sheet image are made visible, displaying the desired text.

The work history graphic works in a similar way, except that its text is prepared in advance and actually painted on the background page image. The main reason the text is not dynamically loaded is that the work history is in a tabbed column format—something that is more complicated than displaying text in labels. To take advantage of this compromise, however, you can choose nicer fonts and create gradient text as shown in Figure 26.13.

FIGURE 26.13.

Using bittmapped text enables the HISTREF.BMP graphic to be specially formatted and embellished.

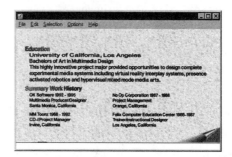

Navigation Graphics

There are also a few button and navigation control images that are actually bitmapped text and graphics pasted on small pieces of the background. One button—the yellow Back button—is toggled off and on depending on where the user is in the interactive flow.

The CD contains copies of these images, which you can use as models to make your own control buttons, headings, or whatever. These background images were produced in Adobe Photoshop, with a few specialized filters that made them very easy to create.

The Main Menu Form

Visual Basic gets its ease and power by combining a visual design environment with event-driven programming. Therefore, building Visual Basic applications involves building visual objects and tying them together with code.

The code and the visual objects are interrelated. If you optimize the visual design—for instance, if you use control arrays—you need less code. Therefore, before you look at some of the programming, look at the visual objects.

The résumé application consists of one form object that contains 12 other objects. Table 26.1 shows the objects placed in the résumé form and also lists some of their relevant characteristics.

Table 26.1. The objects on the résumé form's main menu.

No	Object Name	Control Array	Type	Button Click	Embedded Graphic	Loads Graphic
1	MyResume		form			Yes
2	Highlight	(0-3)	shape			
3	imgBack		image	Yes	Yes	
4	imgButton	(0-3)	image	Yes	——	——
5	imgCore		image		Yes	
6	imgHistRef		image			Yes
7	imgQuit		image	Yes	Yes	
8	imgSample	(0-3)	image			Yes
9	imgStartScrn		image		Yes	
10	imgVitae		image	Yes	Yes	
11	lblCore		label			Loads text
12	lblHeading		label			Loads text
13	OpenAnim		IAnim			Loads animation

The table reveals several things. For instance, most of the objects are images, and many images are used for buttons. These image buttons have code attached to them that is run when the button detects a mouse click. One set of image controls—the imgButton array—does not contain any graphics, and is simply a set of invisible boxes.

As shown in Figure 26.14, the basic menu screen consists of a graphic with four drawn buttons. The transparent `imgButton` controls sit on top of the buttons and respond to mouse movements and mouse clicks. When the user moves a mouse over one of the buttons, the code makes the appropriate Highlight control visible. When the user clicks one of the buttons, the code loads appropriate text into the single Visual Basic label control called `lblCore`.

FIGURE 26.14.

The main résumé screen contains four drawn buttons with transparent `imgButton` *controls on top. Each button responds to mouse movements and mouse clicks.*

The `lblCore` control, which contains the description text, sits on top of the `imgCore` control, which contains the half-page graphic that looks like a piece of paper. When the user clicks an `imgButton`, the application makes both the `imgCore` and `lblCore` objects visible, showing the half-page image loaded with the appropriate text.

Placing transparent or invisible objects directly on the background graphic lets you change the underlying image without changing the functionality. If you change the location of the buttons on the graphic, simply drag the buttons to new locations.

The four `imgSample` controls—`imgSample(0)`, `imgSample(1)`, `imgSample(2)`, and `imgSample(3)`—are loaded with the sample bitmaps—`SAMPLE1.BMP`, `SAMPLE2.BMP`, `SAMPLE3.BMP`, and `SAMPLE4.BMP`. The four sample images overlay each other on the filmstrip fragment. When the user clicks an `imgButton`, the appropriate `imgSample` image box is made visible.

The $1/4$-screen `imgVitae` object is also an image box, which contains the Work History (`HISTREF.BMP`) text bitmap. This object is made visible when the user clicks the `imgVitae` control, which contains the bitmapped text of the word *Vitae*.

Two other controls also sit on the main background. The `imgQuit` control, which exits the program, and the `imgBack` control, containing the word *Back*, is made visible whenever the user selects a menu button or the *Vitae* choice. If the user clicks the `Back` control, the application hides both the half-page and Work History graphics.

Figure 26.15 shows where the various controls sit in relation to one another.

FIGURE 26.15.

The various controls and their relation to one another in design mode, before adding the dynamically loaded images.

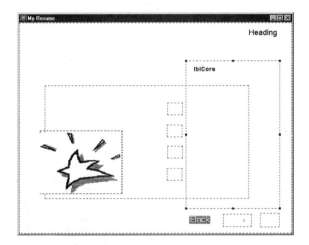

Programming the Résumé Application

If you are familiar with Visual Basic, there is nothing special about the Visual Basic code used in this project. If you are just beginning to learn Visual Basic, the source code for this project is contained on the CD for you to study, use, and modify. Also, if you have not tried to use the résumé engine directly, doing so will help you understand the résumé engine's operation.

Rather than working through the code line by line this chapter will identify the various functional modules and briefly discuss only pieces of code that illustrate each module's function.

An application in Visual Basic is made up of objects and forms that are held together by bits of Visual Basic code. By looking at the visual objects and studying the source code listings, you should be able to understand and modify this project for your own use. The tasks your application must perform follow.

The Application Startup

At startup, the résumé application must be initialized. This means that all variables must be loaded and given starting values, and any files used by the application must be opened and prepared for use. To make your résumé engine directly usable, load both the text descriptions and the graphics, except for the navigation graphics, at startup. This is accomplished by two custom Visual Basic procedures called LoadText and LoadPics, shown in Listing 26.1 and Listing 26.2.

The content of the résumé (the headings and text of the main categories) is contained in a set or array of four element string variables called head(0-3) and core(0-3). These variables are loaded from a specially formatted ASCII text file called RESUME.TXT. The LoadText procedure imports the descriptive information from RESUME.TXT and places it in the string variable arrays. RESUME.TXT must be distributed with the résumé application.

Listing 26.1. The LoadText **procedure imports descriptive information from the** RESUME.TXT **file.**

```
Sub LoadText ()
    ' variables head(0), core(0)... pre-defined
  Dim textfile
  textfile = app.path + "\RESUME.TXT"
      Open textfile For Input As #1
      Input #1, head(0), core(0), head(1), core(1), head(2),
      \\ core(2), head(3), core(3)
      Close #1
End Sub
```

Listing 26.2. The LoadPics **procedure loads the user-specified graphics into the résumé application engine.**

```
Sub LoadPics ()
   Me.Picture = LoadPicture(app.Path + "\mainForm.bmp")
   '
   imgSample(0).Picture = LoadPicture(app.Path +
   \\ "\Sample1.bmp")
   imgSample(1).Picture = LoadPicture(app.Path +
   \\ "\Sample2.bmp")
   imgSample(2).Picture = LoadPicture(app.Path +
   \\ "\Sample3.bmp")
   imgSample(3).Picture = LoadPicture(app.Path +
   \\ "\Sample4.bmp")
   '
   imgHistRef.Picture = LoadPicture(app.Path +
   \\ "\histref.bmp")
End Sub
```

There are advantages and disadvantages to using a dynamic loading method. On the plus side, you can modify the text and graphics shown in the résumé without touching and recompiling the code. On the negative side, this information is sitting unsecured in the open, easy prey for corruption by system errors or cracker intrusion.

Preparing and Playing the Opening Animation

At startup, the animation is loaded into a Motion Tool animation control called OpenAnim (see Listing 26.3) while a black load screen is displayed. The animation starts when the black opening screen is clicked. The click also sets a "watch" variable inside the résumé engine called called AnimStarted to True. We use this variable along with the animation's play event to make sure the animation closes when it is finished playing. Without this "watch" variable, the animation close procedure would run anytime the play status changed—when the animation stopped (which is what we want) and also when the animation started (which is exactly what we do not want.) Using a watch variable such as AnimStarted is called setting a status flag in most event programming circles.

Listing 26.3. This procedure opens the MYOPEN.MWF animation and sets up the AnimStarted flag technique.

```
Sub Form_Load
    ' animation preparation performed at start up
    Dim AnimStarted As Integer    ' used flag animation
                         ' play status
    AnimStarted = False
    OpenAnim.AnimFileName = app.Path + "\myopen.mwf"
    OpenAnim.AnimName = "firstOne"
    OpenAnim.Visible = False
End Sub

Sub OpenAnim_CurFrame (Frame As Integer)
    ' when animation starts AnimStarted is set to True
    If Not (AnimStarted) And OpenAnim.CurFrame > 0 Then
        AnimStarted = True
        End If
End Sub
```

As shown in Listing 26.4, when the play event is triggered, the code checks to see if the animation is starting or stopping . The key to understanding how this flag works is remembering to ask yourself, "What was the value of the AnimStarted variable, *before* the animation play status changed?" AnimStarted = False before the animation plays and AnimStarted = True before the animation stops. The control's Play exit code is run only when the animation is stopping. At this time, the application hides and automatically closes the animation.

Listing 26.4. The animation control makes itself invisible after it plays the animation.

```
' the animation control makes itself invisible
' and inactive once it's played through
Sub OpenAnim_Play (Playing As Integer)
    If AnimStarted And OpenAnim.CurFrame = OpenAnim.MaxFrame Then
        OpenAnim.Visible = False
        End If
End Sub
```

Entering a *wait* Loop on the Main Menu Page

Once the opening animation finishes, the application enters the main application loop and waits for the user to make a request. Basically, the loop works like this: Visual basic displays the main application screen and waits for the user to click one of the "hot" areas—one of the category imgButton controls, the imgVitae control, or the imgQuit control.

The imgButton controls also respond to mouse movement. When the mouse is over a button a highlighted square outline appears around the button. This highlight provides user feedback which makes it easy for the user to see which button will respond to each mouse click. The code for adding this kind of "user feedback" (see Listing 26.5) simply makes the outlining rectangle visible or not, depending on the current mouse position. The code turns the highlight off and hides it whenever the mouse is over the main application form, but not over a button.

Listing 26.5. This code makes the highlight rectangle visible or not, thus providing immediate user feedback.

```
' turns the highlight on over a button
Sub imgButton_MouseMove (index As Integer...)
    highlight(index).BorderColor = &HE0FFFF
    highlight(index).Visible = True
End Sub
' turns all highlights off over any part of the form
Sub Form_MouseMove (Button As Integer, Shift As Integer, X As Single, Y As Single)
    Dim i As Integer
    For i = 0 To 3
        highlight(i).Visible = False
        highlight(i).BorderColor = &HFFFF&
    Next
End Sub
```

Responding to the Selected Option

Once the user selects an option, the application runs a small bit of code that provides the correct response. For the category buttons, the code loads the correct text into both the heading and page labels, loads text into the half-page description, and displays the correct sample graphic (see Listing 26.6).

Listing 26.6. This code loads the appropriate text and graphic information into the selected page.

```
' load correct text into the heading label and show it
lblheading.Caption = head(index)
lblheading.Visible = True
' load correct text into the 1/2 page label and show it
```

continues

Listing 26.6. continued

```
lblCore.Caption = core(index)
lblCore.Visible = True
imgCore.Visible = True
' show appropriate sample graphic
imgSample(index).Visible = True
```

As shown in Listing 26.7, clicking the imgVitae control brings up a similar page but with non-dynamic bitmapped text—the HISTREF.BMP graphic.

Listing 26.7. This code displays the Education/Work History when the Vitae button is clicked.

```
' show the Work History image
imgHistRef.Visible = True
```

At the same time, the résumé is always doing housekeeping to keep the page navigation in sync. For instance, showing the imgBack control (the text button with the word Back on it) is appropriate only while the category half-page or the Work History page are visible. Once the imgBack control is visible, clicking on the Back button triggers code that returns to the first page of the our résumé project (see Listing 26.8). Finally, if the user selects the imgQuit control the application must exit cleanly back to Windows.

Listing 26.8. This code simply returns us to the first page of the résumé.

```
Sub imgBack_Click ()
    ' housekeeping code returns all settings to their
    ' original values

    ' hide the core text and heading images and text
    lblheading.Visible = False
    imgCore.Visible = False
    lblCore.Visible = False
    ' hide sample images
    imgSample(0).Visible = False
    imgSample(1).Visible = False
    imgSample(2).Visible = False
    imgSample(3).Visible = False

    ' hide the Ed/Work history image
    imgHistRef.Visible = False

    ' reset the navigation controls
    imgBack.Visible = False
    imgVitae.Visible = True
End Sub
```

Final Delivery

In a multimedia project the last thing you, as a developer, see is also the first thing your customer or end user sees. To be successful, a multimedia application must also contain an easy-to-use setup routine that walks a novice through a series of Windows screen dialog boxes and sets up the application.

In the old days of DOS and Windows 3.0, you could get by with compressing the files into one large zip file with PKZIP, tell the user to create a directory on the hard drive, unzip the file into it, and run the program from the Windows Program Manager. These days however, because ease-of-use is one of the primary measuring sticks for computer software, it is vitally necessary to provide an easy-to-use, error-free setup program. Up to a few years ago, writing a setup program involved learning how to use Microsoft's setup kit—which could be a week's worth of work in itself.

Fortunately, today there are a number of good install programs available that make writing a setup program much simpler. A demo version of one of the better installers—the Wise Installation System—is included on the CD. With the Wise system, you can create a basic setup program in minutes, and can polish and test a completely professional one in a few hours.

Creating a Professional Installer

With the Wise Installation System, you can create a single installation file that contains the RESUME.EXE engine and all its support files—the bitmaps, text files, sound files, animation files, and library files for Visual Basic and Motion Tool. What's more, this setup file can even create a program group and application icon and place all the files in their rightful places automatically. Finally, the Wise system can compress the over 2MB RESUME application files to just over 600KB—easily small enough to fit on a single floppy.

In Windows, setup programs basically use the same following steps:

1. Display a graphic logo.
2. Display a Welcome message.
3. Prompt the user to select a target directory.
4. Copy files to the target directory.
5. Create program groups and icon launchers.
6. Display a Read Me file or other message.

Because they are so generic, Wise provides a Script Assistant that creates a working installation script by prompting you with a series of dialog boxes. By compiling this script, you can create a full working install program in a matter of minutes. By taking a little more time and modifying this generic script, you could create a customized installer that rivals any program currently available!

Using Script Assistant

Once the Wise Installation System is running, select the Script Assistant item from the File option of the Wise main menu. As show in Figure 26.16 the Script Assistant dialog box appears. Type in My Resume for the Software Title and c:\MyDemo for the Default Directory, as shown. Click the OK button to bring up a second dialog box.

FIGURE 26.16.

The Script Assistant dialog box. Enter the prompts as shown to create a generic setup script for the résumé project.

In this Select Files to Install dialog box, browse to your working résumé project directory—where the RESUME.EXE and all its support files are—using the Directories and File Name list boxes. Click on the drop-down arrow of the List Files of Type list box and select the All Files option. You should see all the files used by the résumé application. Click each necessary file to select it, and press the Add File button to add the files to the installation.

Your list should include these 13 files:

```
MAINFORM.BMP
HISTREF.BMP
SAMPLE1.BMP
SAMPLE2.BMP
SAMPLE3.BMP
SAMPLE4.BMP
RESUME.TXT
MYOPEN.MWF
STING.WAV
RESUME.EXE
IANIM.VBX
PROENG.DLL
VBRUN300.DLL
```

After selecting all the files to be installed, click the OK button to bring up the final Icons dialog box. This dialog box enables you to create a Program Manager group and create icon launchers for the executable files installed into it. As Figure 26.17 shows, for this project you only want to launch RESUME.EXE, the résumé application. You can name the Program Group whatever you'd like.

FIGURE 26.17.

The dialog box to create a Program Manager group and create icon launchers for the executable files installed into it.

After all the necessary files are included you can select the Text item under the Installation option of the Wise main menu. The setup program will run, without copying files, and you can see exactly how the setup flows. After you've made a few test runs, you might wish to reword the setup messages. Like most things about using the Wise installer, you can do this easily.

Modifying the Setup Script

As shown in Figure 26.18, selecting Edit Script Item from the main Wise Installation option brings up the first Welcome dialog box. Here you can edit the wording, add a Message Box icon, and customize this step of the procedure. Every step in the Wise Installation script can be edited in this way. Each script item has an associated dialog box that gives you more than enough options.

FIGURE 26.18.

Every step in a Wise Installation script has an associated dialog box that enables you to easily modify and customize the installation program.

Other than changing the wording to suit your particular style, you can use the setup program pretty much as written. One change that you'll make from the generic script involves the placement of the application's library files (VBXs or DLLs). Although placing everything in one directory is a brute-force way of making sure the application works, an application's library files should really go in the Windows\System directory. What's more, if the files are already there or are newer than the ones you are installing, the setup program should not overwrite them.

If you edit one of the script items that deals with a DLL—say VBRUN300.DLL—you are presented with the Install Files from Installation Executable dialog box. In the Destination box, click the drop-down arrow and select the %SYS%\vbrun300.dll item. In Wise, the pre-defined %SYS% variable represents the Windows system directory on the system being installed. By choosing this item, you are telling Wise to place the source file (VBRUN300.DLL) into a to-be-determined destination (the Windows System directory). For good measure, you can also select the Replace if Existing File Older from the Replacement options (see Figure 26.19) and ensure that you will not overwrite a newer version of your file.

FIGURE 26.19.

How to intelligently copy a DLL file into the target system's Windows\System *directory without overwriting a newer file.*

After you edit the message text, set directories, and test the flow of your installer, you are ready to create an actual installation file. Choose the Compile item from the Installation option on the main menu and Wise will compress and create your final installation file, creating a truly professional installation in record time!

Summary

By now you've learned not only how to create a multimedia résumé, but what's involved in a full-blown multimedia project. You've also learned about working in 256 colors, creating animations, structuring interactivity, and creating a setup program. Multimedia is a multidisciplinary field, and although it's not possible or practical to do it all, a broad understanding of multimedia production will go a long way.

As you work and rework your résumé, you will learn more and more about all the wonderful possibilities New Media offers. And as your experience grows, you'll be able to put bits and pieces of your best work on disk for employers and peers to say "How'd they do that?"

Publishing a Newspaper on the Internet

27

by William R. Stanek

Publishing a newspaper on the Internet is not only possible, it is a reality. Several companies have online versions of their newspapers. Some newspapers are provided free. Others require the reader to have an account at the site and charge readers monthly or annual fees. This chapter is going to take you where no reader has gone before, inside the creation of an actual Internet newspaper called *Internet Daily News*™.

Internet Daily News is a publication of The Virtual Press. *IDN* is one of the most ambitious projects I have ever undertaken. The newspaper has eighteen regular columns and many special weekly columns. Writers from around the world have signed up to be contributing columnists. The development of *IDN* took many months and will debut on the World Wide Web in December 1995.

Although the chapter centers on the development of an Internet newspaper, the design techniques discussed in this chapter can be used for any project designed for the World Wide Web. The purpose of the chapter is to help you develop your design skills through real-life application of the concepts discussed in this book. In the chapter, you will learn many things about developing large projects. The chapter begins with a look at what sparked the idea for the *Internet Daily News.*

A Vision for Success

In March 1994, I founded The Virtual Press. My vision was to create a company that would help launch the careers of aspiring writers. As a veteran writer with little to show for 10 years of writing, I know how difficult it is to break into print. For years I had planned to started up my own press, but traditional small presses are expensive to operate. Eventually, I turned to electronic mediums to publish my works and the works of other authors.

The idea for the *Internet Daily News* was born months before I founded The Virtual Press. If I had started work on *IDN* immediately, the newspaper would have been published on floppy disk and not the Internet. Then, this thing called the World Wide Web was just starting to gain recognition in the Internet community. Fortunately, I realized the timing wasn't right for a newspaper on floppy disk, and I shelved the idea. In 1995, with the World Wide Web spreading like wild fire, I decided it was time to take *IDN* off the shelf.

From the start, *Internet Daily News* was an ambitious project. The goal was to publish a free newspaper seven times a week that would attract regular readers. I planned to obtain material from dozens of freelancers from around the world and organize the material for daily columns, features, and special events. To deliver the news to Internet users for free, I hoped to attract corporate sponsors and advertisers. A few sponsors recognized immediately the tremendous potential for a project of the type I proposed. They knew such a project could attract thousands of readers every day, and they were eager to sign up. Other potential sponsors weren't so eager, and I needed these sponsors to make *IDN* profitable. I knew that to hook these sponsors, I would first have to attract readers, and this is what I set out to do.

An important part of this plan was to enhance TVP's current site at `http://tvp.com/` that already has its own following of 1–2,000 unique visitors a week to attract even more visitors. In this way, the TVP site would have a large readership before *IDN* was implemented. Preliminary marketing and tremendous interest in *IDN* suggest the paper will have 10–20,000 unique visitors a day (50–100,000 hits a day) during its first few weeks in publication. To prepare for this tremendous increase in visitors, I have set up a mirror site for testing purposes at `http://tvpress.com/`.

You can find the *Internet Daily News* front page on the Web at `http://tvp.com/idn.html`. Whether *IDN* sinks or swims, I will consider the project a success because I followed a dream and realized my vision. I followed through with a plan, continued when people told me it was an impossible dream and designed a newspaper that is getting noticed on the Net even before press time. To realize this vision, I followed the steps you will find in this chapter.

You may wonder why you would want to publish a newspaper on the Internet and how you could compete with traditional newspapers like the New York Times or the Chicago Tribune. Publishing a newspaper on the Internet dramatically reduces overhead. You do not need printing presses, and you may not need a full-time in-house staff. Beyond economics, a virtual newspaper is also environment friendly. You do not need paper and your workers will not pollute the environment during their commute to the office. Lastly, in terms of global reach and global power, there is no better medium than Internet publishing to reach a global audience so inexpensively.

Step 1: Organizing Ideas

The first step is to organize your ideas into a plan of action. You should always spend a few hours thinking about something that you may spend years, or certainly months, working on. Getting organized will save you time and help you create a better project.

As the tendency in electronic publishing is to produce an electronic version of the paper-based product, you should begin by following the building blocks for creating effective electronic publications. Think of the creative process as a building process. Just as you build a house one step at a time, you should build the publication one step at a time. The way you organize your thoughts can make the difference between success and failure.

You should begin by managing

- Expectations
- Perceptions
- Strategies
- Goals
- Rules
- Behavior

For a large project such as *Internet Daily News,* initial expectations and perceptions often go beyond reality. You want your publication to be a smashing success, but the more immediate goal should be to get the project started, developed, and operating. If you can do this, you have won 75 percent of the battle. Start by examining the Do and Don't list from Chapter 7, "Organizing Information."

DOS AND DON'TS

DON'T expect the creation and development of the project to flow effortlessly.

DON'T expect first efforts to be perfect.

DON'T expect the completed project to be perfect.

DO expect to make multiple drafts of the project.

DO expect to revise, edit, and proof parts of the project.

DO expect to say the project is "good enough" and that further time spent trying to perfect the project will not be cost-effective.

Here are a do and a don't I'd like to add to the list:

DO have faith in yourself, especially in the tough times.

DON'T listen to the naysayers, especially if your only costs will be time and capital you feel comfortable investing.

When you are working on a large project, adopt strategies that will help you manage the complexity of the project. Do not limit yourself to a few strategies or stick with one strategy when it obviously is not working. The first item on my list of strategies was to break the project down into manageable pieces. Fortunately, I had years of experience with large project management and had already developed the steps for creating electronic publications discussed in Chapter 7. Subsequent sections of this chapter follow each step of the development process and will take you inside my thoughts as I developed the *Internet Daily News.*

Before I started work on the project, I made a commitment to work on the project every day. This was a tall order considering I was already working 80+ hours a week—working full-time, going to graduate school 12 hours a week, running Virtual Press Incorporated, and working on three other projects. Yet I told myself the number of hours I worked on the project wasn't as important as developing a daily routine that involved dedicating time to the project. This dedication of time became my first goal for *IDN* and should also be your first goal for any project you start.

Step 2: Improving Ideas

Although the initial idea for *Internet Daily News* was a good one, it lacked specifics. To improve the ideas for the newspaper, I had to force myself to think about the project in new ways.

Tapping into your creativity is not always easy. People have been trying to figure out how to tap into creativity throughout history. Fortunately, these three key techniques for aiding the creative process have been developed in the past few decades:

- Brainstorming
- Freethinking
- Storyboarding

During each round of brainstorming, you should begin by setting a goal or objective for the session. Start by writing a main topic in the middle of the page, then write down every idea that you think of. You should not evaluate your ideas until the page is full. When the page is full, stop and look for patterns or repeated ideas. You evaluate these patterns or ideas to develop further ideas for the next session.

The first thing I did was find a quiet place where I could think. At the time, the kitchen was the quietest place in the house, so I went to the kitchen. I took with me a notepad and a pen. I wrote "Internet Daily News" in the middle of a blank piece of paper, cleared my thoughts, then promised I would not leave the kitchen until I made three attempts at improving the newspaper idea.

Through practice I learned that for me, three attempts is usually sufficient to substantially improve ideas and that more than three attempts during one session can sometimes be destructive. This is because when you brainstorm you should not evaluate what you put on the page until the session is completed, and after the third round of brainstorming I would start crossing out ideas. If this happens to you after several attempts, you may want to consider taking a break. Do something that will clear your mind like taking a walk, or simply waiting a few hours before trying again.

Figure 27.1 shows how the brainstorming session for *Internet Daily News* progressed. The objective for the first round was to think of topics that would make interesting columns for the newspaper. During the first round, I simply wrote down everything I thought of after I set this objective. Afterward, I drew lines connecting the main ideas.

During the next brainstorming session, I organized the ideas into categories. I came up with seven categories and one new idea:

- Business
- Technology
- Entertainment
- Finance
- Politics
- Publishing
- Reference—"Researcher's Corner"

FIGURE 27.1.

Brainstorming for Internet Daily News.

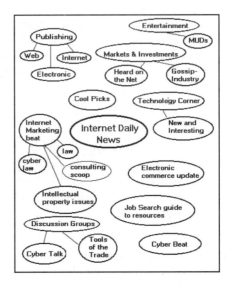

The final session was devoted to expanding the ideas and thinking of names for regular columns and features. Before starting, I decided to refine the categories I had created earlier. As the finance category could be a part of a broad business category, I decided to put the finance ideas in with the business ideas and see what would happen. The politics category I also put in with the business ideas to make sure I focused on politics that could affect Internet business. I renamed the reference section, called it Internet Resources and added technology issues to it. This left me with four categories: publishing, entertainment, business, and Internet resources.

I divided a blank piece of paper into four sections and put the category title at the top of each section. As I started out I told myself, each entry under a category heading would be a possible title for a column. As it happens, I generally wrote three column titles for each entry with the final entry being a refined title that I would probably use in the newspaper. The column titles were sometimes mixed with thoughts going through my mind, which kept my pen moving. Sometimes the original column name I had developed stuck in my mind, and I ended up expanding ideas for the column instead of thinking of a new name for the column.

Here is how the final brainstorming session progressed:

Publishing

Internet Publishing
   Web Publishing
   Web World
   "Web Publisher's Den"

Electronic Publishing
   Electronic Publishing Update
   "The Kitchen Table Publisher"

Publishing
  Broad category Internet
  tools
  "Publishing Update"

Multimedia
  tools
  Multimedia Update
  "Multimedia Corner"

Entertainment

MUDs (Multi-User Dimensions/Multi-User Dungeons)
  Discussing MUDs
  "MUDLand"

Cyber Talk
  Discussion groups
  newsgroups
  mailing lists
  IRCs
  "Cyber Talk"

Multimedia
  Interactive Multimedia
  "Going Interactive"

Cool Picks
  Internet Hot Sites and more
  "Cool Pick Hotel"

Book Reviews

Business

"Electronic Commerce Update"

Cyber Beat
  law and politics in cyberspace
  intellectual property issues
  "Cyber Beat"

Business
 Business gossip on the Net
 "Business Juice"

Marketing, advertising, consulting
 Inside marketing, consulting, and advertising on the Net
 "Inside Scoop"

Finance
 Venture Capital
 investments
 finance
 "Finance Corner"

Internet Resources

Researcher's Paradise
 research resource on the Internet
 "Researcher's Paradise"

Job Hunt
 Job Hunting in Cyberspace
 "Electronic Job Hunt"

Tools of the Trade
 Web and Internet Tools like browser or even Web server talk
 "Tools of the Trade"

Technology Corner
 technology issues
 new and interesting
 "Technology Corner"

Etcetera
 general talk on the Internet
 "Etcetera"

Classifieds

Business advertising

Sponsors

As you can see, the final brainstorming session provided some excellent results. Although the ideas still needed to be refined, the session generated 18 potential topics and column names. There were also a few new ideas that needed to be examined further, such as adding book reviews and advertising. Yet, I now had the beginnings of an Internet newspaper.

Step 3: Developing the Project

Although project development is usually a team effort, many small publishers will find it is largely an individual effort on their part. You will be responsible for creating new material and adapting existing material. For a newspaper project or any project that relies on the work of others, the publisher will be responsible for obtaining material from writers as necessary. Finding this material will be a key part of the later stages of project development.

Project development can be broken down into three processes:

- Composition processes, which include seven activities:

    Planning
    Researching
    Composing
    Evaluating
    Revising
    Editing
    Proofing

- Development processes, which include six phases:

    Requirements phase
    Rapid prototype phase
    Specification phase
    Planning phase
    Design phase
    Implementation phase

- Publishing processes, which include five activities:

    Revision
    Editing
    Proofing
    Testing
    Publishing

The heart of the *Internet Daily News* project is in the development processes. Composition processes will be used as necessary when original material is created. Publishing processes will be used to test the final prototype and will recur every time the newspaper is published.

Requirements Phase

In any project, the first thing you will do is develop a list of things needed to complete the project. If you haven't started a project folder, you should start one now. The project folder will hold everything related to the project. It can have several forms, such as a directory on your hard drive and an actual folder with a three-ring binder. I created a directory called *IDN* on my hard drive and purchased a three-ring binder.

To help you develop a list of the project's needs, you first identify the purpose, scope, and audience for the project:

Internet Daily News

Purpose:	A daily newspaper serving the Internet community.
Scope:	Large project with a broad focus.
Audience:	Internet users who are interested in topics related to the Internet and technology in general.

Next, start a list of constraints for the project. Some projects will have constraints driven by your needs or the needs of the people you are developing the project for. You may want to specify a requirement for project duration, especially if you have a deadline. If you have a set amount of capital to invest in the project, you will want to constrain the project's budget. Capital investments can include time or money. You may also want to limit the size of the project to a certain number of pages or words. In the planning stage you will reevaluate these requirements to see if they are realistic. The initial requirements for the *Internet Daily News* are

Project duration:	No more than 12 months for development.
Project size:	No more than 100 pages with each edition including the Sunday edition.
Project budget:	$XX,XXX. (You would fill in Xs with dollar amount).

Don't let the budget figures alarm you. The project budget is often the most difficult constraint to work with if you are developing the project for your own company. Here, figures for the budget can be listed as time or money. The idea is to start thinking about how much of an investment you really want to make in the project. Remember, your time is money. The amount of time you dedicate to this project detracts from time you could spend on other projects.

If you are incorporated, you may want to charge a reasonable amount for your dedication of time. Under U.S. corporate law, a corporation is a "citizen" with rights recognized under the law. All moneys generated by the corporation belong to the corporation and not to you, the publisher. So the question becomes, how do you get reimbursed for your investment of time? The answer isn't clear cut, but you could start by charging a reasonable amount for your investment of time in the project. Always seek legal council whenever you have a question about the law and your corporation.

By including the budget constraints in the *IDN* project from the beginning, I was telling myself the specific amount of time or money I was comfortable dedicating to the project. I may reach this constraint before *IDN* starts publishing or during the early months after its introduction. However, when I reach this constraint, I will determine if I should close the project or continue.

> **NOTE**
>
> There is no shame in calling it quits when you have reached your budget and decided the project cannot be salvaged. Thousands of companies face this decision every day. The past few years have been particularly hard for software companies that invested in titles for the ill-fated 3DO and Philips Interactive multimedia systems. Several new companies devoted their entire budgets to titles for these systems and lost it all. One of the big losers was a small upstart that lost over four million dollars. Never bet the company on a single project or a single medium. Invest only what you feel comfortable investing and diversify as much as possible.

Finally, you should develop a list of actual needs for the project. These needs can be specific or broad. For the *Internet Daily News*, I wrote down these needs:

Immediate Needs:
   Working capital
   Weekly time investment
   Disk space on hard drive
   Purchase floppy disks to back up project
   Web Browser
   Editor or word processor
   Utility programs for multimedia aspects

Long-term Needs:
   Web site or arrangements with Internet service provider
   Freelancers
   Sponsors and advertisers
   Budget allocation

NOTE

A key point to keep in mind is that nothing you develop in the project is carved in stone. In fact, you should change things. You will notice that throughout the project, there are slight differences as I try out new ideas. You have nothing to lose by trying out new ideas. If in later stages of the project you decide you do not like the changes, you simply go back to the original form.

Rapid Prototype Phase

From the requirements, you may want to develop a rapid prototype. By developing the rapid prototype, you figure out your real needs and find out if you have selected the right tools to carry you through to the completion of the job.

The ideas for *Internet Daily News* were still rough. I knew the current implementation of HTML would not allow me to produce the paper in columnar format, and my most immediate concern became how could I overcome this problem. I decided to keep the rapid prototype simple and use it as a springboard to help me in later stages of project development. I would develop a rough outline for the project in HTML format. To produce the prototype as fast as possible, the documents would contain only text.

The front page for the prototype is depicted in Figure 27.2. During the development of the front page, I adopted a temporary slogan for the paper, "A free daily serving the Internet Community." The phrase was short yet effective. As you will see later, I kept it for the final product as well. The following is the HTML code for the front page:

```
<HTML>
<HEAD><TITLE>Internet Daily News</TITLE></HEAD>
<BODY>
<H1>Internet Daily News</H1>
<P><STRONG>A free daily serving the Internet Community.
</STRONG></P>
<HR>
<H3><A HREF="idnbus.html">Business Section</A></H3>
<H3><A HREF="idnpub.html">Publishing Section</A></H3>
<H3><A HREF="idnent.html">Entertainment Section</A></H3>
<H3><A HREF="idnres.html">Resource Section</A></H3>
<HR>
<P>This page and all contents are Copyright (C) 1995
by The Virtual Press, Hawaii, USA. Internet Daily News
and its respective columns are trademarks of
The Virtual Press.</P>
</BODY>
</HTML>
```

FIGURE 27.2.

Internet Daily News front page prototype.

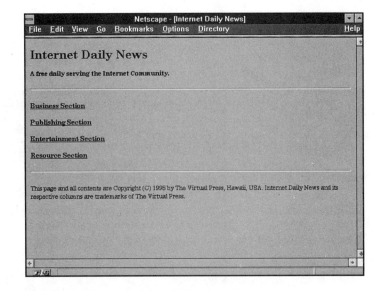

Figure 27.3 depicts the business section of the prototype. Developing the business section forced me to think more carefully about the actual topic each column would cover. In fact, I wrote out a half page summary describing each column. I also started to think about a directory structure and naming system for the paper. At this stage, *IDN* would have its own directory with subdirectories for each section. Because I didn't want to create the directories at this time, I simply put periods in where the slashes might go later. The following is the HTML code for the business section:

```
<HTML>
<HEAD><TITLE>Internet Daily News</TITLE></HEAD>
<BODY>
<H1>Internet Daily News</H1>
<P><STRONG>A free daily serving the Internet Community.
</STRONG></P>
<HR>
<H3>Business Section</H3>
<UL>
<LI><A HREF="projint.bus.ecu.html">Electronic Commerce
Update</A>
<BR>    A daily column devoted to developments in electronic
commerce
<LI><A HREF="projint.bus.cyb.html">Cyber Beat</A>
<BR>      Law & Politics in Cyberspace
<LI><A HREF="projint.bus.ins.html">Inside Scoop</A>
<BR>      Marketing, Consulting & Advertising on the Net
<LI><A HREF="projint.bus.fin.html">Finance Corner</A>
<BR>      Investment opportunities, venture capital firms and
finance on the Net
</UL>
<HR>
<P>This page and all contents are Copyright (C) 1995
```

```
by The Virtual Press, Hawaii, USA. Internet Daily News
and its respective columns are trademarks of
The Virtual Press.</P>
</BODY>
</HTML>
```

FIGURE 27.3.

*Internet Daily News
Business Section prototype.*

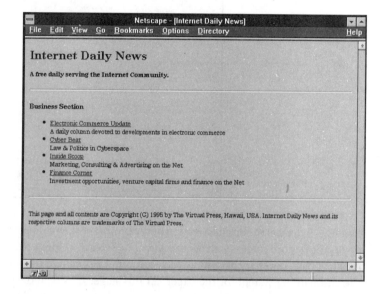

The publishing section for the prototype is depicted in Figure 27.4. In this section, one of the column names changed slightly. The Kitchen Table Publisher became Kitchen Table Publishing. The following is the HTML code for the publishing section:

```
<HTML>
<HEAD><TITLE>Internet Daily News</TITLE></HEAD>
<BODY>
<H1>Internet Daily News</H1>
<P><STRONG>A free daily serving the Internet Community.
</STRONG></P>
<HR>
<H3>Publishing Section</H3>
<UL>
<LI><A HREF="projint.pub.web.html">Web Publisher's Den</A>
<BR>     A daily column devoted to publishing on the Web
<LI><A HREF="projint.pub.ktp.html">Kitchen Table Publishing</A>
<BR>     Covers electronic publishing on CD-ROM and floppy disk
<LI><A HREF="projint.pub.pup.html">Publishing Update</A>
<BR>     Who's who & what's what in publishing
<LI><A HREF="projint.pub.mul.html">Multimedia Corner</A>
<BR>     Multimedia and the publisher: tips, sources & more
</UL>
<HR>
<P>This page and all contents are Copyright (C) 1995
by The Virtual Press, Hawaii, USA. Internet Daily News
and its respective columns are trademarks of
The Virtual Press.</P>
</BODY>
</HTML>
```

FIGURE 27.4.

Internet Daily News publishing section prototype.

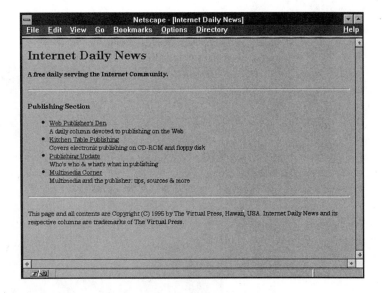

Figure 27.5 shows the entertainment section for the prototype. While I was creating this section, I decided to add a column devoted to reviews of electronic books. The Cyber Talk column was also further defined to include conference rooms. Conference rooms are discussion areas that are growing in popularity on the World Wide Web. The following is the HTML code for the entertainment section:

```
<HTML>
<HEAD><TITLE>Internet Daily News</TITLE></HEAD>
<BODY>
<H1>Internet Daily News</H1>
<P><STRONG>A free daily serving the Internet Community.
</STRONG></P>
<HR>
<H3>Entertainment Section</H3>
<UL>
<LI><A HREF="projint.ent.mud.html">MUDLand</A>
<BR>     Covers the MUD scene.  Tips & talk.
<LI><A HREF="projint.ent.cyb.html">Cyber Talk</A>
<BR>     What's hot & what's not in the land of talk.
<BR>     Covers mailing lists, newsgroups, conference rooms &
IRCs.
<LI><A HREF="projint.ent.int.html">Going Interactive</A>
<BR>     Covers the latest interactive multimedia titles.
<LI><A HREF="projint.ent.cool.html">Cool Pick Hotel</A>
<BR>     Find cool sites on the Internet
<LI><A HREF="projint.ent.rev.html">The Electronic Book
Review</A>
<BR>     Reviews of electronic books.
</UL>
<HR>
<P>This page and all contents are Copyright (C) 1995
by The Virtual Press, Hawaii, USA. Internet Daily News
and its respective columns are trademarks of
```

```
The Virtual Press.</P>
</BODY>
</HTML>
```

FIGURE 27.5.

Internet Daily News entertainment section prototype.

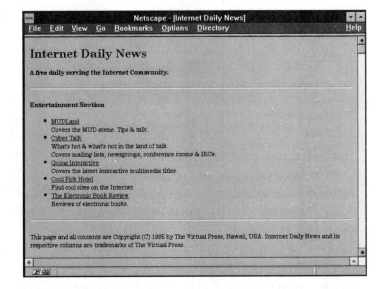

The last page in the prototype was for the resource section shown in Figure 27.6. In this section, I wanted to try some new ideas and see how they would work. This is the HTML code for the resource section:

```
<HTML>
<HEAD><TITLE>Internet Daily News</TITLE></HEAD>
<BODY>
<H1>Internet Daily News</H1>
<P><STRONG>A free daily serving the Internet Community.
</STRONG></P>
<HR>
<H3>Resource Section</H3>
<UL>
<LI><A HREF="projint.res.res.html">Researcher's Paradise</A>
<BR>    We scour the Net for hot resources so you don't have to
<LI><A HREF="projint.res.job.html">On-line Job Hunt</A>
<BR>    A daily column for anyone looking for a job or career
change
<LI><A HREF="projint.res.tool.html">Tools of the Trade</A>
<BR>    Learn about Internet search tools, browsers & more
<LI><A HREF="projint.res.tec.html">Technology Corner</A>
<BR>    What's new & interesting in high-tech
<LI><A HREF="projint.res.etc.html">Etcetera</A>
<BR>    The Internet Daily News classifieds
</UL>
<HR>
<P>This page and all contents are Copyright (C) 1995
by The Virtual Press, Hawaii, USA. Internet Daily News
and its respective columns are trademarks of
```

```
The Virtual Press.</P>
</BODY>
</HTML>
```

FIGURE 27.6.

Internet Daily News resource section prototype.

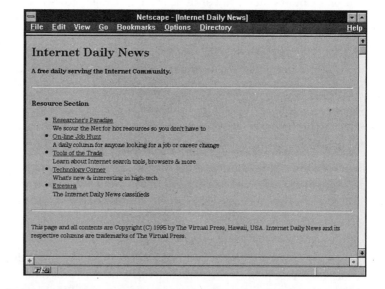

TIP

Although you should include full copyright and trademark information on the front page of your newspaper, ideally this information would not be written out each time it appears on your pages. The information is repeated in the examples you will find throughout this section primarily as a notice the material is an intellectual property created for The Virtual Press yet also to remind you to include this information in your publications as well. As you saw in Chapter 25, "Advertising and Protecting Your Document," providing copyright notice is a first step in protecting your creative works.

The best way to include copyright and trademark information on successive pages of the publication is to abbreviate it and include a link to the full reference. The full reference would be a separate copyright and trademark information page.

Specification Phase

Now that the prototype for the project is developed, you go on to determine specifics about the project. The first thing you would usually do is select target computers and formats for the publication. Yet, because of how HTML and web browsers work, publications designed for the Web can be run on any computer. This means for Web publications, you should focus on format. The hypertext markup language has three levels currently specified. Although HTML level 2 is the current standard, several browsers use the enhancements specified by HTML level 3.

One of the most noteworthy of these is the Netscape browser that takes advantage of many HTML level 3 enhancements and includes some enhancements of its own. If the Netscape browser were an obscure browser, the enhancements specific to it would have little impact on your publication. However, the Netscape browser is already used by more than six million users and is gaining in popularity. For this reason, *Internet Daily News* will include features for Netscape users. These enhancements will be pointed out in the design phase.

Some readers will have text-only browsers or will turn off the automatic-image-loading feature of their browsers. You may also want to add provisions for these users. The *Internet Daily News* will use the ALT attribute of the IMG SRC tag.

In this phase you should also look at how the reader will navigate to the various sections of the publication. HTML makes navigation through the publication easy. The reader will follow links you supply on the page. The *Internet Daily News* will use the anchor tag to specify links.

Next, look at the type of pages, the components and the style for the project. A newspaper published on the World Wide Web is a completely different creature from a traditional print newspaper. The World Wide Web makes it possible for sound, video, audio, and graphics to be included in the publication. Although this allows *IDN* to contain material not possible in a traditional print newspaper, the current structure of HTML does put some limitations on the project. Currently, there is no easy way to produce text in more than one column on the page.

> **NOTE**
>
> In Chapter 20, "Using HTML," I used the <PRE> tag to create text in columns. Although preformatting of text could be used to create columns, this is not practical for *IDN*. Preformatted text is generally displayed in a monospace courier type that, although easy to read, is not as visually appealing as other font types. Also, as I would be preformatting text mostly by hand, this would be time intensive.
>
> Chapter 20 also briefly touched on the table extension for HTML 3.0. Using this extension, I could create tables of text. However, many users do not have browsers capable of displaying tables, which would mean they would see the text all jumbled together. To get around this I could do some creative hacking and add paragraph and line breaks to the table text, but in the end, I decided creating columns would be more work than it was worth. Therefore, I elected not to use tables as well.

To specify the parts of the publication, you could either develop preliminary storyboards or create a list. For *IDN*, I chose to create a list:

Style of Publication:	Modern freelance layout
Type of Pages:	Text pages
	Graphic pages
	Combined text and graphic pages
Publication components:	Front page
	Letters to the Editor page
	Newspaper background page
	Four section overview pages including the following:

                    Business section
                    Publishing section
                    Entertainment section
                    Resource section

18 column pages including the following:

                    Electronic Commerce Update
                    Cyber Beat
                    Inside Scoop
                    Finance Corner
                    Web Publisher's Den
                    The Kitchen Table Publisher
                    Publishing Update
                    Multimedia Corner
                    MUDLand
                    Cyber Talk
                    Going Interactive
                    Cool Pick Hotel
                    The Electronic Book Review
                    Researcher's Paradise
                    On-line Job Hunt
                    Tools of the Trade
                    Technology Corner
                    Etcetera

          Index to Columnists
          Columnist background page (one for each writer)
          Archive index

Finally, for a large project on the Web, readers may want to be able to search through back issues of the publication. Although this is something to write down in your project notebook, it is not something you should worry about developing immediately. Creating a searchable database adds complexity to the publication and should really be a separate project.

Finish the current project before making complex additions or upgrades. Readers of the first issue will not care if a searchable database is available because there will be no back issues to search. The *Internet Daily News* will include provisions for a searchable archive. However, no mechanisms for the archive will be created initially.

Planning Phase

The first thing you should do in the planning stage is to work out a rough schedule for the project. The schedule should contain milestones, goals, and an allocation of time. Use the schedule as a flexible and realistic guideline to help you through to project completion. The purpose of the schedule is to help you start thinking about the project and to formalize the steps necessary to complete the project. The schedule should also help you set regular times to work on the project.

After determining a schedule, you should ask yourself five key questions concerning the project:

- Who are you developing the project for?
- What medium and formats will the project be published on?
- Where will the project be published?
- When will the project be published?
- How will the project be published?

Some of these questions were answered earlier when the requirements were specified. However, you should now reevaluate based on what you now know about the project. Here are the new plans for the *Internet Daily News*:

Audience:
Internet users who are interested in topics related to the Internet and technology in general.

Medium:
World Wide Web

Format:
HTML included enhancements for Netscape browser and provisions for users with text-only browsers.

Site:
Publicly available Web site. Initially project pages will be combined with The Virtual Press project pages with provisions for separate accounts if necessary.

Duration:
Six months for development.

Deadline:
December 1995

Window:
Deadline gives 6–12 month window to produce initial publication.

Project size:
45 pages in HTML format. This includes 18 columnist background pages.
27 pages will not change on a regular basis.
18 pages will change on a regular basis.

NOTE

Using scrollbars on text windows, each page could contain more than one physical page. Therefore, each page corresponds to a full-length article or column of a traditional newspaper.

Critical constraints:
Number of writers critical to implementation.
Number of sponsors and advertisers key to profitability.
$XX,XXX budget, which equates to XXXX hours and a maximum of $XX,XXX in real money. (You would fill in Xs with time and dollar figures.)

Alternate Plans:
Problem: Too few writers.
Solution: Provide *IDN* as a weekly publication.

Problem: Too few sponsors.
Solution: Start aggressively seeking sponsors. Continue operations until another critical constraint is met.

Problem: Nearing budgetary constraints
Solution: Reevaluate project, determine if worthwhile to continue. Possible interim solution is to publish *IDN* as a weekly publication.

Step 4: Designing the Project

Project design is the heart of the project. Every aspect of the *Internet Daily News* will be developed in this stage. This section includes a complete walkthrough of the project:

- Preliminary design using planning sheets
- Design through storyboards
- Logo design
- Page design

Preliminary Design Using Planning Sheets

Storyboards will be used to reduce the complexity of the project. Each page of the presentation will be represented in miniature form on a planning sheet. By adding links to the planning sheet diagrams, the logical flow from page to page can be followed. This will enable you to see the entire newspaper from start to finish, which makes the project more manageable and less mysterious.

You don't have to create the planning sheet on a computer. Often the easiest way to create the planning sheet is by drawing it freehand on the pages of a notepad. Optimally for a large project, you would use a large posterboard or tape several 8 1/2"×11" pieces of paper together.

The initial planning sheet for the *Internet Daily News* is shown in Figure 27.7. From the front page, readers can get to any of the second-level pages. I decided to add another link between the second-level documents that would allow the reader to go to the previous or the next section. At this stage of the design, I wasn't concerned about how this would be done. I focused on the idea that it would be a feature readers may want. This transformed the structure of the storyboards from hierarchical to a combination of linear and hierarchical.

FIGURE 27.7.

Initial planning sheet for Internet Daily News.

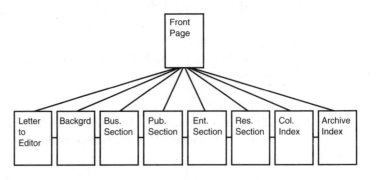

Next, I created a planning sheet for each section of the paper that had levels not seen on the initial planning sheet. Figure 27.8 shows the planning sheet for the resource section. When a reader is on a column page, such as the Online Job Hunt column, I wanted them to be able to go to the previous or next column. I also wanted them to be able to jump to the background page for the writer of the column. This is shown in the links on the planning sheet.

FIGURE 27.8.

Planning sheet for the Resource section.

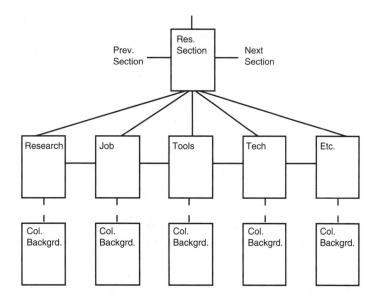

Finally, I created the planning sheet for the index to columnists depicted in Figure 27.9. I wanted readers to be able to go to the previous or next background page. I also wanted readers to able to go to the column written by the columnist they were currently reading about.

As you can see, the combined linear and hierarchical structure for the design of the *Internet Daily News* is extremely flexible, yet still highly structured. High flexibility and structure are the key elements in a sound design. Readers can move forward and backward through sections, columns, and background material. They can go up a level or descend to the next level. They can also follow parallel paths through the document.

Storyboards and Content

After the structure has been designed, the individual parts of the newspaper must be designed. This means developing the content of the storyboards. For a large project, the storyboards will not be developed in depth. The master storyboard concept will be used whenever possible. The master storyboards will form the basis for individual storyboards, which will save many hours of work.

FIGURE 27.9.

*Planning sheet for the
Index to Columnists.*

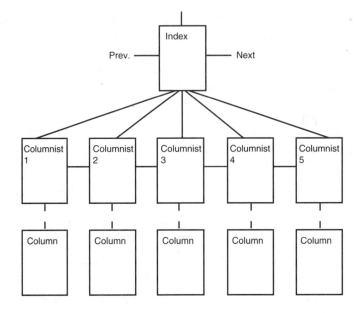

Using the master storyboard method, unique pages and pages with common components are identified. For *Internet Daily News* the unique pages included the following:

- Front page
- Letters to the Editor page
- Newspaper background page
- Index to Columnists
- Archive index

Three possible master storyboards were identified:

- Section overview pages
- Column pages
- Columnist background pages

Internet Daily News has four section overview pages. A representation of the master storyboard developed for these pages is shown in Figure 27.10. This is how you would represent common components on a page. You could draw these freehand and include color coding if you wanted to.

Using the master storyboard, the layout of the overview pages will be the same no matter which page the reader is on. The page will include one common title at the top of the page. Under the first title, there will be a second title. Although this title will be unique to the page, it will always appear in the same place. Each column will have a one-line title associated with it. Column titles will be placed on the page using the LI tag so they are bulleted or as icons. The bottom of the page will have copyright information and possibly a text-based menu.

FIGURE 27.10.

Master storyboard for section overview page.

Internet Daily News has 18 column pages. The master storyboard for these pages is shown in Figure 27.11. The layout of the column pages will be the same no matter which page the reader is on. At the top of the page will be a common title. Under the first title, there will be a second title unique to the page. Beneath the title lines will be an icon or small image. Text will be aligned with the bottom of this image and appear on the same line. The last items on the page will be a text-based menu and the standard copyright information that will appear throughout the publication.

FIGURE 27.11.

Master storyboard for column pages.

The final master storyboard will be for the columnist background page. This is depicted by Figure 27.12. The *Internet Daily News* will have one background page for each of the regular columnists. The layout of the background pages will be uniform throughout the section. The page will include the columnist's name at the top of the page. A photograph of the columnist will be placed under the name. The first line of text will be aligned with the bottom of the image and appear on the same line.

FIGURE 27.12.

Master storyboard for columnist background pages.

Logo Design

Before starting work on the individual pages, I wanted to develop the logo for the *Internet Daily News*. The logo will be a central part in the paper and may appear on most of the pages. You should set aside several hours to work on the logo. To develop the logo for *IDN*, I set aside an afternoon and told myself I would work only on the logo during this time.

The logo should be highly visual in nature. However, you do not need state of the art tools to develop a good logo. To develop *IDN*'s logo, I used two tools:

- Harvard Draw for Windows
- Freeze Frame 2 for Windows

Harvard Draw is a drawing program published by Software Publishing Corporation. I have version 1.01 from 1992. Harvard Draw's features are now a part of Software Publishing Corporation's Harvard Graphics.

Freeze Frame 2 is an excellent commercial tool for manipulating images. FF2 costs $50 and includes design, publishing, file conversion, image manipulation, and screen capture utilities. I use it mostly for file conversion and screen capture.

TIP

Keep in mind my 14-second rule discussed in Chapter 22, "Incorporating Multimedia," when creating your logo. Don't make readers wait too long for any page—even your front page—to download. Develop a logo that has a relatively small file size so you can use it effectively in your publication. If designed well, your logo can be large in size as viewed in the reader's browser, yet small in actual file size and thus quicker in download time.

Remember, slow-loading graphics aren't necessarily large graphics, they are high-resolution graphics or graphics with many colors. A very large two-color image at low resolution will load faster than a small 256-color image at high resolution. In the examples you will see throughout this chapter, there are two sizes for the finished logo for *IDN*. The large logo is less than 6,000 bytes and the small logo is less than 3,000 bytes.

The first step was to select a background for the logo. Using GIF87 or GIF89 formats, I could have used a clear background that would make the image appear to come off the page. However, since I planned to use the Netscape enhancement for backgrounds, I wanted to make sure the logo had a clear background of its own. This ensured there would be no conflict with the color scheme. I selected a clear black background for the logo and drew a rectangular box on the screen. In Figure 27.13, the rectangle is the first item shown.

The second step was to select an image that would be a part of the logo. Because the *Internet Daily News* would serve a global community, I selected an image of the world. This image is the second item shown in Figure 27.13.

FIGURE 27.13.

Creating a logo.

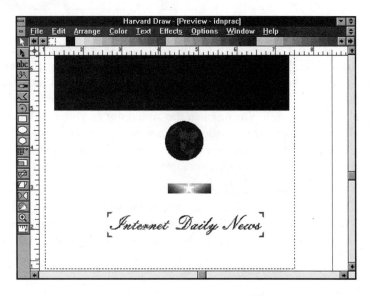

The third step was to create a second image that would be a part of the logo. The purpose of this image was to highlight the central part of the logo, the globe. I created a second rectangular box on the screen and decided to use a radial fill to enhance the image. Using a radial fill, you can select a pattern to be the center of the image you are working with. You also select two colors. The first color is what the image will fade from. The second color is what the image will fade to. Figure 27.14 shows how this was accomplished in the drawing program. I put a five-pointed star in the middle of the box using a radial fill from blue to white. Most drawing programs—even the cheapies—support radial fills.

FIGURE 27.14.

Using radial fills in the logo.

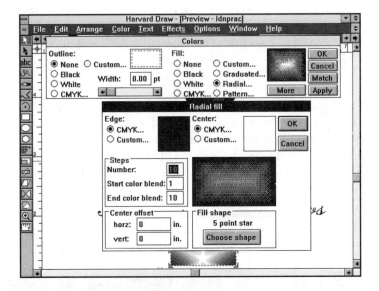

The next part of the logo is the project's title: *Internet Daily News.* Before adding the title, I thought carefully about the proper color for it. The logo already had four colors: black, blue, white, and green. Knowing that too many colors can spoil the effect, I didn't want to use a different color for the title. Black was out, because black text would be unreadable against a black background. Blue or green text would not be visible when used with the image of the globe. All white text on the logo did not look good. To overcome this problem, I selected a radial fill for the text using the same blue and white color scheme I had used earlier. As a result, the title was blue on both ends and white in the middle.

The last step was to combine the four parts of the logo into a single image. Figure 27.15 shows the finished logo. The blue and white box was moved to the middle of the background. The globe was positioned within both boxes, using the white and blue to highlight the globe as planned. Finally, the title was positioned so it was centered in the image and on top of the globe.

FIGURE 27.15.

The completed logo for Internet Daily News.

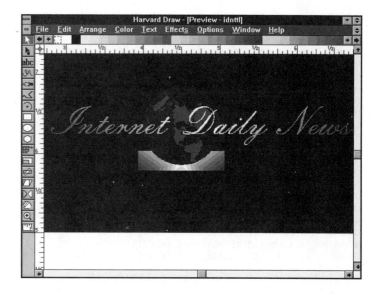

Page Design

This section includes a complete walkthrough of the *Internet Daily News* project. In this stage everything discussed in the chapter comes together, and the paper comes to life. You will find the complete HTML code for every page and accompanying graphics to show what the finished page looks like.

Front Page

The front page follows the hierarchical and linear path structure discussed earlier. All the graphics on the page are clickable. Clicking on the *Internet Daily News* logo shown in Figure 27.16 will take the reader to the paper's background page. Clicking on the section icons will take the reader to the respective section.

Figure 27.17 shows some additions to the front page. A link to a page with site navigation tips was added to help new users maneuver around the site. A text-based menu was also added to provide an additional way to navigate through the paper. The HTML code for the page follows:

```
<HTML>
<HEAD>
<TITLE>Internet Daily News</TITLE>
</HEAD>
<BODY background ="tanpaper.gif">
<CENTER>
<P><A HREF="idnbg.html"><IMG SRC="idnttl3.gif" ALT=""></A></P>
<H1>A free daily serving the Internet Community.</H1>
<HR>
<H3><A HREF="idnbus.html"><IMG SRC="busttl.gif"
```

```
ALT="Business Section"></A>
<A HREF="idnpub.html"><IMG SRC="pubttl.gif"
ALT="Publishing Section"></A>
<A HREF="idnent.html"><IMG SRC="entttl.gif"
ALT="Entertainment Section"></A>
<A HREF="idnres.html"><IMG SRC="resttl.gif"
ALT="Resource Section"></A>
<A HREF="idnedi.html"><IMG SRC="edittl.gif"
ALT="Letter to Editor"></A>
<A HREF="idncol.html"><IMG SRC="colttl.gif"
ALT="Index to Columnists"></A></H3>
</CENTER>
<HR SIZE=4>
<H2><A HREF="idntips.html">Site Navigation Tips</A></H2>
<P><A HREF="idnfp.html">Front Page</A> ¦¦
<A HREF="idnbus.html">Business Section</A> ¦¦
<A HREF="idnpub.html">Publishing Section</A> ¦¦
<A HREF="idnent.html">Entertainment Section</A> ¦¦
<A HREF="idnres.html">Resource Section</A></P>
<P><A HREF="idnedi.html">Letters to Editor</A> ¦¦
<A HREF="idncol.html">Index to Columnists</A></P>
<HR SIZE=4>
<P>This page and all contents are Copyright (C) 1995
by The Virtual Press, Hawaii, USA. Internet Daily News and
its respective columns are trademarks of The Virtual Press.</P>
</BODY>
</HTML>
```

FIGURE 27.16.

Internet Daily News front page.

FIGURE 27.17.

Using icons and text-based menus.

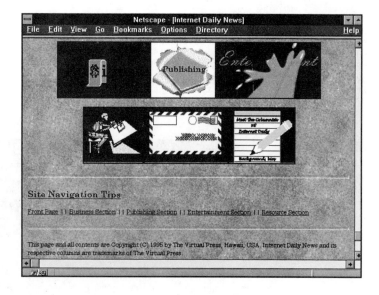

Business Section

The business section also follows the hierarchical and linear path structure discussed earlier. All the graphics on the page are clickable. Figure 27.18 shows a partial view of the business section. Clicking on the section logo will take the reader to the next section. The links to individual columns are included as a text-based list and a text-based menu is also added to provide an additional way to navigate through the paper. The following is the HTML code for the page:

```
<HTML>
<HEAD>
<TITLE>Business Section at Internet Daily News</TITLE>
</HEAD>
<BODY background ="tanpaper.gif">
<CENTER>
<P><A HREF="idnfp.html"><IMG SRC="idnttl3.gif" ALT=""></A></P>
<A HREF="idnpub.html"><IMG SRC="busttl1.gif"
ALT="Business Section"></A>
</CENTER>
<H2>
<UL>
<LI><A HREF="buscyb.html">Cyber Beat</A>
<BR>     Law & Politics in Cyberspace
<LI><A HREF="busecu.html">Electronic Commerce Update</A>
<BR>     The Latest Developments in Electronic Commerce
<LI><A HREF="busins.html">Inside Scoop</A>
<BR>     Marketing, Consulting & Advertising on the Net
<LI><A HREF="busfin.html">Finance Corner</A>
<BR>     Investments, Opportunities & Finance on the Net
</UL>
</H2>
<HR SIZE=4>
<P><A HREF="idnfp.html">Front Page</A> ¦¦
```

```
<A HREF="idnpub.html">Publishing Section</A> ¦¦
<A HREF="idnent.html">Entertainment Section</A> ¦¦
<A HREF="idnres.html">Resource Section</A></P>
<HR SIZE=4>
<P>This page and all contents are Copyright (C) 1995
by The Virtual Press, Hawaii, USA. Internet Daily News and
its respective columns are trademarks of The Virtual Press.</P>
</BODY>
</HTML>
```

FIGURE 27.18.

A partial view of the business section at the Internet Daily News.

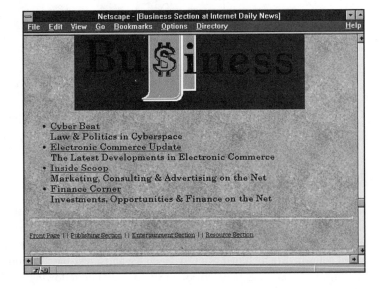

Publishing Section

The publishing section has a structure similar to the business section. This ensures the paper has a uniform look throughout. Clicking on the section logo shown in Figure 27.19 will take the reader to the next section.

As Figure 27.20 shows, the links to columns are put into a list. The text-based menu at the bottom of the page is changed. A link to the business section is added. Finally, a link to the current section is deleted from the menu. Here is the HTML code for the page:

```
<HTML>
<HEAD>
<TITLE>Publishing Section at Internet Daily News</TITLE>
</HEAD>
<BODY background ="tanpaper.gif">
<CENTER>
<P><A HREF="idnfp.html"><IMG SRC="idnttl3.gif" ALT=""></A></P>
<A HREF="idnent.html"><IMG SRC="pubttl2.gif"
ALT="Publishing Section"></A>
</CENTER>
```

```
<H2>
<UL>
<LI><A HREF="pubktp.html">The Kitchen Table Publisher</A>
<BR>     Electronic Publishing on CD-ROM & Floppy Disk
<LI><A HREF="pubmul.html">Multimedia Corner</A>
<BR>     Multimedia and the Publisher: Tips, Sources & More
<LI><A HREF="pubpup.html">Publishing Update</A>
<BR>     Who's Who & What's What in Publishing
<LI><A HREF="pubweb.html">Web Publisher's Den</A>
<BR>     Publishing on the Web
</H2>
</UL>
<HR SIZE=4>
<P><A HREF="idnfp.html">Front Page</A> ||
<A HREF="idnbus.html">Business Section</A> ||
<A HREF="idnent.html">Entertainment Section</A> ||
<A HREF="idnres.html">Resource Section</A></P>
<HR SIZE=4>
<P>This page and all contents are Copyright (C) 1995
by The Virtual Press, Hawaii, USA. Internet Daily News and
its respective columns are trademarks of The Virtual Press.</P>
</BODY>
</HTML>
```

FIGURE 27.19.

Publishing section at the Internet Daily News.

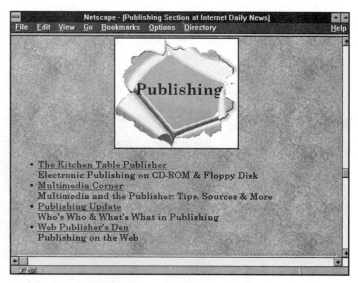

FIGURE 27.20.

Publishing section links.

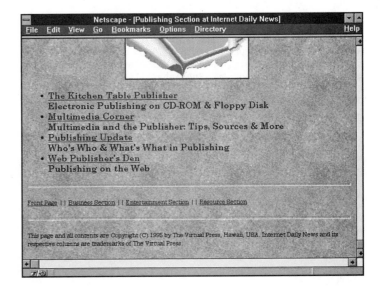

Entertainment Section

The entertainment section shown in Figure 27.21 is designed with fun in mind. This lead to the design of the wonderful paint spill and the dripping letters. In the large graphic featured in the columns, you can clearly read the word entertainment as it spills down the page.

FIGURE 27.21.

Entertainment section at the Internet Daily News.

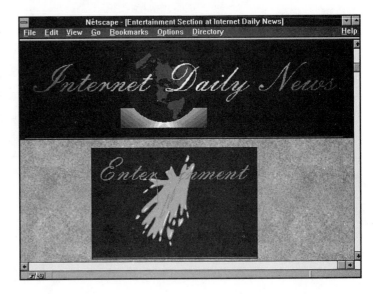

Although clicking on the paper's logo takes readers to the front page, clicking on the section logo will take the reader to the next section. Figure 27.22 shows the links to columns. Much of the information in this section has changed. The descriptions have been cleaned up and one of the section names has been altered. The HTML code for the page is shown here:

```
<HTML>
<HEAD>
<TITLE>Entertainment Section at Internet Daily News</TITLE>
</HEAD>
<BODY background ="tanpaper.gif">
<CENTER>
<P><A HREF="idnfp.html"><IMG SRC="idnttl3.gif" ALT=""></A></P>
<A HREF="idnres.html"><IMG SRC="entttl2.gif"
ALT="Entertainment Section"></A>
</CENTER>
<H2>
<UL>
<LI><A HREF="entmud.html">MUDLand</A>
<BR>      Covers the Multi User Dungeon Scene:  Tips &
Information.
<LI><A HREF="entcyb.html">Cyber Talk</A>
<BR>      What's Hot & What's Not in the Land of Talk.
<BR>      Covers Mailing Lists, Newsgroups, Conference Rooms &
IRCs.
<LI><A HREF="entint.html">Going Interactive</A>
<BR>      Reviews of the Latest Interactive Multimedia Titles.
<LI><A HREF="entcool.html">Cool Pick Hotel</A>
<BR>      Cool Sites & Hot Picks on the Web
<LI><A HREF="entrev.html">The Electric Reviewer</A>
<BR>      Reviews of Electronic Books & Other Non-traditional
Publications.
</UL>
</H2>
<HR SIZE=4>
<P><A HREF="idnfp.html">Front Page</A> ¦¦
<A HREF="idnbus.html">Business Section</A> ¦¦
<A HREF="idnpub.html">Publishing Section</A> ¦¦
<A HREF="idnres.html">Resource Section</A></P>
<HR SIZE=4>
<P>This page and all contents are Copyright (C) 1995
by The Virtual Press, Hawaii, USA.  Internet Daily News and
its respective columns are trademarks of The Virtual Press.</P>
</BODY>
</HTML>
```

FIGURE 27.22.

Entertainment section links.

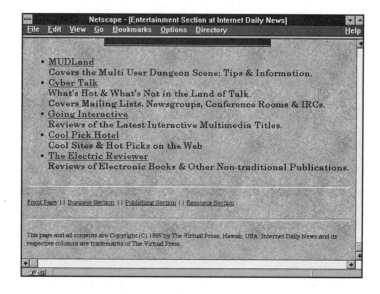

Resource Section

The resource section is shown in Figure 27.23. Clicking on the image of the android will take the reader to the Letter to the Editor section of the paper. The links to the columns are depicted in Figure 27.24. Here is the HTML code for the page:

```
<HTML>
<HEAD>
<TITLE>Resource Section at Internet Daily News</TITLE>
</HEAD>
<BODY background ="tanpaper.gif">
<CENTER>
<P><A HREF="idnfp.html"><IMG SRC="idnttl3.gif" ALT=""></A></P>
<A HREF="idnedi.html"><IMG SRC="resttl2.gif"
ALT="Resource Section"></A>
</CENTER>
<H2>
<UL>
<LI><A HREF="resres.html">Researcher's Paradise</A>
<BR>     We Scour the Net for Great Resources so You Don't
Have to
<LI><A HREF="resjob.html">On-line Job Hunt</A>
<BR> A Column for Anyone Looking for a Job or a Career Change
<LI><A HREF="restool.html">Tools of the Trade</A>
<BR>     Tips & More on the Internet Tools from Browsers to
Search Engines
<LI><A HREF="restec.html">Technology Corner</A>
<BR>     Discover What's New & Interesting in High-Tech
<LI><A HREF="resetc.html">Etcetera</A>
<BR>     The Internet Daily News Classifieds
</UL>
</H2>
<HR SIZE=4>
<P><A HREF="idnfp.html">Front Page</A> ¦¦
```

```
<A HREF="idnbus.html">Business Section</A> ||
<A HREF="idnpub.html">Publishing Section</A> ||
<A HREF="idnent.html">Entertainment Section</A> ||
<A HREF="idnedi.html">Letter to the Editor</A></P>
<HR SIZE=4>
<P>This page and all contents are Copyright (C) 1995
by The Virtual Press, Hawaii, USA.  Internet Daily News and
its respective columns are trademarks of The Virtual Press.</P>
</BODY>
</HTML>
```

FIGURE 27.23.

The Resource section at the Internet Daily News.

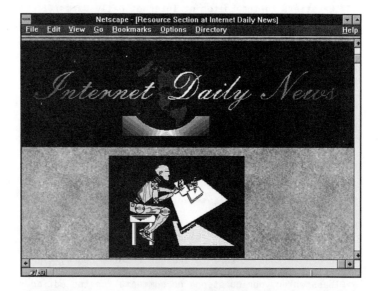

FIGURE 27.24.

Resource section links.

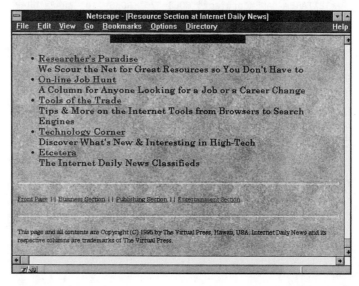

Letter to the Editor

The main features of the Letter to the Editor are shown in Figure 27.25. The section contains an online form that readers can fill out and send using the buttons shown in Figure 27.26. Optionally, the readers can send a direct e-mail message. This is provided because some users cannot use fill-out forms. The HTML code for the page is shown here:

```html
<HTML>
<HEAD>
<TITLE>Letters to the Editor at Internet Daily News</TITLE>
</HEAD>
<BODY background ="tanpaper.gif">
<CENTER>
<P><A HREF="idnfp.html"><IMG SRC="idnttl3.gif" ALT=""></A></P>
<A HREF="idncol.html"><IMG SRC="edittl2.gif"
ALT="Letters to the Editor"></A>
</CENTER>
<H1>
Send a letter to the editor!
<BR>You can use the on-line form below.
<BR>Or send <A HREF="mailto:william@tvp.com" >
<IMG SRC="mail.gif" ALIGN="MIDDLE" ALT="* mail *">
to william@tvp.com.</A>
</H1>
<FORM METHOD="POST"
<FORM ACTION="mailto:william@tvp.com">
<HR SIZE=4>
<P>Your name (First, Middle Initial, Last)
<INPUT NAME="Reader's Name" SIZE="30">
</P>
<P>Address (Please be sure to include country codes) </P>
<P><TEXTAREA NAME="Address" COLS="30" ROWS="5"></TEXTAREA></P>
<P>Please enter your questions or comments for the editor.</P>
<P><TEXTAREA NAME="project" COLS="75" ROWS="10" WRAP="WRAP">
</TEXTAREA></P>
<P><INPUT TYPE="SUBMIT" VALUE="Send Letter to Editor">
<INPUT TYPE="RESET"></P>
</FORM>
<HR SIZE=4>
<P><A HREF="idnfp.html">Front Page</A> ¦¦
<A HREF="idnbus.html">Business Section</A> ¦¦
<A HREF="idnpub.html">Publishing Section</A> ¦¦
<A HREF="idnent.html">Entertainment Section</A> ¦¦
<A HREF="idnres.html">Resource Section</A></P>
<HR SIZE=4>
<P>This page and all contents are Copyright (C) 1995
by The Virtual Press, Hawaii, USA. Internet Daily News and
its respective columns are trademarks of The Virtual Press.</P>
</BODY>
</HTML>
```

FIGURE 27.25.

Letter-to-the-Editor section.

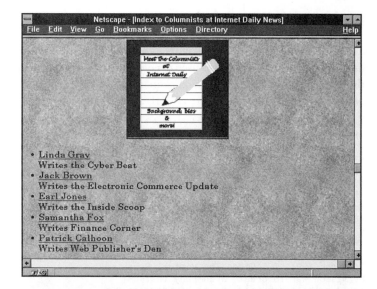

FIGURE 27.26.

Using a fill-out form so a reader can send a letter to IDN's editor.

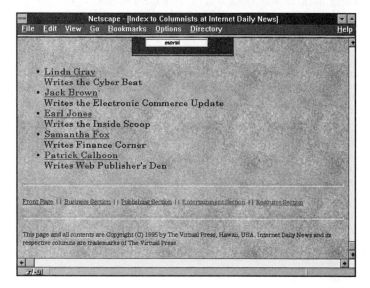

Background Page

The background page shown in Figure 27.27 tells readers briefly about the paper and its publisher. Netscape's CENTER tag was used to give the page a better design. As shown in Figure 27.28 the bottom of the page includes a quick menu. This way readers can jump easily to any section of the paper. The following is the HTML code for the page:

```
<HTML>
<HEAD>
<TITLE>Internet Daily News</TITLE>
</HEAD>
<BODY background ="tanpaper.gif">
<CENTER>
<P><A HREF="idnfp.html"><IMG SRC="idnttl3.gif" ALT=""></A></P>
<H1>
<STRONG>A Brief History</STRONG>
</H1>
<HR>
<P><STRONG>
In March 1994, I founded The Virtual Press.<BR>
My vision was to create a company that<BR>
would help launch the careers of aspiring<BR>
writers. As a veteran writer with little to<BR>
show for 10 years of writing, I knew how<BR>
difficult it was to break into print. For years<BR>
I had planned to start up my own press,<BR>
but traditional small presses are expensive to<BR>
operate. Eventually, I turned to electronic<BR>
mediums to publish my works and the works<BR>
of other authors from around the world.<BR>
<BR>
</STRONG></P>
</CENTER>
<HR SIZE=4>
<P><A HREF="idnfp.html">Front Page</A> ¦¦
<A HREF="idnbus.html">Business Section</A> ¦¦
<A HREF="idnpub.html">Publishing Section</A> ¦¦
<A HREF="idnent.html">Entertainment Section</A> ¦¦
<A HREF="idnres.html">Resource Section</A></P>
<HR SIZE=4>
<P>This page and all contents are Copyright (C) 1995
by The Virtual Press, Hawaii, USA. Internet Daily News and
its respective columns are trademarks of The Virtual Press.</P>
</BODY>
</HTML>
```

FIGURE 27.27.

Internet Daily News background.

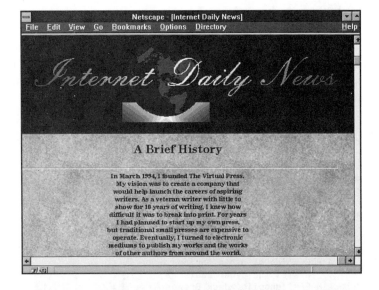

FIGURE 27.28.

Quick menu to the main sections of the paper.

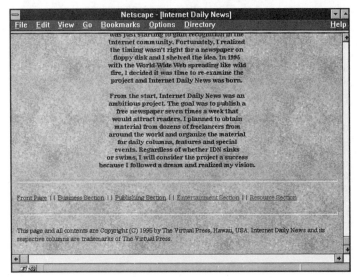

Index to Columnists

The Columnists' index page begins with the image of the notepage shown in Figure 27.29. Using the links shown in Figure 27.30, readers can quickly find a particular writer. The bottom of the page features a text-based menu to the major sections of the paper. Here is the HTML code for the page:

```
<HTML>
<HEAD>
<TITLE>Index to Columnists at Internet Daily News</TITLE>
</HEAD>
<BODY background ="tanpaper.gif">
<CENTER>
<P><A HREF="idnfp.html"><IMG SRC="idnttl3.gif" ALT=""></A></P>
<A HREF="idnbg.html"><IMG SRC="colttl2.gif"
ALT="Index to Columnists"></A>
</CENTER>
<H2>
<UL>
<LI><A HREF="idncollg.html">Linda Gray</A>
<BR>     Writes the Cyber Beat
<LI><A HREF="idncoljb">Jack Brown</A>
<BR>     Writes the Electronic Commerce Update
<LI><A HREF="idncolej.html">Earl Jones</A>
<BR>     Writes the Inside Scoop
<LI><A HREF="idncolsf.html">Samantha Fox</A>
<BR>     Writes Finance Corner
<LI><A HREF="idncolpc.html">Patrick Calhoon</A>
<BR>     Writes Web Publisher's Den
</UL>
</H2>
<HR SIZE=4>
<P><A HREF="idnfp.html">Front Page</A> ¦¦
<A HREF="idnbus.html">Business Section</A> ¦¦
<A HREF="idnpub.html">Publishing Section</A> ¦¦
<A HREF="idnent.html">Entertainment Section</A> ¦¦
<A HREF="idnres.html">Resource Section</A></P>
<HR SIZE=4>
<P>This page and all contents are Copyright (C) 1995
by The Virtual Press, Hawaii, USA. Internet Daily News and
its respective columns are trademarks of The Virtual Press.</P>
</BODY>
</HTML>
```

FIGURE 27.29.

Index to columnists at the Internet Daily News.

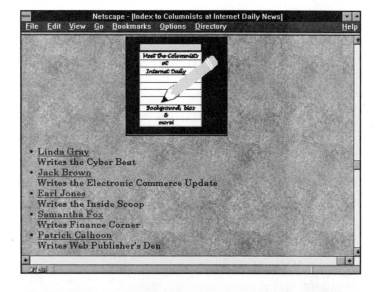

FIGURE 27.30.

Links to individual columnists.

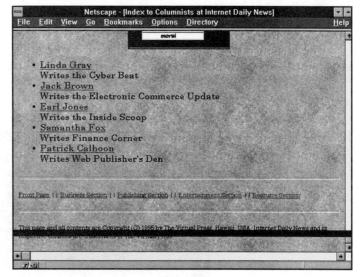

Columns

The next few pages provide a walkthrough of the business section. This will show you how the next level of pages was designed at the *Internet Daily News*. The column pages feature links to the writer's background page using icons and text. Clicking on a section icon will take the reader to the next section.

Figure 27.31 shows the Cyber Beat page. The text-based menu at the bottom of the page will take readers back to the front page or to columns within the business section. Here is the HTML code for the page:

```
<HTML>
<HEAD>
<TITLE>Business Section: Cyber Beat</TITLE>
</HEAD>
<BODY background ="tanpaper.gif">
<CENTER>
<P><A HREF="idnbus.html"><IMG SRC="idnttl3.gif"
ALT=""></A></P>
<P><A HREF="busecu.html">
<IMG SRC="busttl4.gif" ALT="Business Section: Cyber Beat">
</A></P>
</CENTER>
<P><A HREF="idncollg.html"><IMG SRC="colttl3.gif"
ALT="Cyber Beat">
     Written by Linda Gray</A></P>
<P>
<P>Column text goes here</P>
<HR SIZE=4>
<P><A HREF="idnfp.html">Front Page</A> ¦¦
<A HREF="busecu.html">Electronic Commerce Update</A> ¦¦
<A HREF="busins.html">Inside Scoop</A> ¦¦
<A HREF="busfin.html">Finance Corner</A></P>
<HR SIZE=4>
<P>This page and all contents are Copyright (C) 1995
by The Virtual Press, Hawaii, USA.  Internet Daily News and
its respective columns are trademarks of The Virtual Press.</P>
</BODY>
</HTML>
```

FIGURE 27.31.

Cyber Beat column at the Internet Daily News.

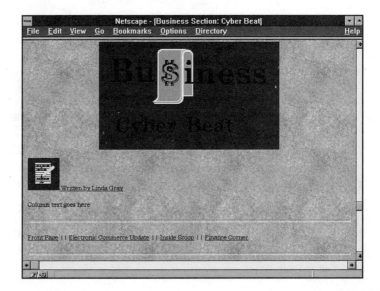

Figure 27.32 shows the Electronic Commerce Update column. The menu at the bottom of the page has been changed to include a link to the Cyber Beat column. The HTML code for the page is shown here:

```
<HTML>
<HEAD>
<TITLE>Business Section: Electronic Commerce Update</TITLE>
</HEAD>
<BODY background ="tanpaper.gif">
<CENTER>
<P><A HREF="idnbus.html"><IMG SRC="idnttl3.gif" ALT=""></A></P>
<P><A HREF="busins.html">
<IMG SRC="busttl3.gif" ALT="Business Section:
Electronic Commerce Update"></A></P>
</CENTER>
<P>
<A HREF="idncoljb.html">
<IMG SRC="colttl3.gif" ALT="Electronic Commerce Update">
     Written by Jack Brown</A>
</P>
<P>
<P>Column text goes here</P>
<HR SIZE=4>
<P><A HREF="idnfp.html">Front Page</A> ¦¦
<A HREF="buscyb.html">Cyber Beat</A> ¦¦
<A HREF="busins.html">Inside Scoop</A> ¦¦
<A HREF="busfin.html">Finance Corner</A><P>
<HR SIZE=4>
<P>This page and all contents are Copyright (C) 1995
by The Virtual Press, Hawaii, USA. Internet Daily News and
its respective columns are trademarks of The Virtual Press.</P>
</BODY>
</HTML>
```

FIGURE 27.32.

Electronic Commerce Update column.

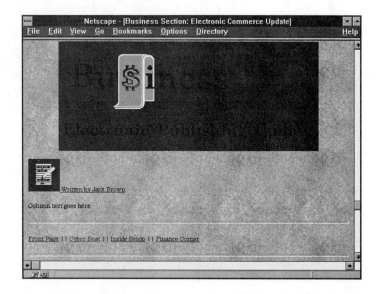

The Inside Scoop column is depicted in Figure 27.33. The uniform look of each section en-sure readers can navigate around the publication easily. The HTML code for this page is

```
<HTML>
<HEAD>
<TITLE>Business Section: Inside Scoop</TITLE>
</HEAD>
<BODY background ="tanpaper.gif">
<CENTER>
<P><A HREF="idnbus.html">
<IMG SRC="idnttl3.gif" ALT=""></A></P>
<P><A HREF="busfin.html">
<IMG SRC="busttl5.gif" ALT="Business Section: Inside Scoop">
</A></P>
</CENTER>
<P><A HREF="idncoljb.html"><IMG SRC="colttl3.gif"
ALT="Inside Scoop">     Written by Earl Jones</A></P>
<P>
<P>Column text goes here</P>
<HR SIZE=4>
<P><A HREF="idnfp.html">Front Page</A> ¦¦
<A HREF="buscyb.html">Cyber Beat</A> ¦¦
<A HREF="busecu.html">Electronic Commerce Update</A> ¦¦
<A HREF="busfin.html">Finance Corner</A></P>
<HR SIZE=4>
<P>This page and all contents are Copyright (C) 1995
by The Virtual Press, Hawaii, USA. Internet Daily News and
its respective columns are trademarks of The Virtual Press.</P>
</BODY>
</HTML>
```

FIGURE 27.33.

Inside Scoop column at the Internet Daily News.

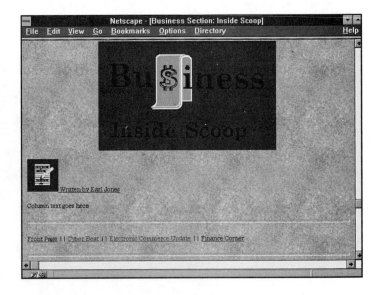

The final column in the business section is Finance Corner. Finance corner is shown in Figure 27.34. Here is the HTML code:

```
<HTML>
<HEAD>
<TITLE>Business Section: Finance Corner</TITLE>
</HEAD>
<BODY background ="tanpaper.gif">
<CENTER>
<P><A HREF="idnbus.html">
<IMG SRC="idnttl3.gif" ALT=""></A></P>
<P><A HREF="buscyb.html">
<IMG SRC="busttl6.gif" ALT="Business Section: Finance Corner">
</A></P>
</CENTER>
<P><A HREF="idncolsf.html">
<IMG SRC="colttl3.gif" ALT="Finance Corner">
    Written by Samantha Fox</A></P>
<P>
<P>Column text goes here</P>
<HR SIZE=4>
<P><A HREF="idnfp.html">Front Page</A> ¦¦
<A HREF="buscyb.html">Cyber Beat</A> ¦¦
<A HREF="busecu.html">Electronic Commerce Update</A> ¦¦
<A HREF="busins.html">Inside Scoop</A></P>
<HR SIZE=4>
<P>This page and all contents are Copyright (C) 1995
by The Virtual Press, Hawaii, USA. Internet Daily News and
its respective columns are trademarks of The Virtual Press.</P>
</BODY>
</HTML>
```

FIGURE 27.34.

Finance Corner column at the Internet Daily News.

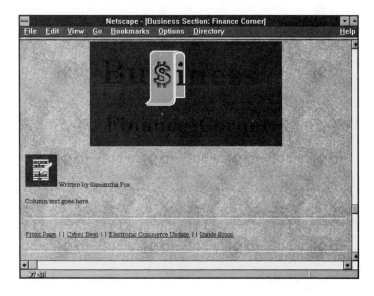

Summary

Any project you start should begin with a vision for success. You have to want to succeed. Follow this vision, with sound planning, development, and design. The first step should be to organize your ideas. Follow organization with an effort to improve your ideas. Next, set aside time to develop your ideas by performing the phases of project development. The last step is to design the project. This is the critical phase of the project where everything you have done comes together.

As you design your own publication, keep in mind the design techniques used to create the *Internet Daily News*. IDN's design is versatile, friendly, and easy to navigate. Readers are provided with multiple navigation mechanisms. They can click on images to go to various sections of the paper. Image links on section pages lead to other sections. Image links on column pages lead to other columns in the section. Readers can also use a text-based menu to quickly navigate to the various sections and columns of the paper. Visit the *Internet Daily News* at `http://tvp.com/idn.html`.

Publishing a Magazine on a Floppy Disk

28

by *William R. Stanek*

Publishing magazines on floppy disk is gaining popularity. A growing number of companies are producing floppy disk versions or extensions to their print versions. Many new publishers are electing to publish exclusively on floppy disk.

The primary reason to publish on floppy disk is that it is a low-cost way to produce a high-quality product. A small publisher with an ordinary PC can produce dazzling productions on floppy disk. You can print additional copies of the edition as necessary and will not be restricted to a dedicated print-run size. In contrast, producing the same magazine as a print edition will cost thousands of dollars more and you will be tied to specific print-run sizes. Additionally, there is little, if any, added cost for including high-resolution images and multimedia features. In traditional print publications adding color costs money. The more colors, the more money the print publication costs to reproduce.

This chapter is going to take you step-by-step through the creation of an actual magazine on floppy disk called *Pulse of the Internet*™. *Pulse of the Internet* is a publication of Virtual Press, Incorporated. *Pulse* is a sister publication to *Internet Daily News*™ and will debut in the first quarter of 1996. Each issue will be loaded with information about the Net from the hottest picks to the hottest trends.

Although the chapter centers on the development of a magazine on floppy disk, the design techniques discussed in this chapter can be used for any publication on floppy disk. The purpose of the chapter is to help you develop your design skills through real-life application of the concepts discussed in this book. In the chapter you will see firsthand how a magazine is developed for publishing on floppy disk. The chapter covers every step from project development to finished design.

A Vision for Success

In March 1994, I founded The Virtual Press. My vision was to create a company that would help launch the careers of aspiring writers. As a veteran writer with little to show for 10 years of writing, I know how difficult it is to break into print. For years I had planned to start up my own press, but traditional small presses are expensive to operate. Eventually, I turned to electronic mediums to publish my works and the works of other authors.

Today, nearly a dozen print magazines are focused specifically on the Internet, and several dozen computer magazines feature regular articles about the Internet. In the summer of 1994, few magazines covered the Internet exclusively, and even computer magazines had sparse coverage of Internet issues. To address the lack of coverage I started work on a project I called *Pulse of the Internet*. The concept behind *Pulse* was a magazine focused on the heartbeat of the Internet. I wanted to cover the issues that were driving changes, growth, and popular culture on the Internet.

Publishing a traditional print magazine was too expensive and restrictive for what I hoped to do with the magazine. I knew at once the medium I wanted to publish *Pulse* on was floppy disk. Publishing on floppy disk was a way to send a message to the world that my magazine was as unique as the Internet itself. Unfortunately, I simply do not have the resources to dedicate my time completely to any single project, and because of this, I am unable to pursue many of my ideas. Yet I did not let a lack of funds or time stop me from expanding my ideas for *Pulse* and investigating the potential marketplace for a magazine on floppy disk. I worked on *Pulse of the Internet* whenever I could which meant stealing time from other projects, working long nights and early mornings and not spending as much time with my family as I would have liked to.

Like *Internet Daily News, Pulse of the Internet* is an ambitious project. I planned to obtain material from dozens of freelancers from around the world and produce the magazine initially as a quarterly. Each issue of the magazine would be packed with useful articles, applications, and multimedia clips. To get a non-traditional magazine into stores, I knew I had to first attract a wide following of readers and advertisers. I also had to make sure *Pulse* was one of the top magazine's covering the Internet. When I set out to do this, I knew it would be a long road to success. My key concept was to dedicate only the time and resources I felt comfortable giving to the project. I focused my vision on success in the long-term and promised to take the project one step at a time.

> **NOTE**
>
> You can subscribe to *Pulse of the Internet* at the special introductory price of $19.95 for a one-year subscription. Canadian orders $25.95. Foreign orders $35.95. This includes 4 quarterly issues, plus the special premiere issue which is included in the base subscription as a bonus for *Electronic Publishing Unleashed* readers. All orders payable in U.S. dollars only. Send check or money order payable to:
>
> Virtual Press, Incorporated
> 408 Division St.
> Shawano, WI 54166
>
> When ordering, please specify your computer system (IBM or Macintosh) and disk type (DD or HD).

Project Development: *Pulse of the Internet* Magazine

As the publisher, you will be responsible for developing the project. This includes creating new material and adapting existing material as necessary. You will develop the heart of the project, the innerworkings. You will also be responsible for obtaining material from writers and attracting the advertisers that will make the magazine profitable.

Project development can be broken down into three processes:

1. Composition processes, which include seven activities:

   Planning

   Researching

   Composing

   Evaluating

   Revising

   Editing

   Proofing

2. Development processes, which include six phases:

   Requirements phase

   Rapid prototype phase

   Specification phase

   Planning phase

   Design phase

   Implementation phase

3. Publishing processes, which include five activities:

   Revision

   Editing

   Proofing

   Testing

   Publishing

The development processes are the focus of this chapter. You use composition processes to create original material. You use publishing processes to test the final prototype and again each time the magazine is published.

Requirements Phase

In the requirements phase, you develop a list of things needed to complete the project. The first item on your list should be a project folder. The *project folder* is a central place to store all materials related to the project. You should create a directory on your hard drive to hold files related to the project. This will ensure you can quickly find text, graphic, sound, and video files used in the project. For this project, I created a directory called PULSE on my hard disk.

You should also purchase a three-ring binder and a filing cabinet or accordion folder to hold important papers related to the project. When subscription orders come in, you will want to keep all orders in one location. A filing cabinet is the best place to keep your records, but an accordion file might suffice.

Identifying the purpose, scope, and audience for the project is a starting point to help you focus on the project and its needs. For *Pulse of the Internet* magazine, I identified the following:

Purpose:	A cutting-edge guide to the Internet
Scope:	Medium-large project with a broad focus
Audience:	Anyone interested in the latest developments on the Internet and not exclusively Internet users

The next step is to start a list of constraints for the project. You will want to specify an optimistic duration for the project that includes everything from initial planning to publishing the first issue. If you have a deadline you must meet, you will want to specify a very specific duration for the project. Don't set yourself up for failure. To ensure you meet the deadline, you should constrict the project duration. If the deadline is 12 months away, set the project duration to 10 months. This will give you a two-month window in case you run into problems. In the planning stage, you will take a close look at all the steps involved in the project and decide if the project duration is realistic.

You might want to constrain the project's budget to ensure your investment in the project is not more than you can afford. Budget constraints can be listed in terms of time or money. Often, you will find that you can only afford to invest a certain amount of time or money in a project. When you reach this constraint, you should reevaluate the project. It makes sense to call it quits when you have reached your budget and decided the project cannot be salvaged.

The size of the project is another key constraint to look at. Every page in the magazine requires an investment of your time. This is true whether you create the material or hire writers. In the planning stage you will reevaluate these requirements to see if they are realistic.

The following are the initial requirements for *Pulse of the Internet* magazine:

Project duration:	10–12 months
Project size:	75–125 pages
Project budget:	$XX,XXX

The last step in the requirements phase is to develop a list of actual needs for the project. These needs can be specific or broad. For *Pulse*, I wrote down these needs:

Immediate Needs:	Working capital
	Weekly time investment
	Disk space on hard drive
	Purchase floppy disks to back up project
	Authoring tools
	Utility programs for multimedia aspects

Long-term Needs: Web site or arrangements with Internet service provider for online promotions

Freelancers

Subscribers

Sponsors and advertisers

Budget allocation

Rapid Prototype Phase

The rapid prototype phase is an optional step in the project development. Using the requirements for the project, you create a working model of the magazine as quickly as possible. The prototype is far from a completed project. Its structure is rather skeletal in that not all the pieces work together, but limited interaction with the model is possible. You use this model to figure out your real needs and to find out whether you have selected the right tools to carry you through to the completion of the job.

When you are done with this phase, you should discard the rapid prototype. If you do not discard the prototype, you may find yourself wasting time trying to continually build and fix the prototype. The purpose of creating the rapid prototype is to help you figure out real needs and save you time. Clinging to the prototype generally defeats the purpose of creating the prototype in the first place.

Figuring out if you should develop a rapid prototype depends on the needs of the project. For every project you must make a decision whether it is in your best interest to develop a rapid prototype or to go on to define the project specifics. For this project, I chose not to develop a rapid prototype, primarily because I wanted to determine the specifics for the project as soon as possible. To reach the widest audience, *Pulse* would be developed for several computer systems and I wanted to take a close look at what I would need to make this possible.

Specification Phase

There are many types of computers on the market. The type of computer for which you design your publication might depend on your target market. However, for a first project, the best system to publish on is the one you are most familiar with. This familiarity will save you time in the development and design stages.

The most popular computers for the home are IBM compatibles using the DOS/Windows operating systems. Although IBM compatibles have a market share many times that of their closest competitors, computer owners of other popular systems represent millions of consumers. Macintosh computers are the next most popular line of PCs. Amiga is another popular computer, especially in Europe. As an Amiga owner, I am a big fan of the Amiga and its capabilities. If you are developing publications for businesses, you will also want to consider the large base of UNIX systems.

After selecting the computer systems you want to develop the project for, you should consider the medium on which you wish to publish. When developing publications for floppy disk, you will want to consider the type of disk you will publish on. Table 28.1 shows the main types of disks. Although 3¹/₂-inch disk drives are in the widest use, 5¹/₄-inch disk drives are often the only floppy drive on older computers. Another thing to keep in mind is that high-density drives are backward-compatible with double-density formats. However, double-density drives cannot read the high-density format.

Table 28.1. Floppy disk types and storage capacities.

Disk Size	Format	Storage Capacity (without compression)
3 ¹/₂ -inch	Double-sided (DS) Double-density (DD)	720KB
3 ¹/₂ -inch	Double-sided (DS) High-density (HD)	1,440KB
5 ¹/₄ -inch	Double-sided (DS) Double-density (DD)	360KB
5 ¹/₄ -inch	Double-sided (DS) High-density (HD)	1,200KB

The final step of the specification phase involves outlining the specific parts of the publication. This means defining the style, the types of pages, and the component parts of the publication. For this project, I created the following list:

Computer System:	IBM compatibles (Macintosh)
Authoring Tool:	NeoBook Professional version (Adobe Acrobat)
Medium:	Floppy Disk
Type of disks:	3 ¹/₂ -inch DD/HD 5 ¹/₄ -inch DD/HD
Style of Publication:	Modern freelance layout
Type of Pages:	Text pages Graphic pages Combined text and graphic pages Multimedia access pages

Publication	Cover page
Components:	Table of contents
	In This Issue—overview page
	Magazine background and contact pages
	Background information
	Contacts for writers and editors
	Subscription information
	Guide to advertising in *Pulse*
	Hot Off the Net—top stories
	3–4 topic pages for features
	Departments
	Net Publishing
	Net Business
	Net Technology
	Net Diversions
	Net Tips and Techniques
	Columns
	3–4 column pages
	Resources
	Marketplace Classifieds
	Net Services
	Net Shopping
	Index to Advertisers
	Product Index

During this stage, I decided to publish the magazine for IBM compatibles and Macintosh systems. Even though I was very familiar with Macintosh computers, I did not own one. This meant an additional investment of capital in the project. I would have to purchase or lease a Macintosh computer. I would also have to buy software and accessories for publishing on the Mac.

At this point, I reviewed the original budget figures for the project. Then I went down to the local computer store to check prices for the equipment and software I would need. The total of the estimate came to $3,500. My original budget figures would accommodate this expenditure, but the working capital I had to dedicate to the project did not allow for this expenditure. Therefore, I decided to hold off on the purchase and look into leasing the Macintosh system.

Planning Phase

Step one in the planning stage is to develop a rough schedule for the project. The schedule should contain milestones, goals, and an allocation of time. The schedule will help you start thinking about the project. Use it as a guide to help you through to project completion.

The next step involves asking yourself five key questions concerning the project:

1. Who are you developing the project for?
2. What medium and formats will the project be published on?
3. Where will the project be published?
4. When will the project be published?
5. How will the project be published?

You answered some of these questions earlier, but you should reevaluate your goals based on what you now know about the project. Here are the initial plans for *Pulse of the Internet* magazine:

Purpose:	A cutting-edge guide to the Internet
Scope:	Medium-large project with a broad focus.
Audience:	Those interested in the latest developments on the Internet including related business, publishing, and technology issues.
Medium:	Floppy disk for DOS/Windows (Floppy disk for Macintosh)
Format	$3^1/_2$-inch DD/HD $5^1/_4$-inch DD/HD
Duration:	Five to six months for development
Deadline:	December, 1995
Window:	Deadline gives 5–12 month window to produce initial publication.
Project size:	28–30 pages 12 pages will not change on regular basis 16–18 pages will change with each edition

> **NOTE**
>
> If you use scrollbars on text windows, each page could contain more than one physical page. Therefore, each page corresponds to a full-length article or column of a traditional magazine.

Critical constraints:	Number of writers critical to implementation. Number of advertisers key to profitability. $*XX,XXX* budget, which equates to *XXXX* hours and a maximum of $*XX,XXX* in real money.

Project Design

Project design is a critical phase of the project. Everything developed before this phase comes together and the actual publication is created. This section includes a complete walkthrough of the design for *Pulse of the Internet* and will look at the following:

- Preliminary design using planning sheets
- Design through storyboards
- Logo design
- Page design

Preliminary Design Using Planning Sheets

An excellent way to reduce the complexity of any project is to design storyboards. When you storyboard, each page of the publication is represented in miniature form on a planning sheet. Links are added to the planning sheet diagrams to show the logical flow from page to page. In this way, you can see at a glance the innerworkings and outline for the entire magazine. An easy way to create a planning sheet is by drawing it freehand on a notepad.

The initial planning sheet for *Pulse of the Internet* is shown in Figure 28.1. The cover page is a starting point for the magazine. From the cover page, the reader can go to the table of contents page and optionally to the main sections of the publication. Once on the table of contents page, the reader can go to any of the sections of the publication. I decided to add links between the section pages to enable readers to go to the previous or the next section. At this stage of the design, I focused on the fact it would be a feature the reader might want and not how this would be accomplished. This transformed the structure of the storyboards from hierarchical to a combination of linear and hierarchical.

The next step is to create planning sheets for each section of the paper that had levels not seen on the initial planning sheet. The planning sheet for the magazine background section is shown in Figure 28.2. Each topic is represented as a separate page, but I put down in the planning notebook that the topics could also be in separate text windows.

The key sections of the magazine contain features or columns. The planning sheet for the department pages is shown in Figure 28.3. Readers can advance through department pages. They can also move quickly to the advertiser or product index. These indexes provide additional information about products or advertisers.

FIGURE 28.1.

The initial planning sheet for Pulse of the Internet.

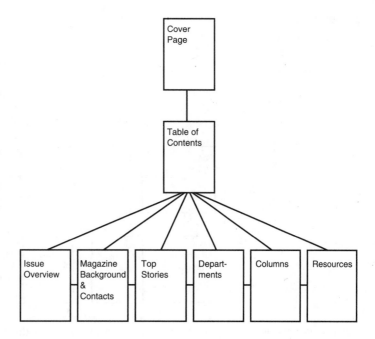

FIGURE 28.2.

The planning sheet for the magazine background and contacts.

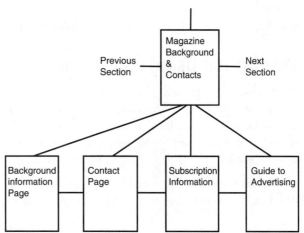

FIGURE 28.3.

The planning sheet for the Departments section.

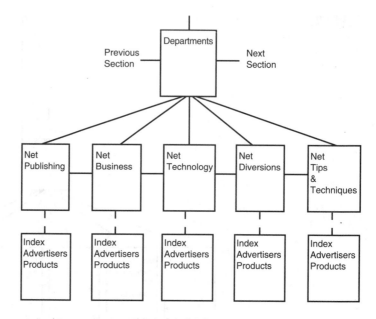

The preliminary design for the *Pulse of the Internet* magazine is flexible, yet still highly structured. Readers can move forward and backward through sections and pages. They can go up a level or descend to the next level. They can also follow parallel paths through the document.

Content Design Using Storyboards

Storyboards are used on planning sheets to aid in designing the structure of the publication. The next type of storyboards concern page content. Usually, storyboards are not developed in-depth unless the project is small or has special concerns. For *Pulse of the Internet,* I chose to use master storyboards whenever possible. The master storyboards will be used as the basis for individual storyboards, which will save many hours of work.

Using the master storyboard method, unique pages and pages with common components are identified. For *Pulse of the Internet,* the unique pages include the following:

- Cover page
- Table of contents
- Magazine background page
- Indexes

The following pages have many items in common:

- Issue overview page
- Features

- Departments
- Columns

After determining the common components of these pages three master storyboards are designed. The initial master storyboard is shown in Figure 28.4. You can draw the common components freehand and include color coding if you want to. The idea is to dedicate time to think about the components of the magazine's pages. By identifying common components and designing the magazine to take advantage of these commonalities, you will save time and create a better design.

FIGURE 28.4.

The initial master storyboard for Pulse.

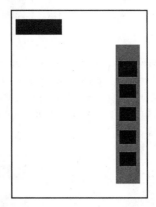

The initial master storyboard will be used on most of the magazine's pages. The page will include one common title in the upper-left corner of the page. The right side of the page will have an on-screen menu. The menu will have the primary navigation features for the magazine.

The features, columns, and departments are the primary pages of the magazine. *Pulse* has 10–12 pages dedicated to each of these sections. The look of these pages should be consistent throughout the magazine. To ensure this, the master storyboard depicted in Figure 28.5 was developed. The top of the page has two titles: the magazine title is in the upper-left corner and a page title is in the middle of the page. Two features will be added to the menu on the right side of the page. The bottom of the menu will have a section title and the page number.

The master storyboard also identifies components that are in common locations on the page but will change. The left side of the page has space assigned for side bars, pictures accompanying the text, and advertising. The space allocated allows for several small sidebars, pictures, or ads. Advertisements can be dynamically linked to pages in the resource section. Beneath the advertising a graphic image will accent the page.

FIGURE 28.5.

The master storyboard for features, columns, and departments.

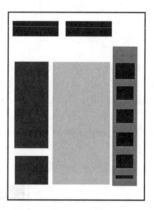

The final master storyboard, as shown in Figure 28.6, is for the marketplace section of the magazine. The marketplace section has the menu and title components from the initial master storyboard. The left side of the page has graphical advertisements. The right side of the page has text windows containing product information. These text windows are placed adjacent to the graphics.

FIGURE 28.6.

The master storyboard for the marketplace section.

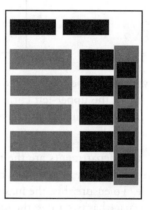

Logo Design

Many magazines feature logos. A logo can be a central part in your magazine's design. Logo design can help you develop a central theme for your magazine project. You should set aside several hours to work on your magazine's logo. To develop the logo for *Pulse of the Internet*, I set aside an afternoon and told myself I would work only on the logo during this time.

The logo should be highly visual, but the design can be pure. You could use letter and color combinations to create a visually stunning but simple design. You don't need state-of-the art tools to develop a good logo. To develop *Pulse's* logo, I used three tools:

- Harvard Draw for Windows
- Windows Paintbrush
- Freeze Frame 2 for Windows

Harvard Draw is a drawing program, which I used to create the original design. Windows Paintbrush is a drawing program that comes with Windows. Although it's a freebie with only the most basic tools, I like to use it for touch-ups because it's so easy to use. In one step I can magnify an image to see a representation of each pixel in the image. I can then touch up the image a pixel at a time quickly and easily.

Freeze Frame 2 (FF2) is an excellent and affordable commercial tool for manipulating images. I used FF2 to capture the area of the screen I was working on. In this way, I could magnify the logo within the drawing program and capture it. This saved me time because I didn't have to create the logo in several sizes. I simply magnified the original logo and captured it at the precise pixel size of my choosing. I could have used other tools to magnify or shrink the logo, but I didn't like the way the logo was distorted by these programs.

After you select the tools, you should design the logo. The first step is to select a background for the logo. I had three colors in mind for the background: silver, gold, and black. I drew one rectangular box on the screen for each color. These are shown in Figure 28.7.

FIGURE 28.7.

Creating a logo.

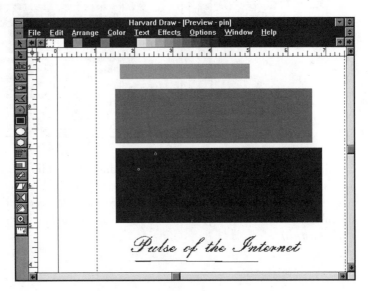

The second step is to design the project's title: *Pulse of the Internet.* Before adding the title, I thought carefully about the style and color of the text. Choosing the style of the text was difficult. I wanted the logo to be simple, but not ordinary. Some font styles do not work well for headlines, and I went through a dozen font styles before selecting a style I liked. Next, I selected a color for the title. Initially, I selected red because it blended well with the three background colors and matched the magazine's theme as the lifeline to the Internet.

The third step is to create an image that will be a part of the logo. The purpose of this image is to enhance the logo and accent the title. My first choice was to draw a thick red line under the title. The line was rather plain and didn't accent the title. To correct this, I transformed the line into a racing stripe. This image is the last item shown in Figure 28.7.

Now that the component parts of the logo were finished, I selected a single background color. I chose the black background because it worked best with the red title. However, the shade of red for the title wasn't deep enough, so I decided to work on the color. I selected a deeper shade of red, and then using a radial fill I faded the title from gold to red, which turned out to be a good balance of light and dark for the logo. Figure 28.8 shows how this was accomplished in the drawing program. Most drawing programs support radial fills.

FIGURE 28.8.

Using radial fills in the logo.

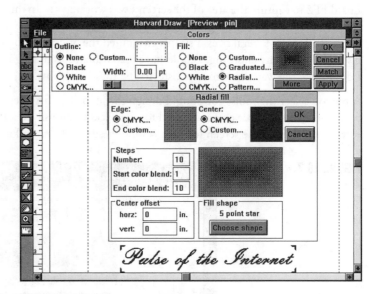

The final step of the logo design is to combine the component parts into a single image. Figure 28.9 shows the finished logo. The title is centered on the black background and the racing stripe is placed under the title. The resulting logo is simple, yet effective. The logo also inspired the color scheme for the magazine. The red, black, and gold (yellow) are used throughout *Pulse of the Internet*.

FIGURE 28.9.

The completed logo for Pulse of the Internet.

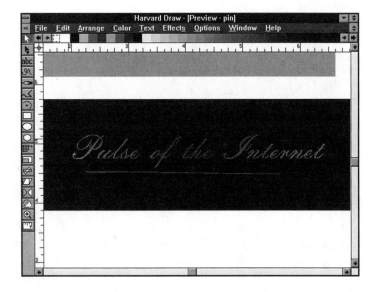

Page Design

The last step in the design process is to develop the pages of the magazine. Readers like pages with high visual impact. High visual impact does not necessarily mean your pages should contain high-resolution graphics. Some of the most visually stunning pages contain no graphics at all. They achieve their impact by using screen space, color, fonts, and headings to their advantage.

This section takes you through every step of the page design for *Pulse of the Internet*. The pictures in this section were taken from a popular authoring tool called NeoBook Professional. NeoBook typifies the authoring tools you should use to develop your projects. I use NeoBook because it has a very straightforward and uncomplicated style. The techniques to add features differ among authoring tools, but the concepts remain the same. An on-screen button is an on-screen button. The way you define attributes for the button might differ, but the types of attributes available will be similar regardless of the authoring tool.

NOTE

NeoBook Professional is one of the most affordable commercial authoring tools available for DOS/Windows. NeoBook Pro is produced by NeoSoft Corporation, which has a technical support staff that is topnotch and friendly. NeoSoft has a complete line of tools to aid in the authoring of electronic publications. The most popular are NeoBook and NeoBook Professional. NeoBook is a basic authoring program that enables you to create everything you will find in this section and is available for $45. NeoBook Professional is an enhanced version of NeoBook that includes support for multimedia and is available for $99.95.

NeoSoft's complete line of products are available for free trial periods. You can find these products on the company BBS at 503-383-7195 and on many on-line services. For more information on NeoSoft call its customer service department at 503-389-5489 or write to

> NeoSoft Corp.
> 354 NE Greenwood Ave., Suite 108
> Bend, Oregon 97701-4631

TIP

When you are creating an electronic publication, always make backups of everything. This will save you time and frustration. Typically, I save my work every 30 minutes. I also use a working file and finished file. I create in the working file and when I design a page I like and know I am going to keep, I save this work to the finished file. This enables me to experiment in the working file, meaning if I make changes I do not like later, I have something to go back to—the finished file. For this project my working file is called PULSEPRA.PUB, and my finished file is called PULSE.PUB.

Designing the Master Page

The master page can be the basis of any page in your publication. In *Pulse of the Internet*, I used master page components on most of the pages, including the following pages:

- Overview page
- Background page
- Table of contents page
- Features pages
- Departments pages
- Columns pages

The first step in designing the master page is to create the features identified in content design as common components. For *Pulse* this included a standard header and an on-screen menu. The menu was formed from a series of buttons. A typical way to create buttons in an authoring tool is shown in Figure 28.10. Buttons have three main attributes: color, border, and font. Each of these attributes can have additional attributes associated with it.

FIGURE 28.10.
Button creation.

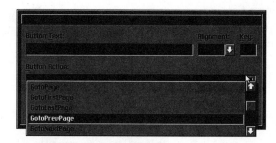

You can fill the button with a solid color, a pattern, or make the button hollow. A hollow button is transparent, meaning it is clear like glass. And like glass, a hollow button will let the reader see anything that is beneath it. The button created for *Pulse of the Internet's* menu is hollow.

You can make the border of the button a specific color, width, and style. By varying color and thickness of the border you can achieve different effects. The style of the border can be solid, dashed, and many other combinations using circles and dashes.

Typically, you select a button tool and place the button on the screen. Afterward, a popup window appears and enables you to select actions for the button. The action for the button being created in Figure 28.10 is to go to the previous page. The button can also have a text label and a quick key associated with it. The text for the button in Figure 28.10 is Prev and P is the quick key.

NOTE

Readers might not want to rely on the mouse. Quick keys enable readers to activate a button using a key on the keyboard. Whenever possible, you should define quick keys. To make it easy for the reader to know what key to press for the button, you should underline a character that corresponds to the quick key.

The way you designate a character to be underlined in Neobook is by preceding it with the caret character (^). For the button in Figure 28.10, the P in the text label is underlined.

After you create the initial button, you should create one additional button for each feature of the menu. The easiest way to do this is to duplicate the original button using the Copy command of the authoring tool. This will ensure the buttons are consistent in size and shape. *Pulse's* menu has five options, and as shown in Figure 28.11, five buttons were created.

FIGURE 28.11.

Building the initial menu components.

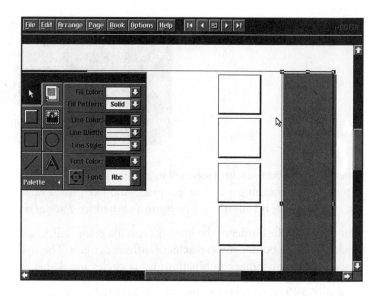

An important part of creating buttons is balancing the size, shape, and number of the buttons. If you have only a few buttons, you can use large buttons. If you have many buttons, you should consider using small buttons. Keep in mind that more than 10 buttons can make a screen look cluttered. If the buttons are not the main feature of the page, consider putting some features on pull-down menus.

After you create the buttons, create a menu bar. As shown in Figure 28.11, the menu bar is colored gray to give the buttons a common background color. Using transparent buttons means changing the color of the menu in the future is a one-step process. To change the menu to blue you only need to change the color of the menu bar.

The next step in the menu design is to add features to the buttons. Select a graphic for each button. As shown in Figure 28.12, the button and the graphic are then arranged into a group. This ensures that the reader can activate the button from anywhere on the button's surface. If the button and the graphic were not grouped, the reader could not click on the area of the button containing the graphic.

The next step of menu creation is to put the components together, which is shown in Figure 28.13. Two additional features were added to the menu bar: a small blue box and a small red box. The blue box is for section titles. The red box is for the page number. Adding page numbers to a publication is usually an automated feature of the authoring tool. By designated a place for page numbers on the master page, any page that includes the menu bar will be numbered appropriately.

FIGURE 28.12.

Adding features to buttons.

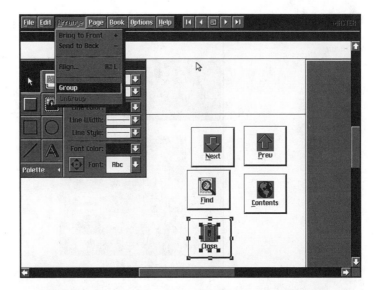

FIGURE 28.13.

Putting components together to form a menu.

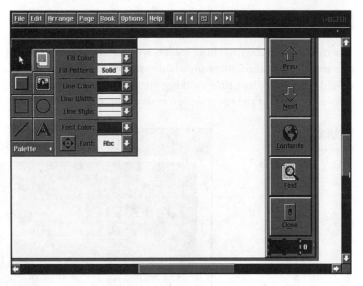

The final master page components are shown in Figure 28.14. A small logo was added to the upper-left corner of the page and a red line was drawn from the logo to the menu bar. Page titles will be added to the empty space above the red line.

FIGURE 28.14.

Adding Final cmponents to the menu.

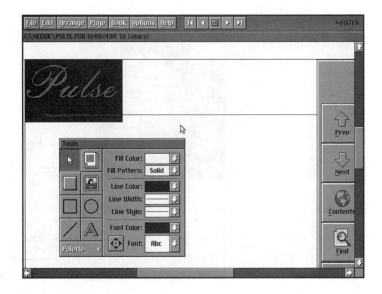

Designing the Cover Page

The cover page is the first thing readers will see when they start the publication. The cover can give readers an immediate impression about the quality of the publication. Consequently, you should spend sufficient time working on the cover. I designed the cover of *Pulse* in two stages. The initial stage of the cover design is shown in Figure 28.15.

FIGURE 28.15.

Creating the cover page.

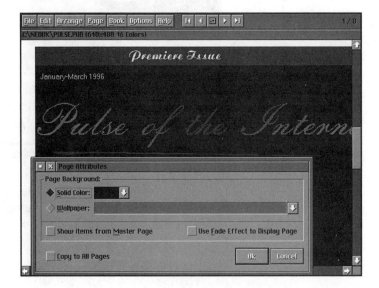

The cover page is a unique page in the magazine and does not include any components of the master page. I created a rectangular box at the top of the page and centered the words *Premiere Issue* within it. Beneath the box I put the date of the issue. Next, I added the magazine's logo.

The cover page's background is set to black to match the background of the logo. This makes the logo blend in with the page. The black background works so well, I decided to use it throughout the publication.

To enable readers to get quickly to any section of the publication, I added a quick menu to the cover. The menu is shown in Figure 28.16. This feature is primarily for readers who aren't reading the magazine for the first time but enable any reader to browse the magazine immediately.

FIGURE 28.16.

Adding a quick menu to the cover.

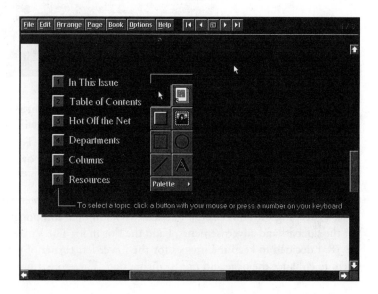

The quick menu is not a table of contents. It has only one option for each major section of the magazine. The purpose of this is to keep the menu simple. A full table of contents will clutter the cover unnecessarily.

Designing the Overview Page

An overview page is a feature you will find in traditional and nontraditional magazines. The purpose of the overview page is to highlight the articles in the issue. Readers can find out what topics are covered in an issue and read a brief synopsis.

The initial stage of the design for *Pulse's* overview page is shown in Figure 28.17. The master page components are added to the page using the Page Attributes window shown previously in Figure 28.15. By selecting the Show Items from Master Page option, the master page components are displayed on the page.

FIGURE 28.17.

Creating the overview page.

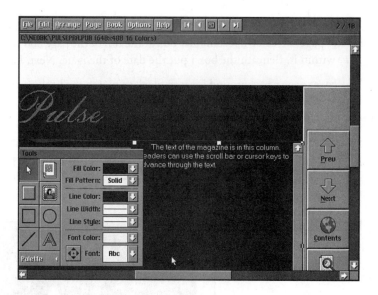

I could have added one text window to the page for each highlighted topic. However, this would mean creating a file for each highlight and updating each file with every issue. Also, the page will get cluttered quickly if too many text windows are added. To solve this problem, I added a single text window to the page. The text window displays an overview of the issue as a letter to readers.

A single text window also follows the design for the second master page I created for the magazine. In keeping with this design, I added two additional components to the page. In the spot for the sidebars and advertisements, I add the slogan for The Virtual Press, as shown in Figure 28.18. I decided to keep the images for the lower-left corner of the magazine simple. I want them to enhance the page and not be distracting. Therefore, I use black and white images.

Designing the Background and Contact Page

The background and contact page give readers important information about the publication. The page should contain subscription, submission, advertising, and contact references. To accomplish this you can add text windows to the background page for each topic.

As shown in Figure 28.19, *Pulse's* background page will have three text windows. A title placed above each text window lets readers quickly determine what type of information the box contains. The first text window contains subscription information. The second text window contains submission information. The third window contains a guide to advertising in the magazine.

FIGURE 28.18.

Adding components to the overview page.

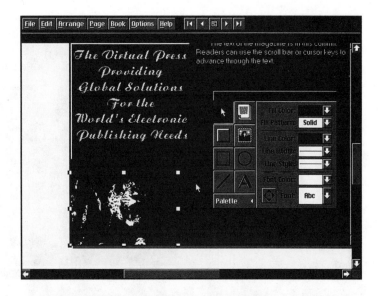

FIGURE 28.19.

Creating the background and contact page.

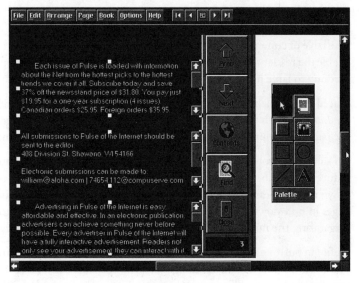

The next step is to use the empty space on the left side of the page. The page looks rather plain with the large empty space. However, with three text windows, titles, and a menu, the background page could easily appear cluttered if the space is filled completely. For this reason, I chose to leave most of the space empty. Brief information about the magazine editor and publishing company is provided adjacent to the text windows. Beneath this, a simple graphic image is added. This is shown in Figure 28.20.

FIGURE 28.20.

Adding components to the page.

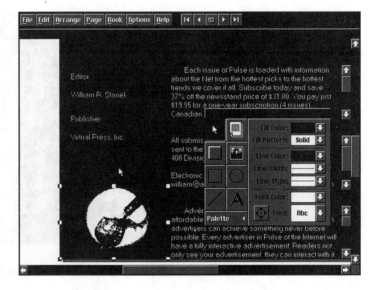

Designing the Table of Contents

The table of contents page in an electronic publication can include hypertext links. These links enable the reader to jump to any page of the publication. Designing the table of contents for a medium to large publication is often difficult because there is so much information to present.

I faced the problem of too much information while designing the table of contents for *Pulse of the Internet.* Each issue of *Pulse* will have 18 or more individual pages. Although I didn't want the page to be cluttered, I did want to give readers as much information as possible.

To solve this problem, I could place the text for each section in pull-down menus. This will reduce the number of components on the page from 18 or more to 6. However, using pull-down menus means readers cannot see all the information at a glance. Instead of putting the pages in pull-down menus by section, I will create on-screen buttons under section headers. Organizing the information helps to clear up the clutter. This is shown in Figure 28.21.

Defining buttons and links in the table of contents is shown in Figure 28.22. In the figure, the Net Business button is being designed. After you add a text label to the button, define the action for the button. When this button is activated, the reader will jump to page nine of the publication. Page nine corresponds to the Net Business page.

Next, add additional components to the page. A title is added to the blue box on the bottom of the menu bar. The red box contains a definition for a page number and is updated automatically. The table of contents is page four of the publication.

Because the reader is already on the table of contents page, this option on the menu bar is ghosted. When you ghost a menu option, you place a button with a different function over the original button. The new button usually has a pattern to obscure the original button text and graphics, as shown in Figure 28.22. The function of the ghost button can be anything from playing a warning tone to displaying text that says you're already on the table of contents page.

FIGURE 28.21.

Creating the table of contents.

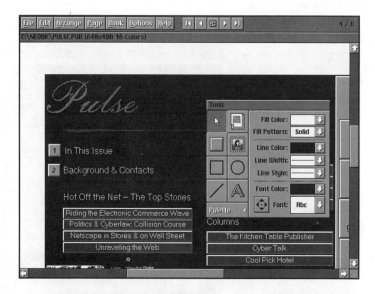

FIGURE 28.22.

Completing the table of contents.

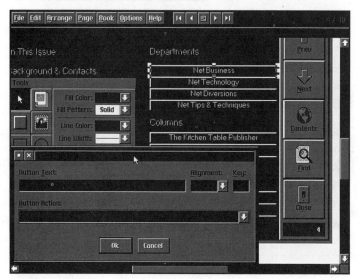

Designing the Central Pages

The features, columns, and departments of *Pulse of the Internet* all have a similar design. These pages follow the design from the second master storyboard developed earlier. This ensures the magazine has a consistent look throughout and makes the pages easy to create. Figure 28.23

shows the page for "The Kitchen Table Publisher" column in *Pulse of the Internet*. A text window has been placed beside the menu bar. A column title has been added to the top of the page centered above the text window.

FIGURE 28.23.

Creating the columns page.

Following the master storyboard's design, an advertisement and an image have been added to the left side of the page. The advertisement is a clickable button on the screen that will take the reader to the marketplace section of the publication.

Designing the Marketplace Page

The marketplace is a key part of the resource section. Here readers can find information on products and advertisers. On one side of the page are graphical advertisements. On the other side of the page are text windows. The text windows can contain any amount of text that the reader can scroll through.

As Figure 28.24 shows, the page title has been added to the top of the page. Advertisements are placed in two columns. In an electronic publication, you are not limited by page constraints. Each advertisement can occupy its own page and have several associated text windows. You can also make the advertisement as interactive as you want, and providing interactive information is the key to the ad's effectiveness.

FIGURE 28.24.

Creating the Marketplace page.

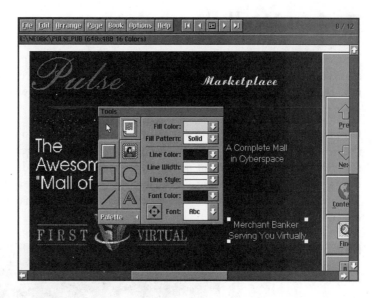

Checking the Page Layout

When the design of the magazine is complete, you should check the page layout for consistency. Most authoring tools feature an easy way to do this. Select Page layout from an option menu and a popup window similar to the one in Figure 28.25 shows you an overview of the layout.

FIGURE 28.25.

Page layout.

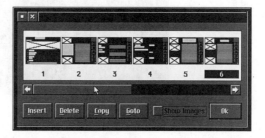

The page layout depicted in Figure 28.25 is for pages 1–6 of *Pulse*. From the graphical representation of the page components, you can see unique and common pages at a glance. The look of pages that follow a particular master storyboard design should be consistent.

Project Walkthrough

This section includes a walkthrough of the *Pulse of the Internet* project. Here everything discussed in this chapter is depicted and page-by-page the magazine comes to life. Sample articles have been placed in some text windows to give you an idea of what the pages will look like when published.

Creating the cover page is the first step toward breathing life into the magazine. Figure 28.26 shows how the components of the cover come together. This page is the first thing readers will see when they start reading your magazine. Set aside at least one day to create the cover. If you design the cover in less time, great. If it takes you longer, set aside additional time as necessary. The great thing about covers is that even though they might change from issue to issue, the design is usually the same.

FIGURE 28.26.

The Pulse of the Internet *cover page.*

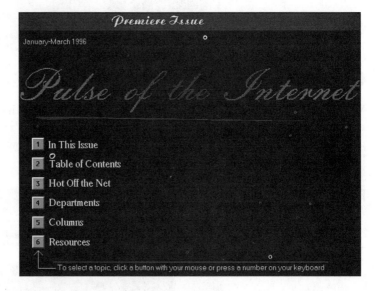

Creating the overview page is the second step toward breathing life into the magazine. Figure 28.27 shows how the components of the overview page have come together. For *Pulse of the Internet*, I called this page "In This Issue" because the overview page should highlight what readers will find in the issue of the magazine. The text on the page is a sample article and not the actual overview page for the premiere issue.

Creating the background page is the third step toward breathing life into the magazine. Figure 28.28 shows how the components of the background page have come together. The page contains subscription, submission, and contact information for the magazine. The information on a background page normally does not change from issue to issue. This means once you design this page, you only have to make minor changes to keep it current.

FIGURE 28.27.

The Pulse of the Internet *issue overview page.*

FIGURE 28.28.

The Pulse of the Internet *background page.*

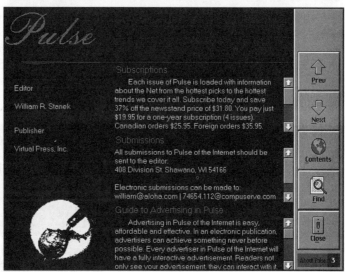

Creating the table of contents is the fourth step toward breathing life into the magazine. Figure 28.29 shows how the components of the table of contents came together. Depending on the design of the page and the style of the magazine, this page can either be mostly static or frequently changing. *Pulse of the Internet's* table of contents page is mostly static. The menu buttons will stay in the same place from issue to issue and only the text labels will change as necessary.

FIGURE 28.29.

The Pulse of the Internet *table of contents.*

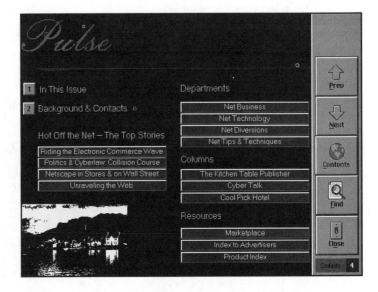

Creating the magazine's central pages is the fifth step. The features, columns, and departments are the heart of *Pulse of the Internet.* Figure 28.30 shows the features page. Figure 28.31 shows the departments page. Figure 28.32 shows the columns page. These are the pages readers will spend most of their time on and as such, the design should be exceptional. Follow the steps outlined in this chapter to develop the master page and its components. Your master page will form the basis of these all-important pages.

FIGURE 28.30.

The Pulse of the Internet *features page.*

FIGURE 28.31.

The Pulse of the Internet *departments page.*

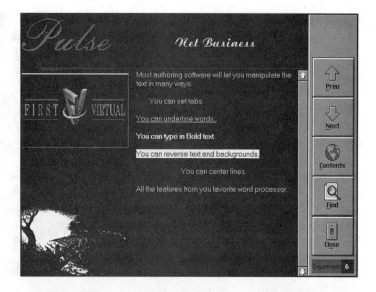

FIGURE 28.32.

The Pulse of the Internet *columns page.*

Creating the resource section is the final step toward breathing life into the magazine. Figure 28.33 shows how the components of the Marketplace page came together. The resource section of the magazine can include many things from advertiser indexes to product indexes. Most magazines feature classifieds and marketplace sections as well.

FIGURE 28.33.
The Pulse of the Internet *marketplace page.*

Summary

Publishing a magazine on floppy disk is a low-cost way to produce a high-quality product. To create your own magazine, follow the development and design concepts in this chapter. Do not rush through the project. The most important thing to keep in mind is to manage your time. Develop the project one step at a time. When you have a clear idea of how you will create the project, begin the design phase. The design phase is where all your planning efforts come together and the project comes to life.

Publishing an Interactive Encyclopedia

29

by Mitch Gould

Because Microsoft, Grolier, and Compton currently have a corner on the market for general-purpose encyclopedias, this chapter is addressed to smaller developers who can compete in the marketplace for *specialty* encyclopedias (for instance, *The Encyclopedia of Horses*) on CD-ROM or for online services. First, this chapter covers general issues common to all encyclopedias and then moves on to practical techniques in multimedia authoring for electronic publishing. It also provides a hands-on experiment with electronic publishing and furnishes a case study of the successful *Grolier Multimedia Encyclopedia*.

Encyclopedia Issues

Before you learn about issues specific to publishing an encyclopedia electronically, you should understand the general issues common to all encyclopedias.

Encyclopedia Defined

Taken together, the Greek words *enkyklios* and *paideia* describe a work that "encircles all knowledge." *Encyclopedia Britannica* reinterprets this ancient concept in more pragmatic terms, pointing out that "people look to encyclopedias to give them an adequate introduction" to a given subject. Various encyclopedias encompass larger or smaller circles of knowledge. Some cover the entire universe (a general multivolume encyclopedia). Others cover such niche topics as American war films, birds, depression, ferns, motor sports, and self-publishing (single-volume specialty encyclopedias found in a local library).

Frankly, the principal criterion that determines whether a subject is suitable for its own encyclopedia is whether a sufficient market exists to support a work devoted to that subject. Once the demand has been determined, the publisher is concerned with establishing sufficient marketplace credibility to justify the customer's investment. The standards for authority differ in the consumer, the literary, and the academic markets. Many consumers are most likely to be impressed by familiar celebrity names; literary customers are swayed by awards and reviews; and academics are influenced by academic affiliations and professional reputation.

An encyclopedia is an example of a reference work: that is, a resource designed to be consulted by many researchers on a relatively frequent basis for several years. For this reason, encyclopedias are not loaned by libraries the way ordinary books are. Because they can provide the first step in a research project, general encyclopedias find a home in even the smallest of public libraries and appeal to parents of school-aged children.

Evolution of Encyclopedias

If we consider only Western Civilization, it seems that perhaps not only the word "encyclopedia," but the concept as well, first appeared among the Greeks in the form of surveys of Platonic and Aristotelian wisdom. The most influential of the subsequent Roman encyclopedists was Pliny the Elder, whose sprawling *Natural History* served as the germ of many other works for the next 1500 years.

In 1620, Francis Bacon published the first volume of a never-finished *Great Insaturation* of knowledge, noteworthy for its division of topics into three categories: the natural world, the human body, and arts and sciences. Gradually, the early attempts at systematically categorizing knowledge proved generally less popular than the more arbitrary alphabetical ordering commonly used today.

Any effort to enumerate all of the encyclopedias that have been published in all languages over the past two thousand years would be doomed to failure, but in English-speaking countries, the *Britannica* rose to a position of prominence in the nineteenth century that is still largely unchallenged. Ironically, the inability of *Britannica's* publisher to produce an electronic version to compete with a new generation of interactive encyclopedias such as Microsoft's, Compton's, and Grolier's, has seriously jeopardized the company itself. This compelling, inexpensive new breed of encyclopedias first appeared with the dawn of the CD-ROM publishing boom in the 1980s.

Grolier was the first publisher to offer its product electronically. Grolier's *Academic American Encyclopedia*, a print set, was developed over a period of ten years and released in 1980. Because Grolier maintained its print encyclopedia in an electronic format, it was able to post the text with an online service in 1982. In 1985, it created the first encyclopedia to appear in a CD-ROM format.

With the emergence of online and CD-ROM markets, Grolier compensated for the decline of its print product by increasing sales of its electronic versions. The company today still offers a print encyclopedia, including a subset of the original, a "family" encyclopedia available for $99 from booksellers Barnes and Noble. Combination sales of the CD and print products are also offered. By contrast, latecomers to the electronic market, such as the publishers of *World Book* and *Encyclopedia Britannica*, were utterly devastated by the marketplace revolution.

In 1993, *Encyclopedia Britannica* offered the *Britannica Instant Research System*, or BIRS, an on-disk version of the entire 32-volume Britannica set, along with the encyclopedia's yearbook edition and a dictionary. The Britannica product is designed for professional researchers and fact-checkers in publishing and journalism. BIRS contains no multimedia elements, runs off a computer's hard disk rather than from a CD, and is available by license only to corporate and institutional users at a hefty annual fee.

In 1994, Britannica released *Britannica CD* for the consumer market, a text-only version of the *New Encyclopedia Britannica*, but tagged the product at $995, effectively pricing itself out of the market. Britannica now faces a turning point in its history, announcing in April 1995 that it was seeking a new infusion of capital to sustain itself in the face of mounting losses, directly attributable to the market in-roads made by electronic media. Analyst Kenneth Kister, author of *Kister's Best Encyclopedia's: A Comparative Guide to General and Specialized Encyclopedias*, summed up the company's plight succinctly, when he said, "How do you sell somebody an encyclopedia that costs in the thousands of dollars when they are getting one for $100 or for free in the box with their new computers?"

Marketplace

Grolier gears its product to a slightly higher-level audience than that of its main competitors, Microsoft *Encarta* and *Compton's Interactive Encyclopedia*. *Compton's* aims at a market ranging from elementary school students to adults, and *Encarta* is written for students slightly above the elementary level. *Grolier's*, on the other hand, addresses the needs of students in high school and beyond. Both *Encarta* and *Compton's* are written for a fourth-grade reading level, whereas *Grolier's* is aimed at a sixth-grade level, more like the daily newspaper. All three products have a suggested retail price of about $100.

Encyclopedia Britannica and *World Book* offer beleaguered alternatives to these successful products. Britannica's strategy has already been mentioned. The *World Book Multimedia Encyclopedia* consists of the complete text of the 20-volume *World Book* set, accompanied by numerous still illustrations, a dictionary, and a respectable number of multimedia assets, including video, animated, and sound clips. Priced slightly higher than the competition at $150, *World Book's* entry is rarely found.

Product Comparison

Microsoft Encarta is based on a Funk and Wagnall's encyclopedia that was originally created in 1912 and sold in supermarkets, whereas Compton's CD encyclopedia is based on a children's print set created in 1922. The origin of *Grolier's* was covered previously.

Grolier's excels at the longer, in-depth article, generally authored by an expert in the field, whereas *Compton's* shines on the snappily written summaries of history, and *Encarta* generally provides its users with more in the way of multimedia assets—899 sound clips, for example, in the 1995 edition of *Encarta*, compared with 507 in the 1995 edition of *Grolier's* and 593 in *Compton's*.

In addition to encyclopedias, other kinds of large reference works are becoming quite popular in interactive format. In 1992, Microsoft integrated Word for Windows with Bookshelf, a bundle containing the *Concise Columbia Encyclopedia*, the *Hammond Atlas*, *The American Heritage Dictionary*, *Roget's Thesaurus*, *The World Almanac and Book of Facts*, *The Concise Columbia Dictionary of Quotations*, and *Barlett's Quotations! Time* has an almanac with the full text of every *Time Magazine* issue from 1989 through 1992. National Geographic has a *Picture Atlas of the World*, and another atlas is a best-selling title: Deforme's *Street Atlas USA*.

Not many specialty encyclopedias are published on CD-ROM yet, but experience has shown that sex sells. Accordingly, Dr. Ruth published an electronic version of her *Encyclopedia of Sex*. For a look at specialty encyclopedias, we might as well turn to a print work better-known to this author, *The Walt Whitman Encyclopedia*, edited by J. R. LeMaster and Donald Kummings. The book, composed of 800 entries on topics that illuminate the poet's life and work, is intended for high school and college students, teachers, scholars, and the general public. It may be especially valuable for graduate students who do not specialize in Whitman. This work is mentioned again in the examples in the following sections.

Overall Structure

The atomic unit of an encyclopedia is the topic or entry—a concise essay on a single person, place, or thing. At first glance, a topic may appear to be a sealed, self-contained fragment, but in the encyclopedia, as in life, one concept is best understood in the context of related concepts. Therefore, entries contain references to related topics. The familiar experience of using an encyclopedia involves browsing webs of interrelated topics. In traditional, printed reference works, this entails searching the shelves for the required volume, hunting alphabetically for the new topic, and locating its cross-linked references, then repeating the cycle. An intent reader might look up at the clock and realize that hours have passed while she navigated Wordsworth's "strange seas of thought, alone." The experience seems to require "weight-lifting" heavy books as well as an intellectual pursuit.

Multimedia's ability to automate browsing is one of the features that makes it so valuable to the modern encyclopedia. The large storage capacity of the CD-ROM enables a multi-volume encyclopedia to be reduced to the size of a single five-inch platter; hence, the original derivation of the term "compact disc." The disc drive's capability to quickly seek a precise location in this massive data store provides effortless browsing.

An entry may provide pictures, maps, charts, and diagrams as well as text. Interactive encyclopedias may add audio, video, and animation. These new media resources make CD-ROMs more interesting to a TV generation with a limited attention span and improve rentention.

Encyclopedias frequently supply generalized information such as bibliographies, atlases, and tables, in addition to topics. The help with foreign languages provided by traditional works can be augmented in the computer version by digitally-recorded pronunciations.

Grolier's Pathmakers feature introduces personal expression into an otherwise objective approach. In the 1996 edition, Pathmakers offers the commentary of "experts" available on selected articles, including such notables as Buzz Aldrin, Kurt Vonnegut, Jr., Stephen J. Gould, Helen Frankenthaler, Jackie Joyner Kersee, and Paul MacCready.

What To Include

Readers come to a topic with varied agendas, including theoretical, pragmatic, social, and historical. They also bring to their studies varying degrees of familiarity with the subject. Encyclopedia entries therefore begin with an introduction general enough to orient a young reader, and then tend to cover the subject's evolution and place in history, its cultural significance, and the kinds of practical facts useful to a researcher beginning in the field. References to important works in the field are often included. If this sounds like a tall order, given the requirement for entries to be concise, it sometimes is. Some researchers even claim that it is easier to write an entire book on a subject than it is to write the ideal encyclopedia entry. Fortunately, the long history of successful encyclopedias provides authors with useful models for almost any subject.

By definition, a multi-volume encyclopedia should cover every topic known to scholars. In practice, of course, coverage is limited to a few thousand of the entries deemed to be either the most important or the most popular with the intended customer.

For the more manageable single-subject encyclopedias, the same philosophy that guides the selection of topics suggests how each topic should be covered; for example, introductory, intermediate, and advanced aspects, theoretical and pragmatic aspects, and cultural and historical aspects.

In *The Walt Whitman Encyclopedia*, for instance, entries start with a concise summary of the theme: an explanation of the subject, factual details, and relevance to Whitman studies. Then, if there is sufficient room, the entry's body presents a coherent presentation on the subject. Finally, the conclusion supplies an assessment of the argument. In addition, authors try to evaluate the strengths and weaknesses of their sources. Each entry provides a bibliography that gives the citations for references, and guides a researcher in learning more.

EXAMPLE

The article entitled "Love," by this author, begins with Whitman's mixed lessons in love from his father, mother, and siblings, as revealed in his poetry and prose. It goes on to show how Whitman's troubled adult love life, as described in the Calamus poems, can be explained as the classic syndrome of an "adult child of an alcoholic." It reveals that the "coming-out" demands in "Song of the Open Road" provided additional stress on his relationship with Fred Vaughan. Then the entry states its central premise: that scholars have been misled by Whitman's well-known failures to secure a primary life-long relationship, when in fact, his relationships—deeply flawed as they were—provided the crucial measure of love he craved. Whitman's most important poems insist that it was in the affirmation of Self he found in his lovers' eyes that he learned to "perceive the universe." The entry concludes that love is the unifying purpose of Whitman's entire poetic career, and that America's acceptance of his "new City of Friends" would be the next great challenge of young American democracy.

Entries on places begin by identifying their geographical locations and must also indicate whether the place is real or imaginary (or both). They provide the unique characteristics of the site, and, ultimately, explain its importance to Whitman. Entries on themes emphasize Whitman's approach to the subject and cover scholarly trends and controversies in understanding his aims and approaches. Entries on Whitman's writings begin with a chronology of their development and publication history, providing any title changes (an important complication in Whitman studies). The body of these entries focuses on theme, style, social connections, and biographical relevance. Their conclusions offer a critical assessment of the work. Entries on people often focus on accomplishments rather than on detailed biographical narratives. The key works or achievements are followed by the date in parenthesis. These entries conclude with a summary of the person's influence and relationship to Walt Whitman.

Authors

The major encyclopedias differ in their attitude towards authors. Many assign the entries to staffers, but a few, such as Compton's, seek out scholars who are recognizable authorities in the given field. A specialty encyclopedia might well be authored by a single authority.

Length and Style

The *Whitman Encyclopedia's* 800 articles vary in length from 350 words to a few thousand words. Authors were asked not to deviate from their assigned lengths by more than 20 percent without first getting permission. All articles were written specifically for the book and will not be published verbatim anywhere else. Authors were asked to conform to the *Chicago Manual of Style* and were given succinct guidelines for manuscript preparation, electronic submissions, headings, names, dates, numbers, and so on. Authors were reminded to avoid personal references ("I" and "we"), unnecessary contractions, and sexist and racist language.

Cross-Referencing

Sometimes the way that knowledge is cross-referenced in an encyclopedia is almost as important as the knowledge itself. Behind the physical instance of every encyclopedia there stands the conceptual model for structuring the relationships between the entries, the taxonomy.

The term *taxonomy* refers to a method for systematically classifying and arranging the body of knowledge.

Grolier uses multiple taxonomies. One prominent feature of *Grolier's Multimedia Encyclopedia* is its Knowledge Tree browser. The Knowledge Tree browser allows a user to select a general topic—for instance, *science*—and proceed down a "branch" of information on this subject, to subtopics on *technology, history, industry and manufacturing, major industry, chemical industry,* and so on—until she finds the subject of interest and summons a list of articles and multimedia assets. The Tree forms an intuitive approach to the knowledge contained in the encyclopedia, as opposed to the class and sub-class hierarchies of traditional taxonomies.

Success in cross-referencing your encyclopedia can make using it a much more absorbing experience for the reader.

Interactive Issues

Now that you know about the concept of an encyclopedia, what makes interactive encyclopedias different? An interactive encyclopedia is often built with an indexed text-retrieval engine, enhanced with an attractive and intuitive user interface, and furnished with such new-media capabilities as audio, animation, and video. Other interactive services may include integration with word processing and communication links to online services. The fast and versatile features of the text-retrieval engine automate browsing and hence form the basis of the encyclopedia's hypertext functions.

Platforms

By the time Windows 95 was released, Windows 3.1 had captured 85 percent of the personal computer marketplace. The introduction of Windows 95 is expected to rapidly increase that percentage. However, a large number of Windows platforms still in use today are older, less powerful machines that lack audio, eight-bit color, and CD-ROMs—and are unsuitable for multimedia. When this segment is taken into account, the number of multimedia-ready PCs that remain does not outnumber multimedia Apple Macintoshes by such a great ratio, and so major publishers make an effort to support both Windows 3.1 and Macintosh platforms.

Developers are now faced with the requirement to support a "third" platform: Windows 95. This is mostly because of the faster 32-bit file system of Windows 95 and the new Direct Draw graphics environment. Windows 95 also supports new 3D extensions, AutoPlay for instant installation of CD-ROMs, and a few other features, such as PolyMIDI. On the other hand, it is important to realize that the multimedia architectures of Windows 3.1 and Windows 95 are largely identical. Multimedia applications written for Windows 3.1, like any other kind of 16-bit application, usually play without a hitch on Windows 95. Within a few years, application developers will stop supporting Windows 3.1 altogether and concentrate on Windows 95.

Authoring Tools

Authoring a comprehensive interactive encyclopedia requires an indexed text-retrieval tool, a user-interface tool, and a media-control tool. In other words, one must not only retrieve the hypertext linkages, but also display them in a versatile and attractive text field and enhance them with audio and video.

Indexed-text retrieval is a specialized task not found in general-purpose authoring tools, such as Macromedia Director, Asymetrix ToolBook, or AimTech IconAuthor. Early windows multimedia titles used Microsoft's simple Windows Help engine. Subsequently, many developers have also turned to Microsoft for a Windows-based text engine called Multimedia Viewer, which is something like a superset of Windows Help. The latest incarnation of Windows Help is MediaView, a version of the Viewer text-retriever minus the Viewer navigation and display functionality. Developers must build their own interfaces to MediaView, using Visual C++ or Visual Basic. Independent software vendors (ISVs) have released products that allow you to port a Multimedia Viewer title over to the Macintosh, and eventually, it will be feasible to port MediaView documents to the Macintosh as well.

Other text-retrieval engines are available from Jouve Software, Inc. (GTI), Knowledge Access (KAware Disk Publisher), Personal Librarian Software (Personal Librarian), and Cognetics Corporation (Hyperties). Important products have recently been released by Foundation Solutions, Inc. (MultiDoc Power Publisher) and Macromedia (Authorware Professional, which integrates the Authorware text engine with Director). MultiDoc was used to produce the Macintosh versions of *Encarta* and *Cinemania*. The most successful of the cross-platform alternatives to Microsoft Viewer, however, have so far been products from Folio (VIEWS), Enigma Retrieval Systems (Insight), and Ntergaid (HyperWriter). Folio's VIEWS has been used to create over 1500 commercially-published titles. Enigma's Insight, the only product to support languages that are read from right to left (Arabic, Hebrew) has been used extensively in Israel for legal titles, financial titles, dictionaries, and education. Ntergaid's HyperWriter has been used to publish the back issues of *WordPerfect Magazine* and *Dr. Dobb's Journal.*

Specialty encyclopedias may not require the massive content bases of general-purpose encyclopedias, so it is feasible to develop them without the high performance of text retrieval engines. What they do require, however, is a cross-platform way to display and navigate through pages of attractive, well-formatted text, supporting a mix of fonts styles and colors. Cross-platform document publishing applications include No Hands Software's Common Ground, Adobe's Acrobat, WordPerfect's Envoy, and Quark's forthcoming multimedia document publisher, code-named "Orion." These are end-user utilities that "print" a document to a device-independent format like PostScript, for display on the screen via a viewer application. These solutions are by no means optimized for fast and versatile text search, the way indexed retrieval engines are.

Other ways to display hypertext involve hypertext add-ons for programming languages, such as Looking Glass Software's RavenWrite VBX, a Windows-only tool that can be used with Visual Basic and Visual C++. RavenWrite not only supports Rich Text Format (RTF), but drop-edge shadows, the use of the entire Windows palette for text colors, and a transparent overlay of text on a graphic background (sometimes called a "virtual watermark"). Looking Glass also sells a hypertext word processor called ViperWrite that makes it very easy to develop hypertext files for use in either the ViperWrite distributable viewer or RavenWrite VBX. Windows 95 also provides a native RTF custom control that allows Visual Basic and Visual C++ developers to display mixed-format text, but it does not support a transparent background or hypertext.

Interactive Graphics

Authoring systems and Windows development languages allow you to create hotspots on graphics so that a graphic acts as a button or a hyperlink. They also allow you to add frame animation to windows in your application. These animations can be controlled by mouse input, enabling the user to interact with the graphics. For example, Visual Basic comes with an animated button custom control that enables you to load an animation into the button frame. You can control the animation programmatically or allow the user to step through it. Indexed-text retrieval engines do not support this functionality, so it must be added to your encyclopedia by multimedia authors. More advanced authoring systems support *sprite* animation, sometimes called "actors"—animated objects with irregular boundaries and transparent regions. Macromedia's Director is the most capable sprite animation editor.

Interactive Audio

Multimedia applications can synchronize audio to user inputs to provide audible feedback when a navigation button is clicked, or to orchestrate sound effects for an animation. Some encyclopedias pronounce words selected by the reader. Others may provide narration synchronized with a subtitle. These features are added through an authoring tool or a programming language. Programming them usually requires expert knowledge of the lower-level multimedia services in the operating system.

Professional-quality audio recording is required to produce multimedia for the consumer marketplace. Improvements in audio compression *codecs* (COder/DECoder techniques) are announced almost every year that make higher-quality audio less and less wasteful of disc space.

Interactive Video

QuickTime and Video for Windows supply highly interactive ways to view digital video. Beyond the standard VCR controls for starting, pausing, rewinding, and stopping video, they offer more sophisticated features, such as subtitling and the processing of timecode, which can be used to synchronize the video with user interface events. The same lower-level programming methods used for audio access can be used to explore video data, but the programming issues become even more complex. The QuickTime and Video for Windows digital video standards are continuing to evolve. Currently both support elementary virtual reality applications.

User Interface

Developers build the user interface for their applications with an authoring tool or a visual programming language. The interface must convey the product's capabilities and choices in an engaging, intuitive, and concise way. The user interface is intimately connected with the underlying messaging functionality of the operating system—the means by which all software objects and hardware devices continuously communicate with one another. Different authoring tools use different paradigms for user access, such as a stack of cards or an animated cartoon.

Navigation

One of the principal roles of the user interface is to enable the user to navigate from topic to topic. Navigation must meet the somewhat contradictory demands of providing great flexibility and at the same time, being easy to understand. Producers must take care that the hypertext links do not lead down too many layers, nor become tangled in a confusing web. Users need to know where they are, where they've been, how to quickly exit, and if desired, get back to where they've just been.

Online Updates

The *Grolier Encyclopedia* has been available online for several years, and the 1996 edition of the CD-ROM enhances this online presence with a CompuServe Connect button. Grolier updates the CompuServe version of its encyclopedia on a quarterly basis, and also supplies it with a weekly feature story called "Background on the News." The backgrounder on June 19, 1995, covered the luxury steamboat, *American Queen,* which ran aground that week on a sand-bar in the Ohio River. The backgrounder was linked to a number of subjects in the database: STEAMBOAT, OHIO RIVER, ROBERT FULTON, and so forth.

This is the first spray from an advancing tidal wave of new services. From the developer's point of view, the online services, including CompuServe, America Online, Prodigy, and Microsoft Network therefore constitute entirely new kinds of platforms for interactive encyclopedias. Moreover, these services are migrating from the sole province of the personal computer to appear on digital settops, delivered to your home TV by cable, telephone, or utility companies. Developers should start today familiarizing themselves with Internet development environments, such as Hypertext Markup Language (HTML), Microware's DAVID settop operating system, and Microsoft's interactive-TV version of Visual Basic.

Hands-On Demo

For a specialty encyclopedia of modest size, it may not be necessary to use a high-powered text-retrieval engine. Other alternatives for hypertext are suitable for multimedia authors who do not have expert programming assistance. Looking Glass Software provides such a product in ViperWrite, a hypertext word processor. ViperWrite allows you to quickly edit, hyperlink, and test a hypertext document. You can then publish the document with a freely-distributable viewer application called ViperPresentation. Better yet, you can glue the hypertext document into a Visual Basic form using another product called RavenWriteVBX. The combination of RavenWrite's elegant hypertext display with Visual Basic's versatile interactivity enables you to create professional-looking multimedia titles of any type.

In this chapter's folder on the CD-ROM, you'll find the VIPRPRES.EXE and CHAPT29.EXE applications. The ViperWrite viewer loads a hypertext *project* file, TIME.HPW. The project file is the initial file for the hypertext display. ViperPresentation displays it against a white background, while providing standardized navigational buttons. CHAPT29.EXE, the version compiled with Visual Basic 3 and the RavenWriteVBX, underlays the hypertext with a graphic, courtesy of a Visual Basic form. Both applications let you explore a sample article for an interactive encyclopedia. Each node in the hypertext database is an .HPW file. The same linking used inside the article to connect these files could obviously be extended to link articles to one another.

The following discussion assumes that you have purchased and installed ViperWrite and Visual Basic version 3 or 4. To give you a feel for the production of this demo, general steps are provided rather than explicit instructions.

Hypertext Word Processing

ViperWrite supports three modes of development: Edit, Present, and Link. In Edit mode, you can edit the text, the embedded buttons, and the embedded graphics. You can alter the text formatting and the page layout. Edit mode also lets you create links to other files or to events— such as the display of graphics or the playback of sound. In Present mode, you can test the application just as the user would. In Link mode, you can change text formatting, test links, and create new links, but you cannot edit the text and graphics.

ViperWrite offers many simple word processor features, including a spell checker. If you prefer to use Microsoft Word for Windows to create your document, go right ahead. Save your documents to rich text file (RTF) format, and load them into ViperWrite. Choose which document is suitable for the initial display and format it inside ViperWrite using the Format menu options, so that it meets the requirements for legibility and attractiveness on the typical target platform, a 640×480 SVGA display. (ViperWrite is an eight-bit color application.) One of the nice features of the Format menu is the Shadow option which allows you to add a drop-edge of variable size to selected text. By specifying the appropriate color to the shadow, you can increase the contrast of your text, and you can add a subtle but effective highlighting to "hot" words.

Once you have edited and formatted the initial document, declare it as your "project" file, using the Edit/Project option. You are given the chance to declare filenames that ViperPresentation will recognize for any optional Content, Glossary, and Index files you create. You can also specify whether ViperPresentation displays its Back, History, Find, and Layer navigation buttons when displaying the application.

You can then load other documents to format and edit each in turn. As you work, you may change the color of certain words, to represent the links. (It's particularly useful to add text in the Microsoft WingDings font, which transforms alphabetical characters into all sorts of symbols and icons—for instance, "E" in WingDings is a left-pointing finger.) Then you select those words, one at a time, and use the Link menu to link that word with another .HPW file, as shown in Figure 29.1.

> **NOTE**
>
> Specialty fonts won't translate if you're publishing for the Web. However, ViperWrite does not generate HTML anyway. It would used to create hyeprtext documents that could only be downloaded and opened by Windows users.

You can also use the native button-building tools to embed buttons into the text. You can also embed graphics into the text, and program them to act as links. More sophisticated applications can make use of ViperWrite's layering capability which acts as filters for different contexts—for instance, you can define one layer for historical references, one layer for footnotes, and still another for term definitions. By turning off different layers, you can keep these levels of additional detail from cluttering the screen.

FIGURE 29.1.

ViperWrite lets you link a "hot word" to another hypertext file.

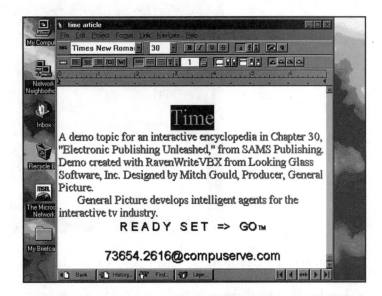

> **NOTE**
>
> As you build your hypertext application, you can switch to the Link mode at any time to test it, and then return to Edit for further changes. When the document is complete, you can bundle it with VIPRPRES.EXE and provide a complete application.

Compiling a Standalone Application

RavenWriteVBX is a *custom control*—in other words, a plug-in software object—for Microsoft Visual Basic. RavenWrite provides both automatic and manual linking to hot spots. In automatic linking, you define the file to be displayed, and RavenWrite opens the file for you. In manual linking, RavenWrite passes you the ID number for the hot spot, and enables you to handle the event in Visual Basic as you see fit. The control supplies a standard Hot Link mode for predefined hot words and a Hot Word mode in which clicking on any word passes that word to Visual Basic. A Select mode allows the user to select text for copying to the Clipboard. The Transparent property gives Visual Basic the ability to display hypertext over a background graphic, as shown in the CHAPT29.EXE demo.

The compiled demo made use of a RavenWriteVBX window over a Visual Basic form designed for 640×480 screens, as shown in Figure 29.2.

FIGURE 29.2.

RavenWriteVBX enables you to interact extensively with the hypertext display.

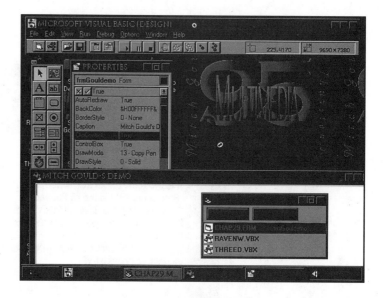

CHAPT29.MAK, a Visual Basic program (also known as a *project*), was inspired by the EDITOR.MAK demo that comes with RavenWriteVBX. CHAPT29.MAK supplied Visual Basic code to handle the tasks given in Table 29.1.

Table 29.1. The procedures used in CHAPT29.EXE.

Procedure	Description
fFormCenter	Centers the form on the screen.
fRavenInit	Sets transparency, turns off scrolling, sets Hot Link mode, and opens the ViperWrite project.
Form_Load	Initializes the VBX when Visual Basic displays the form.
Form_Resize	Centers the form on the screen when it is displayed.
gpb3Exit_Click	Terminates the application.
gpb3Min_Click	Minimizes the application.

(For a further explanation of these simple Visual Basic procedures, see *Windows 95 Multimedia Programming,* by Mitch Gould and Van Thurston, Jr., M&T Books, 1995.)

When the .MAK file is compiled into the standalone .EXE file, the Visual Basic design-time window disappears, as shown in Figure 29.3.

FIGURE 29.3.

CHAPT29.EXE shows a hypertext application suitable for interactive encyclopedias in both Windows 3.1 and Windows 95.

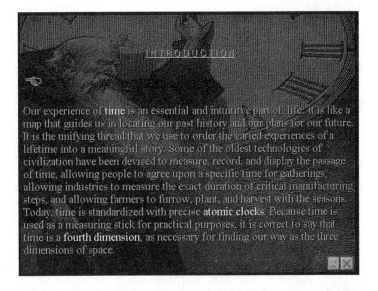

Case Study

The *1996 Grolier Multimedia Encyclopedia*, shown in Figure 29.4, consists of some articles from the print version, as well as additional text commissioned especially for the multimedia version. The new articles appeal to a broad range of users, covering among other things, every U.S. National Park, all the winners of the Nobel Prize, and every member of the Rock 'n Roll Hall of Fame.

FIGURE 29.4.

The Timeline enables users to browse historical connections.

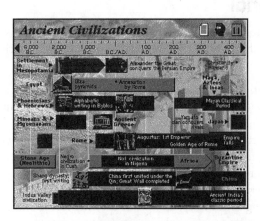

In addition to the new material, *1996 Grolier* contains 6,000 revised and updated articles on such topics and recent events as affirmative action, Bosnia, Chechnya, Oklahoma City, terrorism, and Jacques Chirac.

It contains over 900 maps, including new city maps that expand into greater detail—such as the map of Los Angeles which can be enlarged to detail Beverly Hills. Interactive historical exploration maps now cover North and South America, Africa, and the Arctic and Antarctic. Seventy-seven interactive thematic maps graphically detail such topics as world and continental agriculture, climatic zones, vegetation, population densities, annual precipitation, monthly temperature and rainfall. New Multimedia Maps explore the European and Pacific theaters of World War II using animation, audio, and text.

The disc features overlay art with up to four layers of graphical information which the encyclopedia reader can both see and control. The overlay art feature displays the anatomy of ten animals and the anatomy of a Boeing 747, an Apollo spacecraft, and an Indianapolis 500 race car.

Interactive animations include finger-spelling exercises, different views of the brain, and visualizations of such famous structures as the Statue of Liberty and the Eiffel Tower. These animations allow the reader to control the display and explore different possibilities, encouraging learning by involvement. The Media Gallery provides easy access to video, animations, illustration, and sound clips.

The Yearbook feature offers a detailed view of events from January 1994 through June 1995. It furnishes a survey of the year's major trends and themes, and a description of events on a monthly basis.

The 1996 encyclopedia uses far more music than the previous edition and the full text of 150 historical documents, including the Magna Carta and a number of landmark Supreme Court rulings, as well as hundreds of thousands of true hypertext links.

Editorial

The editors choose experts in the field as their contributors. A majority are degreed professionals, and the 1996 CD-ROM contains more signed articles than *Encarta* and *Compton's* combined.

The continuing national debate over frank discussions of sensitive issues complicates an editor's job in ways from the serious to the absurd. *Grolier's* contains articles on AIDS and abortion, despite complaints from certain critics. The company even received a letter complaining about the naturalist's term *wild ass* from readers who campaigned for the substitution *wild donkey*. The request was not granted. In any event, Grolier needs to handle controversial subjects in order to remain topical. Multimedia developers should note that *Booklist*, the publication of the American Library Association, reviews information products with an eye to currency. In presenting controversy, the editors use only factual material and present opposing viewpoints as opinion, in a manner that is not confrontational.

Beyond these standard editorial duties, the editors also have the responsibility for marking up the articles in Standard Generalized Markup Language and creating the links from each article to other articles and to multimedia assets.

Staffing

The Product Development staff currently consists of about 100 people, divided into six groups:

- Engineering: Creates and maintains the search engine, all human interface code, the internal programmer interfaces, and the installation routines, as well as the editorial tools necessary for generating and testing content.
- Edititorial Databases: Tags all the articles in Structured General Markup Language (SGML), arranges hypertext links.
- Creative/Graphics: Creates user interface objects and all content screens.
- Multimedia Production: Produces and optimizes the encyclopedia's media assets. These employees digitize, edit, and compress pictures, audio, and video, using a broadcast-quality production studio on its premises in Danbury, Connecticut.
- Editorial Content: Continuously develops and refines the content of the encyclopedia.
- Marketing/Product Management: Handles promotion and sales, production of packaging, advertising, public relations, and so on.

As the product nears its release date, ten quality assurance staffers join the team to get the bugs out.

Budgeting and Scheduling

The encyclopedia already contains 34,000 articles, so the annual agenda involves additions of new content, not starting from scratch. Production for the annual update proceeds on parallel tracks: one track for the content of the project—what the end users will read, see, and hear; and the other for the software—the enhanced search engine. The producer outlines the core content of articles and the media assets that will accompany them. At the same time, engineers develop a plan for software changes to be incorporated in the new release.

To estimate the time required to create the new articles for the encyclopedia, the producer allows for the time required to locate, negotiate with, and commission an expert, adding that to the actual research and writing time, and the time editors must spend editing and marking up the text. Numbers drawn from previous experience get plugged into formulas. The producer can multiply the number of new pictures to be incorporated into the 1996 edition by the time historically required to prepare such graphics for use by the engineering department. Estimates based upon the content and assets plans allow the developers to estimate the time required for production and develop a working schedule. The programming plan must deal with all programming issues, minor and major. Because of its abstract, experimental nature, programming's schedule must be looser than editorial's. Once the time has been estimated, the managers break down the content and programming plans into a task list. At this point, a list of resources can be developed and production needs can be fully budgeted.

Acquisitions

Grolier's manager of acquisitions typically employs freelancers—individuals with previous experience and established expertise in the given field of interest, be it the native birds of North America or the folk music of 18th century France. Once the appropriate images or audio tracks are located, negotiations proceed for the right to use them.

Media that predates 1920 usually falls into the public domain and are therefore far more feasible to include. For works such as music copyrighted after 1920, usage rights can become rather expensive. Multimedia producers must acquire both the mechanical rights—the right to reproduce the mechanical recording of the desired piece—and the publisher's right—the performance royalty paid to the publisher. The mechanical right for a modern concert piece, such as Aaron Copland's *Appalachian Spring*, may amount to no more than $200. But the publisher's right constitutes a payment for *every* performance—that is, for each copy of the multimedia piece that is sold. For modern concert pieces, publisher's rights usually go for about seven cents per unit sold. Thus the sale of 200,000 copies of a multimedia encyclopedia containing 20 selections from modern concert masters can cost the company producing it some $13,000 *per piece*, or about $1.5 million. The use of pop music usually doubles these figures, with publisher's rights typically amounting to 13 or 14 cents per unit sold. Further, pop music rights carry what is termed a "most favored nation" clause which states that, should the publisher sell the rights to a piece to another company for more than you paid for it, you must make up the difference between your rate and the new one on copies of your product already sold. For more information on copyright issues, see Chapter 35, "General Laws and Copyright Information."

Tools

Grolier has prototyped concepts with a variety of tools that could work quite well for independent multimedia developers working to bring an encyclopedia to market. These include Microsoft's Visual Basic, Macromedia's Director, Apple's HyperCard, as well as proprietary tools built in-house. For instance, the director of development has employed Visual Basic to develop interface screens and to try out third-part code libraries. He calls it "an absolutely fantastic rapid prototyping tool," and looks forward to the introduction of Visual Basic plug-ins for databases marked in SGML.

The central issue in interactive encyclopedia development, however, is how to get the text content into an easily cross-referenced form, with searching and hyperlinking. Grolier uses various text engines for development, and several staff programmers maintain the interface between the text engine and the output of the Editorial Databases Group, which prepares the text.

The bottom line is this: Users must be able to search for something and find it quickly.

Cross-Platform Issues

Grolier currently serves both Windows 3.1 and Macintosh systems, and treats Windows 95 as a third platform. The porting issues can be complicated for developers both large and small.

Of particular importance for smaller developers is that the need to maintain two sets of assets for different platforms can be costly in terms of both storage and man-hours—two banks of assets entail dual production and quality assurance paths.

An example from Grolier's experience: a newly developed digital sound format, which the company is evaluating, saves space and provides excellent sound, but must be ported to the Macintosh. While Grolier programmers are creating a player to run this format on the Mac, the company has chosen an intermediate course, IMA, using QuickTime™ for both platforms.

Graphics also vary across platforms. For instance, Grolier employs interactive maps, where clicking on a hotspot causes the display of a detail view or graphic. What file format should be used? The GIF format decompresses more slowly than the PCX format, which in turn, is slower than Apple QuickTime graphics.

Grolier employs both QuickTime and Video for Windows. QuickTime has proven to be a more flexible development tool. The QuickTime format compresses easier, and programmers can modify the QuickTime developer's kit for custom approaches.

Human Factors and Usability Testing

Interface concerns occupy a preeminent place in the minds of multimedia producers. Many factors drive interface design decisions, including usability studies and product reviews, not to mention a healthy awareness of what the competition is doing.

The encyclopedia is not a traditional productivity application but a tool for information retrieval. Accordingly, developers have found that the productivity application interface—the standard menu bar of "File-Edit-View" and so on—is not necessarily the best approach for encyclopedia users. Productivity applications are mainly used by office workers, while the multimedia encyclopedia is used by school-aged children and senior citizens alike. For some of these users, a menu option labeled "File" means nothing.

Grolier adopted the SCI model, for Story-Content-Interactivity. Successful, well-designed multimedia products have a good balance among the three areas. Because the story line in an encyclopedia will be weaker than in a narrative product, such as the *Oregon Trail* package, Grolier uses other elements, such as Pathmakers essays, to add story elements. Beyond this innovation, three other principles enhance human factors:

- *Continuously represent the article of interest.* Readers don't want to go through series of menu trees to get to the object of their search. Grolier strives to integrate related pieces of information in all forms and to avoid dead ends in their linkages. Articles continuously link to other articles or media in a virtually unending chain of interconnections.

- *Strengthen the user's ability to directly manipulate the encyclopedia.* End-user studies have proven valuable in this regard. Observation of fifth- and eighth-grade students in New York City found that the students could not decipher the icons employed in previous editions. They simply clicked through the icons in series, from the left side of the screen to the right, to find out what they stood for. So Grolier has replaced these pictures with simply labeled buttons. "If the words are simple enough, most people can read them," says Grolier producer David Wicks.

■ *Enhance the response of the product.* Simply put, respond to all user input in real-time, and make all actions immediately undoable.

Linking

Standard Generalized Markup Language enables the editors to structure documents independently of platform and application. SGML describes documents in terms of titles, paragraphs, sections, illustrations, and so forth, emphasizing content over the metrics of page layout. In addition, SGML can describe hypertext links. The keywords of the link are defined in the DTD, or Document Type Definition, a file read by the SGML interpreter.

The encyclopedia editors speak fluent SGML and use it to create the links that bind the encyclopedia together. Tracking, checking, and editing these becomes a major task in a product with the scope of *1996 Grolier*, which contains 34,000 articles and may link to half a million places. The developers mark up their text in a way that makes linking and moving among the links relatively easy to program, with the emphasis on the word *relatively*. As Wicks says, "It's never really easy." But the editors intend to enable their users to get where they want to go with a reasonable degree of speed and efficiency.

Grolier editors create links with tools that are still somewhat esoteric among most software professionals, though they have been employed in mainstream publishing for some time. Editors double-check the validity of all references, and create links not only to other articles but to multimedia assets as well. To aid them in tracking their work, Grolier editors can generate lists of all the possible links in a given article and can see how many of these links constitute exact matches to other articles, as well as how many of the matches are only probable and how many are guesses. The linking process employs traditional pattern matching, rather than any of the newer techniques of fuzzy logic.

Cross-referencing on the scale of a full-fledged encyclopedia can be a daunting process. During the development process, Grolier editors track their cross references with histograms. Typically, articles will contain, for instance, ten cross references to other articles. But some of the book-length entries can contain as many of 500 links to other articles and assets.

The Jump on TV

Grolier also looks forward to the expansion of online services to include interactive television. Wicks said, "We are preparing for a variety of distribution mechanisms, whether they be set-top, ITV, or satellite-based distribution, in that the background work is already underway in regard to licensing agreements for those particular online media."

Though specific products could not be disclosed, Maryanne Piazza, Grolier Electronic Publishing's director of marketing communications, told us that the company keeps a close eye on developments in this field. "We're never stopping," said Piazza. "Stay tuned."

Summary

An enterprising publisher of specialty works can use this chapter to get a feel for the interactive encyclopedia business. Beginning with the very definition of an encyclopedia in ancient Greece, you traced the development of the encyclopedia from its beginnings to the golden age when *Encyclopedia Britannica* ruled triumphant. You saw the disaster waiting for Britannica when it failed to match its competitors in the race to digitize. Now, Microsoft and Grolier dominate the industry, and by studying the competitive analysis provided in the first part of this chapter, you'll understand why.

You should now have a sense of appropriate content and methodology in commissioning entries for a first-class encyclopedia, and an appreciation for the importance of developing a sound taxonomic model for organizing the links between entries. You'll be prepared to invest serious effort in give the user a coherent, meaningful, and rewarding capacity to browse the interrelated links.

In the second part of the chapter, you had a chance to try ViperWrite, a simple hyperlinking tool that works well quick prototyping of Windows titles, and RavenWrite VBX, an elegant tool for adding hyerptext to Visual Basic applications. Finally, you stepped through the production of a successful major encyclopedia at Grolier's multimedia studio. Best wishes on your electronic publishing venture.

The author acknowledges the contributions of Ed Boggan to this chapter.

Publishing an Electronic Comic Book

Some people say that comics have been around since the earliest cave drawings in the mists of prehistory, arriving at the modern world via hieroglyphics, pre-Columbian manuscripts, the Bayeaux Tapestry and the Gutenberg Press. These people hardly ever get dates and are never invited to the really good parties. Still, it's hardly surprising that many cartoonists see electronic publishing—currently represented by CD-ROMS and the World Wide Web—as just another medium to doodle their scribbles onto. And there are literally hundreds (and in all probability thousands) of tools at their disposal, but cartoonists aren't really heavy into details. We were all too busy drawing funny animals during math class.

However, you need to ask yourself a few questions before taking the plunge into electronic comic publishing. What audience am I writing for? What do I want my computer to do for me? How far do I want to stretch the medium? What am I going to do with that bulk shipment of soap I just received now that I'm not going to get ink on my hands anymore? And shouldn't I be doing something more mature and responsible with my time, like becoming a certified public accountant and suffering a massive coronary by age 43, instead of drawing fuzzy animals and superheroes for a living?

More so than most forms of electronic publishing, putting out a piece of comic art—be it a superhero action adventure, a comic strip, an editorial cartoon or a graphic novel—really lets you pick and choose your own personal method of getting your work online or on-screen. Your main problem won't be finding a way to get it done, but finding what way works best for you and your particular style—oh yeah, and having an absolute blast in the meantime.

Comic art is difficult to define—but you know it when you see it. You don't have to be the world's greatest artist to come up with a great comic, but some of the top comic creators are a among the world's greatest artists. Simple strips like "Dilbert," by Scott Adams, don't require degrees in human anatomy to map out. So what makes a comic?

Cartoons can be anything from stick figures . . .   . . . to comic strip muskrats called "Carson" . . .   . . . to comic books and graphic novels.

So what are your options, assuming you want your comic to go somewhere other than your computer screen? Putting it onto a CD-ROM, or throwing it onto the Internet are the current *modes du jour*. And let's face it, as every newspaper in the country (and quite a few comic strips inside those newspapers as well) will tell you, the Internet and CD-ROMs are as hip, hot, pop-culturally cool and happening as, well, comics themselves.

But Why Publish Electronically in the First Place?

To start out with, there are the potentially massive audiences you can reach with your keen political satire or daring tales of derring-do. And then there are the electronic tricks you can perform, adding a universe of sound and color to your works that will break down boundaries and create new worlds. In all honesty, though, the single benefit of publishing electronically is money.

Lots of money.

Before you start salivating, let us explain. We're not talking about money people will thrust into your welcoming mitts like onrushing manna from heaven, but money you won't have to shell out to publishers, printers, colorists and distributors. Money you won't see leaping from your bank account like so many spawning trout, racing upstream as if your bank account were poison to be fled. Money, in short, you can spend on food and lodging—long considered luxury items to anyone involved in artistic careers over the centuries.

Of course, you could get rich drawing funny animals or superheroes for a living—several people have. But a long time ago, in far ancient days, the dark ages of cartooning—say, five years ago— all artists could really do was send their work to the printers and hope that their kids didn't really have to go to college.

Or a cartoonist could take their masterwork to the local photographer and hope that nobody noticed the results looked like something the cat dragged in after a particularly bad night . . .

Heaven help you—well, heaven help your life's savings, actually—if you want to do something adventurous and, say, add color to your comic. However, the World Wide Web will get your work out and about and viewed in glorious Technicolor™ (well, okay, however many colors your scanner can handle) by a cast of thousands—millions, even, if you're either lucky and/or terribly good at self-promotion. CD-ROMS will now let you throw your comic to an audience about as sophisticated as they come. (True, given the state of television these days, that might not be saying too much. Oh, well, we tried).

A syndicated comic strip can be considered a roaring success if it runs in 40 newspapers. Running in 200 is considered outstanding. But on the World Wide Web, the audience you can potentially reach dwarves even that!

Even bastions of technologically outmoded cartoons (that is, the funny pages) have been jumping on the bandwagon. There's hardly a newspaper around the country without a recent version of Adobe Illustrator and Photoshop to give its graphics some punch. Even if you want to stick with the traditional methods of self-publishing (such as designing a book, printing a book, selling one or two copies of the book, starving), you'll save yourself vast tracts of time and a fortune on aspirin alone if, for example, you do your color separations on Quark XPress and Adobe Separator—even if that's a little like buying a Lambourghini to run down to the corner store for a six-pack.

Hands-on Example 1

You don't even have to be a cartoonist to be a cartoon publisher. Al Gore may not be the next Charles Schulz, but his electronic scrapbook of editorial cartoons can be seen at this Web address:

```
http://www.whitehouse.gov/White_House/EOP/OVP/html/Cartoon.html
```

(We wouldn't dream of trying to lecture the vice-president on how to draw, but we might advise some on his staff to learn how to use a scanner better).

Anyway, with newspapers falling by the wayside or merging every day and with a glut of artists in the comic book market, many cartoonists are turning to CD-ROMS and the World Wide Web as a way to essentially self-syndicate their work. It sure beats beating down editors' doors only to face rejection, humiliation and the resulting waves of angst, existential anguish and self-doubt (not that this has ever happened to us, of course).

Hands-on Example 2

If you want to check out who's already doing what online, you can peruse the Usenet `rec.arts.comics` newsgroup hierarchy. You may have to wade between discussions of "Doonesbury's" liberalism and "Dilbert's" primitivism, but searching diligently through the following sites turns up new self-published comic Web sites all the time:

```
rec.arts.comics.strips
rec.arts.comics.creative
rec.arts.comics.misc
rec.arts.comics.other-media
```

There's a third option, of course. You could turn your artwork into binary code (it's easy—trust us), and post it on one of several Usenet newsgroups themselves (and there's a bridge we'd like to sell you in Brooklyn—trust us). The `alt.binaries` hierarchy is one of the more interesting places on the Internet to explore from time to time, even if you have to avoid groups with names like the following every now and then:

```
alt.binaries.pictures.erotica.hope-you-haven't-had-lunch-yet
```

The downside is that with Web browsers growing more powerful by the month, binary files just don't have the allure they once held. They're clumsy and mistake-prone, and awfully, awfully labor and time intensive, compared to even the slowest Web browser. Also, most people who are likely to stumble across `alt.pictures.cartoons` and its ilk, probably haven't the foggiest notion what to do with that bizarre series of numbers and letters they get when they open up the posting "My Life's Work" that you so lovingly placed there months ago, and your master-piece will go unnoticed.

Hands-on Example 3

But if you have the time and the right programs, dipping into `alt.pictures.anime` and `alt.pictures.cartoons` and converting a couple of binary files to something you can actually view is a fine way to spend an hour or ten. The commercial online services (CompuServe, America Online, and so on) are great places to download UUTool, Graphic Converter, and the Alt.Binary FAQ, all of which you'll need to get anyway.

Good Grief, Now What?

You can use any of three basic ways to get your artwork onto other people's computer screens (without breaking into their offices and attacking their PowerMacs with magic markers, that is). Each has its benefits, and each has its drawbacks. Like everything else that ever had any-thing to do with cartooning (Pen or brush? Pencils or ink? Three-fingered funny animals or four-fingered funny animals?), you'll just have to figure out what suits your style and person-ality best.

Electronic Comics: The Easy Way

Well, it's easy in that all you need to learn is how to operate a scanner. That's right. You don't have to be a techno-nerd to publish your comic electronically. You can sketch it out, ink it up, color it in, slap it on a scanner, and throw it onto a CD-ROM or the Web, and never leave your drawing chair. Just think of the vast sea of electronic publishing resources you can avoid by taking the easy way out. With decent color scanners currently available for under $1,000, you won't even have to sell the kids into indentured servitude to pay for it, either. Best yet, you won't have to delve too deeply into the exciting world of the Internet or CD-ROMs, you won't have to learn the difference between path and pixilation art programs, and you can leave your VCR flashing on "12:00" for as long as your heart desires, as well.

Figure 30.1 shows an editorial cartoon that was scanned in at 400 dpi using a Macintosh ColorOne Mac, untouched, unaltered, and exactly as it appears on the World Wide Web (at `http://www.msn.fullfeed.com/muskrat`, to be precise).

Deep, insightful, and educational, huh?

FIGURE 30.1.
Editorial cartoon.

Hands-On Example 4

United Media has recently started an online service promoting several of their comic artists and creators. You can find their home page at http://www.unitedmedia.com/. Most had probably never heard of the Web until this went up (although we're guessing that Scott Adams would be the exception to that rule).

Electronic Comics: The Current Way

From Disney to "Doonesbury," every other cartoonist under the sun seems to be combining computer-generated art with the honest-to-gosh, old-fashioned, hand-drawn variety these days. The vast majority of people publishing anything use their handy-dandy computers to at least minimally embellish their artwork, even if it's still only seen in newspapers and traditional comic books.

If you wanted to publish a color comic strip even a few years ago, you'd have to cut out sheets of amber lithe (and if you don't know what that is, believe us, you don't want to) or slather various ugly, greyish, smelly photographic paints onto plastic overlays. If you wanted a uniform shade for any kind of cartoon, you'd have to turn to sheets of zip-a-tone dot patterns—and hope your X-acto knife was sharp—or use the equally cumbersome duoshade board. Trust us, if you ever spilled a bottle of developer over one of those things, you welcomed the computer graphics revolution with open arms singing hallelujah.

Now, you can do wonders with programs like Adobe Illustrator or Photoshop. Literally, all you have to do is scan in your drawings, be they black and white or color, and you're in business. You can touch up mistakes on-screen, you can clean up lines, you can even alter text—a real bonus, given cartoonists' reputations for misspellings.

One of the (few) things you'll need to know before leaping into computer cartooning is the difference between path-based programs (such as Illustrator) and pixel-based ones (Photoshop). For straightforward line drawings, where you only need to add flat colors, path programs can take up to ten times less memory—an important consideration, but not the only one to keep in mind. Remember, always do what's right for you.

Abandoned for newer, more sophisticated video games,
Pacman returns to the pack.

David Farley, creator of the World Wide Web comic strip "Doctor Fun," is widely credited as one of the pioneers in putting comics onto the Web. The preceding figure is reprinted with the permission of David Farley and United Media. For more of David's art, visit "Doctor Fun" on the Internet at http://www.unitedmedia.com/.

FARLEY ON DOCTOR FUN

"I started Doctor Fun in 1993 mostly because it seemed liked an obvious thing to do. I had been cartooning for about ten years and had some success at getting published, but had been frustrated by two things, the inability to get my work out in front of people on a daily basis, and the fact that I could do all sorts of neat things with computer graphics which had no audience beyond people who came over and looked at them on my computer. I had had access to the Internet since about 1991, but had not seriously thought about putting a cartoon up until 1993.

"Once I decided I was going to do a regular cartoon on the Internet, a lot of things came into focus. I decided to be worthwhile to myself and my (potential) audience, the cartoon would have to meet a couple requirements: it would have to continue on an ongoing basis, and it would have to take advantage of the medium. Since the cartoon was essentially going to be "published" when people viewed it on their own equipment, I decided to go for broke and create the cartoons in 24-bit color and small enough to fit on a low resolution monitor. After I had done enough cartoons in the format I finally decided on, I realized that it was going to be a real time problem to keep enough cartoons on hand for a daily cartoon, so I decided to cut it down to weekdays. This has worked out well, except for a short break I had to take after I lost several weeks worth of finished cartoons in a serious crash.

"Doctor Fun has kind of been associated with the World Wide Web, although it's also been available on Gopher, Usenet and FTP. (I can claim to have the first cartoon on WWW, but Hans Bjordahl, of "Where the Buffalo Roam," can claim to have the first cartoon on the Internet.) My goal has always been to keep the online format simple and keep developing the cartoon. On my end of things, simply having to finish up a cartoon every day has taught me more about working with images than any course I could have taken the last two years (not that I wouldn't like to study more, given the time). I imagine as long as I keep getting ideas and learning new things, I'll keep drawing.

"After starting at the University of Chicago, then moving to Sunsite at the University of North Carolina, the good people at United Media took an interest in Doctor Fun, and the cartoon is now syndicated through their own Web server. I am quite pleased to be working with United Media, as I think it shows that there is a crossover between the sorts of creative things that have just sprouted and grown on the Internet, and the rest of the publishing world, and it also gives me something of a roadmap for developing Doctor Fun as a career. Whether this will actually happen is still unclear, as we are all in unknown territory today, but it should be interesting."

Electronic Comics: The Way of The Future

Nowadays, you can create a comic right on your computer from start to finish, using programs such as Paint and an electronic artpad. Not too surprisingly, many people who grew up with pen and ink are loath to embrace such changes wholeheartedly. My pal Steve Sack, editorial cartoonist for the *Minneapolis Star-Tribune*, and creator of the comic strip "Professor Doodles," likes having an original physical drawing that he can hold in his hands. But we keep working on him.

With mouse pens and art pads growing more sophisticated, there's very little you can't do on a computer that you can do at your drawing table anymore. And with an entire generation of cartoonists now plugged into the electrosphere, there's little doubt that cartoons conceived, created and finished entirely electronically will be a common feature of the future funny pages (whatever form those take).

Hands-on Example 5

Take a comic you've created, even if you've already enhanced the drawing on computer. Now try and reproduce it entirely on-screen, using your mouse if you haven't got an artpad and mouse pen.

This sketch was scanned in and run through Adobe Streamline and Adobe Illustrator, in roughly the same time it'd take to do a stick figure using the mouse.

The Computer Screen: Panel, Page, or Ghost of Elvis?

Of course, you also have to consider traditional elements of comic art once you make the transition to computer screen. For example, what's the best way to lay out your work? If you're making a comic book, do you want the image that pops up onto people's computer screens to be a single panel with one image? Perhaps you feel more comfortable thinking about the screen as an entire page, with lots of panels that your reader will scroll through, just like a comic book. Composition doesn't just refer to the images inside a frame. What you do with the frame itself can be vitally important.

If this seems like splitting hairs, remember our definition of a comic: sequential art. And in the words of several philosophers (as well as countless stand-up comedians), timing is everything.

For example, imagine this is your computer screen. To get to the next page, you'll have to prompt your computer, whether you're reading a CD-ROM or watching the World Wide Web.

For a really detailed philosophical discourse on the nature of timing, sequence and content, *About Comics*, by Scott McCloud (published by Kitchen Sink, 1993) has everything you need to know, and a lot more.

Doom County, or, Falling into Cartooning Computer Traps

Of course, computers aren't all fun and games (well, okay, so they are. Just don't let on to anybody, or they'll discover our secret). There are some traps you'll probably want to avoid. Ironically, the very ease of creating electronic comics contains its own pitfalls. For example, most comic characters go through a natural process of evolution as the artist changes his or her style slowly over the years. Look at Snoopy from 20 years ago, or Garfield from 15, and you'll see what I mean.

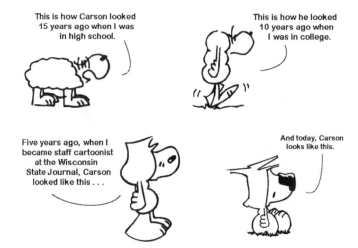

At every stage along the way, I was darned pleased with how I was drawing Carson, and much happier with the drawing than I had been with previous drawings. But had I stored all my drawings on computer discs, and just re-used old drawings for new jokes (as a few cartoonists are experimenting with now), the evolution of my style would have stopped dead.

Every now and then, I'll be really rushed to make a deadline, and the computer helps out enormously. A color separation for a Sunday comic takes from between one to three hours to complete. But as you might guess, the time it took to color the strip shown on the next page was significantly less then usual.

The lesson is, when you really need to, be willing to fall back on every trick in your computing book. But don't let it become too much of a crutch. There's no substitution for perspiration when it comes to creating a comic.

If computers can let you do too little, they can also let you try to do too much. There's no hard and fast rule as to how complex a comic should be: You just draw what feels right to you. Comic strips such as "Jim's Journal" or "Dilbert" are about as simple as they come, but they're effective. Just because you can add dozens of shading patterns with a single keystroke doesn't mean you have to. On the other hand, "Keep it simple," may be equally invalid if your style doesn't lend itself to a few lines. One of the joys of a comic such as "Little Nemo" was the sheer detail Windsor McKay was able to convey. Like so much else, you have to figure out what's best for you.

NOTE

All renderings of Carson in this chapter are copyrighted by John Kovalic.

Like detail, color is something you can add easily, electronically. Unlike detail, it's something not a lot of us have a lot of experience in. If you're like many cartoonists, the closest you've come to publishing something in color probably had something to do with a box of crayons and a homemade Mothers' Day card. Color has always been an expensive proposition for any publisher. It could double, triple or quadruple the cost of putting out a comic book. Now, however, you can add color to any piece of artwork for the price of some more memory.

One of the more fabulously enjoyable aspects of my job is sitting down in front of the latest version of Adobe Illustrator, and spending an hour or two coloring a Sunday strip. Any art program worth its salt will give you a pallet of fixed colors, as well as let you build your own mixtures out of red, blue and yellow screens (okay, magenta, cyan, and yellow, if you want to get technical). When you're starting out, it's a good idea to keep a record of every color you use, so you know whether or not it works in the final 'toon. In other words, will you need to lighten it or darken it the next time around? In the newspapers, for example, I've found that a Caucasian flesh tone works best by building it out of 7% red, 7% yellow and 0% blue. On Netscape, 10%, 10% and 0% works better. And you don't even WANT to know how long it took me to settle on 10% blue, 20% red and 40% yellow for Carson's fur.

(Very) Odds and Ends

We haven't even started to touch on the multimedia aspects of electronic comic-book publishing, yet. Of course, if we want to explore adding sound and animation to your comic, that would be a whole new book. However, if you've got a soundcard and even a simple animation program, there's no end to what you can do. All you have to figure out is where the line between a Comic Book ends and a Saturday Morning Cartoon begins.

Even if you're a purist (like me), and want a comic book that's a Platonic Ideal of what a Comic Book (note the capital letters—that means I took a philosophy class in college) should be, you can still get full use out of the medium you're using. For example, if you have the time (and the memory space, and lots of free Web pages just to cater to your every whim), creating an interactive plot line is easy.

An *interactive* plot line, however, allows the reader to choose what direction the story takes. The simplest of these can be quite straightforward; for example, instead of letting Carson get hit with, say, a brick, we can give the reader other options to choose from.

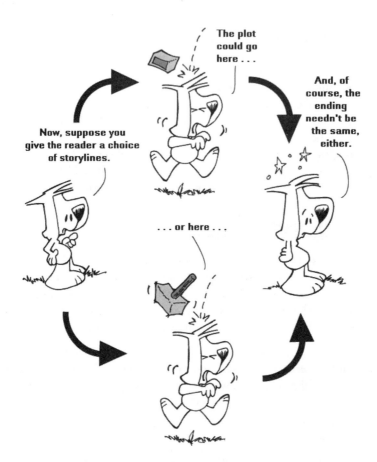

Obviously, you can play fast and loose with the format, supplying alternate endings, alternate events, even alternate characters. In a sense, the work becomes like one big game of "Myst" (minus the point where you pull your hair out), with the reader able to explore the various venues you've created and plotted. The main difference between an interactive comic and a game is that the random events have been removed: The creator, for the most part, is still in charge of the plot, even though a myriad of plots may be available.

Instead of creating three Web pages for the linear plot where Carson is hit by a brick, we simply build a fourth (where he's hit by a hammer) for the interactive version. As long as you map out your plot lines so that *you* know where each one leads, you shouldn't get too confused, either.

Hands-On Example 6

"The Madness of Roland" (HyperBole) was one of the earliest interactive novels to come out on CD-ROM, and it's still one of the best. While creating a unique work of art, the author, Greg Roach, lets the reader take an active part in the storytelling process.

The pitfalls are obvious: Interactivity, no matter how smoothly you get it to flow, can still break the illusion that what the reader is watching is real (yes, even in the comics). How climactic would the finale of *Star Wars*™ have been if Luke jettisoned the bomb, and the audience saw a screen come up that said "Press "A" for the Death Star to be destroyed. Press "B" for the bomb to fail. Press "C" for...." You get the picture. Or rather, the lack of picture, since you're now having to spend time deciding what you want the Movie to do, instead of being entertained by it.

Like color and detail, interactivity and multimedia are options you should explore only if you think your work really needs them.

So Where Do We Go From Here?

Copies of *Teach Yourself Web Publishing with HTML in a Week* by Laura Lemay (Sams Publishing, and *Teach Yourself More Web Publishing with HTML in a Week*, by Laura Lemay (published by sams.net) won't hurt. But it's time for you to grapple with more than that.

So far, this chapter addressed "want-to-be" comic artists, and established comic artists ready for electronic publishing. At this point, you understand what a comic is and isn't. You know how to create a comic, and how to generate computer file images of the comic. Now you can make the transition from paper to electronic media.

The next step is to choose an application software package. This decision depends on your technical expertise, the complexity of the application, and your personal likes and dislikes. Non-technical developers will find it easier to use presentation software or page viewers. The adventurous will want to consider authoring software for more control and sophistication.

Selecting the Application Software

The following is a condensed list of application software. Chapter 5, "Application Tools," and Appendix C, "HTML Commands and Resources," of this book describe more publishing software. The following selections are food for thought. They are programs I have worked with. They present different methods for creating an electronic comic book.

I've divided the application software into four categories: Presentation, Markup Multimedia Authoring, Visual Multimedia Authoring, and Page Viewers.

Presentation

Presentation programs provide one of the simplest solutions to creating an electronic comic book. Two examples are Astound by Gold Disk, and Super Show and Tell by Midisoft. These are multimedia slideshow tools. Think of them as overhead transparencies that move and talk. Typical applications include corporate presentations, multimedia resumes, sales promotions, and so on.

The advantage to these programs is that they are fairly easy, and quick to use. They work well with multimedia elements.

The disadvantage is that presentation programs are geared toward presentation, not publishing. They are excellent programs for their intended applications, and a viable alternative for publishing an electronic comic book.

Markup Multimedia Authoring

Authoring languages such as HTML (HyperText Markup Language) for the World Wide Web, or Multimedia Viewer by Microsoft provide an interesting option for creating an electronic comic book. They are interesting because they're text-based systems versus the visual type development programs. HTML addresses Internet publishing, and Multimedia Viewer addresses CD-ROM publishing.

Advantages to using a markup language include the open authoring environment and the ability to automate markup. An open environment allows developers to use various alternate tools for creating applications. Examples of these tools are text editors, word macros, database management software, graphic programs, and so forth.

It's also possible to speed up and automate the process with markup languages. Manage the information in a database to automate the markup process, or use word macros to generate the markup. Methods for automating markup, by using a database, include reports and merge. Use the database reports to generate marked up text files, or use the database files with word merges to create a marked up document. Methods for using word macros include find, copy, and paste. Used effectively, the macros will greatly reduce markup time.

Markup languages, typically HTML and SGML (Standard General Markup Language), also operate across many computer platforms (DOS, Windows, Macintosh, UNIX, and so on). HTML is the language used with documents on the Internet's World Wide Web. One file is readable on many computer types. SGML is used in the high-end electronic publishing industry. Multimedia Viewer provides for publishing on CD-ROM.

The disadvantage of straight markup languages is that they aren't a WYSIWIG (What You See Is What You Get) visual environment. They are text environments so the text may appear formatted, but the graphics appear as lines of code.

Visual Multimedia Authoring

Authoring tools like Multimedia Toolbook by Asymetric, or Director by Macromedia provide a visual environment (WYSIWYG) for development. They use a script language for controlling events. Scripting is similar to a macro language and programming language.

The major advantage with these tools is the WYSIWYG environment. This allows you to see the media you're working with. Keep in mind that not all screens are alike though. A well-placed image in a screen with resolution settings of 1024×768 might not look so good on a

640×480 screen. The image might not even fit. A comic strip frame might look good spanned across two pages, but it won't look the same on a scrolling screen.

WYSIWYG environments have a slight disadvantage with their proprietary interface. This makes it difficult to automate the development process the way you can with a markup language. These programs are typically self-contained authoring environments.

Page Viewers

Common Ground by Common Ground Software, or Acrobat by Adobe provide the simplest solution to creating an electronic comic book. These programs are page viewing tools, not authoring programs or multimedia tools.

The biggest advantage with these programs is simplicity. Pages are generated using almost any software then printed to a special file format. It's sort of like saving the file to disk, but instead it's printed to disk. Hyperlinks are added to the pages with special viewing software included with the development software.

Simplicity is also a disadvantage. These are page viewers, not authoring programs. They're intended for the easy distribution and printing of information.

Presentation Software in Action

I found it difficult to choose a presentation program to write about. You can pick from a variety of presentation programs. I choose Gold Disk's Astound because I have used it and am familiar with it. It's also a very good program. You may choose another program, such as the newest version of Super Show and Tell and adapt the following exercise accordingly.

Presentation programs are addictive. They're fairly easy to use, and fun to work with. The programs interface well with graphics, animation, audio, and video. They are effective for displaying limited amounts of text.

Initially, I hesitated to categorize presentation programs with electronic publishing. In the 80s I associated paper and text with publishing and desktop publishing. Now I associate information with publishing. Information takes the form of text, graphics, audio, animation, and video. The publishing industry is in the midst of a paradigm shift; we have to recognize how publishing is changing.

The following steps are brief. They outline the basics behind creating a very simple electronic comic book. Astound is fairly simple to use. It's best learned by doing and experimenting.

An Overview of the Process

Here is an overview of the steps for creating a simple electronic comic book.

1. Start the program and create a new presentation with no template.

2. Add a background by selecting Background under the Slide menu, and then choosing a background type. Figure 30.2 shows the menu selections, and optional background types: None, Solid Color, Pattern, Gradient, Picture, or Texture.

FIGURE 30.2.

Adding a background as a starting point.

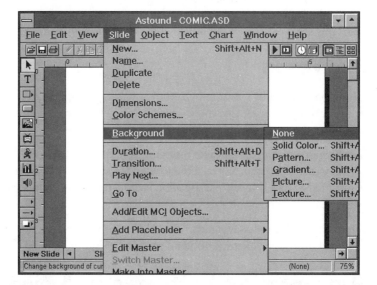

3. Add comic frames to the slide by selecting the Picture button (the mountain top button on the left), or Import under the file menu.

   Complete the screen prompts.

4. Optional: Add a caption to the frame by selecting the Text button, typing the caption, formatting the text, then positioning it on the screen. An advantage to adding text this way is that later on, you can easily edit the text without editing the picture.

5. Add navigation buttons by selecting the Button tool (It's on the left side of screen, and looks like a button) then click and drag a button on the screen.

   Type in a button name.

   Figure 30.3 shows what a screen would look like with one imported picture and two interactive navigation buttons (Next and Previous).

> **NOTE**
>
> Users may wish to overlay text on the picture. This is an option to drawing text in the picture image. The advantage is that its easier to edited text than redrawing images.

6. Add interaction to the on-screen button by selecting the button you wish to add interaction to, then selecting Interaction under the Object menu.

   Select a flow control option to go to a specific slide, the next slide, a previous slide, and so on.

FIGURE 30.3.

Screen with image and buttons.

7. Add more slides (or pages) by selecting New under the Slide menu.

8. Repeat steps 2 through 7 to add other backgrounds, and more comic frame images.

9. Save your application by selecting Save as under the file menu. Several options are available for distributing an application. One of the options provides for creating a self -running application.

CAUTION

Don't go overboard with your project.

You'll find it easy to go overboard using multimedia with presentation programs. Be careful. Tempting options are available to create glitzy transitions, image movement, audio enhancements, animation, interactive choices, and so on.

Remember, we're discussing comic books not cartoons. Animation is a subject on its own.

A Final Word on Presentations

The steps above don't do justice to what you can do with Astound. They only touch the surface. My emphasis is in showing the simplicity in developing an application. There is much more you can do with interaction, and the multimedia elements. Just don't forget where a comic book leaves off, and a cartoon takes over.

Markup Multimedia Authoring

Try Multimedia Viewer if you'd like to experiment with markup authoring, and want to distribute on CD-ROM. It's very much like Microsoft Windows Help, except that it includes full text search, more color (8 bit versus 4 bit), multimedia capabilities, and a few other bells and whistles.

Multimedia Viewer's topic editor integrates with Word for Windows as an authoring tool. On a scale of 1 to 10, Viewer ranks about 5 for difficulty. Run time files, for distributing titles, are royalty free.

The authoring environment is especially open to special development tools. The markup file is a RTF (Rich Text Formatted) file. The RTF file is generated from Word for Window or as text from any text generating tool. A text generating tool is any database system, spread sheet, word processor, macro language, or other tool that is capable of saving a text file.

An Overview of the Process

Developing a Multimedia Viewer title consists of three parts: defining the project, editing the topics, and then compiling the project.

Defining the Project

Here are the steps you should take to define the project.

1. Open the Multimedia Viewer project editor. Figure 30.4 shows the project editor screen.

FIGURE 30.4.

The Project Editor defines the filetype and properties.

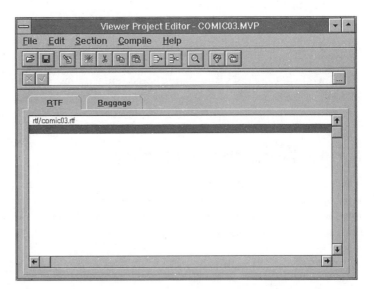

2. Define the window areas by selecting Window definitions from the Section menu. Then select new windows and panes to reflect the following figures.

   Figure 30.5 shows window properties for the "main" screen. This defines the overall window for a Multimedia Viewer title. Experiment with the settings.

FIGURE 30.5.

Define windows with the Window Properties screen.

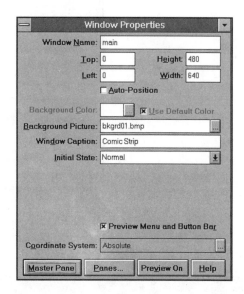

Top and Left define the window starting point from the upper-left corner of your screen. Height and Width define the size of the Viewer screen. The 640×480 size is chosen for simplicity. That way you don't have to worry about fitting images on alternate screen resolutions.

Choosing a background picture is optional. Background pictures are displayed behind the master panes.

Window Caption text is displayed on the window top.

The Absolute Coordinate Systems is checked here for simplicity. With Absolute setting, the window panes are placed in fixed positions. Relative coordinates will position window panes relative to the current screen resolution. Relative is good for full screen displays (that way you don't get that small 640×480 window in a 1024×768 display), but it's also slightly more confusing.

3. Select the Master Pane Button and make the following changes: (We're doing something unusual here to hide the master pane. It will be replaced with a regular pane for cosmetic reasons.) Figure 30.6 shows the master pane properties screen.

   Top and Left are the upper-left corner coordinates for the starting point of the master pane.

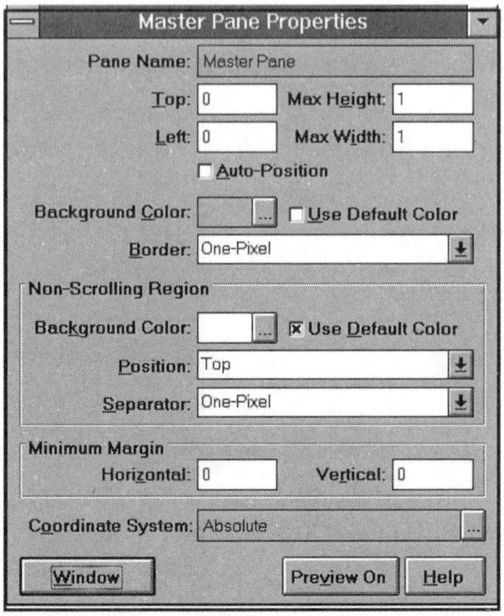

FIGURE 30.6.

*Settings for the Master pane
properties.*

For this example, I chose a Max Width and Height of 1 because I wanted to hide the main window pane. There were cosmetic reasons for this, but that has to do with advanced topics on how window panes act.

> **NOTE**
>
> Remember to make the pane slightly smaller if you want a background picture to show. In this case, we're actually hiding the panes, so we're not concerned.

Light Gray is the selected background color, so it blends into the screen. Another method of hiding things.

The Coordinate System was to Absolute to stay consistent with the window.

4. Define a regular window pane by selecting Window definitions under the Section menu.

Select Panes in the window definitions screen, then New, and then Properties. Figure 30.7 shows the regular pane properties screen.

Top and Left are again the starting point for the upper-left corner of the pane.

Be sure to size the maximum height and width so that your largest image and text fit into the pane (images must be `.bmp` or `.wmf` for Multimedia Viewer). This example uses 350×300 for maximum because the largest image was about that size.

Light Gray was selected for Background color, and None for Border so the panes blends into the background.

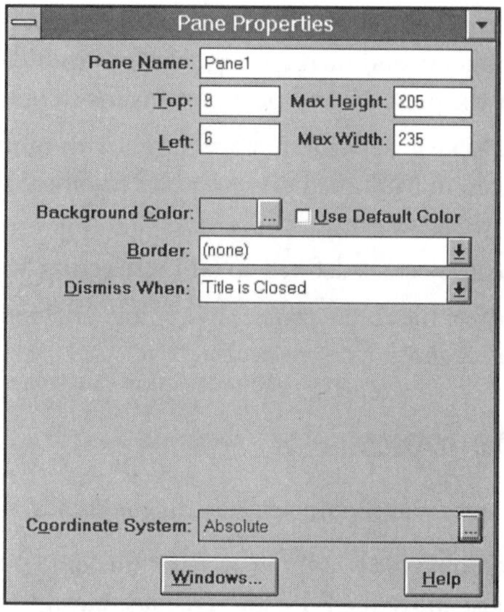

FIGURE 30.7.

Regular pane properties.

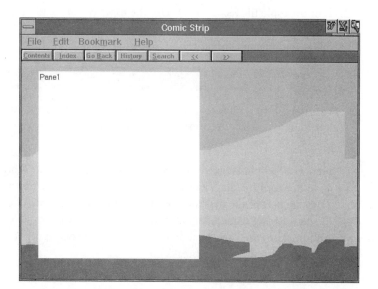

Dismiss When is set to Title is Closed so the panes is visible until we want it to go away.

Coordinate System is set to Absolute to be consistent with other window elements.

This pane is related to the Main Window, so it must be linked to it through the Windows setting.

Figure 30.8 shows what a title screen looks like after the above setting were implemented. This is the Main window, with a hidden Master pane, and a Regular pane displayed.

FIGURE 30.8.

Sample of window with regular pane.

5. Define a group for sequencing the comic frames by selecting Groups under the Section menu, and then define a new group such as group1. Group sequences will activate the previous and next buttons for stepping from page to page.

    Use multiple groups for an application with multi-directional branching. Browse sequences, in Multimedia Viewer, are numbered sequences assigned to the next (>>) and previous buttons (<<).

6. Save the project, as defined so far by selecting Save as from the File menu.

7. Add a topic file to the project by typing a filename, such as comic.rtf, in the text box, then select check mark to accept.

Editing the Topics

Here are the steps you should take to edit the topics.

1. Create a topic file by typing an RTF filename, such as comic.rtf, in browse box. (The box is just above the RTF and Baggage tabs.)

    Press Enter key to accept the filename.

    Double-click your mouse on the select the filename (under the RTF tab window), or select the filename under the Edit menu. This will launch Word for Windows.

> **NOTE**
>
> For Word to launch, be sure the Preferences under Edit menu have a path defined to Word for Windows.

2. Edit the topic file (comic.rtf). Use the topic editor to add topic titles ($), Context strings (#), Topic-entry (!) commands, and Topic Groups (+), or type a sequence of marks and macros similar to the following.

> **NOTE**
>
> The Topic Editor is engaged with a control function. The function is set in the Project Editor Preferences section under Edit along with the path to Word for Windows.

Here is a Sample Word for Windows document with the Word document markup codes for Multimedia Viewer. Don't be confused by the footnote symbols ($#!+). They are part of the markup method for identifying topics, defining keywords indexes, setting sequencing, and so on. Note that the actual text is in the footnote section. Also, the PageBreak lines are for reference purposes only; they indicate where Word for Windows page breaks go.

```
$#!+ Any text.

--------------------------------PageBreak---------------------------------

# {ewc MVBMP2, ViewerBmp2, [caption="\pc;b\cf0;0;0\cb192;192;192Hi Guy!
How you doing?" dither]!comic01.bmp}

--------------------------------PageBreak---------------------------------

$#!+ Any text.

--------------------------------PageBreak---------------------------------

# {ewc MVBMP2, ViewerBmp2, [caption="\pc;b\cf0;0;0\cb192;192;192I'm doing
fine." dither]!comic01.bmp}
----Footnotes for the above footnote symbols $#!+----
$ 1a
# 1a
! PaneID(qchPath, '1b>Pane1', 40)
+ Group1:110
# 1b
$ 2a
# 2a
! PaneID(qchPath, '2b>Pane1', 40)
+ Group1:120
# 2b
```

3. Save the file as an .rtf file by selecting Save as under the File menu, and then making sure the file type is rtf. (Note that the Viewer editors are optimized for Word for Windows version 2.0. Word for Windows 6.0 requires special handling.)

Compile the Project

Complete the title by following these steps:

1. Close the topic file in Word for Windows. Word files can't be open during the compiling process.
2. Save the project file one last time.
3. Select Build under the Compile menu.
4. Choose the Run command from the File menu. Figure 30.9 shows the finished title.

NOTE

As an optional step, you can edit the configuration script under the Section menu to customize the control buttons. This changes the << and >> buttons to say Previous and Next. The following code shows how to do this.

Sample Configuration Script

```
DestroyButton('btn_previous')
DestroyButton('btn_next')
CreateButton('btn_previous', '&Previous Frame', 'Prev()')
CreateButton('btn_next', '&NextFrame', 'Next()')
```

FIGURE 30.9.
Running the finished title.

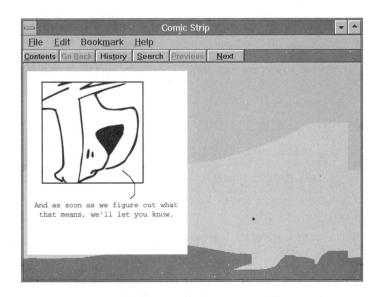

Use a Database to Generate Markup

The initial work, for creating a Multimedia Viewer title, is in the planning and design. Planning is often a major portion of the work. The actual markup is fairly labor intensive, but much of the markup process can be automated after the planning work is completed. This is where a database tool will come in handy.

A database driven project offers several advantages over a project managed by screen pages, flow charts, or mental notes. The advantages are automation, consistency, and very clean markup code with little, if any error.

The following table, database structure, shows how a series of topics is organized. The table is used with Word for Windows merge to create a complete topic file. You'll appreciate the benefit, to using a database, when a project includes several hundred images.

Table 30.1. Sample database structure.

Topic	Image	Caption	Sequence
1	comic01	Hi Guy! How you doing?	Group1:110
2	comic02	I'm fine!	Group1:120
3	comic03	Want to swim in the lake?	Group1:130

Use Word Merge to Generate Markup

Here is a sample of how a Word for Windows merge file might look. This example was used to create the topic file (comic.rtf) described above. It merges data from the data table described above.

This is a sample Word for Windows Merge Document.

```
-----------------------------Body of Document-----------------------------

$#!+fiImagefi
------------------------------------PageBreak------------------------------------

#{ewc MVBMP2, ViewerBmp2, [caption="\pc;b\cf0;0;0\cb192;192;192fiCaptionfi"
dither]!fiImagefi.bmp}

-----------------------------Footnote Section-----------------------------

$ fiTopicfia
# fiTopicfia
! PaneID(qchPath, 'fiTopicfib>PanefiUsePanefi', 40)
+ fiSequencefi
# fiTopicfib
```

Visual Multimedia Authoring

The following steps outline an extremely simple Multimedia Toolbook comic book example. Programs such as Toolbook have far greater power than this example shows. The point to understand is that users don't have to understand the advanced features to build a viable application.

An Overview of the Process

The following procedure provides an overview of the authoring process:

1. Create a new Toolbook file by running Multimedia Toolbook from Program Manager, and then selecting New from the Toolbook file menu. Figure 30.10 shows a blank screen, with the Tool Palette, ready to begin a new project.

2. Add a background, if you wish by selecting Background from the View menu.

   Select Import Graphic from the File menu. Then find your background image in the Import Graphic screen. Figure 30.11 shows a background view with a background image added. It's a basic stripped background that simply breaks up the otherwise solid color background.

3. Add the first comic image by selecting Foreground from the View menu. (Foreground and Background selections interchange with each other in the menu list depending on the current view.)

FIGURE 30.10.
The design screen and Tool Palette.

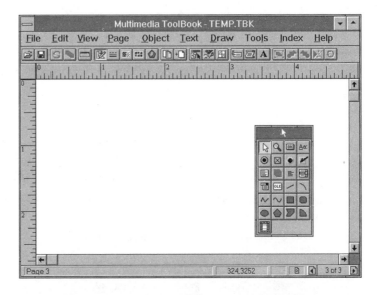

FIGURE 30.11.
Background view.

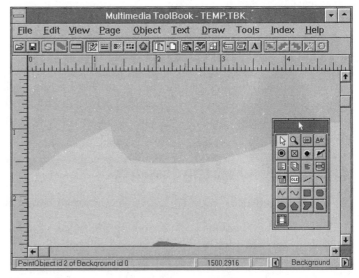

Select Import Graphic from the File menu. Then find your comic image in the Import Graphic screen. Figure 30.12 show the page view of the first page with a comic image added.

FIGURE 30.12.

Foreground view.

4. Add control buttons by selecting Pushbutton from the Tool Palette. (Turn on the Tool Palette from the toolbar.)

   Click and drag a button onto your screen.

   Right-click the button to change the caption.

   Select the Auto script button to add action to the button, such as go to next page, or go to previous page.

   For more control, select hyperlink after right-clicking a button. Set link to one way or two way, and then edit the script to set link to the page ID you want the link to. Find the page ID by going to the page, and then select Page Properties from Object menu.

5. Add additional Toolbook pages with comic frames by selecting New pages from the Object menu, and then repeat steps 3 through 4.

6. Save the project by selecting Save As, or Save As Exe from the File menu. Save as creates a .tbk (toolbook) file which requires Toolbook to execute. Save As Exe creates a stand-alone executable file for distribution to people that don't own Toolbook. A finished page is shown in Figure 30.13.

FIGURE 30.13.

Page with interactive buttons.

Multi-Directional Branching

Some comic books provide alternate directions in the story line. The reader chooses a route to alternate endings. One route might be happy, while the other is sad.

Each of the development tools, described in this chapter, provide interaction and the ability to branch. Multimedia authoring tools with scripting languages, like Toolbook, provide even greater interactive options.

Scripting languages provide both interactive selective branching, and logical branching. Selective branching might be a simple button that goes to a particular page. Logical branching might be a series of pages that are presented as a result of reader defined settings.

I cautioned earlier about going overboard with multimedia. Here I would advise considering the electronic advantage by exploring interaction and branching capabilities of electronic publishing.

Final Remark on Visual Authoring

Visual multimedia authoring programs are extremely powerful tools. A novice can develop a basic application, yet an advanced programmer can create a very sophisticated program. The novice shouldn't be scared off by the authoring script (sort of like programming commands).

Page Viewer

Page viewing programs are made for distributing information, be it text or graphics. Adobe Acrobat creates portable files, Common Ground creates digital paper files. In either case, the process for creating them is as simple as printing a file. In fact, that's exactly what you do from your favorite application—print a file.

An Overview of the Process

Here is the procedure for creating portable files.

1. Print your completed comic frames, or pages, from your favorite application by using the printer setup for Common Ground Maker on Disk. Figure 30.14 shows the Windows printer setup screen with Common Ground in the printers list.

FIGURE 30.14.

Common Ground in the printer selection setting.

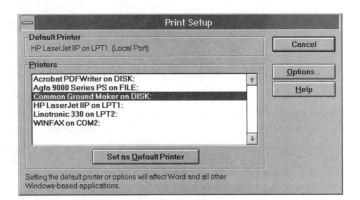

NOTE

Keep in mind that Common Ground is for viewing and printing, not editing. The comic frames, or pages, must be completed before printing to the Common Ground Disk format.

2. Start the Common Ground ProViewer.
3. Open the first frame in your comic book by selecting Open under the File menu.
4. Insert additional comic frames by selecting Pages under the Edit menu, and then inserting the .dp pages created in step 1.
5. Add additional frames by repeating step 3. Add the frame images in the order you want them presented.

6. Save the document by selecting Save as under the File menu, and choosing a new filename. Consider the option for creating a self executing .exe document. This enables users to view your document without installing it. The self-executing feature only adds a little over 250KB to the file.

7. Options for navigating include Create a table of contents and Add hyperlinks, highlights, or bookmarks. The options are access through the button bar, and the Tools menu selections.

   A standard scrollbar, in the Common Ground screen, provides for basic navigation between pages in a document. I suggest adding a table of contents, or other links to navigate between pages. This will make more sense to the end user. Figure 30.15 shows the Common Ground files after bookmarks have been added.

FIGURE 30.15.

View with bookmark list.

Using Multimedia and Other Things

I discussed multimedia with John Kovalic, comic artist and co-author of this chapter on comic books. We came to similar conclusions about using multimedia in comics. Too much multimedia could turn the comic book into a cartoon, overshadow the comic, or simply be a distraction. You'll have to judge for yourself.

More on Multimedia

If you're interested in exploring multimedia, consider buying *Multimedia Madness* by Ron Wodaski (Sams Publishing).

The book reviews multimedia topics (graphics, audio, video, animation), multimedia software & hardware, and just about everything else you'd want to know about multimedia.

Customized Fonts

You can choose from any of the thousands of font typefaces on the market. I half recall seeing a TrueType font called comic. Several libraries and programs are available for those wanting to purchase, modify, or create their own fonts. The Font Company sells libraries of fonts, and Ares Software Corporation sells tools for editing or creating fonts.

Some of the advantages with electronic publishing, over paper, are the choices. There are thousands of font typefaces to choose from, but there are also many ways to implement fonts. Electronic publishing allows you to make text a part of the graphic, a segment within the graphic, overlayed on the graphic, or simply a display heading. Simply put, you don't have to use *white out* and re-draw anymore.

PhotoCD and Portfolio CD

Check into Kodak's Portfolio CD for another interesting way to create a comic book on CD-ROM. The development programs for creating Portfolio CDs use PhotoCD images, add user interactions, and will operate on TVs, PCs, and Macintoshes.

Place It on the WWW

Check out *Teach Yourself Web Publishing with HTML in a Week* by Laura Lemay (Sams Publishing) and *Teach Yourself More Web Publishing with HTML in a Week*, by Laura Lemay (published by sams.net).

These books step you through the process of writing HTML for Web pages, and placing them on the Web.

Summary

Give it a try, go ahead and complain, but don't give up. I'll attest to the fact that complaining is a part of the learning process. I've reviewed software for the past three years, and my normal first reaction is to complain about how the software works. After that, I realize I'm learning.

Choose the software that works best for you. Work should be fun (especially with comic books), so choose the software that makes it fun for you. Page Viewers are the quickest to use and easiest to learn. Presentation programs are the next easiest to learn and perhaps the most fun to use. Authoring programs are more difficult to use, but the added features make them my first choice. Markup multimedia authoring is very interesting because of the environment; it enables you to automate the development process.

Keep in mind, the sequence of comic frames does not have to be linear. Use the interactive capabilities of electronic publishing to enable users to control their destiny. Use links and jumps for branching and non-linear movement. Most publishing programs implement hypertext or hypergraphic links and jumps.

Take advantage of the media. For example, separate the word caption from the comic image. Overlay the caption on the image. This way you can easily modify the caption, without modifying the image. Alternately, generate your graphics with vector drawing programs. That way you can edit any portion of the image later on.

For markup languages, learn to use macros. This speeds up the process of marking documents. Macros also help to write consistent, error-free markup. Use macros to find styles and add markups. Find words, then copy and paste with markup. Use your imagination, and explore the options.

Now do it! Experiment with the steps outlined in this chapter. Use them as guidelines, not as assembly instructions. You'll learn more by doing and experimenting.

PART

VI

Implementation

Testing and Proofing the Publication

31

by William R. Stanek

IN THIS CHAPTER

You have written a book, newsletter, magazine, or other collective work and created an electronic version of it. The document resides on your hard drive, waiting to be published for all the world to see. Getting to this stage in the publishing process has taken many days or weeks. The urge to slap the finished work onto a few hundred disks is almost overpowering, but a voice in the back of your mind keeps you from publishing the document and whisking it out to the world.

You have not worked this hard to fail simply because you didn't proof and test the publication. Ensuring the quality of the project will take only a few hours. That is a small price to pay to ensure the project is the best it can be, especially considering you might have spent hundreds of hours writing and creating the publication. Producing a high-quality product will also help you build credibility. Your credibility as a publisher is a key to your success.

This chapter explores the steps you should take as the publisher to proof and test the publication. You will learn

- What to look for when proofing
- Tips for spell checking the publication
- Tips for grammar checking the publication
- How to catch typos outside the main text
- What to look for when testing
- How to catch inconsistencies
- How to balance the need for perfection with efficiency and timeliness

> **NOTE**
>
> The emphasis in this chapter is on publisher-proofing and testing of electronic publications for CD-ROM and floppy disk. However, you can apply the concepts discussed here to proofing and testing Web publications as well. After all, you should check for spelling and grammar mistakes, look for typos, and inconsistencies, and balance efficiency and timeliness in any electronic publication. User-testing of publications will be discussed in Chapter 32, "User-Testing Your Publication."

What To Look For When Proofing

When you proof something, you are checking the final copy to ensure it is error-free. In the old days, proofing meant there was an ominous stack of freshly typed pages sitting on your desktop. The thicker the stack of pages, the more ominous the proofing process seemed. You hunkered down over your desk with a dozen red pens and toiled for countless hours.

A few days or weeks later those pages no longer looked fresh. They were splattered with red ink from end to end—a dozen or more different proofing symbols you scratched onto the pages. If you were fortunate enough to be the publisher, you could send the work back to the writer. If you were both publisher and writer, you dusted off the typewriter and went to work.

Today, many creative projects will never see the printed page before they are published in finished form. The easily manipulated form of the project in a word processing file make it all too easy to revise online. This is fine most of the time. There is no point in wasting paper printing a publication that will never be seen in printed form. However, in the age of the computerized spelling and grammar checkers, some people even neglect to read their own words for accuracy and consistency. Their editing and proofing process consists entirely of two steps: spell checking and grammar checking. They rely on the spell checker to find their typos and on the grammar checker to catch the remaining mistakes.

Good writers know that no matter what percentage of the errors spelling and grammar checkers claim to find, the critical mistakes will be found only through careful proofing. For example, your spelling checker won't find any of the errors in the following sentences:

The whether outside was sunny and did not altar our plans.

He wade each claws and decided three were knot kneaded.

Who wood have guest what he mite dew.

Not being able to urn a wage is know miner issue.

My spelling checker went through those sentences in less than a second and reported no errors at all. This is because spell checkers do not care if you use the wrong words. They only check for valid words. If a word is valid, they will pass it by.

I decided it might be fun to run the same sentences through my grammar checker. After all, it claims to find 97 percent of the errors I will ever make. Following the advice of the grammar checker, I blindly revised. Each time the grammar checker made a suggestion, I followed it. Here is how the revision progressed, until the grammar checker claimed the paragraph had no errors:

Sentence 1

Original	The whether outside was sunny and did not altar our plans.
Revised	Whether outside was sunny and did not altar our plans.
Revised	Whether outside was sunny, did not altar our plans.
Final	Whether outside was sunny, did not alter our plans.

Sentence 2

Original	He wade each claws and decided three were knot kneaded.
Revised	He wade each claw and decided three were knot kneaded.

Revised	He wades each claw and decided three were knot kneaded.
Revised	He waded each claw and decided three were knot kneaded.
Final	He waded each claw and decided three were not kneaded.

Sentence 3

Original	Who wood have guest what he mite dew.
Revised	Who wood have guested what he mite dew.
Revised	Who woods have guested what he mite dew.
Final	Whom woods have guested what he mite dew.

Sentence 4

Original	Not being able to urn a wage is know miner issue.
Revised	Not could urn a wage is know miner issue.
Final	Not could earn a wage is know miner issue.

Although the results are comical, the truth is not. Grammar checkers follow rules outlined in their programming. The suggestions they offer are also in the programming. Unless someone produces an artificially intelligent grammar-checking program, computer software won't replace the human mind for its ability to reliably check the written word.

Use spelling and grammar checkers to find the tedious errors; the typos or grammar mistakes you made because you were tired, didn't want to break the creative process by reaching for the dictionary, or otherwise. Even though the critical mistakes are up to you to find, you do not have to do so blindly. There are many tips for finding spelling and grammar errors that will save you time and frustration.

Tips for Checking Spelling

Some books on the subject of writing and editing stress the importance of learning the correct spelling of words. They provide dozens of tips and tricks for remembering the spelling of words, stating rules such as "i before e except after c." They provide long lists of commonly misspelled words and advise you to watch out for them. Although spelling is important, it is not so important that it should keep you from creating anything.

To find the common mistakes use a spelling checker. A spelling checker may also be able to help you find inconsistently spelled technical terms. Most word processors include a spelling checker. Remember, the accuracy of the spelling will only be as good as the checker's database of words. Some spelling checkers boast 80,000 to 100,000 word dictionaries. Others have relatively few words. If your spelling checker does not recognize a word, you should consult a dictionary.

TIP

The best dictionary for an electronic publisher is an unabridged dictionary, especially if a spelling checker that has a dictionary of 80,000 or more words is telling you it does not recognize a word. You can find print versions and electronic versions of un-abridged dictionaries.

Unabridged dictionaries often contain a wealth of resources. For example, *Webster's Encyclopedic Unabridged Dictionary of the English Language*, distributed by Crown Publishing Group, is a one-stop resource for spelling and grammar. In addition to over 250,000 words, it contains

- An atlas of the world
- A brief chronology of history
- Important U.S. data from the Constitution to the Declaration of Independence
- A manual of style; rules for grammar
- A bad speller's dictionary
- An abbreviated French-English and English-French dictionary
- An abbreviated German-English and English-German dictionary
- An abbreviated Italian-English and English-Italian dictionary
- An abbreviated Spanish-English and English-Spanish dictionary
- A crossword puzzle dictionary

TIP

After the spelling checker has completed the chore of cleaning up most of the text, you should proof the text and look for incorrect word usage. The primary source of incorrect words will come from words that look alike or sound alike but have different meanings. A grammar checker will catch the commonly confused words if they are used improperly in a sentence. However, if the word seems to be used properly in the sentence, a grammar checker won't find the incorrect word.

Studies have shown that certain words cause more confusion than others. The common ones like set/sit and lay/lie a grammar checker will usually catch. The grammar checker finds errors associated with these words by looking mostly for direct or indirect objects that should accompany these words. Here is a list of commonly confused words that your grammar checker might not catch:

accede	exceed
accept	except
access	excess

adept	adopt	
advice	advise	
affect	effect	
affluent	effluent	
attributed	contributed	
block	Bloc	
cite	sight	site
complement	compliment	
compose	comprise	
confuse	complicate	
demolish	destroy	
describe	prescribe	
discreet	discrete	
elicit	illicit	
eminent	immanent	imminent
faze	phase	
fliers	flyers	
flout	flaunt	
forward	foreword	
imply	infer	
leave	let	
Marshall	marshal	
mean	average	median
moral	morale	
peddle	pedal	
personal	personnel	
precede	proceed	
principal	principle	
quiet	quite	
regulate	relegate	
residence	residents	
respectfully	respectively	
role	roll	
stationary	stationery	
whether	weather	

A good resource to consult for incorrect words is a bad speller's dictionary. The typical bad speller's dictionary will have lists of look-alikes and sound-alikes. Lists will contain pairs of words that can be quickly searched. Each word in the list will have a brief description. Usually, the description is one or two words, which makes the dictionary small and easy to search. Here is an example:

Exercise: practice	Exorcise: drive away evil spirits
Veracity: truth	Voracity: hunger

TIP

If you are looking for interactive resources online, one place to look is the Writer's Gallery. The Writer's Gallery Web site contains a resource listing for reference works available on the Internet. You can find the Writer's Gallery on the Web at

```
http://tvp.com/vpwg.html
```

Some of the listings available include the following:

American English Dictionary

Bartlett's Familiar Quotations

CIA World Factbook

Encyclopedia Britannica

Grammar and style guides

Grolier's Encyclopedia

Handbook of Poetry Terms

Roget's Thesaurus

Webster's Dictionary

World Factbook

Worldwide telephone codes

Tips for Checking Grammar

The English language is one of the most difficult languages on the planet. It is no surprise that English grammar is the most troublesome area of writing. When you write, you have to worry about subject and verb agreement, predicates, punctuation, and more. If you spend too much time worrying about grammar, you probably will get writer's block. As you write, you should concentrate on the creative processes and not editing and proofing processes.

To find the common mistakes use a grammar checker. The best word processors include grammar checkers, but you might have to purchase one separately. Remember, grammar checkers are only as good as the rules they use as the basis for the checking. You can usually follow rule templates based on the style of writing you are working on, such as fiction, nonfiction, or technical. A grammar template for a fiction work will have a set of rules that normally apply to fiction writing.

Grammar checkers will let you customize the rules any way you want. You can turn off rules permanently or only for the session you are currently working on. The more rules you turn off, the lower the efficiency of the check. If you turn off too many rules the grammar checker will be useless. Usually, it is best to follow the grammar templates set up by the experts who created the software. This means if you are working on a general nonfiction work, select the grammar template that applies to general nonfiction.

Although most grammar checkers will also check the spelling of the document, this is often the slowest way to correct typos. Spelling checkers are designed to check spelling quickly and efficiently. Grammar checkers are designed to check grammar quickly and efficiently. Often, the spell checking features of a grammar checker are designed by default. The grammar checking engine needs a database of words and the hierarchy used by spelling checkers is a good way to provide this database.

NOTE

Good resources to consult for grammar questions are style manuals. Styles manuals are the best sources to turn to for grammar, capitalization, and punctuation issues. *The Little Brown Book* by Little Brown and Company is a comprehensive English grammar reference. For technical works, the *Publication Manual of the American Psychological Association*, currently in its fourth edition, is terrific. The *MLA Handbook for Writers of Research Papers* is another good reference.

Styles manuals are also the best sources to turn to for formatting questions. They can answer your questions pertaining to the use of lists, tables, figures, footnotes, equations, and citations. My personal preference out of the many style manuals available is the APA manual mentioned above. The APA manual spells out every point about format clearly and in great detail.

After the grammar checker has found most of your mistakes, follow through by carefully reading the publication. The biggest problem areas are

- Determining the proper case
- Subject-verb agreement
- Noun-pronoun agreement
- Dangling modifiers
- Predicates

Determining the Proper Case

Determining the proper case for pronouns is a common problem area. The *case* of a word refers to the way the word is used in a sentence. There are four cases: nominative, possessive, objective, and reflexive. *Nominative* pronouns are the subject of a clause. *Possessive* pronouns show who or what something belongs to. *Objective* pronouns are objects of verbs or prepositions. *Reflexive* pronouns refer to a noun or pronoun that has already appeared in the sentence. Table 31.1 shows the case for pronouns.

Table 31.1. A guide to correct pronoun case and form.

Pronoun Case	Singular	Plural
Nominative	I, you, he, she, it, one, who	we, you, they
Possessive	my/mine, your/yours, his, her/hers, its, one's, whose	our/ours, your/yours, their/theirs
Objective	me, you, him, her, it, one, whom	us, you, them
Reflexive	myself, yourself, himself, herself, itself, oneself	ourselves, yourselves, themselves

Subject-Verb Agreement

Subjects and verbs agree when they are both singular or both plural. Most problems occur when the subject and verb are separated in the sentence. This separation of the subject and verb even causes problems for grammar checkers, which often assume the subject is the noun that occurs immediately before the verb.

Here is an example:

Incorrect	The children who went to the circus was laughing and playing.
Correct	The children who went to the circus were laughing and playing.

When proofing, match the subject and verb of each sentence about which you have a question. Sometimes it is easier to reword the sentence so the subject and verb are closer together.

Noun-Pronoun Agreement

Nouns and pronouns agree when the pronoun is the same person or number as the noun to which it refers. This means singular pronouns should be used with singular nouns and plural pronouns should be used with plural nouns. The pronoun should be in the same person as the noun when appropriate. Each pronoun should also refer to a specific noun. If it does not, add a noun to correct the problem.

Here is an example:

Incorrect	The captain asked yourself where he had gone wrong.
Correct	The captain asked himself where he had gone wrong.

Dangling Modifiers

Words or phrases that give more information about the subject, verb, or object of a clause are *modifiers*. A dangling modifier occurs when the word being modified does not appear in the independent clause. This problem occurs most often in sentences beginning with a verb that ends in -ing because the modifier must modify the subject of the sentence.

If you have a question about whether a sentence has a dangling modifier, rewrite it. You might find that when you rework the sentence you will add in what was missing from the original sentence.

Here is an example:

Incorrect	Walking home, the truck went up the hill.
Correct	As I walked home, I saw the truck go up the hill.

Predicates

Every sentence contains two basic parts: a subject and a predicate. A *predicate* consists of a verb and all the words modifying or attributed to the verb. These modifying words or attributes are called the *compliment*. The predicate usually states the action performed by the subject or the status of the subject. The verb should describe the action done by or done to the subject.

Here is an example:

Incorrect	The book set down on the table.
Correct	The book is on the table.
Correct	John set the book down on the table.

How To Catch Typos Outside the Main Text Area

When you are proofing the publication, you are looking primarily at the main text areas. An area of the publication that is easily overlooked is the text that occurs outside the main text windows. This text also needs to be checked for typos.

Every button on the screen and menu option contains text. Headings on pages contain text. Images often include captions. This text is easily neglected because you are so familiar with it. After all, you created it and added it to the pages.

Authoring tools that will check the spelling of any text in the publication, let alone all the text in the publication, are rarer than diamonds. This means you will have to check the unique text on every page. Proofreading for typos is hard because people tend to see what should be there and not what is really there.

To catch typos that you might have been staring at and not noticed for weeks as you developed the publication, you should look at the publication in a new way. One way to force yourself to look at the actual text instead of what you believe is there is to go through the publication backward. Start on the last page and work toward the front page.

Remember, you will only have to read unique textual components that are not a part of the text windows you should have already checked. If you used a master page, the task will be much easier than if you did not. This is because you will only have to check a few unique pages or unique features of an individual page. When you check the master page, read the text slowly. Sometimes it helps to read each individual word backward letter by letter. This will help you see the actual word.

Another tip is that if you find a typo on a page, do not relax and think the odds are slim that you will find another typo on the same page. On any page where you find a typo, you should reread the page at least once, and possibly twice. This will ensure you do not miss a typo close to the first typo.

Finally, do not forget to check images, figures, or charts. Text included as part of graphics is easy to neglect, especially if you have to select a page option to view the image. You should do this even for images you believe do not contain text. You might be surprised to find text and greatly relieved when you find and fix a typo you otherwise would have missed.

What To Look for When Testing

Testing traditional computer software is an art form developed over the past 50 years. Programmers have learned many lessons over those years, and electronic publishers will benefit substantially from applying these lessons. Each new advancement in software testing methodology not only saved programmers countless hours of frustration, it often saved their projects from failure as well. Applying some of the same testing methodologies to electronic publications will save you time, and possibly your project as well. This section discusses publisher-testing and not user-testing. User testing is the subject of the next chapter.

Programmers test code in many ways but never 100 percent. The problem with testing every bit of code is that the solution quickly becomes astronomically difficult to achieve. A simple program with six inputs of type A and seven inputs of type B requires the programmers to run 42 test cases to test the code 100 percent. In a program such as a word processor there will be hundreds or thousands of different factors to test. Even in the case where there are only 20 factors, each with five different values, trillions of test cases would have to be run (5^{20} or 9.5×10^{13}).

Publishers could and have tested electronic publications in this straightforward fashion. The reason they did this was based on the faulty assumption that it was the only way to test 100 percent of the publication and that electronic publications were considerably less complex than computer software.

If you agreed with this reasoning, you would test by beginning on page one and choosing every option one at a time. When you were done testing page one, you would go on to test every option on page two, and so on. In a small publication with 50 pages and 10 options on each page, this would mean performing 500 tests and would take hours to test. If you could select each option at a rate of one every 30 seconds, it would take you over four hours to complete the testing.

For a large publication with 300 pages and 25 options on each page, this would mean performing 7,500 tests and would take days to test. If you could select each option at a rate of one every 30 seconds, it would take you $62^1/2$ hours to complete the testing.

As you will see, there are better methods of testing. Programmers developed many techniques to test manageable sets of data. They wanted to test the data to maximize the chances of finding a fault while minimizing the number of test cases. One way to do this is to choose each test case to detect a previously undetected fault. They developed two key methods for testing:

- The black-box method
- The glass-box method

The Black-Box Method

The black-box testing method is one of the two basic ways to systematically test applications. The term *black-box* emerged because of the way this technique is used to test the specifications of a product and not the actual code. Other names for black box testing are data-driven, functional, and input/output-driven testing.

Using the black-box technique, programmers tested boundaries. For example, a piece of software, such as a database, designed to handle one through 10,000 records would be tested as follows:

> The programmers would determine the boundaries for the database. A database with less than one record is below the boundary. A database with 1 to 10,000 records is inside the boundary, and a database with 10,001 records is over the boundary. The programmers would then test a database with zero records, a database with any number of records within the valid range, such as 500, and a database with any number of records over the valid range, such as 10,001.

Over the years, programmers discovered that the probability of detecting a fault was greatly increased if values adjacent to the boundary were also tested. This meant testing the boundary values, values one less than the boundary, and values one more than the boundary. Following this methodology, the programmers of the database would test seven test cases instead of 10,000 test cases. Specifically, the programmers would test the values in Table 31.2.

Table 31.2 Sample test cases to detect faults in database of 10,000 records.

Test Number	Test Type and Size	Significance of Value Tested
1	A database with 0 records	A value one less than the boundary
2	A database with 1 record	The boundary value
3	A database with 2 records	A value one more than the boundary
4	A database with any number	A value of records within the boundaries, such as 500 boundary
5	A database with 9,999 records	A value one less than the boundary
6	A database with 10,000 records	The boundary value
7	A database with 10,001 records	A value one more than the boundary

This testing technique is a key way to test electronic publications as well. In later sections, examples of how to apply this method are explored.

The Glass-Box Method

The glass-box testing method is the second key testing method to systematically test applications. The term "glass-box" emerged because of the way this technique is used to test the logic of a product and when the logic broke down, the glass box broke. Other names for glass box testing are logic-driven and path-oriented testing. With this method, the programmers tested the structure of the software. They did this by ensuring all statements, branches, or paths in the program had been executed properly.

The simplest method was to check to ensure all statements had been executed. Programmers used special testing tools to do this. However, this method proved to be time-consuming.

The next evolution of structure testing involved branch testing. A series of tests were run to ensure each branch of the software had been run. This again was time-consuming.

Finally, programmers developed path-testing techniques. This is the most powerful form of structural testing. There are various forms of path testing; the one that is used most often excludes loops and recursive paths by marking them as checked the first time they are executed. This cleared up one testing problem where the test could get caught in a loop.

For example, when there is a way to get to page two of the publication from page one and a way to get to page one of the publication from page two, a test could potentially be repeated. By indicating that the test has already been done once, a repeat test won't be performed. In this way, you manage the testing process and make it less complex.

This testing technique is an important way to test electronic publications as well. The next section explores examples of how to apply this method and the black-box method.

How To Test Links

You can begin to test the links of your publication by identifying the major components of the publication. These components are the major functions and features you have included in the publication, such as pull-down menus, on-screen menus, and on-screen buttons. A *pull-down menu* is a list of commands that remains hidden until the reader moves the mouse pointer to a keyword designating the menu and clicks it. Before this, only a single summary command for the menu is visible on-screen. An on-screen menu is displayed. The menu is a list of commands or actions that readers can access quickly and efficiently. On-screen buttons represent a single command that will be carried out if the button is activated with key combinations or by clicking it.

If you developed a master page, testing each of these features will be easy because the components of the master page form the basis for the individual pages. The main idea behind master pages is that repetitious or non-unique features of the publication are identified and put on the master page. This way you only have to make minor adjustments to the individual storyboards and can ensure the look of the publication is consistent throughout. Putting non-unique features on the master page also makes testing easy because if a master page component works on page 7, it should also work on page 37.

Following this logic will work in most cases, but problems might arise because each publication is different. A publication with a linear layout is different from a publication with a hierarchical layout. To ensure testing is accurate, you have to define the boundary areas for the publication. Page 7 might be in one boundary area and page 37 might be in another boundary area, depending on how the publication is organized.

To make the testing process manageable no matter the size and organization of the publication, the process can be broken down into several parts. The black-box and glass-box testing techniques can then be applied to these individual parts as necessary:

- Testing internal page navigation mechanisms
- Testing page-turning components
- Testing index components
- Testing search components
- Testing multimedia components
- Testing unique pages

Testing Internal Page-Navigation Mechanisms

You should first test the internal navigation mechanisms within pages. Readers generally select page components using the mouse, cursor controls, quick keys, or the Tab key. Using the mouse, the reader moves the mouse pointer to an option, and then pushes the left mouse button to perform the action. With the cursor keys, the reader can scroll up or down through options or text. Quick keys enable readers to use key combinations to access options. Using the Tab key the reader can also navigate from option to option and select the option by pressing Return.

You will need to test each of the navigation mechanisms you have included in the publication, but the good news is that you should have to do this only one time per mechanism. Select a page in the publication that includes a text window and test the valid ways to manipulate the window's scrollbar. Try to use any of the other mechanisms you permit. If you can use an allowable mechanism on the page, cross the mechanism off your list of things to test. If you cannot use the mechanism on the page because the action is not valid on the particular page, move to a page on which the action is valid. For example, to test the scrollbars on a graphic window, you will need to go to a page with a graphic window. Usually, windows can be manipulated using the mouse or cursor controls.

You usually assign internal navigation mechanisms when you create the publication. For example, you select that you want readers to be able to use the Tab key to navigate between options but not be able to use the Tab key to make a text window active for scrolling with the cursor keys. If a mechanism won't work, you should check the settings you selected in the authoring software when you created the publication.

Testing Page-Turning Components

Page-turning features enable the reader to move quickly around the publication. Readers rely heavily on these features. When you test, you want to make sure these features work as they are supposed to. Common page-turning components you might have in your publications include

- Previous chapter/topic
- Next chapter/topic
- First page
- Previous page/subtopic
- Next page/subtopic
- Last page
- Return to page
- Exit the publication

Your first step should be to determine the boundary areas for the publication. Most publications will have one boundary area encompassing all pages from the first to the last page. Others will have multiple boundary areas. For example, if you include an online help section that is separate from the main pages and can only be accessed by using a Goto Help Index button, this section will also have its own boundaries.

Begin by testing the components of a page within the boundary area. If the previous page feature works on page 9 it should work on page 29. This will be true provided that you use the same mechanism for the previous page function in each case and that the pages are within the same boundary. If a component is from your master page, you can be sure it will have the same functionality throughout the publication.

You will have a problem when page one includes a previous page function. What happens when the reader selects the previous page option? Obviously, there is no previous page to go to, but will the program crash or will it simply ignore the reader's request?

This is why the next step is to test boundary pages. Any features you have included on a boundary page should be individually tested. In particular, you should test features that are not possible, such as a next page feature on the last page of the publication. Again, what happens when this selection is made?

As Chapter 9, "Page Design," discussed, one way to reduce problems is to "ghost" functions that serve no purpose on a particular page. When you ghost a menu option, you place a button with a different function over the original button. The new button usually has a pattern to obscure the original button text and graphics. The reader will then know they cannot select this option. However, you should still assume the reader might try to select a ghosted option and test the ghosted option. A good way to notify the reader that they have made an invalid selection is to design the ghost option so it plays a warning tone.

Testing Index Components

Index features enable the reader to get to special indexes in the publication, such as the table of contents or an online help section. When you test, make sure these features work as they are supposed to. Common index components include

- Go to index
- Go to table of contents
- Go to help index

Follow the steps described in the preceding "Testing Page-Turning Components" section to test the individual pages of the publication. Your first step should be to determine the boundary areas for the publication. These should be the same as the ones you determined earlier. Begin by testing the components of a page within the boundary area, and then test these components in the boundary area. This means if your help index page contains a Goto Help Index option, you should test it even if the option is ghosted.

Because most publications will have a table of contents, an index, and a help index, you will want to test each page individually. Usually, the components that you have added to these pages will be unique. For example, buttons on the table of contents page that enable readers to jump to any individual chapter will probably not occur anywhere else in the publication. The best way to test these unique features is to select them one at a time. Make sure the Goto Chapter 6 option really takes the reader to Chapter 6.

Testing Search Components

Local text search and global text search are used widely in publications. A *local text search* will let the reader search the contents of the main text on the current page. A *global text search* will let the reader search the main text of the entire publication. When you test, make sure these features work as they are supposed to. Follow the steps described in the "Testing Page-Turning Components" section to test the search mechanism on individual pages. Begin by testing the components of a page within the boundary area, and then test the components in the boundary area.

In particular, you will want to test a local search on pages that have no main text, such as graphic pages. On some graphic pages, you might have used the components of the master page. On others, you might have forgotten to remove the text search option from a menu you used elsewhere in the publication and later added to the graphic page. Depending on the results, you might want to ghost the text search option on problem pages.

You should also test the global search option on the last page of the publication. Is the particular software you are using smart enough to continue searching the publication on page one, or does it stop and display no search results when it reaches the bottom of the main text area on the last page? What happens if the last page includes the global search option and there is no text on the page to search? Depending on the results, you might want to ghost the global search option on this page.

Testing Multimedia Components

Multimedia buttons and menus enable readers to access images, sound, and video. Often, these components will enable readers to access unique multimedia items each time they occur; then, you should test each item individually. Other times, the multimedia features will be reused in key locations in the publication. Here you would test each unique item, and then make sure the remaining items access the correct multimedia segments.

When you test multimedia, you will want to make the features work as they are supposed to on all the computer systems with which your publication is supposed to be compatible. If the publication makes limited use of multimedia and is designed to be used on any IBM PC, this does not mean you should test the publication on 286, 386, 486, and Pentium systems. Often, testing the multimedia features of the publication on a low-end computer system and a high-end computer system will suffice.

For publications with advanced multimedia features, you will want to make sure the publication is actually compatible with the monitor, video card, sound card, and computer configurations you claim. Test the publication on a representative cross-section of computer systems. This might mean testing the publication on three or four differently configured systems. Some of these systems should meet the system requirements you specified. Others should exceed or fall short of the requirements you specified. This way, you can verify that the system requirements accurately reflect those actually needed.

Sometimes, you will be unable to test a multimedia publication on different systems. A small publisher or one-person publishing operation simply might not have the resources to test the publication on many different systems. No one is an island. Why not test the publication on a friend or relative's computer system or on the systems of several of your friends or relatives? Where multimedia is concerned, you really want to make sure the system requirements are accurate.

TIP

If you are unsure of what the system requirements should be for the publication you have developed, refer to the authoring software you used to create the publication. The system requirements that the authoring software recommends for you to run the software should also apply to publications you create with the authoring software.

For example, NeoBook Pro states that to use the program, you need the following hardware and software:

- An IBM PC, XT, AT, PS/2, or 100 percent-compatible computer
- EGA, VGA, Hercules monochrome, or compatible graphics card and monitor
- 640KB minimum RAM
- A hard disk
- MS-DOS, PC-DOS, or Novell DOS 3.1 or higher version
- Microsoft, Logitech, or compatible mouse
- Sound Blaster/Sound Blaster Pro or compatible audio card (optional)

For publications created with NeoBook Professional version, readers will need to meet those system requirements. The sound card is optional because your publication might or might not include sound. If you include sound and the reader does not have a compatible sound card the reader's computer system might simply ignore the request to play the sound or it might cause system problems.

Testing Unique Pages

Your publication will probably have several unique pages. These pages will have components that are not included on other pages, and you should test each unique page individually. The unique pages that might be in the publication include

- Startup page
- Overview page
- Table of contents page
- Menu page
- Topic or chapter overview pages
- Index page
- Help index pages
- Credits page

The best way to test unique components is to select them one at a time. Some features included on these pages might be used elsewhere in the publication. If you have already tested an identical feature elsewhere in the publication, you might not have to test it here. Pages in boundary areas, like the start-up page, are exceptions. You will want to test all components of these pages even if you have tested them elsewhere.

How To Catch Inconsistencies

When you are testing buttons, menu options, navigation mechanisms, and other page features, it is easy to miss inconsistencies. After all, you are looking at links, not at material you already proofed. This is why it is easy to miss inconsistencies in the publication. To find something you must first look for it.

Inconsistencies such as typos are easily missed because you are so familiar with the publication. You created every page of the publication and should know it better than anyone else. An example of an inconsistency is a heading that tells the reader this is Chapter @, whereas the main text is from Chapter 3. Unless the text for every chapter begins with a chapter number, this inconsistency is easily missed.

To check for this type of inconsistency, do one of the following:

- If each page of your publication represents a chapter and you included chapter numbers in the text window, you should check chapter numbers in headers and chapter numbers in text windows to be sure they match.
- If each page of your publication represents a chapter and you did not include chapter numbers in the text window, you should check headers and text windows to make sure each chapter is where it is supposed to be.

The inconsistencies are more difficult to trace when each page of your publication represents an actual page. To check for inconsistencies you might have to check hundreds of pages. For example, a duplicate page is often easy to find. However, a missing page is often difficult to notice.

To check for missing or duplicate pages, do one of the following:

- If you included pages numbers outside the text window and inside the text window, make sure the numbers match.

- If you included pages numbers outside the text window, make sure the text in the text window corresponds to the page number.

- If you included pages numbers inside the text window, make sure the pages of the publication are in the proper sequence.

Another area in which inconsistencies can occur is in the placement of unique items on pages. The placement of text and graphic windows can be troublesome because you might not notice small inconsistencies unless you look for them. For example, on page one through six of the publication the text window is aligned with a row of buttons beneath the text window, and then in the rest of the pages the text window was aligned with a column of buttons beside the text window.

The placement of on-screen buttons and menus can also create an inconsistent look in the publication. This is particularly true when you add a few unique buttons to pages of the publication but not to all of the pages. To check for misplaced items, you should move through the pages forward and backward. Concentrate on pages to which you added unique items and move through the pages quickly. Look at the entire page and watch for changes as you move to a new page. A misplaced item should jump out at you because it will be different from other items on the previous page.

When you use multiple fonts in the publication, you can also create inadvertent inconsistencies. Changes in font size can be subtle, but changes in font type should be obvious. Look for inconsistencies in the unique items you added to individual pages, especially when you added components late in the development process. You might have changed fonts when you were working on other parts of the publication. A quick check to ensure the fonts are consistent throughout the publication is a good precaution.

Balancing the Need for Perfection with Efficiency and Timeliness

Creating a publication that has no typos, inconsistencies, or other errors would be a wonderful thing, but in the real world less-than-perfect publications are released every day. At some point, the publisher has to ask herself: How much proofing is enough? How many typos are too many—a hundred, a dozen, less? How much testing is enough? How many inconsistencies or linking problems are acceptable—10, one, or none? When do you stop? When should you stop?

The answers are not easy. Every day a publisher somewhere is making these decisions based on balancing the need for perfection with efficiency and timeliness. Because of their size, some mediums are easier to check for accuracy. A short work, such as a 20-page newsletter, is much easier to proof than a 300-page book. Yet newsletters often contain typos, inconsistencies, and errors.

The real determinant for publications has little to do with size and more to do with timeliness. A monthly magazine must be published monthly. A weekly newsletter must be published weekly. A newspaper must be published every day and in some metropolitan areas twice a day—a morning and an evening edition. At some point, a publisher or editor has to make the decision to tell the writers to print what they have.

Time is also a major factor for publishing books. Some books have to go to the presses in three months to beat the competition. Other books have to go to the presses now or never to tie-in with a current event. Look at the number of books rushed to the press for recent media events. Those books will sell today, but they won't sell in three months when the courtrooms clear.

In the end, your decision might also come down to money. Publishers cannot go on to other moneymaking projects while they are working full-time on a publication. A publication cannot make money unless it is for sale.

You should stop proofing and testing the publication when it makes sense. Base the decision on your needs and the need for perfection in the publication. If necessary, use time and money constraints to help you make the decision to continue checking the publication or to stop.

Summary

Good writers know that the critical mistakes will be found only through careful proofing. When you proof the publication, you look primarily at the main text areas. However, you should also check text that occurs outside the main text windows.

In the area of testing, programmers have learned valuable lessons over the years. Electronic publishers will benefit substantially from applying these lessons. To make the testing process manageable no matter the size and organization of the publication, the process can be broken down into several parts. When you are testing, it is easy to miss inconsistencies. To find inconsistencies you must look for them.

User-Testing Your Publication

32

by Marj Rush-Hovde

IN THIS CHAPTER

There used to be a time when people released publications without user-testing them at all. Audiences had to endure publications that were hard to read and use. That day is past. If you have any competitors, you can be sure that they have tested their publications so that they can satisfy the audience and meet its needs. If your audience members find they can't use your publication easily, they are likely to go to your competition.

User-testing plays an important part in a high-quality development process; it's not merely an option used only if you happen to have enough time for it. The testing you do can give you data about the audience to guide you in making decisions and persuading others about the worth of decisions you have made about the design of the publication. With more and more organizations taking up a "customer focus," user testing can be a powerful way to gather support for an audience-oriented publication.

You can conduct testing at various times throughout the development process in two broad categories: testing for functionality and testing for usability. Testing for functionality is relatively straightforward. You test to see if the software works and responds correctly to user requests. Testing for usability is more complex and is the focus of the bulk of this chapter. The type of testing you conduct depends on your goals and where you are in the development process. Features of each purpose for testing are outlined in Table 32.1.

Table 32.1. Types of testing.

Type of Testing	Goal	At the Beginning of Development	Before Release
Functionality	To determine whether the links and other functions work.	Done only if there is an existing publication to be revised.	Done in-house with a prepared script to test all parts of the publication.
Usability	To learn how users interact with the publication.	Done to help the developer build a model of how users actually use publications in the genre.	Demonstrates whether or not typical users can use the publication effectively for their purposes.

When choosing a method for user testing of your publication, decide on the goals that you want to achieve through the publication, and then test according to the goals. For instance, if you want to find out how easy it is to locate information, design a test that helps you observe how users find information in your publication. If you want to find out how easy your publication is to understand, design a quiz for test users to see how much they understood and can recall. You could potentially perform several dozen kinds of tests, so figuring out the goals and then designing a test helps you to select the testing methods that are most likely to be beneficial.

This chapter describes various types of testing you can do to determine the functionality and usability of your publication. Many of these tests can be conducted at different times within the development process. You learn the goals, advantages, methodology, limitations, and timing for each. These methods and the relevant features are summarized in Table 32.2. Choose the method of user testing that most closely matches your goals.

Table 32.2. Methods of user testing.

Goal: To gain a broad view of audience's opinions.

Goals	*Description*
Research Type	Survey/questionnaire
Advantages	■ Provides information about what a large group of users thinks.
	■ Results can be easily quantified.
	■ Relatively inexpensive to conduct.
Methods	■ Mail survey.
	■ Phone survey.
Limitations	■ May have low response rate, especially from the dissatisfied, and therefore may not give representative sample.
	■ Questions must be designed carefully to encourage an unbiased response.
	■ Respondents may not accurately report what they do.
	■ Doesn't give entire context of use of the publication.
	■ May take a great deal of time to distribute, collect, and analyze.
Timing	■ Early in the design process to find out what the audience wants.
	■ After release to assess effectiveness and future publication design.

Goal: To see how a few people similar to typical users may use the publication.

Research Type	"Lab" observations
Advantages	■ Shows how users actually may use the publication.
	■ Provides for a thorough testing of functionality of the publication.
	■ Allows researcher to focus on specific audience tasks.
Methods	■ Test script prepared beforehand.
	■ Testing room set up with methods to observe users performing tasks.
	■ Out-loud "protocols."

continues

Table 32.2. continued

Goals	Description
	■ Post-test interview.
Limitations	■ May not give a realistic picture of the context of use.
	■ Audience may try to give the tester "right" answers.
	■ Results are difficult to quantify.
	■ May not give a broad picture of many typical users.
Timing	■ Early in the design process if an existing publication needs revising.
	■ Before release with enough time for retesting and revision.

Goal: To determine how a few actual audience members use the publication.

Research Type	Observation at the audience's site
Advantages	■ Gives an in-depth view of how the publication fits into the context of the audience's typical work.
	■ Provides a sense of the limitations within which the audience needs to work.
	■ Creates customer appreciation and "buy-in."
	■ Shows how users understand and interpret the publication.
Methods	■ Observe a few actual audience members in their typical setting for using the publication.
Limitations	■ Observer depends on the goodwill of the audience.
	■ May not provide a broad view of typical use.
	■ Expensive and time-consuming
	■ May need to be done in coordination with organization's client contact people.
Timing	■ Early in design process, whether a publication already exists or not.
	■ Before release, with enough time for retesting and revision.

Goal: To assess how well typical users may understand the publication's content.

Research Type	Reading tests
Advantages	■ May not require a great deal of time and sophisticated equipment.
	■ Allows the tester to ask about specific parts of the publication.
	■ Can provide for testing of multiple readers at the same time.
Methods	■ Test tasks are prepared beforehand.
	■ Users read and give responses about what they understood.

Goals	Description
Limitations	■ May not cover all aspects of use of the publication.
Timing	■ Before release, with enough time for retesting and revision.

Goal: To find out what a broad group of users thinks of the publication.

Research Type	Responses from users
Advantages	■ Gives perspectives on problems that actual users have.
	■ Relatively inexpensive to compile.
Methods	■ Evaluate user response cards.
	■ Look at electronic responses to a Web page.
	■ Analyze phone support logs.
	■ Study reviews in periodicals.
Limitations	■ If this is the only user-testing method used, a seriously flawed publication may be released.
	■ Usually, only people with complaints or problems take time to respond.
Timing	■ After release.

With the information from this chapter in mind, you can customize your testing methods to fit your needs, goals, and constraints. Early in developing your publication, perform tests to help eliminate some of the guesswork in planning (see Chapter 12, "Writing Processes"). If you have an existing publication that you are revising, you can test it on typical users. Even if the existing publication is a paper one, you can still gather information about how users utilize the publication. Later in the development process you can conduct other tests to confirm whether or not the publication achieves its goals for your intended users. With adequate testing appropriately timed, you don't have to guess about how to revise your publication.

If you have an existing publication, you might have already received unsolicited responses from users about its quality, but these responses do not necessarily represent of a broad spectrum of users. Users happy with the publication usually don't take the time to let the company know how well it works. Therefore, of your unsolicited comments, complaints probably outnumber compliments. Take these unsolicited complaints and suggestions for improvement seriously, of course, but also go on to find out what works well in your existing publication.

Methods of Testing Users and Gathering User Information

To find out how audience members use your publication, you can employ several of the methods that are discussed in the following pages. Before you choose your methods, however, consider that the more complex (and expensive) the method, the richer the data it yields. Decide how important audience feedback is to your publication in order to justify the expense and time testing takes. As in any project, the more information you have early in the process, the easier the later phases become.

Gaining a Broad View of Audience Opinions Through a Survey

Many people's first impulse in gathering user information is to take a survey. Surveys can be valuable if done well, but you'll need to be aware of some of the drawbacks to surveys, as well.

Advantages

Well-designed surveys give a broad picture of audience needs, and you can relatively easily turn the results into numbers to guide decisions. They are also one of the least expensive ways to gather information early in the publication development cycle.

Methods

When you do a mail survey, you need a group of people to whom to mail the survey. This might seem obvious, but you need access to a mailing list of current audience members. Sometimes you can pull names from the customer databases of your organization. If you have a large number of audience members to survey, you need to choose a random sample. To encourage participation, some organizations offer small rewards for responding to the survey—a company key chain, a chance to enter a drawing for a large prize, and so on.

However, before you can even mail the survey, you need to design it. Knowing your goals for the publication comes in handy at this point. Determine the most important information you want to collect from your audience. Do you want to know about the publication's usability? Design? Content? Readability?

Once you have decided on the type of information you want from the audience, determine how you want to ask for the information. You can choose questions with open-ended answers or questions that ask for yes/no answers. For an open-ended question, you could ask "What do you like most about the existing publication?" For yes/no answers, which are easier to tabulate, you could ask "Do you think the publication needs revision?" Or instead of questions, you could present statements and then give the audience a scale from 1–4 for "strongly agree" to "strongly disagree." For instance, you might wish to state, "The publication meets my needs at this time," and ask the audience to agree or disagree on the scale. Although yes/no questions and agree/disagree questions are easy to tabulate, you might not gain as much insight as you would from open-ended questions.

The type of questions you choose to include on your survey depends on the kind of information you want and how many resources you can dedicate to tabulating the results. However, it's wise not to mix too many different types of questions in the same survey. The users will become confused by too many types of questions, and tabulating will be more difficult with a mixture.

Questions asking for yes/no answers or a ranking on a scale will be easier to tabulate and quantify, but might not offer as much rich information. Surveys asking for open-ended responses might generate more complex information, but might also take the audience members more time to respond to. Furthermore, the results to open-ended questions are more difficult to quantify. Select the type of questions to use in your survey depending on the type of information you want and what resources you can dedicate to tabulating the results of the survey.

When you are designing survey questions, avoid writing questions that might "lead" the respondents to give the answer they think you want rather than what they really think. For instance, if you ask, "Do you approve of the enhancements we've added?" your respondents might think, "Well, if they're enhancements, I ought to like them" and respond according to what they think they ought to say. If you are not sure whether you are creating leading questions, you can show the survey to an expert in questionnaire design or you can test the questionnaire on a few sample users.

Testing the survey with a few sample users will also let you know how long it takes to fill out the information so that you can let the larger group of respondents know how much time it will take. Generally, you don't want to take more than 10 minutes of your respondent's time for a paper survey, so knowing what topics you want them to cover can help you keep your survey short and increase the chances of a high response rate. (Also, providing free return postage will encourage participants to respond.)

In most instances, you'll want to provide anonymity for respondents, but you might want to give them an option for letting their names be known if they would like to be part of a follow-up of any sort, especially telephone interviews. Showing the survey to a statistician before sending it can also give you guidance in how to design the survey so the quantitative results are useful and easy to handle.

To encourage a hasty response, give respondents a cutoff date; don't just ask them to respond as soon as possible. Once the surveys have been returned, you need to tabulate the results. If you have designed the survey carefully, tabulation should be easier. Once you have the results, you can consult with a statistician for possible ways to interpret the data in creating arguments and making decisions on how to revise a publication for users. The more rigorously designed your survey, the stronger your data. This data is crucial in helping you decide how to redesign your publication.

You might also wish to conduct telephone surveys in addition to or instead of mail surveys. A phone survey can provide rich data and sometimes a higher participation rate. If the respondents to your mail survey have provided their names, you might wish to select a sample of the respondents for a follow-up phone survey. If you are not following up on a mail survey, you select potential respondents in a way similar to selecting those for a mail survey.

In the phone survey, you might wish to get more detailed information from the audience members, particularly if the mail survey asked yes/no or agree/disagree questions. If in the mail survey an audience member indicated dissatisfaction with the publication, you might be able to inquire about exactly what in the publication needs improvement and what improvements have the highest priority in the audience's work.

When you conduct a phone survey, you need to make sure that the people conducting the survey have been adequately trained. The reliability of your results depends on how consistently the questions have been asked of multiple respondents. Also, you don't want the surveyors to alienate clients through inappropriate phone interactions. To make the phone surveys go more smoothly, give the surveyors a way to record responses rapidly so that the client won't have to wait for the caller to write down answers.

As mentioned earlier, phone surveys usually generate a higher response rate than a mail survey. People prefer to take a few minutes to answer questions on the phone rather than take a few minutes to fill out a sheet of paper. However, build in an opportunity at the beginning of the call to allow the potential respondent to decline to be interviewed. Keep track of the number of decliners and acceptors in order to make the data you collect more reliable. One disadvantage to phone surveys over paper surveys is that the respondent might not have enough time to think about responses on the phone, whereas in a paper survey the respondent can think about responses for a couple of days if need be. The final disadvantage is that phone surveys take a great deal of time. Some companies hire and train temporary employees to make the calls, but even this costs more than a paper survey.

Limitations

It's very difficult to force a 100 percent response rate for a survey, so you need to realize that the responses you get will not represent your audience 100 percent. As mentioned earlier, the dissatisfied are also more likely to respond. This low and unrepresentative response becomes problematic when you make decisions about the publication based solely on survey findings. Professional statisticians can help you make your results as reliable as possible and can help you to know whether or not your results are useful. Nevertheless, you would be wise to supplement survey results with at least one of the other methods of user testing discussed later.

As mentioned earlier, it's difficult to design survey questions that don't "lead" the audience to give you the answers which they think you want. Even if the questions aren't leading ones, respondents might not be aware of giving less than precise answers. For instance, if you ask, "How long did it take you to learn how to use this publication?" respondents might say "ten minutes." It might be, however, that it took longer and the respondents might be embarrassed to admit it or might honestly not remember.

A survey also gives you only a limited view of the context of use of the publication. Because surveys shouldn't take a lot of time to complete, they usually focus on only very general information about use and satisfaction. Details are better collected through observations such as those discussed in later sections of this chapter.

Be sure to allow enough time to design, test, and distribute the survey and analyze the results. Many people think taking a survey happens quickly, but a well-designed one can take several months from start to finish.

Timing

If you conduct a survey early in the publication development process, you can ask about an existing publication if one exists. If none exists, you can ask about the typical work that your target audience might do in relation to your publication. I wouldn't recommend a survey in the middle of the development process. Other forms of testing can give you better results at those times. However, after the publication's release, you can conduct a survey to see how satisfied your audience members are with your publication and what suggestions they have for improvements for future editions.

If surveys are well-conducted, whether on phone or paper, they can provide a great deal of data for a relatively low cost. However, from a survey alone you can't always get all the information that you need in order to create or revise a publication. Observing or testing a few users in-depth, as discussed next, can reveal details of how the publication is used.

Testing a Few Typical Audience Members in a "Lab" Setting

Observing how a selected group of typical users encounter your publication in a controlled setting can give you valuable insight into the usability of your electronic publication. Following the advice in this section can help you gain useful information about the usability of your publication.

Advantages

In addition to or instead of a survey of audience members, you might wish to bring a few sample users to a special site early in the development process to observe how they use your publication, if one exists. You can also conduct laboratory tests just before you release a publication. The advantage to a lab test over a survey is that you observe users actually using your publication rather than relying on survey reports of what they say they do. This observation enables you to focus on specific user actions that you might not have learned about from a survey. During these observations you can see whether the publication is functional and also if it is designed for how audiences actually might use it.

Methods

To conduct a laboratory test of your publication, invite a representative sample of users to a designated facility equipped with appropriate technology for running your publication. (If you are unable to bring in typical users, some organizations hire people from a temporary agency who resemble typical users.) Be sure that the technology in the "lab" represents the spectrum of hardware to which your users have access.

Before the sample users arrive, prepare a test "script" based on the goals of your publication for them to follow. This script's design will depend on what you want to find out. If you want to know what the users think of an entire publication, you can design a directive test that moves them through each part of the publication. If you want to observe how users would interact with the publication, design an open-ended test that sets them up with typical tasks. For an example of a directive usability test script, see Table 32.3.

Table 32.3. Usability test script for guiding the user.

Goals of the Publication	Tasks for the User to Perform	Comments for the Test Designer
Users should be able to find desired links within 10 seconds.	**1.** Find the link that takes you to today's edition of the paper.	You can substitute the name of each link if you want to do a thorough test for functionality.
Users should be able to return to the home page without getting lost.	**2.** Select the link you found in task 1. Read the contents and then return to the first page you found.	Be sure your observers don't interfere too much on this type of task. You want to get a sense of how well users can interact with the publication's design.
Users should be able to understand and use the items they find.	**3.** Select the "Tell us what you think" link and send a note to the editor.	If you want to test for understanding of your less interactive links, you can ask users to go to a certain spot and then tell you about what they found there.
After selecting a link, users should be able to tell by reading the first few lines whether or not they want to continue reading.	**4.** Select the "Instant Access" link and read the first few lines. Tell me whether you can figure out what that page contains.	Again, you may want to substitute the names of other pages to see whether or not the first few lines provide adequate guidance to users.

In the directive script, you prepare a scenario that moves users through a fixed set of steps. In the open-ended script, you prepare a looser test that gives a general goal and then asks the users to figure out the steps to achieve the goal. An open-ended user test script provides insight into users' typical patterns of working as it gives users a general task to complete and allows for observation of specific steps they select to complete it. Table 32.4 shows an example of an open-ended script asking the user to follow general directions.

Table 32.4. Open-ended script.

Goals of the Publication	*Tasks for the User to Perform*	*Comments for the Test Designer*
The users will find information their appropriate to topic within one minute without assistance.	**1.** You need to prepare a report on some aspect of Thai culture for a class. Choose one aspect of this culture and find information about it using this CD-ROM encyclopedia.	Allowing the user to select a specific topic can let you see how they conduct a search. You can observe what sort of guesses they make if the first key word produces no "hits."
The user will find information related to a main topic within three minutes of starting to search for it.	**2.** Now that you have found information on your topic, see what other parts of the CD-ROM may provide supplemental information.	Again, allowing them to select their own topics lets you see how they function with little guidance. You'll want to observe what they consider relevant topics.
The user will print selected portions of information that s/he has found.	**3.** When you have found your main information and relevant links, print the information you've found so you can use it for background information as you write your report.	Be careful not to intervene in this task. You want to see how users solve problems when there is no one around to help.
The user should be able to find online help within 30 seconds of encountering a problem.		You may not be able to write a specific task for this goal, but rather you should observe the tasks above to see how long it takes and under what circumstance users try to find online help.

Which type of test you choose depends on what you are testing for and where you are in the development process. If you are testing for functionality late in the development process, you will need a directive script for test users to follow. If you want to test for how users think early in the design process, or for general usability late in the process, an open-ended test works well.

While you are designing the test, especially near the end of the development cycle, determine how successful you want the publication to be. For instance, you might decide beforehand that 90 percent of the test subjects will be able to find their way through it without getting irretrievably lost.

Also, take into account that a huge publication might not be able to be fully tested for usability. In these instances, select a few representative sections or tasks within the publication to test. When you are testing for functionality, however, you'll want to test each part of the publication, no matter how long it takes.

When you set up your laboratory test, consider how many test users you can observe at one time. This number will also be affected by how you choose to collect permanent data during the tests. Ideally, you'd have a video camera and one observer per test subject. But in less ideal circumstances you might need to have one observer for several test subjects at a time. In that situation, the observer would only make notes of times when a user had a problem. The observer would be less able to note normal, trouble-free use of the publication. Some test givers record the users' actions using two video cameras, one trained on the test user and one on the computer.

Even if you do use the video cameras, you probably want at least one observer also taking notes, either in the room or behind a one-way mirror. These notes should cover the following:

- The desired task. For example, perhaps you ask the user to find all information on a certain topic using your publication.
- The user action. Record what observable actions the user takes in order to accomplish the desired task. Remember to note those that fail, as well as those that succeed.
- The computer's response.
- Comments. These are ideas for revisions to the publication that you want to make based on your observation of the test user(s).

Some test users might be nervous about being tested and might try to give you what they think you want. To prevent this, at the beginning of the test clarify to the user that the activity tests the publication, not the user. In other words, the user won't "fail" no matter what. Focusing on the testing of the publication can give you a greater chance to observe what users might typically do with it. Your goal is to observe what people do instead of what you or they think they should do.

You might wish to select a test observer who is not also the designer of the publication, especially if you are testing late in the design process. Not having the designer present prevents the designer from helping the user too much if the user gets lost. If you choose not to have the designer present, you'll still want a way for the designer to observe what happened, perhaps with a one-way glass or a videotape.

The observers of the test should try not to interfere too much. They can learn a great deal by recording how users try to get themselves reoriented after becoming confused. The observers should recommend to the test users that they try to figure out confusing points by themselves before asking for help.

Videotaping and note-taking capture what happens externally, but you might also need a way to capture what the user is thinking while interacting with your publication. Knowing these thoughts can help you understand how users interpret what they see on the screen. However, no machine has yet been designed to capture all of a person's thoughts, so one method that researchers in cognitive psychology have used is called the "think-aloud protocol."

In using think-aloud protocols, you ask the test users to say aloud what's running through their minds as they complete the test. Although this talking might seem a bit strange at first, many test users begin to realize this involves merely articulating the words that run through most people's minds as they solve problems. Naturally, the users could tell you anything whether it's accurate or not, but usually this method gives you at least a partial glimpse into people's ways of representing the task for themselves. The insights gained from these protocols as well as from your observations can help guide your revisions for the publication.

At the end of the test you might find it helpful to interview the test users in order to gain information that you couldn't observe. You might ask about the legibility of the text on the screen, what they saw as the strengths and weaknesses of the publication, or suggestions they would make to improve the publication to fit their needs. You might also focus on discussing places at which they became lost or confused, looking at the reasons for the hitch and discussing what changes in the publication might help to prevent others from encountering that problem.

When you have completed the laboratory testing, sift carefully through the collected data to see if you can spot patterns of use. Especially note when users have had problems with the publication. However, don't assume that simply because one test user had a problem that all users will have that problem in that spot. If more than one user has had the same problem, that can be an indicator that the publication needs changing.

Limitations

When you conduct laboratory testing, you usually don't get a broad spectrum of opinion because usually you have the resources to observe only a few people. In addition, you can't observe how they use your publication in connection with their other activities. Nor do you observe what sort of technology typical users have available to them. You also can't see what types of distractions they might encounter as they work. Finally, because laboratory observation takes a great deal of time, you might not be able to observe many users. Therefore, you might have trouble finding typical patterns of use from a few examples. Nevertheless, the "laboratory" setting enables you to observe users in order to gain a relatively rich picture of how they interact with your publication.

Timing

You can conduct laboratory testing at the beginning of your publication design process and/or at the end. Laboratory testing is especially effective if you want to see how users interact with an existing publication. Even if you have no publication to revise, you can still conduct tests early in the process and observe test users in a laboratory working on a similar task. For instance, perhaps you want to take a paper publication and design an electronic version of it. You can learn a great deal by observing typical users interacting with a paper publication. Or, you may observe them using a publication similar in purpose to the one you wish to create.

Testing an existing publication before revising it can help you plan what revisions to make, given your time and resource constraints. Testing a new or revised publication can help you fine-tune it for the audience. However, you might wish to supplement laboratory testing with observing users in their natural environments to gain even richer of information. Even the best laboratory testing will not give you information about how your publication fits into the context of the audience members' ordinary work. Thus, field observations can give you information you can use to craft your publication for the intended audience.

Gaining Information About Audience Members in Their Natural Settings

Observing users in their natural setting can provide you with the most in-depth information of any method of user testing. However, as with other methods, you'll achieve the most reliable information if you plan the on-site observation carefully, as discussed in this section.

Advantages

Observing users in their natural settings (or field observing, as it's sometimes called) gives you some of the same advantages as observing them in a laboratory setting. You construct a rich picture of users whom you have observed first-hand. You focus on specific aspects of their work, especially how they interpret your publication. Field studies can also show you the limitations within which users work. Finally, if field observations are done well they can help you create audience support and good will because audience members have a sense of having contributed to the publication development.

Method

Field studies yield the most rich and useful data about the usability of your publication, and they cost the most of all methods of user testing. You need to set aside time for people, preferably the publication's designers/writers, to travel to a site or two where audience members use your publication. For instance, if you are designing a CD-ROM publication for library users, you would travel to a library and observe how the users use either your publication or similar publications. Before beginning to observe, clarify what your goals are in observing. You're not just going to the site to "hang out" and hope to stumble upon some insights. Rather, have specific questions in mind for which you want answers. You won't always get anticipated answers, but being prepared can still be helpful.

In addition to observing how the audience members use your publication, notice what sort of computers they use it on and how that affects use. You also want to see when they choose to use the publication—do the library patrons in the preceding example use it only when they have exhausted the possibilities of print materials, or do they go to it first when they have a question?

In addition to observing the interaction between a user and your publication, observe the entire context of where the users work. Where are the computers placed? Can users sit down to use your publication? What might distract the users? Are they limited to a certain length of time to use your publication when others are waiting?

With the permission of the users, observe their actions closely. For instance, if they are doing a keyword search, are they satisfied with the "hits" from their initial keyword, or do they try to refine their search? How do they use on-line help, if at all?

As in laboratory testing, record what you observe. Taking notes is simplest because in many contexts recording devices would make the test subjects self-conscious. (You will, of course, have gotten permission to observe from the person in charge of the site and possibly those you observe.) As in laboratory testing, assure the users that you are testing the publication and not the users.

With field research, it's difficult to test using a prepared script, but not impossible. Whether or not you have a script depends on the goals of your observation. However, without a script you might need to allocate several days for observation in order to see users interacting with all parts of your publication, if that is your goal. As you observe, pay close attention to how your publication fits into the users' usual work. As in laboratory testing, try not to intervene too much when a user encounters a problem.

At the end of your field observations, you can interview the people you observed to find out why they took the actions they did while using your publication or to find out about their past experiences in using the publication. You might also want to ask them what they perceive as the greatest strengths of the publication and what improvements they'd like. Be sure your questions fit the goals of the on-site visit.

Limitations

Because field studies are so time-consuming, you might not be able to conduct many of them. Although you will collect rich data about a few users, their behavior might not be typical of a broad group of users. Therefore, you need to supplement field research with other types of research discussed in this chapter to enhance the reliability of your findings.

When you are observing in the field, you depend on the goodwill of the users. Fortunately, many users want their publications to be designed with them in mind, so cooperation might not be difficult to achieve. However, if your publication is used within an organization that wishes to maintain confidentiality, you might have a more difficult time gaining permission to observe its users. You can deal with this limitation by agreeing up-front to keep the data confidential or even to destroy it once you have learned what you want to learn. You can also deal with this limitation by contacting various organizations that use your publication in case the first one you select doesn't work out.

You can also create and sustain goodwill by being as unobtrusive as possible while observing. This lack of an obvious presence can also help you collect better data about the audience because they might forget from time to time that you are there.

If you are creating the publication within the midst of the organization, the client contact people for your organization might already have relationships established with members of the audience. This can be both a blessing and a curse. It's a blessing because you can find typical audience members easily. It's a curse because the client contact people might be nervous about anyone else interacting with clients, even people from within the organization. This nervousness is understandable, because if client contact people lose an account because of something you did while observing, they get into trouble. To deal with this, you might need to work with the client contact people to plan for field research. You might ask if the two of you could visit the site together. You might also need to persuade them that a publication that has been designed with rich information about the audience in mind will be easier to sell. In addition, client contact people might also learn more about their clients by participating in the field observations. If the client contact person does accompany you, be sure to outline clearly what your goals and methods are for observing. Sales pitches during field research or excessive intervention when the client becomes confused might skew your results. However, even an imperfect field observation can yield a great deal of useful information.

Because field studies are the most expensive and time-consuming studies, you might find it difficult to persuade others within your organization to allow publication designers to conduct these studies. However, the richness of the data that should result in a more appropriately designed publication justifies the time and expense that a field study conducted early in the design process takes. It's less costly to find out about and then design for the users from the start than it is to guess about users and later have to make modifications and staff phone support lines.

Timing

If you want to find out how users typically act, you can observe an existing publication's use during the initial phases of the design process. If no publication exists, you can still observe typical users in their work environments to give you information to guide your design of your publication. After the publication has been designed, some organizations release it to a few test clients (beta testing) and then depend on voluntary response to guide revisions. You might wish to expand on this beta testing by visiting the clients' sites and actually observing use rather than hoping the test users will comment on the topics you want to find out about.

Although field research can be expensive and time-consuming initially, the quality of the data it can provide about users enables you to create an appropriate publication from the start. Otherwise, you might guess wrong and then have to do costly revisions later on. To see how clearly users interpret your words, in addition to surveys and observations of users both in and out of the lab, you can employ readability tests for your publication.

Assessing How Well Typical Users Understand the Publication Through Readability Tests

Readability test differ from the usability tests discussed previously, in that readability tests focus mainly on how your users interpret the words in your publication. Keep in mind the principles covered in this section to make readability tests meet your needs.

Advantages

In order to test typical paper publications, one can conduct reading tests to see how understandable the words are. These tests have some use for electronic publications, especially to see how well users can locate specific information and how well they can understand it. You can also test several users at the same time with readability testing. Readability testing usually does not take a great deal of time or sophisticated equipment. However, an electronic publication usually involves much more than reading straight through a text and grasping it. Therefore, readability tests alone can't give you a sense of how users interact with a publication. Nevertheless, if supplemented by other methods discussed in this chapter, you can use readability tests to provide another useful viewpoint on your publication.

Methods

When you design a test for readability, determine what goals you have for how the audience will process your publication. You might want them to read through all the text and recall it. Thus, you design a test to measure recall. You might want them to be able to find information when they need it; if so, design a test for how easily they find information. You might want them to apply the information they have read and found; if so, design a test that will indicate whether or not they can do what they need to do once they have read the text. Table 32.5 shows a sample set of tasks designed to measure readability; each task is designed depending on the goal for the publication.

Table 32.5. Testing for readability.

Goals of the Publication	Possible Testing Tasks	Comments for the Test Designer
Users should be able to locate information when they need it.	Find the e-mail addresses of the designers of this Web page.	In this case, your readers will use the publication for reference, only looking up what they need to know when they need to know it.
Users should be able to understand and recall the information they have read.	Read the section of this CD-ROM product which tells about family life in Thailand. List three of the five distinguishing features it discusses.	If you want people to remember what they have read, design a test that measures recall. You may not need to test for total recall; sometimes recalling only a portion is acceptable for your goals.
Users should be able to complete a task after reading how to do so.	Read the troubleshooting section of this training publication and take appropriate actions when the gauge on your control panel reaches 4500.	Sometimes after locating and reading information, users need to take action. If they can complete the action, your publication has probably succeeded. (If the users can't, be sure they aren't in any danger.)

In addition to designing your own readability tests, you can also use the software built into many word processors to calculate the readability of the text you create. This software calculates the number of words per sentence and other surface grammatical features of the text. It assesses a score indicating the text's level of difficulty. These electronic readability indexes have limited usefulness (see Chapter 12). They deal only with the readability of the text in isolation from design. In addition, they don't deal with how obscure or common the vocabulary in the text is. Use these readability tools as a starting point for assessing readability, but don't stop with them. Using typical users to test the readability of your publication's text can compensate for some of the limitations of readability software.

Limitations

Electronic publications are meant to be used, not just read. Therefore, readability tests can only measure the quality of the words in the publication. A great part of the communicative power of electronic publications lies in how the visual design communicates. Only usability testing can measure how well users interpret and employ non-verbal symbols. Readability tests also can't ascertain how well a publication functions, whether all the links work as they should, and so on.

As in user observations, you might not be able to test a large cross-section of the typical users. Nevertheless, you can get a sense of how well some people read your publication.

Timing

If you choose to conduct readability tests, test a draft of the publication that is close to being final. You might need to go through several cycles of testing and revising, so allow enough time before your release date for revision after the readability testing. In fact, you might want to conduct readability tests on a new or revised publication before conducting usability tests.

Collecting Reactions from a Broad Group of Users Though Post-Release Testing

As I mentioned at the beginning of this chapter, post-release testing used to be the only kind of testing done for many publications. In too many cases, it's still the only kind, but if you want your publication to meet the needs of your audience and to remain competitive, you'd be wise to supplement post-release testing with one of the types of testing mentioned already.

Advantages

If you use one of the pre-release testing methods, your job isn't necessarily done. If you plan to revise your publication or plan to create similar ones, the results of post-release testing can serve you well for future decision making. Post-release responses can provide relatively inexpensive data about problems that actual users have.

Methods

Post-release testing involves gathering and using responses from the actual audience. You can design deliberate ways to solicit this feedback, or you can simply collect what people choose to tell you.

If you wish to be deliberate, you can design an audience response opportunity into your publication. This might take the form of a mail-back survey with questions about a CD-ROM publication. Or, if you are creating a Web page, you might wish to create a link to a site where audience members can send you messages about the publication electronically. In either case, you'll want to design the questions according to the advice about surveys discussed earlier in this chapter.

Giving audience members a phone help number can also give you data for revising the publication. If your organization's phone support staff members keep logs of their calls from users with problems, you can look over those logs for ideas about not only how well your publication functions, but also about how users interact with it. Talking to the phone support staff yourself can also give you insight as to what they perceive to be the most serious problems with the publication. (However, if you have done extensive audience research and testing before release, the phone support staff might find themselves twiddling their thumbs after release.) Remember that providing extensive phone support after release tends to be much more expensive than creating the publication using a rich picture of the audience in the first place.

A final form of post-release testing might not be available to everyone, but can give you insights. Various periodicals feature reviews of new products. These reviews can give you insight as to what one or two people think of your publication. You can be fairly confident that these reviewers have used your publication extensively.

Limitations

As mentioned earlier in the chapter, if you have guessed incorrectly about audience needs and have conducted no pre-release testing, you will release a publication that does not meet audience needs. You will probably have to re-release an improved version of your publication; thus, a great deal of your development work has been wasted. Nevertheless, post-release testing can supplement pre-release testing.

Allowing audience members to respond when they please can also give you information, but it might be skewed because people with problems are more likely to call or write than those with smooth sailing. Nevertheless, if you see a trend in the reported problems, you might need to make revisions in future publications. Use this unsolicited response wisely; remember that it might well not be representative of all users.

Timing

Naturally, post-release testing comes after your publication has been released. Think of it as part of an on-going conversation with your audience. The pre-release audience data you have collected is probably from only a small sample of users and usually has them trying out an incomplete publication. Your post-release data might involve a broader range and larger number of users working with a polished publication in their daily work over a longer period of time.

Choose the user testing method that suits your needs and goals best, and be aware of the advantages and limitations of each. You might wish to use the methods in combination or modify them to fit your situation. Using as many methods as you can helps you create as rich and accurate a picture of the audience as possible. And remember that you don't have to know everything to know something about your audience. You can use the audience data you have to make decisions about your publication if you avoid the following pitfalls.

Pitfalls to Avoid

In order to get useful results from your testing, you need to make sure that your audience data-gathering techniques avoid the following problems. Although no data-gathering technique gives infallible information, avoiding the following common problem areas can make your data as useful as possible.

Testing Non-Typical Users

As you try to limit the costs of user testing, you might be tempted to test in-house users who might not be typical of your intended audience. Some people who write the publication simply test it themselves. This might work if you are testing for software functionality, but remember these three words if you're thinking of testing non-typical users for usability: Don't do it! You might learn something from testing non-typical users, but it won't give you the right kind of data to enable you to create a publication to meet the needs of your target audience. Even if you have built a rich picture of your audience from other types of research, you never know what users will do until you watch them. Try your best, even if you have limited resources, to test users who are as typical as you can find.

Assuming That One Person's Problem Is Universal

If you receive a complaint from a user or observe one user having a problem with a certain part of your publication, you might think that every user will have this problem. Indeed, that might be the case, but further testing can either confirm or deny this hypothesis. Don't change the publication, especially in major ways, based on only one person's input. That person's needs might not be typical. The more user testing and observation you do, the better your evidence for making changes to the publication.

You are the final decision-maker about the content and the design of the document. Unless your audience members are very rich and can pay for it directly, publications can't be custom-designed for every user. You might have to make difficult choices between the audience's needs and your resources.

Seeing User Actions as Mistakes when They Violate Your Expectations

When you design a publication, you have in mind how you think the audience will use it. However, when you test it on a typical user, you might find that users use it in ways different than you anticipated. They might not be able to discern your intentions from the publication itself. Even if they do, they will interpret the publication based on mental analogies they have to other publications, both paper and electronic. They will also base their interpretations on what they need from your publication. You may be tempted to see their alternative interpretations as mistakes. They're not. People will interpret the way they interpret. The greater the understanding you gain of the analogies they use for interpreting, the better you can design your publication to meet their expectations and ways of encountering new publications.

You can't force the audience to adapt to your design. You can encourage and ease them in certain directions, but users will do things with your publication that you never dreamed of. People readily adapt technology to their needs, but seldom their needs to technology. The more you can adapt to audience needs and their typical ways of interpreting information, the more successful your publication will be.

Not Testing a Publication Before Release

If you test a publication before release, you'll find that you have a better product for your customers. Calls to phone support lines go down, customers buy your future publications, and they recommend them to their friends because they are usable. In addition, you won't need to re-release your publication to make it more usable. You will only need to release a new version when the content needs to be updated. Overall, the image of your organization as one that cares about its audience will be enhanced.

Testing early in the cycle means that you can narrow the publication to fit audience needs from the start, rather than guessing and having to make revisions when you have guessed wrong. Excellent testing will cost something, but not as much in the long run as poor or nonexistent testing.

How To Use the Results of Testing

Whatever type of test you conduct, you will have a lot of information at the end. In order to make decisions about the direction in which to take the publication, you need to interpret the data you have collected and make decisions based on the data and on your circumstances. You might need to persuade others within the organization about the need for proposed changes to the publication, using the data as evidence. Don't assume, however, that research results are the only guideline for decision making. Also, don't assume that the decisions will be clearly indicated by the data you have collected.

For instance, if Test User A has trouble with part 2 of your publication, don't assume that all users will have that problem. Perhaps User A was not typical, and you'll find that Users B, C, and D had no problem. You may need to decide to go with what works for the most typical users rather than the "least common denominator." If your publication appeals to the people with the most basic understanding, you might bore and frustrate those with greater experience, and vice versa. Sometimes it's possible to design a publication that accommodates both, but at other times it's not possible. Having established an intended, primary audience (see Chapter 12) will enable you to argue for decisions about the publication that will meet their needs.

In persuading others within your organization to make changes to the publication, remember to use both the quantitative and the qualitative data you receive through testing. For instance, I once heard of an organization that videotaped the testing of its new software product. Although the testers presented numbers of how many seconds it took for new screens to appear, what really convinced the designers to speed up the processing in the software was the videotaped footage of frustrated test users pretending to crank the computer to make it speed up. As you use the results of your testing, be aware of what will be persuasive to the others within the organization who participate in the decision-making process about the design of the publication.

Summary

User testing can be most enlightening and helpful if it's done well. Choose the testing method based on the goals you have for the publication, the type of information you need, and your resources for conducting the tests. Create new methods if you need to. If you want to have a publication that meets the needs of the users and ways of dealing with information, you need to conduct pre-release testing. Your users will appreciate your careful attention to their needs, and your publication will stand out from your competitors' electronic publications.

Advertising Your Document

33

by William R. Stanek

Advertising is the art of selling your product to consumers. When you advertise your document, you provide information to consumers to help sell the document. The Internet will one day be the most powerful advertising mechanism in the world—in fact, it may already be. Not only can you reach millions of consumers, you can do so at bargain-basement prices. Thousands of businesses have discovered this gold mine. They are online and doing business on the Internet. These businesses are guiding the commercialization of the Internet and changing the way Internet users think about business activities.

Recently a flood of commercial online service users have gained access to the Internet. Companies such as America Online and CompuServe have provided full Internet access to their users. These users have different attitudes toward online businesses. Their online culture sees business as a necessary and important part of the online world. By the end of 1995, over five million commercial online service users will be on the Internet. Add these users to the flood of new users who join through an Internet service provider each month (approximately 175–250,000), and you have an Internet that is rocketing toward commercialization.

As an electronic publisher, you should be at the forefront of the cyberspace advertising movement. The goal of advertising is to help sell your product and you do this by providing key information about the product. This key information is often called the selling points for the product. For example, why would someone want to buy your publication? What would they gain from reading it? Traditional publishers use the front and back covers of their publications to display selling points. Electronic publishers can use the Internet and the Web to provide consumers with the product's selling points and much more.

The Internet empowers you to reach all Internet users via electronic mail and discussion groups. The World Wide Web empowers you to compete on a level with corporate conglomerates and reach consumers in a highly interactive and visual manner that compares with personal sales visits in its effectiveness. In no other medium can the small publisher wield so much power, and you can do so for pennies if you so choose.

On the Internet and the World Wide Web, you can use many ways to spread the word about your products. Your success is tied directly to your advertising approach and the ways in which you advertise. This chapter explains marketing approaches and the successful ways to advertise on the Internet and the World Wide Web, including:

- Advertising on the Internet
- Spreading the word directly via e-mail
- Indirect advertising with e-mail
- Signature files
- Plan files
- Display advertising on the World Wide Web
- Advertising through sponsorship
- Sponsoring discussion groups
- Sponsoring Web pages

Advertising on the Internet

Spreading the word about your products is what advertising is all about. On the Internet, there are many ways to advertise. Some ways are direct: You communicate directly to the prospective customers. Other ways are indirect: You build goodwill, name recognition and sell your products indirectly.

As you saw in Chapter 25, "Advertising and Protecting Your Document," on the direct advertising method is not the best method to use on the Internet today. Direct advertising on the Internet is frowned upon. Internet users do not like receiving the equivalent of electronic junk mail. However, there are times when you can directly advertise to consumers.

While the growing trend is toward commercialization of the Internet, the indirect method of advertising is still the best. You can generate tremendous results with indirect advertising and do so in a way that is unobtrusive. Internet users will recognize that you are trying to be a good citizen, and before you know it, your company will be a welcome member of the Internet community.

Spreading the Word Directly via E-mail

While electronic mail is the most basic tool on the Internet, it is also the most powerful tool in your Internet advertising arsenal. Every Internet user has access to e-mail, and if you wanted to, you could reach them all. You can create messages and send them to one user, two users, or a hundred users. You can receive messages from Internet users and store them in your electronic mail box.

Some mail tools, such as Eudora, will even let you create mailing lists. With a mailing list, you can send a message to a group of Internet addresses quickly and easily. You do this by building a list of everyone you want to send a particular message to and saving it as a mailing list. The next time you want to send a message to the same group of people, you enter the name of the list instead of dozens of user addresses. The mail tool will then send the message to all the users in the list. Mailing lists are great if you plan to create periodicals.

Using Internet directory facilities, such as Netfind and Whois, you could find the addresses of many Internet users. Netfind and Whois let you search through lists of Internet users in ways similar to how you search through the telephone book white pages. With Internet e-mail you can reach users of America Online, CompuServe, MCI Mail, Prodigy, and many other commercial online services, and you do not need an account on any of these systems. For more information on Netfind and Whois, see Chapter 19, "The World Wide Web."

Still, the best thing about Internet e-mail is the cost. Direct mail advertising would cost you at least 25 cents per consumer. This cost includes bulk rate postage, envelopes, paper, and printing costs if you were to do all the work yourself. If you did not do the work yourself, the cost per consumer could be as much as one dollar. This means direct marketing to 1,000 consumers would cost you $250–$1,000.

On the Internet, there is no per unit cost for e-mail and no cost for sending e-mail to multiple consumers. Yet, the key to using e-mail to advertise your products is not through direct advertising. You should only send direct e-mail advertising to consumers who request it. As you build a presence on the Internet through goodwill, community service and participation, you will find that many Internet users will ask you for information about your products. These are the people you will want to send your informational product brochures to. A company with major presence on the Internet, such as Sun Microsystems or Microsoft, receives hundreds of requests every day for product information.

You can use many programs to send e-mail. Popular mail programs include Pine, Elm, and Eudora. Mail programs tend to be very user-friendly. The startup menu for the Pine mail program is depicted in Figure 33.1. To start writing a message using Pine, you would select C. To view messages sent to you, you would select I to view messages in the current folder or L to view a list of folders. A folder is a file where your mail messages are stored. You can store messages in groups by month and various other ways.

FIGURE 33.1.

The Pine Mail program.

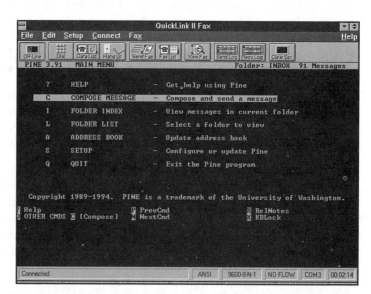

While each mail program is designed somewhat differently, they all let you send e-mail in a similar manner. The organization of a mail message is just like an interoffice memo which has two parts: a header and the message body.

The header usually contains five fields:

To	Who the message is being sent to
From	Who is sending the message

CC	Who should receive a courtesy copy of the message
Date	The current date
Subject	The subject of the message

The message body contains the text of the message. The same is true for an e-mail message except the mail program is smart enough to fill the From and Date fields for you. You only fill the To and the Subject field. In the To field, you type in an e-mail address or group of addresses. In the Subject field, you type in a one line statement about the contents of the message. The CC field is an easy way to send a courtesy copy of the message to other e-mail addresses.

The header may also contain an attachment field. Using the attachment field, you can attach a file to the message. Most e-mail programs will let you attach any type of file, including text and graphics.

In Chapter 19, you saw how addresses are used in the hypertext transfer protocol. The address used with HTTP tells your browser where to look. With e-mail, the address serves the same purpose. It tells the mail program where to send the message.

TIP

The mail address consists of four parts:

- An optional full name of the person you are sending mail to. The mail program will not use this part to address the message, it is simply an eye-pleasing addition to the address.
- The login name of the person you are sending mail to.
- The host computer his or her account is on.
- The domain for the host computer.

An example of a typical e-mail address is

```
William Stanek <william@aloha.com>
```

In the example, the full name of the recipient is William Stanek. The login name is william. The host computer is aloha and the domain is com.

An example e-mail address without the optional full name field is william@aloha.com.

If you know the e-mail address of someone on a commercial online service, you can convert the address to an Internet address, and they can receive a message you sent from the Internet. For example: 74654,112 is my CompuServe address. To convert this to an Internet address I change the comma to a period and put in the host and domain information for CompuServe. A message addressed as 74654.112@compuserve.com would reach my CompuServe mail box.

Indirect Advertising with E-Mail

While you only want to directly advertise to consumers that request information, you can also find many ways to advertise indirectly using e-mail. You will find that indirect or unobtrusive ways of advertising are remarkably effective. Very few Internet users will be offended by indirect advertising. Those few users would probably be offended if you simply mentioned that you are conducting business on the Internet. You cannot please everyone. The best thing you can do is to show those Internet users who dislike commercial enterprises how wrong they are by acting responsibly and in general, you should not waste time responding to them directly.

This section discusses two methods for indirect advertising with e-mail:

- Signature files
- Plan files

Signature Files

Signature files are a very indirect and a highly effective way to advertise. A signature file is a file that can be automatically appended to any message you send via e-mail. This includes standard mail messages and mail messages you post to discussion groups. Messages posted to discussion groups are what make signature files powerful. Thousands of people may read a message you have posted to a discussion group, and every one of them will see your signature.

Signature files are also used widely on the Internet. When you include such a file in a message, it is called your signature because it is the last part of the message. Figure 33.2 depicts one of my signatures. The signature starts from the line with my name then goes on to briefly tell readers of the message about me and The Virtual Press. The message is simple, and if readers want to learn more about TVP or its contests, they can go to the Web site listed or send an e-mail message asking for more information.

Signatures can be wild, elaborate or simple. Some users have signature files that discuss philosophical issues, tell stories or jokes. Other users have elaborate signature files that include ASCII art. The way you use signatures tells people a lot about who you are and what you are about.

On most systems, you can add a signature to your messages simply by creating a file called `.signature`. Adding the signature to your messages is easy. Most browsers check for the `.signature` file and if it exists, they will automatically append it to any message you create. Just because you created a signature file, does not mean you have to use it all the time. In Pine, when you select C, your signature is written to the end of the new mail message immediately. This way you can edit or delete the signature as you wish.

#### Chapter 33

FIGURE 33.2.

Using signatures to advertise.

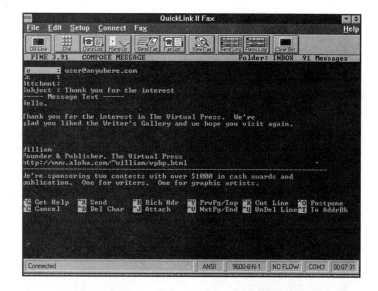

The period before the filename .signature is a UNIX convention signifying that the file is a hidden file. Hidden files are not normally listed unless the user specifically requests to see a listing of all files in a directory.

In the latest version of the Netscape browser, you can select any valid file on your system to be the signature file. If you have the Netscape browser, you can specify a signature file by selecting Preferences under the Options menu. After accessing Preferences, you activate the Set Preferences On menu and select Mail and News. From this screen, you enter the name of the signature file in the Signature File text window.

Many heated debates have started over the issue of signatures and usually not because business persons have used them. Most debates over signatures start because people abuse them. They create signatures that are 50 lines long or are downright rude. The best signatures are six lines or less, which is short enough not to offend others and long enough to make a statement.

Good business signatures do not scream advertisements at Internet users. Nothing will get you in hot water more quickly than blatant advertising in your signature, such as this get-rich-quick scheme:

> Get Rich Quick. Make A Million Dollars. Live In Luxury.
> Send $9.99 To Rip Offs R Us.

The advertising in your signature should not be obtrusive. Hundreds of companies sell products using logos and slogans. Advertisements usually do not tell readers directly to buy now. Often, an ad simply shows the product. A good signature advertising your projects will do the same. If people are interested in purchasing your products, they will follow pointers in your signature or send you e-mail.

A good signature to advertise your publishing projects should contain some of the following items:

- Company slogan or project title with very short description
- Company address
- Phone/fax number
- Pointers to World Wide Web pages
- Pointers to Gopher files

You can have several signatures if you wish. The way to do this using traditional e-mail programs such as Pine is to create several files and copy them to your `.signature` file as you wish to use them. For example, you could create a file called `.signature.business` and a file called `.signature.fun`. When you are conducting business, you copy the `.signature.business` file into your `.signature` file. When you are on your own time, you copy the `.signature.fun` file into your `.signature` file.

Yet if you want to increase the visibility of your business to the fullest, you may want to use a business-oriented signature all the time. I have several signatures that I use depending on whom I am sending a message to. When conducting business with a fellow business person, I use the signature depicted in Figure 33.3. As you see, signatures can be as versatile and effective as you make them.

NOTE

A few Internet users encode their signatures. This way, only the people that want to read the signature will. The most common encoding method is uuencoding. UUENCODE is a simple encoding tool. To decode the signature, you would uudecode it. UUDECODE is a simple decoding tool that will extract the uuencoded text and restore it to its original readable form. Both UUENCODE and UUDECODE are available on the Internet for free. If you see a signature that is unreadable and has many strange characters, it is probably encoded.

FIGURE 33.3.

Be versatile; use more than one signature.

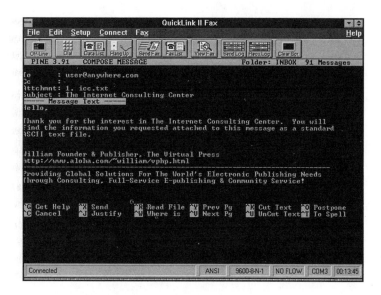

Plan Files

On the Internet you can use several ways to find things out about other users. One of these ways is a program called finger. In its simplest form, the finger command will tell you if someone is currently logged on to his account and what his full name is. By creating a file called plan in your directory, you can increase the functionality of the finger command. Finger looks for this plan file and if it exists, it adds the contents of the file to the normal output. As an electronic publisher, you can use the plan file to advertise information about your publications and to learn more about the people who send you e-mail.

On UNIX systems, .plan is the name of the file you would create. On an IBM PC system, plan.txt would be the name of the file. Plan files are a great way to tell the Internet world more about your publishing projects. They can contain anything you want from product descriptions to prices and background information.

The philosophy pertaining to plan files is this: The plan file is only displayed when someone uses the finger command to try to learn more information about you. If someone is actively seeking information about you, it is perfectly acceptable to advertise to them.

The finger command is virtually universal on the Internet. Finger can be accessed from any standard shell prompt and from World Wide Web gateways. This means anyone can use finger to learn more about you and your products.

Here is a partial plan file from The Virtual Press. The plan gives detailed information about TVP's annual writer's contest. It also contains ordering information for anthologies associated with the contest. To see the entire plan file enter the command, finger william@aloha.com.

The Virtual Press Annual Writer's Contest Rules

Headquarters   Submissions until June 1996

408 Division St.   534 Wright Ave.
Shawano, WI 54166   Wahiawa, HI 96786

The Virtual Press Annual Writer's Contest is an international contest for
unpublished short stories in the English language in three categories:
science fiction, fantasy, and mystery. All submissions should be 5,000 words
or less. Charges $10 entry fee/submission. Awards, in each of the three
categories: $75, $50, $25, $10. Winners will be published in annual
anthology. Runners-up in each of the three categories in 5th through 10th
place will be considered for publication in anthologies in their respective
categories.

Deadline: Nov. 1.

The fastest way to find out if you're a winner is to check The Virtual Press
Home Page on the Internet:

http://tvp.com/

Place an order for The Virtual Press Best Of series now at special discounted
rates for contest entrants! Available on floppy disk!

Order Form (for DOS/Windows version)

_____ The Virtual Press Best Mysteries @ $7.95/each $_____
_____ The Virtual Press Best Fantasy @ $7.95/each $_____
_____ The Virtual Press Best Science Fiction @ $7.95/eac$_____

         Total (US funds/ check or money order) $_____

Preferred format: ____ 3 1/2"   ___ 5 1/4"
                               ____ Double-density (DD) _____ High-density (HD)
                               ____ Standard   _____ Enhanced (VGA/SVGA)

Name: _____
Address: _____
               _____
               _____
Country: _____
Zipcode: _____

TIP

All public Internet systems support `finger`. The syntax from a shell command line is
simple.

To learn more about a user, use this format:

`finger user_name@anywhere.com`

To learn more about an organization or domain, use this format:

`finger @anywhere.com`

On the World Wide Web, there are several finger gateways. One of these gateways is

```
http://www.bprc.mps.ohio-state.edu/cgi-bin/finger.pl
```

Sponsorship

Sponsorship is a way to passively advertise. Whether you have watched the Indianapolis 500, championship ice skating, or a football game, you have seen sponsorship advertising in action. The corporations sponsoring cars, skaters, and teams hang their company logos out where everyone can see them. They put logos on signs that line the fields, rinks, and raceways. They put decals on the racing cars. They put advertising on warm up uniforms or make the uniforms advertising by virtue of the brand name athletes are wearing. Sponsorship of Web pages or Web sites is a great way to promote your products as well.

You can sponsor activities in cyberspace the same way major corporations sponsor sporting events. Two broad sponsorship models are in use on the Internet:

- Direct sponsorship
- Indirect sponsorship

Indirect Sponsorship

A few high-tech companies use the indirect method. One of the biggest providers of indirect sponsorship on the Internet is Sun Microsystems. They offer tremendous support to many new companies by providing the necessary equipment to start Internet Web sites or simply providing a behind the scenes helping hand when one is needed during setup of the site. Many companies would not be in business without this type of sponsorship.

In return for the sponsorship, companies provide notices about where they obtained the equipment. Sun Microsystems provided support for ESPNET SportsZone, which is a service of Starwave Corporation and ESPN. You can view their advertisement by visiting their site: `http://espnet.sportszone.com/`.

Direct Sponsorship

When companies directly sponsor an activity in cyberspace, they do so just like companies do everyday at the raceway. They hang up a sign that tells the world they are the sponsors for this event. When companies indirectly sponsor an activity in cyberspace, they provide support for the activity. They usually do this by donating equipment necessary to conduct the activity much like the warm up suits, footballs, or motor oil sponsors provide.

Most companies prefer direct sponsorship. This way the company's name is openly displayed to consumers. The facilities of the World Wide Web allow you to provide more than the company logo and brief information about the company. You can also provide a hypertext link to your Web pages as part of the advertising. In this way, consumers who want to learn more about your company and products can do so at the touch of a button. They move the pointer to the highlighted text, press the left mouse button and a moment later, they are at your Web site.

The three areas for direct sponsorship are

- Sponsorship of Internet services
- Sponsorship of discussion groups
- Sponsorship of Web sites

Sponsorship of Internet Services

As an electronic publisher, you want to spread the word about your products, and sponsoring Internet services is a great way to do this. Sponsors of Internet services gain visibility in the Internet community. Many services would not be available at all without corporate sponsorship. Internet users recognize this, and the result is that the company builds goodwill.

Community services on the Internet are expensive to maintain. Some of the most expensive services to maintain are databases. Databases on the Web include lists of Web sites, Web resources, Internet users, Gopher sites, Gopher resources, and much more. Sun Microsystems, Computer Storage, Internet Shopping Network, and Frame Technology are the major sponsors for the InfoSeek Web resource database. You can view the InfoSeek Web page at `http://ww2.infoseek.com/doc/help/Sponsors/html`.

At the InfoSeek site, a single sponsor's logo or brief advertisement is displayed with the search results. When the next search is made, a different sponsor's ad is displayed. In this way, each sponsor gets to display its information. Although the InfoSeek sponsors are large corporate sponsors, even the smallest of companies can sponsor Internet services. By sponsoring a service, your publications will gain visibility in the Internet community. You may find the rates are affordable and significantly less than the cost of print advertising.

In the past most Internet services were supported by educational institutions, but the face of the Internet is changing. The Internet is growing explosively, from a community of a few million in 1990 to over 30,000,000 today. University computers cannot handle the strain put on their systems when a service they offer becomes popular on today's Internet.

The universities either have to get funds to update their systems, push the service out into the business sector, or discontinue the service. Recently Stanford University faced this tough decision. A service created by two doctoral candidates was taxing the university's computing resources to the point where little except the service could operate. This service was the Yahoo database of Web resources. Some 200,000 users were using the database every day. The decision to make was whether the service would be discontinued or moved to the commercial sector.

With the help of Netscape Communications Corporation, the database moved to the commercial sector, and Yahoo the corporation was born. Yahoo Corporation plans to follow a sponsorship model similar to the one used by InfoSeek Corporation. Together, these databases claim to attract over 500,000 visitors every day. The volume of visitors to these databases makes them terrific examples of the potential of sponsorship. Sponsorship can be one more way for readers to find out about you and your publications.

Sponsoring Discussion Groups

Discussion groups are another great way to spread the word about your publishing projects. Sponsors of discussion groups gain visibility in the Internet community and build goodwill. The best thing about sponsorship of discussion groups is that it is the most affordable way to passively advertise.

Discussion groups cover just about any topic you can think of. On the Internet, there are thousands of discussion groups, including mailing lists and newsgroups. The most common type of discussion groups are unmoderated discussion groups. Any message sent to an unmoderated group is automatically posted to the group. The other common type of discussion group is the moderated discussion group. All messages posted to a moderated group are screened by the group moderator to ensure they are appropriate to the discussion before they are posted to the group. Because of this screening, moderated groups tend to have the best discussions at the penalty of a slight delay in posting.

Moderating discussion groups takes dedication and time. Many discussion groups are so popular that moderators spend hours every day screening messages or compiling them into a digest for the group's members. Sometimes discussion groups are so popular that moderators could not afford to spend the time to moderate the discussion. When this happens, the moderators either close the discussion group, pass the group on to a new moderator or give up their role as moderator and let the group go on unmoderated.

The Internet community recognizes that something wonderful is lost when a group changes its role or disappears. To ensure this does not happen, a growing trend is to ask for sponsors. With sponsorship, the maintenance of the discussion group is no longer a complete labor of love. Moderators get compensated for their time, and the discussion continues. Everyone wins.

Some discussion groups are sponsored by a single organization. This is true for the `com-priv` discussion group. `Com-priv` discusses issues related to the commercialization and privatization of the Internet. `Com-priv` is a hot group on the Net and is sponsored by Performance Systems International, an Internet access provider. Performance Systems International generates tremendous visibility in the Internet community through its sponsorship of `com-priv`.

On the Internet, many discussion groups are trying the sponsorship model on a temporary basis. The moderators know they have a topic of high interest by the sheer volume of messages posted to the group. As there is an actual list of all members of the group, the moderators also know how many people worldwide are tracking the group's discussion.

A relatively new discussion group trying to get sponsors discusses marketing on the Internet. The group is called internet-marketing. Before trying to attract sponsors, the moderator of the group considered many options, including charging group members an annual membership fee. The concept of charging a membership fee was discussed at length, but most of group's members were opposed to the idea. Currently, internet-marketing is asking companies to sponsor the group for one week at a time. The current sponsor's name is displayed at the top of each day's digest of the discussion. This guarantees the sponsor's information is seen by the thousands of subscribers to the group.

Sponsoring Web Sites

The final way to passively advertise is to sponsor informational and community service areas on the World Wide Web. Some sites on the Web are simply interesting places to visit. The sites are directed at certain groups of users, such as writers. They include valuable information about their topics, areas where Web users can display their ideas or creations, links to resources or to other fun places to visit.

Corporations from around the world are sponsoring Web sites. These companies recognize the value in providing information to the Internet community. They also recognize that it is best to let the experts in an area provide the information users seek. This is especially true when a site has a proven track record.

Web sites can track visitors to the site by many means. The most common way to count visits to a site is to track the number of times each page at the site is accessed. This method of counting is usually referred to as the number of hits at a site. For any site, these numbers can be very misleading. This is especially true for large sites because they may have hundreds of pages. For example, a single visitor to the site accesses 90 pages. Looking only at the number of hits, it looks like 90 visitors came to the site.

Unscrupulous persons seeking sponsorship for their sites will quote extremely high hit rates such as, one million for the year or 250,000 for a one-month period. They will go on to tell potential sponsors that the hit rate represents the number of visitors to the site. Or they will simply not explain the number at all and leave it to the would-be sponsor's imagination.

To ensure hit rates are not misleading, the number of unique visits to the site during a given period should also be given. A unique visit to the site means that if one person visits the site and accesses six pages, the visit only counts once. If the same person returned to the site later the same day or the next day, all pages she visited at that time would count as one unique visit.

Using the number of unique visits you can balance the hit ratio and get a good picture of the number of pages each visitor looks at. A site with 1,000,000 hits annually may have only 100,000 unique visits. This means the average visitor to the site looks at 10 pages before leaving. If you plan to sponsor a Web site ask for the number of hits, the number of unique visits, and the hit to visit ratio. This will give you a better picture of the popularity of the site.

Display Advertising on the World Wide Web

Display advertising on the World Wide Web is the growth area for advertising on the Internet. Nowhere on the Internet will you find more advertising than on the World Wide Web. Almost every major company in the world has a place on the Web. These companies represent many industries: the food and beverage industry, snack foods, consumer goods, traditional publishers and more.

Coca-Cola corporation is one of several companies from the food and beverage industry that are advertising on the Web. The graphics at the Coca-Cola site are dazzling. You can see for yourself by visiting the http://www.cocacola.com/. Coca-Cola generates indirect sales from its display advertising. No one is going to download a can of Coke on the Web, but after visiting the site, they may just visit the refrigerator.

Hershey Corporation represents a company in the snack food industry. Hershey Corporation's home page is available at http://www.microserve.net/~hershey/welcome.html. Hershey's home page invites everyone to visit Chocolate Town. Hershey also generates indirect sales from its display advertising. No one is going to download a Hershey's candy bar on the Web, but after wandering the site, they may go buy a Hershey's chocolate bar.

For a good example of a small publisher, you can visit the Beer magazine Web site at http://www.ambrew.com/btm/. *Beer* magazine is a print magazine for people who love beer and for people who want to brew their own at home. The publishers do not make any money directly by displaying articles from the magazine online, but they do gain tremendous exposure. *Beer* magazine has increased sales and visibility greatly by advertising on the Web.

The list of companies advertising on the Web doesn't end with consumer products or traditional publishers. It includes companies that make their money directly from advertising, such as television and radio stations. The ABC affiliate KGO-TV, serving the San Francisco and Silicon Valley area, has their own Web site at http://www.kgo-tv.com. KGO-TV is not on the Web to sell products to the consumers. However, it is gaining worldwide visibility and most probably attracting new viewers. A larger viewing audience means the company boosts its image and should be able to attract more advertisers.

Government agencies from the CIA to NSA have sites on the Web. NSA's Web site is shown in Figure 33.4. State agencies and cities are advertising on the Web. The City of West Hollywood's Web site, shown in Figure 33.5, has a wealth of information about the city of

West Hollywood. They are advertising to spread the word about their agencies, to build good-will, and to become members of the Internet community. Their sites are informational, but it is advertising just the same.

FIGURE 33.4.

NSA on the Web.

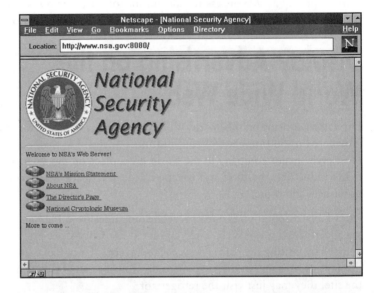

FIGURE 33.5.

The City of West Hollywood on the Web.

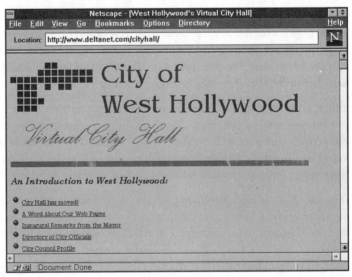

Organizations advertising on the Web have one thing in common, they recognize that Web advertising is an extremely cost-effective way to spread the word about their products. For the cost of a single full-page advertisement in one issue of a major magazine, the company can set up an entire Web site and probably pay the Internet connection charges for an entire year. For the cost of a primetime television commercial thirty seconds in length, the company can pay the salary of a Web administrator for an entire year. The best news is that if you build a hot Web site, you will attract hundreds, and possibly thousands, of visitors every day of the year.

Another great thing about the Web is that you do not need your own Web server to advertise on the Web. A surprising fact is that many major companies lease space from an Internet Service Provider. The Hershey Corporation homepage (`http://www.microserve.net/~hershey/welcome.html`) is on an Internet service provider's Web server.

Using a commercial Web server makes display advertising on the Web the low budget choice. A small site's expenses may be as low as $1 a day. One dollar a day to reach one hundred consumers a day means you're paying a penny per consumer you reach with your message.

However, the per consumer cost of Web advertising is not what makes it so attractive. Television advocates would argue that you could potentially reach one million consumers through a 30-second primetime commercial. While this may be true, on a Web site you will not just catch the consumers' ears as they rush to the refrigerator. You will get their full attention in living color and at their own pace and convenience.

Web advertising is cost-effective because of the high-level of interaction it allows you to have with consumers. Interaction is the key to sales. Interaction puts you on a level close to one you would be on if you personally visited each consumer that visited your site.

Web advertising is sometimes bold and direct, but more often organizations follow an information-based approach to advertising. Visit the sites shown in this section and behind the flashy graphics, you will find information. Information is the key to bringing consumers to your site. The more information you provide to consumers, the better and more popular your site will be.

Summary

Spreading the word about your products is what advertising is all about. There are many direct and indirect ways to advertise on the Internet. Every Internet user has access to e-mail, and if you want to, you can reach them all. However, you should directly advertise only to consumers that request information. You will find that indirect ways of advertising are remarkably effective. Very few Internet users will be offended by indirect advertising.

You can sponsor activities in cyberspace the same way major corporations sponsor sporting events. Sponsorship lets you advertise in a way that is passive and effective. The growth area for advertising on the Internet is the World Wide Web. No where on the Internet will you find more advertising than on the World Wide Web. On the Web, you can display blatant advertising if you want. Yet, the key to advertising on the Internet and the Web is to provide information consumers will value.

Publishing and Marketing Tips

34

by William R. Stanek

Marketing and publishing go hand in hand. A work will not sell unless it is marketed. Before a work is produced, publishers have to consider carefully how they are going to sell the product to the world. To sell the product, the publisher has to adopt a strategy. The strategy you adopt is essential for the success of your project.

Often, publishers begin marketing a publication before it is produced. This gives the publisher a window of opportunity to sell the product to consumers before it is even produced. This window for early marketing of the product is called lead time. Lead time is extremely important, especially if you are depending on sales of the publication. Sales mean money to your publishing operation. Positive cash flow means you can afford to continue publishing the current project and possibly start work on another project.

Because marketing involves selling the product, marketing and advertising are often confused. Advertising is a single activity. The intent of advertising is to help sell the product. Marketing is really a group of activities that includes all steps necessary to get the finished publication to customers. Advertising is one of those activities. Other activities include storing, shipping, and selling the product.

Yet, the most important aspects of marketing are building the image of your projects and establishing a relationship with customers. Behave like an amateur and the public will treat you like an amateur. Act like you do not care about the customer and the customer will not care about you or your ventures. It is fortunate that the modern publisher has such a powerful tool as the Internet available. The Internet has terrific facilities to help you market your projects. These facilities can help you build the image of your projects and establish relationships with customers.

This chapter explores every step of the publishing and marketing process. The chapter will guide you through

- Publishing and beyond
- Marketing the whole story
- Relationship marketing
- Image building
- Getting the word out on the Internet
- Getting the word out on the Web fast

Publishing and Beyond

At this point, the publication is either completed or you have contemplated the steps that will take the project through to completion. Other chapters have discussed ways to create the project and mediums for the project. As you prepare to publish the project, there are many considerations you will want to make, but your primary concern might be to keep expenses as low as possible.

Traditional publishers spend a considerable amount of time calculating the number of works to print. They base the size of the printing on many factors, but the basic factors that determine the print run are the type of publication and the expected demand. Overestimate the demand and the publisher will incur losses. Underestimate the demand and the publisher might lose the opportunity to make a sale.

Even when publishers are sure they have a best-seller on their hands, they do not crank up the printing presses and start printing books. The difference between a product that makes money and one that doesn't has little to do with whether the book was a potential best-seller and more to do with good judgment on the part of the publisher. As ironic as it might seem, best-sellers sometimes lose money. The publisher might have paid the author too large an advance, printed too many books on the first printing, made a subsequent printing too early, or spent too much money advertising and promoting the book.

As a result, a book that should have been a winner was not because of an error in judgment by the publisher. At this point it does not matter if the publication sold one million copies or one. The publication lost money and this error in judgment might have cost the publisher millions of dollars, her job, or the company.

Additionally, traditional publishers incur expenses every time they go back to press. For each printing, there are associated setup fees beyond the printing and material costs for the publication. When a book publisher prints 5,000 books, he or she has to then store those books. The books have to be shipped to distributors and retailers. Books that do not sell might be shipped back to the publisher at the publisher's expense. These costs add up quickly and can also be the reason a work loses money.

Electronic publishers can learn many lessons from traditional publishers. The important thing to keep in mind is that electronic publishing makes it possible for you to have virtually zero overhead. You do not have to publish 5,000 copies of the project even if you have the funds to do so and believe the work will sell 5,000 copies over its life.

Keep in mind that inventory sitting on the shelf costs you money. Every dollar you spend on inventory could be put to better use in other areas of your publishing operation. You could use the money to market the product. You could use the money to start another project, or you could let the money earn interest in the bank. Any use of your material resources is better than letting them sit on your shelves as inventory.

Electronic publishing makes it possible for a print run of any size to be profitable. A small publisher can publish the work one disk at a time. Every time an order is placed, the publisher can turn on the computer, copy the publication onto a new disk, attach a label to the disk, put the disk in packaging, and ship the finished product to the customer. You have low overhead and only have to maintain sufficient supplies in stock to meet the immediate demand.

Do not put your publishing operation in a glass box. Before problems arise you should create a contingency plan. One hundred orders for the publication might come in on the same day, and you might not be able to meet the demand. You might have to order disks, labels, envelopes, or other items. Your printer might malfunction. Your hard disk might crash. There are many things that can and will go wrong.

The contingency plan does not have to be elaborate. It can include

- Ensuring you have multiple copies of the master disks for the publication
- Making provisions to obtain or borrow a computer if your computer breaks down
- Having supplies on hand to meet the demand
- Knowing where you want to order supplies if demand exceeds your supplies

TIP

Never rely on a single point of failure. Back up everything you do in your publishing venture. In the long term this will save you losses and frustration. If you are in the process of creating the publication, make backups of all critical files regularly. If the project is finished, make multiple master copies and store them in several locations.

It might also be a good idea if the places in which you store master copies are geographically separated from each other. If you store master disks in your home office, protect yourself from catastrophic loss by storing copies in a location other than your home.

You should calculate your inventory needs as closely as a publisher calculates print run sizes. Base the size of your inventory on the actual sales you anticipate over a given period and your ability to meet the demand. You should also provide a small reserve inventory in case of emergency.

Figuring out demand and your ability to meet demand is not always easy. This is particularly true if this is your first project. For a first project, the best thing you can do is to obtain the supplies necessary to publish the work and prepare all the go-to-print aspects of the project in electronic form. The supplies you will typically need include

- Disks
- Labels
- Packaging material
- Mailer inserts

Disk Tips

If you haven't already considered the type of disk you plan to publish on, now is the time. The supplies you need to create the finished product are directly related to the type of disc you publish on. You can publish on floppy disk or compact disc.

As Table 34.1 depicts, there are many disk formats and sizes. If you plan to publish on CD-ROM, you might also want to consider releasing the publication on high-density floppy disks. This will ensure the work is available to a wider audience. If you plan to publish on floppy disk, you should publish on $3^1/_2$-inch and $5^1/_4$-inch floppies. Again, this will ensure the work is available to a wider audience.

Each type of disk has a different storage capacity. To lower costs as much as possible, you will want to publish your project on the medium that makes the most sense. The cheapest way to publish is to use as few disks as possible and use the least expensive disk format whenever possible. Because high density drives are backward-compatible with double-density drive formats, always choose double-density over high density if possible and practical. In this way, any computer user with a high-density or a double-density disk drive can use the publication.

Table 34.1. Disk types and storage capacities.

Disk Size	Format	Storage Capacity (without compression)
$3^1/_2$-inch	Double-sided (DS) Double-density (DD)	720KB
$3^1/_2$-inch	Double-sided (DS) High-density (HD)	1,440KB
$5^1/_4$-inch	Double-sided (DS) Double-density (DD)	360KB
$5^1/_4$-inch	Double-sided (DS) High-density (HD)	1,200KB
n/a	CD-ROM	600,000KB

Although publishing on floppy disk is cheap, many consumers prefer CD-ROM. This popularity makes CD-ROM publications more marketable. The problem is that a single CD-ROM might cost a small publisher $7–$15 to produce. Publish on CD-ROM when it makes sense. If the publication requires less than 10MB (10,000KB) of disk space, it might not make sense to publish on CD-ROM. With the many disk compression options available, you should be able to put a 10MB publication on five high-density disks. The cost of five disks is roughly half the cost of a single CD-ROM.

Compression is something you should consider no matter the size of your publication. If you compress the publication you can store it on fewer disks or on a less expensive disk format. Using compression to store the publication on fewer disks makes sense, and many small publishers do this. But do not overlook the savings that will come from storing the publication on a less-expensive disk format. Although it might seem trivial to compress a 1MB publication to 500KB so it can be stored on a double-density disk instead of a high-density disk, the cost savings over time can be tremendous.

One last word of advice on disks is to buy in bulk quantity whenever possible. Table 34.2 shows a cost comparison of disk prices based on quantity and type. Good places to find bulk quantities of disks are office supply stores or mail-order computer stores.

Table 34.2. Disk costs.

Disk Size	Format	Quantity Purchased	Cost/Unit
3$\frac{1}{2}$-inch	DS DD	10	$.75
		100	$.29
3$\frac{1}{2}$-inch	DS HD	10	$.99
		100	$.45
5$\frac{1}{4}$-inch	DS DD	10	$.75
		100	$.22
5$\frac{1}{4}$-inch	DS HD	10	$.95
		100	$.38
——	CD-ROM	1	$14.00
		10	$9.75

Label Tips

When you publish on floppy disk you will want to label the disks. Several manufacturers produce labels designed specifically for disks. These labels come in white, clear, or colors, but often a plain white is the best choice. White labels with black print look professional; and you want to look professional.

Labels for 3$\frac{1}{2}$-inch disks are different from labels for 5$\frac{1}{4}$-inch disks. At 3 to 5 cents each, disk labels aren't cheap, especially when you want to buy thousands of them. When you are just starting out, one box of each type of disk label will probably suffice. You will have 500 to 1000 labels and can buy more when you need them.

> **TIP**
>
> The most popular label maker is the Avery Dennison Corporation. The product code for Avery labels designed for 3$\frac{1}{2}$-inch disks is 5196. The product code for Avery labels designed for 5$\frac{1}{4}$-inch disk is 5197.

Often, what you put on the label is more important than the label itself. Set aside an hour or two to design the labels for the publication. You might want to develop a company logo to print on the labels. You might want to try several design styles. The important information to have on the disk includes

- Company name or logo
- Publication title
- Publication version
- Loading or installation instructions

> **TIP**
>
> Most people will want to load the publication on their hard disk. You might want to create a simple hard disk installation routine. You would include this installation routine with the floppy disk and provide directions on the disk label. For example
>
> Type **INSTALL** to install to hard disk.
>
> or
>
> Type **GO** to run from floppy.

Packaging Tips

The packaging for your publication can be elaborate or simple. The power of an electronic publication is not in a fancy box, it is in the publication itself. Even though many consumers recognize the box is just packaging, some consumers will equate economically designed packaging with a cheap product. Therefore, you should select packaging for the publication that makes sense for the market in which you plan to sell the publication.

If you plan to sell the publication in computer stores or in bookstores, the packaging is important. There are many ready-to-use packaging options from commercial packaging companies. Expect to pay $1 to $3 for each ready-to-use package purchased in small quantities. Before you buy ready-to-use packaging, go to a computer store and look at what publishers of similar products are using.

If you plan to sell the publication through the mail, the packaging really is not important. Many small electronic publishers mail the publication without any special packaging. The 50-cent mailer envelope becomes the product packaging. The small publisher's thoughts on the subject of packaging is this: Books don't need packaging, so why should an electronic book? However, hard-cover books have dust covers and paperbacks have cover art and material on the back cover. Electronic publications at the very least should have mailer inserts.

Mailer Insert Tips

Mailer inserts can be used like the back page of the paperback or the inside cover of a hard-cover book. You can include many things, from promotional material for the book and related projects to instruction manuals. Although a small or easy-to-use publication might not need an instruction manual, you should still include detailed loading instructions. This is true even if you put loading instructions on the disk label. Most first-time users of the product will want detailed instructions.

You can design professional-looking promotional material with your word processor or a desktop publishing program. This material can be a single page or several pages briefly describing the product and its main features. As you create the promotional material for the current project, think of past or future projects related to it. You might want to include promotional material for these additional projects. This is an inexpensive way to spread the word about your work. Promoting your other works to people who have already shown they are interested in the type of project you publish often generates additional sales.

Instruction manuals can also be designed with your word processor or a desktop publishing program. Take a close look at instruction manuals put together by small, and even some large software companies, and you will find they often have a very simple design. The basic component of the manual is ordinary $8^1/_2 \times 11$-inch or $8^1/_2 \times 14$-inch paper folded. Two or three staples inside the fold hold the manual together. The instructions are printed coming down the page on either side of the fold. A cardboard cover is sometimes added to make the manual more durable, but the manual will look fine without it.

The instruction manual for your publication could be 5 to 10 pieces of $8^1/_2 \times 11$-inch or $8^1/_2 \times 14$-inch plain white paper. In your word processor or a desktop publishing program, you would create two columns and set up the page in a landscape orientation. Landscape orientation is turned 90 degrees from the normal portrait orientation. This means if you held the printed page so you could read it, the long side would be horizontal to the ground.

The design of the page in two columns is important. Each column represents opposing pages of the manual. Thus, the columns represent mini pages with appropriate margins on the sides, top and bottom. These margins are often one inch wide but can vary with the style of the manual. When you print the manual, you would also print in landscape orientation.

The cover of the manual can be a thin cardboard or simply a heavy grade of paper. Using cardboard, you can design a professional-looking cover and have a printer print it for you. Using heavy grade paper, you can design and print your own cover.

Marketing the Whole Story

The Internet provides powerful facilities for marketing to millions of consumers, and getting the publication to consumers is what marketing is all about. Although marketing and advertising are often mistakenly thought of as the same process, marketing is much more than advertising. Marketing includes all the steps necessary to sell the project to the consumer. It includes advertising, storing, shipping, and selling. Advertising has been discussed in detail in previous chapters, but the other aspects of marketing haven't.

Fortunately, with an electronic publication there isn't much need to worry about storage. Your filing cabinet, a desk drawer, or a box will store hundreds of disks just fine. Therefore, the focus of this section is on shipping and selling the publication.

Shipping

Shipping the publication is something you might have to do whether you plan to sell through the mail or through retail stores. For any product, even disks, shipping can be expensive. The immediate question you should ask is: Are you going to pay all, part, or none of the shipping charges?

This isn't an easy question to answer. When shipping to retail stores, sometimes the publisher pays and sometimes the retailer pays. When shipping to customers, you will want the customer to pay shipping charges, but customers do not like to pay shipping charges.

A large software publisher with a popular product can charge whatever they feel is reasonable. Some large publishers charge $3.95 to $5.95 to ship a product that is on a single floppy disk. These same publishers charge $20 to $30 to ship products that are part of multidisk sets that include heavy manuals. As a small publisher with a limited track record, you do not have the luxury of charging whatever you feel is reasonable. You should charge what the customer will see as reasonable. Determining what the customer will see as reasonable is difficult at best, and convincing the customer to buy your product and pay shipping charges is a real art.

Street-smart companies that deal through the mail will tell you there are several tradeoffs you can make concerning shipping costs. You could raise the price of the publication, for example, from $7.95 to $9.95 and offer to ship the publication free. You could raise the price of the publication from $7.95 to $8.95 and charge $1.95 for shipping. Or you could keep the price at $7.95 and charge $2.95 for shipping.

All these prices seem reasonable because the prices are low. But if shipping were $5.95 for the same product, the shipping charges might seem unreasonable to consumers. Few consumers would be willing to pay shipping charges of $5.95 for a product that costs $7.95.

Many mail order companies promote the cheap prices of their products and hide high shipping charges away in the fine print. This is an unscrupulous practice by which consumers are rightly outraged. Often, you will receive a product and wonder how the retailer arrived at the shipping charges, especially when the postage charges on the box read $1.95 and you paid $7.95 for shipping.

When figuring shipping charges, you should add in the cost of all packing material and postage. Packing material includes the box, Styrofoam, plastic, and whatever else you ship with the product. You can estimate costs by making a trial run to the local post office. Buy a mailer envelope or a box, packing material, and whatever else you need. Take the package to the post office and see how much postage would be. Then add up all the costs. Be sure to figure in a few cents for the roll of tape you bought to seal the box and a few cents for the labels on the box.

Because you are at the post office, you should find out how much the international postal charges for the product will be. This way you can estimate shipping charges to overseas customers. The costs to ship overseas might surprise you.

You now have a working estimate of the cost of shipping the product nationally and globally. Normally these estimates will be worse-case scenarios because you didn't buy the material in bulk. However, this might be a good price to charge the customer. This way you can be sure you will never pay more to ship the product, and if prices increase, you have a margin to ensure you won't lose money on shipping.

You might also want to use this estimate as a reality check. Consider what the consumer will think is reasonable. If you had planned to charge $3.95 for the publication and it is going to cost $4.95 for shipping, you should either re-evaluate the retail price of the publication or re-estimate shipping costs using cheaper materials or materials bought in bulk.

There are problems associated with buying material in large bulk quantities; this goes back to the idea that inventory on your shelves is money. You can buy 1,000 manila envelopes for 11 cents each, but now you have a $110.00 investment you might not recover. The envelopes could get water damaged. Over time, the envelopes might discolor or you might have to use tape to seal them because the gum won't stick anymore. If this is the case, maybe the 250 envelopes for $39.99 wasn't such a bad deal.

Selling

Selling is the final part of marketing. Although it involves selecting outlets for the product and setting prices, selling is mostly about getting the product into the customer's hands. Don't forget that when you start out, it might take three to six months before you start generating regular sales. The dry period is when you have to work the hardest to spread the word about your company and products.

Your main marketing outlet will probably be mail order sales. On the Internet you will meet people from all around the world. To get your products to them, use standard mail or e-mail. Through standard mail you will have records of the shipment and a way of tracking the product. However, shipping costs can eat up your profits and force consumers to look at local markets.

Shipping the Product on the Internet

Shipping the product to the customer over the Internet is entirely feasible and is done by many companies. A problem arises in ensuring payment and receipt of the product. Not to worry though—electronic commerce is coming into its infancy on the Internet. Companies from around the world are pouring millions of dollars into this area and because of this, it is already possible to make secure money transfers on the Internet. Currently, several hundred companies conduct business on the Internet with electronic currency.

Other Outlets

Other outlets for your products include retail stores, libraries, and conventions. Even though retail stores are common outlets for small publishers, publishers sometimes overlook libraries, conventions, and conferences. The many thousands of libraries around the U.S. and the world buy millions of new books every year. You can generate hundreds or thousands of sales to libraries. Conventions and conferences are also great outlets for the small publisher. If you are attending a conference or a convention you might want to bring samples and flyers. Keep in mind, most of the sales you generate will come in after the conference or convention is over and the attendees have gone home. Be sure to include an order form on your flyers.

When you are trying to promote your products to retailers, look at software stores, bookstores, and possibly, novelty stores. First, try the local bookstores and software stores, and then try the chain stores. Some novelty shops might also be interested in your products. People are always looking for unique gifts and a book on floppy might be what they were looking for. Keep in mind, the pricing schemes and expected discounts can vary greatly depending on the type of store you are trying to sell to.

If you can successfully promote your product to a local software store or chain, the manager will probably be looking for pricing discounts ranging from 10 to 25 percent, depending on the price of the product and the quantity purchased. These are the standard discounts that software companies usually give to retailers. On the other hand, the bookstore manager is accustomed to discounts from 40 to 55 percent. These are the standard discount rates for hardcover books, paperbacks, and even trade books.

Setting prices for electronic publications is often difficult because there are two pricing schemes you could follow. You could price your publications with prices comparable to popular software titles or with prices comparable to traditional print publications. The pricing plan you follow will depend on the style of your publication and your target market.

If the publication is an interactive multimedia title, such as a reference work that includes several disks or a title to be released on CD-ROM, you may be able to charge prices that are at or slightly below a popular software title. If the publication closely resembles the electronic version of a print publication with limited multimedia aspects, you probably should charge prices slightly above that of the publication's traditional print counterpart.

The key is not to price yourself out of business. You do not want to set prices that are too high. If your prices are too high, you will lose sales. You do not want to set prices that are too low. Prices that are too low might rob you of profits and make the customer think of your product as cheap.

Study titles that other software houses or electronic publishers are producing. Look at the features they offer and compare them to your publication. When you find products similar to yours, look at the price these companies are charging, and maybe even purchase their product to compare its functionality to yours. If the products are comparable, you might want to charge a similar price.

Marketing includes advertising, storing, shipping and selling, but it should be much more than a series of activities that you perform in succession. Marketing should have a goal. You should adopt a winning strategy that is going to get your publication into the consumer's hands. The remaining sections of this chapter help you do just that.

Relationship Marketing

Participation in the Internet community is an essential ingredient for success. There are thousands of discussion groups on the Internet. To be sure, one or more of these groups will discuss topics related to your publishing projects. By participating in the Internet community, thousands, and possibly millions, of Internet users will see your name, and through you they will learn about your projects.

Your name and participation in the community can be powerful advertising mechanisms. However, you need to make sure you participate responsibly. Before you actively participate in the discussion, it is best to first be an observer. For a few days or weeks, read material posted by other users. Learn about the group and what is considered acceptable in the group. When you feel confident that you know enough about the group to participate, introduce yourself and join in the discussion.

There are two types of discussion groups on the Internet: mailing lists and newsgroups. You can join mailing lists through e-mail quickly and easily by requesting to subscribe to the list. Any e-mail you send to the list gets sent to all recipients of the list. With newsgroups, you do not receive e-mail from the group, and mail you send to the group is stored in a central location that you can think of as an Internet post office. To access newsgroups, you use special programs called news readers. Some Web browsers have built-in news readers, which makes it easy to participate in newsgroups, and participation is the key to relationship marketing.

Newsgroups offer many advantages over mailing lists. Figure 34.1 shows messages posted to the popular misc.writing newsgroup. Newsgroup messages are organized by subject, or *thread*, as they are called. Threads are topics of discussion. With newsgroups, messages are not thrown out to every member of the group. Readers can select messages they want to read and do not have to wade through hundreds of messages every day. This offers the electronic publisher an advantage because when a member of a newsgroup reads your message, they are usually interested in what you have to say.

FIGURE 34.1.

Newsgroups accessed from the Netscape browser.

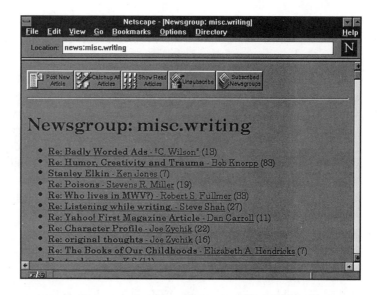

The advantage of reading newsgroup messages while in a Web browser becomes obvious when you come across a message with a URL in it. As Figure 34.2 shows, URLs are highlighted and you can click on them. This enables the reader to instantly jump from the newsgroup to anywhere on the Internet.

FIGURE 34.2.

Newsgroup messages accessed from a browser have clickable URLs.

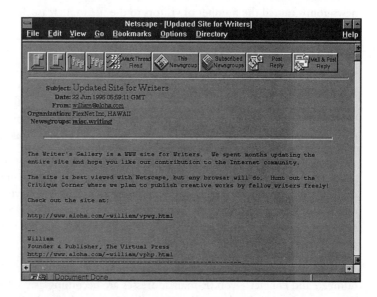

The message displayed in Figure 34.2 is relationship marketing by The Virtual Press. TVP updated its entire site and announced this to groups that would be interested in hearing about it. Notice that the message is not direct advertising concerning the press. The message contains informational material about a service the press offers to the Internet community. Closing the message with a five-line signature tells the reader more about the press and gives them a location for the home page of the press.

URLs are pointers to resources on the Web. Clicking one of the URLs shown in Figure 34.2 will propel you across the World Wide Web (WWW) to The Virtual Press Web site. When you update your Web site, especially if you have community service areas, why not tell the world about it? The Virtual Press redesigned the hundreds of pages at the site during the writing of this book. The amount of information at the site more than doubled and the graphics went from images you would find on your average Web site to fully explosive and highly designed images. A key element is that even though the new graphics were visually powerful they still had small file sizes. This goes back to not frustrating visitors to your Web site with byte-hogging graphics.

A commitment to updating material you publish on the Web is a key strategy to building relationships with Internet users. Your Web publications must not remain static. Static pages do not attract repeat visitors and repeat visitors are the key to establishing relationships.

When you publish material on the Web, plan to have at least one section of the publication that changes often. Tell readers to watch for changes and publish notices of changes. This makes sure your publications grow and attracts visitors to the site. Readers like it when things change. This was evident in the dozens of messages The Virtual Press received praising the redesigned site. A combination of the new Web site design and the messages posted to a handful of newsgroups caused the number of visitors to the site to increase 300 percent for several weeks.

Image Building

Image building is another key to your success. Before or while you market your products you must market yourself. Everything you do as a business person reflects on your products. Behave unprofessionally or produce unprofessional work and consumers will not buy your products. Worse, reviewers and fellow business owners will treat you like an uneducated yokel.

Think of yourself as a company. After you have obtained your business license, act like a company. One of your first acts as an electronic publisher should be to create your company letterhead. Usually, this does not mean going to a print shop and having letterhead made. With your word processor and a high-quality printer, you can produce professional-looking letterhead, which you should use in all company correspondence. This will send a positive message to everyone you correspond with.

You should also print business cards. The card should have the company name, address, phone number, and contact—you. E-mail addresses are becoming as common as FAX numbers on business cards. You should put your e-mail address on the business card and possibly the URL to your home page. Putting home page URLs on business cards has not caught on in the general business community, but many companies that specialize in online services do put a URL on their business cards.

Putting a URL on your business card or letterhead might have interesting results. The person you gave the card or sent the letter to might call or write you asking what the heck is `http://tvp.com/`. Putting this URL on my business cards and letterhead has opened the door for me on many occasions and more than once I was able to start a business relationship from this initial conversation. I have attracted new accounts to my Internet consulting service, been asked to design home pages and sold my press's electronic books based on a conversation that began with a discussion of URLs.

Another part of image building is being prepared to promote your publishing projects whenever the opportunity arises. You should create the following:

- Brochures
- Flyers
- Press packets
- Press reviews

You should store the files containing these promotional materials on your computer. This way, you can easily publish them whether you receive inquiries through the mail or e-mail. If a standard mail inquiry comes in, you print the material and send it out. If an e-mail inquiry comes in, you attach the promotional material to the e-mail message as a standard ASCII text file. The capability to attach files to e-mail messages is a feature widely available in electronic mail programs.

Getting the Word Out on the Internet

Getting the word out about your products through Internet e-mail is essential. One way to do this is by posting press releases to newsgroups. Press releases should be 90 percent informational and 10 percent advertising. The key is to sell the product through information distribution and not direct advertising. Sometimes the line between direct advertising and information distribution is a fine one. Generally, you should not list prices for products in the posting. Instead, give the reader a place to go to get ordering information or additional material related to the work.

The following is a press release for *At Dream's End*, published by The Virtual Press:

> Discover the book thousands of readers have fallen in love with! *At Dream's End* introduces the World of the Paths—a fantasy world 10 years in the making! You'll fall in love with the characters first, but it will be the world that ultimately captures your imagination! You've journeyed across continents to distant worlds and realms, but you've never journeyed along the Path. The Path is dream and reality, three realms intertwined in the very air and under the earth. Vilmos holds the key to unlocking it all, but without Adrina and Seth, the Path will remain forever closed.

Join Adrina, a young princess who yearns to go on a magnificent journey; Vilmos, a young boy who holds the key to forbidden magic; and Seth, a telepath; as they set out on three separate journeys joined only in the web of destiny and soon find their fates in each others' hands.

Fans of fantasy are raving about *At Dream's End* and two independent reviewers have called the book "The best discovery of 1995—A gem waiting to be unearthed by millions of fans of fantasy!" and "A brilliant debut… an absolutely superior tale of fantasy for all tastes!" See for yourself why critics have said, "*At Dream's End* is one of the friendliest and best designed electronic novels on the market today!" Visit the World of the Paths Headquarters on the World Wide Web:

```
http://tvp.com/vpdest1.html
```

The press release is very straightforward. It tells the reader about the publication in a few paragraphs. Brevity is a key point. If readers want additional information, they will contact you directly via e-mail or they will visit your Web site. The press release contains no ordering information or prices. If readers want this information, they will ask for it.

NOTE

The Destiny Chronicles is another one of my many projects. In 1986, I began work on the Destiny Chronicle novels. Early writings started with a chronicle of the history of the world I was creating, a project that took two years to finish. To date I have written four books in the planned eight-book cycle; they include *At Dream's End: A Kingdom in the Balance*, *Unraveling Paths: Dreamers and Mystics*, *Chaos Path: The Hands of Over-Earth*, and *Mid-Path: The Fourth Realm*.

At Dream's End was the test publication for my publishing program at The Virtual Press. For a first attempt at electronic publishing, I expected to sell a few dozen copies of my book to interested readers. In fact, I would have been happy selling two dozen copies because I just wanted to spread the word about something I believed in. Having faith in yourself and your abilities is an all-important first step. If you don't believe in yourself and your work, no one will.

In early 1994, I pre-released *At Dream's End* to test the market for a book on floppy disk. Because the book was well received, I officially released the e-book, and the rest, as they say, is history. A year later and with an advertising budget of $75, *At Dream's End* has sold over 2,500 copies. For a small press with a shoestring budget, selling 2,500 copies of anything is a major success story, and I attribute nearly all of the sales to getting the word out to online users and, of course, good writing. An unexpected fall-out of the visibility the Destiny Chronicles is getting on the Internet is interest from a traditional publisher. However, after years of trying to sell the Destiny Chronicles to publishers and agents who didn't want to bother to read the books, I am not sure I want to see a traditional print version of the books at all.

Getting the word out to Internet users can be the key to your success as well. However, you must follow the guidelines I set forth in Chapter 25, "Advertising and Protecting Your Document," Chapter 33, "Advertising Your Document," and in this chapter on publishing and marketing. Remember, have faith and take the road to publishing success one small step at a time.

This section will show you newsgroups you might want to participate in and post press releases to. Newsgroups are organized by subject hierarchies. They begin with a broad topic, such as

`comp`	Newsgroups that discuss computer-related issues.

Then they go to a more specific topic by further defining a subtopic, such as

`comp.infosystems`	Computer-related newsgroups discussing information system issues.

Then, some groups go on to define a very specific topic, such as

`comp.infosystems.announce`	A group discussing announcements of services or goods related to information systems.

There are many newsgroups discussing computer-related issues. The following are some of the ones you might be interested in as an electronic publisher:

`comp.infosystems.announce`	A group for announcements of new resources.
`comp.infosystems.www.misc`	A group discussing a wide variety of issues related to the World Wide Web that aren't covered in other `comp.infosystems.www` newsgroups.
`comp.infosystems.www.providers`	A group discussing technical issues that Internet service providers and others might face setting up World Wide Web resources or sites.
`comp.infosystems.www.users`	A group discussing technical issues for users of the World Wide Web.
`comp.internet.net-happenings`	A group for announcements of events or happenings on the Internet, including the WWW.
`comp.org.acm`	A group discussing issues related to the ACM (Association for Computing Machinery) organization.
`comp.org.ieee`	A group discussing issues related to the IEEE (Institute of Electrical and Electronics Engineers) organization.

`comp.publish.cdrom.hardware`	A group discussing issues related to publishing on CD-ROM.
`comp.publish.cdrom.multimedia`	A group discussing issues related to multimedia.
`comp.publish.cdrom.software`	A group discussing issues related to software applications on CD-ROM.
`comp.publish.prepress`	A group discussing issues related to publishing and pre-press information.

The alternative newsgroups feature many groups that discuss issues an electronic publisher might be interested in. `Alt` newsgroups are unofficial or temporary topics. They discuss everything imaginable and some things most people cannot imagine.

The following alternative newsgroups discuss issues relating to multimedia, including sound, graphics, and video:

`alt.ascii-art`	A place to find and discuss ASCII art. ASCII art is art designed using the ASCII character set. Some ASCII art is even animated!
`alt.binaries.clip-art`	A place to find and discuss clip art. *Clip art* is graphic images that can enhance your publications.
`alt.binaries.misc`	Discusses miscellaneous types of binaries. *Binaries* are image, sound, or video files. If you can't find what you're looking for in one of the other newsgroups, try here.
`alt.binaries.multimedia`	A great place to discuss multimedia and get help finding multimedia resources.
`alt.binaries.sounds.music`	Discusses digital music modules and other types of music.

Lurk or be an observer for a while before participating in the following discussion group. This way you will learn what other people consider to be the best the Internet has to offer.

`alt.best.of.internet`	A discussion on hot and neat resources on the Net.

Although the following newsgroups are dedicated to specific authors, the topics of conversation don't always revolve around the author or his or her works. If you plan to publish or will publish a work similar in genre or style to the author's works visit the newsgroup. Read the posts to the group for a while, and if the opportunity arises, mention your publication.

`alt.books.anne-rice`	A newsgroup discussing the works of Anne Rice.
`alt.books.isaac-asimov`	A newsgroup discussing the works of Isaac Asimov.
`alt.books.m-lackey`	A newsgroup discussing the works of Mercedes Lackey.
`alt.books.phil-k-dick`	A newsgroup discussing the works of Phil K. Dick.
`alt.books.sf.melanie-rawn`	A newsgroup discussing the works of Melanie Rawn.
`alt.books.stephen-king`	A newsgroup discussing the works of Stephen King.
`alt.books.tom-clancy`	A newsgroup discussing the works of Tom Clancy.

The `alt.fan` newsgroups are for people who are fans of a specific author or world setting. Discussions in these groups range from specifics concerning the topic to general talk among fans to the latest gossip in the publishing community. Some of the `alt.fan` groups are

`alt.fan.douglas-adams`	Fans of Douglas Adams participate in group discussions.
`alt.fan.dragonlance`	Fans of the Dragon Lance series discuss the series and Dungeons and Dragons in general.
`alt.fan.dune`	Fans of Frank Herbert's *Dune* discuss his works and related material.
`alt.fan.eddings`	Fans of Eddings' writing discuss his works and related material.
`alt.fan.heinlein`	Fans of Heinlein's writing discuss his works and related material.
`alt.fan.pern`	Fans of Ann McCaffrey's *Pern* discuss her works and related material.
`alt.fan.piers-anthony`	Fans of Piers Anthony's writing discuss his works and related material.
`alt.fan.tolkien`	Fans of Tolkien's Middle Earth discuss his works and related material.
`alt.fan.tom-clancy`	Fans of Tom Clancy discuss his works and related material.

The following newsgroups are great places to learn about the various commercial online services and what they have to offer electronic publishers. Commercial online services have millions of members around the world. Most commercial online services offer ways for you to advertise on their system. Here are the top five services and their corresponding discussion groups:

`alt.online-service.america-online`	A newsgroup discussing America Online's services.
`alt.online-service.compuserve`	A newsgroup discussing CompuServe's services.
`alt.online-service.delphi`	A newsgroup discussing Delphi's services.
`alt.online-service.genie`	A newsgroup discussing GEnie's services.
`alt.online-service.prodigy`	A newsgroup discussing Prodigy's services.

The following newsgroups discuss books and writing in all its forms. The groups are great places to find people who love to read. They are frequented by journalists, writers, and publishers.

`alt.journalism`	Discusses topics relating to journalism and nonfiction.
`alt.books.technical`	A place for technical book reviews and press releases.
`alt.books.reviews`	A place to find reviews and press releases.
`rec.arts.books`	A discussion on books for readers and writers.
`rec.arts.books.childrens`	A discussion of books for children.
`rec.arts.books.reviews`	Another source for book reviews.
`rec.arts.mystery`	A discussion of mysteries by writers and readers.
`rec.arts.poems`	A discussion of poetry by writers and readers.
`rec.arts.prose`	A discussion of prose by writers and readers.
`rec.arts.sf.reviews`	A place to find reviews of science fiction material.
`rec.arts.sf.written`	A place to discuss writing science fiction.
`misc.books.technical`	A place to discuss technical books and technical writing.
`misc.writing`	A place to discuss writing in all its forms.

Getting the Word Out Fast on the Web

There are no road atlases for the World Wide Web. No one will find out about material you have published on the World Wide Web simply because you have published it. You must publicize on the Web any material you publish to attract visitors to your site. The fastest way to publicize your Web publications is to register them in a Web database. No one is going to register your Web publications in these databases for you. This is something you must do yourself.

Millions of Web users rely on these databases to find the latest resources on the World Wide Web. Popular databases are accessed 100 to 200,000 times a day, so publicizing your Web pages in these databases can have dramatic results. Your site might go from an average of 10 visitors a day to hundreds or thousands of visitors a day.

There are three categories of Web databases:

- Special category link catalogs
- List-based WWW catalogs
- Spider-based WWW catalogs

Special Category Link Catalogs

The Web has many special category link sites. Some of these sites maintain lists of what's popular, new, or cool. Other sites maintain very specific lists, such as lists of publishers or computer companies. Both types of lists are very popular because users know they can rely on these lists to have very specific information and usually up-to-date information.

When you register with a special link catalog, you generally provide a URL and a brief description of your resource. Most of these catalogs have stringent guidelines for the type of links they will accept and publish.

The National Center for Supercomputing Applications (NCSA) maintains the granddad of special link catalogs. Its What's New list introduces new sites on the Web. This list is forever changing and growing. You can find What's New at

```
http://www.ncsa.uiuc.edu/SDG/Software/Mosaic/Docs/whats-new.html
```

You can submit your pages to What's New using a fill-out form at

```
http://www.ncsa.uiuc.edu/SDG/Software/Mosaic/Docs/whats-new-form.html
```

NCSA's list is so popular there is now a What's New Too list. What's New Too capitalizes on the tremendous popularity of NCSA's What's New list, but the site offers a completely different interface and access mechanisms. What's New Too, depicted in Figure 34.3, is one of the second-wave Web resources that takes full advantage of the graphic and search capabilities of the Web. Using a Web search engine, What's New Too gives visitors the option for customizable services. You can add to What's New Too from this page at

```
http://newtoo.manifest.com/WhatsNewToo/submit.html
```

FIGURE 34.3.

What's New Too!

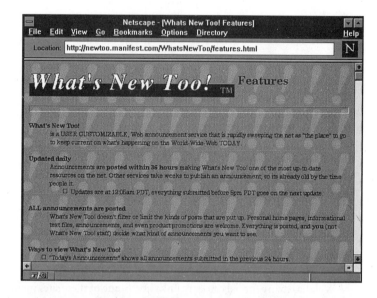

Look at the Web in terms of its development and the design of sites, and two distinct developmental/design styles stand out. Early Web resources simply sought to make information available and were largely textual in nature. These sites represent the first wave of Web site design. Many recently designed sites take full advantage of the graphic and search capabilities of the Web. These sites represent the second wave of Web site design.

Netscape Communications Corporation maintains a What's New and a What's Cool list. The What's New list can be found at http://home.netscape.com/home/whats-new.html. The What's Cool list depicted in Figure 34.4 is a neat idea developed by Netscape Corporation. A team from Netscape wanders the Net looking for cool sites to post to the list. The list is constantly changing and extremely popular. If your site makes the What's Cool list, you've hit the big time.

List-Based WWW Catalogs

Although special category lists might contain a few thousand links, list-based WWW catalogs contain hundreds of thousands of links. A true list-based site like Yahoo maintains its complete database as a series of Web pages. You can search through the directory structure down to specific categories of information. You can add your URL to Yahoo using a form page at http://www.yahoo.com/bin/add. EINet Galaxy also maintains a list catalog. You can submit to EINet using a form page at http://galaxy.einet.net/cgi-bin/annotate.

FIGURE 34.4.
What's Cool?

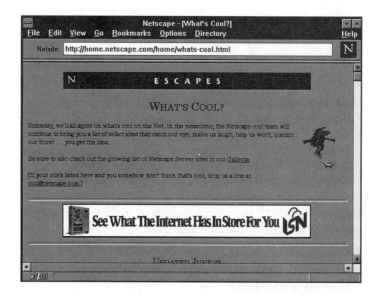

Starting Point is an up-and-coming list-based site. The home page for the site is depicted in Figure 34.5. Notice the heavy use of graphics and clickable icons. This is one of the second wave sites using many features of the World Wide Web to bring resources to users. You can add to the Starting Point list at `http://www.stpt.com/intro.html`.

FIGURE 34.5.
Starting Point.

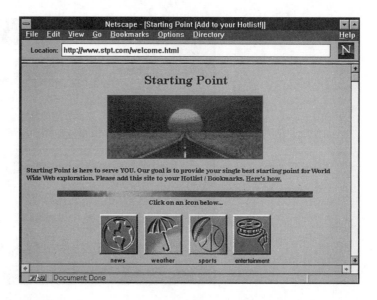

A true list-based structure is difficult to maintain and sometimes difficult to navigate through. The preferred methods for list-based databases are ones that generate Web documents on demand. This lets the reader select parameters for which they want to search and obtain as many results as they want. The InfoSeek database is such a database. It is the largest and easiest to use list site on the Web. You can find submission guidelines for InfoSeek at

```
http://www.infoseek.com:80/doc/FAQ/FAQ_138.html#HEADING139
```

Spider-Based WWW Catalogs

The largest databases on the Web are generated by the spider-based WWW catalog sites. Millions of Web pages are cataloged at these sites. Spider-based catalogs are maintained in a unique and powerful manner. Instead of providing a description of your site, contact points, e-mail addresses, and URLs, all you have to supply is the URL to your site. The site will add your URL to a list of sites it searches. Then once a week or several times a month, the spider goes out across the Web and indexes every page in the catalog. Any word on your page can then be used to match a keyword search by a user.

There are two main spider-based sites on the Web: Lycos and WebCrawler. You should register your URL with both sites. Each site offers unique features and has different searching and cataloging mechanisms.

The Lycos database's home page is depicted in Figure 34.6. Lycos offers a very large database with many search options for users. You can add your URL to the Lycos database by registering it at `http://lycos.cs.cmu.edu/lycos-register.html`. The next time the Lycos spider makes its way across the Web, your pages will be indexed in the database.

FIGURE 34.6.

Lycos spider-based catalog.

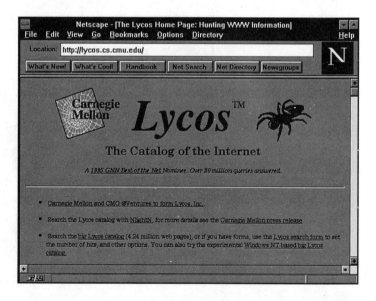

The WebCrawler database's home page is depicted in Figure 34.7. The WebCrawler database isn't as large as Lycos, but it is fast and easy to use. To add your URL to the WebCrawler index, register it on this page at `http://webcrawler.com/WebCrawler/SubmitURLS.html`. The next time the WebCrawler catalogs the Web, your pages will be in the database.

FIGURE 34.7.

The WebCrawler spider-based catalog.

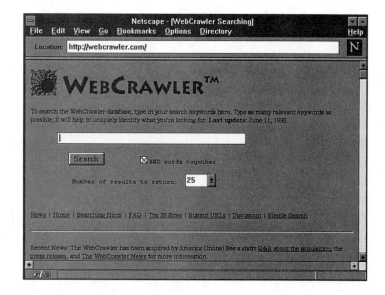

Summary

Electronic publishers can learn many lessons from traditional publishers. The important thing to keep in mind is that electronic publishing makes it possible for you to have virtually zero overhead. Take the time to consider what supplies you will need and order them accordingly. You should also take steps to build the image of you and your company.

Getting the publication to consumers is what marketing is all about. The Internet provides powerful facilities for marketing to millions of consumers. Thousands of businesses have already discovered this. Spreading the word about your products through Internet e-mail is essential to your success. One way to do this is by posting press releases to newsgroups. Press releases should be 90 percent informational and 10 percent advertising. If you publish on the Web, you must publicize this material to attract visitors to the site. The fastest way to publicize your Web publications is to register your links with catalog sites.

General Laws and Copyright Information

35

*by David L.
Gulbransen
and
Lance Rose*

IN THIS CHAPTER

> **CAUTION**
>
> The material presented in this chapter is not meant to be a substitute for legal advice from a licensed attorney at law. This chapter is provided for informational purposes only. If you have concerns about protecting your rights, it is in your best interest to contact a qualified attorney.

Becoming a Publisher

Electronic publishing is a rapidly growing field. Many traditional publishers are making the leap to electronic publishing. For example, there are a couple versions of electronic books on the CD-ROM that accompanies this book. Electronic publishing is unique because of the medium that is employed to publish information; but at the heart of the matter, electronic publishing is still publishing.

In any type of publishing, from books to CD-ROMs, there are issues about the rights to the materials being published, and electronic publishing is no different. The same copyright, trademark, and patent issues apply to electronic publishing. In fact, electronic publishing often raises more issues, such as design patents and ease of reproduction—issues that aren't associated with traditional publishing.

The material presented in this chapter is meant to provide you with the resources to familiarize yourself with some of the legal issues involved in electronic publishing. As mentioned, the material presented here is not meant to be a substitute for professional legal advice. You should approach this chapter as a starting point. With this information, you should be able to find professional legal counsel, and ask intelligent questions to help protect your rights and limit any liability.

Selecting an Attorney

For issues concerning intellectual property rights, there is no substitute for the advice of a licensed, practicing attorney. A lawyer who specializes in copyright, trademark, or patent law will be familiar with the laws of your state, and the federal statutes that can help protect you and your rights. There is no doubt that a good attorney can save you valuable time, and money, by protecting your rights. There is also no doubt that an incompetent attorney might not be such a bargain.

Choosing an attorney can be a difficult task. The amount of trust you need to place in an attorney makes it worth taking the time to do a little research and make a well-informed decision.

Just about anyone could open the yellow pages and let their fingers do the walking. But when it comes to protecting the material you are about to publish or sensitive internal documents, you might want more security than legal roulette.

One way to start narrowing your search for legal counsel is to solicit the recommendation of others in your field. Also, publishers or friends might give you references that will point you in the right direction when finding legal advice.

Many cities and states have referral services. You might glance through the yellow pages to see if your state's Bar Association has a referral service. A quick phone call to a Bar Association referral service can provide you with a list of attorneys who are accepting new clients and who specialize in copyright or patent issues.

After you narrow the field to the final contenders, feel free to make calls and get more information. Any competent attorney should feel comfortable answering questions about their background, education, practice, and specialties. You might be able to make a choice based on this information.

As with many professions, the legal industry has many references available about professional practitioners. One such reference guide is the *Martindale-Hubbell Law Directory* (New York : Martindale-Hubbell Law Directory, Inc.) The *Martindale-Hubbell Law Directory* is a guide that lists information about how long an attorney has practiced, his or her education credentials, and outstanding honors; it also provides a rating for quality of service. You can find the *Martindale-Hubbell Law Directory* in any law library at a college or university, as well as in many local libraries across the country.

After you select an attorney, you should familiarize yourself with the types of protection available for intellectual property. The value of intellectual property has often been overlooked. It is easy to see how an invention or some other physical object may have monetary worth, but ideas can also be valuable. The ideas you have represent possible future physical inventions or might represent valuable artwork. All things created by humans originated as someone's intellectual property. Your ideas and information represent a large investment that needs to be protected.

Copyrights

The most obvious form of protection for published material is the copyright. A copyright involves protection for the author of a variety of works, including written works, performed works (such as musical compositions), and visual works (such as a photograph or painting). These categories are actually much broader than they sound. For example, in computer programs, the code used to create the program and the compiled code are eligible for copyright protection. Copyright protection offers many rights to the original author, including the right to publish the work, perform the work, and transfer the ownership of the work.

Copyright is one of the most basic forms of intellectual property protection. You don't have to have your work published or be a U.S. citizen to be eligible for copyright protection. Any work that is recorded in some form—written, audio/visual recording, or other method of permanently recording the work (such as CD-ROM)—is eligible for copyright protection. Copyright is an inherent right. When your work is created in a permanent form, your copyright protection begins.

Most countries are members of the Berne Convention, which provides international protection for copyrighted works. The Berne Convention helps to provide you with international copyright protection regardless of where the work may have been produced. Under this copyright protection, ownership of material is given when a work is created and recorded in some manner. The ownership, and therefore rights, belong to the creator of the work. So, when you write a story, a song, a program, or even paint a painting, you are automatically considered the owner of the work, and your rights are effective immediately.

There are special cases in which the original author does not retain the ownership of a work. In publishing, some of these conditions are quite common, and special attention should be paid to the nature and conditions under which a work is created.

One case is co-authorship. When two or more persons work collaboratively on a work, both parties can share ownership unless there is an agreement in advance for the transfer of ownership. Because electronic publishing often involves several people working together on a project, this can often be an issue deserving attention.

The other, and very common, case in publishing is works for hire. When a work is created by an employee, the ownership is retained by the employer. For example, at many companies, the code written by a programmer is property of the company, regardless of the nature of the code.

Magazine articles by outside contractors might also be works for hire, and if properly covered by contract, the rights to such works can belong to the publisher. If you intend to hire writers or programmers to develop the content for your work, your contracts should specifically state that you will be the owner of the work. If you are producing content for inclusion in an electronic publishing endeavor, you should also be aware that the rights to your work might not belong to you.

A Case Study

One example of electronic publishing today is the World Wide Web. The World Wide Web offers nearly anyone with a computer and a modem the ability to become an electronic publisher. The WWW can provide information to people around the globe and can help broaden the audience of any material. In the following case study, the Indiana University School of Fine Arts Gallery wished to display artwork on a WWW server to expand the gallery's audience and to explore new methods in electronic art. The idea of publishing artwork in this new electronic media raised several important questions about copyright, reproduction, and fair use. The server is now available at `http://www.fa.indiana.edu/~sofa`.

CASE STUDY: INDIANA UNIVERSITY SCHOOL OF FINE ARTS GALLERY

The Internet is a long established medium for publishing in academic circles. Because the World Wide Web enables the publication of both text and graphic information, it provides a unique medium for the School of Fine Arts Gallery to provide electronic exhibitions.

The School of Fine Arts Gallery has recently begun planning to undertake just such a project. The SOFA On-Line Gallery was designed to provide information about exhibits currently installed in the physical gallery space, and also to provide a medium for artists to explore electronic and interactive arts. Because the actual floorspace available to the SOFA Gallery is limited, an electronic gallery would allow more works to be exhibited, and appeal to a wider audience.

However, the idea of an online gallery raises some very important questions about the intellectual property rights of artist and artwork. For example, with the proper computer equipment, such as a dye sublimation printer, it is possible to output digital images at near photographic quality. The ease of electronic reproduction of artwork raises serious concerns over the artist's control of reproduction—a right granted to the artist under copyright protection. The other concern was with the image format chosen to display the images. Earlier in the year, Unisys—the company that owns the patent in the GIF compression algorithms—announced that it would begin enforcing its rights to claim a royalty fee for use of the image format. The final concern involved the nature of the images to be displayed. Because the World Wide Web is a more public forum than the physical gallery, special attention needed to be given to audience. Although all of the works to be displayed in the gallery are artistic in nature and contain artistic value, there were questions about nudity and subject matter. Several of the works to be displayed in the student section of the gallery also involved parody ads that made subtle, and not so subtle, jokes at large companies.

To solve the first problem, it was decided that artists invited to display their works in the online gallery would need to sign release forms. The release forms stated the artists were aware of the reproduction risks associated with online presentation, and released the School of Fine Arts from any liability concerning unauthorized reproductions of their works. To help protect the artists rights, the school also adopted several policies for the online gallery, which included the following:

■ **Statement of Copyright Notice on the main gallery page.**

   The main WWW Page for the gallery contained information regarding the rights retained by the artist. Similar to a copyright notice in a book or a movie, the notice was designed to inform visitors to the gallery that the images presented were works on exhibition, not public domain works for use in other projects.

■ Low-Resolution Images

To minimize the risks of unauthorized reproductions, the images presented in the gallery were not presented in a high-resolution format. The images were presented at a resolution slightly lower than screen resolution. The lower resolution format effectively prohibited unauthorized production of the works presented while still allowing quality images.

The problem concerning the image format was easily solvable by changing the format of the images to an open standard, such as JPEG. By eliminating the reliance on a proprietary format, the gallery was able to publish the images in a widely popular format without concern of incurring royalty fees.

The final problems faced were endemic to the exhibition of artwork, with added complications because of the electronic publishing medium. The lack of legislation concerning materials available on the Internet creates some serious issues for electronic publishers.

Because no legislation exists and the application of print laws to electronic media is obvious, but not proven, the Gallery decided to proceed cautiously in its presentation of online images.

Information about the exhibits was available to everyone; however, before viewers could access images, it was necessary for them to pass through a disclaimer screen. The disclaimer screen advised viewers that some of the material presented might contain nudity and adult themes. Although the legal aspects of presenting sensitive material on the Internet are still ambiguous, the disclaimer served to warn potential viewers, and ensure that patrons were aware that the materials were artistic—not pornographic.

Fortunately for the students and the gallery, the use of trademarks and copyrighted material in work of an artistic nature or parody are protected by the *fair use* doctrine. The notion of "fair use" can be very ambiguous, but basically works that exercise fair use do the following:

- They contain only a portion of the original work. Reproduction in entirety does not constitute fair use.
- They do not infringe on the earning potential of the original work.

The terms of fair use are very sketchy and are often decided in a court of law. When examining works for fair use, the advice of an attorney is indispensable.

In our case, the images that were created by students were created during the semester in a Fine Arts course and did not damage the value of the original work and could therefore be considered artwork and proper parody.

In the end, the works exhibited drew very positive feedback from the Internet. Students were provided a forum for presenting their artwork to a larger audience, and the school was able to use the publicity generated to plan future projects for the SOFA On-Line Gallery include interactive web pages and full-motion video.

Copyright Protection and Registration

As with many forms of intellectual property rights, copyright protection is often misunderstood. Copyright protection is provided upon the creation of a work, and it is not necessary to register a work to retain copyright. However, registering your material does offer several advantages. Proper registration provides the following benefits:

- Registration serves as a public record of copyright ownership.
- Registered copyright owners can file suit in U.S. Court for copyright infringements.
- Registration serves as valid court evidence of copyright ownership.
- If registration is secured before an infringement occurs, the owner is entitled to attorney fees and court costs. Without prior registration, the owner is entitled to only compensatory damages. Pre-infringement registration also allows the judge to award damages up to the statutory limits.

Clearly, registering your works is the best way to protect your rights. But how do you go about registering your works for copyright protection? Registering your work is not difficult. Begin by protecting your work during the initial stages of creation, before the formal registration process is complete.

First, make sure that a copyright notice accompanies any copies of your work that leave your control. For printed materials, a valid copyright notice contains the copyright symbol, the date of creation, and the copyright owner's name. For example:

© 1995 J. Doe

The copyright notice should appear in a visible place, such as on a title sheet or label, attached to the work.

When your work is complete, you can send the registration materials to the U.S. Copyright Office. Complete the following steps, and you are on your way to having your copyright registered:

1. Complete the Copyright Application Form, available from the U.S. Copyright Office.
2. Submit your application, along with a nonrefundable filing fee of $20 for each application.
3. Include a nonreturnable deposit of the work being registered. The deposit requirements vary in particular situations. The general requirements are
   - If the work is unpublished, one complete copy.
   - If the work was first published in the United States, two complete copies of the best edition.
   - If the work was first published in the United States before January 1, 1978, two complete copies of the work as first published.

■ If the work was first published outside the United States, one complete copy of the work as first published.

You can get detailed information directly from the U.S. Copyright Office. (See the following subsection, Copyright Information from the U.S. Government.)

The terms of your copyright protection are fairly straightforward. The original copyright is awarded for the life of the author, plus 50 years. If the work has coauthors, the copyright applies to the last surviving author. For works owned by a company, the copyright is granted for 75 years after publication, or 100 years after creation, whichever is shorter.

Copyright Information from the U.S. Government

The single biggest source for information regarding copyright issues is the United States government. The U.S. Copyright Office publishes a wealth of material designed to educate the public about copyright laws. The information from the government can help explain complex copyright issues and give you current information regarding copyrights in the United States and abroad.

INFORMATION FROM THE U.S. GOVERNMENT

The United States government can be a great source for useful information about your intellectual property rights. The U. S. Copyright Office publishes a number of circulars that contain very valuable information about the state of copyright laws, and specific information about various forms of copyright (written for the layperson). You can contact the U.S. Copyright Office at

United States Copyright Office
Library of Congress
Washington, DC 20559-6000
(202) 707-3000

Here are some relevant copyright publications:

Circ 1:	*Copyright Basics*
Circ 1b:	*Limitations/Information Furnished by Copyright Office*
Circ 6:	*Access to/Copies of Copyright Records and Deposits*
Circ 15:	*Renewal of Copyright*
Circ 21:	*Reproduction of Copyrighted Works By Educators and Librarians*
Circ 22:	*How to Investigate the Copyright Status of a Work*
Circ 31:	*Ideas, Methods, or Systems*
Circ 40:	*Works of the Visual Arts*
Circ 45:	*Motion Pictures including Video Recordings*

Circ 50:   *Musical Composition*

Circ 55:   *Copyright Registration for Multimedia Works*

Circ 56:   *Copyright for Sound Recordings*

Circ 56a: *Copyright Registration of Musical Compositions*

Circ 61:   *Copyright Registration for Computer Programs*

The U.S. Copyright Office also maintains information available on the Internet at the site `gopher://marvel.loc.gov/11/copyright`.

You can obtain information regarding trademarks and patents from the United States Patent and Trademark Office. The PTO mailing address and phone number is

> U.S. Patent and Trademark Office
> Crystal Plaza 2 9D30
> Washington, D.C. 20231
> (703) 308-0322

Printed copies of any patent, identified by its patent number, can be purchased from the Patent and Trademark Office.

Some other PTO publications include

> Official Gazette of the United States Patent and Trademark Office
>
> Index of Patents
>
> Index of Trademarks
>
> Manual of Classification
>
> Classification Definitions
>
> Title 37 Code of Federal Regulations
>
> Basic Facts about Trademarks
>
> Directory of Registered Patent Attorneys and Agents
>
> Manual of Patent Examining Procedure (MPEP)
>
> The Story of the United States Patent Office

The PTO also maintains a wealth of information available electronically, via the World Wide Web at `http://www.uspto.gov/`.

Using Copyrighted Materials

In addition to copyrighting your own electronically published material, you might want to use materials in your publication that might already be copyrighted by someone else. There are some general guidelines that you can follow to help ensure you won't violate someone else's copyright in your own publication.

Works in the public domain, or those works that have an expired copyright with no renewal, can be used freely. It is a good idea to check thoroughly to see if a work is in the public domain before proceeding. Some vendors offer works (such as image collections) in the public domain for sale that are provided specifically for republication. Some authors of various ShareWare/FreeWare products, which are not in the public domain, also allow for the republication of their works, provided certain guidelines are followed. If you have a piece of software that you would like to distribute and have a question about the right to republish the material, it is best to contact the copyright owner if possible.

For works that are currently under copyright protection, it is possible to get permission from the copyright owner to use a work. Copyright protection is treated as personal property and is transferable. As such, it is generally governed by the personal property laws of individual states. The copyright owner can grant permission for use under the terms of a license contract, and still retain copyright protection. The terms of the contract are subject to negotiation and might include notice of ownership or royalty payments.

If the work you want to include in your publication is being used for educational purposes, a nonprofit organization, or library purposes, it is possible to use a portion of the work under fair use. Fair use is a very ambiguous area of copyright law. Fair use is determined by the courts based on the following criteria:

- Whether the work is used in a publication for profit or nonprofit
- Whether republication of the work will affect its market value
- The amount of original work being used

Fair use can be a great way to quote or make references to a specific work, but it also has the potential to get you into deep trouble. The best example of Fair Use abuse involves copy shops. Many copy shops have established themselves on college campuses as a resource for professors and students. In the past, this also included assembling and binding *readers* for various course offerings. The readers assembled by copy shops were often sections of textbooks or journal articles that a professor wanted to use without forcing students to buy the entire textbook. One such shop, Kinko's Copies, was challenged in a lawsuit brought against them by several textbook publishers on the grounds that the readers did not comply with the terms of fair use. Kinko's defense was based on the idea that the works were not being used for profit and were being used by educational institutions, and therefore, fair use. However, a U.S. court found that Kinko's readers often contained very large sections of original works and could possibly represent a threat to the textbook's sales. Therefore, copy shops must now obtain releases from copyright holders for future editions of any readers. Kinko's was also ordered to pay several million dollars in damages. Fair use can often be a double-edged sword.

You should be aware of all your rights under copyright protection and the fact that these rights extend to others. Copyright protection lets you control your original creations and ensures that you might receive compensation for your work.

Just as you want to protect your rights, the rights of other authors should be respected. If you have a question about using a portion of someone else's work in your own work, it is best to secure the right to do so in writing to protect yourself against possible legal action.

Can You Enforce Your Copyrights Online?

NOTE

Lance Rose, Esq., (elrose@well.com), contributing author to this chapter, is a writer and attorney. He is *of counsel* to Lewis & Roca in Phoenix, Arizona, and co-chair of its Intellectual Property and Technology Group, serving the high-technology, information, and media industries.

It's been said that copyright is all but dead on the Internet—that even if you have a legal copyright, people can freely violate your rights without getting caught. How so?

In the old (pre-Net, pre-Web) days, combating large-scale infringement was understood. Massive copying equipment was needed to copy books and tapes, making it hard for pirates to hide their illicit operations from determined copyright owners. The costs of pursuing pirates could be offset by seizing the large amounts of money they hauled in. And the investment necessary to make and sell large quantities of infringing goods ensured that only a few well-heeled pirates could infringe on a mass level.

In contrast, on the Net it is child's play to commit mass infringements without getting caught. A person can distribute thousands of illegal copies across the vast expanse of the Net for the price of a cup of coffee and hide his or her identity using the anonymous re-mailer services now available online. Now, the copyright owner can neither stop the infringing distribution nor find the joker who did it. Doesn't this render copyright owners helpless to protect their rights?

In fact, copyright is far from dead online. To see why, remember that copyright law is not a theoretical right but a practical tool designed to encourage creators to contribute valuable works to society. To make this happen, copyright law gives creators the ability to charge others to copy, distribute, or alter their works. Perfect enforcement by the owner is not necessary. If the copyright owner receives enough payment to justify the time and effort he put into creating his work, copyright law is working just fine.

Thus, the question of whether people are sending infringements over the Net without penalty is merely academic. The more important point is whether copyright owners are making enough money in the places they can control to justify creating their works in the first place. The general approach to enforcing copyrights online involves four parts:

1. Keep all major venues for the work clear of infringements (large online systems such as CompuServe, America Online, and Prodigy; the World Wide Web; large computer bulletin boards; and so on).

2. Use agent technology to cover the Net. Agent software under development can multiply the investigation efforts of copyright owners on the Net many fold.

3. Symbolic legal actions can scare off infringers: Occasional legal actions and prosecution of major infringers can greatly reduce the attractiveness of violating copyrights.

4. Practical protection technologies, such as software metering. This is not a legal move, but simple self-help—locking up valuable information so only those who paid for the key can get hold of it. This method works better for some kinds of works than others, depending on the market and the kind of work involved.

Any organization following these approaches should not have trouble keeping their copyrighted works protected. What about individuals and small groups that can't afford this approach? Luckily, many creators' rights groups are gearing up to operate on the Net, including well-established groups like the Writer's Guild, ASCAP, and BMI. By combining the interests and resources of many smaller creators, these and other groups should be able to keep the main stream effectively clear of infringements and support healthy market of copyrighted works for small and large creators alike.

Trademarks

A trademark is a symbol, logo, or phrase that is associated with a product or service. Examples of trademarks can be seen in many different areas of commerce. You are probably familiar with the golden arches, or *Coke is it!,* both of which are examples of trademarks and how a trademark can enhance product recognition.

The use of a trademark can be a great way to establish a symbol that will readily be associated with your product or company. You can also protect your rights to use a trademark and prevent other persons or companies from using the same, or confusingly similar, trademark. For example, a certain fast food chain could easily prevent you from using a golden M as the symbol for your restaurant because it would easily be confused with their registered trademark—the golden arches.

It is easy to establish a trademark of your own. One such way is to simply start using the trademark as a symbol associated with your company or product. Trademark registration stipulates that the company that first uses a symbol or slogan has the right to register the trademark. However, you might begin using a trademark and find someone else was using it first. If you are developing a unique product or service, it might be worth the time and effort to register your trademark, and to search to make sure your trademark is unique.

Registering your trademark with the United States Patent and Trademark Office can extend your right to use a trademark, and prevent your competitors from using a similar trademark. The registration process is quite simple. The PTO has trademark repositories available in all 50 states, so you can search for similar trademarks before registering yours. You can apply to register your trademark by completing the application (PTO Form 1478) and sending it in with a $245 fee and a copy of the trademark. You can use a trademark, along with the ™ designation, before the trademark is officially registered. After you have received registration, you use the ® symbol to denote a registered trademark.

If you intend to use a trademark that is not registered to you in an electronic publication, you should secure the rights to do so from the trademark's owner in writing. If you use a trademark without authorization, the owner can sue you for trademark infringement and may be entitled to damages.

Patents

The most complicated form of property rights available to electronic publishers is the patent. The PTO states that a patent is, "a grant of a property right by the Government to the inventor, or his heirs or assignees." (PTO Publication: 003-004-00661-7.) Patents can protect your rights to develop and market an invention or idea that you have invested the time and money in developing. In this manner, patents work to protect your rights by preventing competitors from marketing your ideas without the same investment in research and development.

A patent can protect your ideas and designs in several ways. It can ensure that you have the exclusive rights to market the product you have developed. It grants you the right to sell or license your idea to other companies. It also entitles you to royalties or damages from companies that market your patented ideas without your consent.

Because of the far-reaching implications of being granted a patent, applying for a patent can be a very lengthy and expensive process. To be eligible for a patent, the idea or invention to be patented must be a *novel* idea, as defined by the law.

To qualify as novel, an invention must not

■ Already be patented in any country in the world

■ Appear in any *prior art*

■ Currently be for sale or use in any country in the world

It is possible to market an idea and then apply for a patent, as long as the application is filed within one year of the invention's initial marketing. Prior art is the most difficult requirement of a patent. If an invention or a description of the invention appears in print in any publication in the world, prior art is said to exist and the invention is not patentable.

During the course of examination for a patent, the PTO will conduct a search of all previous U.S. patents and databases from around the world in an attempt to discover prior art. Because of the sheer size and scope of the search, obtaining a patent can become enormously expensive. The fees start with a base that covers the application for up to 20 patents of a similar nature. Additional patents can incur additional fees. There is also a distinction made between large and small entities when applying application fees. Small entities (individuals or small companies) are entitled to application fee discounts.

The patent application process is very long and involved. The process of searching for prior art and approving a patent can take years. Because of the length of time in application for a patent, you might want to market your product before a patent is issued. Applications for patents with the PTO are completely confidential until the patent is issued. Because of this, the choice to market or publicize your unpatented invention is yours. If you have filed an official patent application, you can market your product with the label *Patent Pending,* which is an official designation that you have filed for a U.S. patent. Do not try to protect your rights by marketing a product with the Patent Pending label without first filling an official application.

> **CAUTION**
>
> Using the Patent Pending label without filling an application is considered fraudulent and is subject to severe federal fines.

The complexity of filing for a patent usually warrants hiring a patent attorney or patent agent. Patent attorneys and patent agents are individuals who are officially registered to practice before the PTO. These individuals are governed by the code of conduct as established by the PTO and will offer the most secure route for obtaining your patent. The PTO will not make recommendations of patent attorneys, but it does have a database available of all attorneys and agents authorized to practice before the PTO. You can access the database via the World Wide Web at http://www.uspto.gov/web/attorney/.

After you are granted a patent, you have full property rights to that invention. With a valid patent in hand, you can market your invention, sell the rights to market it, charge royalties for its use, or sell the patent outright. The patent is in effect for 17 years—and in the world of technology, 17 years is a very long time. The patent terms have also recently been altered. The new system, which was signed into law in December 1994, allows for a 20-year patent term. This new 20-year term is now measured from the filing date for the patent, not the issue date. The new changes went into effect in June 1995.

Patent Problems

Patents might seem to be a panacea for protecting your rights to a product, but the U.S. Patent system is suffering from outdated methods that might not prove effective in dealing with the computing industry and software. Unfortunately, you might be running the risk of violating many patents with the creation of your multimedia software.

The current patent system was designed around patenting physical devices, not intellectual property. Because of this, software patents have created some unique problems for the U.S. Patent and Trademark Office. Problems exist in searching for prior art, patent classification, and the very nature of software patents.

Searching for prior art can be very difficult when applied to software patent applications. The problem is that many computing algorithms and sections of code are not published. Software that is compiled from code may be protected by copyright laws, which can prevent illegal copying of a particular product. Obtaining a patent on code, however, can prevent others from developing a similar product entirely. Because code is often developed by individuals or researchers, fairly common algorithms are often discovered and implemented by several individuals at the same time. The nature of computer programming makes the development of similar code to produce similar programs almost inevitable. The problem arises when one individual decides to patent a section of code or a method.

Because a particular piece of code might implement several different techniques, methods, or algorithms, the potential exists for individuals to violate many, possibly hundreds, of patents, without any knowledge. The time and money involved to search for patents is enormous and beyond the reach of most individuals and companies. The problem is compounded by the antiquated system for cataloging patents. A software patent might fall into a category that has little to do with computing based on use in an industrial application. Even the patent title might not accurately reflect the contents of the patent. This leaves potential programmers open to patent infringement unknowingly, without a reliable method for checking their status.

Both the computing world and the U.S. Patent and Trademark Office were shocked by an incredible example of how the current patent system and laws could be abused when, in 1993, Compton's New Media was granted the patent for multimedia technology.

Patent #5,241,671 was granted in August 1993. The patent was submitted by Compton's and included as many as 40 different descriptions of techniques used by a host of multimedia applications. Because of the PTO's inability to find adequate prior art, however, the Compton's patent was issued and Compton's became the defacto inventor of multimedia.

Had it not been for the deliberate gloating on the behalf of Compton's, the problems surrounding their patent might never have come to light. Fortunately, Compton's revealed their patent at Comdex, a computer industry trade show. The president of the company announced that Compton's had the rights to multimedia technology and hinted that the company might require royalty fees from anyone marketing a multimedia product.

The announcement turned the computing industry on its ear. In fact, so much fury was caused over Compton's announcement that the Commissioner of the U.S. Patent Office requested an investigation into the patent. Eventually, with the help of many members of the software industry, adequate prior art was produced to reject Compton's patent claim. Although the world seems safe for multimedia once again, Compton's still has several avenues for appeal—and might still be awarded the patent on multimedia.

The Compton's case is a full-blown example of how software patents are ambiguous and might or might not protect your work. Because the techniques that Compton's used in their multimedia package were industry standards, that had not necessarily been committed to searchable prior art, they were inadvertently granted a patent to technology that was in widespread use. With such mistakes happening on a routine basis, it is easy to see how you might be placing yourself in jeopardy of violating a patent for even the simplest of computer programs.

The concerns over patenting software are valid and serious. If you are developing a custom interface that you feel will revolutionize the dissemination of electronically published material, you might want to consider a patent. However, for most electronic publishers, the techniques and methods used for electronic publishing will be based on well-established industry standards.

For example, if you are creating Internet services, such as in World Wide Web publishing, the real investment on your part is not as much the interface as the content. That is what publishing is about: providing content. Chances are that the interface you choose will be a standard interface in widespread use. After all, an established user base of an interface broadens your potential market. If this is the case, patent protection is probably not warranted. Your best course of action is probably best served by copyright protection.

Determining the Best Method of Protection

When designing your project, it is a good idea to plan the method by which you intend to secure your rights to the material. By planning in advance, or at least before the project is completed, you will be one step closer to securing your rights and releasing your project.

The type of information you are publishing should be your guide to securing intellectual property rights. No matter what you are publishing, you should ensure your rights to the original material. The bulk of the content will most likely fall under copyright protection, as will the medium itself. Copyright protection is certainly the most economical and, for most publishing ventures, is an adequate form of protection. However, if you are developing a multimedia-based project, or customized software or interfaces for your project, you should consider and evaluate patent protection. A patent attorney should be able to provide you with a consultation that will help you determine if your project would benefit from patent protection and help you decide whether the investment in patent protection is worth the risk.

Summary

The area of intellectual property rights in electronic mediums is the subject of frequent debate. There are advocates of information secrecy and freedom. The laws that were set into place hundreds of years ago to deal with printed material and physical inventions are straining to adapt to our electronic world. As an electronic publisher, you have no choice but to protect your work under the current system—or risk losing your investment. You should be aware, however, that the growing popularity of computer networks and electronic publishing will necessitate some changes to intellectual property laws in the future. There is no question that many of today's laws can be applied to electronic publishing. It's also true that with new technologies some laws just will not adapt well. You should be aware of your rights and take an active role in the legislation that will affect your intellectual property rights in the future.

The advice of an attorney specializing in intellectual property rights can help you obtain the best protection under the current laws. You, as an electronic publisher, can help influence the future of electronic intellectual property laws. If freedom of the press belongs to those who own one, electronic publishing pushes those boundaries of freedom just a little bit further.

PART

Appendixes

Resource List of Tools Used in Electronic Publishing

A

by David L. Gulbransen

This list of electronic publishing resources is designed to give you some idea of the common hardware and software packages being used in electronic publishing. Use this list as a starting point for company and product information.

The prices listed in this appendix are based on the list price from the manufacturer. This should give you a starting point to compare mail order and local store prices and make sure you are getting the best deal. Product lines change, so regardless of whether you are buying software or hardware, you should always check the model/version number to make sure you are getting the latest product.

> **CAUTION**
>
> Before purchasing hardware and software, it is always wise to check with the manufacturer for compatibility requirements. Many pieces of hardware listed in this appendix require special controller boards that might not be compatible with all systems. Electronic publishing software is also very resource-intensive, and might not be compatible with some systems, or might require memory upgrades to be used effectively.

Hardware

Because electronic publishing eliminates the need for hardcopy output, the hardware discussed here is largely storage equipment. The volume of information that can be distributed electronically is often so large that traditional means of storage, such as floppy disks, are inadequate. You will find the hardware list divided into three sections: CDR (CD Recordable), MO (Magneto-Optical) drives, and scanners. The CDR drives enable you to publish CD-ROMs for proofing or limited distribution. MO drives provide practical, large-capacity, removable storage, and scanners enable you to input traditional artwork and images.

Recordable CDs

Recordable CD drives enable you to create a CD-ROM that can be passed along to someone with a CD-ROM drive and accessed without requiring special hardware. Recordable CDs are not the most efficient way of mass producing CD-ROMs; however, they are quite useful for producing limited runs of in-house material, promotional material, or working mock-ups before committing to a CD-ROM manufacturing run.

NOTE

Recordable CD drives all have a storage capacity of approximately 650MB. This is due to the formatting requirements of Compact Disk technology. Because there is no variation of capacity among different CDR drives, the major differences among CDR drives will be the speed at which they can write and access data.

Vendor:	**dataDisc, Inc.**
	10334 Battleview Pkwy.
	Manassas, Virginia 22110
	1-800-328-2347
Model:	dataDisc CDR-2x
Suggested Retail Price:	$1,895
Speed:	Double speed
Vendor:	**Eastman Kodak Company**
	343 State St.
	Rochester, New York 14650
	1-800-242-2424
Model:	PCD Writer 225
Suggested Retail Price:	$2,850
Speed:	Double speed
Vendor:	**MicroNet Technology, Inc.**
	80 Technology Dr.
	Irvine, California 92718
	(714) 453-6000
Model:	MCD Pro Quad
Suggested Retail Price:	$4,995
Speed:	Quad speed
Vendor:	**Pinnacle Micro, Inc.**
	19 Technology Dr.
	Irvine, California 92718
	1-800-553-7070
Model:	RCD-1000
Suggested Retail Price:	$1,895
Speed:	Double speed
Vendor:	**Ricoh Corporation**
	5 Dedrick Place
	West Caldwell, New Jersey 07006
	1-800-241-RFMS

Model:	RS-1060C
Suggested Retail Price:	$1,995
Speed:	Double speed

Vendor:	**Sony**
	3300 Zanker Rd.
	San Jose, California 95134
	1-800-352-7669

Model:	CDW-900E
Suggested Retail Price:	$7,500
Speed:	Double speed

Vendor:	**Yamaha**
	100 Century Center Court
	San Jose, California 95112
	1-800-543-7457

Model:	CDR100; CDE100
Suggested Retail Price:	$5,500
Speed:	Quad speed

Magneto-Optical Drives

Magneto-Optical (MO) drives offer a large-capacity removable storage solution. The drives read a storage MO disk that stores information magnetically, but through a laser instead of a traditional magnetic read/write head. They can often be a very cost-effective and reliable way to store large amounts of information. MO drives offer a more stable and reliable backup solution than tape drives and can be very useful for backup or long-term storage. However, because the format for MO drives is not standard, they are not necessarily interchangeable among manufacturers. There are a variety of storage capacities available, but they are not generally useful for distribution purposes.

> **CAUTION**
>
> Although at a glance MO disks bear a keen resemblance to CD-ROMs, the two technologies are very different. MO drives are generally not capable of reading CD-ROMs, and CD-ROM drives are not capable of reading MO disks. If you are looking for a way to record CD-ROMs that can be played back on a standard CD-ROM drive, you should look at recordable CD drives (CDR).

Vendor:	**APS Technologies, Inc.**
	6131 Deramus Ave.
	Kansas City, Missouri 64120
	1-800-235-3707

Model: APS 230 MO
Suggested Retail Price: $600
Storage Capacity: 230MB

Model: APS 1.3GB MO
Suggested Retail Price: $2,000
Storage Capacity: 1.3 GB

Vendor: **Fujitsu**
                          2904 Orchard Pkwy.
                          San Jose, California 95134
                          1-800-626-4686

Model: DynaMO 230
Suggested Retail Price: $749
Storage Capacity: 230MB

Vendor: **Olympus**
                          Two Corporate Center Dr.
                          Melville, New York 11747
                          1-800-347-4027

Model: Deltis 230MO
Suggested Retail Price: $795
Storage Capacity: 230MB

Model: MOS 525E
Suggested Retail Price: $2,300
Storage Capacity: 1.3 GB

Vendor: **Panasonic**
                          2 Panasonic Way
                          Secaucus, New Jersey 07094
                          1-800-742-8086

Model: LF-9000
Suggested Retail Price: $3,995
Storage Capacity: 652MB

Vendor: **Pinnacle Micro, Inc.**
                          19 Technology Dr.
                          Irvine, California 92718
                          800-553-7070

Model: Tahoe-230
Suggested Retail Price: $999
Storage Capacity: 230MB

Vendor:	**Spin Peripherals** 734 Forrest St. Marlborough, Massachusetts 01752 800-466-1200
Model:	Spin 230MB Optical (O)
Suggested Retail Price:	$799
Storage Capacity:	230MB
Vendor:	**FOCUS Enhancements, Inc.** 800 W. Cummings Park, Ste. 4500 Woburn, Massachusetts 01801 800-538-8865
Model:	Focus 1.3 GB MO
Suggested Retail Price:	$2,700
Storage Capacity:	1.3 GB
Vendor:	**FWB, Inc.** 1555 Adams Dr. Menlo Park, California 94025 (415) 325-4392
Model:	hammerDisk230
Suggested Retail Price:	$1,129
Storage Capacity:	230MB
Model:	hammerDisk1300HH
Suggested Retail Price:	$3,289
Storage Capacity:	1.3 GB
Vendor:	**Hewlett-Packard Co.** 5301 Stevens Creek Blvd. Santa Clara, California 95051 1-800-752-0900
Model:	HP C2550A Model 1300T
Suggested Retail Price:	$3,495
Storage Capacity:	1.3 GB
Vendor:	**Hitachi** 2000 Sierra Point Pkwy. Brisbane, California 94005 1-800-HITACHI
Model:	OU152S/D-1
Suggested Retail Price:	$2,880
Storage Capacity:	2 GB

Vendor:	**Iomega Corp.**
	1821 W. Iomega Way
	Roy, Utah 84067
	1-800-777-6654
Model:	Iomega LaserSafe Plus
Suggested Retail Price:	$3,995
Storage Capacity:	1.3 GB
Vendor:	**Sony**
	3300 Zanker Rd.
	San Jose, California 95134
	1-800-352-7669
Model:	SMO-S521
Suggested Retail Price:	$1,995
Storage Capacity:	1.3 GB

Scanners

Scanners are available in a variety of formats, and offer a variety of options. The key elements to a scanner are the image type, resolution, and size. The majority of scanners on the market are flatbed scanners that function similarly to a photocopier. Flatbed scanners are capable of scanning color images at a very high resolution, suitable for a variety of electronic publishing uses. For applications requiring greater quality, 35mm slide scanners can often provide a higher resolution and better quality scan than flatbed scanners.

Manufacturers and retailers also often bundle scanning software with the scanner. The quality of scanning software can range from a stand-alone application, such as OFoto, to "plug-ins" that enable you to operate your scanner from image editing software such as Photoshop. Be sure to inquire about the scanning software bundled with the scanner and compatibility with your system.

> **TIP**
>
> Scanning resolution can often be an ambiguous term. Scanners often have two resolution ratings: one is the optical resolution and the other is an interpolated resolution achieved through software. Optical resolution is the physical resolution that the scanner is capable of achieving. A scanner cannot achieve a resolution higher than it's optical resolution without mathematically manipulating the scanned image. Interpolated resolution is a technique in which the actual scanned information is manipulated mathematically to appear at a higher resolution than it actually is. Some manufacturers will list the interpolated resolution in specifications, which can be misleading when you are evaluating the base quality of each scanner. For evaluating scanners, you should rely on the optical resolution.

CAUTION

Scanners are SCSI devices that might require additional controller boards to work with some systems.

Vendor:	**Apple Computer, Inc.** 1 Infinite Loop Cupertino, California 95014 1-800-776-2333
Model:	Apple Color OneScanner
Suggested Retail Price:	$1,199
Resolution:	300 dpi
Type:	Color
Scan Size:	8.5×14
Vendor:	**Canon** 2995 Redhill Ave. Costa Mesa, California 92626 1-800-848-4123
Model:	IX-3010
Suggested Retail Price:	$569
Resolution:	300 dpi
Type:	Grayscale
Scan Size:	8.5×14
Model:	IX-4015 Color Image Scanner
Suggested Retail Price:	$799
Resolution:	400 dpi
Type:	Color
Scan Size:	8.5×14
Vendor:	**Epson** 20770 Madrona Ave. Torrance, California 90503 1-800-289-3776
Model:	ES-1000C
Suggested Retail Price:	$799
Resolution:	400×800 dpi
Type:	Color
Scan Size:	8.5×14
Model:	ES-1200C PC/Mac
Suggested Retail Price:	$1,049

Resolution: 600 dpi
Type: Color
Scan Size: 8.5×14

Vendor: **Hewlett-Packard Co.**
                     5301 Stevens Creek Blvd.
                     Santa Clara, California 95051
                     1-800-752-0900

Model: HP ScanJet 3c
Suggested Retail Price: $1,179
Resolution: 600 dpi
Type: Color
Scan Size: 8.5×14

Model: HP ScanJet 3p
Suggested Retail Price: $399
Resolution: 300 dpi
Type: Grayscale
Scan Size: 8.5×14

Vendor: **Microtek**
                     3715 Doolittle Dr.
                     Redondo Beach, California 90278
                     1-800-654-4160

Model: ScanMaker IISPX
Suggested Retail Price: $899
Resolution: 1200 dpi
Type: Color
Scan Size: 8.5×14

Vendor: **Mirror Technologies, Inc.**
                     5198 West 76th St.
                     Edina, Minnesota 55439
                     1-800-654-5294

Model: Model 1200
Suggested Retail Price: $1,499
Resolution: 1200 dpi
Type: Color
Scan Size: 8.5×14

Vendor: **PixelCraft, Inc.**
                     130 Doolittle Dr., Ste. 19
                     San Leandro, California 94577
                     1-800-933-0330

Model: Pro Imager 4000
Suggested Retail Price: $2,995
Resolution: 2400 dpi
Type: Color
Scan Size: 8.5×14

Vendor: **Polaroid Corp.**
                          549 Technology Sq.
                          Cambridge, Massachusetts 02139
                          1-800-343-5000
Model: Photo Scanner CS-500/i; CS-500
Suggested Retail Price: $3,995–$4,495
Resolution: 500 dpi
Type: Color
Scan Size: 35mm Slide

Vendor: **UMAX Technologies, Inc.**
                          3353 Gateway Blvd.
                          Fremont, California 94538
                          1-800-562-0311
Model: Vista-S8 LE
Suggested Retail Price: $995
Resolution: 800 dpi
Type: Color
Scan Size: 8.5×14

Software

There are literally hundreds of packages available that can be used for electronic publishing. Because the volume of software tools available is far too large to list in its entirety, this list serves as a selection of some of the most popular and well-received packages. Often, software choices are determined by feature set, platform, environment, and personal preferences. The number of variable in software choices are too numerous to list the complete feature set of each software package available. The contact information provided here will enable you to obtain more information about a specific package and evaluate its feature set against your needs.

THE SHAREWARE CONCEPT

Software is often the most expensive element of any computing environment, and large companies tend to dominate the software industry. Unfortunately, large companies are not always responsive to the needs of individuals or can be slow in updating software packages. There are a number of individuals and smaller software companies that develop packages to fill a certain market niche. Sometimes they develop a custom application that might be useful to others and choose to distribute the software as *shareware* (a term coined by Bob Wallace).

Shareware is based on the idea that you shouldn't have to pay for software that you don't use or that doesn't fit your needs. Software is distributed as shareware based on the honor system. Generally, shareware packages allow a grace period of a week to a month, during which time you might use the software free of charge. If the software does not meet your needs or expectations you can stop using it, with no obligation to pay the author of the software. If you find the software useful and continue to use it, you are expected to pay the licensing, or shareware, fee directly to the author. Shareware fees are usually very reasonable compared to commercial software packages, and shareware applications are often excellent in quality and support.

Shareware can provide great software at affordable prices, but it depends on the honor system. If you use a shareware package, please register it with the author. By supporting the honor system and the small independent developers, shareware will continue to provide good software at reasonable prices.

Page Layout

Page layout programs are traditionally viewed as desktop publishing applications used for preparing traditional print materials. However, as electronic publishing becomes more and more prevalent, it is possible to use these traditional tools to create HTML documents (Hyper Text Markup Language, the format for WWW documents) and PDF files (Portable Document Format, a proprietary format from Adobe Systems, Inc.).

Vendor:	**Adobe Systems, Inc.**
	1585 Charleston Rd.
	Mountain View, California 94039
	1-800-833-6687
Package:	Adobe Acrobat (V.2.0)
Suggested Retail Price:	$195
Requirements:	2MB RAM, 5MB hard disk space
Product Type:	Electronic document publishing tool. Users can create electronic documents that can be displayed by the Acrobat Reader. Also enables the creation of electronic documents from layout programs and word processors.
Package:	Adobe Acrobat Reader (V.2.0)
Suggested Retail Price:	$50/per user; $2,000/50 users
Requirements:	2MB RAM, 5MB hard disk space
Product Type:	Electronic document reader. Used to access PDF files created by Adobe Acrobat.

Package:	Aldus PageMaker (V.6.0)
Suggested Retail Price:	$895
Requirements:	8MB RAM, 15–20MB hard disk space
Product Type:	Page layout program. Used for traditional page layout, creation of PDF documents with Adobe Acrobat, and extensions available for creating HTML.

Package:	Adobe Persuasion (V.3.0)
Suggested Retail Price:	$495
Requirements:	8MB RAM, 20MB hard disk space
Product Type:	Electronic presentation software. Enables user to create electronic presentations that can be played back as movies or projected as large format presentations.

Vendor:	**Frame Technology Corp.**
	333 W. San Carlos St.
	San Jose, California 95110
	1-800-843-7263
Package:	FrameMaker (V.5.0)
Suggested Retail Price:	$895
Requirements:	8MB RAM, 20MB hard disk space
Product Type:	Page layout program. Used for traditional page layout and creation of PDF documents with Adobe Acrobat. FrameMaker has very strong features for formula layout and formatting technical data.

Vendor:	**Manhattan Graphics Corp.**
	250 E. Hartsdale Ave.
	Hartsdale, New York 10530
	1-800-572-6533
Package:	Ready, Set, Go! GX (V.7.0)
Suggested Retail Price:	$395
Requirements:	8MB RAM, 10MB hard disk space, Mac only
Product Type:	Low end/home page layout program. Used for traditional page layout and creation of PDF documents with Adobe Acrobat.

Vendor:	**Microsoft Corp.**
	One Microsoft Way
	Redmond, Washington 98052-6399
	1-800-426-9400
Package:	Microsoft Publisher (V.2.0)
Suggested Retail Price:	$199

Requirements: 4MB RAM, 10MB hard disk space, Windows
Product Type: Low end/home page layout program. Used for tradi-
                           tional page layout and creation of PDF documents with
                           Adobe Acrobat.

Package: Microsoft PowerPoint (V.4.0)
Suggested Retail Price: $395
Requirements: 4MB RAM, 11MB hard disk space
Product Type: Electronic presentation software. Enables user to create
                           electronic presentations that can be played back as
                           movies or projected as large format presentations.

Vendor: **Novell, Inc.**
                           122 East 1700 South
                           Provo, Utah 84606-6194
                           1-800-453-1267
Package: WordPerfect Envoy (V.1.0)
Suggested Retail Price: $189
Requirements: 4MB RAM, 2MB hard disk space
Product Type: Electronic document publishing tool. Users can create
                           electronic documents that can be displayed by the Envoy
                           Reader.

Vendor: **Quark, Inc.**
                           1800 Grant St.
                           Denver, Colorado 80203
                           800-788-7835; 303-894-8888
                           FAX: 303-894-3399
                           Tech support: (303) 894-8888
Package: QuarkXPress (V.3.34)
Suggested Retail Price: $895
Requirements: 4MB RAM, 15MB hard disk space
Product Type: Page layout program. Used for traditional page layout,
                           creation of PDF documents with Adobe Acrobat, and
                           extensions available for creating HTML.

Image Software

Images are a vital part of publishing in any medium. Images might include original illustrations, artwork, or photographs. The software packages list here provide the means to create
custom images, process photo images, and even alter images to fit your specific needs.

NOTE

Image editing software packages are some of the most resource-intensive packages available. They often require great amounts of RAM and hard disk space for the image applications and the images themselves. When purchasing imaging software, keep in mind that the minimum requirements are often sufficient to run an application, but not to accomplish any actual work. If your machine only meets the minimum requirements for these software packages, you should consider upgrading your hardware.

Vendor:	**Adobe Systems, Inc.**
	1585 Charleston Rd.
	Mountain View, California 94039
	1-800-833-6687
Package:	Adobe Photoshop (V.3.0.1)
Suggested Retail Price:	$895
Requirements:	8MB RAM, 150MB hard disk space, CD-ROM
Product Type:	High-end image-editing software. Enables users to manipulate scanned images/photographs and save images in a variety of formats.
Package:	Aldus Photostyler (V.2.0)
Suggested Retail Price:	$795
Requirements:	4MB RAM, 40MB hard disk space
Product Type:	Image-editing software. Enables users to manipulate scanned images/photographs and save images in a variety of formats.

NOTE

Adobe Systems had purchased the Aldus Corporation and its family of products. Many Aldus products may be merged with the Adobe software line.

Package:	Adobe Illustrator (V.5.5)
Suggested Retail Price:	$595
Requirements:	4MB RAM, 12MB hard disk space, CD-ROM
Product Type:	Illustration program. Enables users to create custom illustrations using a variety of graphic design tools.
Vendor:	**Corel Corp.**
	1600 Carling Ave., The Corel Bldg.
	Ottawa, Ontario, Canada K1Z 8R7
	1-800-772-6735

Package: CorelDRAW!5
Suggested Retail Price: $499 (CD-ROM); $649 (disk)
Requirements: 8MB RAM, 20MB hard disk space, Windows
Product Type: Illustration program. Enables users to create custom
                    illustrations using a variety of graphic design tools.

Vendor: **Deneba Software**
                    7400 Southwest 87th Ave.
                    Miami, FL 33173
                    1-800-622-6827
Package: Canvas (V.3.5.2)
Suggested Retail Price: $400
Requirements: 4MB RAM, 5MB hard disk space
Product Type: Drawing/illustration program. Enables users to create
                    custom illustrations using a variety of tools.

Vendor: **Equilibrium Technologies, Inc.**
                    475 Gate Five Road, Suite 225
                    Sausalito, California 94965
                    (415) 332-4343
Package: DeBabelizer (V.1.6)
Suggested Retail Price: $399
Requirements: 8MB RAM, 10MB hard disk space
Product Type: Image conversion program. Allows for batch processing
                    of images. Converts image formats, and allows for batch
                    editing techniques.

Vendor: **Fractal Design Corp.**
                    335 Spreckels Dr., Ste. F
                    Aptos, California 95003
                    1-800-297-2665
Package: Fractal Design Painter (V.3.1)
Suggested Retail Price: $499
Requirements: 8MB RAM, 5MB hard disk space
Product Type: Paint program. Enables users to create custom illustra-
                    tions using a variety of tools similar to traditional artists
                    materials.

Vendor: **Macromedia, Inc.**
                    600 Townsend St., Ste. 310 W
                    San Francisco, California 94103
                    1-800-945-4061
Package: Macromedia FreeHand (V.5.0)
Suggested Retail Price: $595

Requirements:	8MB RAM, 5MB hard disk space
Product Type:	Illustration program. Enables users to create custom illustrations using a variety of graphic design tools.

3D/Animation Software

Vendor:	**Adobe Systems, Inc.**
	1585 Charleston Rd.
	Mountain View, California 94039
	1-800-833-6687
Package:	Adobe Premiere (V.4.0.1)
Suggested Retail Price:	$795
Requirements:	4MB RAM, 80MB hard disk space
Product Type:	Video editing application. Premiere enables the user to edit digitized video and create video clips in a variety of formats.

Vendor:	**Macromedia, Inc.**
	600 Townsend St., Ste. 310 W
	San Francisco, California 94103-4945
	1-800-945-4061
Package:	Director (V.4.0)
Suggested Retail Price:	$699
Requirements:	8MB RAM, 40MB hard disk space
Product Type:	Multimedia authoring software. Enables users to create interactive presentations and animations. Enables users to create stand-alone multimedia applications.

Vendor:	**Specular International, Ltd.**
	479 West St.
	Amherst, Massachusetts 01002
	1-800-433-SPEC
Package:	Infini-D (V.3.0)
Suggested Retail Price:	$699
Requirements:	8MB RAM, 10MB hard disk space
Product Type:	3-D animation package. Enables users to create 3-D models, animations, and presentations.

Vendor:	**Strata, Inc.**
	2 W. St. George Blvd., Ancestor Sq., Ste. 2100
	St. George, Utah 84770
	1-800-869-6855
Package:	Strata StudioPro (V.1.5.2)
Suggested Retail Price:	$1,495

Requirements:	8MB RAM, 10MB hard disk space
Product Type:	High-end 3-D/animation package. Enables users to create 3-D models and animations.

Development Software

Many electronic publishing ventures require custom applications to be designed as a user interface. There are a few applications that enable users to develop custom applications without
a high level of programming knowledge. These programs enable the user to design custom
interfaces and presentations, and then create a stand-alone application that can be distributed
on disk or CD-ROM.

Vendor:	**Allegiant Technologies, Inc.**
	6496 Weathers Place, Ste. 100
	San Diego, California 92121
	1-800-255-8258
Package:	SuperCard (V.2.0)
Suggested Retail Price:	$695
Requirements:	4MB RAM, 2MB hard disk space
Product Type:	Database/file management with custom application building tools. Enables user to create custom applications.

Vendor:	**Apple Computer, Inc.**
	1 Infinite Loop
	Cupertino, California 95014
	1-800-776-2333
Package:	HyperCard (V.2.3)
Suggested Retail Price:	$129
Requirements:	4MB RAM, 5MB hard disk space, Macintosh
Product Type:	Database/file management with custom application building tools. Enables user to create custom stand-alone applications.

Vendor:	**Asymetrix Corp.**
	110 110th Ave., NE, Ste. 700
	Bellevue, Washington 98004-5840
	1-800-448-6543
Package:	ToolBook for Windows (V.3.0)
Suggested Retail Price:	$395
Requirements:	4MB RAM, 2MB hard disk space, Windows
Product Type:	Database/file management with custom application building tools. Enables user to create custom stand-alone applications.

TCP/IP Software

Electronic publishing is commonplace on the Internet, but taking advantage of Internet resources requires special software. The packages listed provide access to Internet services, and come with a variety of applications used to access the Internet. Because this book is concerned with electronic publishing, not Internet access, this section will be brief.

> **TIP**
>
> MacTCP is the TCP/IP software for the Macintosh and is now shipping with Macintosh computers. Telnet, finger, talk, and FTP clients, as well as newsreaders are available as ShareWare from `sumex-aim.stanford.edu`.

> **TIP**
>
> TCP/IP software is now being included in a variety of operating systems. If you have OS/2, Windows NT, or Windows 95, TCP/IP software is built into your operating system. Consult your manuals for installation and usage procedures.

Vendor:	**FTP Software, Inc.**
	100 Brickstone Sq., 5th Fl.
	Andover, Massachusetts 01810
	1-800-282-4FTP
Package:	PC/TCP Network Software (V.3.0)
Suggested Retail Price:	$350
Requirements:	4MB RAM, 4MB hard disk space, Windows
Product Type:	TCP/IP Stack for Windows. Gives user networking capability to use Internet applications. Includes Telnet, Finger, Ping, Talk, and FTP clients.
Vendor:	**Novell, Inc.**
	122 East 1700 South
	Provo, Utah 84606-6194
	1-800-453-1267
Package:	LAN Workplace (V.5.0)
Suggested Retail Price:	$399
Requirements:	4MB RAM, 7MB hard disk space
Product Type:	TCP/IP Stack for Windows and Macintosh. Gives user networking ability to use Internet applications. Includes Telnet, Finger, Ping, Talk, and FTP Clients.

Vendor:	**Trumpet Software International**
	GPO Box 1649
	Hobart
	Tasmania 7001
	Australia
	+61 02 450220
Package:	Trumpet Winsock (V.2.1)
Suggested Retail Price:	$25 ShareWare fee
Requirements:	4MB RAM, 2MB hard disk space, Windows
Product Type:	TCP/IP Stack for Windows. Shareware, does not include client software, but client software is also available as shareware from `ftp.cica.indiana.edu`.

World Wide Web Software

There are three categories of World Wide Web (WWW) software. The first category are *WWW browsers*. WWW browsers are programs that enable you to see the information available from various WWW sites. The browser software downloads HTML documents and formats them for viewing on your PC. The next set of WWW software are *HTML (HyperText Markup Language) authoring tools*. HTML is the language for creating WWW documents. HTML editors enable you to publish HTML documents without becoming lost in the world of HTML programming.

The final category of WWW software are *WWW servers*. WWW servers are software packages that run on a computer connected to the Internet. They enable you to distribute your HTML documents via the World Wide Web.

There are a variety of software packages available for each of the WWW tasks: viewing, authoring, and serving. These packages, however, represent the most popular packages for creating WWW services. Keep in mind that all of these packages require a connection to the Internet to publish documents to the WWW.

World Wide Web Browsers

World Wide Web browsers are software packages that enable you to access the data available on the World Wide Web. There are a variety of packages that enable you to surf the Web, one of the most popular being the Netscape Navigator. Each of the packages available cover the basic tasks required to use the WWW, but some offer a more advanced user interface or a more robust feature set. The choice of WWW browser is largely personal; however, you'll find that many sites on the WWW are geared toward a particular browser, the Netscape Navigator. The Netscape Navigator has enjoyed a more complete feature set for an extended period of time than many browsers, and it has established a firm foothold on the Web. That is not to say that other browsers don't offer similar features, only that Netscape has established a large user base because of its advanced features.

Many web browsers are available for a limited time on a trial basis. This can be a good way to evaluate what each browser offers in features, and it can save you money in the long run by assuring that you get the best product for your needs.

> **TIP**
>
> Mosaic is a free WWW Browser from the National Center for Supercomputing Applications. Because you can use Mosaic free of charge, Mosaic can be a good way to decide if the WWW is worth spending the money on a more full-featured browser, such as Netscape or AIR Mosaic. Both Netscape and AIR Mosaic offer a more complete feature set than Mosaic, so investing in something other than Mosaic is generally advisable.

Vendor:	**Netscape Communications Corp.**
	501 E. Middlefield Rd.
	Mountain View, California 94043
	1-800-NETSITE
Package:	Netscape Navigator (V.1.2)
Suggested Retail Price:	$40, free to educators
Requirements:	4MB RAM, 5MB hard disk space
Product Type:	World Wide Web Browser.
Vendor:	**National Center for Supercomputing Applications**
	605 E. Springfield Ave.
	Champaign, Illinois 61820-5518
	FTP: `ftp.ncsa.uiuc.edu`
Package:	NCSA Mosaic
Suggested Retail Price:	Free
Requirements:	4MB RAM, 3MB hard disk space, Windows
Product Type:	World Wide Web Browser.
Vendor:	**SPRY, Inc.**
	316 Occidental Ave.
	Seattle, Washington 98104
	1-800-SPRY-NET
Package:	AIR Mosaic (V.1.1)
Suggested Retail Price:	$30
Requirements:	4MB RAM, 5MB hard disk space, Windows
Product Type:	World Wide Web Browser.

HTML Editors

The language used to provide information on the World Wide Web is HTML, or Hyper Text Markup Language. HTML is very similar to the older days of typesetting. The code is simply text with formatting information provided by tags. There are a variety of tutorials available on the WWW for learning HTML, but many users will find HTML confusing. Much of this confusion can be eliminated by using an HTML Editor. HTML editors are much like word processors that format your documents in HTML, ready for the Web.

Vendor:	**VPE, Inc.**
	601 Madison St., Ste. 200
	Alexandria, Virginia 22314
	(703) 684-3700
Package:	WebBuilder
Suggested Retail Price:	$2,500
Requirements:	12MB RAM, 4MB hard disk space
Product Type:	Complete Internet services development kit. Enables users to create Internet services and link SQL databases to WWW resources.
Vendor:	**Zandar Corp.**
	P.O. Box 480, South Wardsboro Rd.
	Newfane, Vermont 05345-0480
	(802) 365-9393
Package:	TagWrite for Windows (V.3.2)
Suggested Retail Price:	$199
Requirements:	4MB RAM, 1MB hard disk space
Product Type:	HTML and SGML tagging software. Can translate Microsoft Word RTF documents into HTML.
Vendor:	**Beame & Whiteside Software, Inc.**
	706 Hillsborough St.
	Raleigh, North Carolina 27603-1655
	1-800-INFO-NFS
Package:	Web'd
Suggested Retail Price:	$149
Requirements:	4MB RAM, 5MB hard disk space, Windows
Product Type:	Combines HTML graphic editor with WYSIWYG Web page creation and a WWW server.
Vendor:	**Microsoft Corp.**
	One Microsoft Way
	Redmond, Washington 98052
	800-426-9400

Package: Internet Assistant for MS Word 6.0 (V.1.0)
Suggested Retail Price: Not available at press
Requirements: 4MB RAM, 3MB hard disk space, MS Word
Product Type: Enables user to convert MS Word documents directly
                                into HTML.

Vendor: **Novell, Inc.**
                                122 East 1700 South
                                Provo, Utah 84606-6194
                                1-800-453-1267
Package: Internet Publisher
Suggested Retail Price: $49
Requirements: 4MB RAM, 5MB hard disk space, WordPerfect
Product Type: Enables user to convert WordPerfect documents directly
                                into HTML.

Vendor: **SkiSoft Publishing Corp.**
                                1644 Massachusetts Ave., Ste. 79
                                Lexington, Massachusetts 02173
                                1-800-662-3622
Package: WebPublisher
Suggested Retail Price: $495
Requirements: 4MB RAM, 5MB hard disk space, Windows
Product Type: Enables user to convert a variety of word processing
                                documents directly into HTML. Also has graphics tools
                                for creating new Web pages.

Vendor: **SoftQuad, Inc.**
                                56 Aberfoyle Cresent, Ste. 810
                                Toronto, Ontario, CANADA M8X 2W4
                                1-800-387-2777
Package: HoTMetaL PRO
Suggested Retail Price: $195
Requirements: 4MB RAM, 5MB hard disk space
Product Type: Graphics WYSIWYG HTML editor. Enables users to
                                create Web pages in a word processor-like environment.

WWW Servers

Documents are provided on the World Wide Web through special software packages called servers. Servers are software packages that run continuously on a computer that is connected directly to the Internet, and they monitor for requests from a WWW browser. When the server receives a request for a document, it downloads the information to the browser, and you see the WWW page. Server software varies greatly in complexity and features. The most full-featured servers tend to run on high-end workstations and require a great deal of networking knowledge to operate properly. However, a greater number of personal WWW servers are being made available as ShareWare.

NOTE

Many Internet service providers will make space available on the World Wide Web as a part of your subscription. The installation and maintenance of a commercial Web site is not a task to be taken lightly. In addition to a very strong grasp of the World Wide Web, Web server administration often requires UNIX or Windows NT administration skills. Keeping a Web server up and running can turn into a full-time job.

The Web servers listed here are high-end commercial Web servers. They offer features that enable the easy integration of database services, and often enable secure transactions for Internet commerce. For those readers interested in setting up a personal Web server, see the last three entries.

Vendor:	**Netscape Communications Corp.**
	501 E. Middlefield Rd.
	Mountain View, California 94043
	1-800-NETSITE
Package:	Netscape Publishing System
Suggested Retail Price:	$20,000–$50,000
Requirements:	UNIX system (SunOS, Solaris)
Product Type:	Complete high-end Internet publishing system. Enables users to create and edit a variety of Internet services, include dynamically created WWW pages and database applications. Also enables users to provide secure Internet transactions for Internet commerce.
Package:	Netscape Communications Server (V.1.1)
Suggested Retail Price:	$5,000
Requirements:	UNIX system, Windows NT
Product Type:	High-end World Wide Web server. Provides a variety of tools for Web site administration, as well as server software.

Package: Netscape Commerce Server (V.1.1)
Suggested Retail Price: $25,000
Requirements: UNIX system, Windows NT
Product Type: High-end World Wide Web server. Provides a variety of tools for Web site administration, database integration, as well as server software. Also provides secure transactions for Internet commerce.

Vendor: **Open Market, Inc.**
245 First Street
Cambridge, Massachusetts 02142
(617) 621-9500

Package: Open Market Web Server (V.1.0)
Suggested Retail Price: $4,995
Requirements: UNIX system
Product Type: World Wide Web server software, supports secure transactions for Internet commerce.

Vendor: **O'Reilly & Associates, Inc.**
103 Morris St., Ste. A
Sebastopol, California 95472
1-800-998-9938

Package: WebSite (V.2.0)
Suggested Retail Price: $499
Requirements: Windows NT
Product Type: World Wide Web server software, includes Web browser and basic HTML editor.

Vendor: **Spry, Inc.**
316 Occidental Ave.
Seattle, Washington 98104
1-800-SPRY-NET

Package: Internet Office Server (V.4.0)
Suggested Retail Price: Not available at press
Requirements: UNIX system, Windows NT
Product Type: High-end World Wide Web server. Provides a variety of tools for Web site administration, database integration, as well as server software. Also provides secure transactions for Internet commerce.

TIP

The following Web servers are available free of charge or as shareware. They are designed as Web servers that can be run either on high-performance UNIX systems or on your PC. If you are not interested in Internet commerce, you are on a budget, or you are setting up a personal Web server, these servers offer nearly the same spectrum of services as the commercial packages, with the exception of database integration and secure transactions. Unless your company intends on doing business on the Internet, there is no need to spend a fortune to start publishing your documents on the World Wide Web.

Vendor:	**StarNine Technologies, Inc.**
	2550 Ninth Street, Suite 112
	Berkeley, California 94710
	(510) 649-4949
Package:	MacHTTPD (V.2.2)
Suggested Retail Price:	$95, $75 educational
Requirements:	2MB RAM, 2MB hard disk space
Product Type:	World Wide Web server software. The MacHTTP server runs on both 680x0 Macs and Native for PowerMacs. It provides an easy-to-use interface comparable to any Mac application.
Vendor:	**CERN (European Laboratory for Particle Physics)**
	FTP: `ftp.w3.org`
Package:	CERN HTTPD (V.3.0)
Suggested Retail Price:	Free
Requirements:	Windows, Windows NT, UNIX
Product Type:	World Wide Web server software. The CERN server provides an easy to administer WWW server available for a variety of platforms. The Windows version provides a graphical interface and is available free to the general public.
Vendor:	**National Center for Supercomputing Applications**
	605 E. Springfield Ave.
	Champaign, Illinois 61820-5518
	FTP: `ftp.ncsa.uiuc.edu`
Package:	NCSA HTTPD
Suggested Retail Price:	Free
Requirements:	Windows, Windows NT, UNIX
Product Type:	World Wide Web server. The NCSA WWW server is an easy to administrate WWW server available for a variety of platforms. The Windows version provides a graphical interface and is available free to the general public.

Resource List of CD-ROM Titles

B

by William R. Mann

This appendix consists of a list of CD-ROMs that contain electronically published works. Such works may be based on published books and magazines. They may also come from photographic essays, interviews, or other sources.

Each entry includes the title of the work, and the environment it runs under (DOS, Windows, or Macintosh). Many of the titles are dual platform and will run on Windows machines and the Macintosh. It also includes a few sentences describing the contents of the disc, any special features, and contact information.

20th Century Video Almanac (DOS)

Five-disc video reference to the century. Thousands of photos, hundreds of video clips. Hundreds of thousands of words. A general overview on one disc, with in-depth focuses on the other four. Timeline, On This Day, and other sections allow different approaches to the material.

The Software Toolworks; 60 Leveroni Court; Novato, California 94949; (415) 883-3000.

4 Paws of Crab: An Interactive Thai Cookbook (Macintosh)

Journal entries and photographs provide background on Thailand. Includes a digital version of a Thai cookbook, complete with video clips. Hyperlinks provide information on ingredients.

Live Oak Multimedia; 5901 Christie Avenue, Suite 102; Emeryville, California 94608; (510) 654-7480.

A Brief History of Time (Windows, Macintosh)

Based on the book of the same name. The disc contains the text of the book, with hundreds of images and animations. Narrated by Stephen Hawking himself. Features autoplay mode, background on Hawking, and other related material.

Creative Labs; 1901 McCarthy Boulevard; Milpitas, California 95035; (408) 428-6600.

A Christmas Carol (Windows)

The classic story in text with some illustrations. Fully narrated, with some music. Dictionary for highlighted words. Page history tracks progress through book. Built-in learning guide, index, and music and picture galleries.

EBook, Incorporated; 32970 Alvarado-Niles Road, Suite 704; Union City, California 94587; (510) 429-1331.

A.D.A.M.: The Inside Story (Windows, Macintosh)

A family-oriented anatomy guide. Features animated dissections, narration, and slide shows. Animated Family Scrapbook illustrates important facts. Detailed illustrations; click on them to see medical terms. User-specified race in illustrations. Can lock out sensitive material.

A.D.A.M. Software Incorporated; 1-800-755-2326.

American Heritage Talking Dictionary (Windows)

A talking dictionary with additional features. Includes a word of the day, word search tool, brainstorming tool, anagrams, and more.

Softkey International, Incorporated; 201 Broadway; Cambridge, Massachusetts 02130.

American Sign Language Dictionary (Windows, Macintosh)

Based on the book of the same name. Over 2,200 video clips, with speed control. Divided into sections for ease of use. Includes English, French, and other language versions of the dictionary. Multiple-choice tests, and a game.

HarperCollins Interactive; 10 East 53rd Street; New York, New York 10022; 1-800-424-6234.

American White Pages, 1995 Edition (Windows)

Phone numbers for 70 million homes in the United States. Virtually every listed phone number in the United States is included. Can search by name or location, print information, and download updates.

American Business Information; 5711 South 86th Circle; P.O. Box 27347; Omaha, Nebraska 68127.

Amnesty Interactive: A History and Atlas of Human Rights (Macintosh)

Created with time donated by artists, animators, and musicians. Illustrations and background music. Material divided into five sections. Includes human rights timeline, from Hammurabi to the present.

The Voyager Company; 578 Broadway, Suite 406; New York, New York 10012; 1-800-446-2001.

Annabel's Dream of Ancient Egypt (Windows)

An original story. Reads aloud, accepts electronic bookmarks. Built-in glossary with pronunciation and definitions. Many offline articles and activities for children.

Texas Caviar; 3933 Spicewood Springs Road, Suite E-100; Austin, Texas 78759.

Apollo XIII (Windows, Macintosh)

Documents the ill-fated flight, using actual recordings and video clips. Includes animations of spacecraft flight path. Material divided into six sections for easy access.

Odyssey Interactive; (310) 997-8515.

Berlitz Live! Spanish (Windows, Macintosh)

Spanish language course using Berlitz method. Many images and animations. Background music and folk songs. Includes game that tests your skills, and sends you back to areas that need improvement. Character's lips synched with speech.

Sierra On-Line, Incorporated; P.O. Box 485; Coarsegold, California 93614; 1-800-743-7725.

Berlitz Think & Talk German (Windows, Macintosh)

Nine CD-ROMs with 50 interactive language lessons. Includes a stand-alone bilingual dictionary. CD-quality dialogs, sound effects, music, and other cues to help speed learning. Teaches a vocabulary of over 1,000 words.

Berlitz Publishing Company, Incorporated; 257 Park Avenue South; New York, New York 10010.

Bernard of Hollywood's Marilyn (Windows, Macintosh)

Based on the book of the same name. Over 100 photos and video clips of newsreels. Behind the scenes photos. Transcripts of personal conversations. Can be used as a screen saver.

Corel; 1600 Carling Avenue; Ottawa, Ontario; CANADA K1Z 8R7; 1-800-772-6735.

Better Homes & Gardens Complete Guide to Gardening (Windows, Macintosh)

A book and disc combination. Includes videos and walk-throughs of virtual gardens. A search routine that searches by plant name or type.

Multicom Publishing Incorporated; 1100 Olive Way, Suite 1250; Seattle, Washington; (510) 777-1211.

Better Homes & Gardens New Dieter's Cook Book (Windows, Macintosh)

A book and disc combination. Includes videos, photos, and diet-planning tools. Contains recipes and automatically adjusts shopping lists based on the number of servings desired.

Multicom Publishing Incorporated; 1100 Olive Way, Suite 1250; Seattle, Washington; (510) 777-1211.

Beyond Planet Earth (Windows)

A multimedia exploration of the solar system and beyond. Includes videos from the Discovery channel, hundreds of photographs. Extensive text, and interviews with space science experts. Mission to Mars explores proposals for such a mission.

Discovery Communications, Incorporated; 7700 Wisconsin Avenue; Bethesda, Maryland 20814-3579; (301) 986-1999.

Campaigns, Candidates & the Presidency (Windows)

Based on Simon & Schuster's *Encyclopedia of the American Presidency*, and *Running for President: The Candidates and Their Images*. Studies campaigns of 42 presidents. Hundreds of photos and illustrations. Over 30 minutes of video clips, thousands of facts and quotes.

Compton's New Media; 2320 Camino Vida Roble; Carlsbad, California 92009; (619) 929-2500.

Car & Driver's '95 Buyer's Guide (Windows)

Reviews of 264 new models. Includes 370 articles from the magazine. Over 650 photos, 125 full reports on road and comparison tests. Videos of winners of various Car & Driver awards.

Hachette Filipacchi Productions, LLC.

Club KidSoft (Windows, Macintosh)

A quarterly magazine and disc combination for kids. Includes audio and video clips, as well as multimedia software demos. Contains some games, and locked versions of software that can be unlocked by phone.

KidSoft; 10275 North DeAnza Boulevard; Cupertino, California 95014; 1-800-354-6150.

CNN Newsroom Global View (Windows)

Contains 40 minutes of video, and over 2,000 articles from CNN. Also features hundreds of color maps, the World Clock toolbar (checks latitudes, longitudes, and more). Chartmaker analyzes trends in the CD-ROMs material, creates charts.

Softkey International, Incorporated; 201 Broadway; Cambridge, Massachusetts 02130.

CNN Time Capsule (Windows, Macintosh)

A collection of 100 important news stories. Stories ranked by CNN editors. Also sorted by category. Each story consists of a video clip, caption, and short summary.

Vicarious Entertainment, Incorporated; 2221 Broadway, Suite 205; Redwood City, California 94063; (415) 610-8300.

Complete Multimedia Bible, King James Version (Windows)

The complete King James version of the Bible. Includes 25 minutes of video covering biblical scenes and narratives. James Earl Jones recites The Ten Commandments and other powerful verses. A collection of Biblical maps illustrates important locations.

Compton's New Media; 2320 Camino Vida Roble; Carlsbad, California 92009; (619) 929-2500.

Complete Reference Library (Windows)

Contains 10 full reference works, including dictionary, thesaurus, encyclopedia, directory of addresses, and more. Hundreds of video clips and animations; thousands of photographs.

Mindscape Incorporated; 60 Leveroni Court; Novato, California 94949; (415) 883-3000.

Compton's Interactive Encyclopedia (Windows)

Windows 95 Autoplay ability. Video clips, animations, photos, and sound. Search capability. Contains six interactive environments to explore. Patrick Stewart takes you on a guided tour of the product. Includes an atlas, dictionary, and thesaurus. Small Blue Planet included as a bonus.

Compton's New Media; 2320 Camino Vida Roble; Carlsbad, California 92009; (619) 929-2500.

Compuworks Desktop Bible, King James Version (Windows)

Contains color maps of biblical locations, and the complete text of the King James Bible. Provides detailed chronologies, and allows searches on words, phrases, or verses. Direct access to over 200 parables, events, and miracles.

The WizardWorks Group; Minneapolis, Minnesota 55447.

David Macaulay The Way Things Work (Windows)

Based on the book of the same name. Contains animated movies illustrating the way things work. Over 1,500 screens and popups, and over 1,000 illustrations. 300 animations and 60 minutes of audio. Approximately 70,000 words.

Dorling Kindersley Multimedia; 95 Madison Avenue; New York, New York 10016.

Dead Sea Scrolls (Windows)

Contains color images of the Dead Sea Scrolls, and color photos of people and places related to the scrolls. 70 minutes of video, 3D animated computer reconstructions, interviews, English translations of the scrolls.

Logos Research Systems, Incorporated; 2117 200th Avenue West; Oak Harbor, Washington 98277; (360) 679-6575.

Disney's Animated Storybook, The Lion King (Windows)

Story and games based on the movie. Speech, music, and animations. Pages include hot spots and games. Timon, the meerkat is the guide. Rafiki, the baboon, defines words.

Walt Disney Computer Software, Incorporated; 500 South Buena Vista Street; Burbank, California 91521.

Earthquake (Windows)

Produced by ABC News Interactive. Covers some of the most powerful earthquakes in history, with video clips, text, photos, and animations. Divided into three major sections. Includes narration by Ted Koppel.

Sony Electronic Publishing; Monterey, California; (408) 372-2812.

Eyewitness History of the World (Windows, Macintosh)

Hyperlinked screens provide 27 different approaches to history. Annotated photos, paintings, or sketches, with narration. Biographies, artifacts (some with video clips illustrating their use). Alphabetic index and search tools.

Dorling Kindersley Multimedia; 95 Madison Avenue; New York, New York 10016.

Family Doctor (Windows)

An interactive medical guide based on the work of Dr. Allan Bruckheim. Answers to over 2,000 common questions. Over 300 illustrations. Guides to 1,600 prescription drugs and 900 rare diseases. Video clips, and an animated first-aid guide.

Creative Multimedia Corporation; 514 NW 11th Avenue, Suite 203; Portland, Oregon 97209.

Fodor's Interactive Sports & Adventure Vacations (Windows)

A guide to vacation spots. Contains numerous photos and video clips. Display a vacation destination, then click for a map to it. Background music.

Creative Multimedia Corporation; 514 NW 11th Avenue, Suite 203; Portland, Oregon 97209.

Goldilocks and the Three Bears, in French (Windows)

The classic story, in French, for students of the language. Includes a series of games to reinforce the story. Games have practice screens that give the pronunciation of vocabulary items in pictures.

Syracuse Language Systems, Incorporated; 719 East Genesee Street; Syracuse, New York 13210; (315) 478-6729.

Great Cities of the World, Volume 2 (DOS)

A guide to ten great cities. Fast access to facts, cultural information and more. Includes a travel planner, narrated slide show, and essays by travel experts.

InterOptica Publishing Limited.

Grolier Multimedia Encyclopedia (Windows)

Electronic version of the Academic American Encyclopedia. Video clips, animations, photos, and sound. Search capability. Animated maps that show migrations, and so on. Timeline. Knowledge Explorer with audio video essays.

Grolier Electronic Publishing, Incorporated; Sherman Turnpike; Danbury, Connecticut 06816; (203) 797-3500.

Guiness Multimedia Disc of Records (Windows)

Computerized version of the Guiness book of Records. Pictures and articles from the book. Video clips of certain records. Can organize records by topic, sort by superlatives, or conduct word searches.

Grolier Electronic Publishing, Incorporated; Sherman Turnpike; Danbury, Connecticut 06816; (203) 797-3530.

Haight-Ashbury in the Sixties (Windows, Macintosh)

Photos, video clips, and music from the 1960s. 600 images from behind the scenes of the San Francisco Oracle. Multimedia game to gain enlightenment. Direct access to articles, images, and videos.

Compton's New Media; 2320 Camino Vida Roble; Carlsbad, California 92009; (619) 929-2500.

History Through Art (Windows, Macintosh)

Artworks and information from four historic periods: Ancient Greece, Ancient Rome, the Middle Ages, and the Renaissance. Includes Webster's Dictionary, and ZCI Publishing's Concise Encyclopedia.

ZCI Publishing; 1950 Stemmons, Suite 4044; Dallas, Texas 75207-3109.

Home Repair Encyclopedia (Windows)

Guide to over 100 home repair projects. Includes advice, tips, and reference guides. Some animations and cross-linked explanations. Provides calculator and estimation routines.

Books That Work; 2300 Geng Road, Building 3, Suite 100; Palo Alto, California 94303; 1-800-242-4546.

How Your Body Works, Interactive Encyclopedia of the Human Body (Windows)

Complete information on the human body. Includes 2D and 3D animations, videos of doctors and patients, even a scavenger hunt. Visually explicit sexual material can be disabled.

Mindscape Incorporated; 60 Leveroni Court; Novato, California 94949; (415) 883-3000.

In the Company of Whales (Windows)

A multimedia version of the Discovery channel's documentary of the same name. Video clips of whales in action, with recorded whale songs. A photo and text study of the world of whales. Recordings of a panel of experts answering common whale questions.

Discovery Communications, Incorporated; 7700 Wisconsin Avenue; Bethesda, Maryland 20814-3579; (301) 986-1999.

Interactive Entertainment (Windows)

A monthly multimedia gaming magazine. Articles consist of text or narrated slide shows. Video clips for some product demos and for interviews with gaming experts. Includes demo versions of games in each issue.

Interactive Entertainment; P.O. Box 636; Holmes, Pennsylvania 19043; 1-800-283-3542.

ITN World News (Windows, Macintosh)

Coverage from ITN, the British equivalent of CNN. Each edition covers the previous year. Features graphics and video clips of important stories. Divided geographically, or by subject. Three search tools.

Sony Electronic Publishing; Monterey, California; (408) 372-2812.

Jazz: A Multimedia History (Windows)

A text, video, and music guide to the history of jazz. Each section is separate, but media clips can appear in each. Can search on author's name, words, other options. Includes a glossary, bibliography, index, and discography. Many clips will play on an audio CD player.

Compton's New Media; 2320 Camino Vida Roble; Carlsbad, California 92009; (619) 929-2500.

Julia Child: Cooking with Master Chefs (Windows)

Based on her TV series. Includes 16 chefs from around the world, preparing their favorite dishes. Sound and video. Includes over 100 recipes, 200 cooking tips, and a tour of Julia Child's kitchen.

Microsoft Corporation; One Microsoft Way; Redmond, Washington 98052-6399; 1-800-426-9400.

Kaa's Hunting (Windows, Macintosh)

A multimedia storybook based on Rudyard Kipling's *Jungle Book*. Music and narration for the story. The music can also be played on a standard audio CD player.

EBook, Incorporated; 32970 Alvarado-Niles Road, Suite 704; Union City, California 94587; (510) 429-1331.

Kathy Smith's Fat Burning System (Windows, Macintosh)

A guide to Kathy Smith's exercise and weight-reduction system. Includes video clips and audio from question-and-answer sessions. Interface is divided into a matrix that can be accessed sequentially or randomly.

Xiphias; 8758 Venice Boulevard; Los Angeles, California 90034; (310) 841-2790.

Living Books, Just Grandma and Me (Windows, Macintosh)

An interactive storybook. Offers animation and music, reads text out loud. Click on objects to see additional animations, or hear music. Click on words to hear pronunciation. Read to Me, and Let Me Play modes. English, Spanish, and Japanese text and pronunciation.

Living Books; P.O. Box 6144; Novato, California 94948-6144.

Living Books, The Tortoise and the Hare (Windows, Macintosh)

An interactive storybook. Offers animation and music, reads text out loud. Click on objects to see additional animations, or hear music. Click on words to hear pronunciation. Read to Me, and Let Me Play modes. Supports English and Spanish.

Living Books; P.O. Box 6144; Novato, California 94948-6144.

Material World: A Global Family Protrait (Windows, Macintosh)

Based on Sierra Club book of the same name. Video clips and photos of 30 typical families (and their possessions) from around the world. Includes answers to 60 questions given to each family. Narrated by Charles Kuralt.

StarPress Multimedia; 303 Sacramento Street, 2nd Floor; San Francisco, California 94111; (415) 274-8383.

Mayo Clinic The Total Heart (Windows)

Based on the *Mayo Clinic Heart Book*. Sections replicate material in the book. Click on words for definitions. Animations and sound. Search and print capabilities.

IVI Publishing, Incorporated; 1380 Corporate Center Curve, Suite 305; Eagan, Minnesota 55121.

Mayo Clinic—Family Health Book (Windows)

Created from the book of the same name. Sections replicate material in the book. Click on words for definitions. Atlas of Human Anatomy, with illustrations, photos, and animations. Narrated guide to skin disorders. Search and print capabilities.

IVI Publishing, Incorporated; 1380 Corporate Center Curve, Suite 305; Eagan, Minnesota 55121.

Microsoft Art Gallery, The Collection of the National Gallery, London (Windows)

A computerized picture book. Contains images and artwork for 2,000 works at the National Gallery. Hyperlinks to related articles. Historical atlas and picture types help organize the material. Zoom and print capabilities.

Microsoft Corporation; One Microsoft Way; Redmond, Washington 98052-6399; 1-800-426-9400.

Microsoft Bookshelf (Windows)

A collection of reference works on one CD-ROM. Some references are multimedia. Search program searches across all documents, or just those you specify. Includes dictionary, thesaurus, encyclopedia, atlas, almanac, quotations, and more.

Microsoft Corporation; One Microsoft Way; Redmond, Washington 98052-6399; 1-800-426-9400.

Microsoft Encarta Multimedia Encyclopedia (Windows)

Based on *Funk & Wagnalls' Encyclopedia*. Animation, digitized sound, photos, video clips. Foreign language samples. Search Wizard, timeline, atlas, and gallery browser included.

Microsoft Corporation; One Microsoft Way; Redmond, Washington 98052-6399; 1-800-426-9400.

Microsoft Multimedia Beethoven (Windows)

An illustrated, interactive musical exploration of Beethoven's Ninth Symphony. The Symphony itself, a quick guide, a detailed guide, and a game. Illustrated history of the musician and his times.

Microsoft Corporation; One Microsoft Way; Redmond, Washington 98052-6399; 1-800-426-9400.

Microsoft Multimedia Schubert (Windows)

An illustrated, interactive musical exploration of Schubert's Quintet in A Major. The Quintet, and games based on it. Illustrated history of the musician and his times. The music and supplemental audio can be played on a standard CD player.

Microsoft Corporation; One Microsoft Way; Redmond, Washington 98052-6399; 1-800-426-9400.

Microsoft Wine Guide (Windows)

Narrated wine guide. Video clips with voice. Comprehensive wine encyclopedia and glossary. World Atlas of Wine shows microregions across California, Eastern Europe, and South America. Wine Selector reviews over 5,800 wines and links to atlas.

Microsoft Corporation; One Microsoft Way; Redmond, Washington 98052-6399; 1-800-426-9400.

My First World Atlas (DOS)

A children's atlas. Designed as an adventure into the world of geography.

Interplay Productions; 222 Third Street, Suite 0234; Cambridge, Massachusetts 02142.

My Silly CD of ABC's (DOS, Windows)

Multimedia storybook with many features. Click an object to hear its pronunciation and see it spelled. Tracks words that were clicked on. English or Spanish spelling and pronunciation.

Discis Knowledge Research; P.O. Box 66; Buffalo, New York 14223-0066; 1-800-368-2728.

National Geographic Society's A World of Animals (Windows, Macintosh)

Basic information about several families of animals. Includes narration and photographs. Divided into five books, each covering a class of animal. English or Spanish. Activity guides.

Discis Knowledge Research; P.O. Box 66; Buffalo, New York 14223-0066; 1-800-368-2728.

National Parks of America (Windows, Macintosh)

A photographic guide to the National Parks. Photography by David Muench. Video clips and a guided tour of the program. Includes a travel planner and index. Tracks the material you have viewed. Climactic information.

Multicom Publishing, Incorporated; 1100 Olive Way, Suite 1250; Seattle, Washington 98101.

New York Time Capsule 1994 (Windows, Macintosh)

A collection of seventy-nine 1994 New York State news stories. Each article has a color photo and short video clip. Includes complete index and fast search tool.

Vicarious Entertainment, Incorporated; 2221 Broadway, Suite 205; Redwood City; California 94063; (415) 610-8300.

Normandy: The Great Crusade (Windows)

A multimedia version of the Discovery channel's documentary on the Normandy Invasion in World War II. Over 40 minutes of archival footage from the invasion. Hundreds of photographs, first-person accounts, diaries, letters, background articles, and even radio broadcasts from during the invasion. Animated maps.

Discovery Communications, Incorporated; 7700 Wisconsin Avenue; Bethesda, Maryland 20814-3579; (301) 986-1999.

One World Atlas (Windows)

A world atlas with animated maps. Click on maps to find more details about history, politics, and culture of area clicked. Many photos of locations around the world. Background music.

Virgin Sound and Vision; 122 South Robertson Boulevard; Los Angeles, California 90048; (310) 246-4666.

Passage to Vietnam (Windows, Macintosh)

A photographic tour of Vietnam. Includes background music and sound effects, as well as narration. Contains bios of photographers on the project.

Against All Odds; P.O. Box 629000; El Dorado Hills, California 95762; 1-800-558-3388.

People: 20 Amazing Years of Pop Culture! (Windows, Macintosh)

Based on the last 20 years of *People* magazine. Features over 1,000 magazine covers and their cover stories. A variety of small sections focusing on topics like best and worst dressed. Some video clips, music, and animation. Includes a keyword search ability.

The Voyager Company; 578 Broadway, Suite 406; New York, New York 10012; 1-800-446-2001.

Peter Pan, A Story Painting Adventure (DOS, Macintosh)

An adaptation of the Peter Pan tale, calls on user to help move the story along. Fully animated, with music and speech. More than 30 scenes, each with multiple options for the user.

EA*Kids; 1450 Fashion Island Boulevard; San Mateo, California 94404; 1-800-KID-XPRT.

PhoneDisc Business '95 (Windows)

Complete collection of United States business phone numbers. Extensive searching capabilities. Search on business name, business type, phone number, and address.

Digital Directory Assistance, Incorporated; 6931 Arlington Road, Suite 405; Bethesda, Maryland 20814-5231; 1-800-284-8353.

PhoneDisc Residential '95 (Windows)

Two-CD-ROM set of United States residential phone numbers. Extensive searching capabilities. Search on name, then narrow with state, city, or street information. Cross reference to alternate spellings. Can count people in a specified area with a given name.

Digital Directory Assistance, Incorporated; 6931 Arlington Road, Suite 405; Bethesda, Maryland 20814-5231; 1-800-284-8353.

Popular Mechanics New Car Buyers Guide 1995 (Windows)

Contains specs, reviews, and more for eight hundred 1995 model cars. Includes photographs and hundreds of video clips. Can search and sort, then display detailed report on specific cars. Will calculate invoice and retail prices for cars and option packages.

Books That Work; 2300 Geng Road, Building 3, Suite 100; Palo Alto, California 94303; 1-800-242-4546.

Project Gutenberg (Windows, Macintosh)

Documents taken from Project Gutenberg, a program to bring the text of public domain works onto computers. Contains over 150 works, including the complete works of Shakespeare, Milton's *Paradise Lost*, the U.S. Constitution, and many more.

Walnut Creek CDROM; 1547 Palos Verdes, Suite 260; Walnut Creek, California 94596.

Rand McNally Quick Reference Atlas (Windows)

Contains topographic maps, national flags, facts, and essays. There is an interactive visual glossary. Program can locate cities and calculate the distance between places. Includes a collection of clipart maps.

Rand McNally New Media; 8255 North Central Park Avenue; Skokie, Illinois, 60076-2970.

Reader Rabbit's Interactive Reading Journey (Windows, Macintosh)

A CD-ROM combined with dozens of small books for offline use. Each book is on the disc, where it is read aloud, and the user encouraged to read along. Additional exercises supplement the books.

The Learning Company; 6493 Kaiser Drive; Fremont, California 94555.

Reader Rabbit's Reading Development Library (Windows, Macintosh)

Contains two talking fairy tales. Allows user to see the story form the perspective of any of three characters in the story. Animated, with additional skill-building exercises.

The Learning Company; 6493 Kaiser Drive; Fremont, California 94555.

Sports Illustrated Multimedia Almanac (Windows, Macintosh)

Covers the year in sports. Includes 30 minutes of video, a full year of the magazine, and over 600 photos. Contains statistics and records for NFL, MLB, and NBA players.

StarPress Multimedia; 303 Sacramento Street, 2nd Floor; San Francisco, California 94111; 1-800-782-7944.

Star Trek Omnipedia (Windows, Macintosh)

A voice-activated database of Star Trek material. The material is based on two books: *The Star Trek Encyclopedia*, and the *Star Trek Chronology.*

Simon & Schuster International; 1230 Avenue of the Americas; New York, New York 10020.

Star Trek: The Next Generation Interactive Technical Manual (Windows, Macintosh)

Based on the printed *Star Trek Technical Manual.* Contains 3D rendered graphics of the interior of the ship, and QuickTime movies. Click on objects in rooms to learn more about them. Commander Riker conducts a tour of the ship.

Simon & Schuster International; 1230 Avenue of the Americas; New York, New York 10020.

Street Atlas, USA (Windows, Macintosh)

Contains every street in the United States. Allows zoom for more details. Can search for cities by name, zip, and area codes. Color-coded maps. Can print portions of maps.

DeLorme; P.O. Box 298; Freeport, Maine 04032; (207) 865-1234.

T.J. Finds a Friend (Windows)

A fund-raising disc for the National center for Missing and Exploited Children. Colorful cartoon scenes with text and animated action. Hot spots trigger animations. Mini-encyclopedia for each page.

Media Resources; 640 N. Puente Street; Brea, California 92621; (714) 256-5048.

The Adventure of Pinocchio (Windows)

Contains 270 pages, full-color and narrated. Some pages contain hot spots with animations. On-screen glossary for highlighted words in the text. A quiz at the end of each chapter.

Orange Cherry New Media; 390 Westchester Avenue; Pound Ridge, New York 10576; 1-800-672-6002.

The Essential Frankenstein (Windows)

Based on Mary Shelley's original *Frankenstein*. Adds multimedia effects, and tells the story of Frankenstein, from his creation to today. Sound and animation, with a simple game and other features.

Byron Preiss Multimedia; 24 West 25th Street; New York, New York 10010; (212) 989-6252.

The Face of Life (Windows)

A reference guide to *Life* magazine, 1936 through 1972. Contains 1,800 images of *Life* magazine covers, 4,000 other images, story excerpts, and more. Includes a trivia game and period background music.

Creative Multimedia Corporation; 514 NW 11th Avenue, Suite 203; Portland, Oregon 97209.

The Grammys (Windows, Macintosh)

A guide to the Grammys. Includes 35 short video clips of performances, animations, and special effects. Celebrity interviews and a database of past winner information. Also a trivia game, celebrity interviews, and a studio to create your own Grammy show.

Mindscape Incorporated; 60 Leveroni Court; Novato, California 94949; (415) 883-3000.

The Haldeman Diaries: Inside the Nixon White House (Windows)

Based on H.R. Haldeman's diaries and 8mm home movies. Sixty minutes of video, 900 narrated photos, and many audio clips. Over 1,500 items in all. Includes search capability.

Sony Electronic Publishing; Monterey, California; (408) 372-2812.

The Playboy Interview (Windows)

A collection of 352 interviews from the magazine. Transcripts of articles, hypertext links, and cross references. Material grouped by themes. Includes audio recordings from some interviews.

IBM Multimedia Publishing Studio; 1-800-898-8842.

The Ultimate Human Body (Windows)

A guide to the human body, based on the book. Pronunciations, definitions, and cross references. Over 1,000 illustrations, and detailed microphotography. Includes animations, audio, and over 90,000 words.

Dorling Kindersley Multimedia; 95 Madison Avenue; New York, New York 10016.

Time Almanac of the 1990's (Windows)

Covers the most dramatic events of the decade. Contains every article printed in *Time Magazine*, between 1989 and May 1994. Researcher utility tracks every screen you open. Includes CIA World Factbook, and State Department reports on over 200 countries.

Softkey International, Incorporated; 201 Broadway; Cambridge, Massachusetts 02130.

Total History for Windows (Windows)

A three-CD-ROM set. Contains a multimedia world history, U.S. history, and world factbook. Animations, images, and video clips.

Bureau of Electronic Publishing, Incorporated; 141 New Road; Parsippany, New Jersey 07054; (201) 808-2700.

US Atlas 5.0 (Windows)

A complete atlas with up-to-date maps and statistics. Includes hundreds of photos and video clips.

Mindscape Incorporated; 60 Leveroni Court; Novato, California 94949; (415) 883-3000.

Vivaldi's The Four Seasons (Windows, Macintosh)

Historical essays, biographies, analysis and interpretations of The Four Seasons. Nature scenes as background to music. Forty full-score themes from the work. Can play individual melodies, or full scores. Hot spots provide definitions of terms.

EBook, Incorporated; 32970 Alvarado-Niles Road, Suite 704; Union City, California 94587; (510) 429-1331.

World Atlas 5 (Windows, Macintosh)

Contains maps and other information. Includes statistical charts, video clips, and photographs.

Mindscape Incorporated; 60 Leveroni Court; Novato, California 94949; (415) 883-3000.

World Library's Greatest Books Collection (DOS, Windows)

Contains over 600 complete, unabridged books, stories, plays, poems, religious works, and historical documents. You can search the documents for specific words or phrases. Allows you to open multiple documents on screen, simultaneously.

World Library, Incorporated; 12914 Haster Street; Garden Grove, California 92640; (714) 748-7197.

World View (Windows)

An interactive picture book. Contains 1,000 images in various formats, 25 Video for Windows and MPEG video clips, and 100 music clips. All are royalty free.

Softkey International, Incorporated; 201 Broadway; Cambridge, Massachusetts 02130.

World's Greatest Speeches (Windows)

More than 400 speeches on a wide range of subjects. Pictures, audio clips, video clips. Over 100 biographies of the speakers. Includes search and retrieve capabilities.

Softbit Incorporated; 1 Whitewater; Irvine, California 92715; (714) 251-8600.

HTML Commands
and Resources

C

by Ray Werner

IN THIS CHAPTER

The HTML language is under constant examination and revision. This process is supervised by the Internet Engineering Task Force (IETF), and draft memos are issued from time to time updating the specifications. To learn the current status of any Internet draft, check the 1id-abstracts.txt listing contained in the Internet Drafts Shadow Directories on ftp.is.co.za (Africa), nic.nordu.net (Europe), munnari.oz.au (Pacific Rim), ds.internic.net (US East Coast), or ftp.isi.edu (US West Coast).

The information on document structure contained in this appendix is excerpted from the HTML 2.0 draft dated May 31, 1995. It includes advanced information about the proper syntax and use of the HTML language.

Document Structure

To identify information as an HTML document conforming to the HTML 2.0 specification, each document should start with the following prologue:

```
<!DOCTYPE HTML PUBLIC "-//IETF//DTD HTML 2.0//EN">
```

> **NOTE**
>
> If the body of a text/HTML message entity does not begin with a document type declaration, an HTML user agent (browser) should infer the preceding document type declaration.

A user agent is browser or anything else that interprets HTML. HTML user agents are required to support the preceding document type declaration and the following document type declarations:

```
<!DOCTYPE HTML PUBLIC "-//IETF//DTD HTML 2.0 Level 2//EN">
<!DOCTYPE HTML PUBLIC "-//IETF//DTD HTML 2.0 Level 1//EN">
<!DOCTYPE HTML PUBLIC "-//IETF//DTD HTML 2.0 Strict//EN">
<!DOCTYPE HTML PUBLIC "-//IETF//DTD HTML Strict//EN">
```

They are not required to support other document types, but they can. In particular, they can support other formal public identifiers or other document types altogether. They can support an internal declaration subset with supplemental entity, element, and other markup declarations, or they may not.

Document Element: *<HTML>*

The HTML document element consists of a head and a body, much like a memo or a mail message. The head contains the title and other optional elements. The body is a text flow consisting of paragraphs, lists, and other elements.

Head: *<HEAD>*

The head of an HTML document is an unordered collection of information about the document. For example:

```
<HEAD> <TITLE>Introduction to HTML</TITLE> </HEAD>
```

Title: *<TITLE>*

Every HTML document must contain a <TITLE> element.

The title should identify the contents of the document in a global context. A short title, such as "Introduction" might be meaningless out of context. A title such as "Introduction to HTML Elements" is more appropriate.

> **NOTE**
>
> The length of a title is not limited; however, long titles might be truncated in some applications. To minimize this possibility, titles should be fewer than 64 characters.

A user agent can display the title of a document in a history list or as a label for the window displaying the document.

Base URI: *<BASE>*

The optional <BASE> element specifies the URI (Universal Resource Identifiers) of the document, overriding any context otherwise known to the user agent. The required HREF attribute specifies the URI for navigating the document. The value of the HREF attribute must be an absolute URI.

Keyword Index: *<ISINDEX>*

The <ISINDEX> element indicates that the user agent should allow the user to search an index by typing in keywords.

Link: *<LINK>*

The <LINK> element represents a hyperlink. It is typically used to indicate authorship, related indexes and glossaries, older or more recent versions of material, style sheets, or document hierarchy.

Associated Metainformation: *<META>*

The <META> element is an extensible container for use in identifying, indexing, and cataloging specialized document metainformation. Metainformation does the following:

- Provides a way to discover that the data set exists and how it might be obtained or accessed
- Documents the content, quality, and features of a data set and give an indication of its fitness for use

Each <META> element specifies a name/value pair. If multiple <META> elements are provided with the same name, their combined contents—concatenated as a comma-separated list—is the value associated with that name.

> **NOTE**
>
> The <META> element should not be used where a specific element such as <TITLE> would be appropriate.

The META element is an extensible container. HTTP servers should read the content of the document <HEAD> to generate header fields corresponding to any elements defining a value for the attribute HTTP-EQUIV.

> **NOTE**
>
> The method by which the server extracts document metainformation is unspecified and not mandatory. The META element only provides an extensible mechanism for identifying and embedding document metainformation—how it can be used is up to the individual server implementation and the HTML user agent.

Attributes of the META element:

HTTP-EQUIV   This attribute binds the element to an HTTP header field. An HTTP server can use this information to process the document. In particular, it should include a header field in the responses to GET requests for this document: the header name is taken from the HTTP-EQUIV attribute value, and the header value is taken from the value of the CONTENT attribute. HTTP header names are not case-sensitive.

NAME   The name of the name/value pair. If not present, HTTP-EQUIV
                        gives the name.

CONTENT   The value of the name/value pair.

Some examples follow.

If the document contains the following:

```
<META HTTP-EQUIV="Expires"  CONTENT="Tue, 04 Dec 1993 21:29:02 GMT">
<meta http-equiv="Keywords" CONTENT="Fred, Barney">
<META HTTP-EQUIV="Reply-to"  content="fielding@ics.uci.edu (Roy Fielding)">
```

the server should include the following header fields as part of the HTTP response to a GET or
HEAD request for that document:

```
Expires: Tue, 04 Dec 1993 21:29:02 GMT Keywords: Fred, Barney Reply-to:
fielding@ics.uci.edu (Roy Fielding)
```

When the HTTP-EQUIV attribute is not present, the server should not generate an HTTP response header for the metainformation.

Do not name an HTTP-EQUIV equal to a response header that should normally only be generated
by the HTTP server. Example names that are inappropriate include Server, Date, and Last-
modified—the exact list of inappropriate names depends on the particular server implementation.

Next ID: <NEXTID>

The <NEXTID> element gives a hint for the name to use for an <A> element when editing an
HTML document. The <NEXTID> element should be distinct from all NAME attribute values on
<A> elements. For example:

```
<NEXTID N=Z27>
```

NOTE

Very few Web pages use BASE, LINK, META, or NEXTID. Slightly more, but still very few,
use ISINDEX. These are included here for technical completeness. All Web documents
should have a TITLE element.

Body: <BODY>

The <BODY> element contains the text flow of the document, including headings, paragraphs,
and lists. The following is an example:

```
<BODY> <h1>Important Stuff</h1> <p>Explanation about important stuff... </BODY>
```

Headings: *<H1>* Through *<H6>*

The six heading elements, <H1> through <H6>, denote section headings. Although the order and occurrence of headings is not constrained by the HTML DTD (Document Template Draft), documents should not skip levels (for example, from H1 to H3), because converting such documents to other representations is often problematic. The following is an example of how to use the heading elements:

```
<H1>This is a heading</H1>Here is some text
<H2>Second level heading</H2>Here is some more text.
```

The display of these varies from browser to browser. Example renderings of heading styles include the following:

H1   Bold, large font, centered. One or two blank lines above and below.

H2   Bold, large font, flush-left. One or two blank lines above and below.

H3   Italic, large font, slightly indented from the left margin. One or two blank lines above and below.

H4   Bold, normal font, indented more than H3. One blank line above and below.

H5   Italic, normal font, indented as H4. One blank line above.

H6   Bold, indented same as normal text, more than H5. One blank line above.

Block Structuring Elements

Each of the following elements defines a block structure; that is, they indicate a paragraph break before and after their use.

Paragraph: *<P>*

The <P> element indicates a paragraph. The exact indentation, leading space, and so on of a paragraph is not specified by the Draft and can be a function of other tags, style sheets, or display characteristics of different browsers. Typically, paragraphs are surrounded by a vertical space of one line or half a line. The first line in a paragraph is indented in some cases.

The following is an example of how to use the paragraph element:

```
<H1>This Heading Precedes the Paragraph</H1> <P>This is the text of the first
paragraph. <P>This is the text of the second paragraph. Although you do not
need to start paragraphs on new lines, maintaining this convention facilitates
document maintenance.</P> <P>This is the text of a third paragraph.</P>
```

Preformatted Text: *<PRE>*

The <PRE> element represents a character cell block of text; therefore, it is suitable for text that has been formatted on-screen. Anchor elements and phrase markup may be used within preformatted text, however elements that define paragraph formatting (headings, address, and so on) must not be used. The <PRE> tag can be used with the optional WIDTH attribute. The WIDTH attribute specifies the maximum number of characters for a line and enables the HTML user agent to select a suitable font and indentation.

Within preformatted text, line breaks within the text are rendered as a move to the beginning of the next line.

> **NOTE**
>
> References to "the beginning of a new line" do not imply that the renderer is forbidden from using a constant left indent for rendering preformatted text. The left indent can be constrained by the width required.

> **NOTE**
>
> Within a preformatted text element, the constraint that the rendering must be on a fixed horizontal character pitch might limit or prevent the capability of the HTML user agent to faithfully render phrase markup.

> **NOTE**
>
> Some historical documents contain <P> tags in <PRE> elements. User agents are encouraged to treat this as a line break. A <P> tag followed by a newline character should produce only one line break, not a line break plus a blank line.

The horizontal tab character (encoded in US-ASCII and ISO-8859-1 as decimal 9) must be interpreted as the smallest positive nonzero number of spaces that will leave the number of characters on a line as a multiple of 8.

Here's an example of its use:

```
<PRE> This is an example line. </PRE>
```

> **NOTE**
>
> The characters &, <, and > should be translated into HTML entities even within PRE blocks because some browsers might be confused by them.

Address: *<ADDRESS>*

The <ADDRESS> element specifies such information as address, signature, and authorship, often at the beginning or end of the body of a document. Typically, the <ADDRESS> element is rendered in an italic typeface and might be indented. The following is an example of how to use this element:

```
<ADDRESS> Newsletter editor<BR> J.R. Brown<BR>
JimquickPost News, Jumquick, CT 01234<BR>
Tel (123) 456 7890 </ADDRESS>
```

Block Quote: *<BLOCKQUOTE>*

The <BLOCKQUOTE> element contains text quoted from another source. A typical browser's rendering might be a slight extra left and right indent and/or italic font. The <BLOCKQUOTE> element typically provides space above and below the quote.

Single-font rendition may reflect the quotation style of Internet mail by putting a vertical line of graphic characters, such as the greater than symbol (>), in the left margin. The following is an example of how to use this element:

```
I think the poem ends <BLOCKQUOTE> <P>Soft you now, the fair Ophelia. Nymph,
in thy orisons, be all my sins remembered. </BLOCKQUOTE>, but I am not sure.
```

List Elements

HTML includes a number of list elements. (See the following subsections for examples.) List elements can be used in combination; for example, an <OL> may be nested in an <LI> element of a <UL>.

Unordered List: *<UL>* and *<LI>*

The <UL> represents a list of items with no inherent ordering—typically a bulleted list. This does not mean,however, that the user agent can rearrange the list. The content of a <UL> element is a sequence of <LI> elements; for example:

```
<UL> <LI>First list item
<LI>Second list item
<p>second paragraph of second item
<LI>Third list item </UL>
```

Ordered List: *<OL>*

The <OL> element represents an ordered list of items perhaps sorted by sequence or order of importance. The content of an <OL> element is a sequence of <LI> elements; for example:

```
<OL> <LI>Click the Web button to open the Open the URI window.
<LI>Enter the URI number in the text field of the Open URI window.
```

```
The Web document you specified is displayed. <ol>
<li>substep 1
<li>substep 2 </ol>
<LI>Click highlighted text to move from one link to another. </OL>
```

Directory List: *<DIR>*

The <DIR> element is similar to the <UL> element. It represents a list of short items, typically up to 20 characters each. Items in a directory list can be arranged in columns that are usually 24 characters wide. The content of a <DIR> element is a sequence of <LI> elements. Nested block elements are not allowed in the content of <DIR> elements. The following is an example:

```
<DIR> <LI>A-H<LI>I-M <LI>M-R<LI>S-Z </DIR>
```

Menu List: *<MENU>*

The <MENU> element is a list of items with typically one line per item. The menu list style is usually more compact than the style of an unordered list. The content of a <MENU> element is a sequence of <LI> elements. Nested block elements are not allowed in the content of <MENU> elements. The following is an example:

```
<MENU> <LI>First item in the list.
<LI>Second item in the list.
<LI>Third item in the list. </MENU>
```

Definition List: *<DL>*, *<DT>*, and *<DD>*

A definition list is a list of terms and corresponding definitions. Definition lists are typically formatted with the term flush-left and the definition, formatted paragraph style, indented after the term. The following is an example:

```
<DL> <DT>Term<DD>This is the definition of the first term.
<DT>Term<DD>This is the definition of the second term. </DL>
```

If the DT term does not fit in the DT column (one third of the display area), it can be extended across the page with the DD section moved to the next line, or it can be wrapped onto successive lines of the left-hand column.

The optional COMPACT attribute suggests that a compact rendering be used, because the list items are small and/or the entire list is large. Unless the COMPACT attribute is present, an HTML user agent can leave white space between successive DT DD pairs. The COMPACT attribute can also reduce the width of the left-hand (DT) column.

```
<DL COMPACT> <DT>Term<DD>This is the first definition in compact format.
<DT>Term<DD>This is the second definition in compact format. </DL>
```

Phrase Markup

Phrases can be marked up according to idiomatic usage, typographic appearance, or for use as hyperlink anchors. Available tags include <EM> (emphasis), <STRONG>, <B> (bold), and <I> (italic). Although the <U> (underline) content is part of the specification, it is treated by many browser developers as "optional," and they don't support it.

User agents must render highlighted phrases distinctly from plain text. Additionally, <EM> content must be rendered as distinct from <STRONG> content, and <B> content must rendered as distinct from <I> content.

Phrase elements can be nested within the content of other phrase elements. Here's an example:

```
plain <B>bold <I>italic</I></B>
```

Citation: *<CITE>*

The <CITE> element is used to indicate the title of a book or other citation. It is typically typeset as italics; for example,

```
He just couldn't get enough of <cite>The Grapes of Wrath</cite>.
```

Code: *<CODE>*

The <CODE> element indicates an example of code, typically rendered in a monospaced font. For example:

```
The expression <code>x += 1</code> is short
for <code>x = x + 1</code>.
```

Emphasis: *<EM>*

The <EM> element indicates an emphasized phrase, typically rendered as italics; for example,

```
A singular subject <em>always</em> takes a singular verb.
```

Keyboard: *<KBD>*

The <KBD> element indicates text typed by a user, typically rendered in a monospaced font. This is commonly used in instruction manuals; for example,

```
Enter <kbd>FIND IT</kbd> to search the database.
```

Sample: *<SAMP>*

The <SAMP> element indicates a sequence of literal characters, typically rendered in a monospaced font. For example:

```
The only word containing the letters
<samp>mt</samp> is dreamt.
```

Strong Emphasis: *<STRONG>*

The <STRONG> element indicates strong emphasis, typically rendered in bold. For example:

```
<strong>STOP</strong>, or I'll say "<strong>STOP</strong>" again!.
```

Variable: *<VAR>*

The <VAR> element indicates a placeholder, typically rendered as italic. For example:

```
Take a guess: Roses are <var>blank</var>.
```

Typographic Elements

Typographic elements are used to specify the format of marked text. Typical renderings for idiomatic elements vary between user agents. If a specific rendering is necessary—for example, when the user agent refers to a specific text attribute, as in "The italic parts are mandatory"—a typographic element can be used to ensure that the intended typography is used where possible.

Bold: *<B>*

The <B> element indicates bold text. Where bold typography is unavailable, an alternative representation may be used.

Italic: *<I>*

The <I> element indicates italic text. Where italic typography is unavailable, an alternative representation may be used.

Underline: *<U>*

The <U> element indicates underlined text. (Netscape chooses not to implement this part of the HTML specification.)

Typewriter: <*TT*>

The <TT> element indicates typewriter text. Where a typewriter font is unavailable, an alternative representation may be used.

Anchor: <A>

The <A> element indicates the source and/or destination of a hyperlink. At least one of the NAME and HREF attributes should be given. The following are attributes of the <A> element:

HREF   Gives the destination of a hyperlink.

NAME   Gives the name of the anchor and makes it available as a navigation destination.

TITLE   Suggests a title for the destination resource—advisory only. The TITLE attribute may be used for the following:

- For display prior to accessing the destination resource; for example, as a margin note or on a small box while the mouse is over the anchor or while the document is being loaded.

- For resources that do not specify a title, such as graphics, plain text, and Gopher menus, the TITLE attribute may be used as a window title.

REL   Says what the relationship is that is described by the hyperlink. The value is a whitespace-separated list of relationship names.

REV   Is the same as the REL attribute, but the semantics of the relationship are in the reverse direction. A link from A to B with REL=X expresses the same relationship as a link from B to A with REV=X. An anchor can have both REL and REV attributes.

URN   Specifies a preferred, more persistent, identifier for the destination. The format of URNs is under discussion (1995) by various working groups of the Internet Engineering Task Force.

METHODS   Specifies methods to be used in accessing the destination, as a white space-separated list of names. For similar reasons as for the TITLE attribute, it can be useful to include the information in advance in the link. For example, the HTML user agent may choose a different rendering as a function of the methods allowed; for example, something that is searchable may get a different icon.

Line Break: *
*

The <BR> element specifies a line break between words. For example:

```
<P> Pease porridge hot<BR>
Pease porridge cold<BR>
Pease porridge in the pot<BR>
Nine days old.
```

Horizontal Rule: *<HR>*

The <HR> element is a divider between sections of text; typically, a full-width horizontal rule or equivalent graphic. For example:

```
<HR> <ADDRESS>February 8, 1995, CERN</ADDRESS> </BODY>
```

Image: *<IMG>*

The <IMG> element refers to an image or icon. HTML user agents that cannot process images ignore the <IMG> element.

> **NOTE**
>
> Some HTML user agents can process graphics linked via anchors, but not <IMG> graphics. Therefore, if a graphic is essential, it should be referenced from an <A> element rather than an <IMG> element. If the graphic is not essential, then the <IMG> element is appropriate.

The following are attributes of the <IMG> element:

ALIGN	Alignment of the image with respect to the text baseline. Here are the options:

	TOP	Specifies that the top of the image aligns with the tallest item on the line containing the image.
	MIDDLE	Specifies that the center of the image aligns with the baseline of the line containing the image.
	BOTTOM	Specifies that the bottom of the image aligns with the baseline of the line containing the image.

ALT	Optional alternative text, for use in non-graphical environments, text is displayed if the browser cannot render the graphic image.
ISMAP	Indicates an image map.
SRC	Specifies the URI of the image resource.

Here's an example of its use:

```
<IMG SRC="triangle.xbm" ALT="Warning:"> Be sure to read these instructions.
<IMG SRC="triangle.xbm">Be sure to read these instructions.
<a href="http://machine/htbin/imagemap/sample"> <IMG SRC="sample.xbm" ISMAP> </a>
```

Inserting Special Characters

Every once in awhile you are going to want to include an unusual character in your HTML document. The following table gives you the escape sequence that you need to include to obtain the character.

(This list is derived from "ISO 8879:1986//ENTITIES Added Latin 1//EN.")

Enter this	To get this
&AElig	Capital AE diphthong (ligature)
&Aacute	Capital A, acute accent
&Acirc	Capital A, circumflex accent
&Agrave	Capital A, grave accent
&Aring	Capital A, ring
&Atilde	Capital A, tilde
&Auml	Capital A, dieresis or umlaut mark
&Ccedil	Capital C, cedilla
&ETH	Capital Eth, Icelandic
&Eacute	Capital E, acute accent
&Ecirc	Capital E, circumflex accent
&Egrave	Capital E, grave accent
&Euml	Capital E, dieresis or umlaut mark
&Iacute	Capital I, acute accent
&Icirc	Capital I, circumflex accent
&Igrave	Capital I, grave accent
&Iuml	Capital I, dieresis or umlaut mark
&Ntilde	Capital N, tilde
&Oacute	Capital O, acute accent
&Ocirc	Capital O, circumflex accent
&Ograve	Capital O, grave accent

&Oslash	Capital O, slash
&Otilde	Capital O, tilde
&Ouml	Capital O, dieresis or umlaut mark
&THORN	Capital THORN, Icelandic
&Uacute	Capital U, acute accent
&Ucirc	Capital U, circumflex accent
&Ugrave	Capital U, grave accent
&Uuml	Capital U, dieresis or umlaut mark
&Yacute	Capital Y, acute accent
&aacute	Small a, acute accent
&acirc	Small a, circumflex accent
&aelig	Small ae diphthong (ligature)
&agrave	Small a, grave accent
&aring	Small a, ring
&atilde	Small a, tilde
&auml	Small a, dieresis or umlaut mark
&ccedil	Small c, cedilla
&eacute	Small e, acute accent
&ecirc	Small e, circumflex accent
&egrave	Small e, grave accent
&eth	Small eth, Icelandic
&euml	Small e, dieresis or umlaut mark
&iacute	Small i, acute accent
&icirc	Small i, circumflex accent
&igrave	Small i, grave accent
&iuml	Small i, dieresis or umlaut mark
&ntilde	Small n, tilde
&oacute	Small o, acute accent
&ocirc	Small o, circumflex accent
&ograve	Small o, grave accent
&oslash	Small o, slash
&otilde	Small o, tilde
&ouml	Small o, dieresis or umlaut mark
&szlig	Small sharp s, German (sz ligature)
&thorn	Small thorn, Icelandic
&uacute	Small u, acute accent
&ucirc	Small u, circumflex accent
&ugrave	Small u, grave accent
&uuml	Small u, dieresis or umlaut mark
&yacute	Small y, acute accent
&yuml	Small y, dieresis or umlaut mark

To see a document that shows all of these and more, visit the following site:

```
http://www.well.com/user/rab/entities.html
```

Tables

Tables are not really recognized in the HTML 2.0 specification, but they will be an integral part of the evolving HTML 3.0, which might be formally adopted by the time you read this book. However, tables are so useful that many browsers are recognizing them in advance of the formal adoption of the standard. Here is a list of the commands that you might want to use if you decide to give tables a try. Check out the Netscape home page, `http:\\www.netscape.com`, for information about other new features supported by this fine browser.

Table Tags

Tables, like all other HTML elements, have their own set of tags. The ones that will most likely be included in the finished specification are listed here.

<TABLE ...></TABLE>

This is the "tag team" for all the other table tags, and other table tags will be ignored if they aren't wrapped inside of a TABLE tag.

<TR ...></TR>

This stands for table row. The number of rows in a table is exactly specified by how many TR tags are contained within it, regardless of cells that might attempt to use the ROWSPAN attribute to span into non-specified rows. TR can have both the ALIGN and VALIGN attributes, which if specified become the default alignments for all cells in this row.

<TD ...></TD>

This stands for table data and specifies a standard table data cell. Table data cells must appear only within table rows. Each row need not have the same number of cells specified because short rows will be padded with blank cells on the right. A cell can contain any of the HTML tags normally present in the body of an HTML document. The default alignment of table data is ALIGN=left and VALIGN=middle. These alignments are overridden by any alignments specified in the containing TR tag, and those alignments in turn are overridden by any ALIGN or VALIGN attributes explicitly specified on this cell. By default, lines inside of table cells can be broken up to fit within the overall cell width. Specifying the NOWRAP attribute for a TD prevents linebreaking for that cell.

`<TH ...></TH>`

This stands for table header. Header cells are identical to data cells in all respects, with the exception that header cells are in a bold font, and have a default `ALIGN=center`.

`<CAPTION ...></CAPTION>`

This represents the caption for a table. `CAPTION` tags should appear inside the table but not inside table rows or cells. The caption accepts an alignment attribute that defaults to `ALIGN=top` but can be explicitly set to `ALIGN=bottom`. Like table cells, any document body HTML can appear in a caption. Captions are always horizontally centered with respect to the table, and they can have their lines broken to fit within the width of the table.

Table Attributes

Tables, like text, can have attributes. Here is a list of the available ones.

BORDER

This attribute appears in the `TABLE` tag. If present, borders are drawn around all table cells. If absent, there are no borders, but by default space is left for borders, so the same table with and without the `BORDER` attribute will have the same width.

ALIGN

If appearing inside a `CAPTION`, `ALIGN` controls whether the caption appears above or below the table, and can have the values top or bottom, defaulting to top. If appearing inside a TR, TH, or TD it controls whether text inside the table cell(s) is aligned to the left side of the cell, the right side of the cell, or centered within the cell. Values are left, center, and right.

VALIGN

Appearing inside a TR, TH, or TD, `VALIGN` controls whether text inside the table cell(s) is aligned to the top of the cell, the bottom of the cell, or vertically centered within the cell. It also specify that all the cells in the row should be vertically aligned to the same baseline. Values are top, middle, bottom, and baseline.

NOWRAP

If this attribute appears in any table cell (TH or TD), the lines within this cell cannot be broken to fit the width of the cell. Be careful when you use this attribute because it can result in excessively wide cells.

COLSPAN

This attribute can appear in any table cell (TH or TD), and it specifies how many columns of the table this cell should span. The default COLSPAN for any cell is 1.

ROWSPAN

This attribute can appear in any table cell (TH or TD), and it specifies how many rows of the table this cell should span. The default ROWSPAN for any cell is 1. A span that extends into rows that were never specified with a TR will be truncated.

Background Attribute

Recent versions of the proposed HTML 3.0 specification have added a BACKGROUND attribute to the BODY tag. The purpose of this attribute is to specify a URL that points to an image that is to be used as a background for the document. In Netscape 1.1, this background image is used to tile the full background of the document viewing area. Thus, specifying the following:

```
<BODY BACKGROUND="metal/brushed_aluminum.gif">Document here</BODY>
```

would cause whatever text, images, and so on appeared in that document to be placed on a background.

> **NOTE**
>
> Also available is a BGCOLOR attribute, which specifies the RGB value to use for a background color. `<BODY BGCOLOR="#000ff">` would specify a bright blue background color. See the Netscape page for more details.

Resources and Reading List

Here is a reading list that you might want to refer to for additional information about HTML resources. Items are listed in alphabetical order by topic.

[GOLD90]

C. F. Goldfarb. "The SGML Handbook." Y. Rubinsky, Ed., Oxford University Press, 1990.

[HTTP]

T. Berners-Lee, R. T. Fielding, and H. Frystyk Nielsen. "Hypertext Transfer Protocol -HTTP/1.0." Work in Progress (draft-ietf-http-v10-spec-00.ps), MIT, UC Irvine, CERN, March 1995.

[IANA]

J. Reynolds and J. Postel. "Assigned Numbers." STD 2, RFC 1700, USC/ISI, October 1994.

[IMEDIA]

J. Postel. "Media Type Registration Procedure." RFC 1590, USC/ISI, March 1994.

[ISO-8859-1]

ISO 8859. International Standard—Information Processing—8-bit Single-Byte Coded Graphic Character Sets—Part 1: Latin Alphabet No. 1,

ISO 8859-1:1987. Part 2: Latin alphabet No. 2,

ISO 8859-2, 1987. Part 3: Latin alphabet No. 3,

ISO 8859-3, 1988. Part 4: Latin alphabet No. 4,

ISO 8859-4, 1988. Part 5: Latin/Cyrillic alphabet,

ISO 8859-5, 1988. Part 6: Latin/Arabic alphabet, ISO

8859-6, 1987. Part 7: Latin/Greek alphabet, ISO

8859-7, 1987. Part 8: Latin/Hebrew alphabet, ISO

8859-8, 1988. Part 9: Latin alphabet No. 5, ISO

8859-9, 1990.

[MIME]

N. Borenstein and N. Freed. "MIME (Multipurpose Internet Mail Extensions) Part One: Mechanisms for Specifying and Describing the Format of Internet Message Bodies." RFC 1521, Bellcore, Innosoft, September 1993.

[RELURL]

R. T. Fielding. "Relative Uniform Resource Locators." Work in Progress (draft-ietf-uri-relative-url-06.txt), UC Irvine, March 1995.

[SGML]

ISO 8879. Information Processing—Text and Office Systems—Standard Generalized Markup Language (SGML), 1986.

[SQ91]

SoftQuad. "The SGML Primer." 3rd ed., SoftQuad Inc., 1991.

[URI]

T. Berners-Lee. "Universal Resource Identifiers in WWW: A Unifying Syntax for the Expression of Names and Addresses of Objects on the Network as used in the World Wide Web." RFC 1630, CERN, June 1994.

[URL]

T. Berners-Lee, L. Masinter, and M. McCahill. "Uniform Resource Locators (URL)." RFC 1738, CERN, Xerox PARC, University of Minnesota, October 1994.

[US-ASCII]

US-ASCII. Coded Character Set - 7-Bit American Standard Code for Information Interchange. Standard ANSI X3.4-1986, ANSI, 1986.

Where To Find HTML Editors

HTML is persnickity. Because of this, a lot of programmers have developed editors that will help you construct proper code. The number of editors increases on a regular basis, and any list published here would be out of date before you get it, so check out this site with your WWW browser:

```
http://www.yahoo.com/Computers/World_Wide_Web/HTML_Editors/
```

This Web page is a series of pointers to HTML editors for the following platforms:

DOS
FrameMaker
IRIX
Macintosh
MS Windows
NeXTSTEP
X Window System

What's on the CD-ROM?

D

by Wayne
Blankenbeckler

The CD-ROM included with this book contains a variety of electronic publishing software for IBM-compatible computers.

The demo versions of software on the disc are intended to give you hands-on experience with the capabilities and features of the full software product. These working demos usually work the same as the complete product but with the limitations of not being able to save or print your work; or, they may have a limitation on how long you can use the product. The demos enable you to give these products a good test drive.

The sections that follow describe how Windows users and Macintosh users can use the CD-ROM.

Windows Users

The Windows menu program on the disc enables you to easily navigate through and install the included software. Before you run the menu program, you need to run the disc's setup program, which creates a Program Group.

> **NOTE**
>
> **Windows 95 Users:** When you insert the CD-ROM into your drive, an introductory screen automatically appears and gives you the choice of running the setup program or the CD-ROM menu.

Insert the disc into your CD-ROM drive and start Windows, if you haven't already done so. Follow these steps to create a Program Group:

1. Switch to Program Manager or File Manager. Select **F**ile from the menu, and then select **Run**. **Windows 95 users:** Click on the Start button, and then click on **R**un.

2. In the Run dialog box, type `D:\SETUP.EXE` in the text box and click on OK. If your CD-ROM drive is not drive D, substitute the correct letter. For instance, if your CD-ROM drive is G, type `G:\SETUP.EXE`.

3. The opening screen of the setup program will appear. Click on the Continue button, and follow the directions in the program.

When the setup has completed, double-click the CD-ROM Menu icon to begin your exploration. If you experience problems with the disc, double-click the Troubleshooting icon. Double-click on Read Me First to read a brief guide to using the CD-ROM menu program.

INDEX

ELECTRONIC PUBLISHING UNLEASHED

PLUG YOURSELF INTO...

THE MACMILLAN INFORMATION SUPERLIBRARY™

Free information and vast computer resources from the world's leading computer book publisher—online!

FIND THE BOOKS THAT ARE RIGHT FOR YOU!

A complete online catalog, plus sample chapters and tables of contents give you an in-depth look at *all* of our books, including hard-to-find titles. It's the best way to find the books you need!

- **STAY INFORMED** with the latest computer industry news through our online newsletter, press releases, and customized Information SuperLibrary Reports.

- **GET FAST ANSWERS** to your questions about MCP books and software.

- **VISIT** our online bookstore for the latest information and editions!

- **COMMUNICATE** with our expert authors through e-mail and conferences.

- **DOWNLOAD SOFTWARE** from the immense MCP library:
    - Source code and files from MCP books
    - The best shareware, freeware, and demos

- **DISCOVER HOT SPOTS** on other parts of the Internet.

- **WIN BOOKS** in ongoing contests and giveaways!

TO PLUG INTO MCP: ➔ **WORLD WIDE WEB: http://www.mcp.com**

GOPHER: gopher.mcp.com

FTP: ftp.mcp.com